Value at Risk

VALUE AT RISK

The New Benchmark for Managing Financial Risk

SECOND EDITION

PHILIPPE JORION

McGraw-Hill

New York   San Francisco   Washington, D.C.   Auckland   Bogotá
Caracas   Lisbon   London   Madrid   Mexico City   Milan
Montreal   New Delhi   San Juan   Singapore
Sydney   Tokyo   Toronto

Library of Congress Cataloging-in-Publication Data
Jorion, Philippe
   Value at risk : the new benchmark for managing financial risk / Philippe Jorion.—2nd ed.
     p.   cm.
   ISBN 0-07-135502-2
   1. Financial futures. 2. Risk management. I. Title: The new benchmark for managing
financial risk. II. Title.

HG6024.3.J683 2000
658.15'5—dc21
                                                       00–033239

McGraw-Hill

A Division of The McGraw·Hill Companies

3 4 5 6 7 8 9 0 DOC/DOC 0 6 5 4 3 2 1

ISBN 0-07-135502-2

The sponsoring editor for this book was Catherine Schwent, the editing supervisor was Ruth W. Mannino, and the production supervisor was Elizabeth Strange. It was set in 11/13 Times Roman by ATLIS.

Printed and bound by R. R. Donnelley & Sons Company.

This publication is designed to provide accurate and authoritative information in regard to the subject matter covered. It is sold with the understanding that neither the author nor the publisher is engaged in rendering legal, accounting, or other professional service. If legal advice or other expert assistance is required, the services of a competent professional person should be sought.
    —From a Declaration of Principles jointly adopted by a Committee of the American Bar Association and a Committee of Publishers

McGraw-Hill books are available at special quantity discounts to use as premiums and sales promotions, or for use in corporate training programs. For more information, please write to the Director of Special Sales, Professional Publishing, McGraw-Hill, Two Penn Plaza, New York, NY 10121-2298. Or contact your local bookstore.

 This book is printed on recycled, acid-free paper containing a minimum of 50% recycled de-inked fiber.

Contents in Brief

Preface xxi

PART ONE MOTIVATION 1

Chapter 1 The Need for Risk Management 3
Chapter 2 Lessons from Financial Disasters 31
Chapter 3 Regulatory Capital Standards with VAR 51

PART TWO BUILDING BLOCKS 79

Chapter 4 Measuring Financial Risk 81
Chapter 5 Computing Value at Risk 107
Chapter 6 Backtesting VAR Models 129
Chapter 7 Portfolio Risk: Analytical Methods 147
Chapter 8 Forecasting Risks and Correlations 183

PART THREE VALUE-AT-RISK SYSTEMS 203

Chapter 9 VAR Methods 205
Chapter 10 Stress Testing 231
Chapter 11 Implementing Delta-Normal VAR 255
Chapter 12 Simulation Methods 291
Chapter 13 Credit Risk 313
Chapter 14 Liquidity Risk 339

PART FOUR APPLICATIONS OF RISK-MANAGEMENT SYSTEMS 359

Chapter 15 Using VAR to Measure and Control Risk 361
Chapter 16 Using VAR for Active Risk Management 383
Chapter 17 VAR in Investment Management 407
Chapter 18 The Technology of Risk 431
Chapter 19 Operational Risk Management 447
Chapter 20 Integrated Risk Management 467

PART FIVE THE RISK-MANAGEMENT PROFESSION 481

Chapter 21 Risk Management: Guidelines and Pitfalls 483
Chapter 22 Conclusions 511

References 521

Index 531

Contents

Preface   xxi

Part One.

MOTIVATION   1

Chapter 1.

The Need for Risk Management   3

1.1 Financial Risks   3

     1.1.1 Change: The Only Constant   4

     1.1.2 But Where Is Risk Coming From?   7

     1.1.3 The Toolbox of Risk Management   10

1.2 Derivatives and Risk Management   11

     1.2.1 What Are Derivatives?   11

     1.2.2 Types of Derivatives   12

     1.2.3 Derivatives Markets: How Big?   12

1.3 Types of Financial Risks   15

     1.3.1 Market Risk   15

     1.3.2 Credit Risk   16

     1.3.3 Liquidity Risk   17

     1.3.4 Operational Risk   18

     1.3.5 Legal Risk   20

     1.3.6 Integrated Risk Measurement   21

1.4 In Brief, What Is VAR?   21

     1.4.1 Definition of VAR   22

     1.4.2 Illustration of VAR   22

1.5 VAR and the Evolution of Risk Management   25

Chapter 2.

Lessons from Financial Disasters   31

2.1 Lessons from Recent Losses   32
    2.1.1 Losses Attributed to Derivatives   33
    2.1.2 Perspective on Financial Losses   34
2.2 Case Studies in Risk   36
    2.2.1 Barings's Fall: A Lesson in Risk   36
    2.2.2 Metallgesellschaft   38
    2.2.3 Orange County   40
    2.2.4 Daiwa's Lost Billion   41
    2.2.5 Lessons from Case Studies   42
2.3 Private-Sector Responses   43
    2.3.1 G-30 Report   43
    2.3.2 Derivatives Policy Group   43
    2.3.3 J.P. Morgan's RiskMetrics   44
    2.3.4 Global Association of Risk Professionals (GARP)   45
2.4 The View of Regulators   45
    2.4.1 General Accounting Office (GAO)   46
    2.4.2 Financial Accounting Standards Board (FASB)   46
    2.4.3 Securities and Exchange Commission (SEC)   47
2.5 Conclusions   49

Chapter 3.

Regulatory Capital Standards with VAR   51

3.1 Why Regulation?   52
3.2 The 1988 Basel Accord   55
    3.2.1 The Cooke Ratio   55
    3.2.2 Activity Restrictions   57
    3.2.3 Criticisms of the 1988 Approach   57
3.3 The 1996 Amendment on Market Risks   60
    3.3.1 The Standardized Method   61
    3.3.2 The Internal Models Approach   63
    3.3.3 The Precommitment Model   65

3.3.4 Comparison of Approaches   66

3.3.5 Example   68

3.4 The 1999 Credit Risk Revisions   68

3.4.1 The Revisions   70

3.4.2 Overall Assessment   70

3.5 Regulation of Nonbanks   72

3.5.1 Securities Firms   72

3.5.2 Insurance Companies   74

3.5.3 Pension Funds   75

3.6 Conclusions   75

Part Two.

BUILDING BLOCKS   79

Chapter 4.

Measuring Financial Risk   81

4.1 Market Risks   82

4.2 Probability Distribution Functions   86

4.2.1 A Gambler's Experiment   86

4.2.2 Properties of Expectations   89

4.2.3 The Normal Distribution   91

4.2.4 Other Distributions   93

4.3 Risk   95

4.3.1 Risk as Dispersion   95

4.3.2 Quantiles   95

4.4 Asset Returns   98

4.4.1 Measuring Returns   98

4.4.2 Sample Estimates   101

4.5 Time Aggregation   102

4.5.1 Aggregation with I.I.D. Returns   102

4.5.2 Aggregation with Correlated Returns   104

4.5.3 The Effect of the Mean at Various Horizons   105

Chapter 5.

Computing Value at Risk   107

5.1 Computing VAR   108
    5.1.1 Steps in Constructing VAR   108
    5.1.2 VAR for General Distributions   109
    5.1.3 VAR for Parametric Distributions   110
    5.1.4 Comparison of Approaches   113
    5.1.5 VAR as a Risk Measure   114
5.2 Choice of Quantitative Factors   116
    5.2.1 VAR as a Benchmark Measure   116
    5.2.2 VAR as a Potential Loss Measure   117
    5.2.3 VAR as Equity Capital   117
    5.2.4 Criteria for Backtesting   119
    5.2.5 Application: The Basel Parameters   119
    5.2.6 Conversion of VAR Parameters   121
5.3 Assessing VAR Precision   122
    5.3.1 The Problem of Measurement Errors   122
    5.3.2 Estimation Errors in Means and Variances   123
    5.3.3 Estimation Error in Sample Quantiles   125
    5.3.4 Comparison of Methods   126
5.4 Conclusions   128

Chapter 6.

Backtesting VAR Models   129

6.1 Setup for Backtesting   130
    6.1.1 An Example   130
    6.1.2 Which Return?   131
6.2 Model Backtesting with Exceptions   132
    6.2.1 Model Verification Based on Failure Rates   132
    6.2.2 The Basel Rules   136
    6.2.3 Conditional Coverage Models   140

6.3 Model Verification: Other Approaches 142
    6.3.1 Distribution Forecast Models 142
    6.3.2 Parametric Models 143
    6.3.3 Comparison of Methods 144
6.4 Conclusions 145

Chapter 7.

Portfolio Risk: Analytical Methods 147

7.1 Portfolio VAR 148
7.2 VAR Tools 153
    7.2.1 Marginal VAR 154
    7.2.2 Incremental VAR 155
    7.2.3 Component VAR 159
    7.2.4 Summary 161
7.3 Examples 162
    7.3.1 A Global Portfolio Equity Report 163
    7.3.2 Barings: An Example in Risks 165
7.4 Simplifying the Covariance Matrix 167
    7.4.1 Why Simplifications? 167
    7.4.2 Zero VAR Measures 168
    7.4.3 Diagonal Model 169
    7.4.4 Factor Models 171
    7.4.5 Comparison of Methods 175
7.5 Conclusions 177
    Appendix 7A: Matrix Multiplication 178
    Appendix 7B (Advanced): Principal-Component Analysis 179

Chapter 8.

Forecasting Risks and Correlations 183

8.1 Time-Varying Risk or Outliers? 184
8.2 Modeling Time-Varying Risk 186
    8.2.1 Moving Averages 186
    8.2.2 GARCH Estimation 187
    8.2.3 Long-Horizon Forecasts with GARCH 189
    8.2.4 The RiskMetrics Approach 193

8.3 Modeling Correlation   196

    8.3.1 Moving Averages   196

    8.3.2 Exponential Averages   197

    8.3.3 Crashes and Correlations   198

8.4 Using Options Data   199

    8.4.1 Implied Volatilities   200

    8.4.2 ISD as Risk Forecasts   200

8.5 Conclusions   202

Part Three.

VALUE-AT-RISK SYSTEMS   203

Chapter 9.

VAR Methods   205

9.1 Local versus Full Valuation   206

    9.1.1 Delta-Normal Valuation   206

    9.1.2 Full Valuation   209

    9.1.3 Delta-Gamma Approximations (the "Greeks")   211

    9.1.4 Comparison of Methods   214

    9.1.5 An Example: Leeson's Straddle   215

9.2 Delta-Normal Method   219

    9.2.1 Implementation   219

    9.2.2 Advantages   220

    9.2.3 Problems   220

9.3 Historical Simulation Method   221

    9.3.1 Implementation   221

    9.3.2 Advantages   222

    9.3.3 Problems   223

9.4 Monte Carlo Simulation Method   224

    9.4.1 Implementation   224

    9.4.2 Advantages   225

    9.4.3 Problems   226

9.5 Empirical Comparisons   227

9.6 Summary   229

Chapter 10.

Stress Testing   231

10.1 Why Stress Testing?   232
10.2 Implementing Scenario Analysis   235
10.3 Generating Unidimensional Scenarios   235
    10.3.1 Stylized Scenarios   235
    10.3.2 An Example: The SPAN System   237
10.4 Multidimensional Scenario Analysis   239
    10.4.1 Unidimensional versus Multidimensional   239
    10.4.2 Prospective Scenarios   239
    10.4.3 Factor Push Method   240
    10.4.4 Conditional Scenario Method   240
    10.4.5 Historical Scenarios   242
    10.4.6 Systematic Scenarios   245
10.5 Stress-Testing Model Parameters   245
10.6 Managing Stress Tests   247
    10.6.1 Scenario Analysis and Risk Models   247
    10.6.2 Management Response   247
10.7 Conclusions   248
    Appendix: Extreme Value Theory   249

Chapter 11.

Implementing Delta-Normal VAR   255

11.1 Overview   256
11.2 Application to Currencies   257
11.3 Choosing "Primitive" Securities   259
    11.3.1 Lessons from Exchanges   262
    11.3.2 Specific Risk   263
11.4 Fixed-Income Portfolios   264
    11.4.1 Mapping Approaches   264
    11.4.2 Risk Factors   264
    11.4.3 Comparison of Mapping Approaches   266
    11.4.4 Assigning Weights to Vertices   269
    11.4.5 Benchmarking a Portfolio   271

11.5 Linear Derivatives   274

    11.5.1 Forward Contracts   274

    11.5.2 Commodity Forwards   278

    11.5.3 Forward Rate Agreements   279

    11.5.4 Interest Rate Swaps   282

11.6 Derivatives: Options   285

11.7 Equity Portfolios   287

Chapter 12.

Simulation Methods   291

12.1 Simulations with One Random Variable   292

    12.1.1 Simulating a Price Path   292

    12.1.2 Creating Random Numbers   295

    12.1.3 The Bootstrap   296

    12.1.4 Computing VAR   298

    12.1.5 Risk Management and Pricing Methods   298

12.2 Speed versus Accuracy   299

    12.2.1 Accuracy   300

    12.2.2 Acceleration Methods   301

12.3 Simulations with Multiple Variables   302

    12.3.1 From Independent to Correlated Variables   302

    12.3.2 The Cholesky Factorization   303

    12.3.3 Number of Independent Factors   304

12.4 Deterministic Simulation   306

12.5 Scenario Simulation   307

12.6 Choosing the Model   309

12.7 Conclusions   311

Chapter 13.

Credit Risk   313

13.1 The Nature of Credit Risk   314

    13.1.1 Sources of Risk   314

    13.1.2 Credit Risk as a Short Option   316

    13.1.3 Time and Portfolio Effects   316

13.2 Default Risk   318
    13.2.1 Default Rates   318
    13.2.2 Recovery Rates   321
    13.2.3 Estimating Default Risk   321
13.3 Credit Exposure   323
    13.3.1 Bonds versus Derivatives   323
    13.3.2 Expected and Worst Exposure   325
13.4 Netting Arrangements   327
13.5 Measuring and Managing Credit Risk   329
    13.5.1 Expected and Unexpected Credit Loss   329
    13.5.2 Pricing Credit Risk   330
    13.5.3 Portfolio Credit Risk   332
    13.5.4 Managing Credit Risk   333
    13.5.5 Horizon and Confidence Level   334
13.6 The Basel Risk Charges for Derivatives   334
13.7 Portfolio Credit Risk Models   336
13.8 Conclusions   337

Chapter 14.

Liquidity Risk   339

14.1 Defining Liquidity Risk   340
    14.1.1 Asset Liquidity Risk   340
    14.1.2 Funding Liquidity Risk   342
14.2 Dealing with Asset Liquidity Risk   343
    14.2.1 Bid-Ask Spread Cost   344
    14.2.2 Trading Strategies   346
    14.2.3 Practical Issues   349
14.3 Gauging Funding Liquidity Risk   351
14.4 Lessons from LTCM   352
    14.4.1 LTCM's Leverage   353
    14.4.2 LTCM's "Bulletproofing"   353
    14.4.3 LTCM's Downfall   354
    14.4.4 LTCM's Liquidity   355
14.5 Conclusions   357

Part Four.

APPLICATIONS OF RISK-MANAGEMENT SYSTEMS   359

Chapter 15.

Using VAR to Measure and Control Risk   361

15.1 Who Can Use VAR?   363
    15.1.1 The Trend to Global Risk Management   363
    15.1.2 Proprietary Trading Desks   365
    15.1.3 Nonfinancial Corporations   366
15.2 VAR as an Information-Reporting Tool   370
    15.2.1 Why Risk-Management Disclosures?   371
    15.2.2 Trends in Disclosure   373
    15.2.3 Disclosure Examples   375
15.3 VAR as a Risk-Control Tool   376
    15.3.1 Adjusting Firm-Wide VAR   377
    15.3.2 Adjusting Unit-Level VAR   379
15.4 Conclusions   381

Chapter 16.

Using VAR for Active Risk Management   383

16.1 Risk Capital   384
    16.1.1 VAR as Risk Capital   384
    16.1.2 Choosing the Confidence Level   385
16.2 Risk-Adjusted Performance Measurement   387
16.3 Earnings-Based RAPM Methods   389
16.4 VAR-Based RAPM Methods   391
16.5 Firm-Wide Performance Measurement   394
16.6 VAR as a Strategic Tool   398
    16.6.1 Shareholder Value Analysis   398
    16.6.2 Choosing the Discount Rate   400
    16.6.3 Implementing SVA   401
16.7 Conclusions   402
    Appendix: A Closer Look at Economic Capital   403

Chapter 17.

VAR in Investment Management   407

17.1 Is VAR Applicable to Investment Management?   408
17.2 What Are the Risks?   410
    17.2.1 Absolute and Relative Risks   411
    17.2.2 Policy Mix and Active Management Risk   411
    17.2.3 Funding Risk   413
    17.2.4 Sponsor Risk   414
17.3 Using VAR to Monitor and Control Risks   415
    17.3.1 Using VAR to Check Compliance   416
    17.3.2 Using VAR to Design Guidelines   417
    17.3.3 Using VAR to Monitor Risk   418
    17.3.4 The Role of the Global Custodian   419
    17.3.5 The Role of the Money Manager   420
17.4 Using VAR to Manage Risks   420
    17.4.1 Strategic Asset Allocation   420
    17.4.2 VAR as a Guide to Investment Decisions   422
    17.4.3 VAR for Risk-Adjusted Returns   424
    17.4.4 Risk Budgeting   425
17.5 The Risk Standards   426
17.6 Conclusions   428

Chapter 18.

The Technology of Risk   431

18.1 Systems   432
18.2 The Need for Integration   434
18.3 The Risk-Management Industry   438
18.4 How to Structure VAR Reports   442
18.5 An Application   443
18.6 Conclusions   445

Chapter 19.

Operational Risk Management   447

19.1 The Importance of Operational Risk   448
19.2 Defining Operational Risk   449

19.3 Approaches to Operational Risk   451
19.4 Measuring Operational Risk   452
      19.4.1 Top-Down versus Bottom-Up Approaches   453
      19.4.2 Loss Distributions   453
      19.4.3 The Data Challenge   457
19.5 Managing Operational Risk   459
      19.5.1 Expected versus Unexpected Losses   460
      19.5.2 Controlling Operational Risk   460
      19.5.3 Funding Operational Risk   461
19.6 Conclusions   462
      Appendix: Constructing Loss Distributions   463

Chapter 20.

Integrated Risk Management   467

20.1 The Galaxy of Risks   468
20.2 Event Risks   469
      20.2.1 Legal Risk   469
      20.2.2 Reputational Risk   470
      20.2.3 Disaster Risk   470
      20.2.4 Regulatory and Political Risk   470
20.3 Integrated Risk Management   472
      20.3.1 Measuring Firm-Wide Risk   472
      20.3.2 Controlling Firm-Wide Risk   473
      20.3.3 Managing Firm-Wide Risk: The Final Frontier   474
20.4 Why Risk Management?   475
      20.4.1 Why Bother?   475
      20.4.2 Why Hedge?   477
20.5 Conclusions   478

Part Five.

THE RISK-MANAGEMENT PROFESSION 481

Chapter 21.

Risk Management: Guidelines and Pitfalls 483

21.1 Milestone Documents in Risk Management 484

    21.1.1 "Best Practices" Recommendations from G-30 484

    21.1.2 The Bank of England Report on Barings 486

    21.1.3 The CRMPG Report on LTCM 486

21.2 Limitations of VAR 488

    21.2.1 Risk of Exceedences 488

    21.2.2 Changing Positions Risks 488

    21.2.3 Event and Stability Risks 489

    21.2.4 Transition Risk 491

    21.2.5 Data-Inadequacy Risks 492

    21.2.6 Model Risks 492

21.3 Side Effects of VAR 498

    21.3.1 The "Man in the White Coat" Syndrome 498

    21.3.2 Traders Gaming the System 499

    21.3.3 Dynamic Hedging 502

21.4 Risk-Management Lessons from LTCM 503

    21.4.1 LTCM's Risk Controls 503

    21.4.2 Portfolio Optimization 504

    21.4.3 LTCM's Short Option Position 507

21.5 Conclusions 508

Chapter 22.

Conclusions 511

22.1 The Evolution of Risk Management 512

22.2 The Role of the Risk Manager 513

    22.2.1 Controlling Trading 513

    22.2.2 Organizational Guidelines 514

    22.2.3 Risk Managers 516

22.3 VAR Revisited 517

REFERENCES 521

INDEX 531

PREFACE

THE RISK MANAGEMENT REVOLUTION

Risk management has truly experienced a revolution in the last few years. This was started by *value at risk* (VAR), a new method to measure financial market risk that was developed in response to the financial disasters of the early 1990s. By now, the VAR methodology has spread well beyond derivatives and is totally changing the way institutions approach their financial risk.

The first edition of this book provided the first comprehensive description of value at risk. It quickly established itself as an indispensable reference on VAR, and has been called the "industry standard." Translations into Chinese, Hungarian, Japanese, Korean, Polish, Portuguese, and Spanish soon followed.

The last few years, however, have seen such advances in the field of risk management that a new edition became necessary. Initially confined to *measuring* market risk, VAR is now being used to *control* and *manage* risk actively, both *credit risk* and *operational risk*. The VAR methodology is now leading to the holy grail of firm-wide risk management.

This book is a completely revised version of the previous edition. The revision parallels the enormous increase in the body of knowledge in risk management. Just the number of references, for instance, has ballooned from 80 to more than 200. For many of these, the book now provides Web addresses for convenient updates.

Brand new chapters have been added on the topics of backtesting, stress testing, liquidity risk, operational risk, and integrated risk management. Applications of VAR have also been further developed, with separate chapters on using VAR to measure and control risk, to manage risk, and in investment management. An entire chapter is devoted to the technology of risk. The last chapters describe the rapidly evolving function of the financial risk manager. The text also contains new material on principal components, extreme value theory, and loss distributions.

Since the last edition, unfortunately, there have been new occurrences of financial disasters. This book draws lessons from these crises, in particular from *Long-Term Capital Management* (LTCM). Finally, the book has thoroughly updated the relevant regulatory requirements and now uses terms and definitions that have become industry standards. All in all, the book has been expanded more than 60 percent.

The broader scope of this book is reflected in its new subtitle. It has been changed from *The New Benchmark for Controlling Market Risk* to *The New Benchmark for Managing Financial Risk*.

WHAT IS VAR?

VAR (value at risk) traces its roots to the infamous financial disasters of the early 1990s that engulfed Orange County, Barings, Metallgesellschaft, Daiwa, and so many others. The common lesson of these disasters is that billions of dollars can be lost because of poor supervision and management of financial risks. Spurred into action, financial institutions and regulators turned to value at risk, an easy-to-understand method for quantifying market risk.

What is VAR? VAR is a method of assessing risk that uses standard statistical techniques routinely used in other technical fields. Formally, *VAR measures the worst expected loss over a given horizon under normal market conditions at a given confidence level.* Based on firm scientific foundations, VAR provides users with a summary measure of market risk. For instance, a bank might say that the daily VAR of its trading portfolio is $35 million at the 99 percent confidence level. In other words, there is only 1 chance in a 100, under normal market conditions, for a loss greater than $35 million to occur. This single number summarizes the bank's exposure to market risk as well as the probability of an adverse move. Equally important, it measures risk using the same units as the bank's bottom line—dollars. Shareholders and managers can then decide whether they feel comfortable with this level of risk. If the answer is no, the process that led to the computation of VAR can be used to decide where to trim the risk.

In contrast with traditional risk measures, VAR provides an aggregate view of a portfolio's risk that accounts for leverage, correlations, and current positions. As a result, it is truly a forward-looking risk measure. VAR, however, applies not only to derivatives but to all financial instruments. Furthermore, the methodology can also be broadened from market risk to other types of financial risks.

The VAR revolution has been brought about by a convergence of factors. These include (1) the pressure from regulators for better control of financial risks, (2) the globalization of financial markets, which has led to exposure to more sources of risk, and (3) technological advances, which have made enterprise-wide risk management a not-so-distant reality.

WHO CAN USE VAR?

Basically, VAR should be used by any institution exposed to financial risk. We can classify applications of VAR methods as follows.

- *Passive: information reporting* The earliest application of VAR was for measuring aggregate risk. VAR can be used to apprise senior management of the risks run by trading and investment operations. VAR also communicates the financial risks of a corporation to its shareholders in nontechnical, user-friendly terms.
- *Defensive: controlling risk* The next step was to use VAR to set position limits for traders and business units. The advantage of VAR is that it creates a common denominator with which to compare risky activities in diverse markets.
- *Active: managing risk* VAR is now increasingly used to allocate capital across traders, business units, products, and even to the whole institution. This process starts with adjusting returns for risk. *Risk-adjusted performance measures* (RAPM) automatically correct incentives for traders to take on extra risk due to the optionlike feature of bonuses. Once implemented, risk-based capital charges can guide the institution toward a better risk/return profile. The VAR methodology can also assist portfolio managers in making better decisions by offering a comprehensive view of the impact of a trade on portfolio risk. Ultimately, it will help to create greater *shareholder value added* (SVA).

As a result, VAR is being adopted en masse by institutions all over the world. These include:

- *Financial institutions* Banks with large trading portfolios have been at the vanguard of risk management. Institutions that deal with numerous sources of financial risk and complicated instruments are now implementing centralized risk management systems. Those that do not expose themselves to expensive failures, such as those that occurred with Barings and Daiwa.
- *Regulators* The prudential regulation of financial institutions requires the maintenance of minimum levels of capital as reserves against financial risks. The Basel Committee on Banking Supervision, the U.S. Federal Reserve Bank, the U.S. Securities and Exchange Commission, and regulators in the European Union have converged on VAR as a benchmark risk measure.
- *Nonfinancial corporations* Centralized risk management is useful to any corporation that has exposure to financial risks. Multinationals, for instance, have cash inflows and outflows de-

nominated in many currencies, and suffer from adverse currency swings. "Cash flow at risk analysis" can be used to tell how likely a firm will be to face a critical shortfall of funds.

- *Asset managers*   Institutional investors are now turning to VAR to manage their financial risks. The director of the Chrysler pension fund, for instance, stated that after the purchase of a VAR system, "We can now view our total capital at risk on a portfolio basis, by asset class and by individual manager. Our main goal was to . . . have the means to evaluate our portfolio risk going forward."

VAR also has direct implications for the recent crisis in Asia. One widespread interpretation is that the crisis was made worse by the "opacity" and poor risk-management practices of financial institutions. If this theory is correct, VAR systems would have helped. Professor Dornbusch (1998a) recently argued that "An effective supervisory system would, at the least, put in place a mandatory VAR analysis not only for the individual financial institutions (as is in place in the US, for example) but in fact for the entire country." By drawing attention to potentially dangerous scenarios, a VAR analysis would induce countries to consider hedging foreign currency liabilities, lengthening debt maturities, and taking other measures to reduce risk levels. Some have even proposed judging the credibility of central banks by asking them to report their VAR.[1]

Many derivatives and banking disasters could have been avoided if reporting systems had been more transparent. Time and again, losses are allowed to accumulate because positions are reported at book value, or at cost. When market values are available, this is inexcusable. Simply marking-to-market brings attention to potential problems. VAR goes one step further, asking what could happen under changes in market values.

In the end, the greatest benefit of VAR probably lies in the imposition of a structured methodology for critically thinking about risk. Institutions that go through the process of computing their VAR are forced to confront their exposure to financial risks and set up an independent risk-management function supervising the front and back offices. Thus the process of getting to VAR may be as important as the number itself. Indeed, judicious use of VAR may have avoided many of the financial dis-

---

[1]See Blejer and Schumacher (1999).

asters experienced over the past years. There is no doubt that VAR is here to stay.

PURPOSE OF THE BOOK

The purpose of this book is to provide a comprehensive presentation of the measurement and applications of value at risk. It is targeted to practitioners, students, and academics interested in understanding the recent revolution in financial risk management. This book can also serve as a text for advanced graduate seminars on risk management. The first edition, for instance, has been used in business schools all over the world.

To reap maximum benefit from this book, readers should have had the equivalent of an MBA-level class on investments. In particular, readers should have some familiarity with concepts of probability distribution, statistical analysis, and portfolio risk. Prior exposure to derivatives and the fixed-income market is also a plus. The book provides a brief review of these concepts, then extends the analysis in the direction of measuring aggregate financial risks.

The variety of these topics reflects the fundamental nature of risk management, which is *integration*. Risk managers must be thoroughly familiar with a variety of financial markets, with the intricacies of the trading process, and with financial and statistical modeling. Risk management integrates fixed-income markets, currency markets, equity markets, and commodity markets. In each of these, financial instruments must be decomposed into fundamental building blocks, then reassembled for risk measurement purposes. No doubt this is why risk management has been called "the theory of particle finance." All of this information then coalesces into one single number, a firm's VAR.

The approach to this book reflects the trend and motivation to VAR. As VAR is based on firm scientific foundations, I have adopted a rigorous approach to the topic. Yet the presentation is kept short and entertaining. Whenever possible, important concepts are illustrated with examples. In particular, the recent string of financial disasters provides a wealth of situations that illustrate various facets of financial risks. These can serve as powerful object lessons in the need for better risk management.

STRUCTURE OF THE BOOK

The book is broadly divided into five parts:

1. *Motivation.* Chapters 1 to 3 describe the evolving environment that has led to the widespread acceptance of VAR.
2. *Building blocks.* Chapters 4 to 8 provide a statistical and financial foundation for the quantification of risk.
3. *Value-at-risk systems.* Chapters 9 to 14 compare and analyze in detail various approaches to financial risk measurement.
4. *Applications of risk-management systems.* Chapters 15 to 20 discuss applications of VAR systems, from measuring risk to managing market risk to enterprise-wide risk-management.
5. *The risk-management profession.* Finally, the last two chapters, 21 and 22, discuss common pitfalls in risk management and provide some thought on the rapid evolution of the risk-management profession.

Chapters 6, 10, 14, 16, 17, 18, 19, and 20 are completely new to this edition. Most other chapters have been substantially improved. Chapters 5 and 6, which in the last edition introduced fixed-income markets and derivatives, have been dropped, as they were relatively elementary.

Going into more detail concerning the structure of the book, Chapter 1 paints a broad picture of the evolution of risk management, which is inextricably linked to the growth of the derivatives markets. The chapter describes the types of financial risks facing corporations and provides a brief introduction to VAR.

Chapter 2 draws lessons from recent financial disasters. It presents the stories of Barings, Metallgesellschaft, Orange County, and Daiwa. The only constant across these hapless cases is the absence of consistent risk-management policies. These losses have led to increasing regulatory activity as well as notable private-sector responses, such as J.P. Morgan's RiskMetrics systems.[2]

Chapter 3 analyzes recent regulatory initiatives for using VAR. We discuss the Basel Agreement and the Capital Adequacy Directive imposed by the European Union, both of which use VAR to determine minimum capital requirements for commercial banks. The regulation of other insti-

---

[2]RiskMetrics and CreditMetrics are trademarks of J.P. Morgan. CorporateMetrics is a trademark of the Riskmetrics Group.

tutions, pension funds, insurance companies, and securities firms is also briefly presented.

Chapter 4 explains how to characterize financial risks. We discuss risk and returns and the statistical concepts that underlie the measurement of VAR. Initially, only one source of financial risk is considered.

Chapter 5 turns to a formal definition of VAR. We show how VAR can be estimated from a normal distribution or from a completely general distribution. The chapter also discusses the choice of quantitative parameters, such as the confidence level and target horizon.

Next, Chapter 6 turns to the verification of VAR models. Backtesting consists of systematically matching the history of VAR forecasts with their associated portfolio returns. This process enables the checking of the accuracy of VAR forecasts and also provides ideas for model improvement.

Chapter 7 then turns to analytical methods for portfolio risk. We show how to build VAR using a variance-covariance matrix. To manage risk, however, we also need to understand what will reduce it. Thus the chapter provides a new analysis of VAR tools, such as marginal VAR, incremental VAR, and component VAR. These tools have become essential to control and manage portfolio risk. Given that the dimensions of VAR risk structures can quickly become cumbersome, we also discuss methods to simplify the covariance matrix used in VAR computations.

Chapter 8 discusses the measurement of dynamic inputs. The chapter covers the latest developments in the modeling of volatility and correlations, including moving averages and GARCH. Particular attention is paid to the model used by RiskMetrics.

The next six chapters turn to the measurement of VAR for complex portfolios. Chapter 9 first compares the different methods available to compute VAR. The first and easiest method is the *delta-normal* approach, which assumes that all instruments are linear combinations of primitive factors and relies on delta valuation. For nonlinear instruments, however, the linear approximation is inadequate. Instead, risk should be measured with a full valuation method, such as *historical simulation* or *Monte Carlo simulation*. The chapter discusses the pros and cons of each method, as well as situations where some methods are more appropriate.

Chapter 10 is an entirely new chapter devoted to *stress testing,* which has received increased attention recently and is a complement to traditional probability-based VAR methods.

Chapter 11 develops applications of the delta-normal method, sometimes called the *variance-covariance method*. We show how to decompose portfolios of bonds, derivatives, and equities into sets of payoffs on "primitive" factors for the purpose of computing VAR.

Chapter 12 then turns to simulation methods. Monte Carlo methods simulate risk factors with random numbers, from which complex portfolios can be priced. Because of its flexibility, Monte Carlo is by far the most powerful method to compute value at risk. It can potentially account for a wide range of risks, including price risk, volatility risk, credit risk, and model risk. This flexibility, however, comes at a heavy cost in terms of intellectual and systems development.

Chapter 13 tackles an increasingly important topic, the quantitative measurement of credit risk. Credit risk encompasses both default risk and market risk. The potential loss on a derivatives contract, for instance, depends both on the value of the contract and on the possibility of default. It is only recently that the banking industry has learned to measure credit risk in the context of a portfolio. Once measured, credit risk can be managed and better diversified, like any financial risk.

One of the lessons of the LTCM disaster is the importance of liquidity risk. This is why Chapter 14 is an entirely new chapter devoted to this topic.

The next six chapters are new, dealing with applications of VAR, a topic barely touched upon in the first edition of the book. Applications range from passive to defensive to active. Chapter 15 shows how VAR can be used to quantify and to control risk, while Chapter 16 explains how VAR can be used to manage risk actively. For the first time, institutions have a consistent measure of risk that can be used to compute risk-adjusted performance measures such as risk-adjusted return on capital (RAROC). This is because VAR can be viewed as a measure of "economic" risk capital necessary to support a position.

VAR applications are not limited to the banking sector, however. VAR is now slowly spreading to the investment management industry, as it provides a consistent method for setting risk limits and risk budgeting. Applications, however, must be tailored to the specific needs of this industry.

Chapter 18 discusses the technology of risk, an oft-neglected topic. This ranges from the choice of a spreadsheet to large systems that support strategic business initiatives. Global risk-management systems require a central repository for trades, positions, and valuation models, which allow institutions to measure and manage their risk profile most efficiently.

Chapter 19 then discusses operational risk, which has defied attempts at quantification until recently. We are learning to quantify such risks using tools borrowed from the insurance industry and from VAR techniques. Once quantified, operational risk can be subject to controls and capital charges.

The final step is to put together market, credit, and operational risk. Integration of these risks is important, as financial risks tend to slip toward areas where they are not measured. Thus the ideas behind the VAR revolution are quickly spreading to *enterprise-wide risk management,* which is described in Chapter 20.

For all their technical elegance, VAR methods do not, and are not designed to, measure catastrophic risks. Chapter 21 discusses pitfalls in the interpretation of value at risk. We discuss a notable failure of a supposedly sophisticated risk-management system, that of LTCM. This is why risk management is still as much an art as a science.

Finally, Chapter 22 offers some concluding thoughts. Once the domain of a few exclusive pioneers, risk management is now wholly embraced by the financial industry. It is also spreading fast among the corporate world. As a result, the financial risk manager function is now acquiring strategic importance within the corporate structure.

By promoting sound risk-management practices, this book will hopefully continue to foster a safer environment in financial markets.

Philippe Jorion
Irvine, California

ACKNOWLEDGMENTS

This book has benefited from the comments of numerous practitioners and academics. In particular, I would like to thank James Overdahl, of the Office of the Comptroller and Currency, for his detailed review of the first version of this book. This original project also benefited from the help of Lester Seigel, formerly at the World Bank, and of Jacob Boudoukh, at New York University.

The success of the first edition of this book is also largely attributable to its readers. In particular, the *Global Association of Risk Professionals* (GARP) was kind enough to select this book as the main text for its fast-expanding *Financial Risk Manager* (FRM) examination.

The second edition of this book has also been enriched by discussions with Robert Ceske at NetRisk, Till Guldimann, formerly of J.P. Morgan and now at Infinity, Leo de Bever and his crew at Ontario Teachers' Pension Plan, Raza Hasan at Merrill Lynch, Dan Rosen at Algorithmics, Barry Schachter at Chase Manhattan, Deborah Williams at Meridien Research, and many others. Todd Wolter, now at Credit Suisse Asset Management, provided solid research support during the project. My apologies to anyone I inadvertently missed. Needless to say, I assume responsibility for any remaining errors.

PART ONE

Motivation

CHAPTER 1

The Need for Risk Management

All of life is the management of risk, not its elimination.

Walter Wriston, former chairman of Citicorp

Corporations are in the business of managing risks. The most adept ones succeed; others fail. Whereas some firms passively accept financial risks, others attempt to create a competitive advantage by judicious exposure to financial risks. In both cases, however, these risks should be monitored carefully because of their potential for damage.

This chapter motivates the need for careful management of financial risks. Section 1.1 describes the types of risks facing corporations and argues that financial risks have sharply increased since the breakdown of the fixed exchange rate system. It discusses the factors behind the growth of the risk-management industry. *Risk management* is the process by which various risk exposures are identified, measured, and controlled. Our understanding of risk has been much improved by the development of derivatives markets, which are described in Section 1.2. Value at risk (VAR) is one such recent advance. The main purpose of VAR systems is to assess market risks, which are due to changes in market prices. However, firms are also subject to other types of financial risks, which are discussed in Section 1.3. Finally, Section 1.4 provides a brief introduction to VAR.

1.1 FINANCIAL RISKS

What is exactly risk? *Risk* can be defined as the volatility of unexpected outcomes, generally the value of assets or liabilities of interest. Firms are exposed to various types of risks, which can be broadly classified into business and nonbusiness risks.

3

Business risks are those which the corporation willingly assumes to create a competitive advantage and add value for shareholders. Business, or operating, risk pertains to the product market in which a firm operates and includes technological innovations, product design, and marketing. Operating leverage, involving the degree of fixed versus variable costs, is also largely a choice variable. Judicious exposure to business risk is a "core competency" of all business activity. Business activities also include exposure to *macroeconomic risks,* which result from economic cycles, or fluctuations in incomes and monetary policies.

Other risks, over which firms have no control, can be grouped into *nonbusiness risks.* These include *strategic risks,* which result from fundamental shifts in the economy or political environment. An example is the rapid disappearance of the threat of the Soviet Union in the late 1980s, which led to a gradual decrease in defense spending, directly affecting defense industries. Expropriation and nationalization also fall under the umbrella of strategic risks. These risks are difficult to hedge, except by diversifying across business lines and countries.

Finally, *financial risks* can be defined as those which relate to possible losses in financial markets, such as losses due to interest rate movements or defaults on financial obligations. Exposure to financial risks can be optimized carefully so that firms can concentrate on what they do best—manage exposure to business risks.

In contrast to industrial corporations, the primary function of financial institutions is to manage financial risks actively. The purpose of financial institutions is to assume, intermediate, or advise on financial risks. These institutions realize that they must measure sources of risk as precisely as possible in order to control and properly price risks. Understanding risk means that financial managers can consciously plan for the consequences of adverse outcomes and, by so doing, be better prepared for the inevitable uncertainty.

1.1.1 Change: The Only Constant

The recent growth of the risk-management industry can be traced directly to the increased volatility of financial markets since the early 1970s. Consider the following developments:

- The fixed exchange rate system broke down in 1971, leading to flexible and volatile exchange rates.
- The oil-price shocks starting in 1973 were accompanied by high inflation and wild swings in interest rates.

- On Black Monday, October 19, 1987, U.S. stocks collapsed by 23 percent, wiping out $1 trillion in capital.
- The drive toward monetary unification in Europe was stalled temporarily by the blowup in the European monetary system in September 1992.
- In the bond debacle of 1994, the Federal Reserve Bank, after having kept interest rates low for 3 years, started a series of six consecutive interest rate hikes that erased $1.5 trillion in global capital.
- The Japanese stock price bubble finally deflated at the end of 1989, sending the Nikkei index from 39,000 to 17,000 3 years later. A total of $2.7 trillion in capital was lost, leading to an unprecedented financial crisis in Japan.
- The Asian turmoil of 1997 wiped off about three-fourth of the dollar capitalization of equities in Indonesia, Korea, Malaysia, and Thailand.
- The Russian default in August 1998 sparked a global financial crisis that culminated in the near failure of a big hedge fund, Long Term Capital Management.

The only constant across all these events is their unpredictability. Each time, market observers were aghast at the rapidity of these changes, which in many cases created substantial financial losses. Financial risk management provides a partial protection against such sources of risk.

To illustrate the forces of changes in the last 30 years, Figures 1–1 to 1–4 display movements in exchange rates, in interest rates, in oil prices, and in stock prices since 1962. Figure 1–1 displays movements in the U.S. dollar against the Deutsche mark (DM), the Japanese yen (JY), and the British pound (BP). In 30 years, the dollar has lost about two-thirds of its value against the yen and mark; the yen/$ rate has slid from 361 to less than 100, and the mark/$ rate has fallen from 4.2 to 1.5. On the other hand, the dollar has appreciated by 75 percent against the pound over the same period. In between, the dollar has reached dizzying heights, just to fall to unprecedented lows, in the process creating wild swings in the competitive advantage of nations—and nightmares for unhedged firms.

Figure 1–2 also shows that bond yields fluctuated widely in the 1980s, reflecting creeping inflationary pressures spreading throughout national economies. These were created in the 1960s by the United States,

F I G U R E   1 – 1

Movements in the dollar.

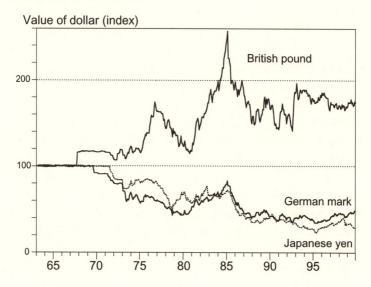

trying to finance the Vietnam War as well as a domestic government-assistance program, and spread to other countries through the rigid mechanism of fixed exchange rates. Eventually, the persistently high U.S. inflation led to the breakdown of the fixed exchange rate system and a sharp fall in the value of the dollar. In October 1979, the Federal Reserve Bank forcefully attempted to squash inflation. Interest rates immediately shot up, became more volatile, and led to a sustained appreciation of the dollar. Bond yields increased from 4 percent in the early 1960s to 15 percent at the height of the monetarist squeeze on the money supply, thereby creating havoc in savings and loans that had made long-term loans, primarily for housing, using short-term funding.

Figure 1–3 shows that oil prices also fluctuated widely. In addition, the sharp oil price increases of the 1970s seem correlated with increases in bond yields. These oil shocks also had an impact on national stock markets, which are displayed in Figure 1–4. Indeed, the great bear market of 1974–1975 was a global occurrence triggered by a threefold increase in the price of crude oil. This episode shows that it is difficult to understand financial risk without a good grasp of the links between interest rates, exchange rates, commodity prices, and stock markets.

FIGURE 1–2

Movements in U.S. interest rates.

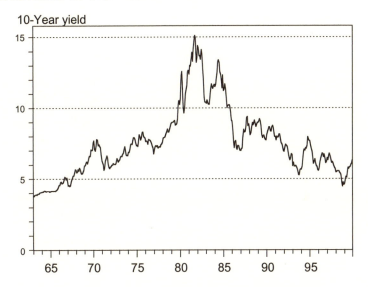

In addition to this unleashed volatility, firms generally have become more sensitive to movements in financial variables. Prior to the 1970s, banks were either heavily regulated or comfortably cartelized in most industrial countries. Regulations such as ceilings on interest rate deposits effectively insulated bankers from movements in interest rates. Industrial corporations, mainly selling in domestic markets, were not too concerned about exchange rates.

The call to reality came with deregulation and globalization. The 1970s witnessed a worldwide movement to market-oriented policies and deregulation of financial markets. *Deregulation* forced financial institutions to be more competitive and to become acutely aware of the need to address financial risk. Barriers to international trade and investment also were lowered. This *globalization* forced firms to recognize the truly global nature of competition. In the process, firms have become exposed to a greater variety of financial risks.

1.1.2 But Where Is Risk Coming From?

This begs the question of the origins of these risks. Risk comes from many sources. Risk can be human-created, such as business cycles, inflation,

FIGURE 1-3

Movements in oil prices.

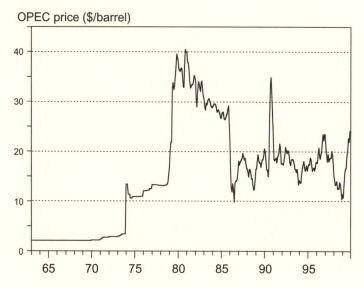

OPEC price ($/barrel)

changes in government policies, and wars. Risk also occurs from unforeseen natural phenomena, including weather and earthquakes. Risk also arises from the primary source of long-term economic growth, technological innovations, which can render existing technology obsolete and create dislocations in employment. Thus risk and the willingness to take risk are essential to the growth of our economy.

Much of the finance and insurance industry has been devoted to the creation of markets to share these risks. At the most basic level, the accumulation of assets, or savings, provides a cushion against income risk. The introduction of personal loans, first recorded in ancient Greece, allows smoothing of consumption through borrowing. Insurance contracts, which have been traced to the Babylonian system of robbery insurance for caravans, use diversification principles to protect against accidents and other disasters. Even the modern publicly held corporations can be viewed as an arrangement that allows investors to spread the risk of ownership in a company across the market as a whole.

Financial markets, however, cannot protect against all risks. Broad macroeconomic risks that create fluctuations in the level of income and

FIGURE 1—4

Movements in stock prices (local currency).

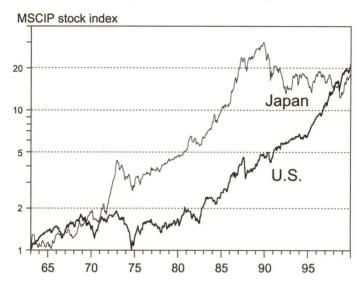

employment are difficult to hedge. This is why governments have created "safety nets" that the private sector cannot provide. In this sense, the welfare state can be viewed as a risk-sharing institution.

Governments, unfortunately, also can contribute to risks. The Asian crisis of 1997, for instance, has been broadly blamed on unsustainable economic policies that created havoc with a fragile financial sector. Time and again, government interference in the banking system seems to lead to systematic misallocation of credit that ultimately leads to banking crises. Also, countries that fix their exchange rate at an unrealistic level create serious imbalances in their domestic economies. This apparent stability encourages institutions to borrow excessively in foreign currencies, creating the conditions for a disaster out of a simple devaluation. This explains why large economies are now either letting their currency float freely or moving toward complete monetary integration, in the form of dollarization or a monetary union, such as in Europe.

A common currency, though, may not provide more stability, since it simply may shift the risk to another location. Giving up fluctuations in currencies in exchange for greater fluctuations in output and employment may not be a bargain.[1]

Going into the debate of the best outlet for these fundamental risks is beyond the scope of this book. These risks manifest themselves in financial risks or macroeconomic risks. What we do know is that fluctuations in market-determined financial prices generally can be hedged in financial markets. These fluctuations, existing or potential, require careful risk management.

1.1.3 The Toolbox of Risk Management

The increased volatility in exchange rates, interest rates, and commodity prices has created the need for new financial instruments and analytical tools for risk management. *Financial risk management* refers to the design and implementation of procedures for controlling financial risks.

Risk management has emerged as a response to the increased volatility in global financial markets. This was made possible through technological innovations.

Technological changes have arisen from advances on two fronts: physical equipment and finance theory. On the one hand, the advent of cheaper communications and computing power has led to innovations such as global 24-hour trading and online risk-management systems. On the other hand, breakthroughs in modern finance theory have allowed institutions to create, price, and control the risks of new financial instruments.

Table 1–1 describes the major developments in financial risk management, starting from the bond duration model and culminating in our current efforts at measuring firm-wide market, credit, and operational risk.

In fact, the methodology behind VAR is not new. It can be traced back to the basic mean-variance framework developed by Markowitz in 1952. What is new is the integration of all risks into a centralized common "metric."

Before we discuss the various types of financial risks that VAR models can and cannot address, we take a short detour explaining derivatives. These essential risk-management tools have helped us to refine our un-

---

1. Much of the discussion of the pros and cons of the European Monetary Union has been devoted to this issue of tradeoffs between various risks in a monetary union. See Paul De Grauwe (1997).

TABLE 1–1

The Evolution of Analytical Risk-
Management Tools

1938	Bond duration
1952	Markowitz mean-variance framework
1963	Sharpe's capital asset pricing model
1966	Multiple factor models
1973	Black-Scholes option pricing model, "Greeks"
1979	Binomial option model
1983	RAROC, risk-adjusted return
1986	Limits on exposure by duration bucket
1988	Risk-weighted assets for banks
	Limits on "Greeks"
1992	Stress testing
1993	Value at risk (VAR)
1994	RiskMetrics
1997	CreditMetrics, CreditRisk+
1998-	Integration of credit and market risk
2000-	Entreprisewide risk management

derstanding of risk. While VAR methods are particularly well suited to measuring derivatives risks, they are much broader than that, however. They truly apply to all financial instruments.

1.2 DERIVATIVES AND RISK MANAGEMENT

1.2.1 What Are Derivatives?

Derivatives are instruments designed to manage financial risks efficiently. A *derivative contract* can be defined generally as a private contract deriving its value from some *underlying* asset price, reference rate, or index—such as a stock, bond, currency, or commodity. Such a contract also specifies a *notional amount,* defined in terms of currency, shares, bushels, or some other unit.

In contrast to *securities,* such as stocks and bonds, which are issued to raise capital, derivatives are *contracts,* or private agreements, between two parties. This distinction is becoming blurred, however, because many securities can have derivatives-like characteristics.[2]

The simplest example of a derivative is a forward contract on a foreign currency, which is a promise to buy a fixed (notional) amount at a fixed price at some future date. Generally, the contract will have an initial value of zero, but it can generate gains or losses as the exchange rate (the underlying) evolves over time.

This derivative is economically equivalent to a position in the cash market, invested in the foreign currency, and financed by a domestic loan. Since there is no upfront cash flow, the instrument is *leveraged,* that is, involves borrowing. Intrinsically, however, it is no more risky than dealing in the underlying cash market. Once this is recognized, the risk of derivatives can be translated into risks of known quantities. This is one of the purposes of VAR.

The leverage, however, is a double-edged sword. It makes the derivative an efficient instrument for hedging and speculation, due to very low transaction costs. On the other hand, the absence of an upfront cash payment makes it more difficult to assess the potential downside. Hence derivatives risks have to be monitored carefully.

1.2.2 Types of Derivatives

Although derivatives have existed since the dawn of civilization, their use has blossomed since the early 1970s. Table 1–2 illustrates their widening coverage.

The breadth of coverage against risks is astonishing. Hedging with derivatives is similar to purchasing insurance; it provides protection against the adverse effect of variables over which businesses or countries have no control. The other side of hedging is that some of their counterparties may be speculators, who provide liquidity to the market in the hope of making profits on their transactions.

1.2.3 Derivatives Markets: How Big?

Derivatives markets can be classified into centralized exchanges, which provide a market for futures and options, and over-the-counter (OTC) mar-

---

2. The Financial Accounting Standards Board (1998) has issued formal definitions of derivatives for accounting purposes.

TABLE 1-2

The Evolution of Derivatives
Markets

1972	Foreign currency futures
1973	Equity options
1975	Treasury bond futures
1981	Currency swaps
1982	Interest rate swaps
	Eurodollar futures
	Equity index futures
	Exchange-listed currency options
1983	Options on equity index
	Options on T-note futures
	Options on currency futures
	Interest rate caps and floors
1985	Eurodollar options
	Swaptions
1987	Compound options
	Average options
1989	Futures on interest rate swaps
	Quanto options
1990	Equity index swaps
1991	Differential swaps
1992	Catastrophe risk insurance options
1993	Captions
1994	Credit default options
1996	Electricity futures
1997	Weather derivatives

kets. These markets are spreading rapidly. As recently as the mid-1980s, the futures industry was largely concentrated in Chicago. Now, futures exchanges can be found all over the world.

Table 1–3 describes the growth of selected derivatives instruments since 1986, focusing only on exchange-traded and swap instruments. The table shows the dollar value of *outstanding positions,* measured in notional amounts, which give some measure of the transfer of risk that occurs between cash and derivatives markets. Since 1986, these markets have grown from $1,083 billion to $72,000 billion currently, that is, $72 trillion.

TABLE 1-3

Global Markets for Selected Derivatives—Outstanding
Contracts ($ Billion)

	1986	1990	1995	1999
Exchange-traded instruments	583	2,292	9,189	13,501
Interest rate futures	370	1,454	5,863	7,897
Interest rate options	146	600	2,742	3,755
Currency futures	10	16	38	37
Currency options	39	56	43	22
Stock index futures	15	70	172	333
Stock index options	3	96	329	1,457
Selected OTC instruments	500	3,450	17,713	58,265
Interest rate swaps	400	2,312	12,811	44,732
Currency swaps	100	578	1,197	3,660
Caps, collars, floors, and swaptions	—	561	3,705	9,873
Total	1,083	5,742	26,902	71,766

Source: Bank for International Settlements. OTC market size is derived from the ISDA survey only. Swap data for 1999
assume the same distribution as in the prior year.

Due to their decentralized nature, data for OTC markets are more
difficult to collect. A more comprehensive survey by the Bank of
International Settlements (BIS) reveals that the total size of the market,
including foreign currency contracts, amounted to about $102 trillion in
December 1999.

On the surface, these numbers are amazing. The annual gross national product of the entire United States was only $9 trillion at the time.
The derivatives markets are greater than the value of global stocks and
bonds, which total around $70 trillion.

For risk-management purposes, however, these numbers are highly
misleading. Notional amounts do not describe market risks. If all these
contracts were canceled—an unlikely event—the BIS estimates that the
replacement value for all OTC contracts would only be 3.2 percent of
their notional amounts, which is $2.8 trillion.

Even this number is still inadequate, since many of these positions
are hedging one another, including cash market risks. In addition, what
matters is not only the current market value but also the potential changes
in market values. This is precisely what VAR attempts to measure.

Nevertheless, the size of this market is astonishing, especially when one considers that financial derivatives have existed only for about 25 years. The first financial futures were launched in Chicago on May 16, 1972. This was a propitious time for currency futures, since exchange rates were just starting to float. Still, many observers were not convinced of the need for derivatives.[3]

By now, most observers realize that these markets provide an essential mechanism to exchange financial risks. Since they allow risks to be transferred to those best able to bear them, one can argue that they actually lower the total amount of risk in the global economy.

On the downside, the technology behind the creation of ever-more complex derivatives instruments seems at times to have advanced faster than our ability to control it. While the 1980s witnessed a proliferation of derivatives, a string of highly publicized derivatives disasters in the early 1990s has led to a much-needed emphasis on risk control. We now turn to a more detailed description of financial risks.

1.3 TYPES OF FINANCIAL RISKS

VAR was developed initially to deal with one aspect of financial risk, market risk. It should be recognized, however, that there are many other aspects of financial risk. Generally, financial risks are classified into the broad categories of market risks, credit risks, liquidity risks, operational risks, and sometimes legal risks.[4] As we will show, these risks may interact with each other.

1.3.1 Market Risk

Market risk arises from movements in the level or volatility of market prices. VAR tools now allow users to quantify market risk in a systematic fashion.

Market risk can take two forms: *absolute risk,* measured in dollar terms (or in the relevant currency), and *relative risk,* measured relative to

---

3. Most notably, Nobel Prize winner Paul Samuelson said the idea of currency futures would fall of its own weight, would tend to create volatility, and would add no net value. Powers (1992) writes a fascinating description of the introduction of currency futures by the Chicago Mercantile Exchange.

4. For an overview of different types of financial risks, see Basel Committee on Banking Supervision (1994), *Risk Management Guidelines for Derivatives.*

a benchmark index. While the former focuses on the volatility of total returns, the latter measures risk in terms of *tracking error,* or deviation from the index.

Market risk can be classified into directional and nondirectional risks. *Directional risks* involve exposures to the direction of movements in financial variables, such as stock prices, interest rates, exchange rates, and commodity prices. These exposures are measured by linear approximations such as *beta* for exposure to stock market movements, *duration* for exposure to interest rates, and *delta* for exposure of options to the underlying asset price.

Nondirectional risks, then, involve the remaining risks, which consist of nonlinear exposures and exposures to hedged positions or to volatilities. Second-order or quadratic exposures are measured by *convexity* when dealing with interest rates and *gamma* when dealing with options. *Basis risk* is created from unanticipated movements in relative prices of assets in a hedged position, such as cash and futures or interest rate spreads. Finally, *volatility risk* measures exposure to movements in the actual or implied volatility.

Market risk is controlled by limits on notionals, exposures, VAR measures, and independent supervision by risk managers.

1.3.2 Credit Risk

Credit risk originates from the fact that counterparties may be unwilling or unable to fulfill their contractual obligations. Its effect is measured by the cost of replacing cash flows if the other party defaults. This loss encompasses the *exposure,* or amount at risk, and the *recovery rate,* which is the proportion paid back to the lender, usually measured in terms of "cents on the dollar."

Losses due to credit risk, however, can occur before the actual default. More generally, *credit risk* should be defined as the potential loss in mark-to-market value that may be incurred due to the occurrence of a credit event. A *credit event* occurs when there is a change in the counterparty's ability to perform its obligations. Thus changes in market prices of debt, due to changes in credit ratings or in the market's perception of default, also can be viewed as credit risk, creating some overlap between credit risk and market risk.

Bonds, loans, and derivatives are all exposed to credit risk. Traditionally, credit exposures could be measured easily as the face value of the debt. With derivatives such as swaps, however, the credit exposure is much less because the initial value of the swap is generally zero. Instead, the exposure is the change in the value of the position, if positive when a default occurs. Thus, measuring credit risk on swaps involves a detailed analysis of the relationship between market risk and credit risk.

Credit risk also includes *sovereign risk*. This occurs, for instance, when countries impose foreign-exchange controls that make it impossible for counterparties to honor their obligations. Whereas default risk is generally company-specific, sovereign risk is country-specific.

One particular form of credit risk is *settlement risk,* which occurs when two payments are exchanged the same day. This risk arises when the counterparty may default after the institution already made its payment. On settlement day, the exposure to counterparty default equals the full value of the payments due. In contrast, the presettlement exposure is only the netted value of the two payments.

Settlement risk is very real for foreign-exchange transactions, which involve exchange of payments in different currencies at different times, such as in the morning in Europe against delivery in the United States later. Indeed, when Herstatt Bank went bankrupt in 1974, it had received payments from a number of counterparties but defaulted before payments were made on the other legs of the transaction, thus potentially destabilizing the global banking system. This bank failure was the impetus for the creation of the Basel Committee on Banking Supervision, which 15 years later promulgated capital adequacy requirements for the banking system.

Credit risk is controlled by credit limits on notionals, current and potential exposures, and, increasingly, credit-enhancement features such as requiring collateral of marking-to-market. The methodologic advances in quantifying market risk are now being extended to credit risk.

1.3.3 Liquidity Risk

Liquidity risk takes two forms, asset liquidity risk and funding liquidity risk. *Asset liquidity risk,* also known as *market/product liquidity risk,* arises when a transaction cannot be conducted at prevailing market prices due to the size of the position relative to normal trading lots. This risk varies across categories of assets and across time as a function of prevailing market conditions. Some assets, such as major currencies or Treasury bonds, have deep markets where most positions can be liquidated easily, with very little price impact. In others, such as exotic OTC derivatives contracts or emerging market equities, any transaction can quickly affect prices. But this is also a function of the size of the position.

Market/product liquidity risk can be managed by setting limits on certain markets or products and by means of diversification. Liquidity risk can be factored loosely into VAR measures by ensuring that the horizon is at least greater than an orderly liquidation period. This is explained in greater detail in a later chapter.

Funding liquidity risk, also known as *cash-flow risk,* refers to the inability to meet payments obligations, which may force early liquidation, thus transforming "paper" losses into realized losses. This is especially a problem for portfolios that are leveraged and subject to margin calls from the lender. Cash-flow risk interacts with product liquidity risk if the portfolio contains illiquid assets that must be sold at less than fair market value.

Indeed, if cash reserves are insufficient, we may have a situation where losses in market values create a need for cash payments, which may lead to an involuntary liquidation of the portfolio at depressed prices. This cycle of losses leading to margin calls and further losses is sometimes described as the "death spiral" (see Box 1–1).

Funding risk can be controlled by proper planning of cash-flow needs, which can be controlled by setting limits on cash-flow gaps, by diversification, and by consideration of how new funds can be raised to meet cash shortfalls.

1.3.4 Operational Risk

Operational risk generally can be defined as arising from human and technical errors or accidents. This includes *fraud* (situations where traders intentionally falsify information), management failure, and inadequate procedures and controls. Technical errors may be due to breakdowns in information, transaction processing, settlement systems, or, more generally, any problem in *back-office operations,* which deal with the recording of transactions and reconciliation of individual trades with the firm's aggregate position.

Operational risks also can lead to market and credit risk. For example, an operational problem in a business transaction, such as a settlement "fail," can create market risk and credit risk, since the cost may depend on movements in market prices.

The valuation of complex derivatives also creates potential operational problems. *Model risk* is the subtle danger that the model used to

BOX 1–1

DAVID ASKIN: A FAILED RISK-NEUTRAL STRATEGY

Some hedge funds lost heavily in the 1994 bond market debacle. David Askin was managing a $600 million fund invested in collateralized mortgage obligations (CMOs). CMOs are securities obtained from splitting up mortgage-backed securities and have characteristics similar to derivatives but are quite complex to price.

He touted his funds to investors as *market-neutral,* in his words, "with no default risk, high triple-A bonds and zero correlation with other assets." David Askin used his proprietary valuation models to identify, purchase, and hedge underpriced securities, with an objective to return 15 percent and more to investors. The $600 million investment, however, was leveraged into a total of $2 billion, which was actually betting on low interest rates. From February to April 1994, as interest rates were being jacked up by the Fed, his funds had to meet increasingly large collateral call payments that in the end could not be met. After the brokers liquidated their holdings, all that was left of the $600 million hedge fund was $30 million—and a bunch of irate investors.

Investors claimed they were misled about the condition of the fund. In the 1994 turmoil, the market for CMOs had deteriorated to a point where CMOs were quoted with spreads of 10 percent, which is enormous. As one observer put it, "dealers may be obliged to make a quote, but not for fair economic value." Instead of using dealer quotes, Askin simply priced his funds according to his own valuation models. The use of model prices to value a portfolio is referred to by practitioners as *marking to model.*

Askin was initially reporting a 2 percent loss in February, but this was later revised to a 28 percent loss. One year later, he was sanctioned by the Securities and Exchange Commission for misrepresenting the value of his funds. He also was barred from the investment industry for a minimum of 2 years.

Askin's investors were victims of market, liquidity, and model risk.

value positions is flawed. Traders using a conventional option pricing model, for instance, could be exposed to model risk if the model is misspecified or if the model parameters are erroneous. Unfortunately, model risk is very insidious. Assessing this risk requires an intimate knowledge of the modeling process. To guard against model risk, models must be subjected to independent evaluation using market prices, when available, or objective out-of-sample evaluations.

The best protection against operational risks consists of redundancies of systems, clear separation of responsibilities with strong internal controls, and regular contingency planning. The industry is currently making great strides in measuring and controlling operational risk. Like market and credit risk, operational risk is now being increasingly quantified.

1.3.5 Legal Risk

Legal risk arises when a transaction proves unenforceable in law. Legal risk is generally related to credit risk, since counterparties that lose money on a transaction may try to find legal grounds for invalidating the transaction (see, for example, Box 1–2).

It also can take the form of shareholder lawsuits against corporations that suffer large losses. After Procter and Gamble announced that it had lost $157 million on complex interest rate swaps entered with Bankers Trust, for example, a disgruntled shareholder filed suit against company executives.

Legal risks are controlled through policies developed by the institution's legal counsel in consultation with risk managers and senior management. The institution should make sure that agreements with counter-

BOX 1–2

CREDIT RISK AND LEGAL RISK

Investors who lose money on a transaction have the nasty habit of turning to courts to invalidate the transaction. One such approach is the *ultra vires* claim used by municipalities to invalidate losing transactions. The legal doctrine underlying this claim is that the investment activity was illegal because it went beyond the municipalities' powers.

The most extreme situation encountered so far is that of interest rate swaps entered by city councils in Britain. The municipalities of Hammersmith and Fulham had taken large positions in interest rate swaps that turned out to produce large losses. The swaps were later ruled invalid by the British High Court. The court decreed that the city councils did not have the authority to enter into these transactions and therefore that the cities were not responsible for the losses. As a result, their bank counterparties had to swallow losses amounting to $178 million.

parties can be enforced before any deal is consummated. Even so, situations that involve large losses often end up in costly litigation simply because the stakes are so large.

1.3.6 Integrated Risk Measurement

The original purpose of VAR systems was to quantify market risk. By now, the industry has converged on a set of risk measures that work reasonably well.

The drawback of focusing on one category of risk only is that institutions may react by moving away from measurable market risk into other types of risks that are more difficult to evaluate. For example, banks that were subject to capital constraints for credit risk soon learned to transfer some of this credit risk into market risk, with a lower capital requirement. Another example is the widespread use of marking-to-market, which decreases credit risk but creates a need for day-to-day handling of cash-flow payments, thereby increasing operational risk.

This is why institutions are now integrating their risk-management systems across the whole enterprise. The market-based VAR methodology is now being extended to measuring integrated market and credit risk. Similarly, *actuarial methods,* which were developed by the insurance industry to measure the distribution of losses from historical experience, are being brought to bear on the measurement of operational risk. The goal is to measure all financial risks on an integrated basis.

After having described the panoply of financial risks, we now turn to a brief introduction of VAR as a method to control market risks.

1.4 IN BRIEF, WHAT IS VAR?

Every morning, Lesley Daniels Webster, head of market risk at Chase Manhattan Bank, receives a neat 30-page report that summarizes the value at risk (VAR) of the bank. The document is generated during the night by computers that quantify the risk of all the trading positions of the bank.

Today, many banks, brokerage firms, investment funds, and even nonfinancial corporations use similar methods to gauge their financial risk. Bank and securities markets regulators and private-sector groups have widely endorsed statistical-based risk-management systems such as VAR. But what is this VAR?

1.4.1 Definition of VAR

VAR can be given the following intuitive definition.

VAR

VAR summarizes the worst loss over a target horizon with a given level of confidence.

More formally, VAR describes the *quantile* of the projected distribution of gains and losses over the target horizon. If c is the selected confidence level, VAR corresponds to the $1 - c$ lower-tail level. For instance, with a 95 percent confidence level, VAR should be such that it exceeds 5 percent of the total number of observations in the distribution.

1.4.2 Illustration of VAR

To illustrate the computation of VAR, consider, for instance, an investor who holds $100 million worth of medium-term notes. How much could the position lose over a month?

To answer this question, we simulate the 1-month return on this investment from historical data, considering only price movements. Figure 1–5 plots monthly returns on 5-year U.S. Treasury notes since 1953. The graph shows returns ranging from below 5 percent to above 5 percent.

BOX 1–3

THE ORIGINS OF VAR

Till Guldimann can be viewed as the creator of the term *value at risk* while head of global research at J.P. Morgan in the late 1980s. The risk-management group had to decide whether *fully hedged* meant investing in long bonds, thus generating stable *earnings,* or investing in cash, thus keeping the market *value* constant. The bank decided that "value risks" were more important than "earnings risks," paving the way for VAR.

At that time, there was much concern about managing the risks of derivatives properly. The Group of Thirty, which had a representative from J.P. Morgan, provided a venue for discussing best risk-management practices. The term found its way through the G-30 report published in July 1993. Apparently, this was the first widely publicized appearance of the term *value at risk.*

FIGURE 1-5

Returns on medium-term bonds.

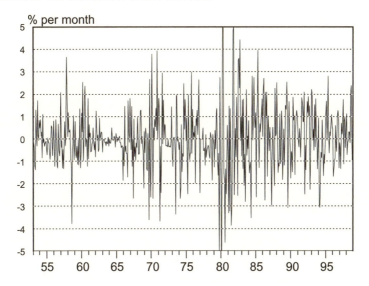

Now construct regularly spaced "buckets" going from the lowest to the highest numbers and count how many observations fall into each bucket. For instance, there are two observations below -5 percent. There is another observation between -5 and -4.5 percent. And so on. By so doing, we construct a *probability distribution* for the monthly returns, which counts how many occurrences have been observed in the past for a particular range. This *histogram,* or frequency distribution, is represented in Figure 1–6.

Next, associate with each return a probability of observing a lower value. Pick a confidence level, say, 95 percent. We need to find the loss that will not be exceeded in 95 percent of cases, or such that 5 percent of observations, that is, 27 of 552 occurrences, are lower. From Figure 1–6, this number is about -2.5 percent.

The choice of the 95 percent level is relatively arbitrary and is discussed in greater detail later. Users now report their VAR with various incompatible parameters. Assuming a normal distribution, however, it is easy to convert all these disparate measures into a common number. If the VAR number is used to assess an appropriate capital cushion, however, the confidence level should be chosen very carefully.

FIGURE 1–6

Measuring value at risk.

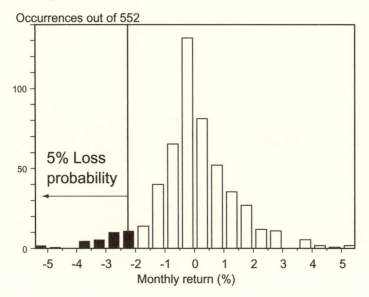

The choice of the holding period, 1 month or 1 day, is also relatively subjective. For a bank trading portfolio invested in highly liquid currencies, a 1-day holding period may be acceptable. For an investment manager with a quarterly rebalancing and reporting focus, a 90-day period may be more appropriate. Ideally, the holding period corresponds to the longest period needed for an orderly portfolio liquidation. A bank trading portfolio, for instance, will be much easier to close out than a portfolio invested in stocks from emerging markets. In the former case, for instance, tens of millions of dollars can be transacted in an instant; in the latter case, the same amount may take days or weeks to find willing counterparts. From the viewpoint of a regulator, the horizon should reflect the tradeoff between the costs of frequent monitoring and the benefits of early detection of potential problems.

We are now ready to compute the VAR of a $100 million portfolio. Based on the preceding analysis, we are 95 percent confident that the portfolio will fall by no more than $100 million times −2.5 percent, or $2.5 million, over a month. Hence the value at risk is about $2.5 million. A similar result would have been obtained by taking the standard deviation of the historical series, which is 1.5 percent, and multiplying it by the 95 percentile of the standard normal distribution, which is 1.645. The result from this normal model is rather close, at $2.4 million.

The market risk of this portfolio can now be communicated effectively to a nontechnical audience with a statement such as this: *Under normal market conditions, the most the portfolio can lose over a month is about $2.5 million at the 95 percent confidence level.*

1.5 VAR AND THE EVOLUTION OF RISK MANAGEMENT

VAR is the latest step in the evolution of risk-management tools. Consider, for instance, a fixed-income portfolio whose value is a function of the current yield.[5]

Figure 1–7 describes the classic risk-management approach. The first step is a valuation problem, which involves solving for the price given the current yield. To understand risk, one could approximate movements in the price through a sensitivity measure. This leads to the concept of duration, which measures the linear exposure of the position to interest rate risk. This approximation can be refined further by convexity, which measures the quadratic, or second-order term. All these are local approximations. Another approach is scenario analysis, which values the portfolio for a series of interest rates, using full valuation.

VAR goes one step further, though. It combines this price-yield relationship with the probability of an adverse market movement. This is shown in Figure 1–8, which describes how the price function is combined with a probability distribution for yields to generate a probability distribution for the bond price. Thus VAR describes the *probability boundary* of potential losses.

VAR is much broader than this simple example, though. Besides interest rates, it can encompass many other sources of risks, such as foreign currencies, commodities, and equities, in a consistent fashion. VAR accounts for leverage and correlations, which is essential when dealing

---

5. See, for instance, Golub and Tilman (2000) for systematic applications to the fixed-income markets.

FIGURE 1-7

Conventional risk-measurement methods.

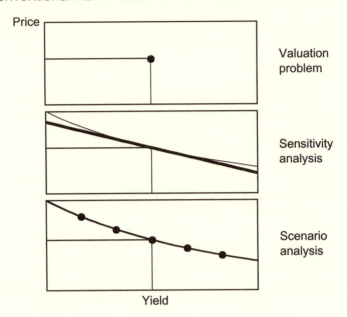

Valuation problem

Sensitivity analysis

Scenario analysis

FIGURE 1-8

Risk measurement with VAR.

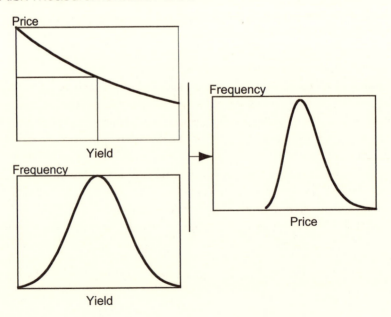

with large portfolios with derivatives instruments. It provides a summary measure of portfolio risk expressed in a probabilistic statement.

In a broad sense, VAR represents an extension of valuation methods for derivatives instruments. Consider the fundamental martingale *valuation* approach, which was a by-product of the Black-Scholes model. To value an asset with payoff that derives from a spot rate S at time T, we simply take the discounted expectation of the future payoff $F(S)$ over the distribution of S:

$$f_t = E^*[e^{-r(T-t)}F(S_T)] \qquad (1.1)$$

where the asterisk is a reminder that the price path is under risk neutrality, i.e., both changing the expected return and the discount rate to the risk-free rate. Instead, VAR measures the *variation* in value of the asset on the target date:

$$\text{VAR}(c,T) = E[F_T] - Q[F_T,c] \qquad (1.2)$$

where $Q[F_T, c]$ is the quantile corresponding to the confidence level c. Both approaches require a pricing function and a model for the distribution of prices.

Figure 1–9 compares the different views of the payoff distribution. Valuation models focus on the mean of the distribution. VAR, on the other

F I G U R E   1–9

Different views of the payoff distribution.

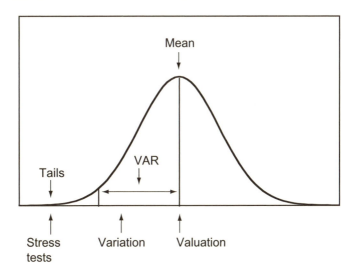

hand, describes the potential variation in the payoffs. At the same time, it seems obvious that VAR measures are not meant to give the worst potential loss. The behavior in the tail can be analyzed through stress-testing techniques, which must be viewed as an indispensible complement to VAR. As we will see, however, it is more difficult to use stress-tests results for capital allocation. Using stress-test results mechanistically has been described as being the rough equivalent of "requiring every resident of an earthquake zone to conduct daily activities as if the earthquake were occurring today." Ordinary business would come to a standstill.

Table 1–4 compares valuation and risk-management approaches. While the two approaches have much methodology in common, there are some notable differences. Valuation methods require more precision, since accurate prices are needed for trading purposes. This is less so for risk-management methods, which simply try to provide a rough measure of downside risk; pricing errors also tend to cancel out. Another difference is that valuation methods operate in a risk-neutral world, whereas risk-management methods deal with actual distributions.

This sudden realization that our vast body of knowledge in the field of derivatives could be put to direct use for risk management explains why VAR has quickly become the "standard benchmark" for measuring financial risks.

No doubt this was helped by the effort of J.P. Morgan, which unveiled its RiskMetrics system in October 1994. Available free on the Internet, RiskMetrics provides a datafeed for computing market risk. The widespread availability of data, as well as a technical manual, immediately engaged the industry and spurred academic research into risk man-

TABLE 1–4

Valuation and Risk Management

	Derivatives Valuation	Risk Management
Principle	Expected discounted value	Distribution of future values
Focus	Center of distribution	Tails of distribution
Precision	High precision needed for pricing purposes	Less precision needed, simply approximate tails
Distribution	Risk-neutral distributions and discounting	Actual, objective distributions

agement. Later, the bank spun off its risk-management group as the RiskMetrics Group, which developed a CreditMetrics system in April 1997 and CorporateMetrics in April 1999. CreditMetrics attempts to measure credit risk in a portfolio framework; CorporateMetrics extends the RiskMetrics approach to a longer horizon, which is more appropriate for nonfinancial corporations.

Lest we forget, VAR is no panacea, however. VAR measures are only useful insofar as users grasp their limitations. As Till Guldimann, then head of J.P. Morgan's global research, described his firm's system: "RiskMetrics isn't a substitute for good management, experience and judgment. It's a toolbox, not a black box." Thus VAR is only an educated estimate of market risk. This does not lessen its value, though. Educated estimates have been used widely in other fields.

Likewise, engineering is sometimes defined as "the art of the approximation" (as opposed to the exact sciences). The same concept can be applied to risk-management systems. Observers who describe risk management as an exact science are doing a disservice to the community.

Overall, VAR should be viewed as a necessary but not sufficient procedure for controlling risk. It must be supplemented by limits and controls, in addition to an independent risk-management function. Indeed, the widespread use of VAR has led to a widespread focus on sound risk-management practices. In my view, this development is beneficial.

CHAPTER 2

Lessons from
Financial Disasters

Experience is a dear school.

Benjamin Franklin

Much like airplane disasters, derivatives have created much anxiety as news of spectacular losses has been splashed across headlines. These losses have spawned a flurry of legislative activity into the regulation of derivatives markets. Wall Streeter Felix Rohatyn has warned that "26-year-olds with computers are creating financial hydrogen bombs." Former House Banking Committee Chairman Henry Gonzalez has claimed that derivatives are "a monstrous global electronic Ponzi scheme." Jim Leach, the succeeding House Banking Committee chairman, took a more balanced approach but still argued that "the sheer size of the market implies that it cannot be ignored." These concerns have led to a number of private-sector initiatives to control financial risks better.

Yet disasters can occur without involvement in derivatives. Section 2.1 provides an overview of recent losses by corporations and in government funds, showing that derivatives losses are small in relation to the size of derivatives markets, to losses in cash markets, and to some other famous financial blunders. Section 2.2 goes over recent case studies in risk, including Barings, Metallgesellschaft, Orange County, and Daiwa. These disasters are instructive, for they have one element in common, poor management of financial risks. The predictable reaction to these losses has been increased scrutiny of financial markets, in particular derivatives, by regulators and legislators. Faced with this "strategic risk," the private sector came up with a number of initiatives toward better risk management. Responses from the private sector and regulators are summarized in Sections 2.3 and 2.4. Regulations specific to financial institutions, because of their importance, are analyzed in the following chapter. Overall, the industry has moved rather fast toward more transparent reporting of risk through marking-to-market and forward-looking measures of risk.

Admittedly, most of the discussion in this chapter involves U.S.-based studies and regulations. This simply reflects the fact that most financial innovations originate in the United States and that U.S. financial markets are, besides the largest, certainly among the most transparent in the world.

2.1 LESSONS FROM RECENT LOSSES

Indeed, losses attributed to derivatives have mushroomed in recent years. Figure 2–1 displays the sum of losses publicly attributed (rightly or wrongly) to derivatives since 1987. These market losses grew sharply in 1994 due to interest rate fluctuations, which created volatility in bond markets. From 1987 to 1998, these losses totaled $28 billion.

FIGURE 2–1

Cumulative losses attributed to derivatives.
(© Capital Market Risk Advisors, Inc.)

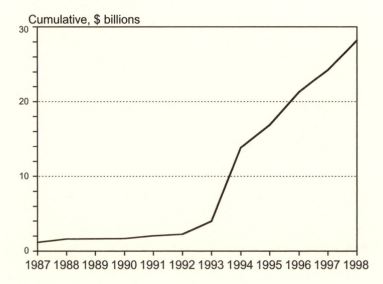

How significant are these losses? In relation to the size of a $90 trillion market, they represent only 0.03 percent of total notional amount, which is quite small in relative terms. On the other hand, the suddenness of losses makes derivatives look particularly dangerous. Much like airplane travel, which is actually safer than most other modes of transportation, derivatives make headlines.

As a result, a few managers, directors, and trustees have taken the extreme step of eliminating all derivatives from their portfolio. Ironically, these operations have in some instances increased the portfolio risk, since derivatives may be used to hedge risks. Further, the remaining portfolios may be producing noncompetitive returns or may be subject to higher costs, given that derivatives offer very low transaction costs. Some of these inconsistencies are apparent from the legislative backlash against derivatives at the state level: Several states have enacted bills that prohibit derivatives in local government investment portfolios yet actively use derivatives to lower their funding costs.

2.1.1 Losses Attributed to Derivatives

Since derivatives are particularly effective tools to hedge and speculate, they can lead to large losses if used inappropriately. Losses from 1993 to 1999 involving derivatives are displayed in Table 2–1.

TABLE 2–1

Losses Attributed to Derivatives: 1993–1999

Corporation	Date	Instrument	Loss ($ million)
Orange County, CA	Dec. 1994	Reverse repos	1,810
Showa Shell Sekiyu, Japan	Feb. 1993	Currency forwards	1,580
Kashima Oil, Japan	Apr. 1994	Currency forwards	1,450
Metallgesellschaft, Germany	Jan. 1994	Oil futures	1,340
Barings, U.K.	Feb. 1995	Stock index futures	1,330
Ashanti, Ghana	Oct. 1999	Gold "exotics"	570
Yakult Honsha, Japan	Mar. 1998	Stock index derivatives	523
Codelco, Chile	Jan. 1994	Copper futures	200
Procter & Gamble, U.S.	Apr. 1994	Differential swaps	157
NatWest, U.K.	Feb. 1997	Swaptions	127

Just focusing on these losses, however, may be misleading for three reasons. First, derivatives positions were taken in some, but certainly not all, situations as a hedge; that is, to offset other business risks. Thus these losses may be offset by operating profits. It has been argued, for instance, that the Metallgesellschaft derivatives losses were offset partially by increases in the value of oil contracts with customers. It is essential, therefore, to distinguish between losses due to outright speculation and losses due to a hedging program.

Second, the size of these losses is directly related to fairly recent large movements in financial markets. In 1994 alone, movements in interest rates created losses for holders of U.S. Treasury bonds of about $230 billion. That is, just by buying and holding "safe" bonds, investors lost a quarter of a trillion dollars. Viewed in this context, these derivatives losses do not seem abnormally high.

Third, we should note the other side of the coin. Derivatives contracts are arrangements between two parties. Because derivatives contracts are zero-sum games, any loss to one party is a gain to the other. Of course, the gainer usually complains less than the loser.

2.1.2 Perspective on Financial Losses

Lest you think that disasters can occur only with derivatives, it is useful to point out other notable financial catastrophes.

- Bank Negara, Malaysia's central bank, lost more than $3 billion in 1992 and $2 billion in 1993 after bad bets on exchange rates. The bank had speculated that the British pound would stay in the European Monetary System (EMS). Instead, the Bank of England, under heavy attack by speculators, let sterling drop out of the EMS in September 1992. Sterling's defense had cost billions to British taxpayers. Some of the winners were hedge funds, one of which (George Soros's) is reported to have made profits of $2 billion.
- In December 1993, the Bank of Spain took control of Banesto, Spain's fifth biggest bank. Banesto had a "black hole" of $4.7 billion in hidden losses, out of a balance sheet of $43 billion; its bad loans and doubtful industrial investments were aggravated by Spain's economic slump. The bank went bust and subsequently was bought by Banco Santander.

- French taxpayers have footed the bill for the biggest-ever bailout of an individual institution. The French government has poured more than $15 billion into Crédit Lyonnais, the country's biggest state-owned bank. The bank's problems stemmed from unfettered expansion and poor management. Notable among its difficulties was its large exposure to French real estate, which suffered huge losses during the 1992–1993 recession. But the bank also suffered from investments in loss-making state-owned companies and even a troubled U.S. film studio. The bank was described as a "monarchy with no checks and balances."

- These losses pale in comparison with the cost of the savings and loans industry in the United States, which is now estimated at $150 billion. In the 1980s, S&Ls were making long-term loans in residential housing that were funded by short-term deposits. As short-term interest rates zoomed up in the early 1980s, S&Ls were squeezed in a "duration gap." Their costs went up more than their revenues, and they started to bleed badly. In a belated and misconceived attempt to repair the damage, Congress deregulated the industry, which then strayed from housing finance into risky investments in commercial real estate and junk bonds. Eventually, a large number of S&Ls became insolvent.

- All this red ink is dwarfed by the financial crisis in Japan, where financial institutions are sitting on a total of perhaps $550 billion in "nonperforming" (euphemism for bad) loans. Particularly troubled are housing loan corporations, which lent heavily during the real estate bubble and collapsed after 1990. The Japanese financial deflation also hit the stock market and, with it, the reserves of the banking system.

Table 2–2 lists the total costs of recent banking disasters, which were borne by taxpayers. The financial burden is often enormous, reaching in some cases more than a third of annual gross domestic product, and translates into permanently lower income for taxpayers. Viewed in this context, the derivatives losses in Table 2–1 appear to be minor incidents.

Instead, the banking system appears to be a systematic source of trouble, nearly always due to *bad loans,* or credit risk gone awry. These problems all reflect a fundamental misallocation of capital that can be ascribed to various causes, some due to the banks themselves, such as insufficient lending standards and poor risk management. More often than

TABLE 2–2

Cost of Financial Insolvencies

Date	Scope	Cost % GDP	Cost $ Billion
Japan, 1990s	Bad loans, property prices	14	550
China, 1990s	4 large state banks insolvent	47	498
U.S., 1984–91	1400 S&Ls, 1300 banks fail	2.7	150
S. Korea, 1998–	Restructuring of banks	28	90
Mexico, 1995–	20 banks recapitalized	17	72
Argentina, 1980–82	70 institutions closed	55	46
Thailand, 1997–	Banking sector	32	36
Spain, 1977–85	Nationalized 20 banks	17	28
Malaysia, 1997–	Banking sector	35	25
Sweden, 1991–94	5 banks rescued	4	15
Venezuela, 1994–	Insolvent banks	20	14
France, 1994–95	Credit Lyonnais	0.7	10
Norway, 1987–93	State takes over 3 banks	8	8
Israel, 1977–83	Entire banking sector	30	8
Chile, 1981–83	8 institutions closed	41	8
Finland, 1991–93	Savings banking sector	8	7
Australia, 1989–92	Two large banks recapitalized	2	6

Source: Data adapted from Caprio and Klingebiel, 1999, "Episodes of Systemic and Borderline Financial Crises," *World Bank Working Paper,* with author's calculations.

not, governments themselves contribute to the risks, through poor bank supervision, ill-advised government intervention, or unsustainable economic policies.

This misallocation of capital can turn into a disaster because banks do not generally diversify their credit risk across countries or industries and are also highly leveraged. A severe downturn in the domestic economy is then fatal. No doubt this explains the recent interest in measuring credit risk more finely.

2.2 CASE STUDIES IN RISK

2.2.1 Barings's Fall: A Lesson in Risk

On February 26, 1995, the Queen of Great Britain woke up to the news that Barings PLC, a venerable 233-year-old bank, had gone bankrupt.

Apparently, the downfall of the bank was due to a single trader, 28-year-old Nicholas Leeson, who lost \$1.3 billion from derivatives trading. This loss wiped out the firm's entire equity capital.[1]

The loss was caused by a large exposure to the Japanese stock market, which was achieved through the futures market. Leeson, the chief trader for Barings Futures in Singapore, had been accumulating positions in stock index futures on the Nikkei 225, a portfolio of Japanese stocks. Barings's notional positions on the Singapore and Osaka exchanges added up to a staggering \$7 billion. As the market fell more than 15 percent in the first two months of 1995, Barings Futures suffered huge losses. These losses were made worse by the sale of options, which implied a bet on a stable market. As losses mounted, Leeson increased the size of the position, in a stubborn belief he was right. Then, unable to make the cash payments required by the exchanges, he simply walked away on February 23. Later, he sent a fax to his superiors, offering "sincere apologies for the predicament that I have left you in."

Because Barings was viewed as a conservative bank, the bankruptcy served as a wakeup call for financial institutions all over the world. The disaster has revealed an amazing lack of controls at Barings: Leeson had control over both the trading desk and the "back office." The function of the back office is to confirm trades and check that all trading activity is within guidelines. In any serious bank, traders have a limited amount of capital they can deal with and are subject to closely supervised "position limits." To avoid conflicts of interest, the trading and back office functions are clearly delineated. In addition, most banks have a separate risk-management unit that provides another check on traders.

The Singapore and Osaka exchanges also drew some attention for their failure to notice the size of positions. On the Osaka exchange, Barings Futures had accumulated 20,000 contracts each worth \$200,000. This was eight times the next largest position of 2500 contracts. Officials at U.S. futures exchanges have stated that such positions would have attracted their attention much sooner had they been in the United States.

One of the reasons Leeson was so unsupervised was his great track record. In 1994, Leeson is thought to have made \$20 million for Barings, or about one-fifth of the total firm's profits. This translated into fat bonuses for Leeson and his superiors. In 1994, Leeson drew a \$150,000 salary with a \$1 million bonus. At some point, the head of Barings Securities,

---

1. Rawnsley (1995) wrote a full account of Barings' fall. For a more partial view, see also Leeson (1996).

Christopher Heath, was Britain's highest paid executive. The problem also was blamed on the "matrix" structure implemented by Barings. Since Leeson's unit reported along both geographic and functional lines, the decentralization inherent in this structure led to poor supervision.

There also were allegations that senior bank executives were aware of the risks involved and had approved cash transfers of $1 billion to help Leeson make margin calls. An internal audit drawn up in 1994 apparently also had been ignored by Barings's top management. The auditor warned of "excessive concentration of power in Leeson's hands."

The moral of this affair is summarized in a February 27, 1995, *Wall Street Journal* article that quotes from the official Bank of England report on Barings:

> Bank of England officials said they did not regard the problem in this case as one peculiar to derivatives. . . . In a case where a trader is taking unauthorized positions, they said, the real question is the strength of an investment houses' internal controls and the external monitoring done by exchanges and regulators.

Barings's shareholders bore the full cost of the losses. The price of Barings's shares went to zero, wiping out about $1 billion of market capitalization. Bondholders received five cents on the dollar. Some of the additional losses were borne by the Dutch financial services group International Nederlanden Group (ING), which offered to acquire Barings for the grand total of one British pound (about $1.50).

Leeson spent 43 months in a Singapore jail and was released in 1999. He then started a new career as a featured speaker, sometimes paid $100,000 a speech. This money, however, will be badly needed to repay a $165 million debt.

2.2.2 Metallgesellschaft

The story of Metallgesellschaft (MG) is that of a hedge that went bad to the tune of $1.3 billion. The conglomerate, Germany's fourteenth largest industrial group with 58,000 employees, nearly went bankrupt following losses incurred by its American subsidiary, MG Refining & Marketing (MGRM), in the futures market.

MGRM's problems stemmed from its idea of offering long-term contracts for oil products. The marketing of these contracts was successful because customers could lock in fixed prices over long periods. By 1993, MGRM had entered into contracts to supply customers with 180 million barrels of oil products over a period of 10 years.

These commitments were quite large, equivalent to 85 days of Kuwait's oil output, and exceeded many times MGRM's refining capacity. To hedge against the possibility of price increases, the company ideally should have entered long-term forward contracts on oil, matching the maturity of the contracts and of the commitments. In the absence of a viable market for long-term contracts, however, MGRM turned to the short-term futures market and implemented a *rolling hedge,* where the long-term exposure is hedged through a series of short-term contracts, with maturities around 3 months, that are rolled over into the next contract as they expire.

Since the 3-month contract eventually will be rolled over into a contract that expires 10 years from now, the profits generated by the rolling hedge should converge (in 10 years) to the profits generated by buying and holding a 10-year forward contract.

In the meantime, the company was exposed to *basis risk,* which is the risk that short-term oil prices temporarily deviate from long-term prices. Indeed, cash prices fell from $20 to $15 in 1993, leading to about a billion dollars of margin calls that had to be met in cash.

Some of these losses may have been offset by gains on the long-term contracts with its customers, since the company could then sell oil at locked-in higher prices. Apparently, however, the German parent did not expect to have to put up such large amounts of cash. Senior executives at the U.S. subsidiary were pushed out, and a new management team was flown in from Europe. The new team immediately proceeded to liquidate the remaining contracts, which led to a reported loss of $1.3 billion. Since then, the liquidation has been severely criticized on the grounds that it effectively realized losses that would have decreased over time.[2] The auditors' report, in contrast, stated that the losses were caused by the size of the trading exposures.

In any event, the loss, the largest German postwar corporate disaster, nearly brought the conglomerate to its knees. Creditors, led by Deutsche Bank, stepped in with a $2.4 billion rescue package. They were asked to write down some of their loans in exchange for equity warrants.

---

2. This line of argument is advanced by Culp and Miller (1995).

Eventually, the stock price plummeted from 64 to 24 marks, wiping out more than half of MG's market capitalization.

2.2.3 Orange County

The Orange County affair perhaps represents the most extreme form of uncontrolled market risk in a local government fund. Bob Citron, the county treasurer, was entrusted with a $7.5 billion portfolio belonging to county schools, cities, special districts, and the county itself. To get a bigger bang for these billions, he borrowed about $12.5 billion, through reverse repurchase agreements, for a total of $20 billion that was invested in agency notes with an average maturity of about 4 years. In an environment where short-term funding costs were lower than medium-term yields, the highly leveraged strategy worked exceedingly well, especially as interest rates were falling.[3]

Unfortunately, the interest rate hikes that started in February 1994 unraveled the strategy. All through the year, paper losses on the fund led to margin calls from Wall Street brokers that had provided short-term financing. In December, as news of the loss spread, investors tried to pull out their money. Finally, as the fund defaulted on collateral payments, brokers started to liquidate their collateral, and Orange County declared bankruptcy. The following month, the remaining securities in the portfolio were liquidated, leading to a realized loss of $1.81 billion.

County officials blamed Citron for undertaking risky investments and not being forthcoming about his strategies. But they also were applauding Citron's track record all along. In his years in office, he returned about $750 million in free money to the county (over and above the state pool). These higher returns simply reflected higher risks.

Citron's mistake was to report his portfolio at cost. He claimed that there was no risk in the portfolio because he was holding to maturity. Since government accounting standards do not require municipal investment pools to record "paper" gains or losses, Citron did not report the market value of the portfolio. This explains why losses were allowed to grow to $1.7 billion and why investors claim they were misled about the condition of the pool.

If his holdings had been measured at current market value, the treasurer may have recognized just how risky his investments actually were.

---

3. Jorion's book (1995b) provides a detailed account of the Orange County story.

Investors, in touch with monthly fluctuations in values, also may have refrained from the "run on the bank" that happened in December 1994. It is fair to surmise that had the VAR of the portfolio been made public, investors probably would have been more careful with their funds.

2.2.4 Daiwa's Lost Billion

Daiwa's case provides a striking counterpart to the Barings disaster. On September 26, 1995, the bank announced that a 44-year-old trader in New York, Toshihide Igushi, allegedly had accumulated losses estimated at $1.1 billion. The losses were of a similar magnitude to those that befell Barings, but Daiwa, the twelfth largest bank in Japan, managed to withstand the blow. The loss "only" absorbed one-seventh of the firm's capital.

Apparently, Igushi had concealed more than 30,000 trades over 11 years, starting in 1984, in U.S. Treasury bonds. As the losses grew, the bank said, the trader exceeded his position limits to make up for the losses. He eventually started selling, in the name of Daiwa, securities deposited by clients at the New York branch. The bank claims that none of these trades were reported to Daiwa and that Igushi falsified listings of securities held at the bank's custodian, Bankers Trust. Apparently, the bank failed to cross-check daily trades with monthly portfolio summaries.

As in the case of Barings, the problem arose because at some point Igushi had control of both the front and back offices. Unlike other Japanese workers who were rotated regularly, he had been hired locally. In their home market, Japanese banks rely on a group spirit that acts as an internal safety mechanism; in overseas operations, such an approach can be fatal.

This loss highlighted the poor risk-management policies of Japanese banks, which already pay a premium rate, up to an extra 0.25 percent, reflecting the nervousness over property losses in Japanese financial institutions. In many ways, the Daiwa case is more worrisome than Barings because the losses were allowed to accumulate over 11 years, not just a few months.

The disclosure of the losses was a delayed reaction to increased supervision of foreign banks in the wake of the Bank of Credit and Commerce International's (BCCI) collapse. The Federal Reserve Board had inspected Daiwa's offices in November 1992 and November 1993. In both instances, the regulators had warned the bank about the risks in its management structure. Daiwa, however, failed to implement major changes and even reported that it deliberately hid records and temporarily removed bond traders in order to pass the 1992 inspection. Under pressure from regulators, Daiwa relegated Igushi to a back office function. Even so, he continued to transact, hiding behind other traders. However, as bank auditors were scrutinizing the New York operation, increased oversight was making it very difficult for him to continue hiding the losses. Igushi confessed his actions in a July 1995 letter to top management.

In response to the loss, Daiwa Bank closed its New York office, and top management announced in October 1995 that it would be stepping down. The bank came under the wrath of U.S. regulators, who ordered the bank to close down its U.S. operations, an unprecedented move. Regulators accused Daiwa of a "pattern of unsafe and unsound banking practices and violations of the law." Officials at the Japanese Ministry of Finance stated: "Clearly, more disclosure is the way to go."

2.2.5 Lessons from Case Studies

All the disasters studied here involve losses in excess of $1 billion. As shown in Table 2–3, these losses were attributed to various causes: primarily rogue traders for Barings and Daiwa, market risks for Metallgesellschaft and Orange County. The only common thread across these hapless cases is the absence of enforced risk-management policies.

Granted, there is no foolproof protection against outright fraud. The checks and balances provided by an additional risk-management system,

TABLE 2–3

Risk Factors in Losses

	Market	Operational	Funding	Lack of Controls
Barings	Yes, Japanese stocks	Yes, rogue trader		Yes
MGRM	Yes, oil		Yes, recapitalization	Yes
O.C.	Yes, interest rates		Yes, default	Yes
Daiwa	Yes	Yes, rogue trader		Yes

as well as uniform treatment of front and back office information, should provide some protection against rogue traders or other operational risks.

2.3 PRIVATE-SECTOR RESPONSES

The string of losses attributed to derivatives, as well as the exponential growth of the market, has attracted the scrutiny of regulators. Perhaps the most memorable warning shot was fired in January 1992 by Gerald Corrigan, president of the New York Fed: "High-tech banking and finance has its place, but it's not all it's cracked up to be. I hope this sounds like a warning, because it is." These comments and the increased flurry of legislative and regulatory activity have led the private sector to come up with its own proposals.

2.3.1 G-30 Report

In 1993, the Group of Thirty (G-30), a consultative group of top bankers, financiers, and academics from leading industrial nations, issued a landmark report on derivatives, "Derivatives: Practices and Principles." The report concludes that derivatives activity "makes a contribution to the overall economy that may be difficult to quantify but is nevertheless both favorable and substantial." The general view of the G-30 is that derivatives do not introduce risks of a greater scale than those "already present in financial markets." The G-30 report also recommends guidelines for managing derivatives, which are described in more detail in Chapter 21. In particular, the G-30 advises to value positions using market prices and to assess financial risks with VAR. These sound practice principles, however, are equally valid for any portfolio, with or without derivatives.

2.3.2 Derivatives Policy Group

The Derivatives Policy Group (DPG) was organized by six major Wall Street firms in August 1994 to address public-policy issues related to the OTC derivatives activities of dealers, which are not subject to the capital requirements of commercial banks.[4]

---

4. These firms, CS First Boston, Goldman Sachs, Lehman Brothers, Merrill Lynch, Morgan Stanley, and Citigroup's Salomon Smith Barney, are the U.S. broker-dealers with the largest OTC derivatives affiliates.

The DPG has established a "Framework for Voluntary Oversight" (1995) that consists of

- *Management controls,* starting with guidelines that clearly define the scope of involvement in derivatives activities, which must be subject to a process for measuring and managing risk.
- *Enhanced reporting,* whereby the institution reports credit exposures as well as financial statements on a regular basis.
- *Evaluation of risk in relation to capital,* using a standardized method to measure market risk with a 99 percent VAR figure measured over a 2-week horizon.
- *Counterparty relationship,* whereby dealers should provide adequate documentation and inform their counterparties of the risks of the transactions.

Accordingly, the DPG firms have given quarterly information about their market and credit risks since 1995 to their regulators. The framework, however, is voluntary and has been limited to the six member firms.[5]

2.3.3 J.P. Morgan's RiskMetrics

Perhaps the most notable of private-sector initiative is that of J.P. Morgan, which unveiled in October 1994 a new system called *RiskMetrics.* The system initially made available risk measures for 300 financial instruments across 14 countries and has been greatly expanded since. Essentially, the data represent an elaborate variance/covariance matrix of risk and correlation measures that evolve through time. To produce their own VAR, users need computer software to integrate the RiskMetrics system with their own positions.

Although the system is available for free, this move is not totally disinterested. RiskMetrics is motivated by a desire to

---

5. The Securities and Exchange Commission (SEC) issued in January 1999 a rule change that creates a class of *OTC derivatives dealers.* The goal was to bring the level of regulation for derivatives' trading U.S. broker-dealers in line with foreign firms or even U.S. commercial banks, which are subject to the Basel capital rules. The new class of OTC derivatives dealers is subject to risk-based capital rules that correspond to the DPG guidelines.

- Promote greater transparency of market risks.
- Make available sophisticated risk-management tools to other potential users, especially those who cannot muster the resources to develop such systems from scratch.
- Establish J.P. Morgan's methodology as an industry standard.

More than any other initiative, RiskMetrics can be credited with providing the impetus for further research in risk management. Indeed, RiskMetrics has spawned an army of system developers and encouraged rival banks to develop new generations of risk-management systems. RiskMetrics also has helped to forestall unnecessary regulatory restrictions on financial markets.

J.P. Morgan later released a system to measure credit risk, called *CreditMetrics,* as well as other versions targeted to the corporate and pension fund markets, CorporateMetrics and PensionMetrics.

2.3.4 Global Association of Risk Professionals (GARP)

The *Global Association of Risk Professionals* (GARP) was established in 1996 to create a forum for communication among worldwide risk professionals. This laudable private-sector initiative, mainly run by volunteers, aims at improving risk-management practices in the industry. The association is Internet-based and run as a not-for-profit group, with membership free of charge. By 2000, GARP had grown to more than 10,000 members.

GARP organizes every year an examination, the *Financial Risk Manager Certificate Program,* whose goal is to establish an industry standard of minimum professional competence in the field. This examination is fast becoming an essential, *sine qua non,* requirement for risk managers.

2.4 THE VIEW OF REGULATORS

The explosive growth of the derivatives markets and well-publicized losses have created much concern for legislators and regulators. In 1993 and 1994, there was a flurry of activity assessing the risks of derivatives, especially in the unregulated OTC swap markets. Since then, the unmistakable trend is toward more transparent reporting of financial risk, notably by the generalized use of VAR measures.

2.4.1 General Accounting Office (GAO)

In May 1994, the General Accounting Office[6] (GAO) issued a widely watched report on derivatives after more than 2 years of study. The report stated that "derivatives serve an important function" but that they require careful management. Among many recommendations, the report advised financial regulators to perform regular evaluations of dealers' risk-management systems and to provide expanded disclosure requirements for derivatives products. The GAO also pointed to gaps in the regulation of OTC derivatives in the United States.

A 1996 follow-up study reported that market participants and regulators had taken a number of actions to improve the management, oversight, and disclosure of derivatives risks since 1994. In particular, the GAO noted that dealers and end-users have strengthened their corporate governance systems and risk-management controls.

2.4.2 Financial Accounting Standards Board (FASB)

The Financial Accounting Standards Board[7] (FASB) has long struggled to set standards for disclosure and accounting treatment of derivatives. For a long time, derivatives have been considered as *off-balance-sheet items,* that is, did not generally appear in balance sheets or earnings. This practice was highly inadequate, since derivatives are, in effect, assets or liabilities, like other balance sheet items. The growth of the derivatives markets made it imperative to revisit its accounting treatment.

In June 1998, the FASB passed a new set of standards, No. 133, "Accounting for Derivative Instruments and Hedging Activities," that unifies derivatives accounting, hedge accounting, and disclosure in a single statement. Effective June 15, 2000, FAS 133 requires derivatives to be recorded on the balance sheet at *fair value,* that is, at quoted market

---

6. The General Accounting Office is the investigative arm of the U.S. Congress, charged with examining all matters relating to the receipt and disbursement of public funds. The GAO performs a variety of services, the most prominent of which are audits and evaluations of government programs and activities.

7. The FASB is an independent agency responsible for developing generally accepted accounting principles. Authority over U.S. accounting rules belongs to the SEC, which has ceded to the FASB, with the occasional threat of intervention. The SEC, however, does prescribe the form of financial statement submitted to it.

prices.[8] Changes in the market value of derivatives must be reported in earnings. For derivatives used (and designated) as a hedge, however, the rules allow the gain or loss to be recognized in earnings at the same time as the hedged item. The new rule also requires reporting entities to describe their risk-management policy for derivatives. The new standards also modify FAS 107, "Disclosure about Fair Value of Financial Instruments," which now encourages (but does not require) entities to disclose information about the market risks of their financial instruments.

Similar progress is made by the International Accounting Standards Committee (IASC), which is developing a set of core *International Accounting Standards* (IAS).[9] In December 1998, it issued IAS 39, which also moves toward marking-to-market, but for all financial assets and liabilities, not only derivatives. By requiring marking-to-market, these new standards confirm the trend toward more transparent reporting.

2.4.3 Securities and Exchange Commission (SEC)

In January 1997, the Securities and Exchange Commission[10] (SEC) issued a ruling that requires companies to disclose *quantitative* information about the risk of derivatives and other financial instruments in financial reports filed with the SEC.[11] This ruling was widely viewed as revolutionary in the sense that companies had to disclose, for the first time, forward-looking measures of risk. The new rules apply to all filings for fiscal years after June 15, 1998.

The rationale behind the SEC's approach is the general feeling by security analysts and accountants that "users are confused." Existing

---

8. The FASB formally defines *fair value* as the "amount at which an asset could be bought or sold in a current transaction between willing parties, that is, other than in a forced or liquidation sale."

9. The purpose of these international standards is to facilitate listing on foreign exchanges. Provided the IAS are adopted by national regulators, companies would only need to submit IAS-compliant financial statements to gain access to foreign markets. Hong Kong and Singapore, for instance, have substantially harmonized their accounting standards with IASC standards.

10. The *SEC* is a federal agency that has wide authority to oversee the nation's security markets. Among other things, it regulates the financial reporting practices of public corporations.

11. The SEC also encourages, but does not require, inclusion of market risk due to nonfinancial assets, liabilities, or transactions, such as inventories or sales commitment. Including these items provides a more complete picture of market risk, although nonfinancial items may be more difficult to measure.

reporting guidelines provide insufficient detail on the scope of involvement in financial instruments and the potential effect of derivatives activity on corporate profits. Indeed, the SEC reviewed *qualitative* disclosure statements by U.S. public corporations and found that the management discussion was typically uninformative. Nearly all companies explain that they use derivatives to "hedge." Few admit to outright speculation, even though the losses incurred by some corporations are *prima facie* evidence to the contrary.[12] As the line between selective hedging and speculation is very thin, such statements shed very little light on the extent and effectiveness of corporate derivatives activities.

To make information reporting more transparent, the SEC now requires registrants to disclose *quantitative* information of market risks using one of three possible alternatives:

1. A *tabular presentation* of expected cash flows and contract terms summarized by risk category.
2. A *sensitivity analysis* expressing possible losses for hypothetical changes in market prices.
3. *Value-at-risk measures* for the current reporting period, which are to be compared to actual changes in market values.

These FASB and SEC rules have generally been welcomed by users of financial statements. The Association for Investment Management and Research (AIMR), a prominent group of financial analysts, for example, commented that the SEC disclosures were "a significant step toward improving investors' ability to assess investment risk." The AIMR even suggested that only one method should be allowed, which would provide more meaningful comparisons across firms.

On the other hand, these rules have been fiercely opposed by the financial industry, which fears that potentially higher volatility in corporate earnings will lead to a reduction in the derivatives business. Apparently, these fears have not materialized. The financial industry has itself converted to these methods, generally preferring value-at-risk reporting, due to the fact that, unlike sensitivity analysis, VAR reveals little information about the direction of exposures.

Admittedly, these rules impose new compliance costs. Corporate users of derivatives are now forced to implement risk-management and

---

12. For instance, the swap positions that led to a loss of $157 million for Procter & Gamble can hardly be described as hedging.

reporting systems that they otherwise may not have. This explains the lack of enthusiasm of corporations for these new rules.[13]

Perhaps the most pointed response to these concerns is a comment from Stern Financial Analysis and Consulting:

> Any registrant who claims excessive financial burden should be required to disclose this, as well as a statement to the effect that he is investing in financial instruments that he cannot monitor nor understand. At least then the investors will be aware that they have invested with a self-professed novice.

2.5 CONCLUSIONS

The derivatives disasters of the early 1990s have led to profound changes in the financial landscape. While unfortunate, none of the derivatives disasters mentioned here has threatened to destabilize the financial system. Instead, these losses served as powerful object lessons in the need to manage financial risks better.

The unifying theme behind these reports and regulations is an increasing emphasis on risk management. In fact, one could argue that better control of market risk through VAR systems is a direct outgrowth of the derivatives markets. By providing tools to control market risk, derivatives will have fulfilled an important social function.

FURTHER INFORMATION

Private Sector

The technical documents for J.P. Morgan's RiskMetrics (now supported by the RiskMetrics Group) are at www.riskmetrics.com.

The Global Association of Risk Professionals can be accessed at www.garp.com.

Probably the most comprehensive annual review of derivatives markets is by Charles Smithson (1997, 1998, 1999).

Also, Capital Market Risk Advisors, a New York–based consulting firm, keeps track of losses attributed to derivatives. Its Web site is at www.cmra.com.

Barry Schachter maintains a comprehensive Web site with VAR publications and other links at www.gloriamundi.org.

---

13. Some corporations also have expressed concerns about being forced to reveal proprietary position information to their competitors. In response, the SEC has allowed registrants to report risk measures that represent averages over the reporting period instead of more timely year-end information.

Essential Regulatory Reports

The text of the Bank of England, G-30, and DPG reports is available on the Web site of the International Finance and Commodities Institute (ICFI), a nonprofit Swiss foundation risk.ifci.ch.

Nonbank Regulators

Information on the FASB's accounting rules, which even includes training programs for FAS 133, can be found at www.fasb.org. The site www.fas133.com is entirely devoted to FAS 133 issues. The International Accounting Standards Committee (IASC)'s site is at www.iasc.org.uk.

For more information on the SEC's market risk disclosure rules, see www.sec.gov. The actual text is at www.sec.gov/rules/final/33-7386.txt. For a good review of disclosure issues, see Linsmeier and Pearson (1997).

The GAO follow-up report (1996) is at www.gao.gov/reports.htm.

CHAPTER 3

Regulatory Capital Standards with VAR

The Committee investigated the possible use of banks' proprietary in-house models for the calculation of market risk capital as an alternative to a standardised measurement framework. The results of this study were sufficiently reassuring for it to envisage the use of internal models to measure market risks. . . .

Basel Committee on Banking Supervision, 1995a

Recent years have witnessed unprecedented changes in financial markets, some of which have been described in the preceding two chapters. As firms have improved their risk-measurement systems, regulators have responded by reexamining capital standards imposed on financial institutions. Indeed, commercial banks, securities houses, and insurance companies are now required to carry enough capital to provide a cushion against unexpected losses. Instead of inflexible rules for capital charges, however, which can lead to adverse "gaming" effects, regulators now favor *risk-based capital* charges that respond more quickly to changes in a firm's risk profile. When firms are exposed to multiple sources of risk, VAR has become a standard benchmark.

The recent impetus behind VAR initially came from bank regulators. In their quest for a "safe and sound" financial system, regulators have grown increasingly worried about the potentially destabilizing effect of expanding trading activities of financial institutions. These worries stem from the increased involvement of banks in the derivatives markets, which are becoming global and more complex and therefore are thought to run the risk of cascading defaults.

The landmark Basel Capital Accord of 1988 provided the first step toward tighter risk management. The so-called Basel Accord sets minimum capital requirements that must be met by commercial banks to guard against credit risks. This agreement was later amended to incorporate market risks. In this amendment, central bankers implicitly recognized that risk-management models in use by major banks were far more advanced than anything they could propose. Banks now have the option to use their own VAR risk-management model as the basis for required capital ratios. Thus VAR is being officially promoted as good risk-management practice. In fact, *soundness,* long a fuzzy concept, can now be measured in terms of probability of insolvency.

Indeed, banks have long recognized that managing financial risks is the natural business of financial institutions. Better risk-management systems allow them to deploy their capital more efficiently and should provide a source of comparative advantage. However, this extends beyond the realm of commercial banks. Securities houses, pension funds, and insurance companies are also in the business of managing financial risks. Here the trend is also, inexorably, to risk-based capital.

This chapter presents regulatory initiatives for VAR. Section 3.1 discusses the rationale behind regulation of the financial sector. The 1988 Basel Accord is summarized in Section 3.2, which is followed by the amendment on market risks in Section 3.3. We compare the Basel-imposed standardized and internal models approaches as well as the pre-commitment approach. Next, Section 3.4 describes the latest proposals for revising the 1988 credit risk charges. Finally, Section 3.5 concludes with the regulation of nonbank financial intermediaries.

3.1 WHY REGULATION?

One could ask at the outset why regulations are necessary. After all, the owners of a financial institution should be free to set their own economic risk capital. *Economic risk capital* is the amount of capital that institutions would devote to support their financial activities in the absence of regulatory constraints, after careful consideration of the risk-return trade-offs involved.

Indeed, shareholders are putting their own capital at risk and suffer the direct consequences of failure to control market risk. Essentially, this is what happened to Barings, where complacent shareholders failed to monitor the firm's management. Poor control over traders led to increasingly risky activities and bankruptcy.

The Bank of England is reported to have agonized over the decision of whether it should bail out Barings. In the end, it let the bank fail. Many observers said this was the correct decision. In freely functioning capital markets, badly managed institutions should be allowed to fail. This failure also serves as a powerful object lesson in risk management.

Nevertheless, regulation generally is viewed as necessary when free markets appear to be unable to allocate resources efficiently. For financial institutions, this is the case for two situations, externalities and deposit insurance.

Externalities arise when an institution's failure affects other firms. Here, the fear is that of systemic risk. *Systemic risk* arises when default by one institution has a cascading effect on other firms, thus posing a threat to the stability of the entire financial system. Systemic risk is rather difficult to evaluate because it involves situations of extreme instability, thus happening infrequently. In recent years, however, two medium-sized institutions, Drexel and Barings, failed without creating other defaults.

Deposit insurance also provides a rationale for regulation. By nature, bank deposits are destabilizing. Depositors are promised to be repaid the full face value of their investment on demand. They may then rationally cause a "run on the bank" if they fear that a bank's assets have fallen behind its liabilities. Given that bank assets can be invested in illiquid securities or in real estate, the run will force liquidation at great costs.

One solution to this problem is government guarantees for bank deposits, which eliminate the rationale for bank runs. These guarantees are also viewed as necessary to protect small depositors who cannot efficiently monitor their bank. Such monitoring is complex, expensive, and time-consuming for the thousands of small depositors who entrust their funds to a bank.

One could argue that deposit insurance could be provided by the private sector instead of the government. Realistically, however, private financial systems may not be able to provide guarantees to investors if large macroeconomic shocks such as the depression of the 1930s occur. Assuming such coverage is desirable, governments can provide this coverage by forcing other sectors of the economy to provide backup capital through taxation.

This government guarantee is no panacea, for it creates a host of other problems, generally described under the rubric of *moral hazard.* Given government guarantees, there is even less incentive for depositors to monitor their banks, but rather to flock to institutions offering high deposit rates. Bank owners are now offered what is the equivalent of a "put" option. If they take risks and prosper, they partake in the benefits. If they lose, the government steps in and pays back the depositors. As long as the cost of deposit insurance is not related to the riskiness of activities, there will be perverse incentives to take on additional risk. These incentives no doubt played a part in the great savings and loans debacle, where total losses are now estimated at $150 billion, most of which was paid for by U.S. taxpayers. The national commission set up to consider the lessons of this fiasco called deposit insurance the "necessary condition" without which this debacle would not have occurred.

The moral hazard problem due to deposit insurance explains why regulators attempt to control risk-taking activities. This is achieved by forcing banks to carry minimum levels of capital, thus providing a cushion to protect the insurance fund. Capital adequacy requirements also can serve as a deterrent to unusual risk taking if the amount of capital to set aside is tied to the amount of risk undertaken.

Still, a remaining issue is the appropriate level of capital required to ensure a "safe and sound" financial system. Historically, regulators have been tempted to set high capital-adequacy levels, just to be safe. Perhaps the best warning against imposing capital standards that are too high was articulated by Alan Greenspan, chairman of the Federal Reserve, in May 1994. He pointed out that

- Bank shareholders must earn a competitive rate of return on capital at risk, and returns are adversely affected by high capital requirements.
- In times of stress, banks can take steps to reduce their exposure to market risks.
- "When market forces . . . break loose of economic fundamentals, . . . sound policy actions, and not just bank capital, are necessary to preserve financial stability."

In Greenspan's view, the management of systemic risk is "properly the job of the central banks," which offer a form of catastrophe insurance against such events.

A more radical approach to the deposit insurance–moral hazard dilemma is to rely on market discipline only. The central bank of New Zealand, for instance, recently has abolished deposit insurance. Thus the Reserve Bank will not bail out failing banks, although it is still responsible for protecting the overall banking system. As a result, depositors must now rely on information provided by commercial banks and ratings agencies to decide whether their funds will be safe. This system puts an increased responsibility on bank directors to ensure that their institution is sound, since failure may lead to creditor lawsuits.

The New Zealand experiment surely will be watched intensely by bank regulators all over the world. In the meantime, the mainstream regulatory path is evolving toward a system where capital requirements are explicitly linked to the risk of activities undertaken by commercial banks.

3.2 THE 1988 BASEL ACCORD

The Basel Accord represents a landmark financial agreement for the regulation of commercial banks. It was concluded on July 15, 1988, by the central bankers from the Group of Ten (G-10) countries.[1]

The main purposes of the accord were to strengthen the soundness and stability of the international banking system by providing a minimum standard for capital requirements and to create a level playing field among international banks by harmonizing global regulations.

The 1988 agreement defined a common measure of solvency (the Cooke ratio, so named after its originator) that only covers *credit risks*. Although not statutory, the new ratios were fully implemented in the G-10 countries by December 1992. By now, over 100 countries have adopted the accord, making for more consistent prudential regulations worldwide.

3.2.1 The Cooke Ratio

The Basel Accord requires capital to be equal to at least 8 percent of the total risk-weighted assets of the bank. Capital, however, is interpreted more broadly than the usual definition of equity book value, since its goal is to protect deposits. It consists of two components:

- *Tier 1 capital, or "core" capital. Tier 1 capital* includes paid-up stock issues and disclosed reserves, most notably from after-tax retained earnings. Such capital is permanent and is regarded as a buffer of the highest quality. This definition is common to all countries' banking systems, and is the most visible basis of capital strength. Of the 8 percent capital charge, at least 50 percent must be covered by tier 1 capital.

---

1. The Basel Committee's members are senior officials from the G-10, Belgium, Canada, France, Germany, Italy, Japan, the Netherlands, Sweden, the United Kingdom, and the United States, plus Luxembourg and Switzerland, who meet four times a year, usually in Basel, under the aegis of the Bank for International Settlements.

- *Tier 2 capital, or "supplementary" capital. Tier 2 capital* includes perpetual securities, undisclosed reserves, subordinated debt with maturity greater than 5 years, and shares redeemable at the option of the issuer. Since long-term debt has a junior status relative to deposits, it acts as a buffer to protect depositors (and the deposit insurer).

Risk capital weights were classified into four categories, depending on the nature of the asset. These *ratios* are described in Table 3–1. For instance, U.S. Treasuries, being obligations of an Organization for Economic Cooperation and Development (OECD) government, are assigned a weight of zero. So is cash and gold held by banks. As the perceived credit risk increases, so does the risk weight. At the other end of the scale, claims on corporations, including loans, bonds, and equities, re-

TABLE 3–1

Risk Capital Weights by Asset Class

Weights (%)	Asset Type
0	Cash held
	Claims on OECD central governments
	Claims on central governments in national currency
20	Cash to be received
	Claims on OECD banks and regulated securities firms
	Claims on non-OECD banks below 1 year
	Claims on multilateral development banks
	Claims on foreign OECD public-sector entities
50	Residential mortgage loans
100	Claims on the private sector (corporate debt, equity, . . .)
	Claims on non-OECD banks above 1 year
	Real estate
	Plant and equipment
0–50	(At national discretion)
	Claims on domestic OECD public-sector entities, e.g., claims on U.S. agencies: 20

Note: The OCED currently consists of Austria, Belgium, Canada, Denmark, France, Germany, Greece, Iceland, Ireland, Italy, Luxembourg, The Netherlands, Norway, Portugal, Spain, Sweden, Switzerland, Turkey, United Kingdom, United States, Japan, Finland, Australia, New Zealand, Mexico, Czech Republic, Hungary, Korea, and Poland, in order of accession.

ceive a 100 percent weight, which means that effectively they must be covered by 8 percent capital.

The *credit risk charge* (CRC) is defined as

$$CRC = 8\% \times (\text{risk} - \text{weighted assets}) = 8\% \times \left(\sum_i w_i \times \text{asset}_i \right) \quad (3.1)$$

where w_i is the risk weight attached to asset i. In addition, these guidelines include capital requirements for the credit exposure of derivatives contracts. The computation of the required capital charges is detailed in the chapter on credit risk.

Signatories to the Basel Accord are free to impose higher capital requirements in their own countries. Accordingly, shortly after the Basel Accord, U.S. legislators passed the Federal Deposit Insurance Corporation Improvement Act (FDICIA) of 1991, aimed at promoting the safety and soundness of American financial institutions. Among the newly established bank capital requirements, U.S. regulators[2] have added the restriction that tier 1 capital must be no less than 3 percent of *total* assets; this ratio can be set higher for banks deemed to be weaker. The European Union (EU) also has issued its own capital requirement rules, known as the Capital Adequacy Directive (CAD), which are in line with the Basel guidelines.

3.2.2 Activity Restrictions

In addition to capital adequacy requirements, the Basel Accord sets limits on "excessive risk takings." These are restrictions on *large risks,* defined as positions that exceed 10 percent of a bank's capital. Large risks must be reported to regulatory authorities. Positions that exceed 25 percent of a firm's capital are not allowed, and the total of large risks must not exceed 800 percent of capital. In practice, however, the rules behind these ratios have not always been defined formally and sometimes need clarification from regulatory authorities. As the example in Box 3–1 shows, clarification came too late to save Barings.

3.2.3 Criticisms of the 1988 Approach

The 1988 Basel regulations have been criticized on several fronts. As is usually the case with binding regulatory requirements, institutions may

---

2. These include the Federal Reserve Board, the Office of the Comptroller of the Currency, and the Federal Deposit Insurance Corporation.

B O X   3-1

BARINGS'S LARGE RISK

Barings went bankrupt because of large positions on the Singapore Monetary Exchange (SIMEX) and on the Osaka Securities Exchange (OSE) that were quite large in relation to the firm's capital. At the time, it was not clear whether Barings's exposure to these exchanges could be classified as quasi-sovereign risk or corporate risk. This was an important issue to resolve because the "large risk" limit does not apply to sovereign risk.

Barings formally requested from the Bank of England (BoE) a clarification as to the status of its exposure to exchanges. The BoE took 2 years to answer. On February 1, 1995, it said that this exposure could not be considered as sovereign and that the 25 percent limit applied. On that day, Barings's exposure to SIMEX was 40 percent of its capital base and to OSE, 73 percent. Eventually, this exposure led to Barings's downfall. Later, a report on the bankruptcy stated that the "delay was unacceptable; the Bank was not entitled to assume that the delay would be inconsequential."

find ways to get around the restrictions or, even worse, may engage in distorted lending patterns. For instance, banks that are subject to binding regulatory capital may move into areas where expected returns from lending exceed regulatory costs in an attempt to equalize regulatory capital with economic capital.

This has led to *regulatory arbitrage,* which generally can be defined as behavior that defeats the regulatory requirements. An example is *securitization,* which transforms loans into tradable securities, some of which can be sold off or moved into the trading books, which lowers the capital requirement without necessarily decreasing the remaining economic credit risk. Indeed, about a quarter of U.S. banks' balance sheets have been securitized in recent years, and the credit quality of loan books has deteriorated. Another example is *credit derivatives,* which are akin to credit insurance and can be used to shuffle credit exposures into areas with lower risk weights.[3]

This problem, however, arises with any regulatory requirements. As William McDonough, chairman of the Basel Committee, has said: "There

---

3. For specific examples, see the International Swap and Derivatives Association (1998) report, the Basel Committee on Banking Supervision working paper (1999a), or Ong (1999).

isn't a system in the world that can't be gamed." The real issue is whether the 1988 guidelines were so grossly out of step with economic charges for credit risk so as to actually induce dangerous behavior. The criticisms of the 1988 Basel Accord can be classified as follows.

- *Inadequate differentiation of credit risks.* The four risk-weight categories are widely viewed as too crude. The same 100 percent ratio, for instance, is applied to low-risk and high-risk borrowers. Thus a loan to General Electric, which is among the biggest corporations in terms of market capitalization with an Aaa credit rating, would require the same regulatory capital as a loan to a near-bankrupt company. Also, the original low capital charge for OECD banks became inadequate as the OECD started to include "emerging" economies with shaky banking institutions. Box 3–2 demonstrates the importance of these issues.

BOX 3–2

PEREGRINE'S DOWNFALL

Peregrine Investments Holdings, one of Hong Kong's leading investment banks, was one of the victims of the Asian crisis of 1997. The bank suffered from losses such as a loan to PT Steady Safe, an Indonesian taxicab operator, that amounted to $235 million, a quarter of the bank's equity capital. After Asian currencies crashed in the summer of 1997, many Asian borrowers were unable to repay their foreign-currency loans. Peregrine's exposure to Asia led to its collapse on January 13, 1998.

While Peregrine was not subject to the capital adequacy requirements of commercial banks, it did not control credit risk adequately. The head of credit-risk management, John Lee, said that he had not even been informed of the the Steady Safe loan, which was the single biggest item in the firm's bond portfolio! The firm's ruin can be traced to insufficient diversification and lack of proper risk-management controls.

The Asian crisis also revealed patterns in bank lending that had become distorted due to the 1988 capital requirements. In 1997, 60 percent of $380 billion bank lending to Asia had a maturity of less than 1 year, which only carries a 20 percent risk weight for non-OECD banks. Asian banks and borrowers buckled under the combined effects of local currency devaluations and liquidity problems due to these short maturities.

- *Nonrecognition of term structure effects.* Even when controlling for the credit rating, the term of the loan is an important factor in measuring credit risk. A 2-year loan to an AA-rated company, for instance, has very little risk of default. In contrast, a 30-year loan to the same company is much riskier.

- *Nonrecognition of risk-mitigation techniques.* These techniques, such as netting or the use of collateral, decrease the economic credit risk but are not recognized under the 1988 rules. *Netting* refers to a legal agreement whereby payment obligations between two parties are amalgamated into one single, net obligation. As a result of netting, counterparty failure will lead to a smaller loss if the amount lent is matched by the amount borrowed. Similarly, credit losses will be lessened if the bank holds collateral. The fact that these prudent risk-mitigation techniques are not recognized under the 1988 Basel Accord is a significant problem because it discourages and even penalizes banks for attempting to control credit risk better.

- *Nonrecognition of diversification effects.* The rules do not recognize that credit risk can, and should, be mitigated through spreading risks across issuers, industries, and geographic locations. As long as correlations between components of the portfolio are below one, simply summing the capital charges will overstate the true risk. Again, this is a significant problem because the 1988 Basel Accord discourages prudent diversification.

- *Nonrecognition of market risk.* Finally, the 1988 Basel Accord did not account for the market risk assumed by banks. This omission was particularly glaring with the growth in *proprietary trading activities* (i.e., trading for their own account) and derivatives. In recognition of this drawback, the Basel Committee has added a capital charge for market risk.

The bottom line is that besides failing to encourage prudent diversification, the 1998 Basel Accord leads to capital charges that have been estimated to be *twice* the economic charges estimated by major U.S. banks.

3.3 THE 1996 AMENDMENT ON MARKET RISKS

In 1996, the Basel Committee amended the Basel Capital Accord to incorporate market risks. This amendment, which came into force at the end of 1997, added a capital charge for market risk based on either of two approaches, the standardized method or the internal models method.

The amendment separated the bank's assets into two categories:

- *Trading book.* This is the bank portfolio containing financial instruments that are intentionally held for short-term resale and typically are marked-to-market.
- *Banking book.* This consists of other instruments, mainly loans.

The amendment adds a capital charge for the market risk of trading books, as well as for the currency and commodity risk of the banking book. The credit risk charge now excludes debt and equity securities in the trading book and positions in commodities but still includes all OTC derivatives, whether in the trading or banking books.

To obtain total capital-adequacy requirements, banks should add their credit risk charge to their market risk charge (MRC):

$$\text{TRC} = \text{CRC} + \text{MRC} \qquad (3.2)$$

In exchange for having to allocate additional capital, banks were allowed to use a new class of capital, *tier 3 capital,* which consists of short-term subordinated debt. The amount of tier 3 capital (tier 2 capital or both) is limited to 250 percent of tier 1 capital allocated to support market risks.

3.3.1 The Standardized Method

The first approach, originally proposed in April 1993, is based on a pre-specified "building-block approach." The bank's market risk is first computed for portfolios exposed to interest rate risk, exchange rate risk, equity risk, and commodity risk using specific guidelines. The bank's total risk is then obtained from the summation of risks across the four categories. Because the construction of the risk charge follows a highly structured and standardized process, this approach is sometimes called the *standardized method.*

For interest rate risk, the rules define a set of maturity bands, within which net positions are identified across all on- and off-balance-sheet items. A duration weight is then assigned to each of the 13 bands, varying from 0.20 percent for positions under 3 months to 12.50 percent for positions over 20 years. The sum of all weighted net positions then yields an overall interest rate risk indicator. Note that the netting of positions within a band and aggregation across bands assume perfect correlations across debt instruments. For currency and equity risk, the market risk capital charge is essentially 8 percent of the net position, whereas for commodities, the charge is 15 percent.[4] In total, the market risk charge is the arithmetic sum of market risk charges for individual positions:

$$\text{MRC}^{\text{STD}} = \sum_i \text{MRC}_i \qquad (3.3)$$

Although this approach aims at identifying banks with unusual exposure, it is still beset by problems. The *duration* of some instruments cannot be identified easily. Mortgages, for instance, contain prepayment options that allow the homeowner to refinance the loan if interest rates fall. This risk is known as *contraction risk*. Conversely, homeowners will make payments over a longer period if interest rates increase. This risk is called *extension risk*. The effective duration of mortgages changes with the level of interest rates and the past history of prepayments for a mortgage pool. Assigning a duration band to one of these instruments becomes highly questionable. More generally, the risk classification is arbitrary. The capital charges of 8 percent are applied uniformly to equities and currencies (and gold) without regard for their actual return volatilities.

Another issue is that the standardized method does not account for *diversification across risks*. Low correlations imply that the risk of a portfolio can be much less than the sum of individual component risks. This diversification effect applies across market risks or across different types of financial risks.

Diversification across market risks is the easiest to measure. Historical data reveal that correlations across markets are not perfect. Investing across global fixed-income markets, for instance, is less risky than investing in a single market. Similarly, exchange rate movements are not perfectly correlated, nor are movements between interest rates and exchange rates. Assuming perfect correlations across various types of risks overestimates portfolio risk and leads to capital adequacy requirements that are too high.

---

4. For precise rules, the reader is referred to the Basel Committee Amendment. In addition to the market risk charge, interest rate and equity positions carry a "specific" risk capital charge, which is intended to cover changes in market values due, for instance, to changes in credit quality.

B O X   3–3

TELESCOPING OF CREDIT AND INTEREST RATE RISK

As an example of a similar telescoping of market and credit risk, consider the overseas debt crisis of the 1980s. American (and other) commercial banks had been eager to lend to developing countries like Brazil and Mexico, but they hoped to escape exposure to currency, interest rate, and credit risk.

An instrument known as the *syndicated Eurodollar loan* seemed to provide the perfect answer. It was denominated in dollars (no currency risk), was payable on a floating-rate basis (no interest rate risk), and was made to governments (which were unlikely to go out of business). However, after U.S. interest rates skyrocketed in the early 1980s, countries like Mexico and Brazil went into default: They were unable to make the (floating) interest payments on their loans. In short, market risk had turned into credit risk—and on a huge scale.

Correlations across different types of risks are more difficult to deal with. Most notably, credit risk may be related to interest rate risk, as shown in Box 3–3. This is true for most floating-rate instruments (such as adjustable-rate mortgages), where borrowers may default should interest rates increase to insufferable amounts. By simply adding up the credit and market risk charges, the Basel Committee has implicitly assumed perfect correlations between these risks, which is the worst-case scenario.

3.3.2 The Internal Models Approach

In response to industry criticisms to the standardized method, the Basel Committee came forth with a major alternative in April 1995. For the first time, it would allow banks the option of using their own risk-measurement models to determine their capital charge. This decision stemmed from a recognition that many banks had developed sophisticated risk-management systems, in many cases far more complex than could be dictated by regulators. As for institutions lagging behind the times, this alternative provided a further impetus to create sound risk-management systems.

To use this approach, banks first have to satisfy various *qualitative requirements*. The bank must demonstrate that it has a sound risk-management system, which must be integrated into management decisions. It must conduct regular stress tests. The bank also must have an independent risk-control unit as well as external audits. When these requirements are satisfied, the market risk charge is based on the following steps:

- *Quantitative parameters.* The computation of VAR shall be based on a set of uniform quantitative inputs:
  - *a.* A horizon of 10 trading days or 2 calendar weeks
  - *b.* A 99 percent confidence interval
  - *c.* An observation period based on at least a year of historical data and updated at least once a quarter.
- *Treatment of correlations.* Correlations can be recognized in broad categories (e.g., fixed income) as well as across categories (e.g., between fixed income and currencies).
- *Market risk charge.* The general market capital charge shall be set at the higher of the previous day's VAR or the average VAR over the last 60 business days times a "multiplicative" factor k. The exact value of this *multiplicative factor* is to be determined by local regulators, subject to an absolute floor of 3. Without this risk factor, a bank would be expected to have losses that exceed its capital in one 10-day period out of a hundred, or about once in 4 years. This does not seem prudent. Also, this factor (sometimes called a *hysteria factor*) is intended to provide additional protection against environments that are less stable than historical data would lead one to believe.[5]
- *Plus factor.* A penalty component, or *plus factor*, shall be added to the multiplicative factor k if backtesting reveals that the bank's internal model incorrectly forecasts risks. The purpose of this factor is to give incentives to banks to improve the predictive accuracy of their models and to avoid overly optimistic projection of profits and losses due to model fitting. Tommasso Padoa-Schioppa, former chairman of the Basel Committee, described this problem as "driving by using the rear-view mirror."

---

5. Studies of bank portfolios based on historical data have shown that while the 99 percent VAR is often exceeded, a multipler of 3 provides adequate protection against extreme losses. See, for instance, Jackson et al. (1997).

Since the penalty factor may depend on the quality of internal controls at the bank, this system is designed to reward truthful internal monitoring, as well as developing sound risk-management systems.

To summarize, the internal models approach (IMA) market risk charge on any day t is

$$\text{MRC}_t^{\text{IMA}} = \max\!\left(k\,\frac{1}{60}\sum_{i=1}^{60}\text{VAR}_{t-i},\ \text{VAR}_{t-1}\right) + \text{SRC}_t \qquad (3.4)$$

where SRC is the specific risk charge.[6] In practice, banks are allowed to base their 10-day VAR from scaling up their 1-day VAR by the square root of 10. Also note that, due to the multiplier, the charge generally will be driven by the 60-day average instead of the latest VAR. The bank would have to experience a sharp increase in its risk positions or in the market volatility for the previous day's VAR to become the dominant factor.

3.3.3 The Precommitment Model

The debate around the choice of capital adequacy levels took another turn as the Federal Reserve Board (1995) proposed a radically different approach to bank regulation, which could become a successor or alternative to the current system.

Under this *precommitment model,* the bank would precommit to a maximum trading loss over a designated horizon. This loss would become the capital charge for market risk. The supervisor would then observe, say, after a quarterly reporting period, whether trading losses exceeded the limit. If so, the bank would suffer a penalty that might include a fine, regulatory discipline, or higher future capital charges. Violations of the limits also would bring public scrutiny to the bank, which provides a further feedback mechanism for good management.

The main advantage of this incentive-compatible approach is that the bank itself chooses its capital requirement. An *incentive-compatible approach* creates incentives for banks to make decisions that produce outcomes consistent with regulatory objectives, eliminating the motive for regulatory arbitrage. As Kupiec and O'Brien (1995, 1997) have shown,

---

6. This charge is explained in more detail in the Basel Committee on Banking Supervision amendment (1996b).

this choice is made optimally in response to regulatory penalties for violations. Regulators can then choose the penalty that will induce appropriate behavior.

This proposal has been welcomed by banking executives, who argued that this approach explicitly recognizes the links between risk-management practices and firm-selected deployment of capital. Bankers also feel that this approach will result in less intrusion by regulators, as well as lower capital requirements. Critics, in contrast, point out that quarterly verification is very slow in comparison with the real-time daily capital requirements of the existing Basel Accord rules. Others worry that imposing a penalty after a bank has incurred a loss could bankrupt the bank or, worse, induce it to "go-for-broke" as it starts losing money.

The approach was subject to a test conducted by the New York Clearinghouse from October 1996 to September 1997. Participants characterized the experiment as a success to the extent that the approach proved operationally workable. Generally, however, regulators are still skeptical. Most probably will want to give sufficient time to the internal models approach to judge how it is working.[7]

3.3.4 Comparison of Approaches

At this point, it is useful to compare the pros and cons of each method. The standardized method is widely viewed as least adequate because of the following factors:

- *Portfolio considerations.* The model ignores diversification effects across sources of risk.
- *Arbitrary capital charges.* The capital charges are only loosely related to the actual volatility of each asset category. This can distort portfolio choices as banks move away from assets for which the capital charge is abnormally high.
- *Compliance costs.* Given that many banks already run sophisticated risk-measurement systems, the standardized method imposes an additional reporting burden.

The second, internal models approach addresses all these issues. It relies on the self-interest of banks to develop accurate risk-management

---

7. The results of the experiment are discussed in Considine (1998) and P. Parkinson (1998).

systems. Internal VAR systems measure the total portfolio risk of the bank, account for differences in asset volatilities, and can be used for regulatory requirements at a small additional cost. In addition, capital requirements will evolve automatically at the same speed as risk-measurement techniques because new developments will be incorporated automatically into internal VARs.

In fact, the standardized approach is so inefficient that according to a recent study, it requires seven times more capital than a 10-day VAR. Even with a multiplicative factor of 3, banks are now able to cut their capital charges in *half* by adopting the internal models approach.

Unfortunately, from the viewpoint of regulators, the internal models method still has some drawbacks:

- *Performance verification.* Supervisors are supposed to monitor whether internal VARs indeed provide good estimates of future market profits and losses. Since capital charges are based on VARs, there may be an incentive to artificially lower the VAR figure to lower capital requirements; thus verification by regulators is important. The problem is that even with a well-calibrated model, there will be instances when losses will exceed the VAR just by chance (e.g., 5 percent of the time using a 95 percent confidence level). Unfortunately, long periods may be needed to distinguish between chance and model inaccuracies, as shown in Chapter 6. This issue makes verification difficult.

- *Endogeneity of positions.* Banks' internal VARs typically measure risk over a short interval, such as a day. Extending these numbers to a 10-day trading period ignores the fact that positions will change, especially in response to losses or unexpectedly high volatility.[8] Therefore, measures of long-horizon exposure ignore efficient risk-management procedures and controls.

Note that these problems do not detract from the usefulness of VAR models for corporate risk management. From the viewpoint of regulators, however, the precommitment approach has much to recommend it because

8. A typical management response is to cut positions as losses accumulate. This pattern of trading can be compared with portfolio insurance, which attempts to replicate a put option. Therefore, attempts by management to control losses will create a pattern of payoffs over long horizons that will be asymmetrical, like options. The problem is that traditional VAR measures are inadequate with highly nonlinear payoffs.

it automatically accounts for changing positions. In addition, the risk coverage level is chosen endogenously by the bank in response to the penalty for failure, which creates fewer distortions in capital markets.

Unfortunately, all models suffer from a performance-verification problem. The regulator can only compare *ex post,* or realized, performance to *ex ante* estimates of risk or maximum loss. Unless the maximum loss is set extremely high, there will always be instances where a loss will exceed the limit even with the correct model. The key, then, for regulators is to separate good intentions and bad luck from reckless behavior.

3.3.5 Example

Table 3–2 provides an example of the computation of the risk charges for J.P. Morgan. The table compares the evolution of assets, equity, and off-balance-sheet instruments. The off-balance-sheet instruments have increased sevenfold over the period, reflecting the huge growth in derivatives markets.

The total risk charge (TRC), or required capital, is computed as

$$\text{TRC} = \text{CRC} + \text{MRC} = 8\% \times \text{risk-adjusted assets} \qquad (3.5)$$

In 1998, total risk-adjusted assets amounted to $140 billion. Using the required 8 percent ratio, this yields a minimum capital of $11.2 billion. The actual capital held by the bank was $16.4 billion, which translates into an actual ratio of 11.7 percent, comfortably above the regulatory minimum. If the bank estimates that its capital exceeds the amount of economic capital required to support its risks, it can shrink its capital base through dividend payments or share repurchases.

It is also informative to break down the required capital into a market and credit risk charge. Assuming a $38 million 95 percent daily VAR, the internal models approach yields a market risk charge of $510 million. This is only 5 percent of the total risk charge of $11.2 billion. Thus the market risk charge is small compared with the credit risk capital requirements.

3.4 THE 1999 CREDIT RISK REVISIONS

Overall, the 1988 Basel Accord was successful in stabilizing the financial system. The accord led to substantial increases in banking capital ratios. Tier 1 capital increased from $840 billion to $1500 billion from 1990 to 1998 for the 1000 largest banks, which have now enough capital to weather most storms.

TABLE 3-2

Computation of Risk Capital

					$ Billions			
	1992	1993	1994	1995	1996	1997	1998
Assets	103.2	133.9	154.9	184.9	204.7	262.2	261.1
Liabilities	95.9	124.0	145.3	174.4	193.9	250.8	249.8
Equity	7.3	9.9	9.6	10.5	10.8	11.4	11.3
Off-balance sheet	1,309	1,680	2,547	3,520	4,795	6,286	8,961
Risk-adjusted assets							
Assets	40.8	46.6	47.4	54.3	68.5	81.0	78.9
Off-balance sheet	33.8	36.8	38.9	48.8	55.4	67.5	61.3
Total	74.6	83.4	86.3	103.1	123.9	148.5	140.2
Risk capital							
Required (8%)	6.0	6.7	6.9	8.2	9.9	11.9	11.2
Actual							
Tier 1	6.6	7.8	8.3	9.0	10.8	11.9	11.2
Tier 2	3.0	3.1	4.0	4.4	4.3	5.8	5.2
Total capital	9.6	10.9	12.3	13.4	15.1	17.7	16.4
Actual ratio	12.9%	13.1%	14.3%	13.0%	12.2%	11.9%	11.7%

While the banking system may now have sufficient overall capital levels, glaring deficiencies have been revealed in the allocation of this capital across credit risks. In response, the Basel Committee proposed new guidelines in June 1999, which have become known informally as *Basel II.*

3.4.1 The Revisions

The proposals are based on three "pillars":

- *Minimum regulatory requirements.* As before, banks are subject to a credit risk charge. Now, however, the charge can be based on *external* credit ratings, for example, issued by the credit rating agencies, or *internal* credit ratings, developed by "sophisticated banks." There is no acceptance yet of internal portfolio credit risk models.

- *Supervisory review.* This is to ensure that banks indeed operate above the minimum regulatory capital ratios, that management develops an internal capital assessment process, and that corrective action is taken as soon as possible.

- *Market discipline.* The goal is to encourage banks to publish information about their exposures, risk profiles, and capital cushion, thus submitting themselves to shareholder scrutiny.

The proposal introduced five categories of risk weights, which are detailed in Table 3–3. These new weights allow better differentiation of credit risk through the use of credit rating agencies or internal ratings.

3.4.2 Overall Assessment

The proposed rules represent a notable improvement over the 1988 Basel Accord, which suffers from a long list of drawbacks, discussed in Section 3.2.3. Indeed, the new risk weights potentially provide much better differentiation of *individual* credit risk.

In some sense, however, the 1999 proposal represents a step backward from the internal models approach for the trading book. By ruling out internal portfolio credit models, the proposal does not reward diversification effects. And we do know that nondiversification has been a leading cause of banking disasters. As with the rigid 1988 rules, Basel II does

TABLE 3-3

Proposed Basel II Risk Weights

	Credit Rating (e.g., Standard and Poor's)					
Claim	AAA to AA−	A+ to A−	BBB+ to BBB−	BB+ to B−	Below B−	Unrated
Sovereign	0%	20%	50%	100%	150%	100%
Banks	20%	50%	50–100%	100%	150%	50–100%
Corporates	20%	100%	100%	100%	150%	100%

not encourage banks to diversify prudently across loans nor to develop comprehensive risk-management systems.

No doubt this is due to the fact that the banking book is typically much larger than the trading book. Thus what may be a small problem with an inadequate market VAR model may develop into a big problem for a credit VAR model. The stakes are simply much higher for the banking book.

Admittedly, portfolio credit models are still in their infancy. As will be seen in a later chapter, these models are much more complex than market VAR systems. They suffer from inadequate availability of data, unresolved conceptual questions, and difficult model validation issues. Backtesting is intrinsically much more difficult than for market risk due to the facts that credit events are more rare, that we have short histories, and that verification needs to cover long periods—ideally, full business cycles. As one regulator put it: "The burden of proof that credit risk modeling works rest firmly with the banks." There is no doubt, however, that VAR-based portfolio models of credit risk should, in theory, provide better allocation of capital.

In the end, these distortions may not matter that much. We can trust the market to align regulatory and economic capital through regulatory arbitrage. As Chairman Greenspan has said, regulatory arbitrage is not necessarily undesirable:

> In many cases, regulatory arbitrage acts as a safety-valve for attenuating the adverse effects of those regulatory capital requirements that are well in excess of the levels warranted by a specific activity's underlying economic risk.

Regulatory arbitrage, unfortunately, may create unnecessary costs for financial institutions, which are passed along to the consumer.

3.5 REGULATION OF NONBANKS

The regulation of nonbank financial intermediaries is fast converging to that of commercial banks. After all, lines of business across the financial industry are becoming increasingly blurred. Commercial banks are now moving into the trading of securities and provide some underwriting and insurance functions. Also, each of these institutions must learn to deal effectively with similar sources of financial risks. The trading portfolio of banks contains assets, liabilities, and derivatives that are no different from those of securities houses.

Table 3–4 compares the structure of balance sheets for financial intermediaries, for which regulations are now discussed in more detail.

3.5.1 Securities Firms

As with banks, the regulation of securities firms is still evolving. Securities broker-dealers hold securities on the asset and liability side (usually called *long* and *short*) of their balance sheet. Regulators require a prudent reserve to cover financial risks. Here, the argument is that regulation is required to protect the firm's customers against a default of their broker-dealer, as well as the "integrity of the markets," a more nebulous concept.

TABLE 3–4

Balance Sheets of Financial Intermediaries

Type	Assets	Liabilities
Banks (banking books)	Loans, securities at book values	Deposits, CDs, subordinated debt
Securities firms	Securities (long)	Securities (short)
Insurance companies	Market value of assets	Actuarial value of insurance payments
Pension funds	Market value of assets	Present value of defined-benefit pensions

Thus capital standards for banks and securities houses have different purposes. Bank capital is designed to maintain the safety and soundness of banks. As such, capital standards for banks are calculated on a going-concern basis. In contrast, capital standards for broker-dealers are calculated on a liquidation basis. Unlike banks, the U.S. securities industry has never required a taxpayer bailout.

In the United States, a broker-dealer must satisfy a minimum capital ratio based on the calculated ratio of capital to debt or receivables.[9] Here, *capital* is defined as the liquid portion of equity book value minus "haircuts" that provide a further margin of safety in case of default and depend on the nature of assets. These haircuts generally are prescribed as a proportion of the notional, such as 15 percent of the market value of the sum of the long and short equity positions.[10] This approach harks back to the early Basel Accord requirements, which imposed capital charges based on a fixed proportion of notional amounts.

Also, regulators have different views as to whether securities firms should hold capital to cover their *gross* positions, consisting of the sum of all long plus short positions, or *net* positions, which allow offsets. The United States and Japan use the gross-position approach, the United Kingdom uses the net-position approach, and the Basel Committee and the European Union (EU) consider a variant of both approaches. The EU, for instance, requires firms to have equity equal to 2 percent of their gross positions plus 8 percent of their net positions.[11]

More recently, the SEC issued in January 1999 a rule change that creates a class of *OTC derivatives dealers,* which are dealers active in OTC derivatives markets. The goal was to bring the level of regulation for derivatives' trading U.S. broker-dealers in line with foreign firms or even U.S. commercial banks, which are subject to the Basel Accord risk-based capital rules. The new class of OTC derivatives dealers is subject

---

9. For instance, the ratio is 6:⅔ percent of aggregate debt, or 2 percent of the total amount of money owed by customers. For a more detailed description, see, for instance, the General Accounting Office (1998) report.

10. The exact rule is 15 percent of the greater of the long and the short plus 15 percent of the portion of the lesser position that exceeds 25 percent of the greater position. One can wonder at the rationale for such rules. For options, though, haircuts are risk-based.

11. Dimson and Marsh (1995) compare the effectiveness of these approaches for a sample of detailed holdings of British market makers. Comparing the riskiness of the portfolio to various capital requirements, they show that the net position approach as required by the United Kingdom dominates the EU and U.S. approaches because it best approximates the actual portfolio risk. The net-position approach comes closest to what portfolio theory would suggest.

to risk-based capital rules that correspond to the DPG guidelines. In other words, the capital charge is now based on internal VAR models.

3.5.2 Insurance Companies

The purpose of capital standards in the case of insurance companies is similar to that of banks. Capital requirements are imposed to try to limit failures of insurance companies so that they can meet policyholders' future claims. Sources of failures for insurance companies can be traced to the market risk of their assets and liabilities, as well as actuarial risk. *Actuarial risk* is the risk of losses that an insurance company takes in exchange for a premium, such as the risk of a premature death for a life insurance company.

Regulation for insurance companies is less centralized than for other financial institutions in the United States, where insurance is regulated at the state level. As in the case of FDIC protection, insurance contracts ultimately are covered by a state guaranty association. State insurance regulators set nationwide standards through the National Association of Insurance Commissioners (NAIC).

In December 1992, NAIC announced new capital adequacy requirements for life insurers. The minimum capital standard is derived from a series of risk factors that are to be applied, as in the early 1988 Basel Accord, to selected assets and liabilities. For instance, no capital is needed to cover holdings of government bonds, and just 0.5 percent is required for mortgages. But 30 percent of the value of equities must be covered. This ratio is much higher than the 8 percent ratio required for banks, which some insurers claim puts them at a competitive disadvantage vis-à-vis other financial institutions that are increasingly branching out into insurance products. NAIC also developed a series of risk factors to protect against actuarial risk.

In the EU, insurance regulation parallels that of banks, with capital requirements, portfolio restrictions, and regulator intervention in cases of violation. For life insurance companies, capital must exceed 4 percent of *mathematical reserves,* computed as the present values of future premiums minus future death liabilities. For non-life insurance companies, capital must exceed the highest of about 17 percent of premiums charged for the current year and about 24 percent of annual settlements over the last 3 years.

These risk-based capital charges generally have been viewed as a step forward by the industry because they represent better, forward-looking measures of risk. Although by no means perfect, these rules are subject to continuous improvement and have raised the awareness of risk in the industry.

3.5.3 Pension Funds

While pension funds are not subject to capital adequacy requirements, a number of similar restrictions govern defined-benefit plans. *Defined-benefit plans* are those where the employer promises to pay retirement benefits according to a fixed formula. The current U.S. regulatory framework was defined by the Employee Retirement Income Security Act (ERISA), promulgated in 1974. Under ERISA, companies are required to make contributions that are sufficient to provide coverage for pension payments. In effect, the minimum capital is the present value of future pension liabilities. The obligation to make up for unfunded liabilities parallels the obligation to maintain some minimal capital ratio. Also, asset risk weights are replaced by a looser provision of diversification and the mandate not to take excessive risks, as defined under the "prudent person rule."

As in the case of banking regulation, federal guarantees are provided to pensioners. The Pension Benefit Guarantee Corporation (PBGC), like the Federal Deposit Insurance Corporation (FDIC), charges an insurance premium and promises to cover defaults by corporations. Other countries have similar systems, although most other countries rely much more heavily on public *pay-as-you-go* schemes, where contributions from current employees directly fund current retirees. The United States, Britain, and the Netherlands are far more advanced in their reliance on private pension funds. Public systems in countries afflicted by large government deficits can ill afford generous benefits to an increasingly aging population. As a result, private pension funds are likely to take on increasing importance all over the world. With those will come the need for prudential regulation.

Like other financial institutions, pension funds recognize the importance of measuring, controlling, and managing their financial risks. Here again, VAR methods can help. An entire chapter in this book is devoted to the application of VAR systems to pension funds.

3.6 CONCLUSIONS

The regulation of financial institutions still varies widely across industries. This is a legacy of differing institutional environments, as well as

TABLE 3–5

Regulation of Financial Intermediaries

Type	Main Risk Factors	Purposes of Regulatory Capital
Banks	Credit risk	Safety and soundness
	Market risk	Protect deposit insurance fund
Securities firms	Market risk	Protect customers
	Liquidity risk	Protect integrity of securities market
Insurance firms	Actuarial risk	Protect claimants
	Market risk	
Pension funds	Market risk	Protect retirees
	Liability risk	Protect pension insurance fund

differing regulatory objectives. Table 3–5 compares the main risk factors for various financial intermediaries, as well as the purposes of regulatory capital.

This table, however, exposes striking similarities between these institutions. All these sectors have to manage multiple sources of financial risk. All the regulatory objectives involve some form of protection. Protection against multiple sources of financial risks is best measured with VAR. This explains why capital requirements are rapidly converging as demarcation lines between banks, securities firms, and insurance companies become increasingly blurred.

The latest manifestation of this merging of business activity is the repeal of the Glass-Steagall Act, which separated banking and securities functions in the United States. Glass-Steagall was enacted in 1933, as the Great Depression was threatening to wipe out the U.S. banking system, with one bank in three failing.[12] Congress then reacted by forcing a separation between commercial and investment banks and instituted federal deposit insurance. While the act succeeded in restoring confidence in the banking system, it quickly became obsolete. It has restricted the ability of U.S. financial institutions to integrate their lines of business and has

---

12. It should be noted that, once again, governments created conditions that contributed to these widespread failures. Banking laws prohibiting interstate banking created a proliferation of small banks that were highly dependent on local economic conditions. Here also, this banking problem can be traced to lack of diversification of credit risk.

hampered their ability to compete with foreign banks and brokerage houses. In recent years, markets effectively got around the restrictions by creating giant financial conglomerates. The most notable was the 1998 merger of a giant commercial bank and an insurance company, Citibank and Travelers. By 1999, the act was repealed.

The merger activity in financial services, however, is creating large conglomerates that need to be subject to consistent capital standards. It is fair to predict that we will observe a further convergence of capital standards to risk-based charges partly based on VAR systems.

FURTHER INFORMATION

The following essential documents have been issued by the Basel Committee on Banking Supervision (BCBS) and are available on the Web site www.bis.org. The original Basel Accord document on credit risk is BCBS (1988). The new capital adequacy framework is in BCBS (1999c). The BCBS (1999a) working paper explores the impact of the Basel Accord. The amendment to the capital accord to incorporate market risks is in BCBS (1996b), with the backtesting framework in BCBS (1996a).

The texts of the EU's capital adequacy directives are:

EU (1989) for the council directive on a solvency ratio for credit institutions, at europa.eu.int/eur-lex/en/lif/dat/1989/en_389L0647.html.

EU (1993) for the council directive on the capital adequacy of investment firms and credit institutions, at europa.eu.int/eurlex/en/lif/dat/1993/en_393L0006.html.

EU (1979) for the council directive on the regulation of life assurance companies, at europa.eu.int/eur-lex/en/lif/dat/1979/en_379L0267.html.

The U.S. General Accounting Office (GAO) has provided a useful comparative overview (1998) of risk-based capital charges in the financial industry. Available at www.gao.gov/reports.htm.

The following document from the International Swaps and Derivatives Association (1998) reviews the 1988 credit risk capital charges. Available at www.isda.org.

The SEC's risk-based rules for OTC derivatives dealers is at www.sec.gov/rules/final/34-40594.txt.

PART TWO

Building Blocks

CHAPTER 4

Measuring Financial Risk

The stock market will fluctuate.

*J.P. Morgan, when asked what the
market was going to do.*

Although in modern parlance the term *risk* has come to mean "danger of loss," finance theory defines *risk* as the dispersion of unexpected outcomes due to movements in financial variables. Thus both positive and negative deviations should be viewed as sources of risk. Countless investors have missed this point as they failed to realize that the superior performance of traders, such as Nick Leeson and Bob Citron, really reflected greater risks. Extraordinary performance, both good and bad, should raise red flags.

To measure risk, one has to define first the variable of interest, which could be portfolio value, earnings, capital, or a particular cash flow. Financial risks are created by the effects of financial factors on this variable.

Since risk needs to be defined rigorously, this chapter lays the probabilistic and statistical foundation of portfolio theory that is behind the use of value at risk (VAR). Readers who are thoroughly familiar with these concepts could skip directly to the next chapter, which formally introduces VAR.

Section 4.1 first discusses various sources of financial risk. The concepts of risk and return are formally defined in Section 4.2, which shows how to use the concept of probability distribution functions to find the probability of a loss. Section 4.3 then turns to the measurement of downside risk. This section also introduces Bankers Trust's RAROC measure of risk-adjusted capital. Potential losses are discussed in terms of quantiles and loss sizes conditional on exceeding the quantile. Section 4.4 discusses the computation of rates of return for financial series. Finally, Section 4.5 explains how to adjust risk measures for different horizons, both with i.i.d. and correlated returns.

4.1 MARKET RISKS

Broadly, there are four different types of financial market risks: interest rate risk, exchange rate risk, equity risk, and commodity risk. Basic analytical tools apply to all these markets. Risk is measured by the standard deviation of unexpected outcomes, or *sigma* (σ), also called *volatility*.

Losses can occur through a combination of two factors: the volatility in the underlying financial variable and the exposure to this source of risk. Whereas corporations have no control over the volatility of financial variables, they can adjust their exposure to these risks, for instance, through derivatives. Value at risk (VAR) captures the combined effect of underlying volatility and exposure to financial risks.

Measurements of linear exposure to movements in underlying risk variables appear everywhere under different guises. In the fixed-income market, exposure to movements in interest rates is called *duration*. In the stock market, this exposure is called *systematic risk*, or *beta* (β). In derivatives markets, the exposure to movements in the value of the underlying asset is called *delta* (Δ). Second derivatives are called *convexity* and *gamma* (Γ) in the fixed-income and derivatives markets, respectively. Convexity measures the change in duration as the interest rate changes; likewise, gamma measures the change in delta as the underlying price changes. Both terms measure the second-order, or quadratic, exposure to a financial variable.

Chapter 1 argues that the increased interest in risk management is partly driven by the increase in volatility in financial variables, which is described in Figures 1-1 to 1-4. These graphs, however, plot movements in the level of financial variables and therefore give only an indirect view of risk.

Risk can be measured more precisely by short-term volatility. Figures 4–1 to 4–4 present the standard deviation of trailing 12-month relative price changes, expressed in percent per annum. Figure 4–1 confirms that the volatility of the DM/$ rate increased sharply after 1973. The demise of the system of fixed exchange rates has added to financial risks. Note that this volatility, on the order of 10 to 15 percent per an-

FIGURE 4-1

Volatility in the German mark/dollar rate.

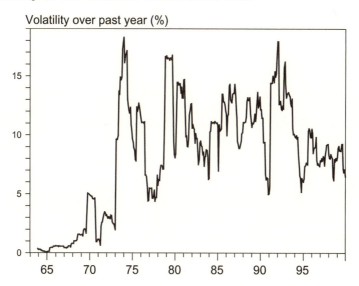

FIGURE 4-2

Volatility in interest rates.

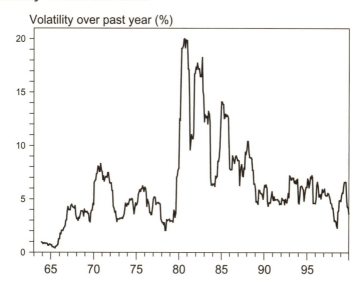

FIGURE 4–3

Volatility in oil prices.

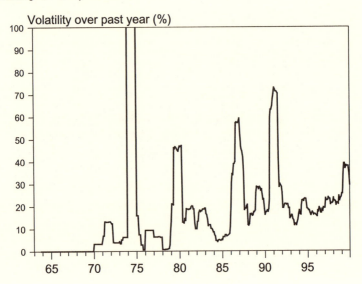

FIGURE 4–4

Volatility in stock prices.

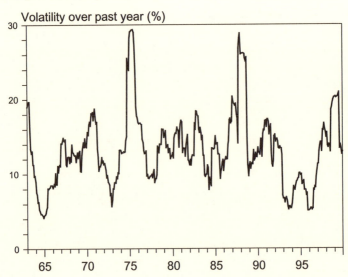

num, is large enough to wipe out typical profit margins for firms with international operations, given that profit margins are also often around 10 to 15 percent.

The measure of risk seems to fluctuate over time, with peaks in 1974 and 1994 and troughs in 1977 and 1991. This begs the question of whether risk is truly unstable over time, or whether these patterns are due to our estimation method and just reflect "noise" in the data. This is an important question to which a whole chapter is devoted later.

The volatility in U.S. bond prices is presented in Figure 4–2. Here, the typical volatility was about 5 percent per annum before 1980. In the 1980s, however, it shot up to 20 percent per annum, only to subside in the 1990s. Figure 4–3 displays the volatility of oil prices. Before 1970, the volatility was very low, since oil was a regulated market. Since then, oil price risk has increased sharply, notably during the OPEC price hikes of 1974 and 1979.

Last, Figure 4–4 measures risk in the U.S. stock market. Volatility appears to be more stable, on the order of 10 to 20 percent per annum. Risk is more consistent in this market, reflecting residual claims on corporations subject to business risks in a mature stock market. Notable peaks in volatility occurred in October 1974, when U.S. stocks went up by 17 percent after three large consecutive drops, and during the October 1987 crash, when U.S. equities lost 20 percent of their value. Volatility therefore occurs because of large unexpected price changes, whether positive or negative. This symmetrical treatment is logical because players in these markets can be long or short, domestic or foreign, consumers or producers. Overall, the volatility of financial markets creates risks (see Box 4–1) and opportunities that must be measured and controlled.

B O X   4–1

RISK

The origins of the word *risk* can be traced to Latin, through the French *risque* and the Italian *risco*. The original sense of *risco* is cut off like a rock, from the latin *re-*, "back," and *secare,* "to cut." Hence the sense of peril to sailors who had to navigate around dangerous, sharp rocks.

4.2 PROBABILITY DISTRIBUTION FUNCTIONS

Risk generally can be defined as the uncertainty of outcomes. It is best measured in terms of probability distribution functions. Probability traces its roots to problems of fair distribution. In fact, in the Middle Ages, the word *probability* meant an "opinion certified by authority." The question of justice led to notions of equivalence between expectations. And work on expectations set the stage for probability theory.

Probability traces its roots to the work of Girolamo Cardano, an Italian who also was an inveterate gambler. In 1565, Cardano published a treatise on gambling, *Liber de Ludo Alae,* that was the first serious effort at developing the principles of probability.

4.2.1 A Gambler's Experiment

Probability theory took another leap when a French nobleman posed a gambling problem to Blaise Pascal in 1654. He wanted to know how to allocate equitably profits in a game that was interrupted. In the course of developing answers to this problem, Pascal laid out the foundations for probability theory.

Cardano and Pascal defined *probability distributions,* which describe the number of times a particular value can occur in an imaginary experiment. Consider, for instance, a gambler with a pair of dice. The dice are fair, in the sense that each side has equal probability, or one chance in six, to come up.

We tabulate all possible outcomes; for example, the combination of (1, 1), or a total of 2, can happen once; a total of 3 can happen twice through combinations of (1, 2) and (2, 1); and so on. Figure 4–5 displays the total distribution for all possible values, which range from 2 to 12.

Table 4–1 summarizes the *frequency distribution* of the total points, which tabulates the number of occurrences of each value. The total number of dice combinations is 36. This first result is not so obvious, for Cardano had to explain to his readers that the total number of possibilities is 36, not 12. Cardano also defined for the first time the conventional format for probabilities expressed as fractions.

Define X as the random variable of interest, the total number of points from rolling the dice. It takes 11 possible values x_i, each with associated frequency n_i. Rescaling the frequencies so that they add up to

FIGURE 4–5

Distribution of payoff.

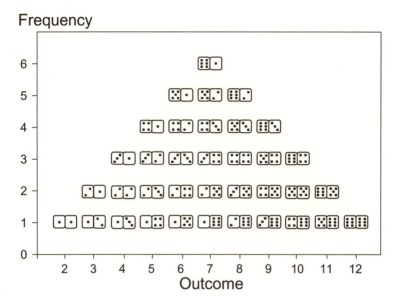

unity, we obtain the associated probability p_i. These probabilities define a *probability distribution function* (pdf) that by construction must sum to unity:

$$\sum_{i=1}^{11} p_i = 1 \tag{4.1}$$

The distribution can be characterized usefully by two variables: its mean and its spread.

The expected value $E(X)$, or *mean,* can be estimated as the weighted sum of all possible values, each weighted by its probability of occurrence:

$$E(X) = \sum_{i=1}^{11} p_i x_i \tag{4.2}$$

To shorten the notation, $E(X)$ is also written as μ. In our example, the summation yields 252/36, which is also 7. Therefore, the expected value from throwing the dice is 7. The figure also shows that this is the value with the highest frequency, defined as the *mode* of the distribution.

TABLE 4–1

Computing Expected Value and Standard Deviation

Value (x_i)	2	3	4	5	6	7	8	9	10	11	12	Total
Frequency of occurrence (n_i)	1	2	3	4	5	6	5	4	3	2	1	36
Probability of occurrence (p_i)	$\frac{1}{36}$	$\frac{2}{36}$	$\frac{3}{36}$	$\frac{4}{36}$	$\frac{5}{36}$	$\frac{6}{36}$	$\frac{5}{36}$	$\frac{4}{36}$	$\frac{3}{36}$	$\frac{2}{36}$	$\frac{1}{36}$	1
Computing $E(X)$: $p_i x_i$	$\frac{2}{36}$	$\frac{6}{36}$	$\frac{12}{36}$	$\frac{20}{36}$	$\frac{30}{36}$	$\frac{42}{36}$	$\frac{40}{36}$	$\frac{36}{36}$	$\frac{30}{36}$	$\frac{22}{36}$	$\frac{12}{36}$	$\frac{252}{36}$
Computing $V(X)$: $p_i[x_i - E(X)]^2$	$\frac{25}{36}$	$\frac{32}{36}$	$\frac{27}{36}$	$\frac{16}{36}$	$\frac{5}{36}$	$\frac{0}{36}$	$\frac{5}{36}$	$\frac{16}{36}$	$\frac{27}{36}$	$\frac{32}{36}$	$\frac{25}{36}$	$\frac{210}{36}$

Next, we would like to characterize the dispersion around $E(X)$ with a single measure. This is done first by computing the *variance,* defined as the weighted sum of squared deviations around the mean[1]:

$$V(X) = \sum_{i=1}^{11} p_i[x_i - E(X)]^2 \qquad (4.3)$$

Note that because deviations from the mean are squared, positive and negative deviations are treated symmetrically. In the dice example, the term that corresponds to the outcome $x_1 = 2$ is $(1/36)(2 - 7)^2 = 25/36$. The table shows that all these add up to $V(X) = 210/36$.

The variance is measured in units of x squared and thus is not directly comparable with the mean. The *standard deviation,* or *volatility,* is then defined as the square root of the variance:

$$SD(X) = \sqrt{V(X)} \qquad (4.4)$$

Again to shorten notation, $SD(X)$ is written as σ. In our example, the standard deviation of future outcomes is $\sqrt{(210/36)} = 2.415$. This number is particularly useful because it indicates a typical range of values around the mean.

---

1. The term *variance* was first introduced by the statistician R. A. Fisher in 1918, in the context of a paper on genetics.

4.2.2 Properties of Expectations

Our gambler's experiment involved a discrete set of outcomes, character-ized by a discrete pdf. For many variables, such as the rate of return on an investment, the range of outcomes is continuous. We therefore rede-fine the pdf as $f(x)$. As in Equation (4.1), it must sum, or integrate, to unity over all possible values, going from $-\infty$ to ∞:

$$\int_{-\infty}^{+\infty} f(x)\, dx = 1 \tag{4.5}$$

By extension, the *cumulative distribution function* (cdf) is the integral up to point x:

$$F(x) = \int_{-\infty}^{x} f(t)\, dt \tag{4.6}$$

The expectation and variance are then, by extension of Equations (4.2) and (4.3),

$$E(X) = \int_{-\infty}^{+\infty} x f(x)\, dx \tag{4.7}$$

$$V(X) = \int_{-\infty}^{+\infty} [x - E(X)]^2 f(x)\, dx \tag{4.8}$$

In what follows, we make extensive use of transformation and combina-tions of random variables. How do these affect expectations and vari-ances?

First, let us define a new random variable as $Y = a + bX$, a linear transformation of the original X. The parameters a and b are fixed. We have, after insertion into Equations (4.7) and (4.8),

$$\begin{aligned}
E(a + bX) &= \int (a + bx)\, f(x)\, dx \\
&= a \int f(x)\, dx + b \int x f(x)\, dx \\
&= a + bE(X)
\end{aligned} \tag{4.9}$$

by Equation (4.5), and

$$\begin{aligned}
V(a + bX) &= \int [a + bx - E(a + bX)]^2 f(x)\, dx \\
&= \int [a + bx - a - bE(X)]^2 f(x)\, dx \\
&= \int b^2 [x - E(X)]^2 f(x)\, dx \\
&= b^2 V(X)
\end{aligned} \tag{4.10}$$

Therefore, the volatility of Y is $\sigma(a + bX) = b\sigma(X)$.

Let us now turn to linear combinations of random variables, such as $Y = X_1 + X_2$, or the payoff on a portfolio of two stocks. Here, the uncertainty is described by a joint pdf of two variables, $f(x_1, x_2)$. If we abstract from the other variable, the distribution for one variable is known as the *marginal distribution*,

$$\int_2 f(x_1, x_2)\, dx_2 = f(x_1) \tag{4.11}$$

The expectation is, by extension of Equations (4.7) and (4.11),

$$
\begin{aligned}
E(X_1 + X_2) &= \int_1 \int_2 (x_1 + x_2)\, f(x_1,x_2)\, dx_1\, dx_2 \\
&= \int_1 \int_2 x_1\, f(x_1,x_2)\, dx_1\, dx_2 + \int_1 \int_2 x_2\, f(x_1,x_2)\, dx_1\, dx_2 \\
&= \int_1 x_1\, [\int_2 f(x_1,x_2)\, dx_2]\, dx_1 + \int_2 x_2\, [\int_1 f(x_1,x_2)\, dx_1]\, dx_2 \\
&= \int_1 x_1\, f(x_1)\, dx_1 + \int_2 x_2\, f(x_2)\, dx_2 \\
&= E(X_1) + E(X_2)
\end{aligned}
$$

$$\tag{4.12}$$

This is remarkably simple: The expectation is a linear operator. The expectation of a sum is the sum of expectations.

Developing the variance, however, is more involved. We have

$$
\begin{aligned}
V(X_1 + X_2) &= \int_1 \int_2 [x_1 + x_2 - E(X_1 + X_2)]^2\, f(x_1,x_2)\, dx_1\, dx_2 \\
&= \int_1 \int_2 \{[x_1 - E(X_1)]^2 + [x_2 - E(X_2)]^2 + 2[x_1 - E(X_1)] \\
&\quad [x_2 - E(X_2)]\} f(x_1,x_2)\, dx_1\, dx_2 \\
&= \int_1 [x_1 - E(X_1)]^2\, f(x_1)\, dx_1 + \int_2 [x_2 - E(X_2)]^2\, f(x_2)\, dx_2 \\
&\quad + 2 \int_1 \int_2 [x_1 - E(X_1)][x_2 - E(X_2)]\, f(x_1,x_2)\, dx_1\, dx_2 \\
&= V(X_1) + V(X_2) + 2\, \text{cov}(X_1,X_2)
\end{aligned}
$$

$$\tag{4.13}$$

where the last term is defined as the *covariance* between X_1 and X_2.

The variance turns out to be a nonlinear operator: In general, the variance of a sum of random variables is not equal to the sum of variances. It involves a cross-product term, which is very important because it drives the diversification properties of portfolios.

However, in the special case where the two variables are independent, which can be written formally as $f(x_1,x_2) = f(x_1) \times f(x_2)$, the last integral reduces to

$$
\begin{aligned}
&\int_1 \int_2 [x_1 - E(X_1)][x_2 - E(X_2)][f(x_1) \times f(x_2)]\, dx_1 dx_2 \\
&= \int_1 [x_1 - E(X_1)]\, f(x_1)\, dx_1 \times \int_2 [x_2 - E(X_2)]\, f(x_2)\, dx_2 \tag{4.14} \\
&= 0
\end{aligned}
$$

since $\int x_1 f(x_1)\, dx_1 = E(X_1)$. The variance of a sum is equal to the sum of variances if the two variables are independent of each other, that is, $V(X_1 + X_2) = V(X_1) + V(X_2)$.

4.2.3 The Normal Distribution

On closer inspection, the distribution in Figure 4–5 resembles the ubiquitous bell-shaped curve proposed two centuries ago by Karl F. Gauss (1777–1855), who was studying the motion of celestial bodies (hence its name, *Gaussian*).[2] The *normal distribution* plays a central role in statistics because it describes adequately many existing populations. Furthermore, P. S. Laplace later proved the *central limit theorem* (CLT), which showed that the mean converges to a normal distribution as the number of observations increases. Also, as the number of independent draws increases (i.e., here increasing the number of dice from two to a large number), the distribution converges to a smooth normal distribution. This explains why the normal distribution has such a prominent place in statistics.

A direct application of these century-old observations is the evaluation of credit risk. Consider the problem of evaluating the capital at risk in a large portfolio containing many small consumer credits. Individually, each loan default can be modeled by a *binomial* distribution, with two realizations only, assuming no partial repayment. In the limit, however, the distribution of a sum of independent binomial variables converges to a normal distribution. Therefore, the portfolio can be modeled by a normal distribution as the number of credits increases. It should be noted that this result relies heavily on the independence of the defaults. If a severe recession hits the economy, it is likely that many defaults will occur at the same time, which invalidates the normal approximation.

A normal distribution has convenient properties. In particular, the entire distribution can be characterized by its first two moments, the mean and variance: $N(\mu, \sigma^2)$. The first parameter represents the location; the second, the dispersion. The distribution function has the following expression:

$$f(x) = \Phi(x) = \frac{1}{\sqrt{2\pi\sigma^2}}\, e^{[-(1/2\sigma^2)(x-\mu)^2]} \tag{4.15}$$

where $e^{(y)}$ represents the exponential of y.

---

2. Galton first coined the term *normal,* which has become almost universal in English, although continental European writers prefer to use the term *Gaussian*.

This function, which is also at the heart of the Black-Scholes option pricing model, could be tabulated for different values of μ and σ. However, this can be considerably simplified by using tables for a normal distribution with mean zero and variance unity, which is called a *standard normal distribution function.*

Start from a *standard* normal variable ϵ such that $\epsilon \approx N(0, 1)$. Next, define X as

$$X = \mu + \epsilon\sigma \qquad (4.16)$$

Going back to Equations (9) and (10), we can show that X has mean $E(X) = E(\epsilon)\sigma + \mu = \mu$, and $V(X) = V(\epsilon)\sigma^2 = \sigma^2$.

The standard normal distribution is plotted in Figure 4–6. Since the function is perfectly symmetrical, its mean is the same as its mode (most likely point) and median (which has a 50 percent probability of occurrence).

About 95 percent of the distribution is contained between values of $\epsilon_1 = -2$ and $\epsilon_2 = +2$. And 66 percent of the distribution falls between values of $\epsilon_1 = -1$ and $\epsilon_2 = +1$. If we want to find 95 percent confi-

FIGURE 4–6

Normal distribution.

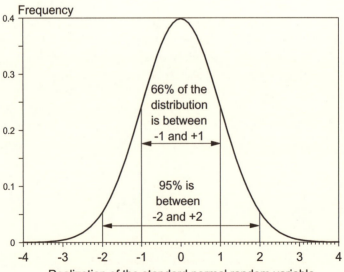

dence limits for movements in an exchange rate, with mean 1 percent and volatility 12 percent, we have

$$X_{min} = 1\% - 2 \times 12\% = -23\%$$
$$X_{max} = 1\% + 2 \times 12\% = +25\%$$

The $[-2, +2]$ confidence interval for ϵ thus translates into $[-23\%, +25\%]$ for the exchange rate movement X.

4.2.4 Other Distributions

The normal distribution is fully described by two parameters only, its mean and standard deviation. For completeness, we also should mention two other moments. *Skewness* describes departures from symmetry. It is defined as

$$\gamma = \left\{ \int_{-\infty}^{+\infty} [x - E(X)]^3 f(x)\, dx \right\} / \sigma^3 \qquad (4.17)$$

The skewness of a normal distribution is 0. Negative skewness indicates that the distribution has a long left tail and hence entails large negative values.

Kurtosis describes the degree of flatness of a distribution. It is measured as

$$\delta = \left\{ \int_{-\infty}^{+\infty} [x - E(X)]^4 f(x)\, dx \right\} / \sigma^4 \qquad (4.18)$$

The kurtosis of a normal distribution is 3. A kurtosis coefficient greater than 3 indicates that the tails decay less quickly than for the normal distribution, implying a greater likelihood of large values, positive or negative. These two measures can be used as a quick check on whether the sample distribution is close to normal.

If not, other parametric distributions can be used. One example is the *Student t* distribution, whose pdf is

$$f(x) = \frac{\Gamma[(n+1)/2]}{\Gamma(n/2)} \frac{1}{\sqrt{n\pi}} \frac{1}{(1 + x^2/n)^{(n+1)/2}} \qquad (4.19)$$

where Γ is the gamma function, and n is a shape-defining parameter known as the *degrees of freedom*.[3] With n very large, this function tends to the

---

3. The gamma function is defined as $\Gamma(n) = \int_0^\infty x^{n-1} e^{-x}\, dx$. See, for instance, Mood et al. (1974).

normal pdf. The Student t pdf has increasingly fatter tails for small values of n. The variance of the variable is $V(X) = n/(n - 2)$.

Another useful distribution is the *generalized error distribution* (GED). Its pdf is

$$f(x) = \frac{\nu}{\lambda 2^{(1+1/\nu)}\Gamma(1/\nu)}\, e^{(-\frac{1}{2}|x/\lambda|^\nu)} \quad \lambda = [2^{-(2/\nu)}\Gamma(1/\nu)/\Gamma(3/\nu)]^{1/2} \quad (4.20)$$

where ν is a shape-defining parameter. This function is convenient because it includes the normal pdf as a special case, with $\nu = 2$. The pdf has fatter tails for values of ν lower than 2. Here, the scaling parameter λ ensures that the variance of X is unity.

Figure 4–7 compares the normal distribution with a Student t distribution with $n = 6$ and a GED distribution with $\nu = 1.3$. These parameters typically describe financial data. We can see that both distributions have fatter tails than the normal distribution. This may be particularly important when assessing the size of potential losses with VAR.

FIGURE 4–7

Comparison of parametric distributions.

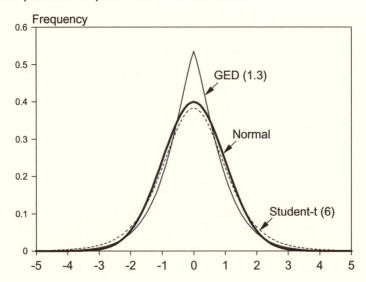

4.3 RISK

4.3.1 Risk as Dispersion

Risk therefore is measured as the dispersion of possible outcomes. A flatter distribution indicates greater risk, and a tighter distribution, lower risk. Figure 4–8 displays the distribution of two exchange rates, the Deutsche mark (DM) and Canadian dollar (C$) against the U.S. dollar. The graph shows the frequency of monthly returns over a recent period, assuming normal distributions. As shown in the figure, the DM/$ rate is riskier than the C$/$ rate because it has a greater range of values.

We now have a measure to compare assets with different risks. Box 4–2 shows how to penalize positions with greater risks using RAROC. Here, the approach assumes that the distribution is normal because it is particularly convenient. Other distributions, however, can be used.

4.3.2 Quantiles

More generally, downside risk can be measured by the quantiles of the distribution. *Quantiles* (also called *percentiles*) are defined as cutoff

FIGURE 4–8

Comparison of currency distributions.

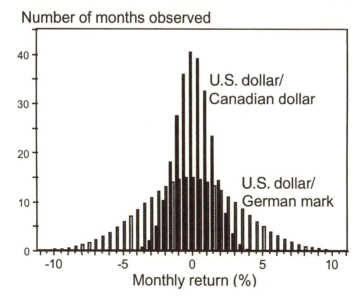

BOX 4—2

RAROC: BANKERS TRUST RISK ADJUSTMENT

Bankers Trust has been a pioneer in risk management, introducing risk measurement through its *risk-adjusted return on capital* (RAROC) system in the late 1970s. The system was inspired by the need to adjust trader profit for risk. Take, for instance, two traders, each of whom makes a profit of $10 million, one in short-term Treasuries and the other in foreign exchange. This raises a number of essential questions: Which trader performed better? How should they be compensated for their profit? And where should the firm devote more capital? RAROC adjusts profits for capital at risk, defined as the amount of capital needed to cover 99 percent of the maximum expected loss over a year. The same 1-year horizon is used for all RAROC computations, irrespective of the actual holding period, to allow meaningful comparisons across asset classes.

To compute the RAROC for the foreign exchange position, assume that the face value of the contracts was $100 million. The volatility of the DM/$ rate is 12 percent per annum. The firm needs to hold enough capital to cover 99 percent of possible losses. Since 1 percent of the normal distribution lies 2.33 standard deviations below the mean, the worst possible loss is $2.33 \times 0.12 \times \$100$ million = $28 million, which is also the capital requirement to sustain this position. Therefore, the RAROC for the foreign exchange trader is $10/$28 = 36 percent. This measure is a reward-to-risk ratio.

Let us now turn to the bond trader. Assume that the gain was obtained with an average notional amount of $200 million and that the risk of these bonds is about 4 percent. The maximum loss is then $2.33 \times 0.04 \times \$200$ million = $19 million. The RAROC for the bond trader is $10/$19 = 54 percent. When adjusted for the capital resources, the bond trader provides a bigger bang for the buck.

RAROC also provides limits on trading. For instance, if a trader loses 10 percent of his or her RAROC capital in a month, he or she must stop trading. Again, RAROC allows meaningful comparisons between different markets.

This adjustment yields a number of essential insights that have shaped the course of Bankers Trust's strategy over the following years. By compensating traders based on their RAROC, risk adjustment permeates the culture of the bank. In the words of the company itself, risk management is practiced "with a holistic approach." Bankers Trust discovered that most of its loan lending was less profitable than other operations and strategically adjusted the direction of the bank into more profitable risk-management functions. This, of course, assumes that the volatility of returns captures all essential aspects of business risks.

values q such that the area to their right (or left) represents a given probability c:

$$c = \text{prob}(X \geq q) = \int_q^{+\infty} f(x)\,dx = 1 - F(q) \qquad (4.21)$$

If the distribution is normal, its quantiles can be found from statistical tables, which report

$$c = \text{prob}(\epsilon \geq -\alpha) = \int_{-\alpha}^{+\infty} \Phi(\epsilon)\,d\epsilon \qquad (4.22)$$

Table 4–2, for instance, reports the quantiles α for a standard normal deviate. To find the number of standard deviations away from the mean for a given confidence level c, choose a number in the first row. For instance, the goal may be to find the VAR at the one-tailed 95 percent confidence level. The table shows that this corresponds to 1.645 standard deviations below the mean.

A complementary measure is the expected value conditional on exceeding the quantile:

$$E(X \mid X < q) = \frac{\displaystyle\int_{-\infty}^q xf(x)\,dx}{\displaystyle\int_{-\infty}^q f(x)\,dx} \qquad (4.23)$$

In other words, we want to know not only the cutoff loss that will happen c percent of the time but also the average size of the loss when it exceeds the cutoff value. This quantity is also called *expected shortfall, tail conditional expectation, conditional loss,* or *tail loss.* In other words, we want to know how much we could lose if we are "hit" beyond VAR.

For a standard normal variable, integrating Equation (4.23) leads to the following formula, which is used in a number of applications later:

$$E(\epsilon \mid \epsilon < -\alpha) = \frac{-\Phi(\alpha)}{F(-\alpha)} \qquad (4.24)$$

For instance, the average of ϵ below zero is

$$E(\epsilon \mid \epsilon < 0) = -\frac{\left(\dfrac{1}{\sqrt{2\pi}}\,e^0\right)}{0.5} = -\sqrt{2/\pi}$$

TABLE 4–2

Lower Quantiles of the Normal Distribution

	Confidence Level (%)								
	99.99	99.9	99	97.72	97.5	95	90	84.13	50
Quantile $(-\alpha)$	-3.715	-3.090	-2.326	-2.000	-1.960	-1.645	-1.282	-1.000	-0.000
$E(\epsilon \mid \epsilon < -\alpha)$	-4.018	-3.370	-2.667	-2.368	-2.338	-2.062	-1.754	-1.525	-0.798

These conditional values are reported in the last line of Table 4–2. It is apparent that the size of the loss, conditional on exceeding the quantile, is not much lower than the quantile itself. For instance, the expected loss conditional on exceeding the 99 percent value of -2.326 is -2.667. This reflects the fact that the tails of the normal distribution decrease at a very fast rate. In fact, the ratio of the tail loss to VAR converges to one as the confidence level increases. For other distributions, the conditional loss can be much farther from its associated quantile.

4.4 ASSET RETURNS
4.4.1 Measuring Returns

In the context of the measurement of market risk, the random variable is taken as the rate of return on a financial asset (although gambling is sometimes an appropriate comparison). The range of possible payoffs on a security also can be described by its probability distribution function.

Define, for instance, the measurement horizon as 1 month. Returns are measured from the end of the preceding month, denoted by the subscript $t - 1$ to the end of the current month, denoted by t. The *arithmetic,* or *discrete,* rate of return is defined as the capital gain plus any interim payment such as a dividend or coupon:

$$r_t = \frac{P_t + D_t - P_{t-1}}{P_{t-1}} \tag{4.25}$$

Note that this definition implies that any income payment is only reinvested at the end of the month.

To focus on long-horizon returns, the practice is to focus on the *geometric* rate of return, which is defined in terms of the logarithm of the price ratio:

$$R_t = \ln \frac{P_t + D_t}{P_{t-1}} \tag{4.26}$$

For simplicity, we will assume that income payments D_t are zero in what follows. Alternatively, one could think of P as the value of a mutual fund that reinvests all dividends.

The advantage of using geometric returns is twofold. First, they may be more economically meaningful than arithmetic returns. If geometric returns are distributed normally, then the distribution can never lead to a price that is negative. This is so because the left tail of the distribution such as $\ln(P_t/P_{t-1}) \rightarrow -\infty$ is achieved as $(P_t/P_{t-1}) \rightarrow 0$ or $P_t \rightarrow 0$.

In contrast, in the left tail of normally distributed arithmetic returns, $r_t = (P_t - P_{t-1})/P_{t-1} \rightarrow -\infty$ is achieved as $(P_t/P_{t-1}) - 1 < -1$ or $P_t < 0$. Economically, this is meaningless. Therefore, imposing a normal distribution on the arithmetic rate of return allows some aberrant behavior in prices.

For some series, using a geometric return also may be more consistent. For instance, exchange rates can be defined in two different base currencies. Using $S(\$/BP)$ as the dollar price of the British pound, the random variable of interest is $x = \ln(S_t/S_{t-1})$. Now, taking the viewpoint of a British investor, who measures asset values in pounds, the variable is $y = \ln[(1/S_t)/(1/S_{t-1})] = -\ln(S_t/S_{t-1}) = -x$. The distributions of x and y therefore are consistent with each other, which is not the case if returns are defined in discrete terms.

Using logarithms is also particularly convenient for converting returns or risk measures into other currencies. Assume that a German investor wants to measure returns in Deutsche marks. This can be derived from dollar-based data, as $\ln[S(DM/BP)] = \ln[S(DM/\$)] + \ln[S(\$/BP)] = -\ln[S(\$/DM)] + \ln[S(\$/BP)]$. The DM-based return is equal to the difference between the dollar-based return on the pound and the dollar-based return on the mark, $z(DM/BP) = x(\$/BP) - x(\$/DM)$, from which variances and correlations immediately follow.

The second advantage of using geometric returns is that they easily allow extensions into multiple periods. For instance, consider the return over a 2-month period. The geometric return can be decomposed as

$$R_{t,2} = \ln(P_t/P_{t-2}) = \ln(P_t/P_{t-1}) + \ln(P_{t-1}/P_{t-2}) = R_{t-1} + R_t \qquad (4.27)$$

This is particularly convenient since the two-month geometric return is simply the sum of the two monthly returns. With discrete returns, the decomposition is not so simple. Thus no rebalancing takes place with geometric returns, whereas arithmetic means correspond to the case of a fixed investment, that is, where gains are withdrawn and losses are added back.

This said, it must be admitted than in many situations the differences between the two returns are small. Consider that $R_t = \ln(P_t/P_{t-1}) = \ln(1 + r_t)$. If r_t is small, R_t can be decomposed into a Taylor series as $R_t = r_t - r_t^2/2 + r_t^3/3 + \cdots$, which simplifies to $R_t \approx r_t$ if r_t is small. Thus, in practice, as long as returns are small, there will be little difference between continuous and discrete returns. This may not be true, however, in markets with large moves such as emerging markets or when the interval horizon is measured in years.

4.4.2 Sample Estimates

In practice, the distribution of rates of return is usually estimated over a number of previous periods, assuming that all observations are *identically* and *independently distributed* (i.i.d.). If T is the number of observations, the expected return, or first moment, $\mu = E(X)$ can be estimated by the sample mean:

$$m = \hat{\mu} = \frac{1}{T} \sum_{i=1}^{T} x_i \qquad (4.28)$$

and the variance, or second moment, $\sigma^2 = E[(X - \mu)^2]$ can be estimated by the sample variance:

$$s^2 = \hat{\sigma}^2 = \frac{1}{(T-1)} \sum_{i=1}^{T} (x_i - \hat{\mu})^2 \qquad (4.29)$$

The square root of σ^2 is the standard deviation of X, often referred to as the *volatility*. It measures the risk of a security as the dispersion of outcomes around its expected value.

Going back to the distribution of monthly exchange rate changes in Figure 4–7, we find that the mean of DM/$ changes was -0.21 percent and that the standard deviation was 3.51 percent. The C$/$ rate displayed a lower volatility of 1.3 percent.

Note that Equation (4.29) can be developed as

$$\hat{\sigma}^2 = \frac{1}{(T-1)} \sum_{i=1}^{T} x_i^2 - \frac{T}{(T-1)} \hat{\mu}^2 \qquad (4.30)$$

This shows that the variance is composed of two terms, the first being the average of the squared returns and the second being the square of the average.

For most financial series sampled at daily intervals, the second term is negligible relative to the first. In the DM/$ example, the squared average return is $(-0.0021)^2 = 0.0000044$, versus a variance term on the order of $(0.0351)^2 = 0.00123$, which is much greater. Therefore, in many situations we can ignore the mean in the estimation of daily risk measures.

The sample skewness of a series can be measured as

$$\hat{\gamma} = \frac{1}{(T-1)} \sum_{i=1}^{T} (x_i - \hat{\mu})^3 / \hat{\sigma}^3 \tag{4.31}$$

Kurtosis is measured as

$$\hat{\delta} = \frac{1}{(T-1)} \sum_{i=1}^{T} (x_i - \hat{\mu})^4 / \hat{\sigma}^4 \tag{4.32}$$

Finally, the covariance between two series i and j can be estimated from sample data as

$$\hat{\sigma}_{ij} = \frac{1}{(T-1)} \sum_{t=1}^{T} (x_{t,i} - \hat{\mu}_i)(x_{t,j} - \hat{\mu}_j) \tag{4.33}$$

4.5 TIME AGGREGATION

Computing VAR requires first the definition of a period over which to measure unfavorable outcomes. This period may be set in terms of hours, days, or weeks. For an investment manager, it may correspond to the regular reporting period, monthly or quarterly. For a bank manager, the horizon should be sufficiently long to catch traders taking positions in excess of their limits. Regulators are now requiring a horizon of 2 weeks, which is viewed as the period necessary to force bank compliance.

To compare risk across horizons, we need a translation method—a problem known as *time aggregation* in econometrics. Suppose that we observe daily data, from which we obtain a VAR measure. Using higher-frequency data is generally more efficient because it uses more available information.

The investment horizon, however, may be 3 months. Thus the distribution for daily data must be transformed into a distribution over a quarterly horizon. If returns are uncorrelated over time (or behave like a random walk), this transformation is straightforward.

4.5.1 Aggregation with I.I.D. Returns

The problem of time aggregation can be brought back to the problem of finding the expected return and variance of a sum of random variables. From Equation (4.27), the two-period return (from $t-2$ to t) $R_{t,2}$ is equal to $R_{t-1} + R_t$, where the subscript 2 indicates that the time interval is two periods. A previous section has shown that $E(X_1 + X_2) = E(X_1) + E(X_2)$ and that $V(X_1 + X_2) = V(X_1) + V(X_2) + 2 \operatorname{cov}(X_1, X_2)$.

To aggregate over time, we now introduce an extremely important assumption: Returns are uncorrelated over successive time intervals. This assumption is consistent with *efficient markets,* where the current price includes all relevant information about a particular asset. If so, all prices changes must be due to news that, by definition, cannot be anticipated and therefore must be uncorrelated over time: Prices follow a *random walk.* The cross-product term $\operatorname{cov}(X_1 X_2)$ must then be zero. In addition, we could reasonably assume that returns are identically distributed over time, which means that $E(R_{t-1}) = E(R_t) = E(R)$ and that $V(R_{t-1}) = V(R_t) = V(R)$.

Based on these two assumptions, the expected return over a two-period horizon is $E(R_{t,2}) = E(R_{t-1}) + E(R_t) = 2E(R)$. The variance is $V(R_{t,2}) = V(R_{t-1}) + V(R_t) = 2V(R)$. The expected return over 2 days is twice the expected return over 1 day; likewise for the variance. Both the expected return and the variance increase linearly with time. The volatility, in contrast, grows with the square root of time.

In summary, to go from annual to daily, monthly, or quarterly data, we can write

$$\mu = \mu_{\text{annual}} T \tag{4.34}$$

$$\sigma = \sigma_{\text{annual}} \sqrt{T} \tag{4.35}$$

where T is the number of years (e.g., 1/12 for monthly data or 1/252 for daily data if the number of trading days in a year is 252).

Square root of time adjustment

Adjustments of volatility to different horizons can be based on a square root of time factor when positions are constant and returns are i.i.d.

As an example, let us go back to the DM/$ rate data, which we wish to convert to annual parameters. The mean of changes is -0.21 percent per month $\times$ 12 $= -2.6$ percent per annum. The risk is 3.51 percent per month $\times \sqrt{12} = 12.2$ percent per annum.

Table 4–3 compares the risk and average return for a number of financial series measured in percent per annum over the period 1973–1998. Stocks are typically the most volatile of the lot (16 percent). Next come exchange rates against the dollar (12 percent) and U.S. bonds (6 percent). Some currencies, however, are relatively more stable. Such is the case for the Canadian dollar/U.S. dollar rate.

TABLE 4-3

Risk and Return: 1973–1998 (% per annum)

	Exchange Rate			U.S. Stocks	U.S. Bonds
	DM/$	C$/$	Yen/$		
Volatility	11.7	4.5	11.8	15.6	5.6
Average	−1.8	1.8	−3.0	14.1	9.0

Note: Total return indices from the S&P 500 stock and Lehman Treasury bond index.

4.5.2 Aggregation with Correlated Returns

So far we have assumed that returns were uncorrelated across periods. For some thinly traded markets, this assumption may not be appropriate. The worry is that when markets are trending, the risk over a longer period may be much higher than from a simple extrapolation of daily risk.

The simplest process is a first-order autoregression, where shocks in returns are related to shocks in the previous period through

$$X_t = \rho X_{t-1} + u_t \tag{4.36}$$

As before, assume that the innovations u_t have the same variance. Additional adjustments must take place if volatility is time-varying.

The variance of the 2-day return is then

$$V(X_t + X_{t-1}) = \sigma^2 + \sigma^2 + 2\rho\sigma^2 = \sigma^2(2 + 2\rho) \tag{4.37}$$

which is higher than in the i.i.d. case if ρ is positive, which is the case if markets are trending. In general, the variance over N periods can be written as

$$V\left(\sum_{i=1}^{N} X_{t+i}\right)$$

$$= \sigma^2[N + 2(N-1)\rho + 2(N-2)\rho^2 + \cdots + 2(1)\rho^{N-1}] \tag{4.38}$$

Figure 4–9 describes the increase in risk as the horizon increases. Starting from, say, a 1 percent daily volatility, risk is magnified to $\sqrt{10} = 3.16$ over a 2-week (10 business days) horizon when $\rho = 0$.

This adjustment, however, understates the true risk in the presence of positive correlation. For instance, with $\rho = 0.2$, the risk measure is in-

FIGURE 4-9

Risk at increasing horizons.

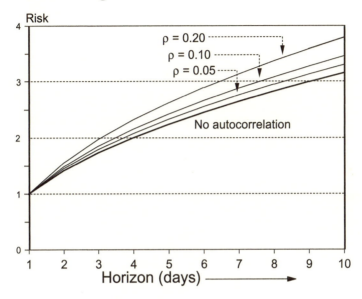

creased to 3.79, which is 20 percent higher than the baseline extrapolation. Hence risk managers have to be careful about assuming independent returns.

4.5.3 The Effect of the Mean at Various Horizons

Note that since the volatility grows with the square root of time and the mean with time, the mean will dominate the volatility over long horizons. Over short horizons, such as a day, volatility dominates. This provides a rationale for focusing on VAR measures that ignore expected returns.

To illustrate this point, consider an investment in U.S. stocks that, according to Table 4–3, returns an average of 14.05 percent per annum with a risk of 15.55 percent. Table 4–4 compares the risks and average returns of holding a position over successively shorter intervals using Equations (4.34) and (4.35). Going from annual to daily and even hourly

TABLE 4-4

Risk and Return over Various Horizons, U.S. Stocks,
1973–1998

Horizon	Years T	Mean m	Risk s	Ratio m /s	Probability of Loss
Annual	1	14.050%	15.55%	0.9035	18.3%
Quarterly	0.25000	3.513%	7.78%	0.4518	32.6%
Monthly	0.08333	1.171%	4.49%	0.2608	39.7%
Weekly	0.01918	0.270%	2.15%	0.1251	45.0%
Daily	0.00397	0.056%	0.98%	0.0569	47.7%
Hourly	0.00050	0.007%	0.35%	0.0201	49.2%

data, the mean shrinks much faster than the volatility. Based on a 252-
trading-day year, the daily expected return is 0.056 percent, very small
compared with the volatility of 0.98 percent.

Table 4–4 can be used to infer the probability of a loss over a given
measurement interval, assuming a normal distribution. For annual data,
this is the probability that the return, distributed $N(\mu = 14.1\%, \sigma^2 = 15.5\%^2)$, falls below 0. Transforming to a standard normal variable, this
is the probability that $\epsilon = (R - 0.141)/0.155$ falls below 0, which is the
area to the left of the standard normal variable $-0.141/0.155 = 0.9035$.
From normal tables, we find that the area to the left of 0.9035 is 18.3 percent. Thus the probability of losing money over a year is 18.3 percent, as
shown in the last column of Table 4–4. In contrast, the probability of losing money over 1 day is 47.7 percent, which is much higher!

This observation is sometimes taken as support for the conventional
wisdom that stocks are less risky in the long run than over a short horizon. Unfortunately, this is not necessarily correct, since the dollar amount
of the loss also increases with time.[4]

By now, we have covered the statistical tools necessary to measure
value at risk (VAR). Computing VAR is the purpose of the next chapter.

---

4. Merton and Samuelson (1974) have written a number of articles denouncing this "fallacy." See
   also Harlow (1991).

CHAPTER 5

Computing Value at Risk

The Daily Earnings at Risk (DEaR) estimate for our combined trading activities averaged approximately $15 million.

J.P. Morgan 1994 Annual Report

Perhaps the greatest advantage of value at risk (VAR) is that it summarizes in a single, easy to understand number the downside risk of an institution due to financial market variables. No doubt this explains why VAR is fast becoming an essential tool for conveying trading risks to senior management, directors, and shareholders. J.P. Morgan, for example, was one of the first users of VAR. It revealed in its 1994 Annual Report that its trading VAR was an average of $15 million at the 95 percent level over 1 day. Shareholders can then assess whether they are comfortable with this level of risk. Before such figures were released, shareholders had only a vague idea of the extent of trading activities assumed by the bank.

This chapter turns to a formal definition of value at risk (VAR). VAR assumes that the portfolio is "frozen" over the horizon or, more generally, that the risk profile of the institution remains constant. In addition, VAR assumes that the current portfolio will be marked-to-market on the target horizon. Section 5.1 shows how to derive VAR figures from probability distributions. This can be done in two ways, either from considering the actual empirical distribution or by approximating the distribution by a parametric approximation, such as the normal distribution, in which case VAR is derived from the standard deviation.

Section 5.2 then discusses the choice of the quantitative factors, the confidence level and the horizon. Criteria for this choice should be guided by the use of the VAR number. If VAR is simply a benchmark for risk, the choice is totally arbitrary. In contrast, if VAR is used to set equity capital, the choice is quite delicate. Criteria for parameter selection are also explained in the context of the Basel Accord rules.

The next section turns to an important and often ignored issue, which is the precision of the reported VAR number. Due to normal sampling variation, there is some inherent imprecision in VAR numbers. Thus, observing changes in VAR numbers for different estimation windows is perfectly normal. Section 5.3 provides a framework for analyzing normal sampling variation in VAR and discusses methods to improve the accuracy of VAR figures. Finally, Section 5.4 provides some concluding thoughts.

5.1 COMPUTING VAR

With all the requisite tools in place, we can now formally define the value at risk (VAR) of a portfolio. *VAR summarizes the expected maximum loss (or worst loss) over a target horizon within a given confidence interval.* Initially, we take the quantitative factors, the horizon and confidence level, as given.

5.1.1 Steps in Constructing VAR

Assume, for instance, that we need to measure the VAR of a $100 million equity portfolio over 10 days at the 99 percent confidence level. The following steps are required to compute VAR:

- *Mark-to-market* of the current portfolio (e.g., $100 million).
- *Measure the variability of the risk factors(s)* (e.g., 15 percent per annum).
- *Set the time horizon,* or the holding period (e.g., adjust to 10 business days).
- *Set the confidence level* (e.g., 99 percent, which yields a 2.33 factor assuming a normal distribution).
- *Report the worst loss* by processing all the preceding information (e.g., a $7 million VAR).

These steps are illustrated in Figure 5–1. The precise detail of the computation is described next.

FIGURE 5-1

Steps in constructing VAR.

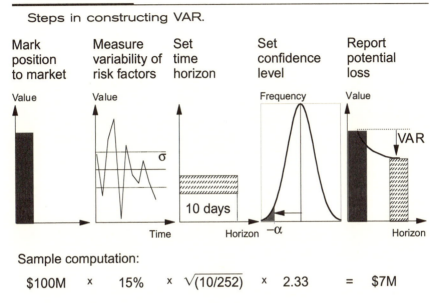

| Mark position to market | Measure variability of risk factors | Set time horizon | Set confidence level | Report potential loss |

Sample computation:

$100M   ×   15%   × $\sqrt{(10/252)}$ ×   2.33   = $7M

5.1.2 VAR for General Distributions

To compute the VAR of a portfolio, define W_0 as the initial investment and R as its rate of return. The portfolio value at the end of the target horizon is $W = W_0 (1 + R)$. As before, the expected return and volatility of R are μ and σ. Define now the lowest portfolio value at the given confidence level c as $W^* = W_0 (1 + R^*)$. The *relative VAR* is defined as the dollar loss relative to the mean:

$$\text{VAR(mean)} = E(W) - W^* = -W_0 (R^* - \mu) \qquad (5.1)$$

Sometimes VAR is defined as the *absolute VAR,* that is, the dollar loss relative to zero or without reference to the expected value:

$$\text{VAR(zero)} = W_0 - W^* = -W_0 R^* \qquad (5.2)$$

In both cases, finding VAR is equivalent to identifying the minimum value W^* or the cutoff return R^*.

If the horizon is short, the mean return could be small, in which case both methods will give similar results. Otherwise, relative VAR is conceptually more appropriate because it views risk in terms of a deviation from the mean, or "budget," on the target date, appropriately accounting for the time value of money. This approach is also more conservative if the mean value is positive. Its only drawback is that the mean return is sometimes difficult to estimate.

In its most general form, VAR can be derived from the probability distribution of the future portfolio value $f(w)$. At a given confidence level c, we wish to find the worst possible realization W^* such that the probability of exceeding this value is c:

$$c = \int_{W^*}^{\infty} f(w) \, dw \tag{5.3}$$

or such that the probability of a value lower than W^*, $p = P(w \leq W^*)$, is $1 - c$:

$$1 - c = \int_{-\infty}^{W^*} f(w) \, dw = P(w \leq W^*) = p \tag{5.4}$$

In other words, the area from $-\infty$ to W^* must sum to $p = 1 - c$, for instance, 5 percent. The number W^* is called the *quantile* of the distribution, which is the cutoff value with a fixed probability of being exceeded. Note that we did not use the standard deviation to find the VAR.

This specification is valid for any distribution, discrete or continuous, fat- or thin-tailed. Figure 5–2, for instance, reports J.P. Morgan's distribution of daily revenues in 1994.

To compute VAR, assume that daily revenues are identically and independently distributed. We can then derive the VAR at the 95 percent confidence level from the 5 percent left-side "losing tail" from the histogram.

From this graph, the average revenue is about $5.1 million. There is a total of 254 observations; therefore, we would like to find W^* such that the number of observations to its left is 254×5 percent $= 12.7$. We have 11 observations to the left of $-\$10$ million and 15 to the left of $-\$9$ million. Interpolating, we find $W^* = -\$9.6$ million. The VAR of daily revenues, measured relative to the mean, is VAR $= E(W) - W^* = \$5.1$ million $- (-\$9.6$ million$) = \$14.7$ million. If one wishes to measure VAR in terms of absolute dollar loss, VAR is then $9.6 million.

5.1.3 VAR for Parametric Distributions

The VAR computation can be simplified considerably if the distribution can be assumed to belong to a parametric family, such as the normal dis-

FIGURE 5-2

Distribution of daily revenues.

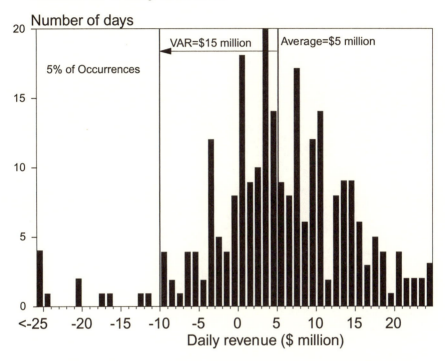

tribution. When this is the case, the VAR figure can be derived directly from the portfolio standard deviation using a multiplicative factor that depends on the confidence level. This approach is sometimes called *parametric* because it involves estimation of parameters, such as the standard deviation, instead of just reading the quantile off the empirical distribution.

This method is simple and convenient and, as we shall see later, produces more accurate measures of VAR. The issue is whether the normal approximation is realistic. If not, another distribution may fit the data better.

First, we need to translate the general distribution $f(w)$ into a standard normal distribution $\Phi(\epsilon)$, where ϵ has mean zero and standard deviation of unity. We associate W^* with the cutoff return R^* such that $W^* = W_0(1 + R^*)$. Generally, R^* is negative and also can be written as $-|R^*|$.

Further, we can associate R^* with a standard normal deviate $\alpha > 0$ by setting

$$-\alpha = \frac{-|R^*| - \mu}{\sigma} \tag{5.5}$$

It is equivalent to set

$$1 - c = \int_{-\infty}^{W^*} f(w)\, dw = \int_{-\infty}^{-|R^*|} f(r)\, dr = \int_{-\infty}^{-\alpha} \Phi(\epsilon)\, d\epsilon \tag{5.6}$$

Thus the problem of finding a VAR is equivalent to finding the deviate α such that the area to the left of it is equal to $1 - c$. This is made possible by turning to tables of the *cumulative standard normal distribution function*, which is the area to the left of a standard normal variable with value equal to d:

$$N(d) = \int_{-\infty}^{d} \Phi(\epsilon)\, d\epsilon \tag{5.7}$$

This function also plays a key role in the Black-Scholes option pricing model. Figure 5–3 graphs the cumulative density function $N(d)$, which increases monotonically from 0 (for $d = -\infty$) to 1 (for $d = +\infty$), going through 0.5 as d passes through 0.

To find the VAR of a standard normal variable, select the desired left-tail confidence level on the vertical axis, say, 5 percent. This corresponds to a value of $\alpha = 1.65$ below 0. We then retrace our steps, back from the α we just found to the cutoff return R^* and VAR. From Equation (5.5), the cutoff return is

$$R^* = -\alpha\sigma + \mu \tag{5.8}$$

For more generality, assume now that the parameters μ and σ are expressed on an annual basis. The time interval considered is Δt, in years. We can use the time aggregation results developed in the preceding chapter, which assume uncorrelated returns.

Using Equation (5.1), we find the VAR below the mean as

$$\text{VAR(mean)} = -W_0(R^* - \mu) = W_0\alpha\sigma\sqrt{\Delta t} \tag{5.9}$$

In other words, the VAR figure is simply a multiple of the standard deviation of the distribution times an adjustment factor that is directly related to the confidence level and horizon.

FIGURE 5–3

Cumulative normal probability distribution.

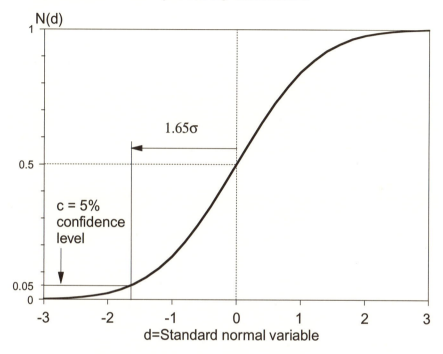

When VAR is defined as an absolute dollar loss, we have

$$\text{VAR(zero)} = -W_0 R^* = W_0(\alpha\sigma\sqrt{\Delta t} - \mu\Delta t) \qquad (5.10)$$

This method generalizes to other cumulative probability functions (cdf) as well as the normal, as long as all the uncertainty is contained in σ. Other distributions will entail different values of α. The normal distribution is just particularly easy to deal with because it adequately represents many empirical distributions. This is especially true for large, well-diversified portfolios but certainly not for portfolios with heavy option components and exposures to a small number of financial risks.

5.1.4 Comparison of Approaches

How well does this approximation work? For some distributions, the fit can be quite good. Consider, for instance, the daily revenues in Figure 5–2. The standard deviation of the distribution is $9.2 million. According

FIGURE 5–4

Comparison of cumulative distributions.

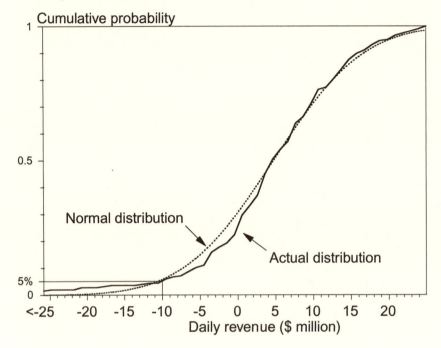

to Equation (5.9), the normal-distribution VAR is $\alpha \times (\sigma W_0) = 1.65 \times$ $9.2 million = $15.2 million. Note that this number is very close to the VAR obtained from the general distribution, which was $14.7 million.

Indeed, Figure 5–4 presents the cumulative distribution functions (cdf) obtained from the histogram in Figure 5–2 and from its normal approximation. The actual cdf is obtained from summing, starting from the left, all numbers of occurrences in Figure 5–2 and then scaling by the total number of observations. The normal cdf is the same as that in Figure 5–3, with the horizontal axis scaled back into dollar revenues using Equation (5.8). The two lines are generally very close, suggesting that the normal approximation provides a good fit to the actual data.

5.1.5 VAR as a Risk Measure

VAR's heritage can be traced to Markowitz's (1952) seminal work on portfolio choice. He noted that "you should be interested in risk as well as return" and advocated the use of the standard deviation as an intuitive measure of dispersion.

Much of Markowitz's work was devoted to studying the tradeoff between expected return and risk in the mean-variance framework, which is appropriate when either returns are normally distributed or investors have quadratic utility functions.

Perhaps the first mention of confidence-based risk measures can be traced to Roy (1952), who presented a "safety first" criterion for portfolio selection. He advocated choosing portfolios that minimize the probability of a loss greater than a disaster level. Baumol (1963) also proposed a risk measurement criterion based on a lower confidence limit at some probability level:

$$L = \alpha\sigma - \mu \qquad (5.11)$$

which is an early description of Equation (5.10).

Other measures of risk have also been proposed, including semideviation, which counts only deviations below a target value, and lower partial moments, which apply to a wider range of utility functions.

More recently, Artzner et al. (1999) list four desirable properties for risk measures for capital adequacy purposes. A risk measure can be viewed as a function of the distribution of portfolio value W, which is summarized into a single number $\rho(W)$:

- *Monotonicity:* If $W_1 \leq W_2$, $\rho(W_1) \geq \rho(W_2)$, or if a portfolio has systematically lower returns than another for all states of the world, its risk must be greater.
- *Translation invariance.* $\rho(W + k) = \rho(W) - k$, or adding cash k to a portfolio should reduce its risk by k.
- *Homogeneity.* $\rho(bW) = b\rho(W)$, or increasing the size of a portfolio by b should simply scale its risk by the same factor (this rules out liquidity effects for large portfolios, however).
- *Subadditivity.* $\rho(W_1 + W_2) \leq \rho(W_1) + \rho(W_2)$, or merging portfolios cannot increase risk.

Artzner et al. (1999) show that the quantile-based VAR measure fails to satisfy the last property. Indeed, one can come up with pathologic examples of short option positions that can create large losses with a low probability and hence have low VAR yet combine to create portfolios with larger VAR. One can also show that the shortfall measure $E(-X|X \leq -VAR)$, which is the expected loss conditional on exceeding VAR, satisfies these desirable "coherence" properties.

When returns are normally distributed, however, the standard deviation–based VAR satisfies the last property, $\sigma(W_1 + W_2) \leq \sigma(W_1) + \sigma(W_2)$. Indeed, as Markowitz had shown, the volatility of a portfolio is less than the sum of volatilities.

Of course, the preceding discussion does not consider another essential component for portfolio comparisons: expected returns. In practice, one obviously would want to balance increasing risk against increasing expected returns. The great benefit of VAR, however, is that it brings attention and transparency to the measure of risk, a component of the decision process that is not intuitive and as a result too often ignored.

5.2 CHOICE OF QUANTITATIVE FACTORS

We now turn to the choice of two quantitative factors: the length of the holding horizon and the confidence level. In general, VAR will increase with either a longer horizon or a greater confidence level. Under certain conditions, increasing one or the other factor produces equivalent VAR numbers. This section provides guidance on the choice of c and Δt, which should depend on the use of the VAR number.

5.2.1 VAR as a Benchmark Measure

The first, most general use of VAR is simply to provide a companywide yardstick to compare risks across different markets. In this situation, the choice of the factors is arbitrary. Bankers Trust, for instance, has long used a 99 percent VAR over an annual horizon to compare the risks of various units. Assuming a normal distribution, we show later that it is easy to convert disparate bank measures into a common number.

The focus here is on cross-sectional or time differences in VAR. For instance, the institution wants to know if a trading unit has greater risk than another. Or whether today's VAR is in line with yesterday's. If not, the institution should "drill down" into its risk reports and find whether today's higher VAR is due to increased volatility or larger bets. For this purpose, the choice of the confidence level and horizon does not matter much as long as *consistency* is maintained.

5.2.2 VAR as a Potential Loss Measure

Another application of VAR is to give a broad idea of the worst loss an institution can incur. If so, the horizon should be determined by the nature of the portfolio.

A first interpretation is that the horizon is defined by the *liquidation period*. Commercial banks currently report their trading VAR over a daily horizon because of the liquidity and rapid turnover in their portfolios. In contrast, investment portfolios such as pension funds generally invest in less liquid assets and adjust their risk exposures only slowly, which is why a 1-month horizon is generally chosen for investment purposes. Since the holding period should correspond to the longest period needed for an orderly portfolio liquidation, the horizon should be related to the liquidity of the securities, defined in terms of the length of time needed for normal transaction volumes. A related interpretation is that the horizon represents the *time required to hedge* the market risks.

An opposite view is that the horizon corresponds to the period over which the portfolio remains relatively constant. Since VAR assumes that the portfolio is frozen over the horizon, this measure gradually loses significance as the horizon extends.

However, perhaps the main reason for banks to choose a daily VAR is that this is consistent with their *daily profit and loss (P&L) measures*. This allows an easy comparison between the daily VAR and the subsequent P&L number.

For this application, the choice of the confidence level is relatively arbitrary. Users should recognize that VAR does not describe the worst-ever loss but is rather a probabilistic measure that should be exceeded with some frequency. Higher confidence levels will generate higher VAR figures.

5.2.3 VAR as Equity Capital

On the other hand, the choice of the factors is crucial if the VAR number is used directly to set a capital cushion for the institution. If so, a loss exceeding the VAR would wipe out the equity capital, leading to bankruptcy.

For this purpose, however, we must assume that the VAR measure adequately captures all the risks facing an institution, which may be a stretch. Thus the risk measure should encompass market risk, credit risk, operational risk, and other risks.

The choice of the confidence level should reflect the degree of risk aversion of the company and the cost of a loss exceeding VAR. Higher risk aversion or greater cost implies that a greater amount of capital should cover possible losses, thus leading to a higher confidence level.

At the same time, the choice of the horizon should correspond to the time required for corrective action as losses start to develop. Corrective action can take the form of reducing the risk profile of the institution or raising new capital.

To illustrate, assume that the institution determines its risk profile by targeting a particular credit rating. The expected default rate then can be converted directly into a confidence level. Higher credit ratings should lead to a higher VAR confidence level. Table 5–1, for instance, shows that to maintain a Baa investment-grade credit rating, the institution should have a default probability of 0.17 percent over the next year. It therefore should carry enough capital to cover its annual VAR at the 99.83 percent confidence level, or 100 − 0.17 percent.

Longer horizons, with a constant risk profile, inevitably lead to higher default frequencies. Institutions with an initial Baa credit rating have a default frequency of 10.50 percent over the next 10 years. The same credit rating can be achieved by extending the horizon or decreasing the confidence level appropriately. These two factors are intimately related.

TABLE 5–1

Credit Rating and Default Rates

	Default Frequency	
Desired Rating	1 Year	10 Years
Aaa	0.02%	1.49%
Aa	0.05%	3.24%
A	0.09%	5.65%
Baa	0.17%	10.50%
Ba	0.77%	21.24%
B	2.32%	37.98%

Source: Adapted from Moody's default rates from 1920–1998.

5.2.4 Criteria for Backtesting

The choice of the quantitative factors is also important for backtesting considerations. Model backtesting involves systematic comparisons of VAR with the subsequently realized P&L in an attempt to detect biases in the reported VAR figures and is described in a later chapter. The goal should be to set up the tests so as to maximize the likelihood of catching biases in VAR forecasts.

Longer horizons reduce the number of independent observations and thus the power of the tests. For instance, using a 2-week VAR horizon means that we have only 26 independent observations per year. A 1-day VAR horizon, in contrast, will have about 252 observations over the same year. Hence a shorter horizon is preferable to increase the power of the tests. This explains why the Basel Committee performs backtesting over a 1-day horizon, even though the horizon is 10 business days for capital adequacy purposes.

Likewise, the choice of the confidence level should be such that it leads to powerful tests. Too high a confidence level reduces the expected number of observations in the tail and thus the power of the tests. Take, for instance, a 95 percent level. We know that, just by chance, we expect a loss worse than the VAR figure in 1 day out of 20. If we had chosen a 99 percent confidence level, we would have to wait, on average, 100 days to confirm that the model conforms to reality. Hence, for backtesting purposes, the confidence level should not be set too high. In practice, a 95 percent level performs well for backtesting purposes.

5.2.5 Application: The Basel Parameters

One illustration of the use of VAR as equity capital is the internal models approach of the Basel Committee, which imposes a 99 percent confidence level over a 10-business-day horizon. The resulting VAR is then multiplied by a safety factor of 3 to provide the minimum capital requirement for regulatory purposes.

Presumably, the Basel Committee chose a 10-day period because it reflects the tradeoff between the costs of frequent monitoring and the benefits of early detection of potential problems. Presumably also, the Basel Committee chose a 99 percent confidence level that reflects the tradeoff between the desire of regulators to ensure a safe and sound financial system and the adverse effect of capital requirements on bank returns.

Even so, a loss worse than the VAR estimate will occur about 1 percent of the time, on average, or once every 4 years. It would be unthinkable for regulators to allow major banks to fail so often. This explains the multiplicative factor $k = 3$, which should provide near absolute insurance against bankruptcy.

At this point, the choice of parameters for the capital charge should appear quite arbitrary. There are many combinations of the confidence level, the horizon, and the multiplicative factor that would yield the same capital charge. The origin of the factor k also looks rather mysterious.

Presumably, the multiplicative factor also accounts for a host of additional risks not modeled by the usual application of VAR that fall under the category of *model risk*. For example, the bank may be understating its risk due to a short sample period, to unstable correlation, or simply to the fact that it uses a normal approximation to a distribution that really has more observations in the tail.

Stahl (1997) justifies the choice of k based on Chebyshev's inequality. For any random variable x with finite variance, the probability of falling outside a specified interval is

$$P(|x - \mu| > r\sigma) \leq 1/r^2 \qquad (5.12)$$

assuming that we know the true standard deviation σ. Suppose now that the distribution is symmetrical. For values of x below the mean,

$$P[(x - \mu) < -r\sigma] \leq \tfrac{1}{2} 1/r^2 \qquad (5.13)$$

We now set the right-hand side of this inequality to the desired level of 1 percent. This yields $r(99\%) = 7.071$. The maximum VAR is therefore $VAR_{max} = r(99\%)\sigma$.

Say that the bank reports its 99 percent VAR using a normal distribution. Using the quantile of the standard normal distribution, we have

$$VAR_N = \alpha(99\%)\sigma = 2.326\sigma \qquad (5.14)$$

If the true distribution is misspecified, the correction factor is then

$$k = \frac{VAR_{max}}{VAR_N} = \frac{7.071\sigma}{2.326\sigma} = 3.03 \qquad (5.15)$$

which happens to justify the correction factor applied by the Basel Committee.

5.2.6 Conversion of VAR Parameters

Using a parametric distribution such as the normal distribution is particularly convenient because it allows conversion to different confidence levels (which define α). Conversion across horizons (expressed as $\sigma\sqrt{\Delta t}$) is also feasible if we assume a constant risk profile, that is, portfolio positions and volatilities. Formally, the portfolio returns need to be (1) independently distributed, (2) normally distributed, and (3) with constant parameters.

As an example, we can convert the RiskMetrics risk measures into the Basel Committee internal models measures. RiskMetrics provides a 95 percent confidence interval (1.65σ) over 1 day. The Basel Committee rules define a 99 percent confidence interval (2.33σ) over 10 days. The adjustment takes the following form:

$$\text{VAR}_{BC} = \text{VAR}_{RM} \frac{2.33}{1.65} \sqrt{10} = 4.45\text{VAR}_{RM}$$

Therefore, the VAR under the Basel Committee rules is more than four times the VAR from the RiskMetrics system.

More generally, Table 5–2 shows how the Basel Committee parameters translate into combinations of confidence levels and horizons, taking an annual volatility of 12 percent, which is typical of the DM/$

TABLE 5–2

Equivalence Between Horizon and Confidence Level, Normal Distribution, Annual Risk = 12 Percent (Basel Parameters: 99 Percent Confidence over 2 Weeks)

Confidence Level c	Number of S.D. α	Horizon Δt	Actual S.D. $\sigma\sqrt{\Delta t}$	Cutoff Value $\alpha\sigma\sqrt{\Delta t}$
Baseline				
99%	-2.326	2 weeks	2.35	-5.47
57.56%	-0.456	1 year	12.00	-5.47
81.89%	-0.911	3 months	6.00	-5.47
86.78%	-1.116	2 months	4.90	-5.47
95%	-1.645	4 weeks	3.32	-5.47
99%	-2.326	2 weeks	2.35	-5.47
99.95%	-3.290	1 week	1.66	-5.47
99.99997%	-7.153	1 day	0.76	-5.47

exchange rate (now the euro/$ rate). These combinations are such that they all produce the same value for $\alpha\sigma\sqrt{\Delta t}$. For instance, a 99 percent confidence level over 2 weeks produces the same VAR as a 95 percent confidence level over 4 weeks. Or conversion into a weekly horizon requires a confidence level of 99.95 percent.

5.3 ASSESSING VAR PRECISION

This chapter has shown how to estimate essential parameters for the measurement of VAR, means, standard deviations, and quantiles from actual data. These estimates, however, should not be taken for granted entirely. They are affected by *estimation error,* which is the natural sampling variability due to limited sample size. Users should beware of the limited precision behind the reported VAR numbers.

5.3.1 The Problem of Measurement Errors

From the viewpoint of VAR users, it is important to assess the degree of precision in the reported VAR. In a previous example, the daily VAR was $15 million. The question is: How confident is management in this estimate? Could we say, for example, that management is highly confident in this figure or that it is 95 percent sure that the true estimate is in a $14 million to $16 million range? Or is it the case that the range is $5 million to $25 million. The two confidence bands give quite a different picture of VAR. The first is very precise; the second is rather uninformative (although it tells us that it is not in the hundreds of millions of dollars). This is why it is useful to examine measurement errors in VAR figures.

Consider a situation where VAR is obtained from the historical simulation method, which uses a historical window of T days to measure risk. The problem is that the reported VAR measure is only an *estimate* of the true value and is affected by sampling variability. In other words, different choices of the window T will lead to different VAR figures.

One possible interpretation of the estimates (the view of "frequentist" statisticians) is that these estimates $\hat{\mu}$ and $\hat{\sigma}$ are samples from an underlying distribution with unknown parameters μ and σ. With an infinite number of observations $T \to \infty$ and a perfectly stable system, the estimates should converge to the true values. In practice, sample sizes are limited, either because some series, like emerging markets, are relatively recent or because structural changes make it meaningless to go back too far in time. Since some estimation error may remain, the natural dispersion of values can be measured by the *sampling distribution* for the parameters $\hat{\mu}$ and $\hat{\sigma}$. We now turn to a description of the distribution of statistics on which VAR measures are based.

5.3.2 Estimation Errors in Means and Variances

When the underlying distribution is normal, the exact distribution of the sample mean and variance is known. The estimated mean $\hat{\mu}$ is distributed normally around the true mean

$$\hat{\mu} \approx N(\mu, \sigma^2/T) \tag{5.16}$$

where T is the number of independent observations in the sample. Note that the standard error in the estimated mean converges toward 0 at a rate of $\sigma\sqrt{1/T}$ as T increases.

As for the estimated variance $\hat{\sigma}^2$, the following ratio has a chi-square distribution with $(T - 1)$ degrees of freedom:

$$\frac{(T - 1)\ \hat{\sigma}^2}{\sigma^2} \approx \chi^2(T - 1) \tag{5.17}$$

In practice, if the sample size T is large enough (e.g., above 20), the chi-square distribution converges rapidly to a normal distribution, which is easier to handle:

$$\hat{\sigma}^2 \approx N\left(\sigma^2, \sigma^4\ \frac{2}{T - 1}\right) \tag{5.18}$$

As for the sample standard deviation, its standard error in large samples is

$$se(\hat{\sigma}) = \sigma\ \sqrt{\frac{1}{2T}} \tag{5.19}$$

For instance, consider monthly returns on the DM/\$ rate from 1973 to 1998. Sample parameters are $\hat{\mu} = -0.15$ percent, $\hat{\sigma} = 3.39$ percent, with $T = 312$ observations. The standard error of the estimate indicates how confident we are about the sample value; the smaller the error, the more confident we are. One standard error in $\hat{\mu}$ is $se(\hat{\mu}) = \hat{\sigma}\sqrt{1/T} = 3.39\sqrt{1/312} = 0.19$ percent. Therefore, the point estimate of $\hat{\mu} = -0.15$ percent is less than one standard error away from 0. Even with 26 years of data, μ is measured very imprecisely.

In contrast, one standard error for $\hat{\sigma}$ is $se(\hat{\sigma}) = \hat{\sigma}\sqrt{1/2T} = 3.39$ $\sqrt{1/624} = 0.14$ percent. Since this number is much smaller than the estimate of 3.39 percent, we can conclude that the volatility is estimated with much greater accuracy than the expected return—giving some confidence in the use of VAR systems.

As the sample size increases, so does the precision of the estimate. To illustrate this point, Figure 5–5 depicts 95 percent confidence bands around the estimate of volatility for various sample sizes, assuming a true daily volatility of 1 percent.

With 5 trading days, the band is rather imprecise, with upper and lower values set at [0.41%, 1.60%]. After 1 year, the band is [0.91%, 1.08%]. As the number of days increases, the confidence bands shrink to the point where, after 10 years, the interval narrows to [0.97%, 1.03%]. Thus, as the observation interval lengthens, the estimate should become arbitrarily close to the true value.

FIGURE 5–5

Confidence bands for sample volatility.

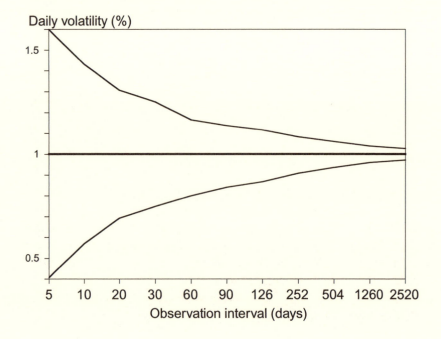

Finally, $\hat{\sigma}$ can be used to estimate any quantile (an example is shown in Section 5.1.4). Since the normal distribution is fully characterized by two parameters only, the standard deviation contains all the information necessary to build measures of dispersion. Any σ-based quantile can be derived as

$$\hat{q}_\sigma = \alpha\hat{\sigma} \tag{5.20}$$

At the 95 percent confidence level, for instance, we simply multiply the estimated value of $\hat{\sigma}$ by 1.65 to find the 5 percent left-tail quantile. Of course, this method will be strictly valid if the underlying distribution is closely approximated by the normal. When the distribution is suspected to be strongly nonnormal, other methods, such as kernel estimation, also provide estimates of the quantile based on the full distribution.[1]

5.3.3 Estimation Error in Sample Quantiles

For arbitrary distributions, the cth quantile can be determined empirically from the historical distribution as $\hat{q}(c)$ (as shown in Section 5.1.2). There is, as before, some sampling error associated with the statistic. Kendall (1994) reports that the asymptotic standard error of $\hat{q}$ is

$$se(\hat{q}) = \sqrt{\frac{c(1 - c)}{T f(q)^2}} \tag{5.21}$$

where T is the sample size, and $f(\cdot)$ is the probability distribution function evaluated at the quantile q. The effect of estimation error is illustrated in Figure 5–6, where the expected quantile and 95 percent confidence bands are plotted for quantiles from the normal distribution.

For the normal distribution, the 5 percent left-tailed interval is centered at 1.65. With $T = 100$, the confidence band is [1.24, 2.04], which is quite large. With 250 observations, which correspond to 1 year of trading days, the band is still [1.38, 1.91]. With $T = 1250$, or 5 years of data, the interval shrinks to [1.52, 1.76].

These intervals widen substantially as one moves to more extreme quantiles. The expected value of the 1 percent quantile is 2.33. With 1 year of data, the band is [1.85, 2.80]. The interval of uncertainty is about

---

1. Kernel estimation smoothes the empirical distribution by a weighted sum of local distributions. For a further description of kernel estimation methods, see Scott (1992). Butler and Schachter (1998) apply this method to the estimation of VAR.

FIGURE 5-6

Confidence bands for sample quantiles.

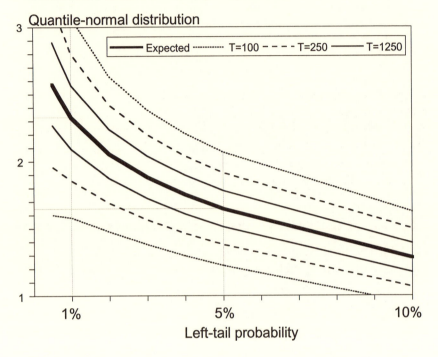

Quantile-normal distribution

twice that at the 5 percent interval. Thus sample quantiles are increasingly unreliable as one goes farther in the left tail.

As expected, there is more imprecision as one moves to lower left-tail probabilities because fewer observations are involved. This is why VAR measures with very high confidence levels should be interpreted with extreme caution.

5.3.4 Comparison of Methods

So far we have developed two approaches for measuring a distribution's VAR: (1) by directly reading the quantile from the distribution $\hat{q}$ and (2) by calculating the standard deviation and then scaling by the appropriate factor $\alpha\hat{\sigma}$. The issue is: Is any method superior to the other?

Intuitively, we may expect the σ-based approach to be more precise. Indeed, $\hat{\sigma}$ uses information about the whole distribution (in terms of all

TABLE 5-3

Confidence Bands for VAR Estimates,
Normal Distribution, $T = 250$

	VAR Confidence Level c	
	99%	**95%**
Exact quantile	2.33	1.65
Confidence band		
Sample $\hat{q}$	[1.85, 2.80]	[1.38, 1.91]
σ-Based, $\alpha\hat{\sigma}$	[2.24, 2.42]	[1.50, 1.78]

squared deviations around the mean), whereas a quantile uses only the ranking of observations and the two observations around the estimated value. And in the case of the normal distribution, we know exactly how to transform $\hat{\sigma}$ into an estimated quantile using α. For other distributions, the value of α may be different, but we should still expect a performance improvement because the standard deviation uses all the sample information.

Table 5–3 compares 95 percent confidence bands for the two methods.[2] The σ-based method leads to substantial efficiency gains relative to the sample quantile. For instance, at the 95 percent VAR confidence level, the interval around 1.65 is [1.38, 1.91] for the sample quantile; this is reduced to [1.50, 1.78] for $\alpha\hat{\sigma}$, which is much narrower than the previous interval.

A number of important conclusions can be derived from these numbers. First, there is substantial estimation error in the estimated quantiles, especially for high confidence levels, which are associated with rare events and hence difficult to verify. Second, parametric methods provide a substantial increase in precision, since the sample standard deviation contains far more information than sample quantiles.

Returning to the $15.2 million VAR figure at the beginning of this chapter, we can now assess the precision of this number. Using the parametric approach based on a normal distribution, the standard error of this number is $se(\hat{q}_\sigma) = \alpha \times se(\hat{\sigma}) = 1.65 \times \$9.2$ million $1/(\sqrt{2\times254}) = \$0.67$. Therefore, a two-standard-error confidence band around the VAR

---

2. For extensions to other distributions such as the Student, see Jorion (1996).

estimate is [$13.8 million, $16.6 million]. This narrow interval should provide reassurance that the VAR estimate is indeed meaningful.

5.4 CONCLUSIONS

In this chapter we have seen how to measure VAR using two alternative methodologies. The general approach is based on the empirical distribution and its sample quantile. The parametric approach, in contrast, attempts to fit a parametric distribution such as the normal to the data. VAR is then measured directly from the standard deviation. Systems such as RiskMetrics are based on a parametric approach.

The advantage of such methods is that they are much easier to use and create more precise estimates of VAR. The disadvantage is that they may not approximate well the actual distribution of profits and losses. Users who want to measure VAR from empirical quantiles, however, should be aware of the effect of sampling variation or imprecision in their VAR number.

This chapter also has discussed criteria for selection of the confidence level and horizon. On the one hand, if VAR is used simply as a benchmark risk measure, the choice is arbitrary and only needs to be consistent. On the other hand, if VAR is used to decide on the amount of equity capital to hold, the choice is extremely important and can be guided, for instance, by default frequencies for the targeted credit rating.

CHAPTER 6

Backtesting VAR Models

Disclosure of quantitative measures of market risk, such as value-at-risk, is enlightening only when accompanied by a thorough discussion of how the risk measures were calculated and how they related to actual performance.

Alan Greenspan (1996)

VAR models are only useful insofar as they predict risk reasonably well. This is why the application of these models always should be accompanied by validation. *Model validation* is the general process of checking whether a model is adequate. This can be done with a set of tools, including backtesting, stress testing, and independent review and oversight.

This chapter turns to backtesting techniques for verifying the accuracy of VAR models. *Backtesting* is a formal statistical framework that consists of verifying that actual losses are in line with projected losses. This involves systematically comparing the history of VAR forecasts with their associated portfolio returns.

These procedures, sometimes called *reality checks,* are essential for VAR users and risk managers who need to check that their VAR forecasts are well calibrated. If not, the models should be reexamined for faulty assumptions, wrong parameters, or inaccurate modeling. This process also will provide ideas for improvement.

Backtesting is also central to the Basel Committee's groundbreaking decision to allow internal VAR models for capital requirements. It is unlikely the Basel Committee would have done so without the discipline of a rigorous backtesting mechanism. Otherwise, banks may have an incentive to understate their reported risk. This is why the system should be designed to maximize the probability of catching banks that willfully understate their risk. On the other hand, the system also should avoid unduly penalizing banks whose VAR is exceeded simply due to bad luck.

The delicate choice is at the heart of statistical decision procedures for backtesting.

Section 6.1 provides an actual example of model verification and discusses important data issues for the setup of VAR backtesting. Next, Section 6.2 presents the main method for backtesting, which consists of counting deviations from the VAR model. It also describes the supervisory framework by the Basel Committee for backtesting the internal models approach. While we can learn much from the Basel Committee framework, it is important to recognize alternative approaches that have proved to be more powerful discriminants of VAR models, as shown in Section 6.3. Finally, Section 6.4 provides some summary conclusions.

6.1 SETUP FOR BACKTESTING

VAR models are only useful insofar as they can be demonstrated to be reasonably accurate. To do this, users must check systematically the validity of the underlying valuation and risk models through comparison of predicted and actual loss levels.

When the model is perfectly calibrated, the number of observations falling outside VAR should be in line with the confidence level. The number of exceedences is also known as the number of *exceptions.* With too many exceptions, the model underestimates risk. This is a major problem because too little capital may be allocated to risk-taking units; penalties also may be imposed by the regulator. Too few exceptions is also a problem because it leads to excess, or inefficient, allocation of capital across units.

6.1.1 An Example

An example of model calibration is described in Figure 6–1, which displays the fit between actual and forecast daily VAR numbers for Bankers Trust. The diagram shows the absolute value of the daily profit and loss (P&L) against the 99 percent VAR, defined here as the "daily price volatility."[1] Observations that lie above the diagonal line indicate days when the absolute value of the P&L exceeded their VAR.

---

1. Note that the graph does not differentiate losses from gains, since companies are usually reluctant to divulge the extent of their trading losses. This illustrates one of the benefits of VAR relative to other methods, namely, that by taking the absolute value, it hides the direction of the positions.

FIGURE 6–1

Model evaluation: Bankers Trust.

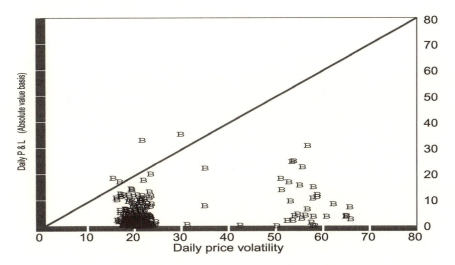

Daily price volatility

Assuming symmetry in the P&L distribution, about 2 percent of the daily observations (both positive and negative) should lie above the diagonal, or about five data points in a year. Here, we observe four exceptions. Thus the model seems to be well calibrated. We could have observed, however, a greater number of deviations simply due to bad luck. The question is: At what point do we reject the model?

6.1.2 Which Return?

Before we even start addressing the statistical issue, a serious data problem needs to be recognized. VAR measures assume that the current portfolio is "frozen" over the horizon. In practice, the trading portfolio evolves dynamically during the day. Thus the actual portfolio is "contaminated" by changes in its composition. The *actual return* corresponds to the actual P&L, taking into account intraday trades and other profit items.

This contamination will be minimized if the horizon is relatively short, which explains why backtesting is usually conducted on daily returns. Even so, intraday trading generally will increase the volatility of revenues. Counterbalancing this is the effect of fee income, which generates steady profits that may not enter the VAR measure.

For verification to be meaningful, the risk manager should track both the actual portfolio return R_t and the hypothetical return R_t^* that most closely matches the VAR forecast. The *hypothetical return* R_t^* represents a frozen portfolio, obtained from fixed positions applied to the actual returns on all securities, measured from close to close. In addition, fee income can be factored in by taking R_t^* as the deviation from the average return.

Sometimes an approximation is obtained by using a *cleaned return,* which is the actual return minus all non-mark-to-market items, such as funding costs, fee income, reserves released, and so on.

Since the VAR forecast really pertains to R^*, backtesting ideally should be done with these hypothetical returns. Actual returns do matter, though, because they entail real profits and losses and are scrutinized by bank regulators. They also reflect the true, *ex post,* volatility of trading returns, which is also informative. Ideally, both actual and hypothetical returns should be used for backtesting, since both sets of numbers yield informative comparisons. For regulatory purposes, however, backtesting applies to actual returns.

6.2 MODEL BACKTESTING WITH EXCEPTIONS

Model backtesting involves systematically comparing historical VAR measures with the subsequent returns. The problem is that since VAR is reported only at a specified confidence level, we expect the figure to be exceeded in some instances, for example, in 5 percent of the observations at the 95 percent confidence level. But surely we will not observe exactly 5 percent excess deviations. A greater percentage could occur due to bad luck, perhaps 6 to 8 percent. At some point, if the frequency of deviations becomes too large, say, 10 to 20 percent, the user must conclude that the problem lies with the model, not bad luck, and undertake corrective action. The issue is how to make this decision. This "accept or reject decision" is a classic statistical decision problem.

6.2.1 Model Verification Based on Failure Rates

The simplest method to verify the accuracy of the model is to record the *failure rate,* which gives the proportion of times VAR is exceeded in a given sample. Suppose a bank provides a VAR figure at the 1 percent left-tail level ($p = 1 - c$) for a total of T days. The user then counts how many times the actual loss exceeds the previous day's VAR. Define N as the number of exceptions and N/T as the failure rate. Ideally, the failure rate should give an *unbiased* measure of p, that is, should converge to p as the sample size increases.

We want to know, at a given confidence level, whether N is too small or too large under the null hypothesis that $p = 0.01$ in a sample of size T. Note that this test makes no assumption about the return distribution. It could be normal, or skewed, or with heavy tails. As a result, this approach is fully nonparametric.

The setup for this test is the classic testing framework for a sequence of success and failures, also called *Bernoulli trials*. The number of exceptions x follows a *binomial* probability distribution:

$$f(x) = \binom{T}{x} p^x (1 - p)^{T-x} \qquad (6.1)$$

We also know that x has expected value of $E(X) = pT$ and variance $V(X) = p(1 - p)T$. When T is large, we can use the central limit theorem and approximate the binomial distribution by the normal distribution:

$$z = \frac{x - pT}{\sqrt{p(1 - p)T}} \approx N(0, 1) \qquad (6.2)$$

which provides a convenient shortcut.

This binomial distribution can be used to test whether the number of exceptions is acceptably small. Figure 6–2 describes the distribution when the model is calibrated correctly, that is, when $p = 0.01$, and when $T = 250$. The graph shows that under the null, we would observe more than four exceptions 10.8 percent of the time. The 10.8 percent number describes the probability of committing a *type 1* error, that is, of rejecting a correct model.

Next, Figure 6–3 describes the distribution of exceptions when the model is calibrated incorrectly, that is, when $p = 0.03$ instead of 0.01. The graph shows that we will not reject the incorrect model more than 12.8 percent of the time. This describes the probability of committing a *type 2* error, that is, of not rejecting an incorrect model.

When designing a verification test, the user faces a tradeoff between these two types of error. Table 6–1 summarizes the two states of the world, correct versus incorrect model, and the decision. For backtesting purposes, users of VAR models need to balance type 1 errors against type 2 errors.

FIGURE 6–2

Distribution of exceptions when the model is correct.

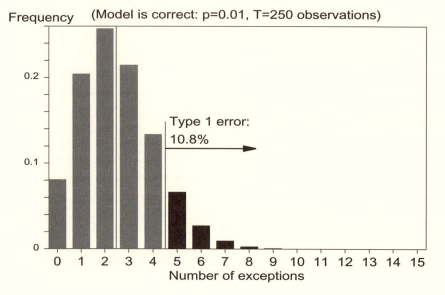

Ideally, one would want to set a low type 1 error and then have a test that creates a very low type 2 error, in which case the test is said to be *powerful*.

Kupiec (1995) develops approximate 95 percent confidence regions for such a test, which are reported in Table 6–2. (It should be noted that the choice of the confidence region for the test is not related to the quantitative level p selected for VAR. This confidence level refers to the decision rule to accept or reject the model.) These regions are defined by the tail points of the log-likelihood ratio:

$$LR_{uc} = -2 \ln[(1 - p)^{T-N} p^N] + 2 \ln\{[1 - (N/T)]^{T-N} (N/T)^N\} \quad (6.3)$$

which is asymptotically distributed chi-square with one degree of freedom under the null hypothesis that p is the true probability.[2] Thus we would reject the null hypothesis if $LR > 3.84$.

For instance, with 2 years of data ($T = 510$), we would expect to observe $N = pT = 1$ percent $\times$ 510 $= 5$ exceptions. But the VAR user

---

2. Statistical decision theory has shown that this test is the most powerful among its class.

FIGURE 6–3

Distribution of exceptions when the model is incorrect.

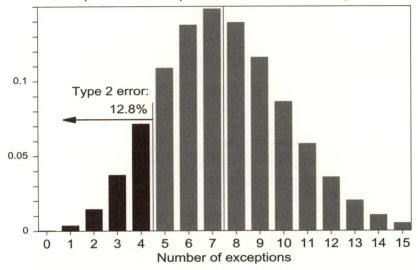

Frequency

(Model is false: p=3%, T=250 observations)

will not be able to reject the null hypothesis as long as N is within the $[1 < N < 11]$ confidence interval. Values of N greater than or equal to 11 indicate that the VAR is too low or that the model understates the probability of large losses. Values of N less than or equal to 1 indicate that the VAR model is overly conservative.

The table also shows that this interval, expressed as a proportion N/T, shrinks as the sample size increases. Select, for instance, the $p = 0.05$ row. The interval for $T = 255$ is $[6/255 = 0.024, 21/255 = 0.082]$; for $T = 1000$, it is $[37/1000 = 0.037, 65/1000 = 0.065]$. Note how the interval shrinks as the sample size extends. With more data, we should be able to reject more easily the model if it is false.

The table, however, points to a disturbing fact. For small values of the VAR parameter p, it becomes increasingly difficult to confirm deviations. For instance, the nonrejection region under $p = 0.01$ and $T = 255$ is $[N < 7]$. Therefore, there is no way to tell if N is abnormally small or the model systematically overestimates risk. Intuitively, detection of systematic biases becomes increasingly difficult for low values of p because these correspond to very rare events. We show later that this approach has a high probability of type 2 errors.

TABLE 6–1

Decision Errors

	Model	
Decision:	**Correct**	**Incorrect**
Accept	OK	Type 2 error
Reject	Type 1 error	OK

This explains why some banks prefer to choose a higher value for p, say, 0.05 (which translates into a confidence level $c = 95$ percent), in order to be able to observe a sufficient numbers of deviations to validate the model. A multiplicative factor is then applied to translate the VAR figure into a safe capital cushion number. Too often, however, the choice of the confidence level appears to be made without regard for the issue of verification.

6.2.2 The Basel Rules

This section now turns to a detailed analysis of the Basel Committee rules for backtesting. While we can learn much from the Basel framework, it

TABLE 6–2

Model Backtesting, 95% Nonrejection Test Confidence Regions

Probability Level p	VAR Confidence Level	Nonrejection Region for Number of Failures N		
		$T = 255$ days	$T = 510$ days	$T = 1000$ days
0.01	99%	$N < 7$	$1 < N < 11$	$4 < N < 17$
0.025	97.5%	$2 < N < 12$	$6 < N < 21$	$15 < N < 36$
0.05	95%	$6 < N < 21$	$16 < N < 36$	$37 < N < 65$
0.075	92.5%	$11 < N < 28$	$27 < N < 51$	$59 < N < 92$
0.10	90%	$16 < N < 36$	$38 < N < 65$	$81 < N < 120$

Notes: N is the number of failures that could be observed in a sample size T without rejecting the null hypothesis that p is the correct probability at the 95 percent level of test confidence.

Source: From Kupiec (1995).

is important to recognize that regulators operate under different constraints from financial institutions. Since they do not have access to every component of the models, the approach is perforce implemented at a broader level. Regulators are also responsible for constructing rules that are comparable across institutions.

The Basel (1996a) rules for backtesting the internal models approach are derived directly from this failure rate test. To design such a test, one has to choose first the type 1 error rate, which is the probability of rejecting the model when it is correct. When this happens, the bank simply suffers bad luck and should not be penalized unduly. Hence one should pick a test with a low type 1 error rate, say, 5 percent (depending on its cost). The heart of the conflict is that, inevitably, the supervisor also will commit type 2 errors due to a bank that willfully cheats on its VAR reporting.

The current verification procedure consists of recording daily exceptions of the 99 percent VAR over the last year. One would expect on average 1 percent of 250, or 2.5 instances of exceptions over the last year.

The Basel Committee has decided that up to four exceptions are acceptable, which defines a "green light" zone for the bank. If the number of exceptions is five or more, the bank falls into a "yellow" or "red" zone and incurs a progressive penalty whereby the multiplicative factor k is increased from 3 to 4, as described in Table 6–3. An incursion into the "red" zone generates an automatic penalty.

TABLE 6–3

The Basel Penalty Zones

Zone	Number of Exceptions	Increase in k
Green	0 to 4	0.00
Yellow	5	0.40
	6	0.50
	7	0.65
	8	0.75
	9	0.85
Red	10+	1.00

Within the "yellow" zone, the penalty is up to the supervisor, depending on the reason for the exception. The Basel Committee uses the following categories:

- *Basic integrity of the model.* The deviation occurred because the positions were reported incorrectly or because of an error in the program code.
- *Model accuracy could be improved.* The deviation occurred because the model does not measure risk with enough precision (e.g., has too few maturity buckets).
- *Intraday trading.* Positions changed during the day.
- *Bad luck.* Markets were particularly volatile or correlations changed.

The description of the applicable penalty is suitably vague. When exceptions are due to the first two reasons, the penalty "should" apply. With the third reason, a penalty "should be considered." When the deviation is traced to the fourth reason, the Basel document gives no guidance, except that these exceptions should "be expected to occur at least some of the time." These exceptions may be excluded if they are the "result of such occurrences as sudden abnormal changes in interest rates or exchange rates, major political events or natural disasters." In other words, bank supervisors want to keep the flexibility to adjust the rules in turbulent times as they see fit.

The crux of the backtesting problem is separating bad luck from a faulty model, or balancing type 1 errors against type 2 errors. Table 6–4 displays the probabilities of obtaining a given number of exceptions for a correct model (with 99 percent coverage) and incorrect model (with only 97 percent coverage). With five exceptions or more, the cumulative probability, or type 1 error rate, is 10.8 percent. This is rather high to start with. In the current framework, one bank out of ten could be penalized even with a correct model.

Even worse, the type 2 error rate is also very high. Assuming a true 97 percent coverage, the supervisor will accept 12.8 percent of banks that have an incorrect model. The framework is therefore not very powerful. And this 99 versus 97 percent difference in VAR coverage is economically significant. Assuming a normal distribution, the true VAR would be 1.237 times greater than officially reported. This understatement would allow, for instance, a reduction in the total capital of $165 billion for the top ten U.S. banks by $39 billion.

TABLE 6-4

Basel Rules for Backtesting, Probabilities of Obtaining Exceptions ($T = 250$)

Zone	Number of Exceptions N	Coverage = 99% Model Is Correct		Coverage = 97% Model Is Incorrect		
		Probability $P(X = N)$	Cumulative (Type 1) (Reject) $P(X \geq N)$	Probability $P(X = N)$	Cumulative (Type 2) (Do Not Reject) $P(X < N)$	Power (1 Type 2) (Reject) $P(X \geq N)$
Green	0	8.1	100.0	0.0	0.0	100.0
	1	20.5	91.9	0.4	0.0	100.0
	2	25.7	71.4	1.5	0.4	99.6
	3	21.5	45.7	3.8	1.9	98.1
Green	4	13.4	24.2	7.2	5.7	94.3
Yellow	5	6.7	10.8	10.9	12.8	87.2
	6	2.7	4.1	13.8	23.7	76.3
	7	1.0	1.4	14.9	37.5	62.5
	8	0.3	0.4	14.0	52.4	47.6
Yellow	9	0.1	0.1	11.6	66.3	33.7
Red	10	0.0	0.0	8.6	77.9	21.1
	11	0.0	0.0	5.8	86.6	13.4

The lack of power of this framework is due to the choice of the high VAR confidence level (99 percent) that generates too few exceptions for a reliable test. Consider instead the effect of a 95 percent VAR confidence level. (To ensure that the amount of capital is not affected, we could use a larger multiplier k.) We now have to decide on the cutoff number of exceptions to have a type 1 error rate similar to the Basel framework. With an average of 13 exceptions per year, we choose to reject the model if the number of exceptions exceeds 17, which corresponds to a type 1 error of 12.5 percent. Here we controlled the error rate so that it is close to the 10.8 percent for the Basel framework. But now the probability of a type 2 error is lower, at 7.4 percent only.[3] Thus, simply changing the VAR confidence level from 99 to 95 percent sharply reduces the probability of not catching an erroneous model.

Another method to increase the power of the test would be to increase the number of observations. With $T = 500$, for instance, we could choose a cutoff number of exceptions of 8, for a type 1 error rate of 13.2 percent and type 2 of 1.7 percent. For about the same type 1 error rate as before, we now have a much lower type 2 error rate, which is a big improvement. With $T = 1000$, we would choose, say, a cutoff of 14 exceptions, for a type 1 error rate of 13.4 percent and type 2 error of 0.03 percent. Increasing the number of observations drastically improves the test. The drawback, of course, is that we may not have that many data points to start with or that the models may have changed.

6.2.3 Conditional Coverage Models

So far the framework focuses on *unconditional coverage,* since it ignores conditioning, or time variation, in the data. Exceptions, however, could "bunch" closely in time, which also should invalidate the model.

With a 95 percent VAR confidence level, we would expect to have about 13 exceptions every year. In theory, these occurrences should be evenly spread over time. If, instead, we observed that 10 of these exceptions occurred over the last 2 weeks, this should raise a red flag. The market, for instance, could experience increased volatility that is not captured by VAR. Or traders could have moved into unusual positions, or risk "holes." Whatever the explanation, a verification system should be de-

---

3. Assuming again a normal distribution and a true VAR that is 1.237 times greater than the reported VAR for an alternative coverage of 90.8 percent.

signed to measure proper *conditional coverage,* that is, conditional on current conditions.

Such a test has been developed by Christofferson (1998), who extends the LR_{uc} statistic to specify that the deviations must be serially independent. The test is set up as follows: Each day we set a deviation indicator to 0 if VAR is not exceeded and to 1 otherwise. We then define T_{ij} as the number of days in which state j occurred in one day while it was at i the previous day and π_i as the probability of observing an exception conditional on state i the previous day. Table 6.5 shows how to construct a table of conditional exceptions.

If today's occurrence of an exception is independent of what happened the previous day, the entries in the second and third columns should be identical. The relevant test statistic is

$$LR_{ind} = -2 \ln[(1 - \pi)^{(T_{00}+T_{10})} \pi^{(T_{01}+T_{11})}]$$
$$+ 2 \ln[(1 - \pi_0)^{T_{00}} \pi_0^{T_{01}}(1 - \pi_1)^{T_{10}} \pi_1^{T_{11}}] \quad (6.4)$$

Here, the first term represents the maximized likelihood under the hypothesis that exceptions are independent across days, or $\pi = \pi_0 = \pi_1 = (T_{01} + T_{11})/T$. The second term is the maximized likelihood for the observed data.

The combined test statistic for conditional coverage is then

$$LR_{cc} = LR_{uc} + LR_{ind} \quad (6.5)$$

TABLE 6-5

Building an Exception Table, Expected Number of Exceptions

| | Conditional | | |
| | Day Before | | |
	No Exception	Exception	Unconditional
Current day:			
No exception	$T_{00} = T_0 (1 - \pi_0)$	$T_{10} = T_1 (1 - \pi_1)$	$T (1 - \pi)$
Exception	$T_{01} = T_0 (\pi_0)$	$T_{11} = T_1 (\pi_1)$	$T (\pi)$
Total	T_0	T_1	$T = T_0 + T_1$

which is now asymptotically distributed $\chi^2(2)$. Thus we would reject at the 95 percent confidence level if $LR > 5.99$. This setup is particularly important given the strong evidence that markets go through periods of calm and turbulence.

During 1998, for instance, J.P. Morgan experienced 20 exceptions, which is far more than the 13 or so it expected with a 95 confidence level. Half of these exceptions were closely "bunched" during the tumultuous period of August to October. As a result, the bank substantially revised its VAR models.

6.3 MODEL VERIFICATION: OTHER APPROACHES[4]

6.3.1 Distribution Forecast Models

Exception-based methods consider only one quantile as opposed to the whole distribution. This may be appropriate for some users, such as bank regulators, who set the capital adequacy charge from this quantile.

For other users, this approach is inefficient. Indeed, Crnkovic and Drachman (1996) argue that institutions are implicitly forecasting the *entire* probability distribution function (pdf) and should assess the quality of the forecast based on the whole pdf instead of one point only.

Their approach extends the exception analysis as follows:

- Select a range of probabilities p between 0 and 1, say, 0.01, 0.02, 0.03, and so on.
- Each day the risk-management system reports a set of VAR numbers for these different confidence levels, say, VAR_1, VAR_2, and so on.
- The following day the risk manager records whether the observed P&L is below VAR_1, VAR_2, and so on.
- At the end of the observation period, the risk manager compiles the total number of observations below VAR_1 as N_1, below VAR_2 as N_2, and so on.

The manager then reports the total proportion of observations $N_i/T = \hat{F}(p_i)$ for each probability level. This is similar to the ratio N/T for exception tests, but for a range of values instead of just one.

---

4. This section is more technical and can be skipped by impatient readers without loss of continuity.

If the distribution was calibrated perfectly, we would find that this empirical distribution, $\hat{F}(p)$, would exactly match p. This leads to a test for checking whether the actual distribution of P&L is consistent with its predicted shape:

$$K = \max_i[\,\hat{F}(p_i) - p_i] + \max_i[p_i - \hat{F}(p_i)] \tag{6.6}$$

which is a Kuiper statistic and has a known distribution. The 95 percent confidence level cutoff value is 0.109 for 250 observations. J.P. Morgan is reported to use a verification system based on this method.

6.3.2 Parametric Models

The distribution-forecast method is still nonparametric, in the sense that it makes no assumption about the pdf. If the risk manager feels confident about the shape of the function, however, more powerful tests can be designed.

For instance, the RiskMetrics approach assumes a normal distribution, which is fully summarized by its mean and standard deviation. If this is the case, there is no point in using the 95 percent quantile because we know that this was derived from a normal pdf. Instead, we should work directly with the standard deviation. This can be extended to more general distributions, as long as the standard deviation can be used as a summary measure of dispersion.

A test can be designed as follows: We would first record the daily return to risk ratio, defined as $\epsilon_t = r_t/s_t$, which is the ratio of the realized daily trading profit over the forecast standard deviation. Next, we would compute the variance of ϵ and multiply it by the number of days T. When the conditional distribution is normal, the statistic

$$V(\epsilon)T \approx \chi^2(T) \tag{6.7}$$

is distributed as a chi-square with T degrees of freedom. With a large number of observations, this can be simplified further to obtain a 95 percent confidence interval of

$$[1 - 1.96\sqrt{2/T} < V(\epsilon) < 1 + 1.96\sqrt{2/T}\,] \tag{6.8}$$

This approach is immensely more efficient than the exception tests. For instance, Table 6–4 shows a type 2 error rate of 12.8 percent for the Basel test, which is quite high. Using the standard deviation test, the error rate falls to 0.02 percent. Further, this error rate is independent of the confidence level p because it is based on the standard deviation, not the quantile. A bank that tries to understate its risk would be immediately caught under this procedure.

The increased power in this verification procedure stems from two sources. First, the method does not focus on a particular quantile but instead on the spread of the distribution, which is measured much more precisely than any specific quantile because it uses all the data, not just the tail points. Second, the method makes a parametric assumption about the distribution, which was assumed to be normal. This can be justified on the grounds that large trading portfolios are subject to many sources of risk, which tend to aggregate to a normal distribution. Indeed, most distributions published in annual reports resemble normal distributions. The methodology, though, can be extended to distributions with heavier tails.

6.3.3   Comparison of Methods

Lopez (1999) provides a systematic comparison of the performance of these tests under realistic assumptions. Table 6–6 illustrates some of the results. Consider a true model with errors that are distributed as a standard normal variable with constant variance. The table examines the power of the tests, or frequency of rejection for various VAR models, and a 95 percent test rejection rule. The experiment is based on $T = 500$ observations.

When the VAR model is the correct one (based on $\sigma = 1.00$), it rejects 5 percent of the time, as we would expect. As the VAR measure de-

T A B L E   6–6

Power of Various Tests, Proportion of Times Model Is Rejected

	True Model Is Standard Normal, with $\sigma = 1.00$ VAR Based on				
	$\sigma = 0.71$	$\sigma = 0.87$	$\sigma = 1.00$	$\sigma = 1.12$	$\sigma = 1.22$
LR_{uc} (99%)	100	55	5	32	70
LR_{cc} (99%)	100	57	5	33	70
Kuiper	100	88	5	61	99

Source: Adapted from Lopez (1999). Sample contains $T = 500$ observations.

viates from the true model, the statistics reject more frequently. The larger the deviation, the more so. For instance, if the VAR is based on $\sigma = 0.87$, the exception test would reject 55 percent of the time. The Kuiper statistic is notably more powerful than the others. In the preceding example, it would reject 88 percent of the time. This shows that the design of the test is quite important.

6.4 CONCLUSIONS

Model verification is an integral component of a systematic risk-management process. Backtesting VAR numbers provides valuable feedback to users about the accuracy of their models. The procedure also can be used to search for possible improvements.

Due thought should be given to the choice of VAR quantitative parameters for backtesting purposes. First, the horizon should be as short as possible in order to increase the number of observations and to mitigate the effect of changes in the portfolio composition. Second, the confidence level should not be too high, since this decreases the effectiveness, or power, of the statistical tests.

Verification tests usually are based on *exception* counts, defined as the number of exceedences of the VAR measure. The goal is to check if this count is in line with the selected VAR confidence level. The method also can be modified to pick up bunching of deviations.

Backtesting involves balancing two types of errors: rejecting a correct model versus accepting an incorrect model. Ideally, one would want a framework that has very high power, or high probability of rejecting an incorrect model. The problem is that the power of exception-based tests is low. The current framework could be improved by choosing a lower VAR confidence level or by increasing the number of data observations. This chapter has presented other methods that should perform better than exception tests.

Adding to these statistical difficulties, we have to recognize other practical problems. Trading portfolios do change over the horizon. Models do evolve over time as risk managers improve their risk-modeling techniques. All of this may cause further structural instability.

Despite all these problems, backtesting has become a central component of risk-management systems. The methodology allows risk managers to improve their models constantly. Perhaps most important, backtesting should ensure that risk models do not go astray.

CHAPTER 7

Portfolio Risk: Analytical Methods

Trust not all your goods to one ship.

Erasmus

The preceding chapters have focused on single financial instruments. Absent any insight into the future, prudent investors should diversify across sources of financial risks. This was the message of portfolio analysis laid out by Harry Markowitz in 1952. Thus the concept of value at risk (VAR), or portfolio risk, is not new. What is new is the systematic application of VAR to many sources of financial risk, or portfolio risk. VAR explicitly accounts for leverage and portfolio diversification and provides one summary measure of risk.

As will be seen in Chapter 9, there are many approaches to measuring VAR. The shortest road assumes that asset payoffs are linear (or delta) functions of normally distributed risk factors. Indeed, the *delta-normal method* is a direct application of traditional portfolio analysis based on variances and covariances, which is why it is sometimes called the *covariance matrix approach.* This approach is *analytical* because VAR is derived from closed-form solutions. The method gives users much control over the measurement of risk, including a simple decomposition of the portfolio VAR.

This chapter shows how to measure and manage portfolio VAR. Section 7.1 details the construction of VAR using information on positions and the covariance matrix of its constituent components.

The fact that portfolio risk is not cumulative provides great diversification benefits. To manage risk, however, we also need to understand what will reduce it. Section 7.2 provides a detailed analysis of VAR tools that are essential to control portfolio risk. These include marginal VAR, incremental VAR, and component VAR. These VAR tools allow users to identify the asset that contributes most to their total risk, to pick the best hedge, to rank trades, or, in general, to select the asset that provides the best risk-return tradeoff. Section 7.3 presents a fully worked out example of VAR computations using Barings' fatal positions.

One drawback of linear VAR models is that the size of the covariance matrix increases geometrically with the number of assets. Section 7.4 discusses practical problems that often occur with empirical measures of the covariance matrix. It also develops simplifications to the covariance matrix based on the diagonal and factor models. Finally, Section 7.5 provides some concluding comments.

7.1 PORTFOLIO VAR

A portfolio can be characterized by positions on a certain number of constituent assets, expressed in the base currency, say, dollars. If the positions are fixed over the selected horizon, the portfolio rate of return is a *linear* combination of the returns on underlying assets, where the weights are given by the relative amounts invested at the beginning of the period. Therefore, the VAR of a portfolio can be constructed from a combination of the risks of underlying securities.

Define the portfolio rate of return from t to $t + 1$ as

$$R_{p,t+1} = \sum_{i=1}^{N} w_i \, R_{i,t+1} \qquad (7.1)$$

where N is the number of assets, $R_{i,t+1}$ is the rate of return on asset i, and w_i is the weight. Weights are constructed to sum to unity by scaling the dollar positions in each asset W_i by the portfolio total market value W. This immediately rules out portfolios that have zero net investment $W = 0$, such as some derivatives positions. But we could have positive and negative weights w_i, including values much larger than one, as with a highly leveraged hedge fund. If the net portfolio value is zero, we could use another measure, such as the sum of the gross positions or absolute value of all dollar positions W^*. All weights would then be defined in relation to this benchmark.

Alternatively, we also could express returns in dollar terms, defining a dollar amount invested in asset i as $W_i = w_i W$. We also will be using x as representing the vector of dollar amount invested in each asset so as to avoid confusion with the total dollar amount W.

It is important to note that in traditional mean-variance analysis, each constituent asset is a security. In contrast, VAR defines the component as a *risk factor* and w_i as the linear exposure to this risk factor. We shall see in Chapter 11 how to choose the risk factors and how to map securities into exposures on these risk factors. Whether dealing with assets or risk factors, the mathematics of portfolio VAR are equivalent, however.

To shorten notation, the portfolio return can be written using *matrix notation*, replacing a string of numbers by a single vector:

$$R_p = w_1 R_1 + w_2 R_2 + \cdots + w_N R_N = [w_1 w_2 \cdots w_N] \begin{bmatrix} R_1 \\ R_2 \\ \vdots \\ R_N \end{bmatrix} = w'R$$
(7.2)

where w' represents the transposed vector (i.e., horizontal) of weights, and R is the vertical vector containing individual asset returns.

By extension of the formulas in Chapter 4, the portfolio expected return is

$$E(R_p) = \mu_p = \sum_{i=1}^{N} w_i \mu_i \tag{7.3}$$

and the variance is

$$V(R_p) = \sigma_p^2 = \sum_{i=1}^{N} w_i^2 \sigma_i^2 + \sum_{i=1}^{N} \sum_{j=1, j \neq i}^{N} w_i w_j \sigma_{ij}$$

$$= \sum_{i=1}^{N} w_i^2 \sigma_i^2 + 2 \sum_{i=1}^{N} \sum_{j<i}^{N} w_i w_j \sigma_{ij} \tag{7.4}$$

This sum accounts not only for the risk of the individual securities σ_i^2 but also for all covariances, which add up to a total of $N(N-1)/2$ different terms.

As the number of assets increases, it becomes difficult to keep track of all covariance terms, which is why it is more convenient to use matrix notation. The variance can be written as

$$\sigma_p^2 = [w_1 \cdots w_N] \begin{bmatrix} \sigma_{11} & \sigma_{12} & \sigma_{13} & \cdots & \sigma_{1N} \\ \vdots & & & & \\ \sigma_{N1} & \sigma_{N2} & \sigma_{N3} & \cdots & \sigma_{N} \end{bmatrix} \begin{bmatrix} w_1 \\ \vdots \\ w_N \end{bmatrix}$$

Defining Σ as the covariance matrix, the variance of the portfolio rate of return can be written more compactly as

$$\sigma_p^2 = w'\Sigma w \tag{7.5}$$

Appendix 7A explains the rules for matrix multiplication. This also can be written in terms of dollar amounts as

$$\sigma_p^2 W^2 = x'\Sigma x \qquad (7.6)$$

So far nothing has been said about the distribution of the portfolio return. Ultimately, we would like to translate the portfolio variance into a VAR measure. To do so, we need to know the distribution of the portfolio return. In the delta-normal model, all individual security returns are assumed normally distributed. This is particularly convenient because the portfolio return, a linear combination of normal random variables, is also normally distributed. If so, we can translate the confidence level c into a standard normal deviate α such that the probability of observing a loss worse than $-\alpha$ is c. Defining W as the initial portfolio value, the portfolio VAR is

$$\text{Portfolio VAR} = \text{VAR}_p = \alpha\sigma_p W = \alpha\sqrt{x'\Sigma x} \qquad (7.7)$$

Diversified VAR

The portfolio VAR, taking into account diversification benefits between components.

At this point, we also can define the individual risk of each component as

$$\text{VAR}_i = \alpha\sigma_i \mid W_i \mid = \alpha\sigma_i \mid w_i \mid W \qquad (7.8)$$

Note that we took the absolute value of the weight w_i because it can be negative, whereas the risk measure must be positive.

Individual VAR

The VAR of one component taken in isolation.

Equation (7.4) shows that the portfolio VAR depends on variances, covariances, and the number of assets. Covariance is a measure of the extent to which two variables move linearly together. If two variables are independent, their covariance is equal to zero. A positive covariance means that the two variables tend to move in the same direction; a negative covariance means that they tend to move in opposite directions.

The magnitude of covariance, however, depends on the variances of the individual components and is not easily interpreted. The *correlation coefficient* is a more convenient, scale-free measure of linear dependence:

$$\rho_{12} = \sigma_{12}/(\sigma_1\sigma_2) \qquad (7.9)$$

The correlation coefficient ρ always lies between −1 and +1. When equal to unity, the two variables are said to be *perfectly correlated*. When 0, the variables are *uncorrelated*.

Lower portfolio risk can be achieved through low correlations or a large number of assets. To see the effect of N, assume that all assets have the same risk, that all correlations are the same, and that equal weight is put on each asset. Figure 7–1 shows how portfolio risk decreases with the number of assets.

Start with the risk of one security, which is assumed to be 12 percent. When ρ is equal to zero, the risk of a 10-asset portfolio drops to 3.8 percent; increasing N to 100 drops the risk even further to 1.2 percent. Risk tends asymptotically to zero. More generally, portfolio risk is

$$\sigma_p = \sigma \sqrt{\frac{1}{N} + \left(1 - \frac{1}{N}\right)\rho} \tag{7.10}$$

FIGURE 7–1

Risk and number of securities.

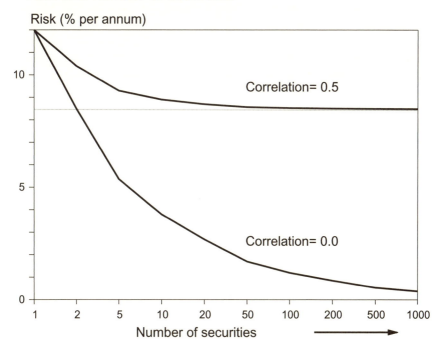

Risk (% per annum)

which tends to $\sigma\sqrt{\rho}$ as N increases. Thus, when $\rho = 0.5$, risk decreases rapidly from 12 to 8.9 percent as N goes to 10 and afterward converges more slowly toward its minimum value of 8.5 percent.

Low correlations thus help to diversify portfolio risk. Take a simple example with two assets only. The "diversified" portfolio variance is

$$\sigma_p^2 = w_1^2\sigma_1^2 + w_2^2\sigma_2^2 + 2w_1w_2\rho_{12}\sigma_1\sigma_2 \qquad (7.11)$$

The portfolio VAR is then

$$\text{VAR}_p = \alpha\sigma_pW = \alpha\sqrt{w_1^2\sigma_1^2 + w_2^2\sigma_2^2 + 2w_1w_2\rho_{12}\sigma_1\sigma_2}W \quad (7.12)$$

This can be related to the individual VAR as defined in Equation (7.8).

When the correlation ρ is zero, the portfolio VAR reduces to

$$\text{VAR}_p = \sqrt{\alpha^2w_1^2W^2\sigma_1^2 + \alpha^2w_2^2W^2\sigma_2^2} = \sqrt{\text{VAR}_1^2 + \text{VAR}_2^2} \quad (7.13)$$

The portfolio risk must be lower than the sum of the individual VARs: $\text{VAR}_p < \text{VAR}_1 + \text{VAR}_2$. This reflects the fact that with assets that move independently, a portfolio will be less risky than either asset.

When the correlation is exactly unity and w_1 and w_2 are both positive, Equation (7.12) reduces to

$$\text{VAR}_p = \sqrt{\text{VAR}_1^2 + \text{VAR}_2^2 + 2\text{VAR}_1\text{VAR}_2} = \text{VAR}_1 + \text{VAR}_2 \quad (7.14)$$

In other words, the portfolio VAR is equal to the sum of the individual VAR measures if the two assets are perfectly correlated. In general, though, this will not be the case because correlations typically are imperfect. The benefit from diversification can be measured by the difference between the *diversified* VAR and *undiversified* VAR, which is typically shown in VAR reporting systems.

Undiversified VAR

The sum of individual VARs, or the portfolio VAR when there is no short position and all correlations are unity.

This interpretation differs when short-sales are allowed. Suppose that the portfolio is long asset 1 but short asset 2 (w_1 is positive and w_2 is negative). This could represent a hedge fund that has $1 in capital and a $1 billion long position in corporate bonds and a $1 billion short position in Treasury bonds, the rationale for the position being that corporate yields are slightly higher than treasury yields. If the correlation is exactly unity, the fund has no risk because any loss in one asset will be offset by a matching gain in the other. The portfolio VAR is then zero.

Instead, the risk will be greatest if the correlation is minus one, in which case losses in one asset will be amplified by the other. Here, the undiversified VAR can be interpreted as the portfolio VAR when the correlation attains its worst value, which is minus one. Therefore, the undiversified VAR provides an upper bound on the portfolio VAR should correlations prove unstable and all move at the same time in the wrong direction. It provides an absolute worst-case scenario for the portfolio at hand.

Example

Consider a portfolio with two foreign currencies, the Canadian dollar (CAD) and the euro (EUR). Assume that these two currencies are uncorrelated and have a volatility against the dollar of 5 and 12 percent, respectively. The portfolio has US$2 million invested in the CAD and US$1 million in the EUR. We seek to find the portfolio VAR at the 95 percent level.

First, we will compute the variance of the portfolio dollar return. Define x as the dollar amounts allocated to each risk factor, in millions. Compute the product

$$\Sigma x = \begin{bmatrix} 0.05^2 & 0 \\ 0 & 0.12^2 \end{bmatrix} \begin{bmatrix} \$2 \\ \$1 \end{bmatrix} = \begin{bmatrix} 0.05^2 \times \$2 + 0 \times \$1 \\ 0 \times \$2 + 0.12^2 \times \$1 \end{bmatrix} = \begin{bmatrix} \$0.0050 \\ \$0.0144 \end{bmatrix}$$

The portfolio variance is then (in dollar units)

$$\sigma_p^2 = x'(\Sigma x) = [\$2 \quad \$1] \begin{bmatrix} \$0.0050 \\ \$0.0144 \end{bmatrix} = 0.0100 + 0.0144 = 0.0244$$

The volatility is $\sqrt{0.0244} = \$0.156205$ million. Using $\alpha = 1.65$, we find $VAR_p = 1.65 \times 156,205 = \$257,738$.

Next, the individual (undiversified) VAR is simply found as $VAR_i = \alpha \sigma_i x_i$,

$$\begin{bmatrix} VAR_1 \\ VAR_2 \end{bmatrix} = \begin{bmatrix} 1.65 \times 0.05 \times \$2 \text{ million} \\ 1.65 \times 0.12 \times \$1 \text{ million} \end{bmatrix} = \begin{bmatrix} \$165,000 \\ \$198,000 \end{bmatrix}$$

Note that these numbers sum to an undiversified VAR of $363,000, which is greater than the portfolio VAR of $257,738 due to diversification effects.

7.2 VAR TOOLS

Initially, VAR was developed as a methodology to measure portfolio risk. There is much more to VAR than simply reporting a single number, however. Over time, risk managers have discovered that they could use the VAR process for active risk management. A typical question may be, "Which position should I alter to modify my VAR most effectively?" Such information is quite useful because portfolios typically are traded incrementally due to transaction costs. This is the purpose of VAR tools, which include marginal, incremental, and component VAR.

7.2.1 Marginal VAR

To measure the effect of changing positions on portfolio risk, individual VARs are not sufficient. Volatility measures the uncertainty in the return of an asset taken in isolation. When this asset belongs to a portfolio, however, what matters is the contribution to portfolio risk.

We start from the existing portfolio, which is made up of N securities, numbered as $j = 1, \ldots, N$. A new portfolio is obtained by adding one unit of security i. To assess the impact of this trade, we measure its "marginal" contribution to risk by increasing w by a small amount, or differentiating Equation (7.4) with respect to w_i:

$$\frac{\partial \sigma_p^2}{\partial w_i} = 2w_i\sigma_i^2 + 2\sum_{j=1, j\neq i}^{N} w_j\sigma_{ij}$$

$$= 2\,\text{cov}\left(R_i, w_iR_i + \sum_{j\neq i}^{N} w_jR_j\right) = 2\,\text{cov}(R_i, R_p) \quad (7.15)$$

Instead of the derivative of the variance, we need that of the volatility. Noting that $\partial \sigma_p^2/\partial w_i = 2\sigma_p\,\partial \sigma_p/\partial w_i$, the sensitivity of the portfolio volatility to a change in the weight is then

$$\frac{\partial \sigma_p}{\partial w_i} = \frac{\text{cov}(R_i, R_p)}{\sigma_p} \quad (7.16)$$

Converting into a VAR number, we find an expression for the *marginal VAR*, which is a vector with component

$$\Delta \text{VAR}_i = \frac{\partial \text{VAR}}{\partial w_i W} = \alpha\,\frac{\partial \sigma_p}{\partial w_i} = \alpha\,\frac{\text{cov}(R_i, R_p)}{\sigma_p} \quad (7.17)$$

Since this was defined as a ratio of the dollar amounts, this marginal VAR measure is unitless.

Marginal VAR
___

The change in portfolio VAR resulting from taking an additional dollar of exposure to a given component. It is also the partial (or linear) derivative with respect to the component weight.

This marginal VAR is closely related to the *beta*, defined as

$$\beta_i = \frac{\text{cov}(R_i, R_p)}{\sigma_p^2} = \frac{\sigma_{ip}}{\sigma_p^2} = \frac{\rho_{ip}\sigma_i\sigma_p}{\sigma_p^2} = \rho_{ip}\frac{\sigma_i}{\sigma_p} \qquad (7.18)$$

which measures the contribution of one security to total portfolio risk. Beta is also called the *systematic risk* of security i vis-à-vis portfolio p and can be measured from the slope coefficient in a regression of R_i on R_p:

$$R_{i,t} = \alpha_i + \beta_i R_{p,t} + \epsilon_{i,t} \qquad t = 1, \ldots, T \qquad (7.19)$$

Using matrix notation, we can write the vector β, including all assets, as

$$\beta = \frac{\Sigma w}{(w'\Sigma w)}$$

Note that we already computed the vector Σw as an intermediate step in the calculation of VAR. Therefore, β and the marginal VAR can be derived easily once VAR has been calculated.

Beta risk is the basis for capital asset pricing model (CAPM) developed by Sharpe (1968). According to the CAPM, well-diversified investors only need to be compensated for the systematic risk of securities relative to the market. In other words, the risk premium on all assets should depend on beta only. Whether this is an appropriate description of capital markets has been the subject of much of finance research in the last 20 years. Even though this proposition is still debated hotly, the fact remains that systematic risk is a useful statistical measure of marginal portfolio risk.

To summarize, the relationship between the ΔVAR and β is

$$\Delta\text{VAR}_i = \alpha(\beta_i \times \sigma_p) = \frac{\text{VAR}}{W} \times \beta_i \qquad (7.20)$$

The marginal VAR can be used for a variety of risk-management purposes. Suppose an investor wants to lower the portfolio VAR and has the choice to reduce all positions by a fixed amount, say, $100,000. The investor should rank all marginal VAR numbers and pick the asset with the largest ΔVAR, since it will have the greatest hedging effect.

7.2.2 Incremental VAR

This methodology also can be used to evaluate the total impact of a proposed trade on the portfolio p. The new trade is represented by the position a, which is a vector of additional exposures to our risk factors, measured in dollars.

Ideally, we should measure the portfolio VAR at the initial position VAR_p and then again at the new position VAR_{p+a}. The incremental VAR is then obtained, as described in Figure 7–2, as

$$\text{Incremental VAR} = VAR_{p+a} - VAR_p \qquad (7.21)$$

This "before and after" comparison is quite informative. If VAR is decreased, the new trade is risk-reducing, or is a hedge; otherwise, the new trade is risk-increasing. Note that a may represent a change in a single component or a more complex trade with changes in multiple components. Hence, in general, a represents a vector of new positions.

Incremental VAR

The change in VAR due to a new position. It differs from the marginal VAR in that the amount added or subtracted can be large, in which case VAR changes in a nonlinear fashion.

The main drawback of this approach is that it requires a full revaluation of the portfolio VAR with the new trade. This can be quite time-

FIGURE 7–2

The impact of a proposed trade with full revaluation.

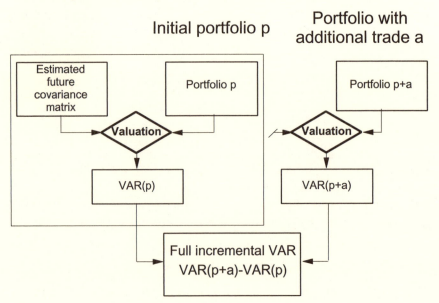

consuming for large portfolios. Suppose, for instance, that an institution has 100,000 trades on its books and that it takes 10 minutes to do a VAR calculation. The bank has measured its VAR at some point during the day. Then a client comes with a proposed trade. Evaluating the effect of this trade on the bank's portfolio would again require 10 minutes using the incremental VAR approach. Most likely, this will be too long to wait to take action.

If we are willing to accept an approximation, however, we can take a shortcut.[1] Expanding VAR_{p+a} in series around the original point,

$$\text{VAR}_{p+a} = \text{VAR}_p + (\Delta\text{VAR})' \times a + \cdots \qquad (7.22)$$

where we ignored second-order terms if the deviations a are small. Hence the incremental VAR can be reported as, approximately,

$$\text{Incremental VAR} \approx (\Delta\text{VAR})' \times a \qquad (7.23)$$

This measure is much faster to implement because the ΔVAR vector is a by-product of the initial VAR_p computation. The new process is described in Figure 7–3.

Here we are trading off faster computation time against accuracy. How much of an improvement is this shortcut relative to the full incremental VAR method? The shortcut will be especially useful for large portfolios where a full revaluation requires a large number of computations. Indeed, the number of operations increases with the square of the number of assets. In addition, the shortcut will prove to be a good approximation for large portfolios, where a proposed trade is likely to be small relative to the outstanding portfolio. Thus the simplified VAR method allows real-time trading limits.

The incremental VAR method applies to the general case where a trade involves a set of new exposures on the risk factors. Consider instead the particular case where a new trade involves a position in one risk factor only (or asset). The portfolio value changes from the old value of W to the new value of $W_N = W + a$, where a is the amount invested in asset i. We can write the variance of the dollar returns on the new portfolio as

$$\sigma_N^2 W_N^2 = \sigma_p^2 W^2 + 2aW\sigma_{ip} + a^2\sigma_i^2 \qquad (7.24)$$

---

1. See also Garman (1996; 1997).

FIGURE 7–3

The impact of a proposed trade with marginal VAR.

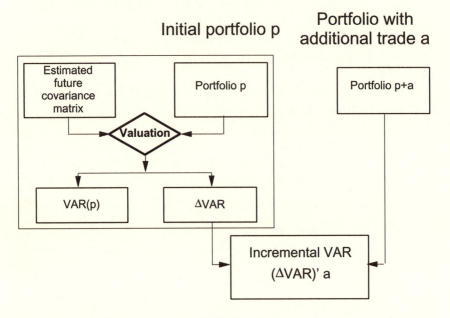

Initial portfolio p   Portfolio with
                           additional trade a

An interesting question for portfolio managers is to find the size of the new trade that leads to the lowest portfolio risk. Differentiating with respect to a,

$$\frac{\partial \sigma_N^2 W_N^2}{\partial a} = 2W\sigma_{ip} + 2a\sigma_i^2 \qquad (7.25)$$

which attains a zero value for

$$a^* = -W\frac{\sigma_{ip}}{\sigma_i^2} = -W\beta_i \frac{\sigma_p^2}{\sigma_i^2} \qquad (7.26)$$

This is the variance-minimizing position, also known as *best hedge.*

Best hedge

Additional amount to invest in an asset so as to minimize the risk of the total portfolio.

Example (continued)

Going back to the previous two-currency example, we are now considering increasing the CAD position by US$10,000.

First, we use the marginal VAR method. We note that β can be obtained from a previous intermediate step as

$$\beta = \frac{\text{cov}(R_i, R_p)}{\sigma_p^2} = \begin{bmatrix} \$0.0050 \\ \$0.0144 \end{bmatrix} / (\$0.156^2) = \begin{bmatrix} 0.205 \\ 0.590 \end{bmatrix}$$

The marginal VAR is now

$$\Delta\text{VAR} = \alpha \frac{\text{cov}(R_i, R_p)}{\sigma_p} = 1.65 \times \begin{bmatrix} \$0.0050 \\ \$0.0144 \end{bmatrix} / \$0.156 = \begin{bmatrix} 0.0528 \\ 0.1521 \end{bmatrix}$$

As we increase the first position by \$10,000, the incremental VAR is

$$(\Delta\text{VAR})' \times a = [0.0528 \; 0.1521] \begin{bmatrix} \$10,000 \\ 0 \end{bmatrix}$$

$$= 0.0528 \times \$10,000 + 0.1521 \times 0 = \$528$$

Next, we compare this to the incremental VAR obtained from a full revaluation of the portfolio risk. We find

$$\sigma_{p+a}^2 = [\$2.01 \; \$1] \begin{bmatrix} 0.05^2 & 0 \\ 0 & 0.12^2 \end{bmatrix} \begin{bmatrix} \$2.01 \\ \$1 \end{bmatrix}$$

which gives $\text{VAR}_{p+a} = \$258,267$. Relative to the initial $\text{VAR}_p = \$257,738$, the exact increment is \$529. Note how close the ΔVAR approximation of \$528 comes to the true value. The linear approximation is excellent because the change in the position is very small.

7.2.3 Component VAR

In order to manage risk, it would be extremely useful to have a *risk decomposition* of the current portfolio. This is not straightforward because the portfolio volatility is a highly nonlinear function of its components. Taking all individual VARs, adding them up, and computing their percentage, for instance, is not useful because it completely ignores diversification effects. Instead, what we need is an additive decomposition of VAR that recognizes the power of diversification.

This is why we turn to marginal VAR as a tool to help us measure the contribution of each asset to the existing portfolio risk. Multiply the marginal VAR by the current dollar position in asset, or risk factor, i:

$$\text{Component VAR} = (\Delta\text{VAR}_i) \times w_i \, W = \text{VAR}\beta_i \, w_i \qquad (7.27)$$

Thus the component VAR indicates how the portfolio VAR would change approximately if the component was deleted from the portfolio. We should note, however, that the quality of this linear approximation improves when the VAR components are small. Hence this decomposition is more useful with large portfolios, which tend to have many small positions.

We now show that these component VARs precisely add up to the total portfolio VAR. The sum is

$$\text{CVAR}_1 + \text{CVAR}_2 + \cdots + \text{CVAR}_N = \text{VAR}\left(\sum_{i=1}^{N} w_i\beta_i\right) = \text{VAR} \quad (7.28)$$

because the term between parentheses is simply the beta of the portfolio with itself, which is unity.[2]

Thus we established that these *component VAR* measures add up to the total VAR. We have an additive measure of portfolio risk that reflects correlations. Components with a negative sign act as a hedge against the remainder of the portfolio. In contrast, components with a positive sign increase the risk of the portfolio.

Component VAR

A partition of the portfolio VAR that indicates how much the portfolio VAR would change approximately if the given component was deleted.

The component VAR can be simplified further. Taking into account the fact that β_i is equal to the correlation ρ_i times σ_i divided by the portfolio σ_p, we can write

$$\text{CVAR}_i = \text{VAR}w_i\beta_i = (\alpha\sigma_p W)w_i\beta_i = (\alpha\sigma_i w_i W)\rho_i = \text{VAR}_i\rho_i \quad (7.29)$$

This conveniently transforms the individual VAR into its contribution to the total portfolio simply by multiplying it by the correlation coefficient.

Finally, we can normalize by the total portfolio VAR and report

$$\text{Percent contribution to VAR of component } i = \frac{\text{CVAR}_i}{\text{VAR}} = w_i\beta_i \quad (7.30)$$

VAR systems can provide a breakdown of the contribution to risk using any desired criterion. For large portfolios, component VAR may be shown by type of currency, by type of asset class, by geographic location,

---

2. This can be proved by expanding the portfolio variance into $\sigma_p^2 = w_1\text{cov}(R_1,R_p) + w_2\text{cov}(R_2,R_p)$ $+ \cdots = w_1(\beta_1\sigma_p^2) + w_2(\beta_2\sigma_p^2) + \cdots = \sigma_p^2(\Sigma_{i=1}^{N}w_i\beta_i)$ [thus the term between parentheses must be equal to one].

or by business unit. Such detail is invaluable for "drill down" exercises, which enable users to control their VAR.

Example (continued)

Continuing with the previous two-currency example, we find the component VAR for the portfolio using $CVAR_i = \Delta VAR_i x_i$,

$$\begin{bmatrix} CVAR_1 \\ CVAR_2 \end{bmatrix} = \begin{bmatrix} 0.0528 \times \$2 \text{ million} \\ 0.1521 \times \$1 \text{ million} \end{bmatrix} = \begin{bmatrix} \$105,630 \\ \$152,108 \end{bmatrix} = VAR \times \begin{bmatrix} 41.0\% \\ 59.0\% \end{bmatrix}$$

We verify that these two components indeed sum to the total VAR of $257,738. The largest component is due to the EUR, which has the highest volatility. Both numbers are positive, indicating that neither position serves as a net hedge for the portfolio.

Next, we can compute the change in the VAR if the EUR position is set to zero and compare with the preceding result. Since the portfolio has only two assets, the new VAR without the EUR position is simply the VAR of the CAD component, $VAR_1 = \$165,000$. The incremental VAR of the EUR position is ($257,738 − $165,000) = $92,738. The component VAR of $152,108 is higher, although of the same order of magnitude. The approximation is not as good as before because there are only two assets in the portfolio, which individually account for a large proportion of the total VAR. We would expect a better approximation as the VAR components are small relative to the total VAR.

7.2.4 Summary

Figure 7–4 presents a graphic summary of our VAR tools for our two-currency portfolio. The graph plots the portfolio VAR as a function of the amount invested in this asset, the euro. At the current position of $1 million, the portfolio VAR is $257,738.

The marginal VAR is the change in VAR due to an addition of $1 in EUR, or 0.1521; this represents the slope of the straight line that is tangent to the VAR curve at the current value.

The incremental VAR is the change in VAR due to the deletion of the euro position, which is $92,738 and is measured along the curve. This is approximated by the component VAR, which is simply the marginal VAR times the current position of $1 million, or $152,108. The latter is measured along the straight line that is tangent to the VAR curve. The graph illustrates that the component VAR is only an approximation to the incremental VAR. These component VAR measures add up to the total portfolio VAR, which gives a quick decomposition of the total risk.

FIGURE 7–4

VAR decomposition.

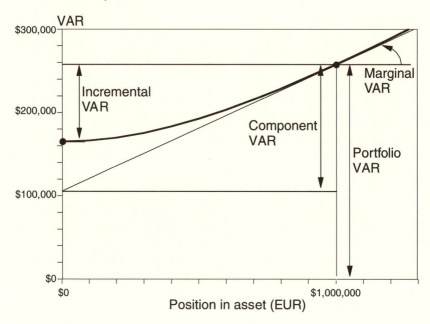

The graph also shows that the best hedge is a net zero position in the euro. Indeed, the VAR function attains a minimum when the position in the euro is zero.

The results are summarized in Table 7–1. This report gives not only the portfolio VAR but also a wealth of information for risk managers. For instance, the marginal VAR column can be used to determine how to reduce risk. Since the marginal VAR for the EUR is three times as large as that for the CAD, cutting the position in the EUR will be much more effective than cutting the CAD position by the same amount.

7.3 EXAMPLES

This section provides a number of applications of VAR measures. The first example illustrates a risk report for a global equity portfolio. The second shows how VAR could have been used to dissect the Barings portfolio.

TABLE 7–1

VAR Decomposition for Sample Portfolio

Currency	Current Position, x_i or w_iW	Individual VAR, $VAR_i =$ $\alpha\sigma_iw_iW$	Marginal VAR, $\Delta VAR_i =$ $VAR\ \beta_i/W$	Component VAR, $CVAR_i =$ ΔVAR_ix_i	Percent Contribution, $CVAR_i/$ VAR
CAD	$2 million	$165,000	0.0528	$105,630	41.0%
EUR	$1 million	$198,000	0.1521	$152,108	59.0%
Total	$3 million				
Undiversified VAR		$363,000			
Diversified VAR				$257,738	100.0%

7.3.1 A Global Portfolio Equity Report

To further illustrate the use of our VAR tools, Table 7–2 displays a risk management report for a global equity portfolio. Here, risk is measured in relative terms, i.e., relative to the benchmark index. The current portfolio has an annualized tracking error, which is also the standard deviation of the difference σ_p, of 1.82 percent per annum. This number can be translated easily into a VAR number using VAR $= \alpha\sigma_pW$. Hence we can deal with VAR or more directly σ_p.

Positions are reported as deviations in percent from the benchmark in the second column. Since the weights of the index and of the current portfolio must sum to one, the deviations must sum to zero.

The next columns report the individual risk, marginal risk, and the percentage contribution to total risk. Positions contributing to more than 5 percent of the total are called *Hot Spots*.[3] The table shows that two countries, Japan and Brazil, account for more than 50 percent of the risk. This is an important but not intuitive result, since the positions in these markets, displayed in the first column, are not the largest. In fact, the United States and United Kingdom, which have the largest deviations from the index, contribute to only 20 percent of the risk. The contribution of Japan and Brazil is high because of their high volatility and correlations with the portfolio.

---

3. Hot Spots is a trademark of Goldman Sachs.

TABLE 7-2

Global Equity Portfolio Report

Country	Current Position (%) w_i	Individual Risk $w_i \sigma_i$	Marginal Risk β_i	Percentage Contribution to Risk $w_i \beta_i$	Best Hedge (%)	Volatility at Best Hedge
Japan	4.5	0.96%	0.068	31.2	−4.93	1.48%
Brazil	2.0	1.02%	0.118	22.9	−1.50	1.66%
U.S.	−7.0	0.89%	−0.019	13.6	3.80	1.75%
Thailand	2.0	0.55%	0.052	10.2	−2.30	1.71%
U.K.	−6.0	0.46%	0.035	7.0	2.10	1.80%
Italy	2.0	0.79%	−0.011	6.8	−2.18	1.75%
Germany	2.0	0.35%	0.019	3.7	−2.06	1.79%
France	−3.5	0.57%	−0.009	3.4	1.18	1.81%
Switzerland	2.5	0.39%	0.011	2.6	−1.45	1.81%
Canada	4.0	0.49%	0.001	1.5	−0.11	1.82%
South Africa	−1.0	0.20%	0.008	−0.7	−0.65	1.82%
Australia	−1.5	0.24%	0.014	−2.0	−1.89	1.80%
Total	0.0			100.0		
volatility:						
Undiversified		6.91%				
Diversified	1.82%					

Source: Adapted from Litterman (1996).

To control risk, we turn to the "Best Hedge" column. The table shows that the 4.5 percent overweight position in Japan should be decreased to lower risk. The optimal change is a decrease of 4.93 percent, after which the new volatility will have decreased from the original value of 1.82 percent to 1.48 percent. In contrast, the 4.0 percent overweight position in Canada has little impact on the portfolio risk.

This type of report is invaluable to control risk. In the end, of course, portfolio managers add value by judicious bets on markets, currencies, or securities. Such VAR tools can be quite useful, however, because analysts can now balance their return forecasts against risk explicitly.

7.3.2 Barings: An Example in Risks

Barings' collapse provides an interesting application of the VAR methodology. Leeson was reported to be long about $7.7 billion worth of Japanese stock index (Nikkei) futures and short $16 billion worth of Japanese Government Bond (JGB) futures. Unfortunately, official reports to Barings showed "nil" risk because the positions were fraudulent.

If a proper VAR system had been in place, the parent company could have answered the following questions. What was Leeson's actual VAR? Which component contributed most to VAR? Were the positions hedging each other or adding to the risk?

The top panel of Table 7–3 displays monthly volatility measures and correlations for positions in the 10-year zero JGB and the Nikkei index. The correlation between Japanese stocks and bonds is negative, indicating that increases in stock prices are associated with decreases in bond prices or increases in interest rates. The next column displays positions that are reported in millions of dollar equivalents.

To compute the VAR, we first construct the covariance matrix Σ from the correlations. Next, we compute the vector Σx, which is in the first column of the bottom panel. For instance, the -2.82 entry is found from $\sigma_1^2 x_1 + \sigma_{12} x_2 = 0.000139 \times (-\$16,000) + (-0.000078) \times \$7700 = -2.82$. The next column reports $x_1 (\Sigma x)_1$ and $x_2 (\Sigma x)_2$, which sum to the total portfolio variance of 256,193.8, for a portfolio volatility of $\sqrt{256,194} = \$506$ million. At the 95 percent confidence level, Barings' VAR was $\$1.65 \times \$506$, or $\$835$ million.

This represents the worst monthly loss at the 95 percent confidence level under normal market conditions. In fact, Leeson's total loss was reported at $1.3 billion, which is comparable with the VAR reported here.

TABLE 7–3

Barings' Risks

	Risk (%) σ	Correlation Matrix		Covariance Matrix Σ		Positions ($ millions) x	Individual VAR $\alpha \sigma x$
10-yr JGB	1.18	1	-0.114	0.000139	-0.000078	($16,000)	$310.88
Nikkei	5.83	-0.114	1	-0.000078	0.003397	$7,700	$740.51
Total						$8,300	$1,051.39

	Total VAR		Marginal VAR		Component VAR	Percent
Asset i	$(\Sigma x)_i$	$x'_i(\Sigma x)_i$	β_i $(\Sigma x)_i/\sigma_p^2$	For $1 million β_i VAR	$\beta_i x_i$ VAR	Contribution
10-yr JGB	-2.82	45,138.8	-0.0000110	($0.00920)	$147.15	17.6%
Nikkei	27.41	211,055.1	0.0001070	$0.08935	$688.01	82.4%
Total		256,193.8			$835.16	100.0%
Risk $= \sigma_p$		506.16				
VAR $= \alpha\sigma_p$		$835.16				

166

The difference is because the position was changed over the course of the 2 months, there were other positions (such as short options), and also bad luck. In particular, on January 23, 1995, one week after the Kobe earthquake, the Nikkei index lost 6.4 percent. Based on a monthly volatility of 5.83 percent, the daily VAR of Japanese stocks at the 95 percent confidence level should be 2.5 percent. Therefore, this was a very unusual move—even though we expect to exceed VAR in 5 percent of situations.

The marginal risk of each leg is also revealing. With a negative correlation between bonds and stocks, a hedged position typically would be long the two assets. Instead, Leeson was short the bond market, which market observers were at a loss to explain. A trader said, "This does not work as a hedge. It would have to be the other way round."[4] Thus Leeson was increasing his risk from the two legs of the position.

This is formalized in the table, which displays the marginal VAR computation. The β column is obtained by dividing each element of Σx by $x'\Sigma x$, for instance, -2.82 by $256,194$ to obtain -0.000011. Multiplying by the VAR, we obtain the marginal change in VAR due to increasing the bond position by $1 million, which is $-\$0.00920$ million. Similarly, increasing the stock position by $1 million increased the VAR by $0.08935.

Overall, the component VAR due to the total bond position is $147.15 million; that due to the stock position is $688.01 million. By construction, these two numbers add up to the total VAR of $835.16 million. The percent contributions are reported in the last column. This analysis reveals that most of the loss was due to the Nikkei exposure and that the bond position, instead of hedging, made things even worse.

7.4 SIMPLIFYING THE COVARIANCE MATRIX

7.4.1 Why Simplifications?

So far we have shown that correlations are essential driving forces behind portfolio risk. When the number of assets is large, however, the measurement of the covariance matrix becomes increasingly difficult. With 10 assets, for instance, we need to estimate $10 \times 11/2 = 55$ different variance and covariance terms. With 100 assets, this number climbs to 5050. The number of correlations increases geometrically with the number of

---

4. *Financial Times* (March 1, 1995).

assets. For large portfolios, this causes real problems: (1) The portfolio VAR may not be positive, and (2) correlations may be estimated imprecisely. This section examines the extent to which such problems can affect VAR measures and proposes some solutions.

In practice, the industry has developed a number of approximations to the covariance matrix. Securities are mapped routinely over general risk factors. These *mapping* procedures replace the exposure profile of a security by that of appropriately chosen indices. The latter are called *general market risks*. In contrast, the remaining risks are called *specific risks*.

Mapping cuts down the computational requirements when there is a large number of positions. In some situations, also, we may not have a complete history of securities data, in which case mapping provides a useful replacement for the security.

7.4.2 Zero VAR Measures

The VAR measure derives from the portfolio variance, which is computed as

$$\sigma_p^2 = w'\Sigma w \tag{7.31}$$

The question is, Is this product guaranteed to be always positive?

Unfortunately, not always.[5] For this to be the case, we need the matrix Σ to be *positive definite*. This can be verified using the singular value decomposition described in Appendix 7B.

A number of conditions must be satisfied for positive-definiteness: The number of historical observations T must be greater than the number of assets N, and the series cannot be linearly correlated. The first condition states that if a portfolio consists of 100 assets, there must be at least 100 historical observations to ensure that whatever portfolio is selected, the portfolio variance will be positive. The second condition rules out situations where an asset is exactly equivalent to a linear combination of other assets.

An example of a non-positive-definite matrix is obtained when two assets are identical ($\rho = 1$). In this situation, a portfolio consisting of $1 on the first asset and −$1 on the second will have exactly zero risk.

In practice, this problem is more likely to occur with a large number of assets that are highly correlated (such as zero-coupon bonds or cur-

---

5. Abstracting from the obvious case where all elements of w are zero.

rencies fixed to each other). In addition, positions must have been matched precisely with assets so as to yield zero risk. This is most likely to occur if the weights have been *optimized* on the basis of the covariance matrix itself. Such optimization is particularly dangerous because it can create positions that are very large yet apparently offset each other with little total risk.

If users notice that VAR measures appear abnormally low in relation to positions, they should check whether small changes in correlations lead to large changes in their VARs.

7.4.3 Diagonal Model

A related problem is that as the number of assets increases, it is more likely that some correlations will be measured with error. Some models can help simplifying this process by providing a simpler structure for the covariance matrix. One such model is the *diagonal model,* originally proposed by Sharpe in the context of stock portfolios.[6]

The assumption is that the common movement in all assets is due to one common factor only, the market. Formally, the model is

$$R_i = \alpha_i + \beta_i R_m + \epsilon_i \qquad E[\epsilon_i] = 0 \qquad E[\epsilon_i R_m] = 0$$
$$E[\epsilon_i \epsilon_j] = 0 \qquad E[\epsilon_i^2] = \sigma_{\epsilon,i}^2 \quad (7.32)$$

The return on asset i is driven by the market return R_m and an idiosyncratic term ϵ_i, which is not correlated with the market or across assets. As a result, the variance can be decomposed as

$$\sigma_i^2 = \beta_i^2 \sigma_m^2 + \sigma_{\epsilon,i}^2 \qquad (7.33)$$

The covariance between two assets is

$$\sigma_{i,j} = \beta_i \beta_j \sigma_m^2 \qquad (7.34)$$

which is solely due to the common factor. The full matrix is

$$\Sigma = \begin{bmatrix} \beta_1 \\ \vdots \\ \beta_N \end{bmatrix} [\beta_1 \cdots \beta_N] \sigma_m^2 + \begin{bmatrix} \sigma_{\epsilon,1}^2 & \cdots & 0 \\ \vdots & & \vdots \\ 0 & \cdots & \sigma_{\epsilon,N}^2 \end{bmatrix}$$

---

6. Note that this model is sometimes referred to as the CAPM, which is not correct. The diagonal model is simply a simplification of the covariance matrix and says nothing about expected returns, whose description is the essence of the CAPM.

Written in matrix notation, the covariance matrix is

$$\Sigma = \beta\beta'\sigma_m^2 + D_\epsilon \qquad (7.35)$$

Since the matrix D_ϵ is diagonal, the number of parameters is reduced from $N \times (N + 1)/2$ to $2N + 1$ (N for the betas, N in D, and one for σ_m). With 100 assets, for instance, the number is reduced from 5050 to 201, a considerable improvement.

Furthermore, the variance of large, well-diversified portfolios simplifies even further, reflecting only exposure to the common factor. The variance of the portfolio is

$$V(R_p) = V(w'R) = w'\Sigma w = (w'\beta\beta'w)\sigma_m^2 + w'D_\epsilon w \qquad (7.36)$$

The second term consists of $\Sigma_{i=1}^{N} w_i^2 \sigma_{\epsilon,i}^2$. But this term becomes very small as the number of securities in the portfolio increases. For instance, if all the residual variances are identical and have equal weights, this second term is $[\Sigma_{i=1}^{N}(1/N)^2]\sigma_\epsilon^2$, which converges to 0 as N increases. Therefore, the variance of the portfolio converges to

$$V(R_p) \to (w'\beta\beta'w)\sigma_m^2 = (\beta_p\sigma_m)^2 \qquad (7.37)$$

which depends on one factor only. Thus, in large portfolios, specific risk becomes unimportant for the purpose of measuring VAR.

As an example, consider three stocks, General Motors (GM), Ford, and Hewlett-Packard (HWP). The top panel in Table 7–4 displays the full covariance matrix for monthly data. This matrix can be simplified by estimating a regression of each stock on the U.S. stock market. These regressions are displayed in the second panel of the table, which shows betas of 0.806, 1.183, and 1.864, respectively. GM has the lowest beta; HWP has the highest systematic risk. The market variance is $V(R_m) = 11.90$. The bottom panel in the table reconstructs the covariance matrix using the diagonal approximation. For instance, the variance for GM is taken as $\beta_1^2 \times V(R_m) + V(\epsilon_1)$, which is $0.806^2 \times 11.90 + 64.44 = 7.73 + 64.44 = 72.17$. The covariance between GM and Ford is $\beta_1\beta_2V(R_m)$, which is $0.806 \times 1.183 \times 11.90 = 11.35$.

The last three columns in the table report the correlations between pairwise stocks. Actual correlations are all positive, as are those under the diagonal model. Although the diagonal model matrix resembles the original covariance matrix, the approximation is not perfect. For instance, the actual correlation between GM and Ford is 0.636. Using the diagonal

TABLE 7–4

The Diagonal Model

	Covariance			Correlations		
	GM	Ford	HWP	GM	Ford	HWP
Full matrix						
GM	72.17			1		
Ford	43.92	66.12		0.636	1	
HWP	26.32	44.31	90.41	0.326	0.573	1
Regression						
β_i	0.806	1.183	1.864			
$V(R_i)$	72.17	66.12	90.41			
$V(\epsilon_i)$	64.44	49.46	49.10			
$\beta_i^2 V(R_m)$	7.73	16.65	41.32			
Diagonal model						
GM	72.17			1		
Ford	11.35	66.12		0.164	1	
HWP	17.87	26.23	90.41	0.221	0.339	1

model, the correlation is driven by exposure to the market, and is 0.164, which is lower than the true correlation. This is so because both stocks have low betas, which is the only source of common variation. Whether this model produces acceptable approximations depends on the purpose at hand; we compute actual VAR numbers in Chapter 11. But there is no question that the diagonal model provides a considerable simplification.

7.4.4 Factor Models

If a one-factor model is not sufficient, better precision can be obtained with multiple factor models. Equation (7.32) can be generalized to K factors

$$R_i = \alpha_i + \beta_{i1}y_1 + \cdots + \beta_{iK}y_K + \epsilon_i \qquad (7.38)$$

where $R_1, \ldots, R_N$ are the N asset returns and $y_1, \ldots, y_K$ are "factors" independent of each other. In the previous three-stock example, the covariance matrix model can be improved with a second factor, such as the transportation industry, that would pick up the higher correlation between GM and Ford. With multiple factors, the covariance matrix acquires a richer structure

$$\Sigma = \beta_1\beta_1'\sigma_1^2 + \cdots + \beta_K\beta_K'\sigma_K^2 + D_\epsilon \qquad (7.39)$$

The total number of parameters is $(N \times K + K + N)$, which may still be considerably less than for the full model. With 100 assets and 5 factors, for instance, the number is reduced from 5050 to 605, which is not a minor decrease.

Factor models are also important because they can help us decide on the number of VAR building blocks for each market. Consider, for instance, a government bond market that displays a continuum of maturities ranging from 1 day to 30 years. The question is, How many VAR building blocks do we need to represent this market adequately?

To illustrate, consider the U.S. Treasury bond market. Table 7–5 presents monthly VARs for 11 zero-coupon bonds as well as correlations for maturities going from 1 to 30 years. Under the RiskMetrics convention, VAR corresponds to 1.65 standard deviations. With strictly parallel moves in the term structure, VAR should increase linearly with maturity. In fact, this is not the case. Longer maturities display slightly less VAR than under a linear relationship. The 30-year zero, for instance, has a VAR of 11.12 instead of the value of 14.09 extrapolated from the 1-year maturity $(0.470 \times 30/1)$.

Particularly interesting are the very high correlations, confirming the presence of one major factor behind bond returns. Correlations are high for close maturities but tend to decrease with the spread between maturities. The lowest value, 0.644, is obtained between the 1- and 30-year zeroes. Could this pattern of correlation be simplified to just a few common factors?

To answer this question, we can turn to the principal-components method. Intuitively, *principal components* attempts to find a series of independent linear combinations of the original variables that provides the best explanation of diagonal terms of the matrix. The methodology is summarized in Appendix 7B.

Another statistical method is *factor analysis*. The latter uses maximum-likelihood techniques to estimate the factor loadings under the restriction that the residual matrix is diagonal and assuming that returns are normally distributed. Factor analysis differs from principal component in that it focuses on the off-diagonal elements of the correlation matrix.

TABLE 7-5

Risk and Correlations for U.S. Bonds (Monthly VAR at 95 Percent Level)

Term (year)	VAR (%)	1Y	2Y	3Y	4Y	5Y	7Y	9Y	10Y	15Y	20Y	30Y
1	0.470	1										
2	0.987	0.897	1									
3	1.484	0.886	0.991	1								
4	1.971	0.866	0.976	0.994	1							
5	2.426	0.855	0.966	0.988	0.998	1						
7	3.192	0.825	0.936	0.965	0.982	0.990	1					
9	3.913	0.796	0.909	0.942	0.064	0.975	0.996	1				
10	4.250	0.788	0.903	0.937	0.959	0.971	0.994	0.999	1			
15	6.234	0.740	0.853	0.891	0.915	0.930	0.961	0.976	0.981	1		
20	8.146	0.679	0.791	0.832	0.860	0.878	0.919	0.942	0.951	0.991	1	
30	11.119	0.644	0.761	0.801	0.831	0.853	0.902	0.931	0.943	0.975	0.986	1

Which method is best depends on the purpose at hand. Wilson (1994) argues that principal components should be used for applications that rely on accurate modeling of volatility, such as simple options. On the other hand, applications for which correlations are critical, such as "diff" swaps, would benefit from factor analysis.

Table 7–6 provides an answer. It shows the first three components for the correlation matrix of U.S. bond returns, based on principal-component analysis. The most striking feature of the table is that the first factor provides an excellent fit to movements of the term structure. The average explanatory power is very high, at 91.9 percent. Since it affects all maturities about equally, this common factor can be defined a yield *level* variable. This explains why duration is a good measure of interest rate risk.

The second factor explains an additional 6.0 percent in movements. Since it has the highest explanatory power and highest loadings for short and long maturities, it describes the *slope* of the term structure. Finally, the last factor is much less important. It seems to be most related to

TABLE 7–6

Principal Components of Correlation Matrix: U.S. Bonds

Maturity (year)	Percentage of Variance Explained by			Total Variance Explained
	Factor 1, Level	Factor 2, Slope	Factor 3	
1	72.2	17.9	9.8	99.8
2	89.7	7.8	0.5	98.0
3	94.3	4.5	0.7	99.5
4	96.5	2.2	1.0	99.7
5	97.7	1.1	0.9	99.7
7	98.9	0.0	0.4	99.3
9	98.2	0.7	0.2	99.1
10	98.1	1.2	0.1	99.4
15	94.1	5.3	0.2	99.6
20	87.2	11.0	0.9	99.1
30	83.6	14.5	0.9	99.0
Average	91.9	6.0	1.4	99.3

1-year rates, perhaps because of different characteristics of money market instruments. Together, the three factors explain an impressive 99.3 percent of all return variation.

This decomposition shows that the risk of a bond portfolio can be usefully summarized by its exposure to two factors only. For instance, the portfolio can be structured so that the net exposure to the two factors is very small. This will improve considerably on duration hedging yet require no forecast of future twists in the yield curve. In other words, we need only two primitive risk factors to represent movements in the yield curve.

7.4.5 Comparison of Methods

The purpose of these various methods is to simplify the computation of the portfolio risk. With hundreds of securities in the portfolio, it may not be feasible to consider each one as an individual risk factor. The question is whether these shortcuts materially affect the VAR measure.

To illustrate, Table 7–7 presents VAR calculations for three portfolios.[7] The first is a diversified portfolio with $1 million equally invested in 10 stocks. The second consists of a $1 million portfolio with 10 stocks all in the same industry, high-technology. The third expands on the diversified portfolio but is market-neutral, with long positions in the first 5 stocks and short the others. VAR is measured with a 1-month horizon at the 95 percent level of confidence using historical data from 1990 to 1999.

To summarize, five methods are examined:

- *Index mapping* replaces each stock by a like position in the index m:

$$VAR_1 = \alpha W \sigma_m$$

- *Beta mapping* also considers the net beta of the portfolio:

$$VAR_2 = \alpha W(\beta_p \sigma_m)$$

- *Diagonal model* considers both the beta and specific risk:

$$VAR_3 = \alpha W \sqrt{(\beta_p \sigma_m)^2 + w' D_\epsilon w}$$

---

7. The diversified portfolio consists of positions in Ford, Hewlett-Packard, General Electric, Procter & Gamble, AT&T, Boeing, General Motors, Disney, Microsoft, and American Express. These are spread among 6 of the 10 industrial sectors in the market. The long-short portfolio is long the first five and short the others. The market index is taken as the S&P 500. This example is similar to that of Beder et al. (1998).

TABLE 7–7

Comparison of VAR Methods

| | Portfolio | | |
Position	Diversified $1,000,000	Hi-Tech $1,000,000	Long-Short $0
VAR			
Index mapping	$63,634	$63,634	$0
Beta mapping	$70,086	$84,008	$298
Industry mapping	$69,504	$90,374	$7,388
Diagonal model	$81,238	$105,283	$41,081
Individual mapping	$78,994	$118,955	$32,598

- *Industry mapping* replaces each stock by a like position in an industry index I:

$$VAR_4 = \alpha W \sqrt{w_I' \Sigma_I w_I}$$

- *Individual mapping* uses the full covariance matrix of individual stocks:

$$VAR_5 = \alpha W \sqrt{w' \Sigma w}$$

This method provides an exact VAR measure over this sample period.

More complex models are certainly possible. For instance, one could model a marketwide effect, then industry effects, and finally assume that remaining terms are uncorrelated.

The table shows that the quality of the approximation depends on the structure of the portfolio. For the first portfolio, all measures are in a similar range, $60,000–$80,000. The diagonal model provides the best approximation, followed by the beta and industry mapping models.

The second portfolio is concentrated in one industry and, as a result, has higher VAR. The index mapping model now seriously underestimates the true risk of the portfolio. In addition, the beta and industry mapping models also fall short. The diagonal model gets close to the true value, as before.

Finally, the third portfolio shows the dangers of simple mapping methods. The index mapping model, given a zero net investment, predicts zero risk. With beta mapping, the risk measure, driven by the net beta, is close to zero, which is highly misleading. The best approximation is again provided by the diagonal model, which considers specific risks.

Otherwise, a shortcut is sometimes used for portfolios with long and short positions. This consists of grouping the long and short positions separately and computing their VAR using beta mapping. Define these as VAR_L and VAR_S. The portfolio VAR is computed as

$$VAR = | VAR_L - VAR_S | + k \times \min(VAR_L, VAR_S) \qquad (7.40)$$

where k is an "offsetting factor." When $k = 0$, for instance, there is full offset between the two, which gives VAR $= VAR_L - VAR_S = \$298$. When $k = 2$, there is no offset at all between specific risks, which gives a very conservative measure, VAR $= VAR_L + VAR_S = \$70,086$. We have partial offset with $k = 1$, which gives VAR $= \max(VAR_L, VAR_S)$, or here, VAR $= VAR_L = \$35,192$, which is not far from the actual value. This ad hoc method is sometimes useful to deal with hedge portfolios.

7.5 CONCLUSIONS

Much of portfolio analysis is based on the fact that fixed portfolios of normally distributed variables are themselves normal. This leads to an analytical approach based on the covariance matrix that is particularly convenient for VAR calculations.

Indeed, closed-form solutions allow us to compute the marginal effect of changing a position and to decompose the current risk into additive components. Armed with these tools, users can better understand and manage their risks.

The disadvantage of these methods is that the covariance matrix quickly increases with the number of securities. This can cause computational problems. As a result, it has become common to model securities risk by "mapping" them over a smaller set of general risk factors.

Mapping, however, forfeits resolution. In most cases, the lack of detail is harmless. We have seen, for example, that for long portfolios, simple mapping methods generally produce acceptable results. Serious shortcomings arise, however, when the portfolio is hedged or uses long and short positions. In such a case, there is a potential for the manipulation of VAR, since simple methods are clearly unable to measure risk properly. This is an example of "gaming the VAR system," which is discussed in a later chapter. In summary, the application of these techniques should be adapted carefully to the portfolio at hand.

APPENDIX 7A: MATRIX MULTIPLICATION

This appendix reviews the algebra for matrix multiplication. Suppose we have two matrices A and B that we wish to multiply to obtain the new matrix C. Their dimensions are $(n \times m)$ for A, or n rows and m columns, and $(m \times p)$ for B.

Note that for the matrix multiplication, the number of columns of A (m) must exactly match the number of rows for B. The dimensions of the resulting matrix C will be $(n \times p)$. Also note that the order of the multiplication matters. The multiplication of B times A is not conformable unless n also happens to be equal to p.

The matrix A can be written in terms of its components a_{ij}, where the first index i denotes the row and the second j denotes the column:

$$A = \begin{bmatrix} a_{11} & a_{12} & \cdots & a_{1m} \\ \vdots & \vdots & \ddots & \vdots \\ a_{n1} & a_{n2} & \cdots & a_{nm} \end{bmatrix}$$

For simplicity, consider now the case where the matrices are of dimension (2×3) and (3×2).

$$A = \begin{bmatrix} a_{11} & a_{12} & a_{13} \\ a_{21} & a_{22} & a_{23} \end{bmatrix}$$

$$B = \begin{bmatrix} b_{11} & b_{12} \\ b_{21} & b_{22} \\ b_{31} & b_{32} \end{bmatrix}$$

$$C = AB = \begin{bmatrix} c_{11} & c_{12} \\ c_{21} & c_{22} \end{bmatrix}$$

To multiply the matrix A by B, we compute each element by taking each row of A and multiplying by the desired column of B. For instance, element c_{ij} would be obtained by multiplying each element of the ith row of A individually by each element of the jth column of B and summing over all of these.

For instance, c_{11} is obtained by taking

$$c_{11} = [a_{11} \quad a_{12} \quad a_{13}] \begin{bmatrix} b_{11} \\ b_{21} \\ b_{31} \end{bmatrix} = a_{11}b_{11} + a_{12}b_{21} + a_{13}b_{31}$$

This gives

$$C = \begin{bmatrix} a_{11}b_{11} + a_{12}b_{21} + a_{13}b_{31} & a_{11}b_{12} + a_{12}b_{22} + a_{13}b_{32} \\ a_{21}b_{21} + a_{22}b_{21} + a_{23}b_{31} & a_{21}b_{22} + a_{22}b_{22} + a_{23}b_{32} \end{bmatrix}$$

APPENDIX 7B (ADVANCED): PRINCIPAL-COMPONENT ANALYSIS

Consider a set of N variables $R_1, \ldots, R_N$ with covariance matrix Σ. These could be bond returns or changes in bond yields, for instance. We wish to simplify, or reduce the dimensions of Σ without too much loss of content, by approximating it by another matrix Σ^*. Our goal is to provide a good approximation of the variance of a portfolio $z = w'R$ using $V^*(z) = w'\Sigma^*w$. The process consists of replacing the original variables R by another set y suitably selected.

The *first* principal component is the linear combination

$$y_1 = \beta_{11}R_1 + \cdots + \beta_{N1}R_N = \beta_1'R \tag{7.41}$$

such that its variance is maximized, subject to a normalization constraint on the norm of the factor exposure vector $\beta_1'\beta_1 = 1$. A constrained optimization of this variance, $\sigma^2(y_1) = \beta_1'\Sigma\beta_1$, shows that the vector β_1 must satisfy $\Sigma\beta_1 = \lambda_1\beta_1$. Here, $\sigma^2(y_1) = \lambda_1$ is the largest *eigenvalue* of the matrix Σ, and β_1 its associated *eigenvector.*

The *second* principal component is the one that has greatest variance subject to the same normalization constraint $\beta_2'\beta_2 = 1$ and to the fact that is must be orthogonal to the first $\beta_2'\beta_1 = 0$. And so on for all the others.

This process basically replaces the original set of R variables by another set of y orthogonal factors that has the same dimension but where the variables are sorted in order of decreasing importance. This leads to the *singular value decomposition,* which decomposes the original matrix as

$$\Sigma = PDP' = [\beta_1 \ldots \beta_N] \begin{bmatrix} \lambda_1 & \cdots & 0 \\ \vdots & & \vdots \\ 0 & \cdots & \lambda_N \end{bmatrix} \begin{bmatrix} \beta_1' \\ \vdots \\ \beta_N' \end{bmatrix} \tag{7.42}$$

where P is an orthogonal matrix, i.e., such that its inverse is also its transpose, $PP' = I$ (or $P^{-1} = P'$) and D a diagonal matrix composed of the λ_i's. The next step would be to give an economic interpretation to the principal components by examining patterns in the eigenvectors.

The definition of P implies that we can write the transformation conveniently as $y = P'R$. Alternatively, if we are given the set of y, we can recover R as $R = Py$. In other words,

$$R_i = \beta_{i1}y_1 + \cdots + \beta_{iN}y_N \qquad (7.43)$$

To each y_j is associated a value for its variance λ_j that is sorted in order of decreasing importance. These eigenvalues are quite useful because they can tell us whether the original matrix Σ truly has N dimensions. For instance, if all the eigenvalues have the same size, then all transformed variables are equally important. In most situations, however, some eigenvalues will be very small, which means that the true dimensionality (or rank) is less than N.

In other cases, some values will be zero or even negative, which indicates that the matrix is not properly defined. The problem is that for some portfolios, the resulting VAR could be negative![8]

If so, we can decide to keep only the first K components, beyond which their variances λ_j can be viewed as too small and unimportant. Thus we replace the previous exact relationship by an approximation:

$$R_i \approx \beta_{i1}y_1 + \cdots + \beta_{iK}y_K \qquad (7.44)$$

Based on this, we approximate the matrix by

$$\Sigma^* = [\beta_1 \ldots \beta_K] \begin{bmatrix} \lambda_1 & \ldots & 0 \\ \vdots & & \vdots \\ 0 & \ldots & \lambda_K \end{bmatrix} \begin{bmatrix} \beta_1' \\ \vdots \\ \beta_K' \end{bmatrix}$$

$$= \beta_1\beta_1'\lambda_1 + \cdots + \beta_K\beta_K'\lambda_K \qquad (7.45)$$

which is very close to Equation (7.39) except for the residual terms on the diagonal. Note that this matrix Σ^* is surely not invertible, since it has only rank of K by construction yet has dimension of N.

The benefit of this approach is that we can now simulate movements in the original variables by simulating movements with a much smaller set of variables y's called *principal components* (PCs).

---

8. It is possible to transform the matrix in a systematic fashion so that it avoids being non-positive-definite. For a review of methods, see Rebonato and Jäckel (2000).

Given a portfolio $z = w'R$, the portfolio can be mapped into its exposures on the principal components:

$$z = \Sigma w_i R_i \approx w_1(\beta_{11}y_1 + \cdots + \beta_{1K}y_K) + \cdots + w_N(\beta_{N1}y_1 + \cdots + \beta_{NK}y_K)$$
$$= (w_1\beta_{11} + \cdots + w_N\beta_{N1})y_1 + \cdots + (w_1\beta_{1K} + \cdots + w_N\beta_{NK})y_K$$
$$= \delta_1 y_1 + \cdots + \delta_K y_K$$

Each term between parentheses represents the weighted exposure to each principal component. For instance, $\delta_1 = w'\beta_1$ would be the portfolio exposure to the first PC. In the stock market, this would be the portfolio total systematic risk. This decomposition is useful for performance attribution because it breaks down the portfolio return into the exposure and return on each PC.

In addition, we can compute the variance of the portfolio directly from Equation (7.45):

$$\sigma^2(z) = w'\Sigma^*w = w'\beta_1\beta_1'w\lambda_1 + \cdots + w'\beta_K\beta_K'w\lambda_K$$
$$= (w'\beta_1)^2\lambda_1 + \cdots + (w'\beta_K)^2\lambda_K$$
$$= \delta_1^2\sigma^2(y_1) + \cdots + \delta_K^2\sigma^2(y_K) \tag{7.46}$$

which is remarkably simple. The variance of the portfolio z is given by sum of the squared exposures δ times the variance of each PC.

Instead of having to deal with all the variances and covariances of R, we simply use K independent terms. For instance, as in the example of a bond market, we can replace a covariance matrix of dimension 11 times 11 with 66 terms by 3 terms in all.

CHAPTER 8

Forecasting Risks and Correlations

Preparing the future is building the present.

Antoine de Saint-Exupéry

Chapter 4 describes the risk of basic financial variables such as interest rates, exchange rates, and equity prices. A reader looking more closely at the graphs would notice that risk appears to change over time. This is quite obvious for exchange rates, which displayed much more variation after 1973. Bond yields also were more volatile in the early 1980s. These periods corresponded to structural breaks: Exchange rates started to float in 1973, and the Fed abruptly changed monetary policies in October 1979. Even during other periods, volatility seems to *cluster,* or group, in a predictable fashion.

The observation that financial market volatility is predictable has important implications for risk management. If volatility increases, so will value at risk (VAR). Investors may want to adjust their portfolio to reduce their exposure to those assets whose volatility is predicted to increase. Also, predictable volatility means that assets depending directly on volatility, such as options, will change in value in a predictable fashion. Finally, in a rational market, equilibrium asset prices will be affected by changes in volatility. Investors who can reliably predict changes in volatility should be able to better control financial market risks.

The purpose of this chapter is to present techniques to forecast variation in risk and correlations. Readers who have no control over the inputs or do not care to know how these were generated could skip this chapter and advance directly to Chapter 9, which compares approaches to VAR.

Section 8.1 motivates the problem by taking the example of a series that underwent structural changes, leading to predictable patterns in volatility. Section 8.2 then presents recent developments in time-series models that capture time variation in volatility. A particular application of these models is the exponential approach adopted by J.P. Morgan for the RiskMetrics system. Section 8.3 extends univariate models to correlation forecasts. Finally, Section 8.4 argues that time-series models are inherently inferior to forecasts of risk contained in option prices.

8.1 TIME-VARYING RISK OR OUTLIERS?

As an illustration, we walk through this chapter focusing on the U.S. dollar/British pound ($/BP) exchange rate measured at daily intervals. Movements in the exchange rate are displayed in Figure 8–1. The 1990–1994 period was fairly typical, covering narrow trading ranges and wide swings. September 1992 was particularly tumultuous. After vain attempts by the Bank of England to support the pound against the German mark, sterling exited the European Monetary System. There were several days with very large moves. On September 17 alone, the pound fell by 6 percent against the mark. Hence we can expect interesting patterns in

FIGURE 8–1

Spot rate: British pound versus dollar.

F I G U R E   8–2

Distribution of the $/BP rate.

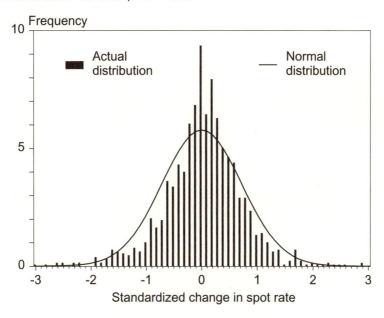

volatility. In particular, the question is whether this structural change led to predictable time variation in risk.

Over this period, the average daily volatility was 0.694 percent, which translates into 11.02 percent per annum (using a 252-trading-day adjustment). This risk measure, however, surely was not constant over time. In addition, time variation in risk could explain the fact that the empirical distribution of returns does not quite exactly fit a normal distribution.

Figure 8–2 compares the normal approximation to the actual empirical distribution of the $/BP exchange rate. Relative to the normal model, the actual distribution contains more observations in the center and in the tails.

These fat tails can be explained by two alternative viewpoints. The first view is that the true distribution is stationary and indeed contains fat tails, in which case a normal approximation is clearly inappropriate. The other view is that the distribution does change through time. As a result, in times of turbulence, a stationary model could view large observations as outliers when they are really drawn from a distribution with temporarily greater dispersion.

In practice, both explanations carry some truth. This is why fore-casting variation in risk is particularly fruitful for risk management. In this chapter we focus on traditional approaches based on *parametric* time-series modeling.[1]

8.2 MODELING TIME-VARYING RISK

8.2.1 Moving Averages

A very crude method, but one that is employed widely, is to use a *moving window* of fixed length for estimating volatility. For instance, a typi-cal length is 20 trading days (about a calendar month) or 60 trading days (about a calendar quarter).

Assuming that we observe returns r_t over M days, this volatility es-timate is constructed from a *moving average* (MA):

$$\sigma_t^2 = (1/M) \sum_{i=1}^{M} r_{t-i}^2 \qquad (8.1)$$

Here we focus on raw returns instead of returns around the mean. This is so because for most financial series, ignoring expected returns over very short time intervals makes little difference for volatility estimates.

Each day, the forecast is updated by adding information from the preceding day and dropping information from $(M + 1)$ days ago. All weights on past returns are equal and set to $(1/M)$. Figure 8–3 displays 20-day and 60-day moving averages for our $/BP rate.

While simple to implement, this model has serious drawbacks. First, it ignores the dynamic ordering of observations. Recent information re-ceives the same weight as older observations in the window that may no longer be relevant.

Also, if there was a large return M days ago, dropping this return as the window moves 1 day forward will substantially affect the volatility es-timate. For instance, there was 3 percent drop on September 17, 1992. This observation will immediately increase the MA forecast, which correctly

---

1. Other methods exist, however. For instance, multivariate density estimation (MDE) is a non-parametric model that appears to be quite flexible, as described by Boudoukh et al. (1995). Also, risk estimators do not have to necessarily rely solely on daily closing prices. Parkinson (1980) has shown that using the information in the extreme values (daily high and low) leads to an estimator that is twice as efficient as the usual volatility; this is so because it uses more information.

FIGURE 8–3

Moving-average (MA) volatility forecasts.

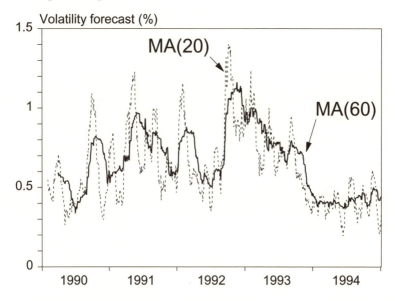

reflects the higher volatility. The MA(20), however, reverts to a lower value after 20 days; the MA(60) reverts to a lower value after 60 days. As a result, moving-average measures of volatility tend to look like *plateaus* of width M when plotted against time. The subsequent drop, however, is totally an artifact of the window length. This has been called the *ghosting* feature because the MA measure changes for no apparent reason.

The figure shows that the MA(60) is much more stable than the MA(20). This is understandable because longer periods decrease the weight of any single day. But is it better? This approach leaves wholly unanswered the choice of the moving window. Longer periods increase the precision of the estimate but could miss underlying variation in volatility.

8.2.2 GARCH Estimation

This is why volatility estimation has moved toward models that put more weight on recent information. The first such model was the *generalized autoregressive heteroskedastic* (GARCH) model proposed by Engle (1982) and Bollerslev (1986). *Heteroskedastic* refers to the fact that variances are changing.

The GARCH model assumes that the variance of returns follows a predictable process. The *conditional* variance depends on the latest innovation but also on the previous conditional variance. Define h_t as the conditional variance, using information up to time $t - 1$, and r_{t-1} as the previous day's return. The simplest such model is the GARCH(1,1) process:

$$h_t = \alpha_0 + \alpha_1 r_{t-1}^2 + \beta h_{t-1} \qquad (8.2)$$

The average, unconditional variance is found by setting $E(r_{t-1}^2) = h_t = h_{t-1} = h$. Solving for h, we find

$$h = \frac{\alpha_0}{1 - \alpha_1 - \beta} \qquad (8.3)$$

For this model to be stationary, the sum of parameters $\alpha_1 + \beta$ must be less than unity. This sum is also called the *persistence,* for reasons that will become clear later on.

The beauty of this specification is that it provides a parsimonious model, with few parameters, that seems to fit the data quite well.[2] GARCH models have become a mainstay of time-series analysis of financial markets, which systematically display volatility clustering. There are literally hundreds of papers applying GARCH models to stock return data (see French et al., 1987), to interest rate data (see Engle et al., 1987), and to foreign exchange data (see Hsieh, 1988; Giovannini and Jorion, 1989). Econometricians also have frantically created many variants of the GARCH model, most of which provide only marginal improvement on the original GARCH model. Readers interested in a comprehensive review of the literature should consult Bollerslev et al. (1992).[3]

The drawback of GARCH models is their nonlinearity. The parameters must be estimated by maximization of the likelihood function, which involves a numerical optimization. Typically, researchers assume that the scaled residuals $\epsilon_t = r_t/\sqrt{h_t}$ have a normal distribution and are independent. If we have T observations, their joint density is the product of

---

2. For the theoretical rationale behind the success of GARCH models, see Nelson (1990).

3. GARCH models have other interesting properties. The returns r_t can be serially uncorrelated but are not independent because they are nonlinearly related through second moments. This class of models is also related to chaos theory. Recent work has revealed that many financial prices display "chaotic" properties. Often, the nonlinearities behind chaos theory can be traced to the time variation in variances. Thus GARCH models explain some of the reported chaotic behavior of financial markets.

the densities for each time period t. The optimization maximizes the logarithm of the likelihood function:

$$\max F(\alpha_0, \alpha_1, \beta \mid r) = \sum_{t=1}^{T} \ln f(r_t \mid h_t) = \sum_{t=1}^{T} \left(\ln \frac{1}{\sqrt{2\pi h_t}} - \frac{r_t^2}{2h_t} \right) \quad (8.4)$$

where f is the normal density function.

Table 8–1 presents the results of the estimation for a number of financial series over the 1990–1999 period. There are wide differences in the level of volatility across series, yet for all these series, the time variation in risk is highly significant. The persistence parameter is also rather high, on the order of 0.97 to 0.99.

Figure 8–4 displays the GARCH forecast of volatility for the $/BP rate. It shows increased volatility in the fall of 1992. Afterward, volatility decreases progressively over time, not in the abrupt fashion observed in Figure 8–3.

The practical use of this information is illustrated in Figure 8–5, which shows daily returns along with conditional 95 percent confidence bands. This model appears to capture variation in risk adequately. Most of the returns fall within the 95 percent band. The few outside the bands correspond to the remaining 5 percent of occurrences.

8.2.3 Long-Horizon Forecasts with GARCH

The GARCH model can be used to extrapolate the volatility over various horizons in a consistent fashion. Assume that the model is estimated using daily intervals. We first decompose the multiperiod return into daily returns as in Equation (4.27):

$$r_{t,T} = r_t + r_{t+1} + r_{t+2} + \cdots + r_T$$

Let us define n as the number of days, or $T - t + 1 = n$.

If returns are uncorrelated across days, the long-horizon variance as of $t - 1$ is

$$E_{t-1}(r_{t,T}^2) = E_{t-1}(r_t^2) + E_{t-1}(r_{t+1}^2) + E_{t-1}(r_{t+2}^2) + \cdots + E_{t-1}(r_T^2)$$

To determine the GARCH forecast in 2 days, we use tomorrow's forecast:

$$E_{t-1}(r_{t+1}^2) = E_{t-1}(\alpha_0 + \alpha_1 r_t^2 + \beta h_t) = \alpha_0 + \alpha_1 h_t + \beta h_t$$

TABLE 8–1

Risk Models: Daily Data, 1990–1999

Parameter	Currency				U.S. Stocks	U.S. Bonds	Crude Oil
	$/BP	DM/$	Yen/$	DM/BP			
Average SD							
σ (% pa)	11.33	10.54	11.78	7.98	14.10	4.07	37.55
GARCH process:							
α_0	0.00299	0.00576	0.01040	0.00834	0.00492	0.00138	0.04153
α_1	0.0379	0.0390	0.0528	0.1019	0.0485	0.0257	0.08348
β	0.9529	0.9476	0.9284	0.8699	0.9459	0.9532	0.9131
Persistence							
$(\alpha_1 + \beta)$	0.9908	0.9866	0.9812	0.9718	0.9944	0.9789	0.9966

FIGURE 8–4

GARCH volatility forecast.

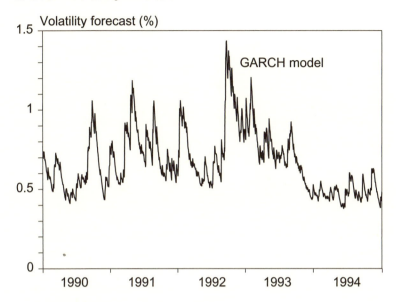

FIGURE 8–5

Returns and GARCH confidence bands.

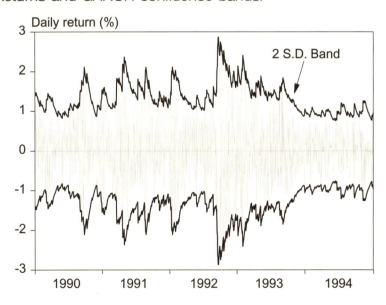

For the next day,

$$E_{t-1}(r_{t+2}^2) = E_{t-1}(\alpha_0 + \alpha_1 r_{t+1}^2 + \beta h_{t+1})$$
$$= \alpha_0 + (\alpha_1 + \beta)[\alpha_0 + (\alpha_1 + \beta)h_t]$$

Substituting n days into the future, the forecast of the "forward" variance at T is

$$E_{t-1}(r_T^2) = \alpha_0 \frac{1 - (\alpha_1 + \beta)^{n-1}}{1 - (\alpha_1 + \beta)} + (\alpha_1 + \beta)^{n-1} h_t \qquad (8.5)$$

The total variance from now to T is then

$$E_{t-1}(r_{t,T}^2) = \frac{\alpha_0}{1 - (\alpha_1 + \beta)}$$
$$\left[(n - 1) - (\alpha_1 + \beta) \frac{1 - (\alpha_1 + \beta)^{n-1}}{1 - (\alpha_1 + \beta)} \right] + \frac{1 - (\alpha_1 + \beta)^n}{1 - (\alpha_1 + \beta)} h_t \qquad (8.6)$$

This shows that the extrapolation of next day's variance to a longer horizon is a complicated function of the variance process and the initial condition. Thus our simple square root of time rule fails due to the fact that returns are not identically distributed.

It is interesting to note that if we start from a position that is the long-run average, $h_t = h = \alpha_0/[1 - (\alpha_1 + \beta)]$, this expression simplifies to

$$E_{t-1}(r_{t,T}^2) = hn \qquad (8.7)$$

Here, the n-day VAR is the 1-day VAR times the square root of n. In other words, the extrapolation of VAR using the square root of time is valid only when the initial position happens to be equal to the long-run value. If the starting position is greater than the long-run value, the square root of time rule will overestimate risk. If the starting position is less than the long-run value, the square root of time rule will underestimate risk.

Figure 8–6 displays the effect of different persistence parameters $(\alpha_1 + \beta)$ on the variance. We start from the long-run value for the variance, 0.51. Then a shock moves the conditional variance to twice its value, about 1.02. High persistence means that the shock will decay slowly. For instance, with persistence of 0.99, the conditional variance is still 0.93 after 20 days. With a persistence of 0.8, the variance drops very close to its long-run value after 20 days only. The marker on each line represents the average daily variance over the next 25 days. High persistence implies that the average variance will remain high.

FIGURE 8-6

Mean reversion for the variance.

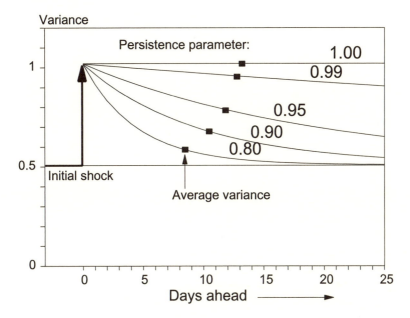

8.2.4 The RiskMetrics Approach

RiskMetrics takes a pragmatic approach to modeling risk.[4] Variances are modeled using an *exponentially weighted moving average* (EWMA) forecast. Formally, the forecast for time t is a weighted average of the previous forecast, using weight λ, and of the latest squared innovation, using weight $(1 - \lambda)$:

$$h_t = \lambda h_{t-1} + (1 - \lambda)r_{t-1}^2 \qquad (8.8)$$

Here, the λ parameter is called the *decay factor* and must be less than unity.

The exponential model places geometrically declining weights on past observations, thus assigning greater importance to recent observations. By recursively replacing h_{t-1} in Equation (8.8), we can write

$$h_t = (1 - \lambda)(r_{t-1}^2 + \lambda r_{t-2}^2 + \lambda^2 r_{t-3}^2 + \cdots) \qquad (8.9)$$

---

4. For more detail on the methodology, see J.P. Morgan's *RiskMetrics Technical Manual* (1995).

FIGURE 8–7

Weights on past observations.

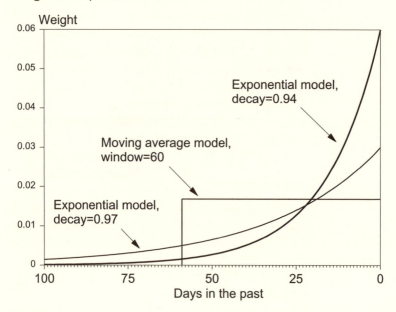

Figure 8–7 displays the pattern of weights for λ = 0.94 and λ = 0.97. For λ = 0.94, the weights decay fairly quickly, dropping below 0.00012 for data more than 100 days old. Thus the number of *effective* observations is rather small.

This model can be viewed as a special case of the GARCH process, where α_0 is set to 0 and α_1 and β sum to unity. The model therefore allows for persistence. As shown by Figure 8–8, the forecasts are nearly identical to those obtained with the GARCH model in Figure 8–4.

The exponential model is particularly easy to implement because it relies on one parameter only. Thus it is more robust to estimation error than other models. In addition, as was the case for the GARCH model, the estimator is *recursive;* the forecast is based on the previous forecast and the latest innovation. The whole history is summarized by one number, h_{t-1}. This is in contrast to the moving average, for instance, where the last M returns must be used to construct the forecast.

The only parameter in this model is the decay factor λ. In theory, this could be found from maximizing the likelihood function. Operationally, this would be a daunting task to perform every day for more than 450 series in the RiskMetrics database. An optimization has other short-

FIGURE 8–8

Exponential volatility forecast.

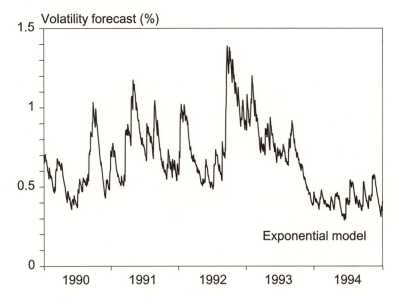

comings. The decay factor may vary not only across series but also over time, thus losing consistency over different periods. In addition, different values of λ create incompatibilities for the covariance terms and may lead to coefficients of correlation greater than unity, as we shall see later. In practice, RiskMetrics only uses one decay factor for all series, which is set at 0.94 for daily data.

RiskMetrics also provides risk forecasts over monthly horizons, defined as 25 trading days. In theory, the 1-day exponential model should be used to extrapolate volatility over the next day, then the next, and so on until the twenty-fifth day ahead, as was done for the GARCH model earlier. Herein lies the rub.

The persistence parameter for the exponential model ($\alpha_1 + \beta$) is unity. Thus the model allows no mean reversion, and the monthly volatility should be the same as the daily volatility. In practice, however, we do observe mean reversion in monthly risk forecasts.

This is why RiskMetrics takes a different approach. The estimator uses the same form as Equation (8.8), redefining r_{t-1} as the 25-day moving variance estimator,

$$h_t^{'} = \lambda h_{t-1}^{'} + (1 - \lambda)s_{t-1}^2 \qquad s_{t-1}^2 = \sum_{k=1}^{25} r_{t-k}^2 \qquad (8.10)$$

In practice, this creates strange "ghost" features in the pattern of monthly variance forecast.[5]

After experimenting with the data, J.P. Morgan chose $\lambda = 0.97$ as the optimal decay factor. Therefore, the daily and monthly models are inconsistent with each other. However, they are both easy to use, they approximate the behavior of actual data quite well, and they are robust to misspecification.

8.3 MODELING CORRELATIONS

Correlation is of paramount importance for portfolio risk, even more so than individual variances. To illustrate the estimation of correlation, we pick two series: the dollar/British pound exchange rate and the dollar/Deutsche mark rate.

Over the 1990–1994 period, the average daily correlation coefficient was 0.7732. We should expect, however, some variation in the correlation coefficient because this time period covers fixed and floating exchange rates regimes. On October 8, 1990, sterling became pegged to the mark within the European Monetary System (EMS). This lasted until the turmoil of September 1992, during which sterling left the EMS and again floated against the mark.

As in the case of variance estimation, various methods can be used to capture time variation in correlation: moving average, GARCH, and exponential.

8.3.1 Moving Averages

The first method is based on moving averages (MAs), using a fixed window of length M. Figure 8–9 presents estimates based on an MA(20) and MA(60). Correlations start low, around 0.5, and then increase to 0.9 as sterling enters the EMS. During the September 1992 crisis, correlations drop sharply and then go back to the pre-EMS pattern. The later drop in correlation would have been disastrous for positions believed to be nearly riskless on the basis of EMS correlations.

These estimates are subject to the same criticisms as before. Moving averages place the same weight on all observations within the moving window and ignore the fact that more recent observations may contain

---

5. See Alexander (1998) for further details.

FIGURE 8–9

Moving-average correlation: $/BP and $/DM.

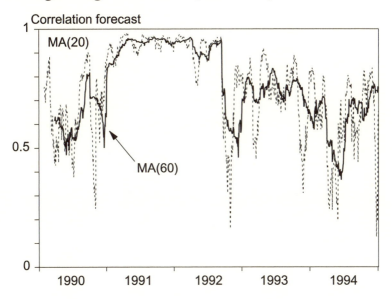

more information than older ones. In addition, dropping observations from the window sometimes has severe effects on the measured correlation.

8.3.2 Exponential Averages

In theory, GARCH estimation could be extended to a multivariate framework. The problem is that the number of parameters to estimate increases exponentially with the number of series. With two series, for instance, we need to estimate nine terms, three α_0, α_1, β parameters for each of the three covariance terms. For larger samples of securities, this number quickly becomes unmanageable.

Here shines the simplicity of the RiskMetrics approach. Covariances are estimated, much like variances, using an exponential weighing scheme:

$$h_{12,t} = \lambda h_{12,t-1} + (1 - \lambda)r_{1,t-1}r_{2,t-1} \qquad (8.11)$$

As before, the decay factor λ is arbitrarily set at 0.94 for daily data and 0.97 for monthly data. The conditional correlation is then

$$\rho_{12,t} = \frac{h_{12,t-1}}{\sqrt{h_{1,t-1}h_{2,t-1}}} \qquad (8.12)$$

FIGURE 8–10

Exponential correlation: $/BP and $/DM.

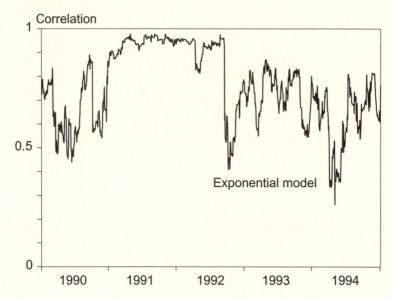

Figure 8–10 displays the time variation in the correlation between the pound and the mark. The pattern of movement in correlations seems not too different from the MA model, plotting somewhere between the MA(20) and MA(60).

Note that the reason why J.P. Morgan decided to set a common factor λ across all series is to ensure that all estimates of ρ are between -1 and 1. Otherwise, there is no guarantee that this will always be the case.

Even so, this method has a small number of effective observations due to the rapid decay of weights. The problem is that in order for the covariance matrix to be positive-definite, we need at least as many time-series observations as number of assets. This explains why the RiskMetrics-provided covariance matrix, with its large number of assets, is typically not positive-definite.

8.3.3 Crashes and Correlations

Low correlations help to reduce portfolio risk. However, it is often argued that correlations increase in periods of global turbulence. If true, such

statements are particularly worrisome because increasing correlations occurring at a time of increasing volatility would defeat the diversification
properties of portfolios. Measures of VAR based on historical data would
then seriously underestimate the actual risk of failure because not only
would risk be understated, but so would correlations. This double blow
could well lead to returns that are way outside the range of forecasts.

Indeed, we expect the structure of the correlation matrix to depend
on the type of shocks affecting the economy. Global factors, such as the
oil crises and the Gulf War, create increased turbulence and increased correlations. Longin and Solnik (1995), for instance, examine the behavior
of correlations of national stock markets and find that correlations typically increase by 0.12 (from 0.43 to 0.55) in periods of high turbulence.
Assuming a large portfolio (where risk is proportional to $\sqrt{\rho}$), this implies that VAR should be multiplied by a factor of $\sqrt{(0.55/0.43)} = 1.13$.
Thus, just because of the correlation effect, VAR measures could underestimate true risk by 13 percent.

The extent of bias, however, depends on the sign of positions. Higher
correlations are harmful to portfolios with only long positions, as is typical of equity portfolios. In contrast, decreasing correlations are dangerous for portfolios with short sales. Consider our previous example where
a trader is long sterling and short mark. As Figure 8–4 shows, this position would have been nearly riskless in 1991 and in the first half of 1992,
but the trader would have been caught short by the September 1992 devaluation of the pound. Estimates of VAR based on the previous year's
data would have grossly underestimated the risk of the position.

Perhaps these discomforting results explain why regulators impose
large multiplicative factors on internally computed VAR measures. But
these observations also point to the need for stress simulations to assess
the robustness of VAR measures to changes in correlations.

8.4 USING OPTIONS DATA

Measures of value at risk (VAR) are only as good as the quality of forecasts of risk and correlations. Historical data, however, may not provide
the best available forecasts of future risks. Situations involving changes
in regimes, for instance, are simply not reflected in recent historical data.
This is why it is useful to turn to forecasts implied in options data.

8.4.1 Implied Volatilities

An important function of derivatives markets is *price discovery.* Derivatives provide information about market-clearing prices, which includes the discovery of volatility. Options are assets whose price is influenced by a number of factors, all of which are observable save for the volatility of the underlying price. By setting the market price of an option equal to its model value, one can recover an *implied volatility,* or implied standard deviation (ISD).[6] Essentially, the method consists of inverting the option pricing formula, finding σ_{ISD} that equates the model price f to the market price, given current market data and option features:

$$c_{market} = f(\sigma_{ISD}) \qquad (8.13)$$

where f represents, for instance, the Black-Scholes function for European options.

This approach can be used to infer a term structure of ISDs every day, plotting the ISD against the maturity of the associated option. Note that σ_{ISD} corresponds to the *average* volatility over the life of the option instead of the instantaneous, overnight volatility. If quotes are only available for longer-term options, we will need to extrapolate the volatility surface to the near term.

Implied correlations also can be recovered from triplets of options on the same three assets. Correlations are also implicit in so-called quanto options, which involve two random variables. An example of a quantity-adjusted option, for instance, would be an option struck on a foreign stock index where the foreign currency payoff is translated into dollars at a fixed rate. The valuation formula for such an option also involves the correlation between two sources of risk. Thus options potentially can reveal a wealth of information about future risks and correlations.

8.4.2 ISD as Risk Forecasts

If options markets are efficient, the ISD should provide the market's best estimate of future volatility. After all, options trading involves taking

---

6. One potential objection to the use of option volatilities is that the Black-Scholes (BS) model is, *stricto sensu,* inconsistent with stochastic volatilities. Recent research on the effect of stochastic volatilities, however, has shown that the BS model performs well for short-term at-the-money options. For other types of options, such as deep out-of-the-money options, the model may be less appropriate, creating discrepancies in implied volatilities known as the *volatility smile.* For further details, see Bates (1995), Duan (1995), and Heston (1993).

FIGURE 8–11

Volatility forecasts: DM/pound.

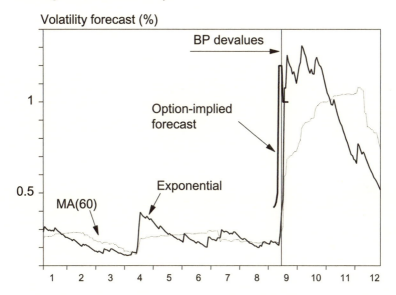

volatility bets. Expressing a view on volatility has become so pervasive in the options markets that prices are often quoted in terms of bid-ask volatility. Since options reflect the market consensus about future volatility, there are sound reasons to believe that options-based forecasts should be superior to historical estimates.

The empirical evidence indeed points to the superiority of options data.[7] An intuitive way to demonstrate the usefulness of options data is to analyze the September 1992 breakdown of the European Monetary System (EMS). Figure 8–11 compares volatility forecasts during 1992, including the implied from DM/BP cross-options, the RiskMetrics volatility, and a moving average with a window of 60 days.

As sterling came under heavy selling pressures by speculators, the ISD moved up sharply, anticipating a large jump in the exchange rate. Indeed, sterling went off the EMS on September 16. In contrast, the RiskMetrics volatility moved up only after the first big move, and the MA

---

7. Jorion (1995a), for instance, shows that for currency futures, options-implied volatilities subsume all information contained in time-series models. Campa and Chang (1998) find that the implied correlation for the dollar/mark and dollar/yen rates outperforms all historical models.

volatility changed ever so slowly. As options traders rationally anticipated greater turbulence, the implied volatility was much more useful than time-series models.

Overall, the evidence is that options contain a wealth of information about price risk that is generally superior to time-series models. This information is particularly useful in times of stress, when the market has access to current information that is simply not reflected in historical models. Therefore, my advice is as follows: *Whenever possible, value at risk should use implied parameters.*

The only drawback of options-implied parameters is that the menu of traded options is not sufficiently wide to recover the volatility of all essential financial prices. Even fewer cross-options could be used to derive implied correlations. As more and more options contracts and exchanges are springing up all over the world, however, we will be able to use truly forward-looking options data to measure risk. In the meantime, historical data provide a useful alternative.

8.5 CONCLUSIONS

Modeling time variation in risk is of central importance for the measurement of VAR. This chapter has shown that for most financial assets, volatility varies in a predictable fashion. This variation can be modeled using time-series models such as moving average, GARCH, and exponential weights. These models adapt with varying speeds to changing conditions in financial markets. They also can be extended, with some difficulties, to modeling correlations across assets.

The drawback of historical models, unfortunately, is that they are always one step too late, starting to react *after* a big movement has occurred. For some purposes, this is insufficient, which is why volatility forecasts ideally should be obtained from options prices.

PART THREE

Value-at-Risk Systems

CHAPTER 9

VAR Methods

In practice, this works, but how about in theory?

Attributed to a French mathematician

Value at risk (VAR) has become an essential component in the toolkit of risk managers because it provides a quantitative measure of downside risk. In practice, the objective should be to provide a reasonably accurate estimate of risk at a reasonable cost. This involves choosing among the various industry standards a method that is most appropriate for the portfolio at hand. To help with this selection, this chapter presents and critically evaluates various approaches to VAR.

Approaches to VAR basically can be classified into two groups. The first group uses local valuation. *Local-valuation methods* measure risk by valuing the portfolio once, at the initial position, and using local derivatives to infer possible movements. The delta-normal method uses linear, or delta, derivatives and assumes normal distributions. Because the delta-normal approach is easy to implement, a variant, called the "Greeks," is sometimes used. This method consists of analytical approximations to first- and second-order derivatives and is most appropriate for portfolios with limited sources of risk. The second group uses full valuation. *Full-valuation methods* measure risk by fully repricing the portfolio over a range of scenarios. The pros and cons of local versus full valuation are discussed in Section 9.1. Initially, we consider a simple portfolio that is driven by one risk factor only.

This chapter then turns to VAR methods for large portfolios. The best example of local valuation is the delta-normal method, which is explained in Section 9.2. Full valuation is implemented in the historical simulation method and the Monte Carlo simulation method, which are discussed in Sections 9.3 and 9.4.

This classification reflects a fundamental tradeoff between speed and accuracy. Speed is important for large portfolios exposed to many risk factors, which involve a large number of correlations. These are handled most easily in the delta-normal approach. Accuracy may be more important, however, when the portfolio has substantial nonlinear components.

An in-depth analysis of the delta-normal and simulation VAR methods is presented in following chapters, as well as a related method, stress testing. Section 9.5 presents some empirical comparisons. Finally, Section 9.6 summarizes the pros and cons of each method.

9.1 LOCAL VERSUS FULL VALUATION

9.1.1 Delta-Normal Valuation

Local-valuation methods usually rely on the normality assumption for the driving risk factors. This assumption is particularly convenient because of the invariance property of normal variables: Portfolios of normal variables are themselves normally distributed.

We initially focus on *delta valuation,* which considers only the first derivatives. To illustrate the approaches, take an instrument whose value depends on a single underlying risk factor S. The first step consists of valuing the portfolio at the initial point

$$V_0 = V(S_0) \qquad (9.1)$$

along with analytical or numerical derivatives. Define Δ_0 as the first partial derivative, or the portfolio sensitivity to changes in prices, evaluated at the current position V_0. This would be called *modified duration* for a fixed-income portfolio or delta for a derivative. For instance, with an at-the-money call, $\Delta = 0.5$, and a long position in one option is simply replaced by a 50 percent position in one unit of underlying asset. The portfolio Δ simply can be computed as the sum of individual deltas.

The potential loss in value dV is then computed as

$$dV = \frac{\partial V}{\partial S}\Big|_0 \, dS = \Delta_0 \times dS \qquad (9.2)$$

which involves the potential change in prices dS. Because this is a linear relationship, the worst loss for V is attained for an extreme value of S.

If the distribution is normal, the portfolio VAR can be derived from the product of the exposure and the VAR of the underlying variable:

$$\text{VAR} = |\Delta_0| \times \text{VAR}_S = |\Delta_0| \times (\alpha\sigma S_0) \qquad (9.3)$$

where α is the standard normal deviate corresponding to the specified confidence level, e.g., 1.645 for a 95 percent confidence level. Here, we take $\sigma(dS/S)$ as the standard deviation of *rates* of changes in the price. The assumption is that rates of changes are normally distributed.

Because VAR is obtained as a closed-form solution, this method is called *analytical*. Note that VAR was measured by computing the portfolio value only once, at the current position V_0.

For a fixed-income portfolio, the risk factor is the yield y, and the price-yield relationship is

$$dV = -D^*V\,dy \qquad (9.4)$$

where D^* is the *modified duration*. In this case, the portfolio VAR is

$$\text{VAR} = (D^*V) \times (\alpha\sigma) \qquad (9.5)$$

where $\sigma(dy)$ is now the volatility of changes in the *level* of yield. The assumption is that changes in yields are normally distributed, although this is ultimately an empirical issue.

This method is illustrated in Figure 9–1, where the profit payoff is a linear function of the underlying spot price and is displayed at the upper left side; the price itself is normally distributed, as shown in the right panel. As a result, the profit itself is normally distributed, as shown at the bottom of the figure. The VAR for the profit can be found from the exposure and the VAR for the underlying price. There is a one-to-one mapping between the two VAR measures.

How good is this approximation? It depends on the "optionality" of the portfolio as well as the horizon. Consider, for instance, a simple case of a long position in a call option. In this case, we can easily describe the distribution of option values. This is so because there is a one-to-one relationship between V and S. In other words, given the pricing function, any value for S can be translated into a value for V, and vice versa.

This is illustrated in Figure 9–2, which shows how the distribution of the spot price is translated into a distribution for the option value (in the left panel). Note that the option distribution has a long right tail, due to the upside potential, whereas the downside is limited to the option premium. This shift is due to the nonlinear payoff on the option.

FIGURE 9-1

Distribution with linear exposures.

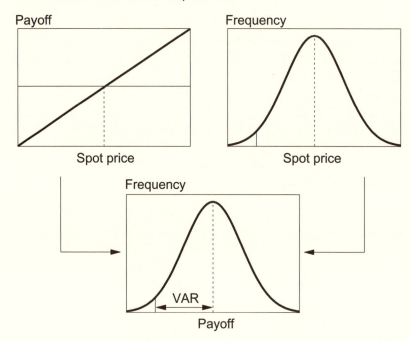

Here, the cth quantile for V is simply the function evaluated at the cth quantile of S. For the long-call option, the worst loss for V at a given confidence level will be achieved at $S^* = S_0 - \alpha\sigma S_0$, and

$$VAR = V(S_0) - V(S_0 - \alpha\sigma S_0) \qquad (9.6)$$

The nonlinearity effect is not obvious, though. It also depends on the maturity of the option and on the range of spot prices over the horizon. The option illustrated here is a call option with 3 months to expiration. To obtain a visible shift in the shape of the option distribution, the volatility was set at 20 percent per annum and the VAR horizon at 2 months, which is rather long.

The figure also shows thinner distributions that correspond to a VAR horizon of 2 weeks. Here, the option distribution is indistinguishable from the normal. In other words, the mere presence of options does not necessarily invalidate the delta-normal approach. The quality of the approximation depends on the extent of nonlinearities, which is a function of the

FIGURE 9-2

Transformation of distributions.

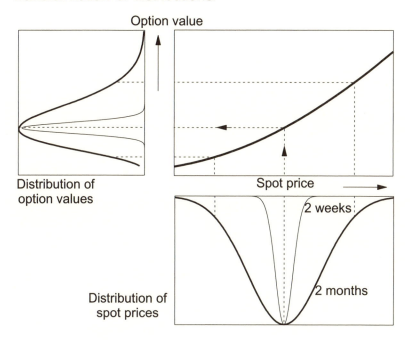

type of options, of their maturities, as well as of the volatility of risk factors and VAR horizon. The shorter the VAR horizon, the better is the delta-normal approximation.

9.1.2 Full Valuation

In some situations, the delta-normal approach is totally inadequate. This is the case, for instance, when the worst loss may not be obtained for extreme realizations of the underlying spot rate. Also, options that are near expiration and at-the-money have unstable deltas, which translate into asymmetrical payoff distributions.

An example of this problem is that of a long *straddle*, which involves the purchase of a call and a put. The worst payoff, which is the sum of the premiums, will be realized if the spot rate does not move at all. In general, it is not sufficient to evaluate the portfolio at the two extremes. All intermediate values must be checked.

The *full-valuation approach* considers the portfolio value for a wide range of price levels:

$$dV = V(S_1) - V(S_0) \qquad (9.7)$$

The new values S_1 can be generated by simulation methods. The *Monte Carlo simulation approach* relies on prespecified distributions. For instance, the realizations can be drawn from a normal distribution,

$$dS/S \approx N(0, \sigma^2) \qquad (9.8)$$

Alternatively, the *historical simulation approach* simply samples from recent historical data.

For each of these draws, the portfolio is priced on the target date using a full-valuation method. This method is potentially the most accurate because it accounts for nonlinearities, income payments, and even time-decay effects that are usually ignored in the delta-normal approach. VAR is then calculated from the percentiles of the full distribution of payoffs. Computationally, this approach is quite demanding because it requires marking-to-market the whole portfolio over a large number of realizations of underlying random variables.

To illustrate the result of nonlinear exposures, Figure 9–3 displays the payoff function for a short straddle that is highly nonlinear. The resulting distribution is severely skewed to the left. Further, there is no direct way to relate the VAR of the portfolio to that of the underlying asset.

The problem is that these simulation methods require substantial computing time when applied to large portfolios. As a result, methods have been developed to speed up the computations.

One example is the *grid Monte Carlo approach*, which starts by an exact valuation of the portfolio over a limited number of grid points.[1] For each simulation, the portfolio value is then approximated using a linear interpolation from the exact values at the adjoining grid points. This approach is especially efficient if exact valuation of the instrument is complex. Take, for instance, a portfolio with one risk factor for which we require 1000 values $V(S_1)$. With the grid Monte Carlo method, 10 full valuations at the grid points may be sufficient. In contrast, the full Monte Carlo method would require 1000 full valuations.

---

1. Picoult (1997) describes this method in more detail.

FIGURE 9–3

Distribution with nonlinear exposures.

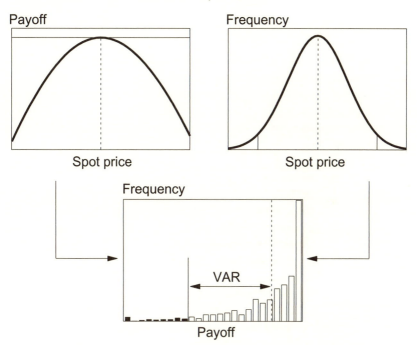

9.1.3 Delta-Gamma Approximations (the "Greeks")

It may be possible to extend the analytical tractability of the delta-normal method with higher-order terms. We can improve the quality of the linear approximation by adding terms in the Taylor expansion of the valuation function:

$$dV = \frac{\partial V}{\partial S}\, dS + \frac{1}{2}\, \frac{\partial^2 V}{\partial S_2}\, dS^2 + \frac{\partial V}{\partial t}\, dt + \cdots$$

$$= \Delta dS + \frac{1}{2}\, \Gamma\, dS^2 + \Theta\, dt + \cdots \quad (9.9)$$

where Γ is now the second derivative of the portfolio value, and Θ is the time drift, which is deterministic.

For a fixed-income portfolio, the price-yield relationship is now

$$dV = -(D^*V)\, dy + \frac{1}{2}\, (CV)\, dy^2 + \cdots \qquad (9.10)$$

where the second-order coefficient C is called *convexity* and is akin to Γ.

Figure 9–4 describes the approximation for a simple position, a long position in a European call option. It shows that the linear model is valid only for small movements around the initial value. For larger movements, the delta-gamma approximation creates a better fit.

We use the Taylor expansion to compute VAR for the long-call option in Equation (9.6), which yields

$$\begin{aligned}
\text{VAR} &= V(S_0) - V(S_0 - \alpha\sigma S_0) \\
&= V(S_0) - [V(S_0) + \Delta(-\alpha\sigma S) + 1/2\Gamma(-\alpha\sigma S)^2] \qquad (9.11) \\
&= |\,\Delta\,|\,(\alpha\sigma S) - 1/2\Gamma(\alpha\sigma S)^2
\end{aligned}$$

This formula is actually valid for long and short positions in calls and puts. If Γ is positive, which corresponds to a net long position in options, the second term will decrease the linear VAR. Indeed, Figure 9–4

F I G U R E   9–4

Delta-gamma approximation for a long call.

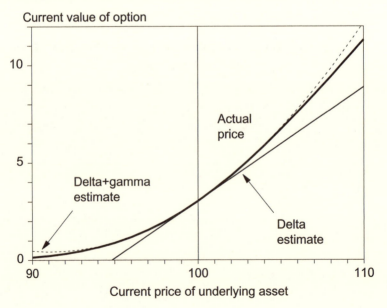

shows that the downside risk for the option is less than that given by the delta approximation. If Γ is negative, which corresponds to a net short position in options, VAR is increased.

This transformation does not apply, unfortunately, to more complex functions $V(S)$, so we have to go back to the Taylor expansion [Equation (9.9)]. The question now is how to deal with the random variables dS and dS^2.

The simplest method is called the *delta-gamma-delta method*. Taking the variance of both sides of the quadratic approximation [Equation (9.9)], we obtain

$$\sigma^2(dV) = \Delta^2\sigma^2(dS) + (1/2\Gamma)^2\sigma^2(dS^2) + 2(\Delta 1/2\Gamma)\ \text{cov}(dS,\ dS^2) \quad (9.12)$$

If the variable dS is normally distributed, all its odd moments are zero, and the last term in the equation vanishes. Under the same assumption, one can show that $V(dS^2) = 2V(dS)^2$, and the variance simplifies to

$$\sigma^2(dV) = \Delta^2\sigma^2(dS) + 1/2[\Gamma\sigma^2(dS)]^2 \quad (9.13)$$

Assume now that the variables dS and dS^2 are jointly normally distributed. Then dV is normally distributed, with VAR given by

$$\text{VAR} = \alpha\ \sqrt{(\Delta S\sigma)^2 + 1/2(\Gamma S^2\sigma^2)^2} \quad (9.14)$$

This is, of course, only an approximation. Even if dS was normal, its square dS^2 could not possibly also be normally distributed. Rather, it is a chi-squared variable.

A further improvement can be obtained by accounting for the skewness coefficient ξ, as defined in Chapter 4.[2] The corrected VAR, using the so-called *Cornish-Fisher expansion,* is then obtained by replacing α in Equation (9.14) by

$$\alpha' = \alpha - \frac{1}{6}(\alpha^2 - 1)\xi \quad (9.15)$$

There is no correction under a normal distribution, for which skewness is zero. When there is negative skewness (i.e., a long left tail), VAR is increased.[3]

The second method is the *delta-gamma–Monte Carlo method,* which creates random simulations of the risk factors S and then uses the Taylor

---

2. Skewness can be computed as $\xi = [E(dV^3) - 3E(dV^2)E(dV) + 2E(dV)^3]/\sigma^3(dV)$ using the third moment of dV, which is $E(dV^3) = (9/2)\Delta^2\Gamma S^4\sigma^4 + (15/8)\Gamma^3 S^6\sigma^6$.

3. See also Zangari (1996).

approximation to create simulated movements in the option value. This method is also known as a *partial-simulation approach*. Note that this is still a local-valuation method because the portfolio is fully valued at the initial point V_0 only. The VAR can then be found from the empirical distribution of the portfolio value.

In theory, the delta-gamma method could be generalized to many sources of risk. In a multivariate framework, the Taylor expansion is

$$dV(S) = \Delta'dS + 1/2(dS)'\Gamma(dS) + \cdots \qquad (9.16)$$

where dS is now a vector of N changes in market prices, Δ is a vector of N deltas, and Γ is an N by N symmetrical matrix of gammas with respect to the various risk factors. While the diagonal components are conventional gamma measures, the off-diagonal terms are *cross-gammas,* or $\Gamma_{i,j} = \partial^2 V/\partial S_i \partial S_j$. For instance, the delta of options also depends on the implied volatility, which creates a cross-effect.

Unfortunately, the delta-gamma method is not practical with many sources of risk because the amount of data required increases geometrically. For instance, with $N = 100$, we need 100 estimates of Δ, 5050 estimates for the covariance matrix Σ, and an additional 5050 for the matrix Γ, which includes second derivatives of each position with respect to each source of risk. In practice, only the diagonal components are considered. Even so, a full Monte Carlo method provides a more direct route to VAR measurement for large portfolios.

9.1.4 Comparison of Methods

To summarize, Table 9–1 classifies the various VAR methods. Overall, each of these methods is best adapted to a different environment:

- For large portfolios where optionality is not a dominant factor, the delta-normal method provides a fast and efficient method for measuring VAR.
- For portfolios exposed to a few sources of risk and with substantial option components, the "Greeks" method provides increased precision at a low computational cost.
- For portfolios with substantial option components (such as mortgages) or longer horizons, a full-valuation method may be required.

It should be noted that the linear/nonlinear dichotomy also has implications for the choice of the VAR horizon. With linear models, as we

TABLE 9—1

Comparison of VAR Methods

Risk Factor Distribution	Valuation Method	
	Local Valuation	Full Valuation
Analytical	Delta-normal	Not used
	Delta-gamma-delta	
Simulated	Delta-gamma-MC	Monte Carlo (MC)
		Grid MC
		Historical

have seen in Chapter 4, daily VAR can be adjusted easily to other periods by simple scaling by a square root of time factor. This adjustment assumes that the position is constant and that daily returns are independent and identically distributed.

This time adjustment, however, is not valid for options positions. Since options can be replicated by dynamically changing positions in the underlying assets, the risk of options positions can be dramatically different from the scaled measure of daily risk. Therefore, *adjustments of daily volatility to longer horizons using the square root of time factor are valid only when positions are constant and when optionality in the portfolio is negligible.* For portfolios with substantial options components, the full-valuation method must be implemented over the desired horizon instead of scaling a daily VAR measure.

9.1.5 An Example: Leeson's Straddle

The Barings' story provides a good illustration of these various methods. In addition to the long futures positions described in Chapter 7, Leeson also sold options, about 35,000 calls and puts each on Nikkei futures. This position is known as a *short straddle* and is about delta-neutral because the positive delta from the call is offset by a negative delta from the put, assuming most of the options were at-the-money.

Leeson did not deal in small amounts. With a multiplier of 500 yen for the options contract and a 100-yen/$ exchange rate, the dollar exposure of the call options to the Nikkei was delta times $0.175 million. Initially, the market value of the position was zero. The position was

FIGURE 9–5

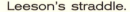

Leeson's straddle.

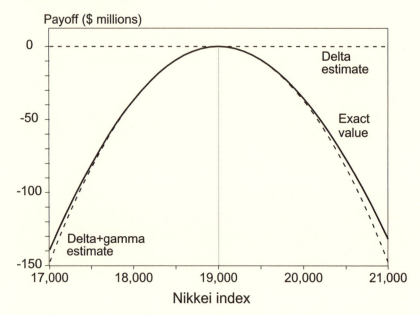

designed to turn in a profit if the Nikkei remained stable. Unfortunately, it also had an unlimited potential for large losses.

Figure 9–5 displays the payoffs from the straddle, using a Black-Scholes model with a 20 percent annual volatility. We assume that the options have a maturity of 3 months. At the current index value of 19,000, the delta VAR for this position is close to zero. Of course, reporting a zero delta-normal VAR is highly misleading. Any move up or down has the potential to create a large loss. A drop in the index to 17,000, for instance, would lead to an immediate loss of about $150 million. The graph also shows that the delta-gamma approximation provides increased accuracy. How do we compute the potential loss over a horizon of, say, 1 month?

The risks involved are described in Figure 9–6, which plots the frequency distribution of payoffs on the straddle using a *full Monte Carlo simulation* with 10,000 replications. This distribution is obtained from a revaluation of the portfolio after a month over a range of values for the Nikkei. Each replication uses full valuation with a remaining maturity of

FIGURE 9–6

Distribution of 1-month payoff for straddle.

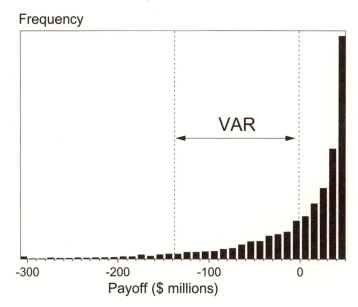

2 months (the 3-month original maturity minus the 1-month VAR horizon). The distribution looks highly skewed to the left. Its mean is $-\$1$ million, and the 95th percentile is $-\$139$ million. Hence the 1-month 95 percent VAR is $138 million.

How does the "Greeks" method fare for this portfolio? First, let us examine the delta-gamma-delta approximation. The total gamma of the position is the exposure times the sum of gamma for a call and put, or $0.175 million $\times$ 0.000422 = $0.0000739 million. Over a 1-month horizon, the standard deviation of the Nikkei is σS = 19,000 $\times$ 20 percent/$\sqrt{12}$ = 1089. Ignoring the time drift, the VAR is, from Equation (9.13),

$$\text{VAR} = \alpha \sqrt{\tfrac{1}{2}[\Gamma(\sigma S)^2]^2} = 1.65 \sqrt{\tfrac{1}{2}(\$0.0000739 \text{ million} \times 1089^2)^2}$$
$$= 1.65 \times \$62 \text{ million} = \$102 \text{ million}$$

This is substantially better than the delta-normal VAR of zero, which could have fooled us into believing the position was riskless.

Using the Cornish-Fisher expansion and a skewness coefficient of -2.83, we obtain a correction factor of $\alpha' = 1.65 - \tfrac{1}{6}(1.65^2 - 1)(-2.83)$

= 2.45. The refined VAR measure is then 2.45 × \$62 million = \$152 million, much closer to the true value of \$138 million.

Finally, we can turn to the delta-gamma–Monte Carlo approach, which consists of using the simulations of S but valuing the portfolio on the target date using only the partial derivatives. This yields a VAR of \$128 million, not too far from the true value. This variety of methods shows that the straddle had substantial downside risk.

And indeed the options position contributed to Barings' fall. As January 1995 began, the historical volatility on the Japanese market was very low, around 10 percent. At the time, the Nikkei was hovering around 19,000. The options position would have been profitable if the market had been stable. Unfortunately, this was not so. The Kobe earthquake struck Japan on January 17 and led to a drop in the Nikkei to 18,000, shown in Figure 9–7. To make things worse, options became more expensive as market volatility increased. Both the long futures and the straddle positions lost money. As losses ballooned, Leeson increased his exposure in a desperate attempt to recoup the losses, but to no avail. On February 27, the Nikkei dropped further to 17,000. Unable to meet the mounting margin calls, Barings went bust.

FIGURE 9–7

The Nikkei's fall.

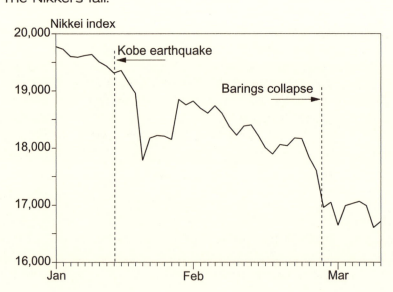

9.2 DELTA-NORMAL METHOD

9.2.1 Implementation

If the portfolio consisted of only securities with jointly normal distributions, the measurement of VAR would be relatively simple. The portfolio return is

$$R_{p,t+1} = \sum_{i=1}^{N} w_{i,t} R_{i,t+1} \qquad (9.17)$$

where the weights $w_{i,t}$ are indexed by time to recognize the dynamic nature of trading portfolios.

Since the portfolio return is a linear combination of normal variables, it is also normally distributed. Using matrix notations, the portfolio variance is given by

$$\sigma^2(R_{p,t+1}) = w_t' \Sigma_{t+1} w_t \qquad (9.18)$$

where Σ_{t+1} is the forecast of the covariance matrix over the VAR horizon.

The problem is that VAR must be measured for large and complex portfolios that evolve over time. The delta-normal method, which is explained in much greater detail in a subsequent chapter, simplifies the process by

- Specifying a list of risk factors
- Mapping the linear exposure of all instruments in the portfolio onto these risk factors
- Aggregating these exposures across instruments
- Estimating the covariance matrix of the risk factors
- Computing the total portfolio risk

This mapping produces a set of exposures $x_{i,t}$ aggregated across all instruments for each risk factor and measured in dollars. The portfolio VAR is then

$$\text{VAR} = \alpha \sqrt{x_t' \Sigma_{t+1} x_t} \qquad (9.19)$$

Within this class of models, two methods can be used to measure the variance-covariance matrix Σ. It can be solely based on historical data using, for example, a model that allows for time variation in risk. Alternatively, it can include implied risk measures from options. Or it can

FIGURE 9–8

Delta-normal method.

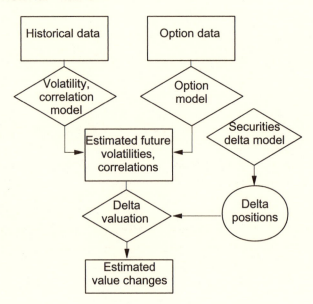

use a combination of both. As we saw in the preceding chapter, options-implied measures of risk are superior to historical data but are not available for every asset, let alone for pairs of assets. Figure 9–8 details the steps involved in this approach.

9.2.2 Advantages

The delta-normal method is particularly *easy* to implement because it involves a simple matrix multiplication. It is also *computationally fast,* even with a very large number of assets, because it replaces each position by its linear exposure.

As a parametric approach, VAR is easily *amenable to analysis,* since measures of marginal and incremental risk are a by-product of the VAR computation.

9.2.3 Problems

The delta-normal method can be subject to a number of criticisms. A first problem is the existence of *fat tails* in the distribution of returns on most financial assets. These fat tails are particularly worrisome precisely because VAR attempts to capture the behavior of the portfolio return in the left tail. In this situation, a model based on a normal distribution would underestimate the proportion of outliers and hence the true value at risk. As discussed in Chapter 8, some of these fat tails can be explained in terms of time variation in risk. However, even after adjustment, there are still too many observations in the tails. A simple ad hoc adjustment consists of increasing the parameter α to compensate, as is explained in Chapter 5.

Another problem is that the method inadequately measures the risk of *nonlinear instruments*, such as options or mortgages. Under the delta-normal method, options positions are represented by their "deltas" relative to the underlying asset. As we have seen in the preceding section, asymmetries in the distribution of options are not captured by the delta-normal VAR.

Lest we lead you into thinking that this method is inferior, we will now show that alternative methods are no panacea because they involve a quantum leap in difficulty. The delta-normal method is computationally easy to implement. It only requires the market values and exposures of current positions, combined with risk data. Also, in many situations, the delta-normal method provides adequate measurement of market risks.

9.3 HISTORICAL SIMULATION METHOD
9.3.1 Implementation

The historical simulation method provides a straightforward implementation of full valuation (Figure 9–9). It consists of going back in time, such as over the last 250 days, and applying current weights to a time-series of historical asset returns:

$$R_{p,k} = \sum_{i=1}^{N} w_{i,t} R_{i,k} \qquad k = 1, \ldots, t \qquad (9.20)$$

Note that the weights w_t are kept at their current values. This return does not represent an actual portfolio but rather reconstructs the history of a hypothetical portfolio using the current position. The approach is sometimes called *bootstrapping* because it involves using the actual distribution of recent historical data (without replacement).

More generally, full valuation requires a set of complete prices, such as yield curves, instead of just returns. Hypothetical future prices for scenario k are obtained from applying historical changes in prices to the current level of prices:

$$S^*_{i,k} = S_{i,0} + \Delta S_{i,k} \qquad i = 1, \ldots, N \qquad (9.21)$$

FIGURE 9–9

Historical simulation method.

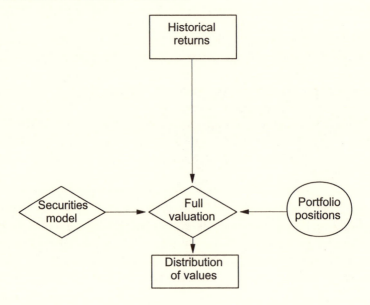

A new portfolio value $V^*_{p,k}$ is then computed from the full set of hypothetical prices, perhaps incorporating nonlinear relationships $V^*_k = V(S^*_{i,k})$. Note that to capture *vega risk,* due to changing volatilities, the set of prices can incorporate implied volatility measures. This creates the hypothetical return corresponding to simulation k:

$$R_{p,k} = \frac{V^*_k - V_0}{V_0} \qquad (9.22)$$

VAR is then obtained from the entire distribution of hypothetical returns, where each historical scenario is assigned the same weight of $(1/t)$.

As always, the choice of the sample period reflects a tradeoff between using longer and shorter sample sizes. Longer intervals increase the accuracy of estimates but could use irrelevant data, thereby missing important changes in the underlying process.

9.3.2 Advantages

This method is relatively *simple to implement* if historical data have been collected in-house for daily marking-to-market. The same data can then be stored for later reuse in estimating VAR.

Historical simulation also short-circuits the need to estimate a co-variance matrix. This *simplifies the computations* in cases of portfolios with a large number of assets and short sample periods. All that is needed is the time series of the aggregate portfolio return.

The method also deals directly with the *choice of horizon* for measuring VAR. Returns are simply measured over intervals that correspond to the length of the horizon. For instance, to obtain a monthly VAR, the user would reconstruct historical monthly portfolio returns over, say, the last 5 years.

By relying on actual prices, the method allows nonlinearities and nonnormal distributions. *Full valuation* is obtained in the simplest fashion: from historical data. The method captures gamma, vega risk, and correlations. It does not rely on specific assumptions about valuation models or the underlying stochastic structure of the market.

Perhaps most important, it can account for *fat tails* and, because it does not rely on valuation models, is not prone to model risk. The method is robust and intuitive and, as such, is perhaps the most widely used method to compute VAR.

9.3.3 Problems

On the other hand, the historical simulation method has a number of draw-backs. First, it assumes that we do have a *sufficient history* of price changes. To obtain 1000 independent simulations of a 1-day move, we require 4 years of continuous data. Some assets may have short histories, or there may not be a record of an asset's history.

Only *one sample path* is used. The assumption is that the past represents the immediate future fairly. If the window omits important events, the tails will not be well represented. Vice versa, the sample may contain events that will not reappear in the future.

And as we have demonstrated in Chapter 8, risk contains significant and predictable time variation. The simple historical simulation method presented here will miss situations with temporarily elevated volatility.[4] Worse, historical simulation will be very slow to incorporate *structural breaks,* which are handled more easily with an analytical methods such as RiskMetrics.

---

4. A simple method to allow time variation in risk proceeds as follows: First, fit a time-series model to the conditional volatility and construct historical scaled residuals. Second, perform a historical simulation on these residuals. Third, apply the most recent volatility forecast to the scaled portfolio volatility. For applications, see Hull and White (1998).

This approach is also subject to the same criticisms as the *moving-window estimation of variances*. The method puts the same weight on all observations in the window, including old data points. The measure of risk can change significantly after an old observation is dropped from the window.[5]

Likewise, the *sampling variation* of the historical simulation VAR will be much greater than for an analytical method. As is pointed out in Chapter 5, VAR is only a statistical estimate and may be subject to much estimation error if the sample size is too short. For instance, a 99 percent daily VAR estimated over a window of 100 days produces only one observation in the tail, which necessarily leads to an imprecise VAR measure. Thus very long sample paths are required to obtain meaningful quantiles. The dilemma is that this may involve observations that are not relevant.

A final drawback is that the method quickly becomes *cumbersome for large portfolios* with complicated structures. In practice, users adopt simplifications such as grouping interest rate payoffs into bands, which considerably increases the speed of computation. Regulators also have adopted such a "bucketing" approach. But if too many simplifications are carried out, such as replacing assets by their delta equivalents, the benefits of full valuation can be lost.

9.4 MONTE CARLO SIMULATION METHOD

9.4.1 Implementation

Monte Carlo (MC) simulations cover a wide range of possible values in financial variables and fully account for correlations. MC simulation is developed in more detail in a later chapter. In brief, the method proceeds in two steps. First, the risk manager specifies a stochastic process for financial variables as well as process parameters; parameters such as risk and correlations can be derived from historical or options data. Second, fictitious price paths are simulated for all variables of interest. At each horizon considered, the portfolio is marked-to-market using full valuation as in the historical simulation method, $V_k^* = V(S_{i,k}^*)$. Each of these "pseudo" realizations is then used to compile a distribution of returns,

---

5. To alleviate this problem, Boudoukh et al. (1998) propose a scheme whereby each observation R_k is assigned a weight w_k that declines as it ages. The distribution is then obtained from ranking the R_k and cumulating the associated weights to find the selected confidence level.

FIGURE 9–10

Monte Carlo method.

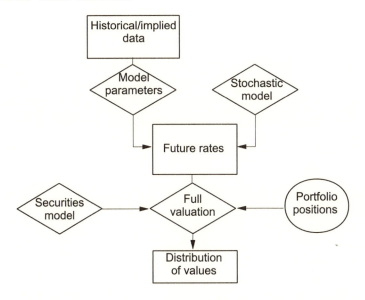

from which a VAR figure can be measured. The method is summarized in Figure 9–10.

The Monte Carlo method is thus similar to the historical simulation method, except that the hypothetical changes in prices ΔS_i for asset i in Equation (9.20) are created by random draws from a prespecified stochastic process instead of sampled from historical data.

9.4.2 Advantages

Monte Carlo analysis is by far the most *powerful method* to compute VAR. It can account for a wide range of exposures and risks, including *nonlinear price risk,* volatility risk, and even model risk. It is flexible enough to incorporate time variation in volatility, *fat tails,* and extreme scenarios. Simulations generate *the entire pdf,* not just one quantile, and can be used to examine, for instance, the expected loss beyond a particular VAR.

MC simulation also can incorporate the *passage of time,* which will create structural changes in the portfolio. This includes the time decay of options; the daily settlement of fixed, floating, or contractually specified cash flows; or the effect of prespecified trading or hedging strategies.

These effects are especially important as the time horizon lengthens, which is the case for the measurement of credit risk.

9.4.3 Problems

The biggest drawback of this method is its *computational time*. If 1000 sample paths are generated with a portfolio of 1000 assets, the total number of valuations amounts to 1 million. In addition, if the valuation of assets on the target date involves itself a simulation, the method requires a "simulation within a simulation." This quickly becomes too onerous to implement on a frequent basis.

This method is the most *expensive to implement* in terms of systems infrastructure and intellectual development. The MC simulation method is relatively onerous to develop from scratch, despite rapidly falling prices for hardware. Perhaps, then, it should be purchased from outside vendors. On the other hand, when the institution already has in place a system to model complex structures using simulations, implementing MC simulation is less costly because the required expertise is in place. Also, these are situations where proper risk management of complex positions is absolutely necessary.

Another potential weakness of the method is *model risk*. MC relies on specific stochastic processes for the underlying risk factors as well as pricing models for securities such as options or mortgages. Therefore, it is subject to the risk that the models are wrong. To check if the results are robust to changes in the model, simulation results should be complemented by some sensitivity analysis.

Finally, VAR estimates from MC simulation are subject to *sampling variation,* which is due to the limited number of replications. Consider, for instance, a case where the risk factors are jointly normal and all payoffs linear. The delta-normal method will then provide the correct measure of VAR, in one easy step. MC simulations based on the same covariance matrix will give only an approximation, albeit increasingly good as the number of replications increases.

Overall, this method is probably the most comprehensive approach to measuring market risk if modeling is done correctly. To some extent, the method can even handle credit risks. This is why a full chapter is devoted to the implementation of Monte Carlo simulation methods.

9.5 EMPIRICAL COMPARISONS

It is instructive to compare the VAR numbers obtained from the three methods discussed. Hendricks (1996), for instance, calculated 1-day VARs for randomly selected foreign currency portfolios using a delta-normal method based on fixed windows of equal weights and exponential weights as well as a historical simulation method.

Table 9–2 summarizes the results, which are compared in terms of percentage of outcomes falling within the VAR forecast. The middle column shows that all methods give a coverage that is very close to the ideal number, which is the 95 percent confidence level. At the 99 percent confidence level, however, the delta-normal methods seem to underestimate VAR slightly, since their coverage falls short of the ideal 99 percent.

Hendricks also reports that the delta-normal VAR measures should be increased by about 9 to 15 percent to achieve correct coverage. In other words, the fat tails in the data could be modeled by choosing a

TABLE 9–2

Empirical Comparison of VAR Methods:
Fraction of Outcomes Covered

Method	95% VAR	99% VAR
Delta-normal Equal weights over		
50 days	95.1%	98.4%
250 days	95.3%	98.4%
1250 days	95.4%	98.5%
Delta-normal Exponential weights:		
$\lambda = 0.94$	94.7%	98.2%
$\lambda = 0.97$	95.0%	98.4%
$\lambda = 0.99$	95.4%	98.5%
Historical simulation Equal weights over		
125 days	94.4%	98.3%
250 days	94.9%	98.8%
1250 days	95.1%	99.0%

distribution with a greater α parameter. A Student t distribution with four to six degrees of freedom, for example, would be appropriate.

As important, when the VAR number is exceeded, the tail event is, on average, 30 to 40 percent greater than the risk measure. In some instances, it is several times greater. As Hendricks states, "This makes it clear that VAR measures—even at the 99th percentile—do not bound possible losses."

This empirical analysis, however, examined positions with *linear* risk profiles. The delta-normal methods could prove less accurate with options positions, although it should be much faster. Pritsker (1997) examines the tradeoff between speed and accuracy for a portfolio of options.

Table 9–3 reports the accuracy of various methods, measured as the mean absolute percentage error in VAR, as well as their computational times. The table shows that the delta method, as expected, has the highest average absolute error, at 5.34 percent of the true VAR. It is also by far the fastest method, with an execution time of 0.08 seconds. At the other end, the most accurate method is the full Monte Carlo, which comes arbitrarily close to the true VAR, but with an average run time of 66 seconds. In between, the delta-gamma-delta, delta-gamma–Monte Carlo, and grid Monte Carlo methods offer a tradeoff between accuracy and speed.

An interesting but still unresolved issue is, How would these approximations work in the context of large, diversified bank portfolios? There is very little evidence on this point. The industry initially seemed to prefer the analytical covariance approach due to its simplicity. With the rapidly decreasing cost of computing power, however, there is now

TABLE 9–3

Accuracy and Speed of VAR Methods:
99 Percent VAR for Option Portfolios

Method	Accuracy: Mean Absolute Error in VAR (%)	Speed: Computation Time, s
Delta	5.34	0.08
Delta-gamma-delta	4.72	1.17
Delta-gamma-MC	3.08	3.88
Grid Monte Carlo	3.07	32.19
Full Monto Carlo	0	66.27

a marked trend toward the generalized use of historical simulation methods.

9.6 SUMMARY

We can distinguish a number of different methods to measure VAR. At the most fundamental level, they separate into local (or analytical) valuation and full valuation. This separation reflects a tradeoff between speed of computation and accuracy of valuation.

Delta models can use parameters based on historical data, such as those implemented by RiskMetrics, or on implied data, where volatilities are derived from options. Both methods generate a covariance matrix, to which the "delta" or linear positions are applied to find the portfolio VAR. Among full-valuation models, the historical simulation method is the easiest to implement. It simply relies on historical data for securities valuation and applies the most current weight to historical prices. Finally, the most complete model, but also the most difficult to implement, is the Monte Carlo simulation approach, which imposes a particular stochastic process on the financial variables of interest, from which various sample paths are simulated. Full valuation for each sample path generates a distribution of portfolio values.

Table 9–4 describes the pros and cons of each method. The choice of the method largely depends on the composition of the portfolio. For portfolios with no options (nor embedded options) and whose distributions are close to the normal pdf, the delta-normal method may well be the best choice. VAR will be relatively easy to compute, fast, and accurate. In addition, it is not too prone to model risk (due to faulty assumptions or computations). The resulting VAR is easy to explain to management and to the public. Because the method is analytical, it allows easy analysis of the VAR results using marginal and component VAR measures. For portfolios with options positions, however, the method may not be appropriate. Instead, users should turn to a full-valuation method.

The second method, historical simulation, is also relatively easy to implement and uses actual, full valuation of all securities. However, its typical implementation does not account for time variation in risk, and the method relies on a narrow window only.

In theory, the Monte Carlo approach can alleviate all these technical difficulties. It can incorporate nonlinear positions, nonnormal distributions, implied parameters, and even user-defined scenarios. The price to pay for this flexibility, however, is heavy. Computer and data require-

T A B L E 9–4

Comparison of Approaches to VAR

Features	Delta-Normal	Historical Simulation	Monto Carlo Simulation
Positions			
Valuation	Linear	Full	Full
Distribution			
Shape	Normal	Actual	General
Time-varying	Yes	Possible	Yes
Implied data	Possible	No	Possible
Extreme events	Low probability	In recent data	Possible
Use correlations	Yes	Yes	Yes
VAR precision	Excellent	Poor with short window	Good with many iterations
Implementation			
Ease of computation	Yes	Intermediate	No
Accuracy	Depends on portfolio	Yes	Yes
Communicability	Easy	Easy	Difficult
VAR analysis	Easy, analytical	More difficult	More difficult
Major pitfalls	Nonlinearities, fat tails	Time-variation in risk, unusual events	Model risk

ments are a quantum step above the other two approaches, model risk looms large, and value at risk loses its intuitive appeal. As the price of computing power continues to fall, however, this method is bound to take on increasing importance.

In practice, all these methods are used. A recent survey by Britain's Financial Services Authority has revealed that 42 percent of banks use the covariance matrix approach, 31 percent use historical simulation, and 23 percent use the Monte Carlo approach. The delta-normal method, which is the easiest to implement, appears to be the most widespread.

All these methods present some advantages. They are also related. Monte Carlo analysis of linear positions with normal returns, for instance, should yield the same result as the delta-normal method. Perhaps the best lesson from this chapter is to check VAR measures with different methodologies and then to analyze the sources of differences.

CHAPTER 10

Stress Testing

> This is one of those cases in which the imagination is baffled by the facts.
>
> *Winston Churchill*

The main purpose of value-at-risk (VAR)–type risk measures is to quantify potential losses under "normal" market conditions. In principle, increasing the confidence level could progressively uncover large but unlikely losses. The problem is that VAR measures based on recent historical data can fail to identify extreme unusual situations that could cause severe losses. This is why VAR methods should be supplemented by a regular program of stress testing.

Stress testing is indeed required by the Basel Committee as one of seven conditions to be satisfied to use internal models. It is also endorsed by the Derivatives Policy Group and by the G-30 (in recommendation 6). Unfortunately, stress-testing guidelines generally are vague. There is also much confusion in the industry about the application and use of stress testing.

Stress testing can be described as a process to identify and manage situations that could cause extraordinary losses. This can be made with a set of tools, including (1) scenario analysis, (2) stressing models, volatilities, and correlations, and (3) policy responses.

Scenario analysis consists of evaluating the portfolio under various states of the world. Typically, these involve large movements in key variables, which require the application of full-valuation methods. The first applications of stress tests consisted of sequentially moving key variables by a large amount. This, however, ignores correlations. More generally, scenarios provide a description of the joint movements in financial variables and can be either *historical* or *prospective,* i.e., drawn from historical events or from plausible economic and political developments.

More recently, the industry has realized that the identification of scenarios should be driven by the particular portfolio at hand. For example, a highly leveraged portfolio with a long position in corporate bonds offset by a short position in Treasuries could suffer sharp losses if correlations broke down. The scenario should then be structured to create unusual decreases in correlations. Other portfolios will be vulnerable under other situations.

Whenever the stress tests reveal some weakness, management must take steps to handle the identified risks. One solution could be to set aside enough capital to absorb potential large losses. Too often, however, this amount will be cripplingly large, reducing the return on capital. Alternatively, positions can be altered to reduce the exposure. The goal is to ensure that the institution can ride out the turmoil. In other words, stress testing can help to guarantee the very survival of the institution.

Section 10.1 discusses why stress testing is required at all. In theory, extreme events could be identified by increasing the confidence level of VAR measures. Section 10.2 shows how to use scenarios to generate portfolio losses. Sections 10.3 and 10.4 then examine scenario analysis in great detail. Next, Section 10.5 turns to stress testing of the model parameters. Section 10.6 then discusses management actions that can be taken in response to stress-test results.

10.1 WHY STRESS TESTING?

Compared with VAR methods, stress testing appears refreshingly simple and intuitive. The first step is scenario analysis, which examines the effect of simulated large movements in key financial variables on the portfolio. Due to its simplicity, this approach actually predates VAR methods.

To understand the need for scenario analysis, consider, for instance, the stock market crash of October 19, 1987. Figure 10–1 displays the distribution of U.S. daily stock returns using data from 1984 to 1998. Over this period, the average volatility was about 1 percent per day. On Monday October 19, the S&P index lost 20 percent of its value.

Even if there was some time variation in volatility, this 20 standard deviation event was so far away in the tail that it should have never happened under a normal distribution. The figure also shows that a standard 99 percent VAR interval would have totally missed the magnitude of the actual loss.

FIGURE 10–1

Distribution of daily U.S. stock returns, 1984–1998.

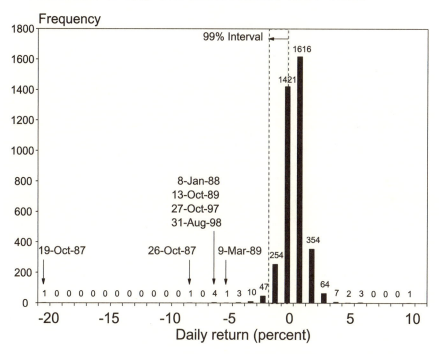

More generally, Bookstaber (1997) says that

> A general rule of thumb is that every financial market experiences one or more daily price moves of 4 standard deviations or more each year. And in any year, there is usually at least one market that has a daily move that is greater than 10 standard deviations.

These remarks, however, are an indictment of the distributional assumption rather than VAR itself. In theory, one could fit a better distribution to the data and vary the confidence level so as to cover more and more of the left-tail events. This can be accomplished with historical simulations or, if a smoother distribution is required, through the use of extreme value theory (EVT), which is described in the appendix to this chapter. In other words, the generation of a scenario is akin to a particular point in the distribution drawn from historical data. So what is special about stress testing?

The goal of stress testing is to identify unusual scenarios that would not occur under standard VAR models. Berkowitz (2000) classifies these scenarios into the following categories:

1. Simulating shocks that have never occurred or are more likely to occur than historical observation suggests
2. Simulating shocks that reflect permanent structural breaks or temporarily changed statistical patterns

The first reason to stress test is that VAR measures typically use recent historical data. Stress testing, in contrast, considers situations that are absent from historical data or not well represented but nonetheless likely. Alternatively, stress tests are useful to identify states of the world where historical relationships break down, either temporarily or permanently.

B O X   10–1

VICTOR NIEDERHOFFER: THE EDUCATION OF A SPECULATOR

Victor Niederhoffer outlined his investment philosphy in his book, *Education of a Speculator,* which quickly became a best-seller. An eccentric and brilliant investor, he was a legend of the hedge fund business. Indeed, he had compiled an outstanding track record—a 32 percent compound annual return since 1982.

Niederhoffer's mission was to "apply science" to the market. Although he had a Ph.D. in business from the University of Chicago, he did not believe in efficient markets and traded on statistical anomalies. He believed, for instance, that the market would never drop by more than 5 percent in a single day. Putting this theory into practice, Niederhoffer sold naked out-of-the-money puts on stock index futures. When the stock market plummeted by 7 percent on October 27, 1997, he was unable to meet margin calls for some $50 million. His brokers liquidated the positions, wiping out his funds.

Apparently, his views were narrowly based on recent history. It is true that the worst loss had been 3.1 percent in the previous 5-year period. Larger losses do occur once in a while, however. Most notably, the market lost 20.4 percent on October 19, 1987.

A direct example of the need for stress testing is Niederhoffer's belief, described in Box 10–1, that the market would not drop by more than 5 percent in a day. Indeed, this did not happen from 1990 to October 1997. This does not mean that a loss of this magnitude can never happen.

Another illustration is a breakup of a fixed exchange rate system. In the summer of 1992, it would have been useful to assess potential vulnerabilities in the European Monetary System. Indeed, in September 1992, the Italian lira and the British pound abandoned their fixed exchange rates, which led to a disastrous fall in their value. Historical volatilities based on the previous 2 years would have completely missed the possibility of a devaluation. Thus scenario analysis forces managers to consider events they might otherwise ignore.

10.2 IMPLEMENTING SCENARIO ANALYSIS

We now consider the implementation of scenario analysis. Define s as a selected scenario. This is constructed as a set of changes in risk factors $\Delta f_{k,s}$ for various k. Based on the new hypothetical risk-factor values $f_{k,0} + \Delta f_{k,s}$, all the securities in the portfolio are then revalued, preferably using a full-valuation method. The portfolio return is derived from the individual changes in securities values $R_{i,s}$ as

$$R_{p,s} = \sum_{i=1}^{N} w_{i,t} R_{i,s} \qquad (10.1)$$

Note that this process is akin to the historical simulation method, except that the scenario is indexed by time and all scenarios are given the same probability in the other method. Figure 10–2 details the steps involved in this approach. The question is how to generate realistic scenarios.

10.3 GENERATING UNIDIMENSIONAL SCENARIOS

10.3.1 Stylized Scenarios

The traditional approach to scenario analysis focuses on one variable at a time. For instance, the Derivatives Policy Group provides specific guidelines for scenarios. It recommends focusing on a set of specific movements:

1. Parallel yield curve shifting by ± 100 basis points
2. Yield curve twisting by ± 25 basis points

FIGURE 10-2

Scenario analysis approach.

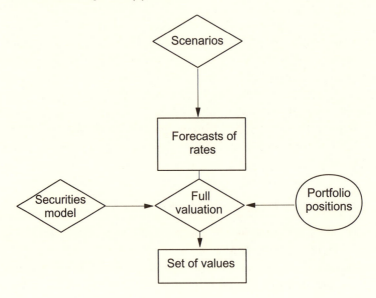

3. Each of the four combinations or yield curves shift and twist
4. (Implied) volatilities changing by ±20 percent of current values
5. Equity index values changing by ±10 percent
6. Currencies moving by ±6 percent for major currencies and ±20 percent for others
7. Swap spreads changing by ±20 basis points

While these movements are quite large for a daily horizon, the DPG's goal was to provide comparable results across institutions in order to assess zones of vulnerabilities. By specifying consistent guidelines, it tried to ensure that all the models used by brokers "possess broadly similar performance."

These scenarios shock risk factors one at a time (apart from the third scenario). This method is appropriate in situations where the portfolio depends primarily on one source of risk. The Office of Thrift Supervision (OTS), for instance, uses scenario analysis to assess the market risk of savings and loan associations (S&Ls).[1] The OTS requires institutions to estimate what would happen to their economic value under parallel shifts in the yield curve varying from −400 to +400 basis points. The OTS recently has imposed a risk-based capital requirement directly linked to the interest-rate exposure of supervised institutions.

10.3.2 An Example: The SPAN System

The Standard Portfolio Analysis of Risk (SPAN) system is a good example of a scenario-based method for measuring portfolio risk. SPAN was introduced in 1988 by the Chicago Mercantile Exchange (CME) to calculate collateral requirements on the basis of overall portfolio risk. Since its inception, SPAN had become widely used by futures and options exchanges as a mechanism to set margin requirements.

The objective of the SPAN system is to identify movements in portfolio values under a series of scenarios. SPAN then searches for the largest loss that a portfolio may suffer and sets the margin at that level. The SPAN system only aggregates futures and options on the same underlying instrument. It uses full-valuation methods, given the emphasis on options.

Consider, for instance, a portfolio of futures and options on futures involving the \$/€ exchange rate. SPAN scans the portfolio value over a range of prices and volatilities. These ranges are selected so that they cover a fixed percentage of losses, e.g., 99 percent. Consider, for instance, a contract with notional of €125,000 and current price of \$1.05/€. Assuming a 12 percent annual volatility, the price range is set at the daily VAR:

$$\text{Price range} = 2.33 \times (12 \text{ percent}/\sqrt{252})$$
$$\times (€125,000 \times 1.05\$/€) = \$2310$$

This is indeed close to the daily margin for a futures position. Next, the volatility range is set at 1 percent.

Table 10–1 presents an example of scenario generation. We select scenarios starting from the initial rate plus and minus three equal steps that cover the price range, as well as an up and down move for the volatility. In addition, to provide protection for short positions in deep out-of-the-money options, two scenarios are added with extreme price

---

1. The OTS is a U.S. agency created in 1989 to supervise S&Ls.

T A B L E 10–1

Example of SPAN Scenario System

	Scenario			Gain/Loss	
	Fraction Considered for P&L	Price Scan	Volatility Scan (expressed in range)	Long Call	Long Futures
1	100%	0	1	$198	$0
2	100%	0	−1	−$188	$0
3	100%	+1/3	1	$395	$767
4	100%	+1/3	−1	−$21	$767
5	100%	−1/3	1	$23	−$767
6	100%	−1/3	−1	−$332	−$767
7	100%	+2/3	1	$615	$1533
8	100%	+2/3	−1	$170	$1533
9	100%	−2/3	1	−$132	−$1533
10	100%	−2/3	−1	−$455	−$1533
11	100%	+1	1	$858	$2300
12	100%	+1	−1	$388	$2300
13	100%	−1	1	−$268	−$2300
14	100%	−1	−1	−$559	−$2300
15	35%	+2	0	$517	$1610
16	35%	−2	0	−$240	−$1610
Ranges:		$0.0061	1%		

Note: Euro-FX futures and option on futures with notional of €125,000, spot of 1.05$/€, strike of $1.10, 12 percent annual volatility, 90 days to maturity, and interest rate of 5 percent.

movements, defined as double the maximum range. Since these price changes are so rare, the margin required is 35 percent of the resulting loss. The value of each option and futures position is calculated under each scenario, using full valuation. The table presents calculations for two positions only, long a call and long a futures, under each of the 16 scenarios.

The long call position would suffer the most under scenario 14, with a large downward move in the futures accompanied by a drop in the volatility. Similarly, the worst loss for a long futures position also occurs under a large downward move. This analysis is repeated for all options and futures in the portfolio and aggregated across all positions. Finally, the margin is set to the worst portfolio loss under all scenarios.

The SPAN system is a scenario-based approach with full valuation. Its systematic scanning approach is feasible because it considers only two risk factors. The number of combinations, however, would soon become unmanageable for a greater number of factors. This is perhaps the greatest hurdle to systematic scenario analysis.

Another drawback is that the approach essentially places the same probability on most of the scenarios, which ignores correlations between risk factors. And as we have seen, correlations are an essential component of portfolio risk.

10.4 MULTIDIMENSIONAL SCENARIO ANALYSIS

10.4.1 Unidimensional versus Multidimensional

Unidimensional scenarios provide an intuitive understanding of the effect of movements in key variables, using a bottom-up approach. The problem is that they do not account for correlations. This is where multidimensional scenarios are so valuable. The process consists of (1) positing a state of the world and (2) inferring movements in market variables as in a top-down approach.

10.4.2 Prospective Scenarios

Prospective scenarios represent hypothetical one-off surprises that are studied for their implications for financial markets. One might want to examine, for instance, the effect of an earthquake in Tokyo, of Korean reunification, of a war in an oil-producing region, or of a major sovereign default. The definition of scenarios should be done with input from top managers, who are most familiar with the firm's business and extreme events that may affect it.

Let us go back to the example of a scenario analysis for a potential breakup in the Exchange Rate Mechanism (ERM), evaluated as of summer 1992. The risk manager could hypothesize a 20 percent fall in the value of the lira against the mark. One could further surmise that if the Italian central bank let the lira float, short-term rates could likewise drop and the stock market would rally. Beyond the effect on Italian interest rates and equity prices, however, it may not be obvious to come up with plausible scenarios for other financial variables. The problem is that the portfolio may have large exposures to these other risk factors that remain hidden. Thus this type of subjective scenario analysis is not well suited to large, complex portfolios.

10.4.3 Factor Push Method

Some implementations of stress testing try to account for multidimensionality using a rough two-step procedure. First, push up and down all risk-factor variables individually by, say, 2.33 standard deviations, and then compute the changes to the portfolio. Second, evaluate a worst-case scenario, where all variables are pushed in the direction that creates the worst loss. For instance, variable 1 could be pushed up by $\alpha\sigma_1$, whereas variable 2 is pushed down by $\alpha\sigma_2$, and so on.

This approach is very conservative but completely ignores correlations. If variables 1 and 2 are highly and positively correlated, it makes little sense to consider moves in opposite directions. Further, looking at extreme movements may not be appropriate. Some positions such as combinations of long positions in options will lose the most money if the underlying variables do not move at all.

10.4.3 Conditional Scenario Method

There is a systematic method, however, to incorporate correlations across all variables consistently. Let us represent the "key" variables that are subject to some extreme movements as R^*. The other variables are simply represented by R. The usual approach to stress testing focuses solely on R^*, setting the other values to zero. Let us call this the *narrow stress loss* (NSL) = $\Sigma_i w_i^* R_i^*$.

To account for multidimensionality, we first regress the R variables on the controlled R^* variables, obtaining the conditional forecast from

$$R_j = \alpha_j + \sum_i \beta_j R_i^* + \epsilon_j = E(R_j \mid R^*) + \epsilon_j \qquad (10.2)$$

This allows us to predict other variables conditional on movements in key variables using information in the covariance matrix.

We can construct a *predicted stress loss* as PSL = $\Sigma_i w_i^* R_i^*$ + $\Sigma_j w_j E(R_j \mid R^*)$. This can be compared with the realized, *actual stress loss,* which is ASL = $\Sigma_i w_i^* R_i^* + \Sigma_j w_j R_j$.

Kupiec (1998) illustrates this method with 102 episodes of large moves from April 1993 to January 1998 using a \$1 million portfolio invested in eight equity markets and four bond markets. Table 10–2 presents typical results. For the Philippine peso, for instance, the narrow stress loss is \$3070. The predicted and actual losses are much smaller, due to

TABLE 10-2

Comparison of Forecast Losses on a $1 Million Portfolio

Key Variable	Period	Event Size (σ)	Position Key Variable	Narrow	Stress Loss	
					Predicted	Actual
Philippine peso	11 Jul. 1997	-5.50	$40,700	-$3,070	$43	$190
Japanese equities	23 Jan. 1995	-5.23	$72,120	-$2,700	-$7,730	-$11,700
U.S. equities	27 Oct. 1997	-4.93	$136,480	-$6,650	-$5,330	-$5,420
U.K. bonds	29 Dec. 1994	-4.84	$122,910	-$2,640	-$3,550	-$3,030
U.S. bonds	20 Feb. 1996	-4.86	$122,970	-$1,210	-$7,070	-$10,380

the fact that other markets (including Philippine equities) move in the opposite way. In contrast, the $2700 loss for Japanese equities is made much worse by movements in other markets.

In all cases, the predicted stress loss produces results that are much closer to the actual stress loss than in the simple, narrow model that zeroes out nonkey variables. The conclusion is that the covariance matrix, which is at the core of conditional normal VAR modeling, does provide useful information for stress-testing analysis. It is only in cases where correlations totally break down that the method can fail to predict losses.

10.4.5 Historical Scenarios

Alternatively, scenario analysis can examine historical data to provide examples of joint movements in financial variables. The role of the risk manager is to identify scenarios, such as those listed in Table 10–3, that may be outside the VAR window. Each of these scenarios will then yield a set of joint movements in financial variables that automatically takes correlations into account.

For instance, Table 10–4 looks at the stock market crash of October 1987. On Monday October 19, the S&P index lost more than 20 percent of its value. The sheer size of this movement had dramatic effects on other prices. The next day, the Nikkei fell by 15 percent. In order to forestall the failure of financial institutions, the Federal Reserve injected liquidity in the financial system, pushing short-term interest rates down by 91 ba-

TABLE 10–3

Examples of Historical Scenarios

Scenario	Period
Oil price stock	January 1974
Stock market crash	October 1987
European Monetary System crisis	September 1992
Bond market crash	April 1994
Mexican devaluation	December 1994
Asian currency crisis	Summer 1997
Russian credit crisis	August 1998

TABLE 10–4

October 1987 Market Crash: Change in Market Variables

Date	Equities				Fixed Income			Currencies	
	U.S., S&P	Japan, Nikkei	U.K., FTSE	Germany, DAX	Fed Funds	3-mo T-Bill	30 yr T-Bond	Yen/$	DM/$
Oct 19	−20.4%	−2.4%	−9.1%	−9.4%	−0.14 bp	−0.52 bp	0.01 bp	−0.2%	−1.3%
Oct 20	5.3%	−14.9%	−11.4%	−1.4%	−0.77 bp	−0.62 bp	−0.76 bp	1.5%	1.7%

FIGURE 10–3

Monthly U.S. stock returns, 1900–1998.

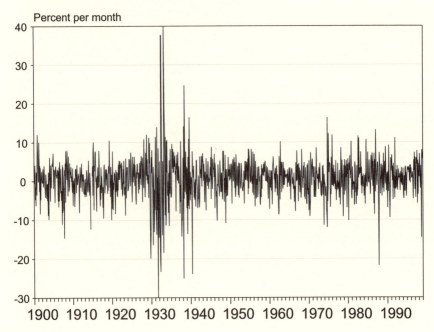

sis points in 2 days. This chaos, however, had apparently little effect on currency markets.

Historical scenarios are quite useful to measure joint movements in financial variables. Their drawback, from the risk manager's perspective, is the limited number of extreme events. Whenever possible, very long histories should be considered. These give a long-term perspective that may be absent from recent data.

The October 1987 crash, for instance, is widely viewed as an extremely unusual event. Perhaps so if one looks only at recent data. On the other hand, a different perspective is offered by Figure 10–3, which reports monthly returns on U.S. stocks since the beginning of the century. The figure shows that if one goes back sufficiently in time, there have been many other instances of losses exceeding 20 percent over a month and that the recent past has not been unusually volatile.

Likewise, events such as sovereign defaults are extremely rare. Recently, however, Russia defaulted on its domestic debt and Ecuador on its Brady bonds.[2] One would need to go back to the 1930s to encounter sovereign defaults on external debt. Defaults should be expected to occur, however. Otherwise, there would be no rationale for the wide yield spread observed on some sovereign debt.

10.4.6 Systematic Scenarios

Historical or prospective stress tests, while intuitive, may not reveal the most dangerous states of the world. With large, complex portfolios, losses can arise from unexpected combinations of financial risk factors.

Another practical method relies on the output from a VAR Monte Carlo analysis. Instead of focusing on a particular quantile, the risk manager could examine the worst losses from the simulation. These should reveal the particular combinations of risk factors that could spell danger for the institution. The question is whether the combination of variables could occur with even greater impact. In any case, such analysis provides valuable insight into the vulnerabilities of a particular portfolio.

Another approach is the *maximum-loss criterion*. This aims at identifying the worst loss through an optimization that respects the correlations between the risk-factor movements Δf:

$$ML = \min \text{loss}(\Delta f) \qquad \text{subject to} \qquad \Delta f' \Sigma^{-1} \Delta f \leq c \qquad (10.3)$$

where $\text{loss}(\Delta f)$ is a loss value that depends on the realization of Δf, Σ is the covariance matrix of the risk factors, and c is a confidence level that can be changed as needed. Studer (1999) provides examples of such an optimization.

10.5 STRESS TESTING MODEL PARAMETERS

Going back to the schematics of scenario analysis in Figure 10–2, we should critically examine all the steps in the generation of risk measures. A stress-testing process should consider not only movements in market variables but also the other components of the risk-management system, i.e., the securities valuation models and the risk engine.

A distinction is usually made between *sensitivity analysis,* which examines the effect of changing the functional form of the model, and stress testing *model parameters,* which are inputs into the model.

---

2. *Brady* bonds are dollar-denominated sovereign bonds issued principally in exchange for Latin American bank loans of the 1980s.

Let us consider sensitivity analysis first. Derivatives securities can be priced using a variety of models. Interest rate derivatives, for instance, can be valued using one- or multiple-factor models, with parameters typically estimated from historical data. Mortgage-backed securities must in addition model prepayments. All these assumptions introduce insidious risks. Current model prices may fit the current market data but may not provide a good approximation under large movements in key variables. The Askin story (see Box 1–1) provides an example of an MBS portfolio that was thought to be hedged but led to large losses under severe interest rate shocks. Pricing models may fail in changing environments.

Likewise, simplifications in the risk-measurement system also may create hidden risks. For example, bond mapping replaces a continuous-yield curve by a finite number of risk factors. If there is insufficient *granularity,* or detail, in the choice of the risk factors, the portfolio could be exposed to losses that are not measured by the risk-management system.

Turning to *model parameters,* pricing and risk-management systems rely on particular input data, such as a set of volatilities and correlations. Correlations, however, may deviate sharply from historical averages in times of stress. A key issue is whether a traditional variance-covariance–based VAR system provides adequate measures of risk when historical correlation patterns break down.

To some extent, this question can be answered directly by scenario analysis based on historical data. It is also informative, however, to check how sensitive a VAR number is to changes in the risk measures. As will be seen in the example of LTCM, this is especially important if the same period is used to measure risk and optimize the portfolio, given random estimation error in correlations.

As an example, consider a covariance matrix measured with recent data that shows a high correlation between two series. The risk manager, however, cannot believe that this high correlation will remain in the future and could alter the covariance matrix toward values that are considered reasonable.[3] The stress test then compares the new VAR measure with the original one.

---

3. This is no easy matter, since changing some entries manually could produce an inconsistent matrix, which is not positive-semidefinite (see Chapter 7). A positive-semidefinite matrix ensures that for any value of the vector w, the product $w'\Sigma w$ will never be negative. Rebonato and Jäckel (1999) describe methods to ensure that this will be the case.

In all these cases, there is no simple rule to follow for stress testing. Rather, the risk manager must be aware of limitations, assumptions, and measurement errors in the system. Stress testing can be described as the art of checking whether the risk forecasts are robust to changes in the structure of the system.

10.6 MANAGING STRESS TESTS

10.6.1 Scenario Analysis and Risk Models

One important but often ignored issue is how to incorporate stress-test results into traditional risk models. Consider, for instance, a single-scenario analysis, to which the risk manager assigns a probability π. This measure can be subjective or modeled in some fashion. For instance, the probability of a devaluation can increase as a currency becomes overvalued according to some fundamental indicator, such as purchasing power parity, or perhaps some global index of volatility.

To recognize how scenario analysis can be folded into a new distribution, consider that a traditional historical simulation simply assigns a weight of $(1/T)$ to all returns, where T is the number of observations. Berkowitz (2000) argues that the most consistent method to incorporate stress tests is to construct a new probability distribution from the combination of the usual distribution with weight $(1 - \pi)$ and the stress-test loss with weight π.

If the stress test is well designed, the new distribution will represent prospective losses better. The question is what to do if the size of the losses appears unacceptably large.

10.6.2 Management Response

This is the crux of the issue with stress testing. Too often stress-testing results are ignored because they involve large losses that are dismissed as irrelevant.

Indeed, institutions do not need to withstand every single state of the world. Central banks, in particular, are supposed to provide protection against systemic banking crises. Likewise, there is little point in trying to protect against a widespread nuclear war.

Relevant scenarios, however, require careful planning. One response is for the institution to set aside enough capital to absorb the worst losses revealed by stress tests. In many cases, however, this amount may be much too large, which will make setting it aside uneconomical.

A number of other actions can be considered, though. The institution could

- Purchase protection or insurance for the events in question (although this may transform market risk into counterparty risk)
- Modify the portfolio to decrease the impact of a particular event through exposure reduction or diversification across assets
- Restructure the business or product mix for better diversification
- Develop a plan for a corrective course of action should a particular scenario start to unfold
- Prepare sources of alternative funding should the portfolio liquidity suffer

This plan of action should help ensure that the institution will survive this scenario as shown in Box 10–2.

10.7 CONCLUSIONS

While VAR focuses on the dispersion of revenues, stress testing instead examines the tails. Stress testing is an essential component of a risk-management system because it can help to ensure the survival of an in-

---

B O X   10–2

STRESS TESTING'S BENEFITS

A risk manager at a U.S. investment bank recalls that in December 1997, stress tests showed that the firm could be put in jeopardy should Russia default on its debt.* The firm reduced its exposure to Russia and purchased credit derivatives.

The bank was able to ride the turmoil but still suffered losses due to the fact that some counterparties defaulted on the credit protection. This illustrates that stress testing is generally useful but is still a subjective exercise that cannot possibly cover all contingencies.

---

*Risk Magazine, December 1998.

stitution in times of market turmoil. The methodology of stress testing also applies to credit and operational risks.

In some sense, stress testing can be viewed as an extension of the historical simulation method at increasingly higher confidence levels. Stress testing, however, does provide a useful complement to standard VAR methods because it allows users to include scenarios that did not occur over the VAR window but nonetheless are likely. It also allows risk managers to assess "blind spots" in their pricing or risk-management systems. The main benefit of stress testing is to identify vulnerabilities in an institution's position.

The drawback of the method is that it is highly subjective. Bad or implausible scenarios will lead to wrong measures of VAR. The history of some firms has shown that people may be very bad at predicting extreme situations. Generally, stress-test results are presented without an attached probability, which makes them difficult to interpret. Unlike VAR, stress testing can lead to a large amount of unfiltered information. There may be a temptation for the risk manager to produce large numbers of scenarios just to be sure any likely scenario is covered. The problem is that this makes it harder for top management to decide what to do.

Overall, stress testing should be considered a complement to rather than a replacement for other measures of VAR. Stress testing is useful to evaluate the worst-case effect of large movements in key variables. This is akin to drawing a few points in the extreme tails: useful information, but only after the rest of the distribution has been specified. Still, stress testing provides a useful reminder that VAR is no guarantee of a worst-case loss.

APPENDIX: EXTREME VALUE THEORY

Extreme value theory (EVT) has been used widely in applications that deal with the assessment of catastrophic events in fields as diverse as reliability, reinsurance, hydrology, and environmental science. Indeed, the impetus for this field of statistics came from the collapse of sea dikes in the Netherlands in February 1953, which flooded large parts of the country, killing over 1800 people.

After this disaster, the Dutch government created a committee that used the tools of EVT to establish the necessary dike heights. As with VAR, the goal was to choose the height of the dike so as to balance the cost of construction against the expected cost of a catastrophic flood.

EVT extends the central limit theorem, which deals with the distribution of the *average* of i.i.d. variables drawn from an unknown distribution to the distribution of their *tails*.[4]

Gnedenko (1943) proved the celebrated *EVT theorem,* which specifies the shape of the cumulative distribution function (cdf) for the value
x beyond a cutoff point *u*. Under general conditions, the cdf belongs to
the following family:

$$F(y) = 1 - (1 + \xi y)^{-1/\xi} \qquad \xi \neq 0$$
$$F(y) = 1 - \exp(-y) \qquad \xi = 0 \qquad\qquad (10.4)$$

where $y = (x - u)/\beta$, with $\beta > 0$ a *scale* parameter. For simplicity, we
assume that $y > 0$, which means that we take the absolute value of losses
beyond a cutoff point. Here, ξ is the all-important shape parameter that
determines the speed at which the tail disappears. We can verify that as
ξ tends to zero, the first function will tend to the second, which is exponential. It is also important to note that this function is only valid for *x*
beyond *u*.

This distribution is defined as the *generalized Pareto distribution* because it subsumes other known distributions, including the Pareto and normal distributions as special cases. The normal distribution corresponds to
$\xi = 0$, in which case the tails disappear at an exponential speed. For typical financial data, $\xi > 0$ implies *heavy tails* or a tail that disappears more
slowly than the normal. Estimates of ξ are typically around 0.2 to 0.4 for
stock market data. The coefficient can be related to the Student *t*, with
degrees of freedom approximately $n = 1/\xi$. Note that this implies a range
of 3 to 6 for *n*.

Heavy-tailed distributions do not necessarily have a complete set of
moments, unlike the normal distribution. Indeed, $E(X^k)$ is infinite for $k \geq$
$1/\xi$. For $\xi = 0.5$ in particular, the distribution has infinite variance (like
the Student *t* with $n = 2$).

In practice, EVT estimators can be derived as follows: Suppose that
we choose *u* to represent the 95th percentile. The EVT distribution then
provides a parametric distribution of the tails above this level. We first
need to use the actual data to compute the ratio of observations in the tail

---

4. For a good introduction to EVT in risk management, see McNeil (1999). Embrechts et al. (1997)
   have written a book that provides a complete and rigorous exposition of the topic. For applications using a different approach based on block maxima, see Longin (2000) and Danielsson
   and de Vries (1997), among others.

beyond u, or N_u/N, which is required to ensure that the tail probability sums to unity. We also need to estimate the parameters β and ξ; Longin (1996) presents various methods to do so. We can then estimate the tail cdf as

$$\hat{F}(y) = 1 - (N_u/N)\left[1 + \hat{\xi}\frac{(x - u)}{\beta} \right]^{-1/\hat{\xi}} \qquad (10.5)$$

The VAR at the cth level of confidence is obtained by setting $\hat{F}(y) = c$, which yields

$$\text{VAR} = u + \frac{\hat{\beta}}{\hat{\xi}} \{[(N/N_u)(1 - c)]^{-\hat{\xi}} - 1\} \qquad (10.6)$$

This provides a *quantile estimator* of VAR based not only on the data but also on our knowledge of the parametric distribution of the tails.

Figure 10–4 illustrates the fitting of the lower tails of S&P 500 daily returns. The normal cdf drops much faster than the empirical distribution

F I G U R E   10–4

Distribution of S&P 500 lower-tail returns: 1984–1998.

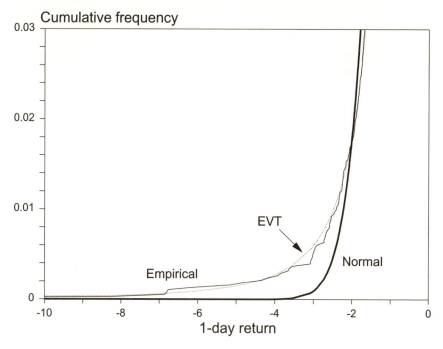

and assigns very low probability to extreme values. In contrast, the empirical (or historical simulation) method follows the data more faithfully. Its drawback, however, is that the quantiles are very imprecisely estimated. Instead, the EVT tails provide a smoother, parametric fit to the data without imposing unnecessary assumptions.

More generally, the approach can be extended to time variation in the scale parameter, in effect augmenting a GARCH process by an EVT distribution. The estimation proceeds in two steps: (1) fitting a GARCH model to the historical data using a (pseudo) maximum likelihood method and (2) fitting the EVT distribution to the scaled residuals. McNeil and Frey (1998) show that this approach provides better tail coverage than the static EVT or the GARCH-normal models.

Another issue is that of *time aggregation*. When the distribution of 1-day returns is normal, we know that the distribution of 10-day returns is likewise, with the scaling parameter adjusted by the square root of time, or $T^{1/2}$, where T is the number of days. EVT distributions are stable under addition, i.e., retain the same tail parameter for longer-period returns. Danielsson and de Vries (1997), however, have shown that the scaling parameter increases at the approximate rate of T^ξ, which is slower than the square root of time adjustment. For instance, with $\xi = 0.22$, we have $10^\xi = 1.65$, which is less than $10^{0.5} = 3.16$. Intuitively, because extreme values are more rare, they aggregate at a slower rate than the normal distribution as the horizon increases.

These results are illustrated in Table 10–5, which compares VAR estimates across various confidence levels and across days. The table confirms that for 1-day horizons, the EVT VAR is higher than the normal VAR, especially for higher confidence levels. At the 99.9 percent confidence level, the EVT VAR is 2.5, against a normal VAR of 1.9. This effect, however, is offset by time aggregation. The 10-day EVT VAR is 4.3, which is now less than the normal VAR of 5.9. For longer horizons, therefore, the conclusion is that the usual Basel square-root-of-time scaling factor may provide sufficient protection.

To summarize, the EVT approach is most useful for estimating tail probabilities of extreme events. For routine confidence levels such as 90, 95, and perhaps even 99 percent, conventional methods may be sufficient. At higher confidence levels, however, the normal distribution underestimates potential losses. The historical simulation method provides an improvement but still suffers from lack of data in the tails, which makes it difficult to estimate VAR reliably. This is where EVT comes to the res-

TABLE 10–5

The Effect of Fat Tails and Multiple Periods on VAR

	Confidence				
	95%	99%	99.5%	99.9%	99.95%
Extreme value					
1-Day	0.9	1.5	1.7	2.5	3.0
10-Day	1.6	2.5	3.0	4.3	5.1
Normal					
1-Day	1.0	1.4	1.6	1.9	2.0
10-Day	3.2	4.5	4.9	5.9	6.3

Source: Danielsson and de Vries (1997).

cue. EVT helps us draw smooth curves through the extreme tails of the distribution based on powerful statistical theory.

The EVT approach need not be difficult to implement. For example, the Student *t* distribution with 4 to 6 degrees of freedom is a simple distribution that adequately describes the tails of most financial data.

Even so, we should recognize that fitting EVT functions to recent historical data is still fraught with pitfalls. The most powerful statistical techniques cannot make short histories reveal once-in-a-lifetime events. This is why, for all the new techniques behind EVT, stress testing remains a delicate art form.

CHAPTER 11

Implementing Delta-
Normal VAR

The second [principle], to divide each of the difficulties under examination into as many parts as possible, and as might be necessary for its adequate solution.

René Descartes

Among various approaches to measuring value at risk (VAR), the delta-normal method is the easiest to implement. Portfolios that are linear combinations of normally distributed risk factors are themselves normally distributed. Thus all that is required is the combination of exposures and the variance-covariance matrix. The VAR measure is obtained from a simple matrix multiplication.

This method is important not only for its own sake but also because it illustrates the "mapping" principle in risk management. Even the more sophisticated simulation methods cannot possibly model the enormous number of risk factors in financial markets. They have to rely on simplifications. Hence the first step in understanding risk is to decompose financial instruments into their fundamental building blocks, which is the primary purpose of this chapter.

This chapter goes through several VAR examples presented in order of increasing complexity. Section 11.1 first reviews the basic principle behind the delta-normal VAR method. Section 11.2 then shows how to quantify VAR for a very simple portfolio, which represents the cash flows of a multinational corporation in different currencies. In this example, each position corresponds to one risk factor exactly. In general, however, this is not the case, since the number of risk factors in the covariance matrix is simplified into a limited set of "primitive" factors. Section 11.3 explains how to choose such a set of factors.

We then proceed to illustrate cases where securities are broken down into their constituent components. The following three sections explain how to decompose financial assets into cash-flow positions that we assign to various risk factors. Section 11.4 deals with fixed-income instruments, Section 11.5 with linear derivatives, and Section 11.6 with options. Last, Section 11.7 deals with equity risks.

11.1 OVERVIEW

Figure 11–1 describes a typical implementation of the delta-normal method. The first component is provided by a datafeed system, such as the RiskMetrics system currently available on the Internet. The second component must reside locally and consists of a "mapping system" that transforms the portfolio positions into weights on each of the securities for which risk is measured. The estimated change in value, or VAR, results from the combination of these two components.

So far we have assumed that every security in the portfolio was one of those for which risk and correlation data are made available. Save for the simplest portfolios, this is impractical. With tens of thousands of outstanding stocks and bonds and an almost infinite variety of derivatives, there is no way to cover the existing universe of securities.

FIGURE 11–1

Implementation of the delta-normal method.

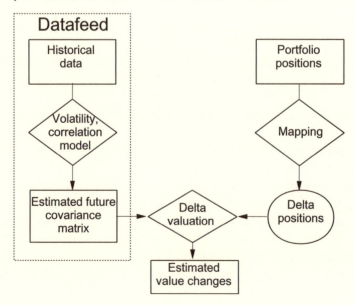

As important, even a complete history of all securities would not be relevant. The risk characteristics of bonds, for instance, change as they age. The risk of options depends on the current price of the underlying asset. Thus past history may not be a useful guide to future risks.

This is why risk typically is measured for a set of "primitive" factors such as foreign currencies, zero-coupon bonds, national equity markets, and commodities. For portfolios invested in these primitive factors only, VAR can be computed directly from the covariance matrix of factors and the vector of positions.

In most cases, portfolios also contain more complex assets. This chapter shows how to decompose securities into building blocks with delta-positions x aligned on each of the primitive risk factors and measured in dollars. Once these are obtained, the VAR of the portfolio can be computed from the covariance matrix over the target horizon Σ and the number of standard deviations corresponding to the specified confidence level:

$$\text{Value at risk} = \alpha\sqrt{x'\Sigma x} \qquad (11.1)$$

For instance, α is set at 1.65 for a one-tail 95 percent confidence level. Alternatively, the covariance matrix is sometimes presented in terms of the correlation matrix R and individual volatilities σ, $\Sigma = S'RS$, where S is a matrix with the volatilities on its diagonal but zeroes everywhere else. The "risk" factor is then measured directly as the vector $V = (\alpha\sigma)$. VAR is then calculated as

$$\text{VAR} = \sqrt{x'(\alpha S'RS\alpha)x} = \sqrt{(x \times V)'R(x \times V)} \qquad (11.2)$$

The RiskMetrics system provides estimates of V and R, from which VAR can be calculated by pre- and postmultiplying the correlation matrix R by the appropriate vector.

11.2 APPLICATION TO CURRENCIES

VAR can be used to determine the exposure to financial risks such as currency risks. As an illustration, let us consider the case of a U.S. automobile manufacturer with a total of $52 billion in annual sales. The corporation has assembly facilities in Canada, which export $9.2 billion worth of vehicles to the United States annually. Direct exports from the United States to Germany amount to $1.4 billion and to Japan $1.3 billion.

Focusing solely on exchange rates, the question is, What is the VAR of the company's cash flows over a monthly horizon? The corporation's exposure derives from the currency denomination of its costs and revenues. Simplifying to the extreme, we can translate annual cash flows into monthly numbers: $-\$767$ million in Canadian dollars (CAD), $\$117$ million in German marks (DEM), and $\$108$ million in Japanese yen (JPY).

The top part of Table 11–1 shows the risk and correlation of these three currencies. The volatility of the mark and yen is more than twice that of the Canadian dollar. In addition, these two currencies are highly correlated with each other. By way of contrast, the Canadian dollar is negatively correlated with the other two currencies.

The next three panels detail the steps in the computation:

1. Compute the risk matrix $(\alpha S)'R(S\alpha)$.
2. Postmultiply by the positions $[(\alpha S)'R(S\alpha)]x$.
3. Premultiply by the positions $x'[(\alpha S)'R(S\alpha)x]$.

The final number is the squared VAR, multiplied by 10,000 because we measured volatilities in percent. Taking the square root and dividing by 100, we find VAR = $\$28.5$. Therefore, the company could lose as much as $\$28.5$ million over a monthly horizon at the 95 percent confidence level.

We also can use the VAR tools developed in Chapter 7 to understand the sources of risk better. The computations for component VAR are displayed in the table. First, we need to compute the β_i of each cash flow, which is obtained by dividing each element in the first column by the total VAR squared (e.g., $-6717/8,146,136 = -0.00082$). The component VAR is then ($\beta_i \times x_i \times$ VAR).

The component VAR for the Canadian dollar position is $\$18.0$ million, against $\$4.7$ million and $\$5.8$ million for the mark and yen. It is much higher for the first currency because the position is greater, even though the Canadian dollar is less volatile than the others. All the component VARs are positive, which indicates that no hedging takes place. Intuitively, the negative correlations indicate that the best diversification benefits would have been obtained with positions of like signs in Canadian dollars and other currencies. Unfortunately, this is not the case. Expenses are in Canadian dollars, and revenues are in other currencies. The signs of these flows increase the overall cash-flow VAR.

Overall, in relation to the company's total annual profits of $\$5.8$ billion, the risk of losses due to exchange rates is small. Other companies are not so lucky. Toyota, for instance, sells 49 percent of its vehicles outside Japan yet produces only 20 percent outside Japan. As a result, for every fall of Y1 in the yen/$ rate, the company's profits decrease by $100 million. Exposure to exchange rates has had a significant effect on Toyota's bottom line.

This type of information is essential to the decision of whether or not this exposure should be hedged. Hedging can be achieved with financial instruments or, in the long run, by altering marketing strategies or shifting production and sourcing across countries. Thus VAR is an essential first step toward an informed risk management system.

The next logical step in risk management is the measurement of economic risks due to financial variables, not just cash-flow risks. This is much more complex for a number of reasons. First, the previous analysis assumes that quantities do not change with prices. In practice, changing prices in the foreign currency may affect demand and thus total revenues. Second, the currency of denomination is not necessarily the same as the currency of determination. For instance, the price for parts used for construction in Canada could fluctuate in line with the U.S. dollar, even though prices are invoiced in Canadian dollars. Third, and more generally, even domestic operations could be affected by exchange rates. The resurgence of U.S. automobile manufacturers can be attributed in part to the sustained appreciation of the yen, which has made Japanese cars more expensive in America. Whether these financial risks should be hedged is a more complex matter that is discussed in a later chapter. Still, this method allows institutions to estimate a global measure of their financial risks.

11.3 CHOOSING "PRIMITIVE" SECURITIES

The preceding example was straightforward because currencies are basic risk factors. In general, portfolios must be reduced to positions on a "primitive" set of securities. To a large extent, the choice of these primitive risk factors is arbitrary. More factors lead to tighter risk measurement. The tradeoff is that the marginal improvement may not be worth the additional cost and complexity.

In the bond market, for instance, a one-factor model may provide a good first approximation to risk for some portfolios. For more precision, more factors can be added. The need for additional coverage depends on the complexity of the exposure to financial risk. Simple portfolios may be described adequately by one interest rate factor. More complex positions, such as those run by government securities dealers, should account

TABLE 11-1

Computing the VAR of Multinational Cash Flows (Monthly VAR at 95 Percent Level)

Input Data

	Risk (%) $V = \alpha\sigma$	Correlation (R)			Cash Flow x
		CAD	DEM	JPY	
CAD	2.747	1	−0.208	−0.216	−$767 million
DEM	6.220	−0.208	1	0.787	$117 million
JPY	8.046	−0.216	0.787	1	$108 million

Step 1: Computing the Risk Matrix $(\alpha S)'\,R(\alpha S)$

$(\alpha S)'$			R			(αS)			= Result		
2.75	0.	0.	1	−0.208	−0.216	2.75	0.	0.	7.55	−3.55	−4.77
0.	6.22	0.	−0.208	1	0.787	0.	6.22	0.	−3.55	38.69	39.39
0.	0.	8.05	−0.216	0.787	1	0.	0.	8.05	−4.77	39.39	64.74

Step 2: Postmultiplying by x

$(\alpha S)'\,R(\alpha S)$			x	= Result
7.55	−3.55	−4.77	−767	−6,717
−3.55	38.69	39.39	117	11,505
−4.77	39.39	64.74	108	15,269

Step 3: Premultiplying by x'

x'		(αS)' R(αS) x	= Result (VAR)²
−767	117	108	−6,717	8,146,136
			11,505	
			15,269	

Accessory Step: Computing Component VAR

(αS)' R(αS)x	Divide by (VAR)²	Compute β	Multiply by xVAR	Component VAR =βxVAR
−6,717	1/8146136	−0.00082	−767 ($28.5)	$18.0
11,505	1/8146136	0.00141	117 ($28.5)	$4.7
15,269	1/8146136	0.00187	118 ($28.5)	$5.8

Final Report

	Individual VAR (| x | V)	Component VAR (βxVAR)
CAD	$21.0 million	$18.0 million
DEM	$7.3 million	$4.7 million
JPY	$8.7 million	$5.8 million
Undiversified	$37.0 million	
Diversified		$28.5 million

for every twist and shape of the yield curve. The degree of leverage in such portfolios is such that tracking error can be magnified to create large losses.

Another rationale for the choice of risk factors is to define sources of risk that can be readily hedged using existing exchange-listed futures contracts. This leads into the next step following exposure measurement, hedging. Sources of risk that can be hedged easily are particularly useful to identify.

11.3.1 Lessons from Exchanges

A side benefit of futures contracts is that they reveal what the market views as primitive factors. This choice is not obvious, for there are few successful derivatives contracts.[1] The key to explaining the success of exchange-listed contracts lies in understanding their economic function. Successful contracts require the following conditions:

- *Large underlying cash markets.* A large underlying cash market demonstrates interest in the underlying asset. It also provides reassurance that the contract can be priced fairly in relation to the underlying asset.

- *Large volatility of underlying asset.* High volatility leads to hedging needs for business-related financial risks and also creates the possibility of fast profits for speculators. Indeed, the empirical evidence points to a strong relationship between trading volume and volatility.

- *Lack of close substitutes.* Derivatives generally are successful when they provide a means to hedge price risks that cannot be met with existing contracts. If the prices on two assets move in similar fashion, for instance, one derivative contract may be sufficient to hedge the two price risks. The residual risk, known as *basis risk,* may be enough to warrant trading in a new contract, especially if it is less liquid.

All these conditions are directly relevant to the choice of primitive factors for risk management. At the very least, risk factors should include exchange-listed instruments, which have revealed their economic importance.

---

1. Silber (1981), for instance, reports that the success rate of contracts is only one out of four.

11.3.2 Specific Risk

The choice of primitive risk factors also will influence the size of specific risks. *Specific risk* can be defined as risk that is due to issuer-specific price movements, after accounting for general market factors. Hence the definition of specific risk depends on that of general market risk.

For equities, for instance, we have seen from Equation (7.36) that if one defines the general market risk as driven by the stock market index, the portfolio variance is

$$V(R_p) = w'\Sigma w = (\beta_p^2)\sigma_m^2 + \sum_{i=1}^{N} w_i^2 \sigma_{\epsilon i}^2 \qquad (11.3)$$

where the second component is the aggregate of firm-specific risk for the entire portfolio. Ignoring this term will understate the portfolio risk.

Alternatively, consider a corporate bond portfolio. Our primitive risk factors could be movements in a set of J government bond yields z_j and in a set of K credit spreads s_k sorted by credit rating. We then model the movement in each corporate bond yield dy_i by a movement in z at the closest maturity and in s for the same credit rating. The remaining component is ϵ_i, which is assumed to be independent across i.

The portfolio price movement is then

$$dV = \sum_{i=1}^{N} DVBP_i dy_i = \sum_{j=1}^{J} DVBP_j dz_j$$
$$+ \sum_{k=1}^{K} DVBP_k ds_k + \sum_{i=1}^{N} DVBP_i d\epsilon_i \qquad (11.4)$$

where $DVBP$ is the total dollar value of a basis point for the associated risk factor. For instance, we may have $N = 100$ corporate bonds in the portfolio and only $J = 10$ government maturities. The 10 values for $DVBP_j$ then represent the summation of the DVBP across all individual bonds for each associated government maturity.

This leads to a total-risk decomposition of

$$V(dV) = \text{general risk} + \sum_{i=1}^{N} DVBP_i^2 \, V(d\epsilon_i) \qquad (11.5)$$

A greater number of general risk factors should create less residual risk. Even so, we need to ascertain the size of the second, specific risk term. In practice, there may not be sufficient history to measure the specific risk of individual bonds, which is why it is often assumed that all issuers within the same risk class have the same risk.

11.4 FIXED-INCOME PORTFOLIOS

11.4.1 Mapping Approaches

Bond positions describe the distribution of money flows over time by their amount, timing, and the credit quality of issuer. This creates a continuum of risk factors, going from overnight to long maturities for various credit risks. In practice, we have to restrict the number of risk factors to a small set. For some portfolios, one risk factor may be sufficient. For others, 15 maturities may be necessary. For portfolios with options, we need to model movements not only in yields but also in their implied volatilities.

Once the risk factors have been selected, the question is how to "map," or summarize, the portfolio positions into exposures on these risk factors. We can distinguish three mapping systems: principal, duration, and cash flows. With *principal mapping,* the bond risk is associated with the maturity of the principal payment only. With *duration mapping,* the risk is associated with that of a zero-coupon bond with maturity equal to the bond duration. With *cash-flow mapping,* the risk of fixed-income instruments is decomposed into the risk of each of the bond cash flows. In each case, mapping should preserve the market value of the position as well as its market risk.

11.4.2 Risk Factors

We start by describing the risk factors using RiskMetrics data. Table 11–2 presents monthly VARs of zero-coupon bonds as well as correlations for maturities going from 1 month to 30 years. Here, VAR corresponds to a 1.65 standard deviation movement.

Duration is a measure of linear exposure to changes in yields. The duration approximation assumes parallel moves in the term structure. Hence all yields should have the same volatility and be perfectly correlated with each other. Hence the VAR of zero-coupon bonds should be proportional to their maturity. The table shows that this is not the case. The 30-year VAR, for instance, is less than three times the 10-year VAR. Also, correlations are below unity, sometimes significantly so.

TABLE 11–2

Risk and Correlations for U.S. Zeroes (Monthly VAR at 95 Percent Level)

Vertex	VAR (%)	1m	3m	6m	1Y	2Y	3Y	4Y	5Y	7Y	9Y	10Y	15Y	20Y	30Y
1m	0.021	1													
3m	0.064	0.56	1												
6m	0.162	0.50	0.69	1											
1Y	0.470	0.51	0.67	0.87	1										
2Y	0.987	0.45	0.52	0.80	0.90	1									
3Y	1.484	0.44	0.50	0.79	0.89	0.99	1								
4Y	1.971	0.42	0.47	0.76	0.87	0.98	0.99	1							
5Y	2.426	0.41	0.46	0.74	0.86	0.97	0.99	1.0	1						
7Y	3.192	0.39	0.44	0.70	0.83	0.94	0.97	0.98	0.99	1					
9Y	3.913	0.37	0.42	0.66	0.80	0.91	0.94	0.96	0.98	1.0	1				
10Y	4.250	0.36	0.41	0.65	0.79	0.90	0.94	0.96	0.97	0.99	1.0	1			
15Y	6.234	0.33	0.38	0.61	0.74	0.85	0.89	0.92	0.93	0.96	0.98	0.98	1		
20Y	8.146	0.30	0.35	0.55	0.68	0.79	0.83	0.86	0.88	0.92	0.94	0.95	0.99	1	
30Y	11.119	0.26	0.31	0.51	0.64	0.76	0.80	0.83	0.85	0.90	0.93	0.94	0.98	0.99	1

11.4.3 Comparison of Mapping Approaches

As an example, Table 11–3 describes a two-bond portfolio consisting of a $100 million 5-year 6 percent issue and a $100 million 1-year 4 percent issue. Both issues are selling at par, implying a market value of $200 million. The portfolio has an average maturity of 3 years and a duration of 2.733 years. The table lays out the present value of all portfolio cash flows discounted at the appropriate zero-coupon rate.

Principal mapping considers the timing of redemption payments only. Since the average maturity of this portfolio is 3 years, the VAR can be found from the risk of a 3-year maturity, which is 1.484 percent. The VAR is then $200 million × 1.484 percent = $2.97 million. The only positive aspect of this method is its simplicity. This approach overstates the true risk because it ignores intervening coupon payments. It does not preserve the portfolio's risk.

The next step in precision is duration mapping. We replace the portfolio by a zero-coupon bond with maturity equal to the duration of the portfolio, which is 2.733 years. We discuss in the next section how to allocate the portfolio to the adjoining 2- and 3-year vertices. Using a linear interpolation for duration for the VARs, we find a risk of 0.987 + (1.484 − 0.987) × (2.733 − 2) = 1.351 percent for this hypothetical zero. With a $200 million portfolio, the duration-based VAR is $2.70 million, slightly less than before.

TABLE 11–3

Mapping for a Bond Portfolio

Term (year)	Cash Flows 5-Year	Cash Flows 1-Year	Spot Rate	Mapping (PV) Principal	Mapping (PV) Duration	Mapping (PV) Cash Flow
1	$6	$104 million	4.000	.00	.00	$105.77
2	$6	0	4.618	.00	.00	$5.48
2.733	—	—		—	$200.00	—
3	$6	0	5.192	$200.00	.00	$5.15
4	$6	0	5.716	.00	.00	$4.80
5	$106	0	6.112	.00	.00	$78.79
Total				$200.00 million	$200.00 million	$200.00 million

Finally, the cash-flow mapping method consists of grouping all cash flows on term structure "vertices," which correspond to maturities for which volatilities are provided. Each cash flow is represented by the present value of the cash payment, discounted at the appropriate zero-coupon rate.

Coupon-paying bond $=$ Cash flow PV on vertex 1
$+$ Cash flow PV on vertex 2 $+ \cdots +$ Principal PV on last vertex

---

Table 11–4 shows how to compute the portfolio VAR using cash-flow mapping. The second column reports the cash flows x from Table 11–3. The third column presents the product of these cash flows with the risk of each vertex $V = \alpha\sigma$ (at the 95 percent confidence level), which represents the individual VARs.

With perfect correlation across all zeroes, the VAR of the portfolio would be

$$\text{Undiversified VAR} = \sum_{i=1}^{N} \mid x_i \mid V_i$$

which is $2.63 million. This number is close to the VAR obtained from the duration approximation, which was $2.70 million.

The right side of the table presents the correlation matrix of zeroes for maturities ranging from 1 to 5 years. To obtain the portfolio VAR, we premultiply and postmultiply the matrix by the dollar amounts (xV) at each vertex. Taking the square root, we find a VAR measure of $2.57 million. This is the most the portfolio could lose over a 1-month horizon at the 95 percent confidence level.

Note that the duration VAR was $2.70 million and the diversified VAR $2.57 million. These differences are due to two factors. First, risk measures are not perfectly linear with maturity, which should be the case if term structure shifts were strictly parallel. Second, correlations are below unity, which reduces risk even further. Thus, of the $130,000 difference in the extreme VARs ($2.70 million $-$ $2.57 million), $70,000 is due to differences in yield volatility ($2.70 million $-$ $2.63 million), and $60,000 is due to imperfect correlations.

Table 11–5 presents another approach to VAR, which is directly derived from movements in the value of zeroes, as in stress testing. Assume

TABLE 11–4

Computing the VAR of a $200 Million Bond Portfolio (Monthly VAR at 95 Percent Level)

Term (year)	Cash Flows x	Individual VAR (%) x × V	Correlation Matrix R					Component VAR
			1Y	2Y	3Y	4Y	5Y	
1	$105.77	49.66	1					$0.45
2	$5.48	5.40	0.897	1				$0.05
3	$5.15	7.65	0.886	0.991	1			$0.08
4	$4.80	9.47	0.866	0.976	0.994	1		$0.09
5	$78.79	191.15	0.855	0.966	0.988	0.998	1	$1.90
Total	$200.00 million	263.35						
VAR ($ million)								
Undiversified		$2.63 million						
Diversified								$2.57 million

TABLE 11–5

Computing VAR from Change in Prices of Zeroes

Term (year)	Cash Flows ($ million)	Old Zero Value	Old PV of Flows	Zero Risk (VAR)	New Zero Value	New PV of Flows
1	110	0.9615	$105.77	0.4696	0.9570	$105.27
2	6	0.9136	$5.48	0.9868	0.9046	$5.43
3	6	0.8591	$5.15	1.4841	0.8463	$5.08
4	6	0.8006	$4.80	1.9714	0.7848	$4.71
5	106	0.7433	$78.79	2.4261	0.7252	$76.88
Total			$200.00 million			$197.37 million
Loss						$2.63 million

that all zeroes were perfectly correlated. Then we could decrease all ze-roes' values by their VAR. For instance, the 1-year zero is worth 0.9615. Given the VAR in Table 11–5 of 0.4696, a 95 percent probability move would be for the zero to fall to $0.9615 × (1 − 0.4696 percent) = 0.9570. If all zeroes are perfectly correlated, they should all fall by their respec-tive VAR. This generates a new distribution of present value factors, which can be used to price the portfolio. Table 11–5 shows that the new value is $197.37 million, which is exactly $2.63 million below the original value. This number is exactly the same as the one obtained in the preceding para-graph, with correlations set to unity.

The two approaches illustrate the link between computing VAR through matrix multiplication and through movements in underlying prices. Computing VAR through matrix multiplication is much more di-rect, however, and more important, because it also allows nonperfect cor-relations across different sectors of the yield curve.

11.4.4 Assigning Weights to Vertices

The preceding example of duration mapping showed that, in general, cash flows fall between the selected vertices. In our example, the portfolio con-sists of one cash flow with maturity of $D_p = 2.7325$ years and present value of $200 million. The question is, How should we allocate the $200 million to the adjoining vertices in a way that best represents the risk of the original investment?

A simple method consists of allocating funds according to *duration matching*. Define x as the weight on the first vertex and D_1, D_2 as the duration of the first and second vertices. The portfolio duration D_p will be matched if

$$xD_1 + (1 - x)D_2 = D_p \qquad (11.6)$$

or $x = (D_2 - D_p)/(D_2 - D_1)$. In our case, $x = (3 - 2.7325)/(3 - 2) = 0.2675$, which leads to an amount of \$200 million $\times$ 0.2675 = \$53.49 million on the first vertex. The balance of \$146.51 million is allocated to the 3-year vertex.

Unfortunately, this approach may not create a portfolio with the same risk as the original portfolio. The second method aims at *variance matching*. Define σ_1 and σ_2 as the respective volatilities and ρ as the correlation. The portfolio variance is

$$V(R_p) = x^2\sigma_1^2 + (1 - x)^2\sigma_2^2 + 2x(1 - x)\rho\sigma_1\sigma_2 \qquad (11.7)$$

which we set equal to the variance of the zero-coupon bond falling between the two vertices. By linear interpolation of the price volatilities for 2- and 3-year zeroes, the portfolio volatility is $\sigma_p = 1.351$ percent, as we have done before.[2] Therefore, the weight x that maintains the portfolio risk to that of the initial investment is found from solving the quadratic equation

$$(\sigma_1^2 + \sigma_2^2 - 2\rho\sigma_1\sigma_2)x^2 + 2(-\sigma_2^2 + \rho\sigma_1\sigma_2)x + (\sigma_2^2 - \sigma_p^2) = 0 \qquad (11.8)$$

The solution to the equation $ax^2 + 2bx + c = 0$ is $x = (-b \pm \sqrt{b^2 - ac})/a$, which leads to the two roots $x_1 = 0.2635$ and $x_2 = 5.2168$. We choose the first root, which is between zero and unity. As shown in Table 11–6, this translates into a position of \$52.71 million on the 2-year vertex and \$147.29 million on the 3-year vertex.

In this example, the difference between the two approaches is minor. The VAR from variance matching is \$2.702 million, versus \$2.698 million when duration matching. In fact, the duration approximation is

---

2. Another approach is to interpolate yield volatilities, from which the price volatility can be obtained. Unfortunately, this method does not ensure a solution x that is always such that $0 < x < 1$. Also, there is no theory to suggest that interpolating yield volatilities is more appropriate than interpolating price volatilities.

TABLE 11–6

Assigning Weights to Vertices

Term (year)		Variance Matching			Duration Matching	
	VAR (%)	Correlation	Weight	Amount	Weight	Amount
2	0.9868		0.2635	$52.71	0.2675	$53.49
3	1.4841	0.9908	0.7365	$147.29	0.7325	$146.51
2.7325	1.3510					
Total			1.0000	$200.00 million	1.0000	$200.00 million
VAR				$2.702 million		$2.698 million

exact under two conditions: (1) the correlation coefficient is unity, and (2) the volatility of each vertex is proportional to its duration ($\sigma_1 = \sigma D_1$, $\sigma_2 = \sigma D_2$, $\rho = 1$). Under these conditions, Equation (11.7) simplifies to

$$V(R_p) = x^2\sigma^2 D_1^2 + (1 - x)^2\sigma^2 D_2^2 + 2x(1 - x)\sigma^2 D_1 D_2$$
$$= \sigma^2[xD_1 + (1 - x)D_2]^2 \quad (11.9)$$

which equals $(\sigma D_p)^2$ if $[xD_1 + (1 - x)D_2] = D_p$. In other words, duration matching is perfectly appropriate under these conditions. In more general cases, especially if ρ is much lower than 1, the duration approximation will fail to provide a portfolio with the same risk as that of the original portfolio.

11.4.5 Benchmarking a Portfolio

Finally, we illustrate how to compute VAR in relative terms, i.e., relative to a performance benchmark. Table 11–7 presents the cash-flow decomposition of the J.P. Morgan U.S. bond index, which has a duration of 4.62 years. Assume that we are trying to benchmark a portfolio of $100 million. Over a monthly horizon, the VAR of the index at the 95 percent confidence level is $1.99 million. This is about equivalent to the risk of a 4-year note. The undiversified VAR is $2.07 million, slightly higher.

Next, we try to match the index with two bonds. The rightmost columns in the table display the positions of two-bond portfolios with duration matched to that of the index. Since no zero-coupon has a maturity

TABLE 11-7

Benchmarking a $100 Million Bond Index (Monthly VAR at 95 Percent Level)

Vertex	Risk (%)	Position: JPM/U.S. Index ($ Million)	Position: Portfolio				
			1 ($ Million)	2 ($ Million)	3 ($ Million)	4 ($ Million)	5 ($ Million)
≤1m	0.022	1.05	0.0	0.0	0.0	0.0	84.8
3m	0.065	1.35	0.0	0.0	0.0	0.0	0.0
6m	0.163	2.49	0.0	0.0	0.0	0.0	0.0
1Y	0.470	13.96	0.0	0.0	0.0	59.8	0.0
2Y	0.987	24.83	0.0	0.0	62.6	0.0	0.0
3Y	1.484	15.40	0.0	59.5	0.0	0.0	0.0
4Y	1.971	11.57	38.0	0.0	0.0	0.0	0.0
5Y	2.426	7.62	62.0	0.0	0.0	0.0	0.0
7Y	3.192	6.43	0.0	40.5	0.0	0.0	0.0
9Y	3.913	4.51	0.0	0.0	37.4	0.0	0.0
10Y	4.250	3.34	0.0	0.0	0.0	40.2	0.0
15Y	6.234	3.00	0.0	0.0	0.0	0.0	0.0
20Y	8.146	3.15	0.0	0.0	0.0	0.0	0.0
30Y	11.119	1.31	0.0	0.0	0.0	0.0	15.2
Total		100.0	100.0	100.0	100.0	100.0	100.0
Duration		4.62	4.62	4.62	4.62	4.62	4.62
VAR ($million)							
Absolute		1.99	2.25	2.16	2.04	1.94	1.71
Relative		0.00	0.43	0.29	0.16	0.20	0.81

of exactly 4.62 years, the closest portfolio consists of two positions, each in a 4- and a 5-year zero. The respective weights for this portfolio are $38 million and $62 million.

Define the new vector of positions for this portfolio as x and for the index as x_0. The VAR of the deviation relative to the benchmark is

$$\text{Relative VAR} = \alpha \sqrt{(x - x_0)'\Sigma(x - x_0)} \qquad (11.10)$$

After performing the necessary calculations, we find that the relative VAR of this duration-hedged portfolio is $0.43 million. Thus the maximum deviation between the index and the portfolio is at most $0.43 million under normal market conditions. This potential shortfall is much less than the $1.99 million absolute risk of the index. The remaining tracking error is due to nonparallel moves in the term structure.

Relative to the original index, the tracking error can be measured in terms of variance reduction, similar to an R^2 in a regression. The variance improvement is

$$1 - \left(\frac{0.43}{1.99}\right)^2 = 95.4 \text{ percent}$$

which is in line with the explanatory power of the first factor in the variance decomposition of bond returns detailed in Chapter 7.

Next, we explore the effect of altering the composition of the tracking portfolio. Portfolio 2 widens the bracket of time vertices; it consists of positions in years 3 and 7. Its tracking error VAR is $0.29 million, which is an improvement over the previous number.

Portfolio 3 consists of positions in years 2 and 9. This comes the closest to approximating the cash-flow positions in the index, which has the greatest weight on the 2-year vertex. The tracking error VAR is reduced further to $0.16 million. Portfolio 4 consists of positions in years 1 and 10. Now the VAR increases to $0.20 million. This mistracking is even more pronounced for a portfolio consisting of 1-month bills and 30-year zeroes, for which the residual VAR increases to $0.81 million.

Among the portfolios considered here, the lowest tracking error is obtained with portfolio 3. Note that the absolute risk of these portfolios is lowest for portfolio 5. As correlations decrease for more distant maturities, we should expect that a duration-matched portfolio should have the lowest absolute risk for the combination of most distant maturities, such as a barbell portfolio of cash and a 30-year zero. However, minimizing absolute market risk is not the same as minimizing relative market risk.

This example demonstrates that duration hedging only provides a first approximation to interest rate risk management. If the goal is to minimize tracking error relative to an index, it is essential to use a fine decomposition of the index by maturity. Among the combinations considered here, the lowest tracking error is attained for a portfolio with cash positions that are closest to those of the index.

11.5 LINEAR DERIVATIVES

11.5.1 Forward Contracts

Forward and futures contracts are the simplest types of derivatives. Since their value is linear in the underlying spot rates, their risk can be easily constructed from basic building blocks. Assume, for instance, that we are dealing with a forward contract on a foreign currency. The basic valuation formula can be derived from an arbitrage argument.[3]

To establish notations, define

S_t = spot price of one unit of the underlying cash asset

K = contracted forward price

r = domestic risk-free rate

y = income flow on the asset

τ = time to maturity.

When the asset is a foreign currency, y represents the foreign risk-free rate r^*. For convenience, we assume that all rates are compounded continuously.

We seek to find the current value of a forward contract f_t to buy one unit of foreign currency at K after time τ. To do this, we consider the fact that investors have two alternatives, which are economically equivalent: (1) Buy $e^{-r^*\tau}$ units of the asset at the price S_t and hold for one period, or (2) enter a forward contract to buy one unit of the asset in one period. Under alternative (1), the investment will grow, with reinvestment of dividend, to exactly one unit of the asset after one period. Under alternative (2), the contract costs f_t upfront, and we need to set aside enough cash to pay K in the future, which is $Ke^{-r\tau}$. After 1 year, the two alternatives lead to a position in one unit of the asset. Therefore, their initial cost must be

---

3. For a systematic approach to pricing derivatives, see, for instance, the excellent book by Hull (2000).

identical. This leads to the following valuation for outstanding forward contracts:

$$f_t = S_t e^{-y\tau} - K e^{-r\tau} \qquad (11.11)$$

Note that we can repeat the preceding reasoning to find the current forward rate F_t that would set the value of the contract to zero. Setting $K = F_t$ and $f_t = 0$ in Equation (11.11), we have

$$F_t = (S_t e^{-y\tau}) e^{r\tau} \qquad (11.12)$$

This allows us to rewrite Equation (11.11) as

$$f_t = F_t e^{-r\tau} - K e^{-r\tau} = (F_t - K) e^{-r\tau} \qquad (11.13)$$

In other words, the current value of the forward contract is the present value of the difference between the current forward rate and the locked-in delivery rate. If we are long a forward contract with contracted rate K, we can liquidate the contract by entering a new contract to sell at the current rate F_t. This will lock in a profit of $(F_t - K)$, which we need to discount to the present time to find f_t.

Let us examine the risk of a 1-year forward contract to purchase DEM 100 million in exchange for \$70.880 million. Table 11–8 displays pricing information for the contract (current spot, forward, and interest rates), risk, and correlations. The first step is to find the market value of the contract. We can use Equation (11.11), accounting for the fact that the quoted interest rates are discretely compounded, as

$$f_t = \$0.6962 \, \frac{1}{(1 + 3.9375 \text{ percent})} - \$0.7088 \, \frac{1}{(1 + 5.8125 \text{ percent})}$$
$$= \$0.6699 - \$0.6699 = 0$$

TABLE 11–8

Risk and Correlations for Components (Monthly VAR at 95 Percent Level)

			Correlations		
Component	Price	VAR (%)	DEM Spot	DEM 1Y	USD 1Y
DEM spot	\$0.6962	6.2201	1	0.1912	0.0400
Long DEM bill	3.9375%	0.2876	0.1912	1	0.2937
Short USD bill	5.8125%	0.4696	0.0400	0.2937	1
Fwd	\$0.7088				

Thus the initial value of the contract is zero. This value, however, may change, creating market risk.

Among the three sources of risk, the volatility of the spot contract is the highest by far, with a 6.22 percent VAR (corresponding to 1.65 standard deviations over a month for a 95 percent confidence level). This is much greater than the 0.29 percent VAR for the DEM 1-year bill or even the 0.47 percent VAR for the USD bill. Thus most of the risk of the forward contract is driven by the cash DEM position.

But risk is also affected by correlations. The positive correlation of 0.19 between the DEM spot and bill positions indicates that when the DEM goes up in value against the dollar, the value of a 1-year DEM investment is likely to appreciate. Therefore, higher values of the DEM are associated with lower DEM interest rates.

This positive correlation increases the risk of the combined position. On the other hand, the position is also short a 1-year USD bill, which is positively correlated with the other two legs of the transaction. This should decrease the risk of the transaction. The issue is, What will be the net effect on the risk of the forward contract?

VAR provides an exact answer to this question, which is displayed in Table 11–9. But first we have to compute the positions x on each of

TABLE 11–9

Computing VAR for a DEM 100 Million Forward Contract (Monthly VAR at 95 Percent Level)

Position	Present Value Factor	Cash Flows	PV of Flows x	Individual VAR $|x| V$	Component VAR βxVAR
DEM spot			$66.99	$4.167	$4.155
Long DEM bill	0.962116	DM100.00	$66.99	$0.193	$0.041
Short USD bill	0.945067	−$70.88	−$66.99	$0.315	$0.007
VAR					
Undiversified				$4.675 million	
Diversified					$4.203 million

the three building blocks of the contract. By taking the partial derivative of Equation (11.11) with respect to the risk factors, we have

$$df = \frac{\partial f}{\partial S}\, dS + \frac{\partial f}{\partial r^*}\, dr^* + \frac{\partial f}{\partial r}\, dr$$

$$= e^{-r^*\tau}\, dS - Se^{-r^*\tau}\, \tau dr^* + Ke^{-r\tau}\, \tau dr \quad (11.14)$$

Here, the building blocks consist of the spot rate and interest rates. Alternatively, we can replace interest rates by the price of bills. Define these as $P = e^{-r\tau}$ and $P^* = e^{-r^*\tau}$. We then replace dr by dP using $dP = (-\tau)e^{-r\tau}dr$ and $dP^* = (-\tau)e^{-r^*\tau}\, dr^*$. The risk of the forward contract becomes

$$df = (Se^{-r^*\tau})\frac{dS}{S} + (Se^{-r^*\tau})\frac{dP^*}{P^*} - (Ke^{-r\tau})\frac{dP}{P} \quad (11.15)$$

This shows that the forward position can be separated into three cash flows, (1) a long spot position in DEM, worth DEM 100 million = $70.88 million in a year or $(Se^{-r^*\tau}) = \$66.99$ million now, (2) a long position in a DEM investment, also worth $66.99 million now, and (3) a short position in a USD investment, worth $70.88 million in a year or $(Ke^{-r\tau}) = \$66.99$ million now. Thus a position in the forward contract has three building blocks:

Long forward contract = long foreign currency spot
   + long foreign currency bill + short U.S. dollar bill

Considering only the spot position, the VAR is $66.99 million times the risk of 6.22 percent, which is $4.167 million. To compute the diversified VAR, we use the risk matrix from the data in Table 11–8, and pre- and postmultiply by the vector of positions (PV of CF column in the table). The total VAR for the forward contract is $4.203 million. This number is about the same size as that of the spot contract because exchange rate volatility so dominates bond volatility.

The risk of a forward contract includes both currency and interest rate risk. Longer maturities are exposed to greater interest rate risk. For instance, changing the maturity in our example from 1 to 10 years would increase the VAR from $4.203 million to $4.867 million.

More generally, the same methodology can be used for long-term currency swaps, which are equivalent to portfolios of forward contracts. For instance, a 10-year contract to pay dollars and receive marks is equivalent to a series of 10 forward contracts to exchange a set amount of dollars into marks. To compute the VAR, the contract must be broken down into a currency risk component and a string of USD and DEM fixed-income components. As before, the total VAR will be driven primarily by the currency component.

11.5.2 Commodity Forwards

The valuation of forward or futures contracts on commodities is substantially more complex than for financial assets such as currencies, bonds, or stock indices. Such financial assets have a well-defined income flow y, called the *foreign interest rate,* the *coupon payment,* or the *dividend yield,* respectively.

Things are not so simple for commodities, such as metals, agricultural products, or energy products. Most products do not make monetary payments but instead are consumed, thus creating an implied benefit. This flow of benefit is loosely called *convenience yield* to represent the benefit from holding the cash product. This convenience yield, however, is not tied to another financial variable, such as the foreign interest rate for currency futures. It is also highly variable, creating its own source of risk.

As a result, the risk measurement of commodity futures uses Equation (11.13) directly, where the main driver of the value of the contract is the current forward rate for this commodity. As we have seen in the preceding section, the effects of interest rate movements are usually negligible for short maturities.

Table 11–10 illustrates the term structure of volatilities for selected energy products and base metals. First, we note that monthly VAR measures are very high, ranging from 9 to 18 percent for near contracts. In contrast, currency and equity market VAR are typically around 6 percent. Thus commodities are much more volatile than typical financial assets.

Second, we observe that volatilities decrease with maturity. The effect is strongest for less storable products such as energy products and less so for base metals. It is actually imperceptible for precious metals, which have low storage costs and no convenience yield. For financial assets, volatilities are primarily driven by spot prices, which implies basically constant volatilities across contract maturities.

TABLE 11—10

Volatility of Commodity Contracts (Monthly VAR at 95 Percent Level)

	Energy Products			
Maturity	Natural Gas	Heating Oil	Unleaded Gasoline	Crude Oil-WTI
1-month	17.94	10.01	10.81	9.14
3-month	11.28	8.46	8.19	7.77
6-month	8.30	6.77	7.26	6.50
12-month	7.55	6.26	3.87	5.37
	Base Metals			
Maturity	Aluminum	Copper	Nickel	Zinc
Cash	10.24	10.04	13.25	8.50
3-month	9.55	8.25	12.95	8.22
15-month	7.95	7.49	12.85	7.29
27-month	9.66	8.53		9.15

Let us now say that we wish to compute the VAR for a 12-month forward position on 1 million barrels of oil, priced at \$16.8 per barrel. Using the present value factor in Table 11–9, this translates into a current position of \$15,877,000.

Differentiating Equation (11.13), we have

$$df = \frac{\partial f}{\partial F} dF = e^{-r\tau} F \frac{dF}{F} \tag{11.16}$$

The contract VAR is therefore

$$\text{VAR} = \$15,877,000 \times 5.37 \text{ percent} = \$853,000$$

In general, the contract cash flows will fall between the maturities of the risk factors, and present values must be apportioned accordingly.

11.5.3 Forward Rate Agreements

Forward rate agreements (FRAs) are forward contracts that allow users to lock in an interest rate at some future date. The buyer of an FRA locks in a borrowing rate; the seller locks in a lending rate. In other words, the "long" receives a payment if the spot rate is above the forward rate.

Consider, for instance, a contract where the short leg of the FRA is defined by τ_1 year and the long leg by τ_2 year. Assume linear compounding for simplicity. The forward rate can be defined as the rate that equalizes the return on a τ_2-period investment with a τ_1-period investment rolled over at the forward rate:

$$(1 + R_2\tau_2) = (1 + R_1\tau_1)[1 + F_{1,2}(\tau_2 - \tau_1)] \qquad (11.17)$$

For instance, suppose that you sold a 6×12 FRA on \$100 million. This is equivalent to borrowing \$100 million for 6 months and investing the proceeds for 12 months. When the FRA expires in 6 months, assume that the prevailing 6-month spot rate is higher than the locked-in forward rate. The seller then pays the buyer the difference between the spot and forward rates applied to the principal. In effect, this payment offsets the higher return that the investor would otherwise receive, thus guaranteeing a return equal to the forward rate. Therefore, an FRA can be decomposed into two zero-coupon building blocks.

Long 6×12 FRA = long 6-month bill + short 12-month bill

Table 11–11 provides a worked-out example. If the 360-day spot rate is 5.8125 percent and the 180-day rate is 5.625 percent, the forward rate must be such that

$$(1 + F_{1,2}/2) = \frac{(1 + 5.8125 \text{ percent})}{(1 + 5.625 \text{ percent}/2)}$$

or $F = 5.836$ percent. The present value of the notional \$100 million in 6 months is $x = \$100/(1 + 5.625 \text{ percent}/2) = \$97.264$ million. This amount is invested for 12 months. In the meantime, what is the risk of this FRA?

Table 11–11 displays the computation of the value at risk for the FRA. The VAR of 6-month and 12-month zeroes is 0.1629 and 0.4696, respectively, with a correlation of 0.8738. Applied to the principal of \$97.26 million, the VAR of single zeroes would be \$0.158 million and \$0.457 million, respectively. If the two zeroes were not correlated, the to-

TABLE 11-11

Computing the VAR of a 100 Million FRA (Monthly VAR at 95 Percent Level)

Position	PV of Flows x	Risk (%) V	Correlation Matrix R		Individual VAR | x | V	Component VAR βxVAR
180 days	−$97.264	0.1629	1	0.8738	$0.158	−$0.116
360 days	$97.264	0.4696	0.8738	1	$0.457	$0.444
VAR						
Undiversified					$0.615 million	
Diversified						$0.327 million

tal VAR of the FRA would be obtained from the square root of the sum of variances, which is $0.484 million.

Fortunately, the correlation, substantially lowers the FRA risk. As the table shows, the largest amount the position can lose over a month at the 95 percent level is $0.327 million, which is less than the risk of a 12-month zero.

11.5.4 Interest Rate Swaps

Interest rate swaps allow investors to exchange interest rate flows from fixed to floating, or vice versa. Swaps can be decomposed into two legs, a fixed leg and a floating leg. The fixed leg can be priced as a coupon-paying bond; the floating leg is equivalent to a floating-rate note.

To illustrate, let us compute the VAR of a $100 million 5-year interest rate swap. We enter a dollar swap that pays 6.195 percent annually for 5 years in exchange for floating-rate payments indexed to London Interbank Offer Rate (LIBOR). Initially, we consider a situation where the floating-rate note is about to be reset. Just before the reset period, we know that the coupon will be set at the prevailing market rate. Therefore, the note carries no market risk. Its market value can be mapped on cash only. Right after the reset, however, the note becomes similar to a bill with maturity equal to the next reset period.

Interest rate swaps can be viewed in two different ways, as (1) a combined position in a fixed-rate and in a floating-rate bond or (2) a portfolio of forward contracts. We first value the swap as a position in two bonds, using the risk measures in Table 11–2. Details are in Table 11–12.

The second and third columns lay out the payments on both legs. The next column lists the spot rate for maturities going from 1 to 5 years. The fifth column reports the present value of the net flows, fixed minus floating. The last column presents the component VAR, which adds up to a total diversified VAR of $2.152 million. The undiversified VAR is obtained from summing all individual VARs; as usual, the value of $2.160 million somewhat overestimates risk.

This swap also can be viewed as the sum of five forward contracts, as shown in Table 11–13. The 1-year contract promises payment of $100 million plus the coupon of 6.195 percent; discounted at the spot rate of 5.813 percent, this yields a present value of −$100.36 million. This is in exchange for $100 million now, which has no risk.

TABLE 11-12

Computing the VAR of a $100 Million Interest Rate Swap (Monthly VAR at 95 Percent Level)

| Term (year) | Cash Flow | | Rate (%Pa) | PV of Flows | Individual VAR | Component VAR |
	Fixed	Float				
1	−6.195	0	5.813	−$5.855	$0.027	$0.024
2	−6.195	0	5.929	−$5.521	$0.054	$0.053
3	−6.195	0	6.034	−$5.196	$0.077	$0.075
4	−6.195	0	6.130	−$4.883	$0.096	$0.096
5	−106.195	0	6.217	−$78.546	$1.905	$1.905
Total				−$100.00		
VAR						
Undiversified					$2.160 million	
Diversified						$2.152 million

283

TABLE 11–13

An Interest Rate Swap Viewed as Forward Contracts

| Term (year) | PV of Flows: Contract | | | | | VAR |
	1	1 × 2	2 × 3	3 × 4	4 × 5	
1	–100.36					
2		94.50				
		–94.64	89.11			
3			–89.08	83.88		
4				–83.70	78.82	
5					–78.55	
VAR	$0.471 million	$0.571 million	$0.488 million	$0.446 million	$0.425 million	
Undiversified						$2.401 million
Diversified						$2.152 million

The next contract is a 1×2 forward contract, which promises to pay the principal plus the fixed coupon in 2 years, or $-\$106.195$ million; discounted at the 2-year spot rate, this yields $-\$94.64$ million. This is in exchange for $100 million in 1 year, which is also $94.50 million discounted at the 1-year spot rate. And so on until the fifth contract, a 4×5 forward contract.

Table 11–13 shows the VAR of each contract. The undiversified VAR of $2.401 million is the result of a simple summation of the five VARS. It overstates the true risk of the position because it assumes perfect correlation between all five forward contracts, which is not the case. The fully diversified VAR is $2.152 million, exactly the same as in the preceding table. This demonstrates the equivalence of the two approaches.

Finally, we examine the change in risk after the first payment has just been set on the floating-rate leg. The floating-rate note (FRN) then becomes a 1-year bond initially valued at par but subject to fluctuations in rates. The only change in the pattern of cash flows is to add $100 million to the position on year 1 (from $-\$5.855$ to 94.145). The resulting VAR then decreases from $2.152 million to $1.763 million. More generally, the swap's VAR will converge to zero as the swap matures, dipping each time a coupon is set.

11.6 DERIVATIVES: OPTIONS

A warning flag should be raised at the outset: The delta-normal method may poorly measure the market risk of options. This is so because options are nonlinear instruments, whereas the delta-normal method is fundamentally linear.

To simplify, consider the Black-Scholes (BS) model for European options. The model assumes, besides perfect capital markets, that the underlying spot price follows a continuous *geometric brownian motion* with constant volatility $\sigma(dS/S)$. Based on these assumptions, the Black and Scholes (1973) model, as expanded by Merton (1973), gives the value of a European call as

$$c = c(S,K,\tau,r,y,\sigma) = Se^{-y\tau} N(d_1) - Ke^{-r\tau} N(d_2) \qquad (11.18)$$

where $N(d)$ is the cumulative normal distribution function described in Chapter 5 with arguments

$$d_1 = \frac{\ln(Se^{-y\tau}/Ke^{-r\tau})}{\sigma\sqrt{\tau}} + \frac{\sigma\sqrt{\tau}}{2} \qquad d_2 = d_1 - \sigma\sqrt{\tau}$$

where K is now the *exercise price* at which the option holder can, but is not obligated to, buy the asset. As before, we use y and r^* interchangeably.

Changes in the value of the option can be approximated by taking partial derivatives:

$$dc = \frac{\partial c}{\partial S} dS + \frac{1}{2} \frac{\partial^2 c}{\partial S^2} dS^2 + \frac{\partial c}{\partial r^*} dr^* + \frac{\partial c}{\partial r} dr + \frac{\partial c}{\partial \sigma} d\sigma + \frac{\partial c}{\partial t} dt \quad (11.19)$$

$$= \Delta dS + \frac{1}{2} \Gamma dS^2 + \rho^* dr^* + \rho dr + \Lambda d\sigma + \Theta dt$$

The advantage of the BS analytical formulation is that it leads to closed-form solutions for all these partial derivatives. Table 11–14 gives typical values for 3-month options with various exercise prices.

It is instructive to consider only the linear effects of the spot rate and two interest rates:

$$dc = \Delta dS + \rho^* dr^* + \rho dr$$

$$= [e^{-y\tau} N(d_1)]dS + [-Se^{-y\tau} \tau N(d_1)]dr^* + [Ke^{-r\tau} \tau N(d_2)]dr$$

$$= [Se^{-y\tau} N(d_1)] \frac{dS}{S} + [Se^{-y\tau} N(d_1)] \frac{dP^*}{P^*} - [Ke^{-r\tau} N(d_2)] \frac{dP}{P}$$

$$(11.20)$$

TABLE 11–14

Derivatives for a European Call (Parameters: S = \$100, σ = 20%, r = 5%, y = 3%, τ = 3 months)

			Exercise Price		
	Variable	Unit	$K = 90$	$K = 100$	$K = 110$
c		Dollars	11.02	4.22	1.05
		Change per:			
Δ	Spot price	Dollar	0.868	0.536	0.197
Γ	Spot price	Dollar	0.020	0.039	0.028
Λ	Volatility	(% pa)	0.103	0.198	0.139
ρ	Interest rate	(% pa)	0.191	0.124	0.047
ρ^*	Asset yield	(% pa)	−0.220	−0.135	−0.049
Θ	Time	Day	−0.014	−0.024	−0.016

This formula bears a striking resemblance to that for foreign currency forwards, as in Equation (11.15). The only difference is that the position on the spot foreign currency and on the foreign currency bill is now multiplied by $N(d_1)$, and the position on the dollar bill is multiplied by $N(d_2)$.

In the extreme case, where the option is deep in the money, both $N(d_1)$ and $N(d_2)$ are equal to unity, and the option behaves exactly like a position in a forward contract. In this case, the BS model reduces to $c = Se^{-y\tau} - Ke^{-r\tau}$, which is indeed the valuation formula for a forward contract, as in Equation (11.11).

Also note that the position on the dollar bill $Ke^{-r\tau} N(d_2)$ is equivalent to $Se^{-y\tau} N(d_1) - c = S\Delta - c$. This shows that the call option is equivalent to a position of Δ in the underlying asset plus a short position of $(\Delta S - c)$ in a dollar bill:

Long option = Long Δ asset + Short $(\Delta S - c)$ bill

For instance, assume that the delta for an at-the-money call option on an asset worth \$100 is $\Delta = 0.536$. The option itself is worth \$4.2. This option is equivalent to a \$53.6 position in the underlying asset financed by a loan of \$49.4.

Thus, when $N(d)$ is relatively stable, the risk of option positions can be constructed from component building blocks using the delta-normal approach. The main drawback of this approach, of course, is that deltas dynamically change over time, and therefore, the approximation is valid only for small movements in the underlying asset or for options with small gammas.

11.7 EQUITY PORTFOLIOS

Stock portfolios can be rather large, often with positions in excess of hundreds of securities. This motivates models for simplifying the covariance matrix. Chapter 7 examines a number of such models. The issue is whether simplifications of the "full" model cause material errors in the measurement of VAR.

The simplest model is the diagonal model, where the variance of the portfolio return R_p is, as in Equation (7.36):

$$V(R_p) = (x'\Sigma x) = (x'\beta\beta'x)\sigma_m^2 + x'D_\epsilon x \qquad (11.21)$$

To compute portfolio risk, one needs the vector of betas, which represents the systematic risks relative to a market index m, the variance of the market index σ_m^2, and the residual variances, which are captured by the diagonal matrix D_ϵ.

A further simplification obtains if one ignores the residual risk. RiskMetrics, for instance, provides risk measures for a number of stock markets. Since the portfolio beta is

$$\beta_p = \sum_{i=1}^{N} x_i \beta_i = x'\beta \tag{11.22}$$

the portfolio VAR is $\text{VAR}_p = \text{VAR}_m \beta_p$. In effect, this approximation consists of ignoring the second term in Equation (11.21). We referred to this model as the *beta model*.

TABLE 11–15

Computing the VAR of a $100 Million Stock Portfolio (Monthly VAR at 95 Percent Level)

	Position	Covariance Matrix			VAR
		GM	**FORD**	**HWP**	
VAR (%)		14.01	13.41	15.68	
Beta		0.806	1.183	1.864	
Cov. matrix					
Full					
GM	$33.33 million	72.17	43.92	26.32	$11.76 million
FORD	$33.33 million	43.92	66.12	44.31	
HWP	$33.33 million	26.32	44.31	90.41	
Diagonal					
GM	$33.33 million	72.17	11.35	17.87	$10.13 million
FORD	$33.33 million	11.35	66.12	26.23	
HWP	$33.33 million	17.87	26.23	90.41	
Beta					
GM	$33.33 million	7.73	11.35	17.88	$7.30 million
FORD	$33.33 million	11.35	16.65	26.24	
HWP	$33.33 million	17.88	26.24	41.32	
Undiversified					
GM	$33.33 million	72.17	69.08	80.78	$14.37 million
FORD	$33.33 million	69.08	66.12	77.32	
HWP	$33.33 million	80.78	77.32	90.41	

Finally, regulators are considering a measure of VAR that is undiversified, i.e., where all correlations are set to unity. The issue is, What is the effect of these approximations on the portfolio VAR?

As an example, let us go back to the three-stock portfolio described in Chapter 7. A total of $100 million is invested equally in GM, Ford, and Hewlett Packard (HWP). The VAR is computed over a monthly horizon at the 95 percent confidence level. The first line in Table 11–15 shows the VAR of each individual stock, which ranges from $13.41 million to $15.68 million for a $100 million position.

Next, the table displays four covariance matrices: the full model, the diagonal model, the beta model, and the undiversified model. Their respective VARs are $11.76, $10.13, $7.30, and $14.37. These numbers indicate that the diagonal model provides a good approximation of the actual portfolio VAR, although slightly on the low side. The beta model, in contrast, substantially underestimates the true VAR because it ignores residual risk.

Finally, the undiversified VAR is too conservative. The value of $14.37 is also obtained from adding the individual VARs, $33.33 × 14.01 percent + $33.33 × 13.41 percent + $33.33 × 15.68 percent = $14.37. This measure of risk fails to recognize the diversification properties of portfolios.

As the number of stocks in the portfolio increases from three to hundreds, we would expect that the VAR from the diagonal model will provide an increasingly better approximation of the actual VAR. This is so because the total portfolio risk decreases as the number of assets increases.

CHAPTER 12

Simulation Methods

Deus ex machina

Wall Street is often compared to a casino. The analogy is appropriate in one respect: Securities firms commonly use simulation techniques, known as *Monte Carlo methods,* to value complex derivatives. Simulation methods approximate the behavior of financial prices by using computer simulations to generate random price paths.

Numerical simulations were first used by atom bomb scientists at Los Alamos in 1942 to crack problems that could not be solved by conventional means. The name *Monte Carlo* was derived from the name of a famous casino established in 1862 in the south of France (actually, in Monaco). What better way to evoke random draws, roulette, and games of chance?

These methods are used to simulate a variety of different scenarios for the portfolio value on the target date. These scenarios can be generated in a random fashion (as in Monte Carlo simulation), or from historical data (as in historical simulation), or in other, more systematic ways. The portfolio value at risk (VAR) can then be read off directly from the distribution of simulated portfolio values.

Because of its flexibility, the simulation method is by far the most powerful approach to value at risk. It potentially can account for a wide range of risks, including price risk, volatility risk, and nonlinear exposures. In principle, simulations can be extended to longer horizons, which is important for credit risk measurement, and to the interaction of assets and liabilities. It also can measure operational risk.

This approach, however, involves costly investments in intellectual and systems development. It also requires substantially more computing power than simpler methods. Time requirements, however, are being whittled down by advances in computers and faster valuation methods.

This chapter shows how simulation methods can be used to uncover VAR. The first section introduces a simple case with just one random variable. Section 12.2 then discusses the tradeoff between speed and accuracy. The case with many sources of risk is discussed in Section 12.3. Next, Sections 12.4 and 12.5 turn to newer methods, deterministic simulations, and scenario simulations. The choice of models is reviewed in Section 12.6. Finally, Section 12.7 provides some concluding thoughts.

12.1 SIMULATIONS WITH ONE RANDOM VARIABLE

The basic concept behind the Monte Carlo approach is to simulate repeatedly a random process for the financial variable of interest, covering a wide range of possible situations. These variables are drawn from prespecified probability distributions that are assumed known. Thus simulations recreate the entire distribution of portfolio values.

We first concentrate on a simple case with just one random variable.

12.1.1 Simulating a Price Path

The first, and most crucial, step in the simulation consists of choosing a particular stochastic model for the behavior of prices. A commonly used model is the *geometric brownian motion* (GBM), which underlies much of option pricing theory. The model assumes that innovations in the asset price are uncorrelated over time and that small movements in prices can be described by

$$dS_t = \mu_t S_t dt + \sigma_t S_t dz \qquad (12.1)$$

where dz is a random variable distributed normally with mean zero and variance dt. This variable drives the random shocks to the price and does not depend on past information. It is *brownian* in the sense that its variance continuously decreases with the time interval, $V(dz) = dt$. This rules out processes with sudden jumps, for instance. The process is also *geometric* because all parameters are scaled by the current price S_t.

The parameters μ_t and σ_t represent the instantaneous drift and volatility at time t, which can evolve over time. For simplicity, we will assume in what follows that these parameters are constant over time. But since μ_t and σ_t can be functions of past variables, it would be easy to simulate time variation in the variances as in a GARCH process, for example.

In practice, the process with infinitesimally small increment dt can be approximated by discrete moves of size Δt. Define t as the present time, T as the target time, and $\tau = T - t$ as the (VAR) horizon. To generate a series of random variables S_{t+i} over the interval τ, we first chop up τ into n increments, with $\Delta t = \tau/n$.[1]

Integrating dS/S over a finite interval, we have approximately

$$\Delta S_t = S_{t-1}(\mu\Delta t + \sigma\epsilon\sqrt{\Delta t}) \tag{12.2}$$

where ϵ is now a standard normal random variable, i.e., with mean zero and unit variance. We can verify that this process generates a mean $E(\Delta S/S) = \mu\Delta t$, which grows with time, as does the variance $V(\Delta S/S) = \sigma^2\Delta t$.

To simulate the price path for S, we start from S_t and generate a sequence of epsilons (ϵ's) for $i = 1, 2, \ldots, n$. Then S_{t+1} is set at $S_{t+1} = S_t + S_t(\mu\Delta t + \sigma\epsilon_1\sqrt{\Delta t})$, S_{t+2} is similarly computed from $S_{t+1} + S_{t+1}(\mu\Delta t + \sigma\epsilon_2\sqrt{\Delta t})$, and so on for future values, until the target horizon is reached, at which point the price is $S_{t+n} = S_T$.

Table 12–1 illustrates a simulation of a process with a drift (μ) of zero and volatility (σ) of 10 percent over the total interval. The initial price is \$100, and the interval is cut into 100 steps. Therefore, the local volatility is $0.10 \times \sqrt{1/100} = 0.01$.

The second column starts with the initial price. The next column displays the realization of a standard normal variable. With no drift, the increment in the following column is simply ($\epsilon \times 0.01$). Finally, the last column computes the current price from the previous price and the increment. The values at each point are conditional on the simulated values at the previous point. The process is repeated until the final price of \$91.06 is reached at the 100th step.

Figure 12–1 presents two price paths, each leading to a different ending price. Given these assumptions, the ending price must follow a normal distribution with mean of \$100 and standard deviation of \$10.[2] This

---

1. The choice of number of steps should depend on the VAR horizon and the required accuracy. A smaller number of steps will be faster to implement but may not provide a good approximation to the stochastic process.
2. In fact, the ending distribution is actually log normal, since the price can never fall below 0.

TABLE 12-1

Simulating a Price Path

Step i	Previous Price S_{t+i-1}	Random Variable ϵ_i	Increment ΔS	Current Price S_{t+i}
1	100.00	0.199	0.00199	100.20
2	100.20	1.665	0.01665	101.87
3	101.87	−0.445	−0.00446	101.41
4	101.41	−0.667	−0.00668	100.74
⋮				
100	92.47	1.153	−0.0153	91.06

FIGURE 12-1

Simulating price paths.

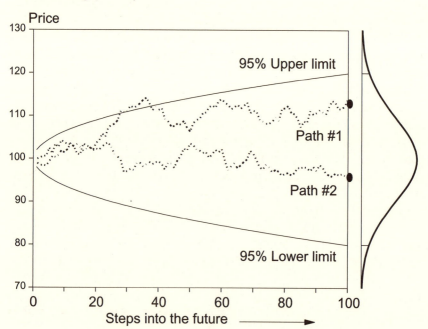

distribution is illustrated on the right side of the figure, along with 95 percent confidence bands, corresponding to two standard deviation intervals.

But the distribution also is known at any intermediate point. The figure displays 95 percent confidence bands, which increase with the square root of time until they reach $\pm 2 \times 10$ percent. In this simple model, risk can be computed at any point up to the target horizon.

12.1.2 Creating Random Numbers

Monte Carlo simulations are based on random draws ϵ from a variable with the desired probability distribution. The numerical analysis usually proceeds in two steps.

The first building block for a random number generator is a uniform distribution over the interval [0, 1], which produces a random variable x. More properly speaking, these numbers are "pseudo" random because they are generated from an algorithm using a predefined rule. Starting from the same "seed" number, the sequence can be repeated at will.

The next step is to transform the uniform random number x into the desired distribution through the inverse cumulative probability distribution function (pdf). Take the normal distribution. By definition, the cumulative pdf $N(y)$ is always between 0 and 1. Therefore, to generate a normally distributed random variable, we compute y such that $x = N(y)$, or $y = N^{-1}(x)$.[3] More generally, any distribution function can be generated as long as the function $N(y)$ can be inverted. Figure 12–2 illustrates the transformation.

At this point, an important caveat is in order. It seems easy to generate variables that are purely random, but in practice, it is quite difficult. A well-designed algorithm will generate draws that "appear" independent over time. Whether this sequence is truly random is a philosophical issue that we will not address. Good random number generators must create series that pass all conventional tests of independence. Otherwise, the characteristics of the simulated price process will not obey the underlying model.

Most operating systems, unfortunately, provide a random number generator that is simple but inaccurate. All algorithms "cycle" after some

---

3. Moro (1995) shows how to use approximations to the function N^{-1} to accelerate the speed of computation.

FIGURE 12-2

Transformation from uniform to normal.

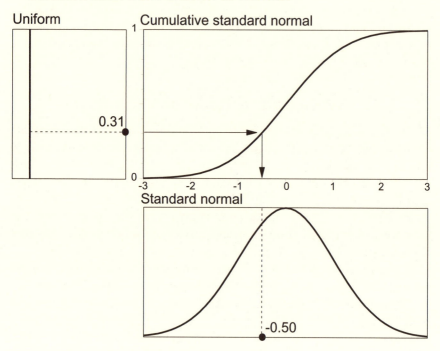

iterations; i.e., they repeat the same sequence of pseudorandom numbers. Good algorithms cycle after billions of draws; bad ones may cycle after a few thousand only.

If the cycle is too short, dependencies will be introduced in the price process solely because of the random number generator. As a result, the range of possible portfolio values may be incomplete, thus leading to incorrect measures of VAR. This is why it is important to investigate the qualities of the algorithm, which, after all, drive the entire result.

12.1.3 The Bootstrap

An alternative to generating random numbers from a hypothetical distribution is to sample from historical data with replacement. Thus we are agnostic about the distribution. For example, suppose we observe a series of M returns $R = \Delta S/S$, $\{R\} = (R_1 \ldots R_M)$, which can be assumed to be i.i.d. random variables drawn from an unknown distribution. The historical simulation method consists of using this series once to generate pseudore-turns. But this can be extended much further.

The bootstrap estimates this distribution by the empirical distribu-tion of R, assigning equal probability to each realization. The method was proposed initially by Efron (1979) as a nonparametric randomization tech-nique that draws from the observed distribution of the data to model the distribution of a statistic of interest.[4]

The procedure is carried out by sampling from $\{R\}$, with replace-ment, as many observations as necessary. For instance, assume that we want to generate 100 returns into the future, but we do not want to im-pose any assumption on the distribution of daily returns. We could pro-ject returns by randomly picking one return at a time from the sample over the past $M = 500$ days, with replacement. Define the index choice as $m(1)$, a number between 1 and 500. The selected return is then $R_{m(1)}$, and the simulated next-day return is $S_{t+1} = S_t(1 + R_{m(1)})$. Repeating the operation for a total of 100 draws yields a total of 100 pseudovalues S_{t+1}, . . ., S_{t+n}.

An essential advantage of the bootstrap is that it can include fat tails, jumps, or any departure from the normal distribution. For instance, one could include the return for the crash of October 19, 1987, which would never (or nearly never) occur under a normal distribution. The method also accounts for correlations across series, since one draw consists of the si-multaneous returns for N series, such as stock, bonds, and currency prices.

The bootstrap approach, it should be noted, has limitations. For small sample sizes M, the bootstrapped distribution may be a poor approxima-tion to the actual one. Therefore, it is important to have access to suffi-cient data points. The other drawback of the bootstrap is that is relies heavily on the assumption that returns are independent. By resampling at random, any pattern of time variation is broken.

The bootstrap, however, also can accommodate some time variation in parameters as long as we are willing to take a stand on the model. For instance, the bootstrap can be applied to the normalized residuals of a GARCH process:

$$\epsilon_t = \frac{r_t}{\sqrt{h_t}}$$

---

4. The asymptotic properties of the bootstrap for commonly used statistics such as the mean, me-dian, variance, and distribution quantiles have been studied by Bickel and Freedman (1981).

where r_t is the actual return, and h_t is the conditional variance from the estimated GARCH process. To recreate pseudoreturns, one would then first sample from the historical distribution of ϵ and then reconstruct the conditional variance and pseudoreturns. Given that the purpose of VAR is to capture behavior in the tails and that historical data display fatter tails than in normal distributions, the bootstrap is ideally suited to VAR methods.

12.1.4 Computing VAR

Once a price path has been simulated, we can build the portfolio distribution at the end of the selected horizon. The simulation is carried out by the following steps:

1. Choose a stochastic process and parameters.
2. Generate a pseudosequence of variables $\epsilon_1, \epsilon_2, \ldots, \epsilon_n$, from which prices are computed as $S_{t+1}, S_{t+2}, \ldots, S_{t+n}$.
3. Calculate the value of the asset (or portfolio) $F_{t+n} = F_T$ under this particular sequence of prices at the target horizon.
4. Repeat steps 2 and 3 as many times as necessary, say, $K = 10,000$.

This process creates a distribution of values $F_T^1, \ldots, F_T^{10,000}$. We can sort the observations and tabulate the expected value $E(F_T)$ and the quantile $Q(F_T,c)$, which is the value exceeded in c times 10,000 replications. VAR is then

$$\mathrm{VAR}(c,T) = E(F_T) - Q(F_T,c) \qquad (12.3)$$

12.1.5 Risk Management and Pricing Methods

It is interesting to note that the Monte Carlo method was proposed originally in the context of option valuation.[5] Simulations are particularly useful to evaluate options that have no closed-form solution. Under the risk-

---

5. See Boyle (1977) and, more recently, a review by Boyle et al. (1997).

neutral valuation method, Monte Carlo simulation consists of the following steps:

1. Choose a process with a drift equal to the risk-free rate, i.e., with $\mu = r$ in Equation (12.1).
2. Simulate prices to the horizon S_T.
3. Calculate the payoff of the derivative at maturity T, $F(S_T)$.
4. Repeat these steps as often as needed.

The current value of the derivative is obtained from discounting at the risk-free rate and averaging across all experiments:

$$f_t = E^*[e^{-r\tau} F(S_T)] \qquad (12.4)$$

where the expectation indicates averaging and the asterisk is a reminder that the price paths are under risk-neutrality, i.e., both changing the expected return and the discount rate to the risk-free rate.

This method is quite general and can be applied to options that have price-dependent paths (such as lookback options or average rate options) or strange payoffs at expiration (such as nonlinear functions of the ending price). Its main drawback is that it cannot price options accurately where the holder can exercise early. Also, the distribution of prices must be finely measured to price options with sharp discontinuities, such as binary options, which pay a fixed amount if the price ends up above or below the strike price. With large "holes" in the price distributions, the payoffs on combinations of binary options simply could not appear in the final portfolio distribution. Thus highly complex payoffs can be handled with increased precision.

Monte Carlo methods also allow users to measure vega risk, or exposure to changes in volatility. All that is required is to repeat the simulation with the same sequence of ϵ values but with another value for σ. The change in the value of the asset due solely to the change in the volatility measures vega risk.

12.2 SPEED VERSUS ACCURACY

The main drawback of Monte Carlo (MC) methods is their computational time requirements. Consider, for instance, a portfolio exposed to one risk factor only. Say we require 10,000 replications of this risk factor for acceptable accuracy. If the portfolio contains 1000 assets, we will need 10,000,000 full valuations.

If, in addition, the portfolio contains complex instruments, such as mortgages or exotic options, whose valuation itself requires a simulation. Measuring risk at a target date then requires "a simulation within a simulation":

- For valuation (i.e., from the VAR horizon to the maturity of the instrument)
- For risk management (i.e., from the present time to the VAR horizon)

Without shortcuts, the number of required simulations can soon reach astronomical values. This is why the industry is busily developing methods to cut down the number of simulations without too much loss in accuracy.

12.2.1 Accuracy

Simulations inevitably generate *sampling variability,* or variations in summary statistics due to the limited number of replications. More replications lead to more precise estimates but take longer to estimate. Define K as the number of *replications,* or pseudorandom trials. To choose K, it is useful to assess the tradeoff between precision and the number of replications.

Figure 12–3 illustrates the convergence of the empirical distribution toward the true one. With $K = 100$, the histogram representing the distribution of the ending price is quite irregular. The histogram becomes smoother with 1000 replications, even more so with 10,000 replications, and eventually should converge to the continuous distribution in the right panel. One advantage of the MC method is that the user can evaluate the increase in accuracy directly as the number of replications increases.

If the underlying process is normal, the empirical distribution must converge to a normal distribution. In this situation, Monte Carlo analysis should yield exactly the same result as the delta-normal method: The VAR estimated from the sample quantile must converge to the value of $\alpha\sigma$.

Any deviation must be due to sampling variation. Assuming no other source of error, this effect can be measured by the asymptotic standard error reported in Equation (5.21), which shows that the standard error is inversely related to the square root of K. This is illustrated in Table 12–2,

FIGURE 12–3

Convergence to true distribution.

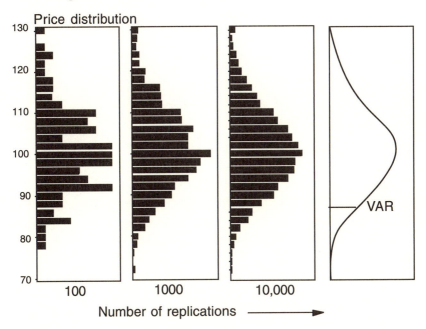

which provides the results of 100 simulation runs of a standard normal distribution with an increasing number of replications.

The table shows that for a 99 percent VAR with 100 replications, the standard error of the estimate around 2.33 is 0.42, rather high. In our sample of 100 runs, the VAR estimate ranged from a low of −1.67 to a high of −3.47. This dispersion is clearly unacceptable. To increase VAR precision by a factor of 10, we need to increase the number of replications by a factor of 100, for a total of 10,000.

12.2.2 Acceleration Methods

Researchers are busily developing methods to accelerate computations. One of the earliest, and easiest, is the *antithetic variable technique,* which consists of changing the sign of all the random samples ε. This creates twice the number of replications for the risk factors at little additional cost. We still need, however, twice the original number of full valuations on the target date.

TABLE 12–2

Convergence Statistics

		Standard Error of Quantile		
		Replications:		
Left Tail	**Expected Quantile**	**100**	**1000**	**10,000**
1%	−2.326	0.418	0.112	0.036
5%	−1.645	0.228	0.062	0.021
10%	−1.282	0.164	0.052	0.016

This method also can be applied to the historical simulation method, where we can add a vector of historical price changes with the sign reversed. This is also useful to eliminate the effect of trends in the recent historical data.

Glasserman et al. (1999) discuss *importance sampling techniques,* which attempt to sample along the paths that are most important for the problem at hand. The idea is that if our goal is to measure a tail quantile accurately, there is no point doing simulations that will generate observations in the center of the distribution. The method involves shifts in the distribution of random variables. These authors show that relative to the usual MC method, the variance of VAR estimators can be reduced by a factor of at least 10. Other techniques are discussed later in this chapter.

12.3 SIMULATIONS WITH MULTIPLE VARIABLES

12.3.1 From Independent to Correlated Variables

In practice, portfolios contain more than one source of financial risk. Even simple securities such as convertible bonds depend on a combination of two or more financial variables. The simulation methodology can be extended easily to the more general multivariate case, which considers N sources of risk.

Simulations handle well portfolios that depend on more than one state variable. This is so because the computation time increases linearly with N, whereas the time for other methods such as the binomial method or the finite-difference method increases geometrically with N.

If the variables are uncorrelated, the randomization can be performed independently for each variable:

$$\Delta S_{j,t} = S_{j,t-1}(\mu_j \Delta t + \sigma_j \epsilon_{j,t} \sqrt{\Delta t}) \tag{12.5}$$

where the ϵ values are independent across time period and series $j = 1, \ldots, N$.

Generally, however, variables are correlated. To account for this correlation, we start with a set of independent variables η, which are then transformed into the ϵ. In a two-variable setting, we construct

$$\begin{aligned} \epsilon_1 &= \eta_1 \\ \epsilon_2 &= \rho\eta_1 + (1 - \rho^2)^{1/2}\eta_2 \end{aligned} \tag{12.6}$$

where ρ is the correlation coefficient between the variables ϵ. First, we verify that the variance of ϵ_2 is unity:

$$V(\epsilon_2) = \rho^2 V(\eta_1) + [(1 - \rho^2)^{1/2}]^2 V(\eta_2) = \rho^2 + (1 - \rho^2) = 1$$

Then we compute the covariance of the ϵ as

$$\text{cov}(\epsilon_1, \epsilon_2) = \text{cov}[\eta_1, \rho\eta_1 + (1 - \rho^2)^{1/2}\eta_2] = \rho\,\text{cov}(\eta_1, \eta_1) = \rho$$

This confirms that the ϵ variables have correlation of ρ. The question is, How was the transformation (Equation 12.6) chosen?

12.3.2 The Cholesky Factorization

More generally, suppose that we have a vector of N values of ϵ, which we would like to display some correlation structure $V(\epsilon) = E(\epsilon\epsilon') = R$. Since the matrix R is a symmetrical real matrix, it can be decomposed into its *Cholesky* factors

$$R = TT' \tag{12.7}$$

where T is a lower triangular matrix with zeros in the upper right corners.

Then start from an N vector η, which is composed of independent variables all with unit variances. In other words, $V(\eta) = I$, where I is the identity matrix with zeros everywhere except on the diagonal. Next, construct the variable $\epsilon = T\eta$. Its covariance matrix is $V(\epsilon) = E(\epsilon\epsilon') =$

$E(T\eta\eta'T') = TE(\eta\eta')T' = TIT' = TT' = R$. Thus we have confirmed that the values of ϵ have the desired correlations.

As an example, consider the two-variable case. The matrix can be decomposed into

$$\begin{bmatrix} 1 & \rho \\ \rho & 1 \end{bmatrix} = \begin{bmatrix} a_{11} & 0 \\ a_{12} & a_{22} \end{bmatrix} \begin{bmatrix} a_{11} & a_{12} \\ 0 & a_{22} \end{bmatrix} = \begin{bmatrix} a_{11}^2 & a_{11}a_{12} \\ a_{11}a_{12} & a_{12}^2 + a_{22}^2 \end{bmatrix}$$

Because the Cholesky matrix is triangular, the factors can be found by successive substitution by setting

$$a_{11}^2 = 1$$
$$a_{11}a_{12} = \rho$$
$$a_{12}^2 + a_{22}^2 = 1$$

which yields

$$\begin{bmatrix} 1 & \rho \\ \rho & 1 \end{bmatrix} = \begin{bmatrix} 1 & 0 \\ \rho & (1 - \rho^2)^{1/2} \end{bmatrix} \begin{bmatrix} 1 & \rho \\ 0 & (1 - \rho^2)^{1/2} \end{bmatrix}$$

And indeed, this is how Equation (12.6) was obtained:

$$\begin{bmatrix} \epsilon_1 \\ \epsilon_2 \end{bmatrix} = \begin{bmatrix} 1 & 0 \\ \rho & (1 - \rho^2)^{1/2} \end{bmatrix} \begin{bmatrix} \eta_1 \\ \eta_2 \end{bmatrix}$$

This explains how a multivariate set of random variables can be created from simple building blocks consisting of i.i.d. variables. In addition to providing a method to generate correlated variables, this approach generates valuable insight into the random number generation process.

12.3.3 Number of Independent Factors

For the decomposition to work, the matrix R must be positive-definite. Otherwise, there is no way to transform N independent source of risks into N correlated variables of ϵ.

As discussed in Chapter 7, this condition can be verified with the singular value decomposition. This alternative decomposition of the covariance matrix provides a check that the matrix is well behaved. If any of the eigenvalues is zero or less than zero, the Cholesky decomposition will fail.

When the matrix R is not positive-definite, its *determinant* is zero. Intuitively speaking, the determinant d is a measure of the "volume" of a matrix. If d is zero, the dimension of the matrix is less than N. The determinant can be computed easily from the Cholesky decomposition into two matrices. Since the matrix T has zeros above its diagonal, its determinant reduces to the product of all diagonal coefficients, $d_T = \Pi_{i=1}^{N} a_{ii}$. The determinant of the covariance matrix R is then $d = d_T^2$.

In our two-factor example, the matrix is not positive-definite if $\rho = 1$, which implies that the two factors are really the same. The Cholesky decomposition then yields $a_{11} = 1$, $a_{12} = 1$, and $a_{22} = 0$, and the determinant $d = (a_{11}a_{22})^2$ is 0. As a result, the second factor η_2 is never used, and ϵ_1 is always the same as ϵ_2. The second random variable is totally superfluous. In this case, the covariance matrix is not positive-definite and has rank of one, or only one meaningful risk factor.

These conditions may seem academic but, unfortunately, soon become very real with simulations based on a large number of factors. The RiskMetrics covariance matrix, for instance, is routinely non-positive-definite due to the large number of assets. These problems can arise for a number of reasons. Perhaps this is simply due to the large number of correlations. With $N = 450$, for instance, we have about 100,000 correlations with rounding errors. This also could happen when the effective number of observations T is less than the number of factors N. One drawback of time-varying models of variances is that they put less weight on older observations, thereby reducing the effective sample size. Or the correlations may have been measured over different periods, which may produce inconsistent correlations.[6] Another reason would be that the series are naturally highly correlated (such as the 9-year zero coupon bond with the adjoining maturities) or that some series were constructed as a linear combination of others (such as a currency basket).

For simulations, this may be a blessing in disguise, since fewer numbers of variables are sufficient. In Chapter 7, we gave the example of 11 bonds for which the covariance matrix could be reduced without much loss of information to two, or perhaps three, principal components. Thus the problem can be solved using a matrix of smaller dimensions, which considerably speeds up the computation. This illustrates that the design of simulation experiments, including the number of risk factors, is critical.

---

6. Consider three assets. We have 1 year of data for assets A and B and a high correlation. For asset C, we only have 1 month of data. If asset C has a high observed correlation with A and a low enough correlation with B, the correlation matrix will be inconsistent.

12.4 DETERMINISTIC SIMULATION

Monte Carlo simulations methods generate independent, pseudorandom points that attempt to "fill" an N-dimensional space, where N is the number of variables driving the price of securities. Researchers now realize that the sequence of points does not have to be chosen randomly.

Indeed, it is possible to use a *deterministic* scheme that is constructed to provide a more consistent fill to the N-space. The choice must account for the sample size, dimensionality of the problem, and possibly the shape of the function being integrated. These deterministic schemes are sometimes called *quasi-Monte Carlo,* although this is a misnomer because there is nothing random about them. The numbers are not independent but rather are constructed as an ordered sequence of points.

To illustrate, Figure 12–4 compares a distribution for two variables only (after all, this is the number of dimensions of a page). The figure shows, on the left, pseudorandom points and, on the right, a deterministic, *low-discrepancy* sequence obtained from a so-called Sobol procedure.[7]

The left graph shows that the points often "clump" in some regions and leave out large areas. These clumps are a waste because they do not contribute more information. The right panel, in contrast, has more uni-

---

7. This algorithm is described in Press et al. (1992).

FIGURE   12–4

Comparison of distributions.

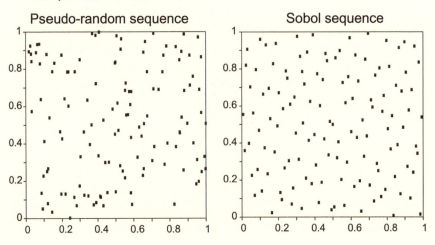

form coverage. Instead of drawing independent samples, the deterministic scheme systematically fills the space left by the previous numbers in the series.

Quasi-random methods have the desirable property that the standard error shrinks at a faster rate, proportional to close to $1/K$ rather than $1/\sqrt{K}$ for standard simulations. Indeed, a number of authors have shown that deterministic methods provide a noticeable improvement in speed.[8] Papageorgiou and Paskov (1999) compare the computation of VAR for a portfolio exposed to 34 risk factors using 1000 points. They find that the deterministic sequence is 10 times more accurate than the Monte Carlo method.

One drawback of these methods is that since the draws are not independent, accuracy cannot be assessed easily. There is no doubt, though, that these methods provide a substantial acceleration in the computations. Since this is currently an active field of research, we can expect further progress in these methods.

12.5 SCENARIO SIMULATION

We can go one step further in the design of the simulations by decreasing even further the number of points. *Scenario simulation* is a method introduced by Jamshidian and Zhu (1997) that uses information about the structure of the problem to design a very efficient simulation with a limited number of scenarios.

Consider, for instance, the problem of estimating the distribution of a 10-year interest rate swap values. This involves perhaps 12 risk factors, key rates along the yield curve. The first step consists of using principal-component analysis, developed in Chapter 7, to reduce the dimensionality of the problem. We have seen that two or three independent factors are in fact sufficient.

The second step consists of building scenarios for each of these factors, approximating a normal distribution by a binomial distribution with a small number of states. If $m + 1$ states are selected, the probability of state i is

$$P(i) = 2^{-m}\left(\frac{m!}{i!(m-i)!}\right) \qquad i = 0, \ldots, m \qquad (12.8)$$

---

8. See, for example, Boyle et al. (1997) for call options and Paskov and Traub (1995) for mortgage securities.

For instance, we could select seven states for the first factor with probabilities given by

$$\frac{1}{64}, \quad \frac{6}{63}, \quad \frac{15}{64}, \quad \frac{20}{64}, \quad \frac{15}{64}, \quad \frac{6}{64}, \quad \frac{1}{64}$$

Since the second and third factors are less important, we can use fewer scenarios, say, five and three, respectively. Since factors are independent, we can find their joint distribution from the total of $7 \times 5 \times 3 = 105$ scenarios.

The first scenario, for instance, would involve the lowest values for the variables and a probability of $1/64 \times 1/16 \times 1/4 = 0.00024$. We then transform the principal-component variables into 12 changes along the yield curve, which we use to value the swap. After having priced all scenarios, we combine the probability of each scenario with the swap value to build a probability distribution function.

As Table 12–3 shows, this method produces results very close to a Monte Carlo analysis with 20,000 replications. With only 105 valuations, this method is much more efficient. Intuitively, this is so because the method leverages the dimensionality of the problem. The approach would be very poor with only one risk factor but is increasingly better as N increases.

In addition, the method gives much better control over the extreme values. The probability of large moves can be altered manually for stress-testing purposes.

Indeed, this method was used to calculate the risk exposure of the derivative product subsidiary of Sakura Global Capital, which involves a large multicurrency portfolio of swaps.

TABLE 12–3

Risk Profile of a $100 Million 10-Year Swap 30-Day Horizon

Method	Standard Deviation	97.5% VAR	99.0% VAR
Two-factor (5 × 3)	$2723		
Three-factor (7 × 5 × 3)	$2727	$6764	$9020
Monte Carlo	$2711	$7154	$8682

12.6 CHOOSING THE MODEL

These simulation methods, however, are prone to model risk. If the stochastic process chosen for the price is unrealistic, so will the estimate of VAR. This is why the choice of the underlying process is particularly important.

For example, the geometric brownian motion model in Equation (12.1) adequately describes the behavior of some financial variables, such as stock prices and exchange rates, but certainly not that of fixed-income securities. In the brownian motion model, shocks to the price are never reversed, and prices move as a random walk. This cannot represent the price process for default-free bond prices, which must converge to their face value at expiration.

Another approach is to model the dynamics of interest rates as

$$dr_t = \kappa \, (\theta - r_t)dt + \sigma r_t^{\gamma} dz_t \qquad (12.9)$$

This class of model includes the Vasicek (1977) model when $\gamma = 0$; changes in yields are then normally distributed, which is particularly convenient because this leads to many closed-form solutions. With $\gamma = 0.5$, this is also the Cox, Ingersoll, and Ross (1985) model of the term structure (CIR). With $\gamma = 1$, the model is log normal.[9]

This process is important because it provides a simple description of the stochastic nature of interest rates that is consistent with the empirical observation that interest rates tend to be mean reverting. Here, the parameter $\kappa < 1$ defines the speed of mean reversion toward the long-run value θ; situations where current interest rates are high, such as $r_t > \theta$, imply a negative drift $\kappa(\theta - r_t)$ until rates revert to θ. Conversely, low current rates are associated with positive expected drift. Also note that with $\gamma = 0.5$, the variance of this process is proportional to the level of interest rates; as the interest rate moves toward 0, the variance decreases, so r can never fall below 0.

Equation (12.9) describes a one-factor model of interest rates that is driven by movements in short-term rates dr_t. In this model, movements in longer-term rates are perfectly correlated with movements in this short-term rate through dz. The correlation matrix of zero-coupon bonds consists of ones only. This may be useful to describe the risks of some simple portfolios but certainly not for the leveraged fixed-income portfolios of financial institutions.

---

9. Bliss and Smith (1998) show that $\gamma = 0.5$ provides a good fit to U.S. short-term interest rates.

For more precision, additional factors can be added. Brennan and Schwartz (1979), for example, proposed a two-factor model with a short and long interest rate modeled as:

$$dr_t = \kappa_1(\theta_1 - r_t)dt + \sigma_1 dz_{1t} \qquad (12.10)$$

$$dl_t = \kappa_2(\theta_2 - l_t)dt + \sigma_2 dz_{2t} \qquad (12.11)$$

where the errors have some correlation. Generalizing, one could use the full covariance matrix along some 14 points on the yield curve as provided by RiskMetrics. In theory, *finer granularity* should result in better risk measures, albeit at the expense of computational time. In all these cases, the Monte Carlo experiment consists of first simulating movements in the driving risk factors and then using the simulated term structure to price the securities at the target date.

Here is where risk management differs from valuation methods. For short horizons (say, 1 day to 1 month), we could assume that changes in yields are jointly normally distributed. This assumption may be quite sufficient for risk-management purposes. Admittedly, it would produce inconsistencies over long horizons (say, beyond a year) because each yield could drift in different directions, creating term structures that look unrealistic.[10]

With longer horizons, the drift term in Equation (12.10), for example, becomes increasingly important. To ensure that the two rates cannot move too far away from each other, one could incorporate into the drift of the long rate an *error-correction term* that pushes the long rate down when it is higher than the short rate. For instance, one could set

$$dr_t = \kappa_1[\theta_1 - (r_t - l_t)]dt + \sigma_1 dz_{1t} \qquad (12.12)$$

Indeed, much work has been devoted to the analysis of time-series that are *cointegrated*, i.e., that share a common random component.[11] J.P. Morgan's CorporateMetrics, for instance, relies on cointegration relationships to project long-term variables. These error-correction mecha-

---

10. This explains why the Black model is often used to price short-term options on long-term bonds. Although theoretically inconsistent, it produces good results because the maturity of the option is so short relative to that of the underlying.

11. Much of the ground-breaking work in cointegration was done by Engle and Granger, of the University of California at San Diego. See, for instance, Engle and Granger (1991), a good review book.

nisms can be applied to larger-scale problems, thus making sure our 14 yields move in an admissible fashion.

Furthermore, over shorter horizons, the distinction between equilibrium models and arbitrage models loses its importance. Equilibrium models postulate a stochastic process for some risk factors, which generates a term structure. This term structure, however, will not fit exactly the current term structure, which is not satisfactory for fixed-income option traders. Traders argue that if the model does not even fit current bond prices, it cannot possibly be useful to describe options. This is why *arbitrage models* take today's term structure as an input (instead of output for the equilibrium models) and fit the stochastic process accordingly.

For instance, a one-factor no-arbitrage model is

$$dr_t = \theta(t)dt + \sigma dz_t \qquad (12.13)$$

where the function $\theta(t)$ is chosen so that today's bond prices fit the current term structure. This approach has been extended to two-factor Heath-Jarrow-Morton (1992) models, but their estimation is computer-intensive and has been described as "at the very boundaries of feasibility."[12]

For risk-management purposes, what matters is to capture the richness in movements in the term structure, not necessarily to price today's instruments to the last decimal point. Thus the "art" of risk management lies in deciding what elements of the model are important.

12.7 CONCLUSIONS

Simulation methods are now widely used for risk-management purposes. Interestingly, these methods can be traced back to the valuation of complex options, except that there is no discounting. Thus the investment in intellectual and systems development for derivatives trading can be used readily for computing value at risk. No doubt this is why officials at the Fed have stated that derivatives ". . . have had favorable spill-over effects on institutions' abilities to manage their total portfolios."

Simulation methods are quite flexible. They can either postulate a stochastic process or resample from historical data. They allow full valuation on the target date. On the downside, they are more prone to model risk, due to the need to prespecify the distribution, and are much slower and less transparent than analytical methods.

---

12. See Rebonato (1996).

TABLE 12–4

Comparison of VAR Methods

Risk-Factor Distribution	Valuation Method	
	Local Valuation	Full Valuation
Variance-covariance	Delta-normal	
Binomial scenarios		Scenario simulation
Deterministic simulation		Full simulation
Monte Carlo simulation or historical simulation	Delta-gamma-MC	Full Monte Carlo or grid MD (interpolation)

In recent years, a number of simulation methods have developed. These are listed in Table 12–4 in order of increasing time requirement.

The Monte Carlo method generates random draws for the risk factors from prespecified distributions. The historical simulation method simply uses changes that appeared in recent history. While flexible, these methods create substantial sampling variation in the measurement of VAR. Greater precision comes at the expense of vastly increasing the number of replications, which slows down the process.

In contrast with these "random" approaches, new methods impose more structure on the simulation. Deterministic simulations create more systematic coverage of the risk factors and allow greater precision for the same number of data points. Scenario simulations reduce the dimensionality of the problem even further.

Overall, simulation methods are likely to become ubiquitous tools in risk management. With the ever decreasing cost of computing power and advances in scientific methods, we can expect to see vast improvements in the delivery of results.

CHAPTER 13

Credit Risk

Don't focus on derivatives.
One of the most dangerous activities of banking is lending.

Ernest Patakis, Federal Reserve Bank of New York

Credit risk can be broadly defined as the risk of financial loss due to counterparty failure to perform their obligations. As Chapter 2 has shown, the historical record of financial institutions proves that credit risk is far more important than market risk.

Time and again, lack of diversification of credit risk has been the primary culprit for bank failures. The dilemma is that banks have a comparative advantage in making loans to entities with whom they have an ongoing relationship, thereby creating excessive concentrations in geographic or industrial sectors.

It is only recently that the banking industry has learned to measure credit risk in the context of a portfolio. These newer models truly started to blossom as a result of the risk-management revolution started by value at risk (VAR). After all, VAR aggregates risks across an institution, taking into account portfolio effects. Once measured, credit risk can be managed and better diversified, like any financial risk. This is why the banking sector is busily developing sophisticated *internal models* for credit risk.

These recent developments can be traced to the risk analysis of swaps, by now the largest class of derivatives. Initially, swaps were arranged between top-rated credit risks, and margins were fat enough to absorb the very few defaults in these markets. Later, as the market matured, greater volumes exposed participants to deteriorating credit risks. This led to a need for more precise measurement of credit risk.

Credit risk, unfortunately, is much more difficult to quantify than market risk. There are many more factors driving credit risk, some of which are extremely difficult to measure due to their infrequency. This includes default probabilities, their correlations, and recovery rates. In addition, credit risk models suffer from a verification problem. Unlike market risk, for which backtesting can be performed on a daily basis, the longer horizon of credit risk models makes it difficult to compare risk forecasts with their realization.

Nevertheless, the industry has made important strides in the direction of greater diversification of credit risk across geographic and industrial sectors, which ultimately should lead to a safer financial environment. The test of these recent models, however, will truly come during the next economic downturn.

This chapter provides an introduction to credit risk. The quantification of credit risk has by now become a large subject area, and a whole book could be devoted to this topic alone (see the References at the end of the book). Instead, the emphasis is on the extension of traditional risk-management methods to credit risks.

Section 13.1 compares the management of credit risk with that of market risk. We then explore the two major components of credit risk, default risk and exposures, in Sections 13.2 and 13.3. Section 13.4 discusses the effect of netting arrangements and illustrates bank disclosures about credit risks. Next, Section 13.5 shows how to combine this information to measure and manage credit risk. The following section presents the Basel charges for credit risk. These are compared with the very recently developed portfolio credit risk models in Section 13.7. Finally, Section 13.8 provides some concluding comments.

13.1 THE NATURE OF CREDIT RISK

13.1.1 Sources of Risk

Credit can be ascribed to two factors:

1. *Default risk,* which is the objective assessment of the likelihood that a counterparty will default, or *default probability,* combined with the *loss given default*
2. *Market risk,* which drives the market value of the obligation, also known as *credit exposure*

Consider, for instance, the credit risk of a forward contract on a foreign currency. The credit exposure is the positive value of the contract, whose value depends on movements in exchange rates. Thus credit risk involves both default and market risk.

As a result, the risk-management function for credit risk focuses on issues that are quite different from those facing market risk managers, as shown in Table 13–1. First, credit risk deals with the combined effect of market risk and default risk. Second, risk limits apply to different units. For market risk, limits apply to levels of the trading organization (such as business units, trading desks, or portfolios); for credit risk, limits apply to the total exposure to each counterparty, a legally defined entity. Third, the time horizon is generally quite different, usually very short (days) in the case of market risk but much longer (years) for credit risk. This longer horizon makes it important to consider changes in the portfolio, as well as any mean reversion in the risk factors. Fourth, legal issues are very important for evaluating credit risk, whereas they are not applicable for market risk. Recovery from credit losses depends on national laws and on the application of bankruptcy rules.

Overall, credit risk is much less amenable to precise measurement than market risk, for all the reasons listed above. In addition, due to their infrequent nature, default probabilities and their correlations are much more difficult to measure than dispersion in market movements.

TABLE 13–1

Comparison of Value at Risk to Credit Risk

Item	Value at Risk	Credit Risk
Source of risk	Market risk	Market risk and default
Unit to which risk limits apply	Some level of trading organization	Legal entity of counterparty
Time horizon	Short term (days)	Long term (years)
	Static portfolio	Dynamic portfolio
	Mean reversion not important	Mean reversion essential
Legal issues	Not applicable	Very important

Source: Adapted from Evan Picoult, Citibank.

13.1.2 Credit Risk as a Short Option

For default risk to create losses, two conditions must be satisfied. First, there must be a net claim against the counterparty (or credit exposure) and, second, that counterparty must default.

Traditionally, credit risk only applied to bonds and loans, for which the exposure is simply the face value of the investment. Derivatives, in contrast, can have either positive value (a net asset to the solvent party) or negative value (a liability of the solvent party). There is credit exposure when the contract has positive value, or is *in-the-money.*

In effect, the loss due to default is much like that of an option. Define V_t as the current, or replacement, value of the asset to the solvent party. Assuming no recovery in case of default, the loss is the *current exposure* V_t, if positive:

$$\text{Loss}_t = \max(V_t, 0) \tag{13.1}$$

This asymmetric treatment stems from the fact that if the counterparty defaults while the contract has negative value, the solvent party is typically not free to "walk away" from the contract, as shown in Box 13–1. In contrast, a loss may occur if the defaulting party goes bankrupt, in which case payment will be only a fraction of the funds owed. Therefore, the current exposure from default has an asymmetrical pattern, like a short position in an option.

13.1.3 Time and Portfolio Effects

Credit risk, however, should include not only the current replacement value but also the *potential,* or future, loss from default. Indeed, the G-30 report recommends that users "measure credit risk in two ways: (1) current exposure and (2) potential exposure, which is an estimate of the future replacement cost of derivative transactions." The *peak credit exposure* is often measured as

$$\text{Peak credit exposure}_t = \max(V_t + \Delta V_\tau, 0) \tag{13.2}$$

where ΔV_τ represents the maximum increase in value over the horizon τ at a specified confidence level c.

This approach has the merit of simplicity. Unfortunately, it ignores the time variation of credit exposure as well as that of the default proba-

B O X   1 3 – 1

WALK-AWAY FEATURES IN DREXEL'S COLLAPSE

The collapse of the Drexel Burnham Lambert Group (DBL Group) in 1990 provides an illustration of the asymmetry in payoffs when default occurs.*

DBL Group's bankruptcy placed its swap subsidiary, DBL Products, in default. Most of DBL's swap agreements contained a walk-away clause that permitted the solvent party to cease payment even if it owed money to the defaulting party (the standard documentation for swaps has been changed since).

Even so, nearly all counterparties paid DBL Products the money they owed, for a number of reasons. DBL Products threatened to challenge the right to walk away through litigation. Counterparties settled to avoid expensive litigation, since there were unresolved legal issues as to the enforceability of these contracts. A number of counterparties also feared that other institutions would be less likely to do business with them if they took advantage of the walk-away clause with Drexel. As a result, DBL was paid 100 percent of what is was owed but negotiated to pay only about 70 percent of the value of the contracts that were in-the-money for the solvent parties.

---

*For more details, see the U.S. Congress (1993) hearings on derivatives.

---

bility. Credit exposures can evolve in complicated ways over time. Also, a counterparty with a high credit rating has low default risk initially but higher risk later.

More sophisticated approaches rely on the *potential exposure profile,* which describes the worst potential loss, measured at some confidence level, at a set of future dates (e.g., monthly intervals). The pattern of dynamic credit exposure can be combined with future default probabilities to create a credit risk profile across time.

Even with these adjustments, the traditional approach is on a *transaction-by-transaction basis,* which essentially ignores portfolio effects. Consider, for instance, a portfolio consisting of a long yen forward position and a short yen forward with two different counterparties. The portfolio is hedged as to market risk. The transaction-by-transaction approach would consider the effect of default on each position separately. A loss on the long position occurs if the yen appreciates and the first counterparty defaults; a loss on the short position occurs if the yen depreciates and the second counterparty defaults. In this approach, the potential credit losses from the two positions are added up.

Since appreciation and depreciation of the yen are two mutually exclusive events, however, this method overstates the true potential loss from credit risk. Instead, a *portfolio approach* would take into account interactions between market movements and then determine the potential loss. In this case, assuming equal probability of appreciation/depreciation and of default by the two counterparties, the potential loss is only half the previous measure.

Accounting for time and portfolio effects, however, is no simple matter. This requires Monte Carlo simulation methods that combine market risk with credit risk. The benefits of an integrated portfolio approach can be substantial, though. In one case, a large U.S. financial institution calculated a $27 billion peak credit exposure using traditional methods. Using simulations, the firm found a peak portfolio exposure over all time horizons of $5.5 billion only.[1] This substantially lowered the amount of economic capital required to support the transactions.

Thus it is essential to measure credit risk within the context of a portfolio, which is the purpose of internal portfolio credit risk models. We now turn to the various components of credit risk.

13.2 DEFAULT RISK

13.2.1 Default Rates

Perhaps the most delicate part of credit risk modeling consists of assessing default probabilities. These can be based on actuarial models or market prices.

Actuarial models forecast objective default probabilities by analyzing factors associated with historical default rates. One such approach is that of *credit-rating agencies,* which classify issuers by *estimated default frequencies* (EDFs). If useful, these classifications should be related to actual default rates. Indeed, Table 13–2 shows historical default rates reported by Standard and Poors' for various credit ratings. A borrower with an initial rating of BBB, for example, had an average 0.24 percent default rate over the next year and 5.03 percent over the next 10 years.

---

1. This example is provided by Algorithmics, a vendor that provides software to measure integrated credit and market risk.

TABLE 13-2

Standard and Poors' Cumulative Default Rates (Percent)

Rating	Year									
	1	2	3	4	5	6	7	8	9	10
AAA	0.00	0.00	0.05	0.11	0.17	0.31	0.47	0.76	0.87	1.00
AA	0.00	0.02	0.07	0.15	0.27	0.43	0.62	0.77	0.85	0.96
A	0.04	0.12	0.21	0.36	0.56	0.76	1.01	1.34	1.69	2.06
BBB	0.24	0.54	0.85	1.52	2.19	2.91	3.52	4.09	4.55	5.03
BB	1.01	3.40	6.32	9.38	12.38	15.72	17.77	20.03	22.05	23.69
B	5.45	12.36	19.03	24.28	28.38	31.66	34.73	37.58	40.02	42.24
CCC	23.69	33.52	41.13	47.43	54.25	56.37	57.94	58.40	59.52	60.91

Note: Static pool average cumulative default rates, 1981–1998 (adjusted for "not rated" borrowers.)

The table shows that lower-rated borrowers have higher default rates. Thus, we could use this information as estimates of default risk for an initial rating class. It should be recognized, however, that these numbers are just estimates and could be quite imprecise, especially for better credit risks. As we have seen in Chapter 5, estimation of low-probability events is problematic due to the sample sizes involved.

Table 13–2 reports *cumulative* default rates c_n, which represent the total probability of defaulting at any time between now and year n. This information can be used to recover *marginal* or annual default rates d_i during year i. This represents the proportion of firms that default in year i from the set that is still alive at the end of the previous year.

Figure 13–1 shows that for a firm to survive year n, it needs to have survived up to year $n - 1$ and not defaulted in year n. Hence we can write the survival rate up to year n as

$$(1 - c_n) = (1 - c_{n-1})(1 - d_n) = \prod_{i=1}^{n}(1 - d_i) \qquad (13.3)$$

which can be used to solve recursively for d_i. For example, for year 1 of our BBB-rated credit, $c_1 = d_1 = 0.24$ percent. Solving for year 2, we set $(1 - 0.54 \text{ percent}) = (1 - 0.24 \text{ percent})(1 - d_2)$, which yields $d_2 = 0.302$ percent, and so on.

FIGURE 13–1

Sequential default process.

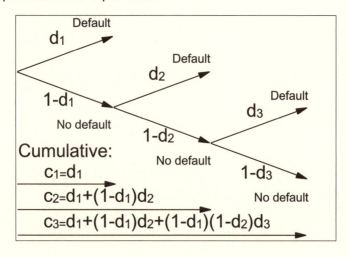

We also can compute the total probability of defaulting exactly in year i, starting from now, as

$$k_i = (1 - c_{i-1})d_i \qquad (13.4)$$

13.2.2 Recovery Rates

The other component of default risk is the *recovery rate*. This represents the fraction recovered given default, or one minus the loss given default (LGD). This depends on whether the debt is secured or not and on the status of the creditor in bankruptcy. Table 13–3 displays typical recovery rates for U.S. debt. The average recovery rate for senior unsecured debt, for instance, has been estimated at $f = 51$ percent. As an example, the expected credit loss on a BBB-rated $100 million 5-year bond would be $100 million $\times$ 2.19 percent $\times$ (1 − 51 percent) = $1.07 million. Typically, derivatives would have the same status as senior unsecured debt, and the same recovery rate can be used. This number, however, varies widely, creating another source of uncertainty.

13.2.3 Estimating Default Risk

An alternative source of information for default risk is market yields on bonds issued by the counterparty. Figure 13–2 describes a simplified default process for a credit-risky bond over one period. At maturity, the bond

TABLE 13–3

Historical Recovery Rates for U.S. Corporate Debt

	Recovery Rates	
Ranking	**Average**	**SD**
Senior secured bank loans	70%	21%
Senior secured bonds	55%	24%
Senior unsecured bonds	51%	26%
Subordinated bonds	32%	21%
All bonds	45%	27%

Source: Moody's, from 1977–1998 defaulted bond prices.

FIGURE 13–2

A simplified bond default process.

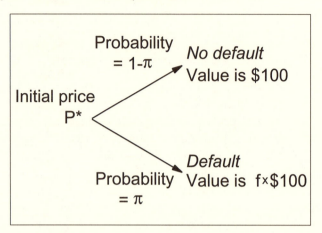

can either be in default or not. Its value is $f \times \$100$ if default occurs and $100 otherwise. Define $c = \pi$ as the cumulative default rate until maturity.

If bond prices carry no risk premium, the current price must be the mathematical expectation of the discounted values in the two states. Define y^* and y as the yields on the credit-risky bond and on an otherwise identical risk-free bond. Hence

$$P^* = \frac{\$100}{(1 + y^*)} = \frac{\$100}{1 + y} \times (1 - \pi) + \frac{f \times \$100}{1 + y} \times \pi \quad (13.5)$$

Note that we discounted at the risk-free rate y because we assumed that there was no risk premium. After rearranging terms,

$$1 + y = (1 + y^*)[1 - \pi(1 - f)] \quad (13.6)$$

To simplify, let us drop second-order terms. We find

$$y^* \approx y + \pi(1 - f) \quad (13.7)$$

Hence the credit spread $y^* - y$ measures the probability of default π times the loss given default $(1 - f)$. We can use the information in yields to measure credit risk.

If, however, investors require an additional compensation for bearing this default risk, the credit spread also will include a risk premium.

This method, obviously, is useful only if the counterparty has issued publicly traded bonds for which meaningful market prices exist.

An alternative is to turn to default risk models based on stock prices, which are available for a larger number of companies and are more actively traded than corporate bonds. The Merton (1974) model views equity as akin to a call option on the assets of the firm, with an exercise price given by the face value of debt. If the value of the assets is less than the promised payments, the firm defaults. The current stock price, therefore, embodies a forecast of default probability, in the same way that an option embodies a forecast of being exercised. Developing this approach, however, is well beyond the scope of this book.

In addition to measuring individual default risk, we also need to measure the correlation of defaults. As we have seen in the case of market risk, correlations are the most important drivers of portfolio risk. Equation (7.10) shows that in large portfolios, the portfolio volatility tends to the average volatility times the square root of the correlation coefficient.

A number of approaches have been proposed to measure these default correlations. CreditMetrics, for instance, maps each borrower onto an industry and country index and infers a default correlation from the exposure and correlations of risk factors.

13.3 CREDIT EXPOSURE

Credit exposure is defined as the replacement value of the asset, if positive, on the target date. This is also the market price. Its distribution can be usefully characterized by an expected value and worst value at some confidence level.

13.3.1 Bonds versus Derivatives

In the case of risky debt, credit exposure at expiration is the principal. Before expiration, the exposure can vary if the market value of the bond changes, but overall, this will be close to the principal, or notional.

With derivatives, in contrast, credit exposure is much more complex. The exposure represents the positive value of the contract, which is much less than the notional amount. Consider, for instance, a fixed-to-floating interest rate swap. There is no exchange of principal at initiation or at expiration. Each period, payments are netted and represent small

FIGURE 13–3

Exposure profile for a 5-year interest rate swap.

Swap value, percent of notional

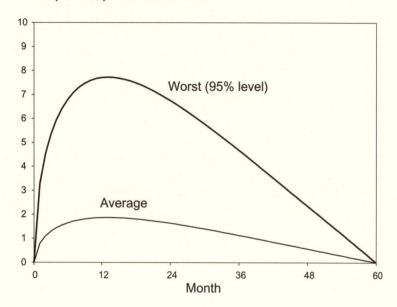

proportions of the principal. The exposure stems from the fact that the rate on the fixed payments may differ from prevailing market rates. At maturity, this risk is zero because there are no remaining coupon payments.

To illustrate, Figure 13–3 presents the exposure profile of a 5-year interest rate swap.[2] Initially, the exposure is 0 if the contract is fairly priced. After 1 year, the average exposure rises to about 2 percent of the notional. Eventually, the value of the swap converges to 0 at maturity because there is no exchange of principal. This profile is a combination of two factors, the *amortization effect,* which decreases risk as the maturity nears, and the *diffusion effect,* which increases the dispersion of interest rates as time goes by. Over long horizons, it is important to factor in mean reversion effects, which can dramatically affect the extent of this dispersion. The graph also shows that the worst exposure, measured at the 95 percent confidence level, peaks at about 8 percent of the notional after 1 year.

---

2. This is based on the one-factor Vasicek model in Equation (12.9) with mean reversion $\kappa = 0.04$ and volatility $\sigma = 0.30$ percent per month. These are typical parameters for recent U.S. interest rate data.

FIGURE 13–4

Exposure profile for a 5-year currency swap.

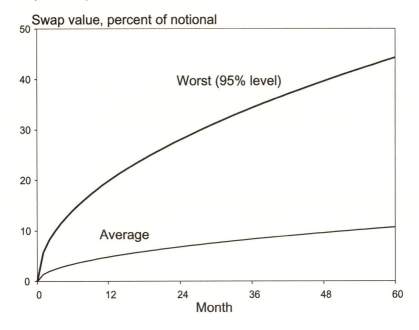

In contrast, the exposure on a currency swap increases steadily with the passage of time. This is so because exchange rate risk applies to all coupon payments and also to the principal, since the principal is exchanged in two different currencies. There is no amortization effect and, in addition, very little mean reversion in exchange rates. Figure 13–4 shows an average exposure of about 10 percent at maturity.[3] The maximum exposure can be quite large.

13.3.2 Expected and Worst Exposure

Expected credit exposure (ECE) is the expected value of the asset replacement value x, if positive, on a target date:

$$\text{Expected credit exposure} = \int_{-\infty}^{+\infty} \max(x, 0) f(x) \, dx \qquad (13.8)$$

---

3. The exposure profile in the figure considers currency risk only, using a normal model with no mean reversion and an annual volatility of 15 percent.

where $f(x)$ is the distribution function of x. Note that the credit exposure is intertwined with market risk. This formula is also akin to an option.

Worst credit exposure (WCE) is the largest (worst) credit exposure at some level of confidence c. This is also sometimes defined as *credit at risk* (CAR). Like VAR, it is implicitly defined as the largest value such that

$$1 - c = \int_{CAR}^{\infty} f(x)\, dx \tag{13.9}$$

As an example, suppose that the payoff is normally distributed. The expected credit exposure is then ECE $= 1/2E(x \mid x > 0) = \sigma/\sqrt{2\pi}$.[4] The worst credit exposure at the 95 percent confidence level is given by WCE $= 1.65\sigma$.

Consider, for instance, an outstanding forward or swap contract. If the current in-the-money value of the contract is x_0, we have

$$\text{ECE} = \text{notional}(x_0 + \sigma/\sqrt{2\pi}) \tag{13.10}$$

For a bond or a loan, we could assume that changes in the market value are small relative to the principal:

$$\text{ECE} = \text{principal} \tag{13.11}$$

This also applies to *receivables, trade credits* (where default applies to the face amount at maturity), and *financial letters of credit,* which are guarantees against default and are fully drawn when default occurs. For *short* positions in options, for which the premium already has been paid, the option contract can expire either as worthless or as a liability. Hence there is no credit exposure to the counterparty:

$$\text{ECE} = 0 \tag{13.12}$$

For *long* positions in options, the current exposure is the value of the option.[5] All the instruments with the same counterparty should be analyzed in this fashion.

---

4. This can be obtained from the formula on the expected loss conditional on being below zero (Equation 4.24) after further dividing by two because there is a 50 percent chance of being in the money.
5. Some option features, however, can mitigate credit risk. If a swap contains an American option, the holder of an in-the-money swap may want to exercise early if the credit rating of its counterparty starts to deteriorate.

More generally, exposure should take into account *exposure modifiers,* which attempt to decrease the exposure to the counterparty.[6] These include *recouponing,* where a regular coupon payment brings the value of the swap back to zero, or *exposure limits,* which, when reached, require a payment from the counterparty. *Collateral* also can be held as a means to reduce exposure. The ultimate form of credit exposure reduction is *daily marking-to-market,* in which case any changes in the value of the derivative are settled daily, reducing the exposure to intraday volatility. This, of course, creates other types of risk, liquidity and operational risk, because the cash flows must be managed daily.

13.4 NETTING ARRANGEMENTS

An important method to control credit risk exposures is netting agreements. The purpose of *netting* is to offset transactions between two parties with settlement of the *net* difference in cash flows across all contracts covered by a netting agreement. Closeout netting is by now a standard provision in the legal documentation of OTC derivative contracts, which has been helped by a standardized agreement established in 1992 by the *International Swaps and Derivatives Association* (ISDA).

Netting decreases credit risk by lowering credit exposure. Bilateral closeout netting agreements cover a set of N derivatives contracts between two parties. In case of default, a counterparty cannot stop payments on contracts that have negative value while demanding payment on positively valued contracts. Essentially, these agreements stipulate that the net loss in case of default is the positive sum of the market value of *all* contracts in the agreement:

$$\text{Net loss} = \max(V, 0) = \max\left(\sum_{i=1}^{N} V_i, 0\right) \qquad (13.13)$$

In contrast, without a netting agreement, the potential loss is the sum of all positively valued contracts:

$$\text{Loss} = \sum_{i=1}^{N} \max(V_i, 0) \qquad (13.14)$$

This is always greater than the loss under netting agreements. At worst, the two calculations will be the same if all payoffs are perfectly corre-

---

6. See, for instance, Wakeman (1998).

lated. For a given total notional, the benefit from a netting agreement depends on the number of contracts N and the extent to which contract values covary with each other. The larger is N and the lower is the correlation, the greater is the benefit from netting.

The effect of netting is most easily demonstrated for current exposure. Without netting agreements or collateral, the derivatives-related *gross replacement value* (GRV) is the sum of the worst-case loss over all counterparties K:

$$\text{GRV} = \sum_{k=1}^{K} \text{loss}_k = \sum_{k=1}^{K} \left[\sum_{i=1}^{N_k} \max(V_i, 0) \right] \qquad (13.15)$$

With netting agreements and collateral, the exposure is defined as the *net replacement value* (NRV):

$$\text{NRV} = \sum_{k=1}^{K} \text{net loss}_k = \sum_{k=1}^{K} \left[\max\left(\sum_{i=1}^{N_k} V_i, 0 \right) - \text{collateral}_k \right] \qquad (13.16)$$

To illustrate the importance of netting, Table 13–4 compares derivatives information provided in annual reports for a group of major banks.

TABLE 13–4

Derivatives Credit Risk: 1998 (Billions of Dollars)

			Derivatives		
Bank	Capital	Notional	Gross Replacement Value	Net Replacement Value	Ratio NRV/ Notional
Bank America	57.1	4,285	16.5	15.2	0.4%
Bankers Trust	8.5	2,448	53.9	12.8	0.5%
Citicorp	55.0	7,987	69.2	37.4	0.5%
Chase	26.1	10,353		33.3	0.3%
J.P. Morgan	16.4	8,741		48.1	0.6%
Merrill Lynch	10.1	3,470	28.6	18.3	0.5%
Morgan Stanley	14.1	2,860		21.4	0.7%
Salomon	8.8	4,442	14.3		0.3%
CSFP	10.2	4,649	87.0	31.3	0.7%
Deutsche Bank	34.3	4,100	91.1	45.5	1.1%
UBS	29.3	11,149		123.4	1.1%
Barclays	20.9	2,845		23.1	0.8%

In line with the size of the derivatives market, the notional amounts in the third column are quite large, all in excess of a trillion dollars.

A more appropriate measure of exposure is the net replacement value, or current exposure. This summarizes the potential loss if all counterparties defaulted at the same time, and is computed in two steps.

First, the bank computes the gross replacement value of its derivatives position, which is the sum of the positive replacement costs of all items in the portfolio. This represents a worst-case scenario where every single counterparty against which derivatives are in the money would default. Positions where the bank has a negative position, or owes money to the other party, are not considered.

In the second step, the bank makes an allowance for master netting agreements and collateral. These netting agreements reduce the exposure to one party by collapsing a set of contracts with the same party into one agreement. Default then involves losing only the net replacement value minus any collateral held and applied, if positive. Typically, banks also break down information about the credit quality of counterparties and maturity profile of the derivatives portfolio.

For Bankers Trust, for instance, the notional portfolio is $2448 billion, which appears to be huge compared with capital of only $8.5 billion. Relative to notionals, however, the bank has a much smaller GRV of $53.9 billion and even lower NRV of $12.8 billion. On average, the NRV is only a small fraction, 0.5 percent, of these enormous notional amounts. Even so, this worst-case measure still fails to capture credit risk properly because it ignores the probability of default, potential future exposure, and diversification effects.

13.5 MEASURING AND MANAGING CREDIT RISK

13.5.1 Expected and Unexpected Credit Loss

The exposure profile can be combined with default and recovery rates to yield the expected and unexpected credit loss. The first step consists of chopping up the horizon into time intervals, say, 1 year.

Expected credit loss (ECL) at each point in time t is defined as

$$\text{Expected credit loss}_t = \text{ECE}_t \times \text{prob(default)}_t \times (1 - f) \quad (13.17)$$

where f is the fractional recovery rate, and the probability of default is the probability of defaulting during the year ending at t, measured as $(1 - c_{t-1})d_t$. The ECL number provides essential information for pricing purposes. It can be used as the basis for computing a minimum bid-ask spread and a credit provision. It should be deducted from revenues when computing risk-adjusted return on capital measures.

Next, the *unexpected credit loss* (UCL) is defined as

$$\text{Unexpected credit loss}_t = \text{CAR}_t \times \text{prob(default)}_t \times (1 - f) \quad (13.18)$$

This is the maximum default loss at the selected level of confidence. This number, also known as *default VAR,* can be used to establish the amount of capital required to support the transaction.

This leads to a shortcut to the measurement of default VAR. If the initial value of the position is zero (as in a swap contract), the amount at risk will be the future profit. If we also assume that the recovery rate is zero, then the default VAR is

$$\text{Default VAR} = \text{VAR} \times \text{prob(default)} \quad (13.19)$$

We can then integrate market risk and credit risk as

$$\text{Total VAR} = \text{VAR} \times [1 + \text{prob(default)}] \quad (13.20)$$

ignoring the dispersion in defaults.

13.5.2 Pricing Credit Risk

The preceding example focuses on a fixed horizon, say, 1 year. Often, credit risk managers select an annual horizon because it leaves room for corrective action should the counterparty start to develop problems.

For pricing purposes, we need to consider the total credit loss over the life of the asset. This involves the time variation in the exposure and in the probability of default and a discounting factor. Define PV_t as the present value of a dollar paid at t. The *present value of expected credit losses* (PVECL) can be obtained as the sum of the discounted expected credit losses:

$$\text{PVECL} = \sum_t \text{ECL}_t \times \text{PV}_t$$
$$= \sum_t [\text{ECE}_t \times \text{prob(default)}_t \times (1 - f)] \times \text{PV}_t \quad (13.21)$$

A shortcut consists of taking the average default probability and the average exposure:

$$\text{PVECL}_2 = \left(\sum_t \text{PV}_t\right) \text{ave(ECE}_t) \, \text{ave[Prob(default)}_t] \, (1 - f) \quad (13.22)$$

This, however, may be oversimplifying if the default probabilities or exposure profiles change over time in a related fashion. For currency swaps with highly rated counterparties, for instance, both the exposure and the default probability increase with time. Taking the average will understate the credit risk.

Finally, the *present value of unexpected credit loss* (PVUCL) can be obtained as the sum of the discounted unexpected credit losses:

$$\text{PVUCL} = \sum_t \text{UCL}_t \times \text{PV}_t \qquad (13.23)$$

As an example, consider a 5-year interest rate swap with a counterparty initially rated BBB and a notional of $100 million. The discount factor is 6 percent, and the recovery rate 51 percent. Table 13–5 illustrates the computation of PVECL.

The first column reports the cumulative default probability from Table 13–2, expressed in percent. The second column shows the marginal probability, and the third column shows the probability of defaulting in each year, conditional on not having defaulted before. The next column reports the annual ECE for this swap. Combining with the PV factor and multiplying by $(1-0.51)$ leads to the entry in the last column. Since c was in percent, the total is $0.0071 million on a swap with notional of $100 million, which is close to 1 basis point. Thus the expected credit loss is quite low for this swap. It would be much greater, about a hundred times so, for a bond with the same characteristics.

TABLE 13–5

Computation of Expected Credit Loss

Year	c_t	d_t	Prob	ECE	PV	Factor
1	0.24	0.240	0.240	1.862	0.9434	0.2066
2	0.54	0.301	0.300	1.631	0.8900	02134
3	0.85	0.312	0.310	1.130	0.8396	0.1441
4	1.52	0.676	0.670	0.569	0.7921	0.1480
5	2.19	0.680	0.670	0.000	0.7473	0.0000
Total			2.190			0.7120

13.5.3 Portfolio Credit Risk

Once information has been gathered on the exposures, default probabilities, and recovery rates for all the assets in the portfolio, the distribution of losses due to credit risk can be described as

$$L = \sum_{i=1}^{N} \text{CE}_i \times (1 - f_i) \times b_i \qquad (13.24)$$

where CE_i is the credit exposure, f_i is the recovery rate, and b_i is a random variable that takes the value of 1 if default occurs and 0 otherwise, with probability p_i.

Table 13–6 gives an example of a $100 million portfolio with three issuers, rated BB, B, and C, respectively. For simplicity, assume that the exposures are constant, that there is no recovery, and that default events are independent across issuers. The top of the table displays exposures and default probabilities over the next year. The bottom part lists all possible states. In the first state, there is no default, which happens with probability given by $(1 - p_1)(1 - p_2)(1 - p_3) = 0.714$. In the second state,

TABLE 13–6

Portfolio Exposures, Default Risk, and Credit Losses

Issuer	Exposure	Probability
A	$35	0.0101
B	$40	0.0545
C	$25	0.2369

Default	Loss	Probability
None	$0	0.714224
A	$35	0.007287
B	$40	0.041169
C	$25	0.221727
A,B	$75	0.000420
A,C	$60	0.002262
B,C	$65	0.012781
A,B,C	$100	0.000130

only the first issuer defaults, with probability $p_1(1 - p_2)(1 - p_3) = 0.007$. And so on.

We can then tabulate the frequency of credit losses. From the distribution, we can compute the expected loss, which is \$8.5 million, and the worst loss at the 95 percent confidence level, which is about \$43 million. More generally, numerical simulation methods are needed to take into account many more assets, varying exposures, uncertain default probabilities and recovery rates, and correlated defaults.

13.5.4 Managing Credit Risk

We are now ready, at last, to use this information for management purposes. Figure 13–5 shows a typical distribution of credit losses, which is heavily skewed to the left. Note that this pattern is akin to a short position in an option.

The *credit reserve* (CR) is the amount to set aside in anticipation of expected credit losses. This can be found from the present value of expected credit losses.

The *equity reserve* is the amount to set aside as a buffer to cover unanticipated credit losses, as in the case of market VAR. This can be set

FIGURE 13–5

Measuring credit risk.

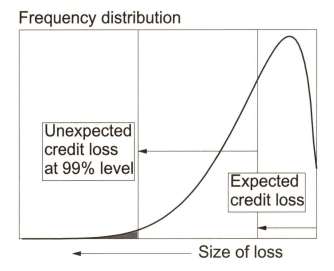

Frequency distribution

Unexpected credit loss at 99% level

Expected credit loss

Size of loss

to the difference between the PVUCL and the credit reserve for the whole portfolio. (Normally, the pricing of credit instruments should also incorporate the renumeration of the equity reserve.)

As in the case of market VAR, the methodology can be used to optimize the portfolio. The first step consists of measuring the expected net profit on the portfolio, accounting for the yield spread and expected credit losses. Each portfolio can then be evaluated by comparing its expected net profit to its total risk, the goal being to achieve the best risk-return profile.

13.5.5 Horizon and Confidence Level

So far we have not discussed the choice of the horizon or confidence levels. Credit risk models, such as CreditMetrics, commonly choose a 1-year horizon. In the case of market risk, a 10-day horizon was selected by the Basel Committee. Since credit events are much less frequent than market events, a longer horizon is warranted. A 1-year horizon also corresponds to the minimum interval to report default rates. The choice of a longer horizon also means that if risk-mitigating actions can be undertaken as a problem develops, the worst risk rarely will be attained.

As in the case of the VAR parameters, the choice of the confidence interval is also somewhat arbitrary. Given a longer horizon, however, a lower confidence interval can be selected, perhaps 95 percent instead of the 99 percent level for market risk. In fact, this implies one exceedence every 20 years, which is even safer than the one exceedence every 4 years for typical market risk parameters.

13.6 THE BASEL RISK CHARGES FOR DERIVATIVES

As explained in Chapter 3, the primary purpose of the ground-breaking 1988 Basel Accord was to ensure consistent minimum capital standards as a buffer for credit risk. The rules require capital to be equal to at least 8 percent of the total risk-weighted assets of the bank, including off-balance-sheet items (see BCBS, 1995c).

To account for derivatives, for which notionals are not really meaningful, the rules define a *credit exposure* as the sum of the current replacement value plus an *add-on* that is supposed to capture the potential exposure:

$$\text{Credit exposure} = \text{NRV} + \text{add-on}$$
$$\text{Add-on} = \Sigma[\text{notional} \times \text{add-on factor} \times (0.4 + 0.6 \times \text{NGR})] \quad (13.25)$$

TABLE 13–7

Add-on Factors for Potential Credit Exposure (Percent of Notional)

Residual Maturity (tenor)	Contract				
	Interest Rate	Exchange Rate, Gold	Equity	Precious Metals, but Not Gold	Other Commodities
<1 year	0.0	1.0	6.0	7.0	10.0
1–5 years	0.5	5.0	8.0	7.0	12.0
>5 years	1.5	7.5	10.0	8.0	15.0

where the add-on factor depends on the tenor and type of contract, as listed in Table 13–7. NGR is the *net-to-gross ratio,* or ratio of current net market value to gross market value, which is always between 0 and 1.

The add-on factor roughly accounts for the maximum credit exposure, such as described in Figures 13–2 and 13–3, which depends on the volatility of the risk factor and the maturity. This explains why the add-on factor is greater for currency swaps than for interest rate instruments. Finally, the purpose of the NGR factor is to reduce the capital requirement for contracts that fall under a netting agreement.

Risk-weighted assets are then obtained by applying counterparty risk weights to the credit exposure, which is placed on the same footing as the face value of loans. For instance, take a $100 million interest rate swap with a domestic corporation. With a residual maturity of 4 years, the typical current market value of the swap is $1 million. Using the 0.5 percent add-on factor, the total credit exposure is CE = $1 million + $100 million × 0.5 percent = $1.5 million. This number must be multiplied by the counterparty-specific risk weight and 8 percent to derive the minimum level of capital needed to support the swap.[7]

In the case of J.P. Morgan, for instance, Table 13–4 shows an NRV of $48.1 billion. With the add-on, this translates into risk-adjusted assets for off-balance sheet items (see Table 3–2) of $61.3 billion, which is close to half the total risk-adjusted assets of the bank.

In the Basel framework, credit risk is evaluated on a *transaction-by-transaction basis.* Default risk is taken into account indirectly through

---

7. Since most counterparties for such transactions tend to be excellent credits, counterparties that would attract a risk weight of 100 percent are given a weight of 50 percent instead.

the risk weights, which vary across types of counterparties. The main drawback of this approach, of course, is that it completely ignores the potential for diversification across time and counterparties.

13.7 PORTFOLIO CREDIT RISK MODELS

This is what led to the development of internal credit risk models. Although the Basel approach has the advantage of simplicity, portfolio credit risk models are much more satisfactory. They can account for the time profile of credit exposure, for realistic default rates, and for correlations. Netting and other exposure modifiers can be modeled explicitly.

This is generally achieved through simulation methods, which explicitly model movements in asset prices, changes in exposure, defaults, and losses across the whole portfolio. Such methods can account for the legal structure of transactions by assigning individual transactions to master netting agreements, master netting agreements to counterparties, and even counterparties to countries. Perhaps the greatest advantage of these methods is that they account for portfolio diversification effects across transactions and counterparties. And we do know that banks have time and again suffered losses due to lack of diversification. Portfolio credit risk models, by inducing banks to diversify their portfolios, will accomplish an important purpose.

Table 13–8 compares the leading credit risk models. The models differ in a number of key dimensions.

- *Risk definitions.* Models can define credit risk as either the occurrence of default or, more generally, as any change in the market value of the asset that is due to changing perceptions of default.
- *Risk drivers.* Credit risk can be modeled as being driven by changes in asset values, by fundamental macroeconomic factors, or from a statistical model.
- *Correlations.* Correlations between default risks can come from comovements between equities with similar exposures or from macroeconomic factors.
- *Recovery rates.* Recovery rates can be taken as random or constant.
- *Solution.* The solution can be analytical or based on simulations.

TABLE 13–8

Comparison of Credit Risk Models

	CreditMetrics	CreditRisk+	CreditPortfolioView
Originator	J.P. Morgan	Credit Suisse	McKinsey
Philosophy	Merton model, microeconomic causal	Actuarial top-down, no causality	Econometric, macroeconomic causal
Risk definition	Market value	Default losses	Market value
Risk drivers	Asset values	Default rates	Macro factors
Correlation	From equities	Default process	Factor model
Recovery rates	Random	Constant	Random
Solution	Simulation/ analytical	Analytical	Simulation

While these models seem to have taken disparate approaches to credit risk, in fact, they have a very similar underlying mathematical structure.[8]

In the end, these portfolio approaches, which fully account for diversification across instruments and counterparties, have many advantages. They can help banks to decide whether to extend credit based on the incremental credit VAR, as opposed to decisions made on a stand-alone basis. They allow banks to manage their credit risk better by identifying concentrations of credit risk by name, industry, country, or product. By assessing credit risk more finely, they make it possible to carry a smaller level of economic capital, increasing returns to the remaining capital.

13.8 CONCLUSIONS

Credit risk in derivatives has two distinguishing characteristics. The first is the need to quantify exposure, or market risk. In traditional banking, the credit exposure is determined easily. For a bond or loan contract, it is measured as the outstanding principal plus any accrued interest. With derivatives, the exposure is much more complex. It depends on whether the contract has positive or negative market value, both current and future.

---

8. See, for instance, the comparative analyses in Gordy (2000) and Koyluoglu and Hickman (1999).

The second characteristic is the potential for diversification across counterparties and portfolios of instruments. If exposures tend to offset each other, the risk of the portfolio will be considerably less than the sum of each credit exposure. Similarly, if default risk is diversified in terms of geographic and industrial classification of counterparties, losses are less likely to occur all at once.

In recent years, financial institutions have learned to quantify the credit risk of their portfolios and to integrate market and credit risk. This has a number of advantages. Better measurement leads to more efficient use of capital. It also allows banks to price credit at a transaction level, thereby gaining an advantage over the competition. In this process, we should gain a safer banking system.

FURTHER INFORMATION

The field of credit risk has witnessed startling developments in the last 5 years. Before that, the focus was on individual credit risk, i.e., default rates and recovery on bonds. The more recent models emphasize that credit risk should be viewed in a portfolio context.

Books
The following books provide good overviews of portfolio credit risk: Ong (1999), Saunders (1999), Caouette et al. (1998). Useful compilations of articles can be found in Risk Publications (1995) and Shimko (1999).

Models
The technical documents for J.P. Morgan's CreditMetrics (now supported by the RiskMetrics Group) are at www.riskmetrics.com. A description of Credit Suisse's CreditRisk+ system is at www.csfp.co.uk.

Reports
The Basel Committee has produced a number of useful reports that describe credit risk models, such as BCBS (1999b). They can be found at www.bis.org. The International Swaps and Derivatives Association has a report on credit risk, ISDA (1998), at www.isda.org.

CHAPTER 14

Liquidity Risk

LTCM then faced severe market liquidity problems when its investments began losing value and the fund attempted to unwind some of its positions.

President's Working Group on Financial Markets, 1999

Traditional value at risk (VAR) models rely on market prices, since marking-to-market is widely viewed as the ultimate discipline. VAR, however, assumes that the portfolio is "frozen" over the horizon and that market prices represent achievable transaction prices. This marking-to-market approach is adequate to quantify and control risk but may be more questionable if VAR is supposed to represent the worst loss over a liquidation period.

The question is how VAR can be adapted to deal with liquidity considerations. As we saw in Chapter 1, liquidity risk can be grouped into asset liquidity and funding liquidity risk. The former relates to the risk that the liquidation value of the assets differs significantly from the current mark-to-market value. The latter refers to the risk that an institution could run out of cash and is unable to raise new funds to meet its payment obligations, which could lead to formal default. Thus liquidity considerations should be viewed in the context of liabilities.

This chapter discusses recent developments that adapt traditional VAR measures to liquidity considerations. First, Section 14.1 analyzes asset and funding liquidity risk in some detail. Asset liquidity risk can be evaluated by the price impact of the liquidation. Funding liquidity risk, in contrast, deals with cash resources as well as potential cash requirements.

Next, Section 14.2 provides insight into asset liquidity risk by comparing liquidation strategies. One strategy is immediate liquidation, which may incur very large costs due to the price impact but insulates the portfolio from price volatility risk. Another strategy is that of liquidation at a constant rate, which minimizes trading costs but leaves the portfolio exposed to volatility risk. Optimal execution strategies best balance these low-cost and volatility requirements.

Section 14.3 then discusses measures of funding liquidity risk proposed by the Counterparty Risk Management Policy Group (CRMPG). These measures show that even though an institution can have zero traditional VAR, different swap credit terms can generate very different cash requirements.

Next, Section 14.4 is devoted to an analysis of the Long-Term Capital Management (LTCM) debacle. LTCM failed because of its lack of diversification and funding liquidity risk and asset liquidity risk, which were simply due to its sheer size. Finally, Section 14.5 provides some concluding comments.

14.1 DEFINING LIQUIDITY RISK

14.1.1 Asset Liquidity Risk

Asset liquidity risk, sometimes called *market/product liquidity risk,* arises when a transaction cannot be conducted at prevailing market prices due to the size of the position relative to normal trading lots.

Liquidity can be measured by a price-quantity function. This is also known as the *market impact effect.* Highly liquid assets, such as major currencies or Treasury bonds, are characterized by *deep markets,* where positions can be offset with very little price impact. *Thin markets,* such as exotic OTC derivatives contracts or emerging market equities, are those where any transaction can quickly affect prices.

This price function is illustrated in Figure 14–1.[1] The starting point is the current *mid price,* which is the average of the bid and ask quotes and is generally used to mark the portfolio to market. The bid-ask spread is $0.25, valid up to some limit, say, 10,000 shares. This is sometimes called the *normal market size.* For quantities beyond this point, however, the sale price is a decreasing function of the quantity, reflecting the price pressure required to clear the market. Conversely for the purchase price.

---

1. In what follows, we ignore the fixed component of trading costs, i.e., commissions and taxes.

F I G U R E   14–1

Price-quantity function.

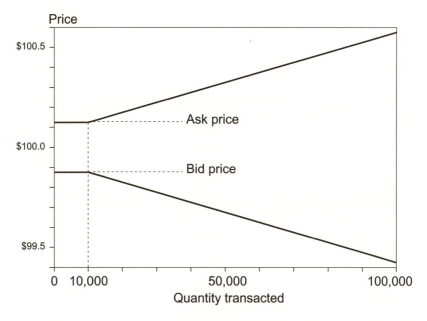

The relationship is assumed to be linear, although it could take another shape with parameters that vary across assets and, possibly, across time.

In this case, selling 100,000 shares would incur a cost of about 60 basis points per share. In practice, the size of the sale would have to be measured relative to some metric such as the median daily trading volume. For a widely traded stock such as IBM, for instance, selling 4 percent of the daily trading volume incurs a cost of about 60 basis points.

Here, liquidity can be measured usefully by the price-quantity function combined with the existing position of the institution. If the position is below 10,000 shares, then market liquidity is not a major issue. In contrast, if the institution holds a number of shares worth several days of normal trading volume, liquidity should be of primary concern.

In addition to varying across assets, liquidity is also a function of prevailing market conditions. This is more worrying, because markets seem to go through regular bouts of liquidity crises. Most notably, liquidity in bond markets dried up during the summer of 1998 as uncertainty about defaults led to a "flight to quality," i.e., increases in the prices of Treasuries relative to those of other bonds. A similar experience occurred during the 1994 bond market debacle, at which time it became quite difficult to deal in eurobonds or mortgage-backed securities.

Traditionally, asset liquidity risk has been controlled through position limits. The goal of *position limits* is to limit the exposure to a single instrument, even if it provides diversification of market risk, in order to avoid a large market impact in case of forced liquidation.

14.1.2 Funding Liquidity Risk

Cash-flow/funding liquidity risk refers to the inability to meet payment obligations when the institution runs out of cash and is unable to raise additional funds. Often, this forces unwanted liquidation of the portfolio. It should be noted that funding risk arises from the use of *leverage,* whereby institutions borrow to expand their assets. This type of risk must be analyzed in the context of the asset and liability structure of the institution.

Looking at the asset side, potential demands on cash resources depend on

- *Variation margin requirements,* due to marking-to-market
- *Mismatch in the timing of collateral payments,* due to the fact that even if an institution is perfectly matched in terms of market risk, it may be forced to make a payment on a position without having yet received an offsetting payment on a hedge
- *Changes in collateral requirements,* due to requests by lenders to increase the amount of collateral they require

Here, some words of explanation are in order. An example of mismatch in cash flows is an institution that has two economically hedged positions structured with different credit terms, such as a one-way mark-to-market swap and a two-way mark-to-market swap. In the former, the institution is required to make payments if the position loses money; it will not, however, receive intermediate payments if the position gains. In contrast, under two-way swaps, payments can be made or received if the position loses or gains money. Because of the asymmetry in the hedge, the institution will be subject to mismatches in the timing of collateral payments if the first swap loses money. Even with two-way mark-to-market agreements, there can be some uncertainty in the cash-flow payments due to operational errors or discrepancies in the valuation of the swaps.

Next, changes in collateral requirements can arise due to requests by lenders to raise their haircuts. Normally, brokers require collateral that is worth slightly more than the cash loaned, by an amount known as a *haircut,* designed to provide a buffer against decreases in the collateral value. Unless contract terms forbid it, brokers can raise their haircuts if the market becomes more volatile, creating demands on cash.

These examples provide yet another illustration of the complex interaction between different types of risks. Marking-to-market has been developed primarily to control credit risk. The problem is that it may create another risk, cash-flow risk. Further, if the institution does not carry enough cash to meet its margin calls, it may be forced to liquidate holdings at depressed prices, thereby creating asset liquidity risk.

Looking at the liability side is also important, however. The institution may be able to meet margin calls by raising funds from another source, such as a line of credit or new equity issues. The problem is that it may be difficult to raise new funds precisely when the institution is faring badly and needing it most.

Conversely, the institution also must evaluate the likelihood of redemptions, or cash requests from equity holders or debt holders. However, this is most likely to occur when the institution appears most vulnerable, thereby transforming what could be a minor problem into a crisis. It is also important to avoid debt covenants or options that contain "triggers" that would force early redemption of the borrowed funds.

14.2 DEALING WITH ASSET LIQUIDITY RISK

Trading returns typically are measured from midmarket prices. This may be adequate for measuring daily profit and loss (P&L) but may not represent the actual fall in value if a large portfolio were to be liquidated. The question is how to measure risk more properly, which can give insights into how to manage this risk.

Traditional adjustments are done on an ad hoc basis. Liquidity risk can be loosely factored into VAR measures by ensuring that the *horizon* is at least greater than an orderly liquidation period. Generally, the same horizon is applied to all asset classes, even though some may be more liquid than others.

Sometimes, longer liquidation periods for some assets are taken into account by artificially increasing the volatility. For instance, one could mix a large position in the dollar/yen with another one in the dollar/Polish zloty, both of which have an annual volatility of 10 percent, by artificially increasing the second volatility in the VAR computations.

14.2.1 Bid-Ask Spread Cost

More formally, one can focus on the various components of liquidation costs. The first and most easily measurable is the quoted bid-ask spread, defined in relative terms, that is,

$$S = \frac{[P(\text{ask}) - P(\text{bid})]}{P(\text{mid})} \tag{14.1}$$

Table 14–1 provides typical spreads. We see that spreads vary from a low of about 0.05 percent for major currencies, large U.S. stocks, and on-the-run Treasuries to much higher values when dealing with less liquid currencies, stocks, and bonds. Treasury bills are in a class of their own, with extremely low spreads. These spreads are only indicative, since they depend on market conditions. Also, marketmakers may be willing to trade within the spread.

TABLE 14–1

Typical Spreads and Volatility

Asset	Spread, % (Bid-Ask)	Volatility, % Daily	Volatility, % Annual
Currencies			
Major (euro, yen, etc.)	0.05–0.20	0.3–1.0	5–15
Emerging (floating)	0.50–1.00	0.3–1.9	5–30
Bonds			
On-the-run Treasuries	0.03	0.0–0.7	0–11
Off-the-run Treasuries	0.06–0.20	0.0–0.7	0–11
Corporates	0.10–1.00	0.0–0.7	0–11
Treasury bills	0.003–0.02	0.0–0.1	0–1
Stocks			
U.S.	0.05–5.00	1.3–3.8	20–60
Average, NYSE	0.20	1.0	15
Average, all countries	0.40	1.0–1.9	15–30

Note: Author's calculations. Cost of trades excludes broker commissions and fees. See also *Institutional Investor* (November 1999).

At this point, it is useful to review briefly the drivers of these spreads. According to market microstructure theory, spreads reflect three different types of costs: order-processing costs, asymmetric information costs, and inventory-carrying costs.

Order-processing costs cover the cost of providing liquidity services and reflect the cost of trading, the volume of transaction, the state of technology, and competition. With fixed operating costs, these order-processing costs should decrease with transaction volumes. *Asymmetric information costs* reflect the fact that some orders may come from informed traders, at the expense of marketmakers who can somewhat protect themselves by increasing the spread. Finally, *inventory-carrying costs* are due to the cost of maintaining open positions, which increases with higher price volatility, higher interest rate carrying costs, and lower trading activity or turnover.

If the spread were fixed, one could simply construct a liquidity-adjusted VAR from the traditional VAR by adding a term:

$$\text{LVAR} = \text{VAR} + L_1 = (W\alpha\sigma) + 1/2(WS) \qquad (14.2)$$

where W is the initial wealth, or portfolio value. For instance, if we have $1 million invested in a typical stock, with a daily volatility of $\sigma = 1$ percent and spread of $S = 0.25$ percent, the 1-day LVAR at the 95 percent confidence level would be

$$\text{LVAR} = (\$1 \text{ million} \times 1.645 \times 0.01) + 1/2(\$1 \text{ million} \times 0.0025)$$
$$= \$16,450 + \$1250 = \$17,700$$

Here, the correction factor is relatively small, accounting for 7 percent of the total.

This adjustment can be repeated for all assets in the portfolio, leading to a series of add-ons, $\frac{1}{2}\Sigma_i \mid W_i \mid S_i$. This sequence of positive terms increases linearly with the number of assets, while the usual VAR benefits from diversification effects. Thus the relative importance of the correction factor will be greater for large portfolios.

A slightly more general approach is proposed by Bangia et al. (1999), who consider the uncertainty in the spread. They characterize the distribution by its mean $\bar{S}$ and standard deviation σ_S. The adjustment considers the worst increase in the spread at some confidence level:

$$\text{LVAR} = \text{VAR} + L_2 = (W\alpha\sigma) + \frac{1}{2}[W(\bar{S} + \alpha'\sigma_S)] \qquad (14.3)$$

At the portfolio level, one could theoretically take into account correlations between spreads. In practice, summing the individual worst spreads provides a conservative measure of the portfolio worst spread.

Although this approach has the merit of considering some transaction costs, it is not totally satisfactory. It only looks at the bid-ask spread component of these costs, which may be appropriate for a small portfolio but certainly not when liquidation can affect market prices. Also, if the decision is taken to liquidate the portfolio immediately, the VAR horizon should be very short. What is needed is a model that takes into account the cost and benefit of trading strategies.

14.2.2 Trading Strategies

The extension based on bid-ask spreads, while an improvement over traditional VAR calculation, very much ignores the market impact factor, which can be significant. To some extent, this can be mitigated by suitable execution strategies. These should be taken into account when computing a liquidity-adjusted VAR.

To simplify, let us assume a linear price-quantity function. For a sale,

$$P(q) = P_0(1 - kq) \qquad (14.4)$$

Assume that $P_0 = \$100$ and $k = 0.5 \times 10^{-7}$. Say that we start with a position of 1 million shares of the stock. If we liquidate all at once, the price drop will be $P_0 kq = \$100 \times (0.5 \times 10^{-7}) \times 1,000,000 = \$5$, leading to a total price impact of $5 million. In contrast, we could decide to work the order through at a constant rate of 200,000 shares over 5 days. Define n as the number of days to liquidation. In the absence of other price movements, the price drop will be $1.0, leading to a total price impact of $1 million, much less than before.

Immediate liquidation creates quadratic costs:

$$C_1(W) = q \times [P_0 - P(q)] = kq^2 P_0 \qquad (14.5)$$

whereas *uniform liquidation* creates lower costs:

$$C_2(W) = q \times [P_0 - P(q/n)] = k(q^2/n)P_0 \qquad (14.6)$$

The drawback of liquidating more slowly is that the portfolio remains exposed to price risks over a longer period. The position profiles are illustrated in Figure 14–2. Under the immediate sale, the position is liquidated before the end of the next day, leading to a high cost but min-

FIGURE   14–2

Profile of execution strategies.

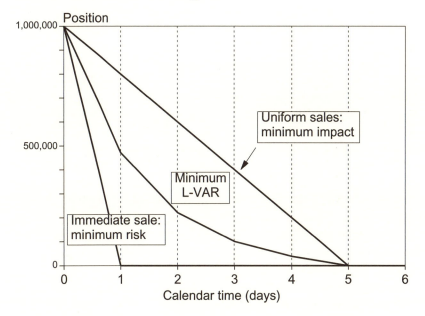

imum risk. Under the uniform sale, the position is sold off in equal-sized lots, leading to low costs but high risk. The key is to choose a strategy that offers the best cost-risk tradeoff.

To analyze the risk profile of these strategies, define σ as the daily volatility of the share price, in dollars. We assume that sales are executed at the close of the business day, in one block. Hence, for the immediate sale, the price risk or variance of wealth is zero, $V_1(W) = 0$. For the uniform sale, the portfolio variance can be computed assuming independent returns over n days as

$$V_2(W) = \sigma^2 q^2 \left\{ \left(1 - \frac{1}{n}\right)^2 + \left(1 - 2\frac{1}{n}\right)^2 + \cdots + \left[1 - (n-1)\frac{1}{n}\right]^2 \right\}$$

$$= \sigma^2 q^2 \left[n\frac{1}{3}\left(1 - \frac{1}{n}\right)\left(1 - \frac{1}{2n}\right) \right] \quad (14.7)$$

For example, with $n = 5$, the correction factor between braces is 1.20. Thus constant liquidation over 5 days is equivalent to the marking-to-market risk of a position held over 1.2 days. It is interesting to note that the 10-day fixed horizon dictated by the Basel Committee is equivalent to a constant liquidation over 31 days.

Execution strategies need not be limited to these two extreme cases. More generally, we can choose a strategy x that leads to an optimal trade-off between execution costs and price risk:

$$\min_x[C_x(W) + \lambda V_x(W)] \tag{14.8}$$

where λ reflects the aversion to price risk.

Lawrence and Robinson (1997), for instance, propose a simple solution, which is to minimize over n, using Equations (14.7) and (14.6). Almgren and Chriss (1999) provide a more complete closed-form solution for efficient execution strategies in the cost-risk plane. An optimal trajectory is described in Figure 14–2. Note that the strategy can be described by its *half-life,* which is the time required to liquidate half the portfolio. For the optimal strategy here, this takes 1 day.

This leads to the concept of liquidity-adjusted VAR, or *implementation shortfall,* which is

$$\text{LVAR} = \alpha\sqrt{V(W)} + C(W) \tag{14.9}$$

where α corresponds to the confidence level c. In other words, this LVAR measure takes into account not only liquidation costs but also the best execution strategy such that LVAR will not be exceeded more than a fraction c of the time.

Figure 14–3 compares various VAR measures for different speeds of execution. The "static" 1-day and 5-day VARs correspond to the usual mark-to-market VAR measures with 30 percent annual volatility. Under these conditions, the daily volatility is 1.9 percent, and the 1-day VAR is $3.1 million for this $100 million portfolio. With a 25-basis-point spread and no market impact, the spread adjustment is small, at $125,000 only. This, however, ignores price impact.

Instead, the LVAR measure incorporates the total execution cost and price risk components in a consistent fashion. As we extend the length of liquidation, the execution cost component decreases, but the price risk component increases. Here, the total LVAR is minimized at a half-life of 1 day. In this case, a 5-day static VAR would provide a conservative measure of liquidation VAR.

The real benefit of this approach is that it draws attention to market impact effects in portfolio liquidation. It also illustrates that execution strategies should account for the tradeoff between execution costs and price volatility.

FIGURE 14–3

Liquidity-adjusted VAR.

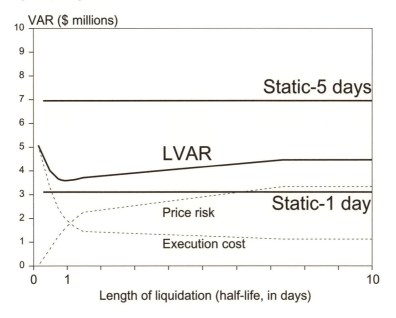

For instance, there are other ways to implement the liquidation. In the case of stock portfolios, for example, the portfolio manager could cut its price risk by immediately putting in place a hedge with stock index futures. In this case, the remaining price risk is "specific" to the security. Orders to sell could then be transmitted so as to minimize their price impact.

14.2.3 Practical Issues

In practice, the computational requirements to adjust the conventional VAR numbers are formidable. The method requires a price-quantity function for all securities in the portfolio. Combined with the portfolio position, this yields an estimate of the price impact of a liquidation, as well as the optimal time to liquidation.

Table 14–2 provides an example of such an analysis, as provided by Morgan Stanley (MS) for a four-country $50 million equity portfolio. The data for Switzerland are expanded at the individual stock level. To estimate the total impact cost, we need information about the historical bid-ask spreads, the median trading volume, and recent volatility. The

TABLE 14–2

Market Impact Cost Report

Asset	Portfolio				Cost Analysis			Impact Cost (bp)
	Value (US$)	Shares Held	Price	Spread (bp)	Median Volume	Shares/ Volume		
France	19,300,182	184,063	104.9	19.9		1.3%		18.2
Germany	19,492,570	322,550	60.4	26.1		2.5%		29.3
Switzerland	19,300,182	9,355	572.1	12.5		1.1%		9.5
Novartis	5,351,851	1,630	1,453.6	11.7	123,554	1.3%		8.8
Swatch	64,678	400	161.7	32.9	42,559	0.9%		15.5
Nestle	1,752,009	935	1,873.8	6.4	76,004	1.2%		7.3
CS Group	1,165,797	6,390	182.4	22.2	978,168	0.7%		14.1
U.K.	5,860,371	424,373	13.8	20.2		0.6%		17.6
Total	50,004,974	940,341	53.2	21.6		1.7%		21.5

Source: Morgan Stanley (1999).

portfolio relative *size* is then defined as the number of shares held as a percentage of median trading volume. MS then computes the total impact cost as a function of half the bid-ask spread and of this size variable.

Here, the total cost of immediate (1-day) liquidation is estimated to be 21.5 basis points. This can be compared to the daily marking-to-market volatility of this portfolio, which is 110 basis points. Thus, if the portfolio were to be liquidated at the end of the next day, the worst LVAR loss at the 95 percent confidence level would be about $50 million $\times$ (1.65 $\times$ 1.1 percent + 0.22 percent) = $50 million $\times$ 2.0 percent = $1.0 million. The relative importance of liquidity would no doubt be much greater for a larger portfolio. In addition, the framework presented in the preceding section allows the investor to evaluate the cost and risk of various trading strategies.

14.3 GAUGING FUNDING LIQUIDITY RISK

Measuring funding liquidity risk involves examining the asset-liability structure of the institution and comparing potential demands on cash with the available supply of equivalent instruments. Some lessons are available from the Counterparty Risk Management Policy Group (CRMPG), which was established in the wake of the LTCM near failure to strengthen practices related to the management of market, counterparty credit, and liquidity risk.[2]

The CRMPG proposes to evaluate funding risk by comparing the amount of cash an institution has at hand with to what it could need to meet payment obligations. It defines *cash liquidity* as the ratio of cash equivalent over the potential decline in the value of positions that may create cash-flow needs.

Table 14–3 illustrates an example of an institution that has a position in two offsetting swaps. Since it is perfectly hedged, it has zero traditional VAR, or market risk. Yet different swap credit terms create funding risk.

In the case where the two swaps are both marked-to-market, any cash payment in one swap must be offset by a receipt on the other leg. The only risk is that of a delay in the receipt. Assume the worst move on a $100 million swap at the 99 percent level over 1 day is $1.1 million.

---

2. The CRMPG consists of senior-level practitioners from the financial industry, including many banks that provided funding to LTCM.

TABLE 14–3

Computing Funding Liquidity Ratio

	Case 1	Case 2
Assets		
Cash	$5	$5
Liabilities		
Equity	$5	$5
Derivatives		
Long 10-year swap	$100, two-way marked-to-market	$100, unsecured
Short 10-year swap	$100, two-way marked-to-market	$100, two-way marked-to-market
Cash equivalent	$5	$5
Funding VAR	$1.1 (1-day)	$3.5 (10-day)
Ratio	4.5	1.4

Let us consider this is the worst cash need. The funding ratio is then $5/$1.1 = 4.5, rather high, which indicates sufficient cash coverage.

In the case where one of the swaps is not secured by marking-to-market, the risk is that of a decrease in the value of the mark-to-market swap, which would not be offset by a cash receipt on the other leg until settlement. We now need to consider a longer horizon VAR, say, 10 days, which gives $3.5, for a funding ratio of 1.4. This seems barely enough to provide protection against funding risk. Thus some of the elements of traditional VAR can be used to compute funding risk, which can be quite different from market risk when the institution is highly leveraged.

14.4 LESSONS FROM LTCM[3]

The story of Long-Term Capital Management (LTCM) provides a number of lessons in liquidity risk. LTCM was founded by Meriwether in 1994, who left Salomon Brothers after the 1991 bond scandal. Meriwether took with him a group of traders and academics and set up a hedge fund that tried to take advantage of "relative value" or "convergence arbitrage" trades, betting on differences in prices, or spreads, among closely related securities.

---

3. This draws on Philippe Jorion, "How Long-Term Lost Its Capital," *Risk* (September 1999).

14.4.1 LTCM's Leverage

Since such strategies tend to generate tiny profits, leverage has to be used to create attractive returns. By December 1997, the total equity in the fund was $5 billion. LTCM's balance sheet was about $125 billion. This represented an astonishing leverage ratio of 25:1. Even more astonishing was the off-balance-sheet position, including swaps, options, and other derivatives, that added up to a notional amount of $1.25 trillion. This represents the total of *gross positions,* measured as the sum of the absolute value of the trade's notional principals.

To give an idea of the magnitude of these positions, the BIS reported a total swap market of $29 trillion in 1998. Hence LTCM's swap positions accounted for 2.4 percent of the global swap market. Many of these trades, however, were offsetting each other, so this notional amount is practically meaningless. What mattered was the net risk of the fund. LTCM, however, failed to appreciate that these gross positions were so large that attempts to liquidate them would provoke large market moves.

14.4.2 LTCM's "Bulletproofing"

LTCM was able to leverage its balance sheet through sale-repurchase agreements (repos) with commercial and investment banks. Under repo agreements, the fund sold some of its assets in exchange for cash and a promise to purchase them back at a fixed price on some future date. Normally, brokers require collateral that is worth slightly more than the cash loaned, by an amount known as a *haircut,* designed to provide a buffer against decreases in the collateral value. LTCM, however, was able to obtain unusually good financing conditions, with next-to-zero haircuts, since it was widely viewed as "safe" by its lenders. In addition, the swaps were subject to two-way marking-to-market.

On the supply side, LTCM also had "bulletproofed" itself against a liquidity squeeze. LTCM initially had required investors to keep their money in the fund for a minimum of 3 years. The purpose of this so-called lockup clause, which was very unusual in the hedge fund industry, was to avoid forced sales in case of poor performance. LTCM also secured a $900 million credit line from Chase Manhattan and other banks.

Even though LTCM had some protection against funding liquidity risk, it was still exposed to market risk and asset liquidity risk.

FIGURE 14–4

LTCM's returns.

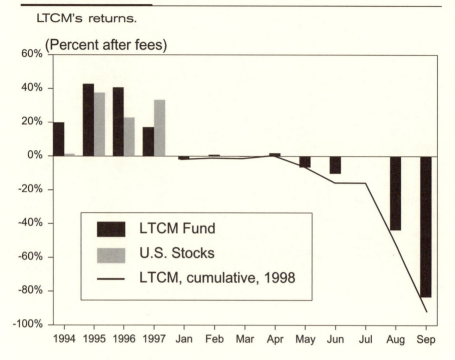

14.4.3 LTCM's Downfall

LTCM's strategy profited handsomely from the narrowing of credit spreads during the early years, leading to after-fees returns above 40 percent, as shown in Figure 14–4.

Troubles began in May and June of 1998. A downturn in the mortgage-backed securities market led to a 16 percent loss in LTCM's capital. Then came August 17. Russia announced that it was "restructuring" its bond payments—de facto defaulting on its debt. This bombshell led to a reassessment of credit and sovereign risks across all financial markets. Credit spreads, risk premia, and liquidity spreads jumped up sharply. Stock markets dived. LTCM lost $550 million on August 21 alone.

By August, the fund had lost 52 percent of its December 31 value. With assets still at $126 billion, the leverage ratio had increased from 28:1 to 55:1. LTCM badly needed new capital. It desperately tried to find new investors, but there were no takers.

In September, the portfolio's losses accelerated. Bear Stearns, LTCM's prime broker, faced a large margin call from a losing LTCM

T-bond futures position. It then required increased collateral, which de-pleted the fund's liquid resources.

LTCM was now caught in a squeeze between *funding risk,* as its re-serves dwindled, and *asset risk,* as the size of its positions made it im-practical to liquidate assets.

From the viewpoint of the brokers, a liquidation of the fund would have forced them to sell off tens of billions of dollars of securities and to cover their numerous derivatives trades with LTCM. Because lenders had required next-to-zero haircuts, there was a potential for losses to accrue while the collateral was being liquidated.

The potential disruption in financial markets was such that the New York Federal Reserve felt compelled to act. On September 23, it orga-nized a bailout of LTCM, encouraging 14 banks to invest $3.6 billion in return for a 90 percent stake in the firm. These fresh funds came just in time to avoid meltdown. By September 28, the fund's value had dropped to $400 million only. Investors had lost a whopping 92 percent of their year-to-date investment.

14.4.4 LTCM's Liquidity

LTCM failed because of its inability to measure, control, and manage its risk. This was due in no small part to the fact that LTCM's trades were rather undiversified. LTCM was reported to have lost about $1.5 billion from interest rate swaps positions and a similar amount from short posi-tions on equity volatility. As we show later, this was a result of an ill-fated attempt to manage risk through portfolio optimization.

Table 14–4 describes the exposure of various reported trades to fun-damental risk factors. All the trades were exposed to increased market volatility. Most were exposed to liquidity risk (which is itself positively correlated with volatility). Many were exposed to default risk.

To illustrate the driving factor behind LTCM's risks, Figure 14–5 plots the monthly returns against monthly changes in credit spreads. The fit is remarkably good, indicating that a single risk factor would explain 90 percent of the variation up to the September bailout. Thus there was little diversification across risk factors.

In addition, LTCM was a victim of both asset and funding liquidity risk. Although it had taken some precautions against withdrawal of funds, it did not foresee that it would be unable to raise new funds as its performance dived. The very size of the fund made it difficult to organize an orderly portfolio liquidation.

TABLE 14-4

Exposure of LTCM's Portfolio to Risk Factors

	Loss If Risk Factor Increases		
Trade	Volatility	Default	Illiquidity
Long interest rate swap	Yes	Yes	Yes
Short equity options	Yes		
Long off-the-run/short on-the-run Treasuries			Yes
Long mortgage-backed securities (hedged)	Yes		Yes
Long sovereign debt	Yes	Yes	Yes

FIGURE 14-5

Explaining LTCM returns.

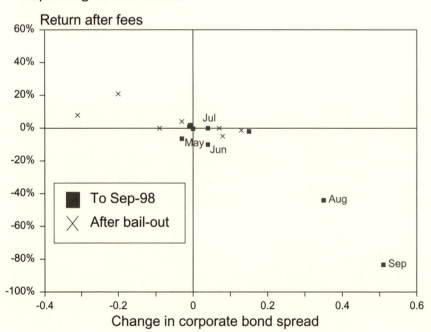

The episode also raised questions about the soundness of the brokers' risk-management systems. The brokers lulled themselves into thinking that they were protected because their loans were "fully collateralized." Even so, their loans carried no haircuts and were exposed to the risk that LTCM could default at the same time as the collateral lost value. One of the lessons of this near disaster was to accelerate the integration of credit and market risk management.

14.5 CONCLUSIONS

This chapter has shown how to account for liquidity risk. Originally, the implicit assumption behind VAR was that the assets can be liquidated before they have moved by more than the amount estimated.

In practice, this concept can be refined to account for liquidity risk. Asset liquidity risk can be traced to the price impact of the liquidation of a large position relative to normal market sizes. We have seen that different execution strategies can be compared on the basis of a liquidity-adjusted VAR, which requires an estimate of the price impact function.

Funding liquidity risk, in contrast, considers the available supply of cash equivalents as well as potential claims that may arise due to leverage. Here again, the VAR concept can be altered to estimate the risk that a portfolio could run out of cash.

Whether liquidity risk is relevant very much depends on the liability structure of the investment. Consider, for instance, an investment in "illiquid" assets such as exotic collateralized mortgage obligations. If the investment is funded by short-term borrowing, the investor runs a liquidity risk and should mark the investment at its liquidation value. In contrast, if the investment is funded by unleveraged equity, marking-to-market is an appropriate measure of risk.

As for other applications of VAR, the main benefit of these analyses is not so much to come up with one summary risk number but rather to provide a systematic framework to think about alternative execution strategies or marking-to-market arrangements.

While LVAR may be somewhat difficult to measure, some rules of thumb are useful. We do know that bid-ask spreads are positively correlated with volatility. A position in illiquid assets will incur greater execution costs as volatility increases. Thus liquidity risk can be mitigated by taking offsetting positions in assets, or businesses, that benefit from increased volatility or have positive vega.

PART FOUR

Applications of Risk-Management Systems

CHAPTER 15

Using VAR to Measure and Control Risk

At the close of each business day, tell me what the market risks are across all businesses and locations.

Dennis Weatherstone, J.P. Morgan

So far this book has discussed the motivation, building blocks, and various approaches to value-at-risk (VAR) systems. It is now time to turn to the implementation and applications of VAR.

By now VAR has established itself as a key building block of financial risk-management systems. VAR is ideally suited to institutions that have leverage and that are exposed to multiple sources of risks. This includes institutions that engage in proprietary trading but also asset managers and nonfinancial corporations such as multinationals.

At the time VAR burst on the scene, in 1994, it was devised initially as a method to report financial risks. Institutions have established global risk-management committees that aggregate company-wide risks into a single VAR measure that is easy to communicate to top management and shareholders. For most users, however, VAR was simply a *passive* application. They were content to use VAR to report "risk numbers" to stakeholders. Since then, VAR has evolved into much more than risk quantification.

Institutions have learned to apply VAR as a risk-control tool. Once a global risk-management system is in place, it can be used to control risk more tightly than before. For instance, position limits for traders can be complemented by VAR limits that properly account for the leverage and changing risk of various instruments. At the firm-wide level, VAR allows the institution to monitor its global risk exposure, taking into account diversification across business units. The firm can identify whether too many

FIGURE 15–1

Evolution of VAR applications.

bets create unacceptable risks and, if so, reverse engineer the VAR process to identify where to cut risks. This second stage of applications represents a notable improvement over the passive reporting of risk. It is still *defensive* in nature, however.

Most recently, VAR has developed into an *active* risk-management tool. With VAR tools on hand, institutions can decide how to trade off risk and return. Economic capital can be allocated as a function of business risks. Traders can be evaluated in terms of their risk-adjusted performance. Among the most advanced institutions, VAR systems are now used to identify areas of competitive advantage, or sectors where they add risk-adjusted value. The evolution of VAR applications is described in Figure 15–1.

This chapter deals with the passive and defensive applications of VAR systems. Section 15.1 first reviews factors that create a need for global risk systems. It discusses situations where VAR systems are likely to be more valuable. Applications of VAR as an information-reporting tool and as a risk-control tool are analyzed in Sections 15.2 and 15.3.

The active risk-management function, because it is so important, is examined in the following chapter. We also examine the application of

VAR to asset managers in a separate chapter. VAR-type approaches are being extended beyond market risk to the management for firm-wide risks. This very recent trend toward firm-wide risk management is explained in a later chapter.

15.1 WHO CAN USE VAR?

15.1.1 The Trend to Global Risk Management

VAR methods represent the culmination of a trend toward *centralized* risk management. For a number of years, financial institutions have maintained local risk-management units, especially around derivatives that need to be carefully controlled because of their leverage. But only recently have institutions started to measure risk on a global basis.

This trend to global risk management is motivated by two driving factors, exposure to *new sources of risk* and the *greater volatility* of new products. While 20 years ago most securities traded by banks consisted of "plain vanilla" bonds, nowadays products such as derivatives on 30-year municipal indices or exotic options are common. With the globalization of financial markets, investors are now exposed to new sources of risk such as foreign currency risk. Greater volatility is induced by greater risk in some underlying variables, such as exchange rates, or by the design of products that are more sensitive to financial variables.

This trend toward centralized risk management goes back to the creation of customized OTC derivatives, such as swaps, in the 1980s. Initially, these OTC derivative transactions were immediately offset with opposing transactions, i.e., swaps with similar credit risks. Intermediaries were essentially acting as brokers. Later, derivatives were *warehoused,* i.e., kept in inventory with dealers temporarily hedging the transaction until an offsetting transaction could be found. This led to the need for a good inventory system, as well as a good accounting system to track transactions. The next step was the transition to a *portfolio approach*. Each transaction was disaggregated into component cash flows and aggregated with other instruments in the portfolio. This is what started the process of computing VAR.

For credit risk management, centralization is also essential. The continued expansion of derivatives markets has created new entrants with lower credit ratings and greater exposure to counterparties. A financial institution may have a myriad of transactions with the same counterparty, coming from various desks, such as currencies, fixed income, commodities, and so on. Even though all the desks may have a reasonable exposure when considered on an individual basis, these exposures may add up to an unacceptable risk. Moreover, with netting agreements, the total exposure depends on the net current value of contracts covered by the agreements. All of which becomes intractable unless a global measurement system for credit risk is in place.

Financial institutions were the first to monitor on a centralized basis counterparty exposure, country, and market risks across all products and geographic locations. Asset managers and nonfinancial corporations, however, also would benefit from global risk-management systems.

Implementing a global risk-management system, however, is no small feat. It involves integrating systems, software, and database management, which can be very expensive. In addition, it requires substantial investment in intellectual and analytical expertise. As such, it may not be appropriate for all institutions (see, for instance, Box 15–1). This is why it is useful to delineate factors that favor the development of such systems.

BOX   15–1

MERRILL'S APPROACH

Merrill's approach to global risk management differs from that of other banks. A much smaller proportion of revenues is generated by position trading. Most of its profits come from customer orders, which are generally hedged immediately.

Given Merrill's large volume of trading, VAR reports produced at the close of the previous day quickly become outdated. Perhaps this explains why Merrill's risk managers do not rely much on computer models. In their view, their best risk-management tool is "distribution."

Merrill also takes the view that it has natural "business" exposure to volatility that offsets the exposure of its financial portfolio. When volatility increases, more customer orders flow in, which generates additional profits. These profits offset potential falls in the value of its inventory. The firm also keep a positive vega (long volatility) position on its option books, just to be sure.

Diversity of Risk

Institutions exposed to a diversity of financial risks, interest rates, exchange rates, and commodity prices would certainly benefit from a global risk-management system. They need a system that consistently accounts for correlations, various exposures, and volatility across risk factors. This is especially so when the institution has a large number of independent risk-taking units whose risks need to be aggregated at the highest levels. In contrast, institutions that are exposed to one source of risk only may not require a sophisticated global risk-management system. If their leverage is not too high, a simple duration measure may be sufficient.

Amount of Proprietary Trading

Firms that take aggressive proprietary positions do require the discipline imposed by a global risk-management system, especially if their leverage is high. On the other hand, firms that routinely match all trades have less of a need for such a system. One such example is foreign exchange "brokers," who simply match buyers and sellers without ever taking positions. For them, a VAR system is not essential.

Complexity of Instruments

Firms that deal with complex instruments do require a centralized risk-management system that allows consistent measures and controls of risk. Another benefit is that such a system requires a central repository for all trade processing, price quotes, and analytics. This provides some protection against operational risk, including fraud and model risk.

15.1.2 Proprietary Trading Desks

Proprietary trading desks are the prime example of institutions that satisfy all the criteria listed above. Their business has become exposed to global sources of risk. At the same time, the desks can take aggressive positions, can operate generally independently of each other, and can deal with complex products.

Consider, for instance, an investment bank where traders are awaiting U.S. unemployment numbers. Currency traders may short the dollar; they bet on unexpectedly high figures, leading to a fall in U.S. interest rates that should push the dollar down. Bond traders also may expect joblessness to rise and go long Treasury bonds. The fall in inflationary expectations may push commodity traders to short gold. Individually, these risks may be acceptable, but as whole, they sum to a sizable bet on just one number. Global risk management provides a uniform picture of the bank's risk. It fully accounts for correlations across locations and across asset classes. It allows firms to understand their risk better and therefore to hedge and price their risk better.

One of the earliest applications is the famous 4:15 P.M. report at J.P. Morgan. Table 15–1 shows the global trading business of the bank in 1994. Trading activities are grouped into seven business areas, each of them active in up to 14 locations. Altogether, the bank has 120 independent risk-taking units that handle over 20,000 transactions per day with a total volume exceeding $50 billion. Although decentralized trading appears very profitable, strong central risk controls are essential to understanding the global risk exposure of the bank.

At the end of the day, all trading units report their estimated profit and loss for the day, their position in a standardized mapping format, and their estimated risk profile over the next 24 hours. Corporate risk management then aggregates the information with centrally administered volatilities and correlations. This leads to the global consolidated 4:15 P.M. report, which is discussed by business managers before being sent to the board's chair. Before such reports became commonplace, banks essentially were ignorant of their aggregate risk.

15.1.3 Nonfinancial Corporations

VAR is also taking hold in the corporate world, albeit more slowly than for financial institutions. The main issue with corporates is the greater focus on cash flows rather than market values of assets and liabilities. The problem is that relationships between cash flows and financial market variables may be more difficult to assess.

The VAR methodology can be modified to measure what has been called *cash flow at risk* (CFAR).[1] The first step consists of delineating business exposures, which can be done with various levels of complexity. Consider first *contractual cash flows,* such as a contract to sell goods in a foreign currency, say, the euro (€). This contract can be "mapped" to a long position in the euro with an exposure equal to the notional amount. *Anticipated exposures* are similar except that they involve some

---

1. See, for instance, Turner (1996). CorporateMetrics, launched by the RiskMetrics Group in April 1999, is such an application.

TABLE 15–1

J.P. Morgan's Trading Business

	Fixed Income	Currency	Commodities	Derivatives	Equities	Emerging Markets	Proprietary	Total
Number of active locations	14	12	5	11	8	7	11	14
Number of independent risk-taking units	30	21	8	16	14	11	19	120
Thousands of transactions per day	>5	>5	<1	<1	>5	<1	<1	>20
$ Billions in daily trading volume	>10	>30	1	1	<1	1	8	>50

TABLE 15-2

Cash-Flow Exposure

	Period				
	1	2	3	4	Total
Cash flow (euro million)	2	2.1	1.5	2.5	8.1
Exchange rate ($ / euro)	1.02	1.04	1.06	1.08	
Cash flow ($ million)	2.04	2.18	1.59	2.70	8.51

uncertainty as to the actual payment; this risk can be factored in by setting the exposure to a fraction of the notional.

Suppose, for instance, that a U.S. corporation exports to Europe and is planning to receive a series of four quarterly payments, as described in Table 15–2. The table also reports the budgeted exchange rate and the total cash flow in dollars, which is $8.51 million.

The next step consists of setting up simulations to model the behavior of key financial variables, commodity prices, exchange rates, and interest rates. The horizon selected needs to match that of the business planning cycle. Note that with longer horizons, the modeling of expected returns is increasingly important, justifying the use of cointegration techniques described in Chapter 12. This is not such a problem with short-term VAR measures because volatility dominates expected returns over short horizons.

Finally, these financial variables need to be combined with business exposures. This is akin to attaching a simulation engine to the business cash-flow model. In the preceding example, if we assume an annual volatility of 12 percent and a trend given by the budgeted rates, simulations yield an average cash flow of $8.52 million and a 95 percent lower value of $7.40 million. Hence the worst cash-flow shortfall, or CFAR, is $1.12 million.

This approach can be generalized to all earnings, not just specific cash flows, in which case the risk measure is *earnings at risk* (EAR). Financial variables affect *operating cash flows* through quantities sold, sales revenues, the cost of goods sold, and other costs, as shown in Figure 15–2. For instance, costs may be affected by commodity prices or, if imported, exchange rates. Sales revenues may be affected by exchange rates, if exported. This shows the need to model *economic exposures,* which

Measuring cash flow at risk.

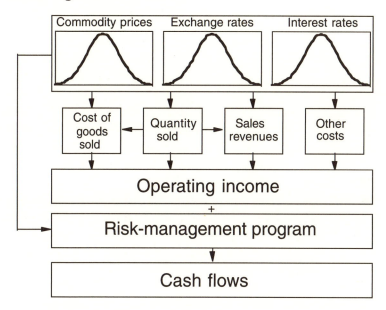

represent the sensitivity of cash flows to movements in the price of the financial variable.

Exposures can be complex, though. They depend on notional amounts as well as on the competitive environment in which the firm operates. Consider, for instance, a U.S. exporter to Europe. This company will have low currency exposure if it competes with other U.S. firms, since all products are priced in dollars. In contrast, if the exporter competes with foreign firms, the exposure can be substantial.

To be more specific, we can write export revenues as a function of foreign currency prices P^*, of quantities sold Q, and of the exchange rate S expressed in dollars. Now define the *elasticity* of P^* with respect to S as the ratio of the percentage change of P^* for a given percentage change of S:

$$\frac{(P_1^* - P_0^*)}{P_0^*} = \eta \; \frac{(S_1 - S_0)}{S_0} = \eta\delta \qquad (15.1)$$

We can write revenues as

$$R = P_1^* Q S_1 = P_0^*(1 + \delta\eta)QS_0(1 + \delta) \qquad (15.2)$$

If the U.S. exporter has no market power in the foreign market, $\eta = 0$, and U.S. revenues will fall by the full amount of the depreciation in S. This is the example in Table 15–2. In contrast, if prices are set in dollars all over the world, the elasticity $\eta = -1$ and dollar revenues are not affected. In the intermediate case, with local competition, the U.S. exporter will raise prices only partially to offset the fall in the exchange rate. We may then have $\eta = -0.5$. The simulation can be modified to take into account this business exposure.

Even more generally, there is no reason to focus on cash flows alone. Losses can occur if the value of inventories, or balance sheet positions, fluctuates due to financial variables. For some items on the balance sheet, such as commodity positions, this effect can be measured readily. For other items, this may be more questionable.

Also difficult to assess are the effect of *strategic options,* whereby firms can alter their marketing strategy (product or pricing) or production strategy (such as product sourcing or plant location) over the horizon in response to movements in financial variables. These options, as in the case of stop-loss or other risk-mitigating techniques, in general will reduce market risk.

Once this model is constructed, risk can be measured using the VAR of the operating cash flows. A risk-management program can then be set up with derivatives to lower this risk, as shown in Figure 15–2. The effectiveness of the hedging program will be measured by the reduction in VAR.

Although cash flow at risk is certainly not easy to measure, there is no question that the gathering of current company-wide information provides useful information. Indeed Box 15–2 illustrates the benefits of VAR in a Treasury operation.[2]

15.2 VAR AS AN INFORMATION-REPORTING TOOL

By now VAR has become the standard method to report financial market risks. VAR is a user-friendly method to present concise reports on risk to shareholders. VAR is also used to apprise senior management of the risks run by the trading and investment operations.

---

2. See also "The World According to Jerome Lienhard," *Derivatives Strategy* (January 1999).

B O X   15–2

TOYOTA'S VAR

Toyota Motor Credit Corporation (TMCC) is one of the largest corporate issuers in the global bond markets. Its goal is to facilitate the sale of Toyota cars to U.S. consumers. The company raises about $7 billion a year to provide funds for car leases, which typically involve level payments over a 3-year period.

TMCC simply could lock in fixed rates to cover its assets and liabilities. The treasury manager, Jerome Lienhard, however, takes the view that raising funds at floating rates is cheaper in a positively sloped yield curve environment.

This, however, involves taking some interest rate risk, which is measured using value at risk. TMCC runs Monte Carlo simulations of its cash inflows and outflows and discounts them to the present. These simulations allow realistic interest rate paths as well as the inclusion of caps, or call options, that provide protection if floating rates increase. TMCC tapped Tokai Bank's risk-management practice group, some of whom had Bankers Trust experience.

VAR is computed using a 95 percent confidence interval over a 30-day period. This horizon gives the treasurer enough time to react if rates increase unexpectedly. Since TMCC put its VAR system in place, the portfolio VAR has been reduced from $85 million to about $30 million. This represents 1.3 percent of its capital of about $2 billion. Furthermore, TMCC estimates that hedging expenses have been reduced by $10 million, or 20 percent. Says Lienhart, "There is no question that we have gained enormous understanding of risk through the process of creating an in-house system."

15.2.1 Why Risk-Management Disclosures?

Indeed, disclosure is improving rapidly. A recent report by banking and securities industry regulators finds that 66 financial institutions provided quantitative information on VAR in their 1998 annual reports, compared with only 4 firms in 1993.[3] No doubt this was in response to prodding from the Basel Committee (1995b), who states that disclosure

---

3. The joint report was issued by the Basel Committee and the International Organisation of Securities Commissions (IOSCO), which represents securities regulators from major industralized countries.

. . . can reinforce the efforts of supervisors to foster financial market stability in an environment of rapid innovation and growing complexity. If
provided with meaningful information, investors, depositors, creditors and
counterparties can impose strong market discipline on financial institutions
to manage their trading and derivatives activities in a prudent fashion and
in line with their stated business objectives.

The view is that disclosure of quantitative information about market risk is an effective means of *market discipline,* or scrutiny by shareholders, debtors, and financial analysts. Firms that fail to reveal this information may be susceptible to market rumors, possibly resulting in loss
of business or funding difficulties. Market discipline should manifest itself by requiring "a higher return from funds invested in, or placed with,
a bank that is perceived to have more risk."[4] Disclosure of market risks
is also one of the three pillars of the new Basel Committee (1999b) guidelines on credit risk.

Transparency also should lead to more *financial market stability.*
Indeed, the LTCM saga is a perfect illustration of how an institution can
build up unreasonable amounts of leverage while disclosing very little information to the rest of the world, subsequently creating a near disaster
in financial markets.[5]

Arguments for disclosure also apply to nonfinancial institutions. Lev
(1988) develops a theory that rationalizes *mandated* disclosure requirements. The gist of the argument is that disclosure may be in the best interest of the company itself. The reason is that uninformed investors who
feel they are not receiving enough information from a company can react
by choosing to do less trading in that company's stock. Thus *asymmetric
information* leads to lower trading volumes, higher trading costs, and perhaps lower equity values, which is not socially optimal.

Indeed, the industry often fails to make voluntary disclosures of information that would be relevant to investors. For instance, a *coordination problem* arises if each firm benefits from disclosure only if all other
firms likewise disclose. If so, this market failure may require disclosure
regulations. Indeed, we find that disclosure regulations are present "across
practically all free-market economies."

---

4. See the report, "Enhancing Bank Transparency," by the Basel Committee (1998b).
5. The report also notes that public disclosure may have undesirable effects, particularly with weak
institutions that run the risk of a liquidity crisis even when solvent in terms of net assets.
Disclosure, however, lessens the risk of a systemic crisis. It also should provide an incentive
for corrective action at an earlier stage.

The issue then boils down to an evaluation of whether the benefits of disclosure of market risks are greater than the cost imposed on corporations. A recent evaluation by the Securities and Exchange Commission (SEC, 1998) finds that its new market risk disclosures "provide investors and analysts with new and useful information." For example, analysts said that disclosures may allow investors to avoid investments in companies that are deemed too risky. A bank also said that it is now using the new market risk disclosure in its evaluation of loan applications. On the cost side, companies required to disclose found the rules "not terribly costly," with estimates ranging from $10,000 to $50,000.

Thus not only do these quantitative disclosure rules provide information on market risk otherwise difficult to assess, but they also bring some reassurance that a risk-management system is in place.

15.2.2 Trends in Disclosure

Disclosure about trading and derivatives activity usually appears in two places in annual reports:

- *Management discussion and analysis.* This section typically contains a narrative statement of the types of risks the firm is exposed to. More detailed information includes a qualitative description of risk-management procedures, objectives, and strategies for using derivatives and quantitative information about market and credit risks.

- *Financial statements.* This section describes the financial position of the firm and, depending on national accounting rules, can include information about derivatives positions in footnotes. Annual financial statements and footnotes are *audited* by independent accountants.

Table 15–3 provides a summary of disclosure of market risks. Of the 71 banks and securities firms surveyed, 66 report VAR data, but only 27 report the actual change in portfolio value corresponding to the reported VAR. This information is also important because it enables users to assess the effectiveness of risk-management systems. More firms disclose information about trading income, although few bother to give details about lines of activity.

The earliest such survey revealed wide discrepancies in information disclosure across national borders, with U.S. banks in the vanguard of

TABLE 15-3

Disclosure of Market Risks: 1998

Country	Total Examined	Disclosed VAR Data	Disclosed Daily P&L with VAR	Disclosed Information on Trading Income
		Number of Institutions		
Belgium	3	3	1	2
Canada	6	6	2	5
France	6	6	2	4
Germany	6	5	2	4
Italy	6	5	2	6
Japan, banks	7	7	6	7
Japan, securities houses	2	1	0	2
Luxemburg	2	2	0	0
Netherlands	3	3	0	2
Sweden	2	2	0	1
Switzerland	3	3	3	3
U.K.	7	7	1	7
U.S., banks	9	9	3	8
U.S., securities houses	9	7	5	3
Total in 1998	71	66	27	56
Memo, 1997	78	63	21	74
Memo, 1996	79	50	18	69
Memo, 1995	79	36	11	64
Memo, 1994	79	18	5	59
Memo, 1993	79	4	0	48

Source: Basel Committee surveys.

risk-management practices. By now, banks in most of the industrialized countries shown in Table 15–3 provide similar levels of information. Banks in most other countries, however, are still less forthcoming. It is fair to predict that the pressure will be on marginal players to improve disclosure.

Even among industrialized countries, there is room for improvement. A recent Basel Committee report (1999d) promulgated "best practices" guidelines for public disclosure of trading and derivatives activities. At the top of the list comes a description of the organizational risk-management structure and control processes. It also recommends detailed qualitative and quantitative disclosures of risk-management practices, including market, credit, liquidity, and other risks (classified as operational, legal, and reputational risks). Earnings also should be discussed and broken down by risk category or major product lines.

The guidelines advise banks and securities houses to disclose more than end-of-period VAR, which just reveals market risk at one point in time. Instead, institutions should provide summary VAR figures on a daily, weekly, or monthly basis, perhaps in a graph. They also should compare their daily P&L information to VAR numbers to give some indication of the effectiveness of the risk-management system.

15.2.3 Disclosure Examples

Table 15–4 compares the information provided in annual reports for a group of global financial institutions. The table shows daily VARs reported

TABLE 15–4

VAR Reporting in 1998

| | | Average 1-Day VAR | | | |
| | | | | MR | Risk |
Institution	Confidence Level	VAR ($MM)	99% VAR ($MM)	Charge ($MM)	Capital ($MM)
Bank America	97.5%	45	53	504	57,055
Bankers Trust	99%	51	51	484	8,540
Citicorp	97.7%	18	21	199	55,008
Chase	99%	26	26	244	26,161
J.P. Morgan	95%	38	54	511	16,454
Deutsche Bank	99%	43	43	408	34,303
UBS	99%	51	51	479	29,322
Barclays	98%	35	39	374	20,953
Bear Stearns	95%	14	20	192	4,955*
Merrill Lynch	99%	41	40	384	10,132*
Morgan Stanley	99%	43	43	408	14,119*
Salomon	99%	71	71	674	8,768*
CSFP	99%	71	71	671	10,257*

Source: Bank financial reports.
*Refers to equity capital only.

BOX 15–3

MOBIL'S DISCLOSURE

Mobil Corporation, a multinational company, is exposed to interest rates, exchange rates, and oil and gas prices. In its annual reports, the company states that "it has significant exposure to these risks" but that "if Mobil did not use derivatives instruments, its exposure to market risk would be higher." Its total notional amount in derivatives stood at $15.4 billion at the end of 1998. This number itself, however, has little meaning in terms of potential losses.

Mobil defines its risk with respect to benchmarks defined as 100 percent floating rate for interest rate risk, fully hedged for currency risk, and based on spot prices for commodity risks. Using a daily VAR at the 99.7 percent confidence level, Mobil reports its VAR as $4 million for interest rate risk and $8 million for commodity risk. Commodity risk includes physical commodities and derivatives, since this risk is managed on a combined basis. These numbers seem quite manageable when compared with the company's annual income of about $2 billion.

at various confidence levels. Since disclosure is voluntary, standards vary. Assuming a normal distribution, however, translation into a common standard is straightforward.

For J.P. Morgan, for example, the average 95 percent 1-day VAR is $38 million, which translates into a market risk charge (MRC) of $3 \times \sqrt{10} \times \$54 = \$511$ million. This is a small fraction of its total risk-based capital of $16,454 million. Of course, the total capital primarily must absorb credit risks.

As for nonfinancial corporations, they are finally starting to provide quantitative information on their financial market risk, as required by the SEC. Disclosures for Mobil, for example, are illustrated in Box 15–3.

15.3 VAR AS A RISK-CONTROL TOOL

VAR is not only useful for reporting purposes but also as a risk-control tool. VAR limits can be used to control the risk of traders, as a supplement to traditional limits on notional amounts. Such limits also can be used at the level of the overall institution.

Often, the mere act of quantifying risk is sufficient to provoke the institution into risk reduction. Goldman Sachs, the U.S. investment bank, for instance, was caught by the U.S. interest rate hikes of 1994. In response, it developed what is considered one of the best risk-management groups on Wall Street. Interestingly, its VAR chart showed a much lower risk profile after risk-management measures were in place. Yet the company made more money than ever.

15.3.1 Adjusting Firm-Wide VAR

These VAR limits also can be adjusted as a function of the perceived return-to-risk tradeoff. In the face of an increasingly volatile environment, for instance, a sensible response is to scale down positions. An example of this reaction is presented in Figure 15–3, which plots the evolution of the daily VAR for Bankers Trust's combined portfolio during 1994.

The figure shows that the bank's VAR started at about $70 million at the beginning of January 1994, then declined sharply during February to about $30 million, and except for minor fluctuations, remained at that level for the rest of the year.

FIGURE   15–3

Bankers Trust's VAR.

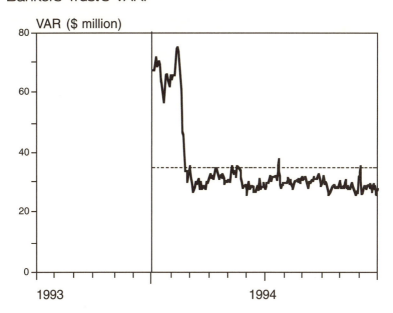

Bankers Trust explains this drastic change as follows:

> The year began with a sharp, global increase in interest rates. . . . The Corporation responded to this adverse and unsettled market environment through an orderly withdrawal in the first quarter of 1994 from substantial market positions. . . . The risk reduction that occurred during February 1994 reflected the Corporation's decision to reduce its exposure in its Trading and Positioning accounts due to fluctuations in interest rates. . . . Also, interest rate risk was the single largest source of market risk during the year with an average Daily Price Volatility of $29 million. In comparison, the Corporation's average Daily Price Volatility across all market risks was $35 million in 1994.

In other words, this withdrawal is rationalized by the increased volatility of the fixed-income market, which was a substantial contributor to the overall risk of the corporation in 1994. Figure 15–4 shows the level and expected volatility of short-term interest rates during the same period. As interest rates started to rise in February 1994, volatility also increased. In response, Bankers Trust scaled down its positions substan-

FIGURE 15–4

Interest rates: Level and volatility.

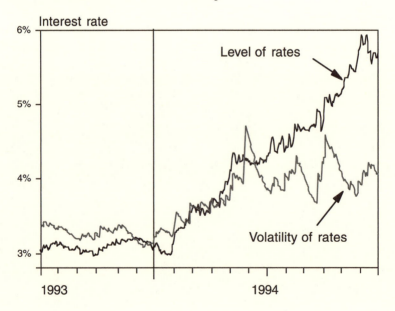

tially, by an amount that must have more than offset the increase in volatility. Thus VAR can help as a guide to decide how much exposure to financial risks should be allowed.

15.3.2 Adjusting Unit-Level VAR

At the business area or unit level, VAR also can be used to set position limits for traders and to decide where to allocate limited capital resources. A great advantage of VAR is that it creates a common denominator with which to compare various risky activities.

Traditionally, position limits are set in terms of notional exposure. A trader, for instance, may have a limit of $10 million on overnight positions in 5-year Treasuries. The same limit for 30-year Treasuries or in Treasury bond futures, however, is substantially riskier. Thus notional position limits are not directly comparable across units.[6] Instead, VAR provides a common denominator to compare various asset classes and can be used as a guide to set position limits for business units.

In addition, since VAR accounts for correlations, position limits can be set such that the risk limit at higher levels can be lower than the sum of risk limits for individual units. As Figure 15–5 shows, diversification allows the risk limit for business group A to be $60 million, which is less than the sum of $75 million for units A1, A2, and A3, due to diversification benefits.

Figure 15–6 gives an example of a summary position report for a firm with exposure to foreign currencies and fixed-income markets. The two business units have differing positions in U.S. dollars, euros, and yen. All positions and risk measures are expressed in millions of dollars.

The chart shows the FX position for each unit as well as the estimated VAR and the VAR limit. For instance, unit A has a 1-day VAR at the 95 percent confidence level of $1.28 million, against a limit of $2 million. Unit B has a higher FX VAR of $2.73 million and limit of $3 million. Note that the total FX VAR for the two units, $1.94 million, is substantially lower than the sum of individual VARs because of diversification. The total FX VAR limit of $4 million also reflects diversification.

The next panel shows the bond positions, expressed in 2-year equivalents. The total interest rate VAR is $0.81 million, below its limit of $4

---

6. Stop-loss limits allow comparability across positions but are not forward-looking.

FIGURE 15—5

Setting VAR limits.

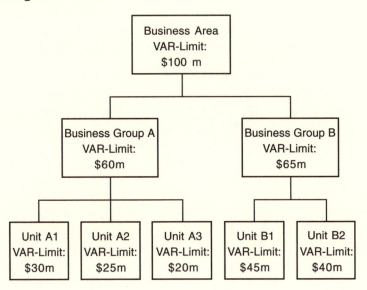

FIGURE 15—6

Example of VAR reports.

	Unit A	Unit B		Total
FX Position	-150	120	$	-30
(spot equiv. $MM)	100	80	Euro	˙180
	50	-200	Yen	-150
VAR	$1.28	$2.73		$1.94
Limit:	*$2.00*	*$3.00*		*$4.00*
Interest Rate Position	-300	0	$	-300
(2-year equiv. $MM)	90	150	Euro	240
	100	-500	Yen .	-400
VAR	$0.68	$0.67		$0.81
Limit:	*$2.00*	*$3.00*		*$4.00*
Total Position				
VAR	$1.27	$2.74		$2.01
Limit:	*$3.00*	*$4.50*		*$5.00*

million. Finally, the last lines display the VAR for each unit, their limits, and the total portfolio VAR, which is only $2.01 million. Such a report gives a broad perspective on positions and risk profiles. Because it contains the essential information in a simple summary form, any exceedence of limit can be detected quickly.

VAR limits, however, cannot be the sole deciding factor for positions. If market volatility jumps up suddenly, the risk manager may want to give some leeway in the enforcement of limits or even increase the VAR limit accordingly. Otherwise, it may prove too costly to liquidate positions under difficult market conditions. It is also useful to bear in mind that various VAR models have different responses to temporarily higher volatility. The RiskMetrics model, for instance, has a very fast and permanent response to changes in risk. In contrast, the Basel model is designed to have a slower reaction time. Thus implementation of limits should be subject to the educated judgment of the risk manager.

Swiss Bank Corporation (SBC) and Goldman Sachs, for instance, take a different approach to their trader risk limits. While SBC imposes hard limits, Goldman Sachs is more flexible and allows traders to renegotiate their limits. The latter approach seems to be more appropriate, in the spirit of an optimal risk-return tradeoff, as long as traders are penalized for their increased risk.

15.4 CONCLUSIONS

VAR represents the culmination of an unstoppable march toward global risk measurement. In contrast with previous measures, VAR provides a prospective description of the portfolio's risk profile aggregated at the highest level in a comprehensive and consistent fashion. This need for global risk-management systems is rationalized by the fact that institutions are now exposed to more sources of risk and to more complex financial instruments. By now, VAR has become a standard benchmark to quantify market risk. Only four financial institutions disclosed VAR data in 1993. Five years later, a full 66 of the 71 surveyed did so.

The use of VAR, however, has gone beyond simple risk measurement. Many institutions now use it to control their trading risk, as a supplement to traditional limits on notional amounts. Here again, VAR allows consistency and comparability across various units. It should be noted that VAR does not alleviate the need for traditional, notional, or stop-loss-based position limits. VAR systems do have deficiencies, which are summarized in a later chapter. As a result, it is still advisable to maintain other types of limits in order to avoid situations where traders can game the "blind spots" of VAR systems.

Finally, VAR is starting to be used as an active management tool for the allocation of capital. This is the subject of the next chapter.

CHAPTER 16

Using VAR for Active Risk Management

> Returns these proprietary businesses produce look very different on a risk-adjusted basis.
>
> *Analyst's comment at the announcement that Travelers was disbanding*
> *Salomon's bond arbitrage unit*

Investors have long recognized that financial management is about balancing return against risk. Before the widespread application of value at risk (VAR), however, institutions did not have the tools to evaluate the risk-return tradeoff for business lines. Banks relied on measures such as return on assets (ROA) or return on book equity (ROE) that totally ignored differences in the risk of various activities. Since then, risk-adjusted performance measures based on VAR have become a key building block for modern financial risk management.

This chapter discusses how VAR can be used to manage risk actively. Active risk-management functions include performance evaluation, capital allocation, and strategic business decisions.

The chapter starts by showing how VAR can be viewed as a measure of "economic" risk capital necessary to support a position. This generalization of the equity investment concept is driven by the complexity and leverage of financial products and institutions. This has made it necessary to evaluate activities that require little upfront capital but create contingent liabilities. Section 16.1 shows how such activities can be charged risk-based capital.

Assigning economic risk capital to a trading activity allows risk-adjusted performance measurement (RAPM), as shown in Section 16.2. Next, we discuss two approaches for measuring risk-adjusted returns. Earnings-based methods are presented in Section 16.3, whereas asset-based methods (such as VAR) are discussed in Section 16.4.

The purpose of these methods is to provide a uniform yardstick to measure the performance of traders or business units but also to guide investment decisions, or capital allocation, into new business areas. Capital allocation is the process by which a firm assigns economic capital to transactions, products, or business lines. In this context, Section 16.5 discusses whether risk adjustments should take into account correlations with other business units.

Of course, VAR is only one facet of capital decisions. It just quantifies the existing risk. It does not tell us whether we should or should not take a risk. To answer this question, we need to also account for expected profits. The tradeoff between profits and risks can be analyzed using the framework of shareholder value added (SVA), which is explained in Section 16.6.

16.1 RISK CAPITAL

16.1.1 VAR as Risk Capital

VAR can be viewed as a measure of *risk capital,* or economic capital required to support a financial activity. This resolves the paradox of how to calculate rates of return on investments that require no upfront investment, like futures. Consider, for instance, a bank with one investment only, a futures position with a notional of $100, a margin of $10, and a payoff (or dollar return) of $5. This example is not unlike the situation of highly leveraged financial institutions such as commercial banks, investment banks, and hedge funds.

How do we compute the rate of return on this $5 payoff, to compare it with other investments? In other words, what is the relevant denominator? The notional is not relevant, since it is never paid. Nor is the margin, which is a performance bond and may not provide the cushion desired by the bank.

Instead, we could consider the amount of *equity capital* that needs to be set aside to cover most of the potential losses at a predetermined confidence level. Taking into account only market risks, this equity capital is basically a market VAR measure. Therefore, VAR measures the *economic capital* (EC), defined as the aggregate capital required as a cushion against unexpected losses:

$$EC = VAR \qquad (16.1)$$

Note that this economic capital may differ from the bank's book capital.

FIGURE   16–1

Equity capital as a VAR measure.

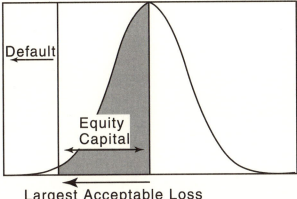

Largest Acceptable Loss

Suppose, for instance, that VAR is estimated to be $10 at the 99 percent level. As before, VAR is interpreted as the "largest" acceptable loss the bank is willing to suffer. To cover this loss, the bank must maintain adequate equity capital. In other words, VAR is the amount of capital a firm allocates to self-insurance. This is illustrated in Figure 16–1. The appendix to this chapter shows how to translate the VAR measure on the target horizon to a current amount of economic capital.

Note that this capital is leveraged. That is, the equity is supported by borrowing. Ideally, the bank should select the amount of leverage to balance the marginal benefits of increased leverage with the marginal costs of increased default probability.[1] In this case, the rate of return on equity is $5/$10 = 50 percent. With a lower capital base, the rate of return would be even higher. The drawback, of course, is that the investment is more risky. The choice of this optimal capital structure should be reflected in the choice of the confidence level.

16.1.2 Choosing the Confidence Level

This interpretation of VAR also helps to determine the appropriate confidence level. Consider a hypothetical bank for which all the risks are cap-

---

1. For a commercial bank, the benefits of leverage can be classified into (1) tax advantages due to the deductibility of interest payments, (2) low-cost access to funds through bank deposits, and (3) strengthening managers' incentives to invest in positive NPV projects. Costs can be attributed to (1) default and reorganization costs and (2) liquidity constraints that could disrupt business activities.

tured by the VAR measure. A 1-year horizon is selected, assuming it corresponds to the horizon needed to adjust the level of capital, i.e., to raise additional equity. If the bank suffers a loss greater than the VAR within a year, its equity capital is wiped out, and the bank defaults.

The bank can then set the VAR confidence level in relation to the desired credit rating. This is illustrated in Table 16–1, which reports the relationship between the credit ratings supplied by a rating agency, Moody's, and their historical 1-year default probabilities. The last columns report the *equity coverage,* measured as the number of standard deviations necessary to achieve the desired credit rating.

TABLE 16–1

Choosing Equity Coverage from the Credit Rating (Multiples of Standard Deviation Assuming Various Distributions)

Desired Rating (Moody's)	1-Year Probability of Default	Equity Coverage (Multiple of SD)	
		Normal	**Student *t***
Aaa	0.01%	3.72	9.08
Aa1	0.02%	3.54	8.02
Aa2	0.02%	3.54	8.02
Aa3	0.03%	3.43	7.46
A1	0.05%	3.29	6.79
A2	0.06%	3.24	6.56
A3	0.07%	3.19	6.37
Baa1	0.13%	3.01	5.67
Baa2	0.16%	2.95	5.44
Baa3	0.70%	2.46	4.01
Ba1	1.25%	2.24	3.52
Ba2	1.79%	2.10	3.23
Ba3	3.96%	1.76	2.62
B1	6.14%	1.54	2.30
B2	8.31%	1.38	2.08
B3	15.08%	1.03	1.65

Note: Equity coverage is defined as the number of standard deviations (SD) necessary to achieve desired default probability. Two distributions are used, the standard normal and Student *t* with 6 degrees of freedom.

Choice of confidence level

VAR can be set at a value such that the probability of losses exceeding VAR is equal to the probability of default for this risk class.

As an example, assume that the market risk of the bank is such that the annual standard deviation of profits and losses is $1 billion. How much capital should the bank set aside to achieve an Aaa credit rating? The table shows that if the distribution of losses is normally distributed, the required amount of equity is 3.72 times $1 billion, or $3.72 billion. If, however, the bank estimates that the distribution of losses has fatter tails than the normal distribution, it could select the multiplier from a Student t distribution, for example. In this case, the required amount of equity is higher, at $9.08 billion.

Suppose, for instance, that the bank wants to maintain an Aa credit rating and sets its equity capital to 8 times its annual standard deviation of profit and loss (P&L), or $8 billion. It has $4 billion in debt. With a loss equal to $8 billion, the value of equity is wiped out. With a loss equal to $12 billion, bondholders are also wiped out. With a greater loss, depositors, or the government deposit insurance fund, are also at risk.

Box 16–1 shows how Bank of America linked its desired credit rating to a confidence level and to a multiple of standard deviations.[2]

16.2 RISK-ADJUSTED PERFORMANCE MEASUREMENT

Armed with this measure of risk capital, the VAR methodology allows us to compare traders, or business units, or investment portfolios, that generate large revenues with little apparent need for capital. The VAR number can be viewed as the amount of risk capital necessary to support the position and therefore is akin to an upfront investment. In the preceding example, we computed a risk-adjusted performance measurement (RAPM) as the dollar profit over the dollar VAR, which is $5/$10, or 50 percent.

RAPM allows institutions to compare units that have very different risk capital needs. Let us go back, for instance, to the example of traders in Chapter 4 (Box 4–2). Two traders achieved profits of $10 million each over the last year. How do we compare their performance? How do we

---

2. See Zaik et al. (1996) and James (1966).

BOX 16–1

RISK MANAGEMENT AT BANK OF AMERICA

In 1993, Bank of America decided to implement risk-adjusted performance measurement throughout the organization. The bank identified major categories of risk for which unexpected losses required holding economic capital.

The amount of economic capital attributed to all business units was set so as to guaranteee the solvency of the bank at a 99.97 percent confidence level over one year. This 0.03 percent probability of default was determined to reduce the risk of the bank to the level of AA-rated companies.

The time horizon was set at 1 year as a compromise betwen the time frame for credit risk and market risk. While relatively arbitrary, the most important aspect of this choice was to ensure consistency across all business units and sources of risk.

For most market risks, with normal distributions, the bank estimated a capital coverage of 3.4 times the standard deviation of unexpected losses. For asymmetric risks such as credit risks, the capital coverage was set at 6 standard deviations.

---

decide which unit should be given additional risk capital? Table 16–2 shows how RAPM helps to answer this question.

Assume a constant notional amount of $100 million and $200 million for the FX and bond traders, respectively, and an annual volatility in currency and bond markets of 12 and 4 percent. We can compute the risk capital at the 99 percent level over 1 year as $28 million and $19 million for the two traders, as shown in Table 16–2.

TABLE 16–2

Computing RAPM

	Profit	Notional	Volatility	VAR	RAPM
FX trader	$10 million	$100 million	12%	$28 million	36%
Bond trader	$10 million	$200 million	4%	$19 million	54%

The risk-adjusted performance is then measured as the profit divided by the economic capital risk charge:

$$\text{RAPM} = \frac{\text{profit}}{\text{EC}} \qquad (16.2)$$

To translate into annual numbers, one can take the annual profit and the average of the daily VAR numbers.

The table shows that the bond trader has a higher RAPM than the currency trader, at 54 versus 36 percent, due to the lower risk capital requirement. Thus this trader makes better use of scarce equity capital.

This adjustment is the essence of the *risk-adjusted return on capital* (RAROC) developed by Bankers Trust in the late 1970s. Bankers computes a "RAROC risk factor" using a weekly standard deviation σ_w,

$$\text{RAROC risk factor} = 2.33 \times \sigma_w \times \sqrt{52} \times (1 - \text{tax rate}) \qquad (16.3)$$

that is applied to the notional amount to measure the capital charge. Apart from the tax factor, which determines the amount required on an after-tax basis, this is essentially a VAR measure.

RAROC is formally defined as

$$\text{RAROC} = \frac{(\text{profit} - \text{risk adjustment})}{\text{capital}} \qquad (16.4)$$

where profits are charged a cost for immobilizing capital, of the form $k \times$ capital, where k is a discount rate that is discussed later in the chapter.[3]

16.3 EARNINGS-BASED RAPM METHODS

Another widely used risk-adjusted performance measure is based on earnings instead of assets. From the history of realized profits and losses, we can measure the standard deviation of daily profits. Define this as the *earnings at risk* (EAR) over 1 day, EAR(1-day). The EAR over an annual period is computed from applying the square root of time rule, $\text{EAR} = \text{EAR(1-day)} \times \sqrt{252}$, assuming 252 trading days in a year. The earnings-based RAPM consists of profits divided by the EAR measures.

---

3. Other methods have been proposed, such as return on risk-adjusted capital (RORAC), which puts the adjustment in the numerator. These are all variations on the same theme. Matten (1996) lists various methods.

Earnings-based methods are easy to implement because they only require historical data on trader or unit performance. They also give some indication of the risks undertaken.

This approach, however, has shortcomings. First, EAR measures historical risks rather than giving a forward-looking measure of risk. It reflects past decisions rather than current profiles. Second, the risks that are not realized over the sample period will be missed by the EAR approach. As Box 16–2 shows, this approach is also prone to model risk if it relies on the trader's valuation model or parameters to measure profits. Finally, focusing on earnings does not help to understand the drivers of risk, nor does it provide tools to control volatility.

On the other hand, earnings-based measures are more useful at a broader level of aggregation, e.g., when analyzing business units or when

BOX 16–2

THE DANGER OF RELYING ON EARNINGS MEASURES

In 1987, Bankers Trust had a close encounter with disaster. Apparently, the firm had enjoyed profits of $600 million from foreign currency trading, half of which were attributed to Andy Krieger, its star trader, who specialized in selling long-dated currency options. He was so successful that he was given a trading limit of $700 million that represented a quarter of the bank's capital. The problem was that the positions were illiquid and difficult to value.

After he left, the firm unraveled his trades and then realized that his trading revenues had to be lowered by $80 million. The bank also was shocked to learn that it sometimes had $2 billion at risk. "Its whole future was riding on the judgment and trades of one 32-year-old banker," an executive said.

The bank vowed this would never happen again. Top management put in place more robust risk-control systems and made sure traders were evaluated on their risk-adjusted performance.

This episode illustrates the shortcoming of earnings-based volatility measures. Marking-to-market positions are notoriously difficult in illiquid markets such as long-dated options in exotic currencies. Even if measured correctly, the profit pattern of short options positions gives a misleading picture of the true risk. These positions generate small stable profits as long as markets behave normally but can lose large amounts of money in times of increased volatility.

TABLE 16–3

Comparing Asset- and Earnings-Based VAR

	Asset-Based	Earnings-Based
Approach	Structural model: bottom-up	Aggregate model: top-down
Horizon	Forward-looking: uses current profile	Backward-looking: uses historical data
Best application	Similar businesses such as trading	Disparate activities such as fee income
Usefulness for control	Very useful: details risk drivers	Not so useful: no info on risk drivers
Ease of implementation	Difficult to set up: process data	Easy to calculate: use P&L time series
Coverage	Covers only modeled risks (e.g., market)	Captures all risks (historical data only)

comparing disparate business activities. Because they focus on the actual earnings volatility, such measures cover all sources of risk, including business and operational risks, that cannot be measured easily with structural asset-based models, which are best developed for measuring market risks.

Earnings-based measures also provide a link between required risk capital and the perception of risk by investors, earnings volatility. The methodology developed in the following sections, however, applies as well to asset-based (VAR) and to earnings-based risk measures. Table 16–3 summarizes the pros and cons of asset- and earnings-based VAR measures.

16.4 VAR-BASED RAPM METHODS

Based on VAR, the RAPM approach allows managers to adjust the profit performance of traders for the risk they are taking. The VAR approach offers a standardized base for comparing markets with different risk characteristics.

RAPM uses the dollar profit divided by its associated VAR. For unit i,

$$\text{RAPM}_i = \frac{\text{profit}_i}{\text{VAR}_i} \qquad (16.5)$$

More specifically, a trading business can be decomposed into various components such as customer execution, customer positioning, and house positioning. Each of these must be assigned revenues and costs. For instance, the revenue component of customer execution consists of commissions and bid/ask spreads; the cost component includes operating and clearance costs.[4] In addition to direct expenses and costs, the system also should account for transfer pricing allocations and charges for overhead and tax allocations.

The conventional RAPM measure considers the total profit over the period under consideration, typically a year, divided by the average of the daily VAR over the same year.[5]

A major benefit of RAPM is that the risk adjustment provides a solution to the moral hazard problem inherent in linking trader bonuses to profits. Without controlling for risks, traders may have an incentive to take more aggressive positions. This is due to the asymmetrical payoff profile of a trader's compensation. Traders typically receive a percentage of (or bonus based on) profits, which can be quite large. In contrast, if they lose a large amount of money, they still draw their base salary. The worst penalty they can suffer is to be fired. This limited liability profile is described in Figure 16–2.

This payoff profile is akin to a long position in an option. Since option values increase with volatility, traders have an incentive to increase the risk of their positions. Such behavior may be optimal for them but not for the corporation (see Box 16–3). As with risk-based capital requirements for financial institutions, imposing an *ex ante* penalty for higher risk attempts to curb this behavior.

The great advantage of this RAPM method is that it creates a natural incentive for traders to take a position only when they have strong

---

4. For further analysis of performance measurement in the trading room, see Bralver and Kuritzkes (1993).

5. In practice, the VAR measure may be adjusted for a "management intervention factor." Whenever a trader starts to lose money, management intervenes by lowering the position limits. If the trader continues to lose money, he or she may be terminated, in which case performance evaluation is not an issue. On the other hand, if the trader recovers, the trading limits can be relaxed. This is modeled by running simulations of a controlled diffusion process initially with some uptrend representing expected profits. In the simulations, if the process falls below some value, the process then switches to another with a lower trend and variance, representing the tighter trading limits. After improvement, the process can then return to its original specification. The simulations then provide a ratio of "controlled VAR" to the usual VAR, which can be applied as a correction factor to the trader's VAR.

FIGURE 16-2

The optionlike bonus profile.

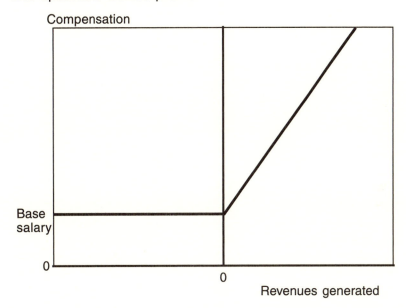

views on markets. If they have no views, they will optimally abstain from investing.

More generally, RAPM should take into account other financial risks. It can be measured as

$$\text{RAPM} = \frac{\text{revenues} - \text{costs} - \text{expected losses}}{\text{VAR}} \qquad (16.6)$$

where

$$\text{VAR} = \text{market VAR} + \text{credit VAR}$$
$$+ \text{operational VAR} - \text{diversification} \quad (16.7)$$

This definition includes not only market but also credit and operational risks and possibly diversification benefits. Expected losses cover statistically expected credit and operational losses and are usually called *credit reserves*. Here, VAR measures the capital necessary to cushion against unexpected market, credit, and operational risks and can be defined as *overall economic capital*.

BOX 16-3

THE DIFFICULTY OF ADJUSTING BONUS STRUCTURES

Currently, most traders are compensated as a function of their profits only. Attempts at changing the typical compensation structure have so far met with little success.

One such experiment was attempted by Warren Buffett, as part of his efforts to reshape Salomon Brothers after he became chairman in 1991. Buffett pledged to curb the excesses of what he called an "irrational" compensation system.

Salomon cut bonuses paid to managing directors by an average of 25 percent. At the same time, a bigger share of the bonus was paid in company stock rather than in cash.

These changes, however, were undermined by competitors willing to pay top dollars to attract the most talented individuals. Several Salomon managers walked out, and the new structure had to be scrapped.

Regulators have complained that this system encourages excessive risk-taking. They have not taken action so far, due to the global nature of trading. The Bank of England, for instance, has recognized that any regulatory action on this front simply will prompt trading business to move to another jurisdiction.

More fundamentally, it is up to the shareholders to decide whether they want to be in the business of granting a license to speculate to their traders. No doubt this explains why the famous U.S. bond arbitrage unit at Salomon was disbanded in 1998. The Travelers group, the parent company that had just acquired Salomon, was unwilling to accept the high profit volatility in the bond arbitrage business.

16.5 FIRM-WIDE PERFORMANCE MEASUREMENT

RAPM methods represent a generalization of a well-known performance measure, the *Sharpe ratio,* developed by William Sharpe in 1966. This ratio measures the ratio of average return, in excess of the risk-free rate, to the total volatility of returns:

$$S_i = \frac{\overline{R_i} - R_F}{\sigma(R_i)} \qquad (16.8)$$

where $\overline{R_i}$ is the average return on asset i and $\sigma(R_i)$ its volatility. RAPM generalizes this formula to dollar numbers, using risk capital instead of an upfront investment.

The performance-measurement literature, however, has long recognized that this risk adjustment ignores diversification considerations. The Sharpe ratio is appropriate when total risk matters, i.e., when all an investor's wealth is invested in this asset. When the asset, however, is considered only in relation to a large, diversified portfolio, measuring risk by total volatility is inappropriate.

To address this problem, Treynor (1965) proposed an alternative performance measure emphasizing systematic rather than total risk. The *Treynor ratio* is the ratio of average return, in excess of the risk-free rate, to the contribution of this asset to the portfolio's total risk:

$$T_i = \frac{\overline{R}_i - R_F}{\beta_i} \tag{16.9}$$

where β_i is the systematic risk of asset i relative to the total bank's portfolio p.

Similarly, the conventional RAPM definition is not entirely appropriate, due to the fact that the trader's risk is only one component of the bank's total risk. Generally, trading profits may be related to the risks of other departmental units. Consider, for instance, an institution with two units, a bond trading desk and a futures desk. If both departments take long positions in anticipation of a decrease in interest rates, the total risk to the corporation will be very large. In contrast, if the futures desk goes short, the combined positions may be nearly risk-free; this may be the case, for instance, when the two desks engage in arbitrage between the cash and futures markets. Applying VAR separately to each unit overstates their combined risk.

We now need to transform the Treynor measure into dollar numbers. This can be done using the concept of *marginal VAR,* which is developed in Chapter 7. We defined the marginal VAR for security i, ΔVAR_i, as the change in total VAR due to an increase in the allocation to i. This can be generalized to the level of the business unit, or trader. The marginal RAPM measure is now

$$\text{Marginal RAPM}_i = \frac{\text{profit}_i}{(\Delta\text{VAR}_i)} = \frac{\text{profit}_i}{(\text{VAR} \times \beta_i)} \tag{16.10}$$

This measure can be used as a guide to make decisions to enter or exit a particular business line. Its drawback, however, is that it does not fully allocate all the bank capital to each unit.

To do this, we need to resort to the previously defined concept of *component VAR,* which provides a partition of the firm's VAR into various components. The component RAPM measure (sometimes called *diversified*) is now

$$\text{Component RAPM}_i = \frac{\text{profit}_i}{(\text{CVAR}_i)} = \frac{\text{profit}_i}{(\text{VAR} \times w_i \beta_i)} = \frac{\text{profit}_i}{(\text{VAR}_i \times \rho_i)}$$

$$(16.11)$$

where all the CVAR_i measures are ensured to sum to the firm's total VAR. The *percent VAR* is then simply the ratio of CVAR_i to total VAR.

Table 16–4 gives an example of a bank with four lines of trading activity. The data represent the actual quarterly earnings of a large bank. The first column reports the annual profit, the second the quarterly volatility. This can be translated into an annual VAR at the 99 percent confidence level by multiplying by 2.33 times the square root of 4, making the usual assumption of normal distributions.

The conventional RAPM measure is based on the individual (sometimes called *undiversified*) VAR. Here, the return-to-risk ratio for the interest rate desk appears to be much higher than that of other units.

The bank's total VAR is only about half the sum of the units' VAR, due to diversification effects. The next column reports the correlation of each unit with the total. The interest rate desk displays a high correlation, whereas the FX desk has a negative correlation.

The percent VAR analysis indeed shows that about 80 percent of the bank's VAR is due to the interest rate desk. In addition, the FX desk serves as a hedge against other risks. Its component VAR is actually negative.[6] Thus additional capital should be allocated in priority to this unit because this will decrease the total risk of the bank.

This example illustrates that the application of VAR in performance measurement depends on its intended purposes.

- *Internal performance measurement* aims at rewarding units that produce the best performance within their allowed parameters. It requires a risk measure that does not depend on what other units do. For instance, the composition of a bonus pool should only depend on actions that a unit has full control over. Here, the individual (undiversified) VAR seems the appropriate choice.

---

6. This points to another practical difficulty with marginal VAR measures. Measurement error in the β sometimes can lead to situations where the value of β is very low, which creates abnormally high performance measures when dividing by marginal VAR.

T A B L E 16–4

Profit and Risk Measures ($ Millions)

Unit	Annual Profit	Quarterly Volatility	Individual VAR	RAPM	Correlation	Component VAR	Percent VAR
Interest rate	$1636	$152	$708	2.31	0.851	$603	79.9%
FX	$381	$92	$426	0.89	−0.131	($56)	−7.4%
Equity	$123	$71	$332	0.37	0.554	$184	24.4%
Commodity	$50	$16	$74	0.68	0.322	$24	3.1%
Sum			$1541				
Diversification			($786)				
Total	$2189	$162	$755	2.90		$755	100.0%

- *External performance measurement,* in contrast, aims at allocation of existing or new capital to existing or new business units. Such decisions should be made with the help of marginal and component (diversified) VAR measures.

In practice, for performance-measurement purposes, risk capital typically is allocated according to the unit's own risk. The bank then reaps the benefits of diversification, which are allocated to the central unit. Indeed, this central unit is directly responsible for setting position limits for each unit and for deciding how much to allocate across business units. This method has the advantage of being robust and easy to implement.

16.6 VAR AS A STRATEGIC TOOL

More generally, VAR also can be useful at the strategic level. Risk-adjusted performance measures can be used to identify where shareholder value is being added throughout the corporation.

The objective is to help management make decisions about which business lines to expand, maintain, or reduce, as well as about the appropriate level of capital to hold.

16.6.1 Shareholder Value Analysis

Indeed, the purpose of *shareholder value analysis* (SVA) is to maximize the total value to shareholders. The framework is that of a net present value (NPV) analysis, where expected free cash flows are discounted at the appropriate interest rate k. This hurdle rate must necessarily reflect the risks of the project, as perceived by shareholders.

SVA dictates that any project must be undertaken only when it generates a positive NPV. Alternatively, if the corporation cannot generate such profitable projects, it simply should return capital to its shareholders in the form of dividends or share buybacks. Or the capital could be used for acquisitions. Indeed, this focus on SVA explains why many banks have been repurchasing their shares recently.

Here, a key factor is the choice of the discount rate. Activities that generate large profits but with much variability may not be very attractive if cash flows are discounted at a high rate, reflecting the fact that investors dislike volatility. On the other hand, activities with steady returns may look more attractive once their risk profile is taken into account.

Bankers Trust, for instance, expanded into businesses that provide a high RAROC, such as asset management and MBS processing, both of which produce stable income. Perhaps this is why the asset-management business, which produces stable profits, is typically characterized by higher price/earnings ratios than trading businesses, which have high earning volatility.

SVA is consistent with a more recent variation, called *economic value added* (EVA).[7] EVA focuses on the creation of value during a particular period, measuring "residual" economic profits as

$$\text{EVA} = \text{profit} - (\text{capital} \times k) \qquad (16.12)$$

where profits are adjusted for the cost of economic capital, using k as the appropriate discount rate. EVA is also consistent with RAROC, given that the profit measure in Equation (16.4) imputes a charge for capital.[8] If so, EVA is simply the numerator in RAROC.

Indeed, RAROC-type methods are being used increasingly for strategic decisions. Zaik et al. (1996), for example, explain that Bank of America compares each business unit's RAROC to the cost of the bank's equity, which is the minimum rate of return required by shareholders. If RAROC is greater, the unit is deemed to add value to shareholders.[9]

Initially, RAROC was designed for performance measurement. As such, it focuses on past performance. Similarly, EVA measures the economic value added during the reporting period.

These measures also can be used to compare prospective investments. The main difference is that the profit measure is projected, instead of realized, and that multiple periods have to be considered. In other words, SVA is a prospective multiperiod measure, whereas EVA is a one-period measure. The two methods, however, are consistent with each other and lead to similar decision rules provided the same inputs are used.[10]

---

7. EVA is a trademark of Stern Stewart & Co.
8. Stoughton and Zechner (1999) discuss the link between RAROC and EVA within the context of optimal capital allocation.
9. Crouhy et al. (1999) provide detailed comparisons of project valuation methods and find that under certain conditions, RAROC equals the firm's equity cost of capital. They also explain problems with the RAROC methodology.
10. Assuming that capital is fully invested or that excess capital has zero return, the one-period NPV criterion maximizes (profit + capital)/(1 + k) − capital = (profit − k × capital)/(1 + k), which is equivalent to maximizing EVA.

16.6.2 Choosing the Discount Rate

The choice of the capital charge, or of the discount rate k, however, is a complex issue. The preceding section has shown that the capital charge can be a function of the unit's undiversified VAR or of the component VAR. The rationale for the latter choice is that the component VAR measures the effect on the bank's total risk.

It is not obvious, however, that the bank should focus on its total risk. If the bank's shareholders are well diversified, they should penalize the bank for its marginal contribution to the "market" portfolio volatility instead of its total risk. This insight forms the basis for the capital asset pricing model (CAPM), which holds that shareholders only worry about systematic risk. The CAPM states that the required return on a project, or hurdle rate k_i, should be constructed as the sum of the risk-free rate R_F and of the market risk premium times the project's systematic risk β_i^m:

$$k_i = R_F + [E(R_m) - R_F]\beta_i^m \qquad (16.13)$$

If so, the risk penalty should measure the unit's systematic risk vis-à-vis the market, not the bank.

As with all financial theories, the usefulness of the CAPM is that it forces us to identify conditions under which its precepts may not hold. One could say, for instance, that empirical tests do not entirely support the CAPM and that earnings volatility does seem to matter to investors. Alternatively, we could look into the literature that tries to rationalize why firms do seem to hedge financial risks. The fact that firms do undertake hedging activities has presented somewhat of a puzzle to finance researchers. Indeed, with "perfect" capital markets, there would be no need to hedge. This produces profits or losses that should average out to zero over the long run. In the meantime, hedging simply lowers the variability of outcomes. Firms could decide not to hedge and simply raise external funds whenever they are subject to unfavorable financial shocks. As predicted by the Miller-Modigliani theorem, hedging does not provide any benefits under these conditions.

Thus hedging theories argue that there are some "frictions" in capital markets that make hedging worthwhile. (In fact, most bankers would argue that their very raison d'être stems from inefficiencies in capital markets.) One such theory is that reducing the bank's volatility is important due to the high costs of financial distress.

Other theories have to do with financial market imperfections. If raising external capital is much more costly than using internal cash, then the bank should try to smooth out its earnings so as to provide steady investments from internal funds. Froot and Stein (1998) show that with such capital constraints, the hurdle rate the bank should impose on investment projects takes the form of

$$k_i = R_F + c_1\beta_i^m + c_2\beta_i \qquad (16.14)$$

which now depends not only on the market beta but also on the beta of the project with respect to the bank's existing portfolio β_i.

Finally, some factors are specific to financial institutions. A unique aspect of commercial banks is that they face regulatory constraints that link their capital to their risk level. Assuming these constraints are binding, it then makes sense for the bank to allocate its precious capital as a function of each unit's marginal contribution to the bank's risk. For investment banks, financial distress can prove very expensive. They are as leveraged as commercial banks but do not have access to low-cost deposits as a source of funds. As a result, they have to rely on short-term funding. In times of distress, liquidity constraints can cause major disruptions because funding sources can quickly dry up.

In practice, banks seem to worry mainly about their total risk, instead of their systematic risk, perhaps for all the reasons listed above.

16.6.3 Implementing SVA

Institutions have found that a strong capital allocation process produces substantial benefits. The fact that there are various approaches should not be a deterrent to the application of SVA/EVA/RAROC models.

Experience has shown that the main benefit of these methods is that the process itself nearly always leads to improvements. Financial executives are forced to examine prospects for revenues, costs, and risks in all their business activities. Invariably, managers learn things about their business they did not know.

One bank consultant study, for example, has found that typical banks have only one-third of their business with high risk-adjusted returns, one-third with returns around 12 percent, and fully one-third with returns below 8 percent. Without a risk-adjustment method, it is not easy to tell where a particular business line or product would fit.

Even though this approach is a first step toward better business decisions, other factors must be considered. Customer satisfaction and repeat business are important considerations that are better captured by a

B O X   16–4

SVA IN ACTION

After it merged with Chemical Bank, Chase Manhattan Bank implemented SVA to improve its profitability in 1998. The bank required all managers to deduct an explicit charge for the cost of capital from the net income they produced. This capital cost was set at a deliberately high rate of 13 percent so as to weed out marginal businesses. To make its point, the bank announced that managers' pay would be tied to their SVA.

By the end of the year, the results had been dramatic. While Chase's earnings continued to grow at 15 percent, asset growth stopped. Managers were quick to pull out of businesses with marginal SVA, which allowed capital to be reallocated more efficiently. Profit margins went up from 11.2 to 13.7 percent, and the stock price zoomed up by 30 percent.

---

multiperiod model. Development cycles are also overlooked in single-period models. EVA systems also ignore business synergies. For instance, businesses with low returns may have cross-selling benefits that make them worth keeping. Still, RAPM methods represent a big improvement in the allocation of capital. In practice, these methods are proving successful (see Box 16–4).

16.7 CONCLUSIONS

Financial institutions are realizing that efficient allocation of capital must be supported by risk-adjusted performance measures. The starting point for these methods is VAR, which measures the amount of economic capital necessary to support a business activity. This leads the way for RAPM methods, such as RAROC, which deduct risk charges from profits.

This approach provides a poweful mechanism to counterbalance the structural incentive of traders to take on more risk than they should. Thus we should hope that "risk penalties" will become a common element of trader's compensation structure.

RAPM-based methods are entirely in line with shareholder value analysis, which carefully balances profits against risks. For the first time, we now have the tools to apply risk-management analysis to the level of the whole firm and to make strategic decisions based on the best return-to-risk ratio. There is no doubt that these developments have been made possible by the widespread use of VAR.

APPENDIX: A CLOSER LOOK AT ECONOMIC CAPITAL

This appendix gives a more formal but technical interpretation of VAR as economic capital. Originally, VAR was developed as a method to measure short-term risks. For longer horizons, however, discounting or trends become an issue. VAR, which is a shortfall measure on a target horizon, needs to be converted into economic capital valued in *current* dollars.

This link is best explained in the Merton (1974) framework that views equity as a call option on the value of an indebted firm. The debt is risky, since there is no guarantee that the value of the firm will be sufficient to repay the face value of the debt, which plays the role of the strike price. Define

$$
\begin{aligned}
S_t &= \text{value of equity} \\
B_t &= \text{value of debt} \\
V_t = S_t + B_t &= \text{value of the firm} \\
K &= \text{face value of debt} \\
\mu &= \text{expected return on } V \\
r &= \text{risk-free rate} \\
\sigma &= \text{volatility of } V \\
T &= \text{length of horizon}
\end{aligned}
$$

To briefly summarize the essence of option pricing theory, we can price an option in a *risk-neutral world* by (1) assuming that all assets grow at the risk-free rate and (2) discounting at the same risk-free rate. This explains why the actual growth μ does not appear in the Black-Scholes model. This shortcut does not mean that investors are risk-neutral but instead happens to provide the correct solution.

Now, if the value of the firm follows a log-normal process, we can write

$$
\ln(V_T) = \ln(V_t) + (\mu - \tfrac{1}{2}\sigma^2)T + \sigma\sqrt{T}\epsilon \tag{16.15}
$$

Note that the $\tfrac{1}{2}\sigma^2$ term is due to the transformation of arithmetic returns to logarithms (see, for instance, Hull, 2000). We can find the break-even level such that the probability of falling below V^* is equal to the desired value of p:

$$
p = P(V_T \leq V^*) = P\{\epsilon \leq [\ln(V^*/V_t) - (\mu - \tfrac{1}{2}\sigma^2)T]/\sigma\sqrt{T}\}
$$

$$
= P(\epsilon \leq -\alpha) \tag{16.16}
$$

where ϵ is a standard normal variable and α is the deviate corresponding to the probability p. Note that μ is the actual (i.e., objective instead of risk-neutral) trend in V. This break-even level defines the VAR on the target date as

$$\text{VAR}_T = E(V_T) - V^* \tag{16.17}$$

If the value of the firm drops below V^*, the firm defaults.

Once the strike price is set, the amount of economic capital required to provide the desired confidence level can be calculated as the value of the stock, or a call option on the firm with strike price $K = V^*$:

$$\text{EC} = S_t = C(V_t, K, T, r, \sigma) = V_t N(d_1) - Ke^{-rT} N(d_2) \tag{16.18}$$

with the usual notations.

Example

Consider a firm with initial value $V_t = \$100$, parameters $\mu = 8$ percent, $r = 5$ percent, and $\sigma = 30$ percent. The firm is financed with a mix of equity and zero-coupon debt. We wish to find the economic capital such that the probability of default is 1 percent over $T = 1$ year.

Solving Equation (16.16) with the associated deviate $\alpha = 2.33$,

$$[\ln(V^*/V_t) - (\mu - \tfrac{1}{2}\sigma^2)T]/\sigma\sqrt{T} = -2.33$$

we find $V^* = \$51.48$. We can now compute the value of equity in the capital structure, using Equation (16.18), which gives $S_t = \$51.09$. Debt must account for the remainder, or $B_t = \$100 = \$51.09 = \$48.91$.

Hence the economic capital required to achieve this default probability should be $\$51.09$, expressed in current dollars. The VAR at the 1-year horizon is

$$\text{VAR}_T = E(V_t) - V^* = V_t e^{\mu T} - V^* = \$108.33 - \$51.48 = \$56.85$$

Note that this says nothing yet about how much economic capital should be held at the present time.

Suppose that, mistakenly, this VAR number is taken as the current equity capital. If so, the actual probability of default will be lower than 1 percent.[11] This bias increases for longer horizons and greater expected returns.

---

11. Kupiec (1999) illustrates the biases that can occur when this method is not applied properly.

We can take a shortcut to translate the VAR number into economic capital. When the probability of default is very low, $N(d_1)$ and $N(d_2)$ are close to unity, and the Black-Scholes model collapses to

$$S_t \approx V_t - Ke^{-rT} = e^{-rT}(V_t e^{rT} - V^*)$$
$$= e^{-rT}[E^{RN}(V_T) - V^*] = e^{-rT}\,\text{VAR}_T^{RN} \quad (16.19)$$

where the expectation is taken with respect to the risk-neutral measure, i.e., assuming that V_t will grow at the risk-free rate. Thus VAR_T^{RN} is the VAR on the target date, assuming that the value of the firm grows at the risk-free rate. To translate this VAR into a current number, we simply discount at the risk-free rate.

In our example, this yields

$$\text{VAR}_T^{RN} = V_t e^{rT} - V^* = \$105.13 - \$51.48 = \$53.65$$

and

$$S_t \approx e^{-0.05} \times \$53.65 = \$51.03$$

which is quite close to the true value of $51.09. This shows that equity capital should be viewed as a VAR measure discounted into the present.

CHAPTER 17

VAR in Investment Management

> We have a standard deviation for our total plan, but it only tells you what happened in the past. By contrast, VAR looks forward.
>
> *Director of Chrysler's pension fund*

By now, value at risk (VAR) has spread well beyond the Wall Street trading departments where it originated. The investment management industry is also discovering the benefits of VAR systems.

Many of the reasons that made VAR successful in the banking industry also apply to asset managers. VAR is a forward-looking measure of the risk profile of the fund. The more traditional returns-based approach, in contrast, is purely historical; it does not offer timely measurement of risk.

VAR is comprehensive, since it accounts for leverage and diversification. VAR is an intelligible measure of risk that can be explained easily to plan managers and trustees. VAR also leads to better control and management of financial risks. As a bonus, comprehensive risk-management systems provide some protection against rogue traders, thereby helping to avoid embarrassing financial losses.

VAR systems also can be used to set consistent guidelines. Typically, investment managers operate under a myriad of constraints, delineated in a list of prohibited investments and limits on notional amounts. Originally, the goal of these guidelines was to contain risk. Controlling positions by limits, however, does not account for diversification or new instruments and may not be consistent across markets.

This chapter shows how VAR can benefit investment managers. Section 17.1 discusses the application of risk-management systems to the asset-management industry. It focuses primarily on pension funds, which constitute the largest segment of the industry and were the first to embrace VAR methods. Globally, pension funds account for a massive $15 trillion out of a securities market valued at around $50 trillion.

Traditionally, the investment-management industry has faced a greater number of definitions of risk, which are summarized in Section 17.2. Section 17.3 shows how to use VAR to monitor and control risk. More recently, VAR is being used to manage portfolios actively, as discussed in Section 17.4. Finally, Section 17.5 describes the recently developed "Risk Standards," which establish risk-management guidelines for institutional investors.

17.1 IS VAR APPLICABLE TO INVESTMENT MANAGEMENT?

The investment-management industry consists of institutional and individual investors. *Institutional investors* include investment companies, such as mutual funds, pension funds, insurance companies, endowment funds, and private partnerships, such as hedge funds. This group is part of the "buy side" of Wall Street, in contrast with banks, the "sell side" that developed VAR.

Whereas VAR has been widely, and rather quickly, accepted by the banking industry, it is taking longer to gain acceptance in the investment-management industry. Perhaps this is so because investment management differs in many fundamental respects from the fast-paced trading environment of dealing banks. Table 17–1 compares the characteristics of the buy side with those of the sell side.

VAR is particularly appropriate for a trading environment, where the horizon is short and turnover high. In this case, historical measures of risk are basically useless, since yesterday's portfolio profile may have nothing to do with today's. In fast-moving markets, even a daily VAR calculation may not be sufficient.

In an investment environment, in contrast, the horizon, as measured by the portfolio evaluation period, is much longer, monthly or quarterly. Positions change more slowly. In particular, passive funds have very low turnover, perhaps 5 percent over a year. Even rather active funds typically turn over at an annual rate of 100 percent only. This implies that over the course of a month, only 8 percent of the portfolio will have changed. This is much less than the frenetic day-to-day trading of commercial banks.

Bank trading portfolios are also highly leveraged, which makes it

TABLE 17-1

Risk Management for the Sell and Buy Sides

Characteristic	Sell Side (e.g., Banks)	Buy Side (e.g., Investors)
Horizon	Short-term (1 day, intraday)	Long-term (month, quarter, years)
Turnover	Rapid	Slow
Leverage	High	Low
Risk measures	VAR	Asset allocation
	Stress tests	Tracking error
Risk controls	Position limits	Diversification
	VAR limits	Benchmarking
	Stop-loss rules	Investment guidelines

particularly important to control their risk. A sequence of adverse events could easily bankrupt the portfolio, as shown by the Barings crisis. In contrast, pension funds, whose positions are guided by a "prudent investor" philosophy, do not allow leverage. Thus there is a less fundamental need to control the downside risk.

Hedge funds, however, are a category apart. They may have high leverage and greater turnover than traditional managers. Long-Term Capital Management is an extreme example of a hedge fund that went nearly bankrupt due to its huge leverage. Such hedge funds are more akin to the trading desks of investment banks than to pension funds. As such, they should use similar risk-management systems.

Another difference with the trading environment is that some VAR techniques are notably less effective for long horizons. With a short horizon, it is essential to capture changes in asset volatility. There is indeed strong empirical support for the hypothesis that volatility changes predictably over short horizons. Shocks to volatility, however, have fairly rapid decay times.[1] In practice, GARCH effects are hardly perceptible in monthly data.

In sum, the daily application of VAR for bank trading portfolios is essential. Portfolios change quickly. So does risk. The situation is quite

---

1. For instance, the half-life of a GARCH process with a decay factor of 0.97 is about 20 trading days. This means that a given increase in variance will be cut in half after a month.

B O X   17–1

LESSONS FROM WISCONSIN

In March 1995, the State of Winsconsin Investment Board, which controls over \$34 billion in assets, revealed that it had lost \$95 million on currency and interest rate swaps. While the loss was small in relation to the asset pool, it led to great embarrassment.

Of the total loss, \$35 million came from just one contract, an interest rate swap that paid

$$\$10 \text{ million} \times (2.95 \text{ percent} - \text{MexSpread})/2.95 \text{ percent}$$

where MexSpread was defined as the yield spread between Mexican and U.S. government bonds. Apparently, the staff had not done a proper sensitivity analysis of the value of the swap and thought that the amount at risk was only \$10 million. In fact, it was much greater due to the leverage effect induced by the denominator. This loss would have been avoided had the swap been marked-to-market or, even better, evaluated with a VAR method.

---

different with investment portfolios, which change slowly and are less exposed to variations in risk.

Overall, these differences may explain why the application of VAR has spread more slowly among pension funds than banks. This does not mean, however, that VAR systems are not useful for investment portfolios. To the contrary, VAR systems will bring about better control and management of financial risks. As Box 17–1 shows, it is especially important to understand the risk of derivatives positions.

One could argue that institutional investors have too many measures of risk. These include "prudent investor" rules, diversification principles, benchmarking, and investment guidelines. In contrast, VAR provides a simple, transparent, and consistent measure of overall risk. The only advantage of this multiplicity of risk controls is that it is probably more robust to model misspecifications than quantitative measures such as VAR.

17.2 WHAT ARE THE RISKS?

First, we have to define the risks in investment management. Risk can be clearly defined for a bank trader. It is the risk of loss on the mark-to-market position. For asset managers, however, the definition may not be so simple. Pension fund sponsors and managers use a variety of definitions for risk.

17.2.1 Absolute and Relative Risks

Risk can be defined as the possibility of asset losses in the base currency, dollar or other. This is the most common definition of risk. For managers who have a mandate to beat a benchmark, however, risk must be measured in relative terms. We can distinguish between two definitions:.

- *Absolute risk,* which is the risk of a dollar loss over the horizon. This is the usual definition of risk in a trading environment. Sometimes, this is called *asset risk.* The relevant rate of return is R_{asset}.

- *Relative risk,* which is the risk of a dollar loss in a fund relative to its benchmark. This shortfall is measured as the dollar difference between the fund return and that of a like amount invested in the benchmark. The relevant return is the *tracking error* $E = R_{asset} - R^b$, which is the excess return of the asset over the benchmark. If this is normally distributed, VAR can be measured from the standard deviation of the tracking error σ_E as $VAR = \alpha W_0 \sigma_E$.

17.2.2 Policy Mix and Active Management Risk

The absolute performance of the fund can be broken down into two components, one due to policy (or benchmark) choice and the other to active management. Hence total asset risk also can be attributed to two sources, the risk of the total policy mix and the risk of total active manager deviations from the policy mix.

- *Policy mix risk,* which is the risk of a dollar loss due to the policy mix selected by the fund. Since the policy mix generally can be implemented by investing in passive funds, this risk represents that of a passive strategy.

- *Active management risk,* which is the risk of a dollar loss due to the total deviations from the policy mix. This represents the summation of profits or losses across all managers relative to their benchmark. Thus there may be diversification effects across managers, depending on whether they have similar styles or not. In addition, the current asset allocation mix temporarily may deviate from the policy mix.

The absolute risk can be measured from fund returns and defined as

$$R_{\text{asset}} = \sum_i w_i R_i \qquad (17.1)$$

where w_i is the weight on fund i, with return R_i. This can be decomposed into

$$R_{\text{asset}} = R_{\text{policy mix}} + R_{\text{active mgt.}} = \sum_i w_i R_i^b + \sum_i w_i(R_i - R_i^b) \qquad (17.2)$$

where R_i^b represents the return on the benchmark for fund i. If the pension plan deviates from its policy mix, the active management portion can be further decomposed into a term that represents policy decisions and manager performance.

The fund's total VAR can be obtained from the policy mix VAR, the active management VAR, and a cross-product term. As an example, the Ontario Teachers' Pension Plan Board (OTPPB) estimates that its annual VAR at the 99 percent level of confidence can be decomposed as follows (in percent of the initial fund value):

Source of Risk	VAR
Policy mix VAR	19.6%
Active mgt. VAR	1.6%
Asset VAR	19.3%

This table points to a number of interesting observations. First, most of the downside risk is due to the policy mix. This well-known result was first shown by Brinson et al. (1986), who demonstrated that most of the variation in portfolio performance can be attributed to the choice of asset classes. In other words, the choice of mix of stocks and bonds will have more effect on the portfolio performance than the choice of a particular equity or bond manager.

The second interesting result is that the VAR due to active management is rather small. Apparently, the fund diversifies away much of the risk of managers deviating from their benchmarks through a careful choice of various styles or, simply, many managers. Another explanation is that most of the assets are invested in indexed or closely indexed funds.

Finally, the table shows that the policy mix VAR and active management VAR do not add up to the total asset VAR. In fact, there is a slightly negative correlation between the two, leading to a lower overall asset VAR. If so, active managers could take substantially greater deviations from their benchmark without affecting the plan's total VAR.

This analysis is a good example of insights created by a VAR analysis. The decomposition into sources of risks can help plan sponsors to make more informed decisions.

17.2.3 Funding Risk

Focusing on the volatility of assets, however, may not be appropriate if investor's liabilities also matter. For a pension fund with defined benefits, the key issue is whether there is sufficient money to pay the promised benefits if the plan were terminated. In other words, risk should be viewed in an *asset/liability management* (ALM) framework.

Funding Risk

Funding risk is the risk that the value of assets will not be sufficient to cover the liabilities of the fund. The relevant return is that of the *surplus* $S = R_{asset} - R_{liabilities}$.

This funding risk represents the true long-term risk to the owner of the fund, the corporation. Sometimes this is called *surplus at risk,* where the surplus refers to the difference between the value of assets and liabilities. If the surplus turns negative, the corporation will have to provide additional contributions to the fund.

While the volatility of assets can be measured by marking-to-market, the volatility of liabilities is more difficult to gauge. Typically, liabilities can be assessed from *accumulated benefit obligations,* which measure the present value of pension benefits owed to employees discounted at an appropriate interest rate.

Since liabilities consist mainly of nominal payments, their value will in general behave like a short position in a long-term bond. Thus decreases in interest rates, while beneficial for equities on the asset side, can increase even more the value of liabilities, thereby negatively affecting the surplus.[2] The minimum risk position then corresponds to an immunized

---

2. For instance, 1995 was a great year for U.S. stocks, which jumped by more than 34 percent. Pension fund assets grew by 29 percent. During 1995, however, bonds also experienced the largest decrease in yields of the decade, with a drop of 1.8 percent. As a result, liabilities rose by 41 percent, more than wiping out the increase in assets.

BOX 17–2

SURPLUS AT RISK AT AT&T

The AT&T pension plan determines its investment policy based on a surplus-at-risk rule. The $20 billion plan was enjoying a surplus of about $6 billion as of 1998.

AT&T trustees want to be 95 percent confident that the company's pension plan will still be fully funded at a 5-year horizon. The plan then chooses the asset mix that generates the highest expected return, provided this minimum funding level is met.

---

portfolio, where the duration of the assets matches that of liabilities. The VAR methodology can be extended to simulate the effect of market factors on the pension fund surplus, as shown in Box 17–2.

For longer horizons, the usual VAR approach may no longer be appropriate because it assumes that the current portfolio is static. Ideally, the investor should account for changing positions. For instance, the risk profile of the fund could be altered as a function of the size of the surplus. In this situation, long-term shortfall risk becomes much more complex to model.

A simple example of such dynamic rebalancing is a call option, which can be viewed as a specific investment rule where the position in the underlying asset decreases as its price gets closer to the strike price. To generate the distribution of payoffs, the investor needs to model the asset value and to define the dynamic investment rule. More generally, such dynamic decision rules can be uncovered by a technique known as *stochastic programming*. This extension of traditional VAR has been applied with some success by some pension plans.[3] The technique, however, is computationally very cumbersome and, like Monte Carlo simulations, is subject to model risk.

17.2.4 Sponsor Risk

This notion of surplus risk can be extended to the risk to the owner of the fund, the plan sponsor, who ultimately bears responsibility for the pension fund. One can distinguish between the following risk measures:

---

3. See, for instance, Muralidar and Van Der Wouden (2000) for a practical application to the World Bank pension fund. Ziemba and Mulvey (1998) contains a collection of useful studies on this topic.

■ *Cash-flow risk,* which is the risk of year-to-year fluctuations in contributions to the pension fund. Plan sponsors that can absorb greater variations in funding costs, for instance, can adopt a more volatile risk profile, leading to greater expected returns.

■ *Economic risk,* which is the risk of variation in total economic earnings of the plan sponsor. The surplus risk may be reduced, for instance, if falls in the pension plan surplus are offset by greater operating profits.

From the viewpoint of the plan sponsor, risk is not only measured by movements in the assets, or even the surplus, but rather by the ultimate effect on the economic value of the firm. Thus pension plan management should be integrated with the overall financial goals of the plan sponsor. This is in line with the trend to enterprise-wide risk management, which is analyzed in a later chapter.

17.3 USING VAR TO MONITOR AND CONTROL RISKS

Generally, investment decisions for pension funds are implemented in two steps. In the first step, the board or a consultant provides a strategic, long-term asset allocation study, usually based on mean-variance portfolio optimization, also taking into account liabilities. This study determines the amounts to be invested in various asset classes, e.g., domestic stocks, domestic bonds, foreign stocks, foreign bonds, and perhaps additional classes such as emerging markets, real estate, and venture capital.

In the second step, the fund may delegate the actual management of funds to a stable of outside managers, which is periodically reviewed for performance relative to its benchmark. The managers will be given specific guidelines defining the universe of assets they can invest in, with some additional restrictions such as duration, maximum deviations from equity sector weights, or maximum amounts of foreign currency to hedge or cross-hedge. Typically, risk is only measured ex post, i.e., after the facts from historical data.

The problem with this approach lies in its static nature. Because the assets of the fund are dispersed over a number of managers, it is difficult to create a current picture of the overall risk of the fund. During a quarter, for instance, many fund managers may have increased their exposure to one particular industry. Taken separately, these risks may be acceptable, but as a whole, they may amount to an unsuspected large bet on one source of risk.

In addition, money managers sometimes change their investment strategy, either deliberately or inadvertently. If so, the fund should be able to detect and correct such changes quickly. As in the case of bank trading portfolios, the increased exposure of investment funds to more sources of risk and more complex instruments has created a need for better risk control.

This is the very purpose of VAR. In addition to providing improved measures of market risk, VAR systems allow finer control of risks, as well as some protection against operational risk. Investors can use real-time VAR measurements to check whether short-term risk deviates from long-term targets. VAR systems also can be used to design investment guidelines.

17.3.1 Using VAR to Check Compliance

The impetus for centralized risk management in the investment-management industry came from the realization that the industry is not immune to the "rogue trader" syndrome that has plagued the banking industry. Indeed Box 17–3 explains how the Common Fund lost $138 million due to unauthorized trading. The lessons from this loss are applicable to any "manager of managers," i.e., a manager who delegates the actual investment decisions to a stable of managers.

More generally, the fear is that an investment manager's deviation from guidelines may cause a large loss. But even more worried are pension plan directors in the United Kingdom, who have become personally liable for inappropriately managed accounts since the Maxwell pension fraud.[4]

While rogue traders are, fortunately, rare, minor violations of investment guidelines occur routinely. Some securities may be prohibited because of their risks or for other reasons (e.g., political or religious). Bank custodians, however, indicate that fund managers sometimes trade in and out of unauthorized investments before the client realizes what happened. With monthly reporting, it is hard to catch such movements. Centralized risk-management systems, in contrast, can monitor investments in real time.

---

4. Robert Maxwell was the owner of the Mirror Group publishing empire. After his mysterious death in November 1991, it was revealed that the "robber baron" had stolen £450 million from 30,000 Mirror and Maxwell company pensioners.

BOX 17-3

RISK CONTROLS AT THE COMMON FUND

In 1995, the Common Fund, a nonprofit organization that manages about $20 billion on behalf of U.S. schools and universities, announced that it had lost $138 million due to unauthorized trading by one of its managers. Apparently, Kent Ahrens, a trader at First Capital Strategies, had deviated from what should have been a safe index-arbitrage strategy between stock index futures and underlying stocks. One day he failed to complete the hedge and lost $250,000. He then tried to trade his way out of this loss but with little success. The growing loss was concealed for 3 years until Ahrens confessed in June 1995.

This loss was all the more disturbing because after the Barings affair, the Common Fund had specifically asked First Capital to demonstrate that a rogue trader could not do the same thing at First Capital. The firm answered that market neutrality was being verified daily. In this case, it seems that proper checks and balances were not in place.

Although the dollar loss was not large compared with the size of the asset pool, it severely damaged the reputation of the Common Fund. Several fund investors left, taking $1 billion with them. The fallout also led to the resignation of the president of the Common Fund.

In retrospect, the Common Fund realized that running an operation with a large number of fund managers requires strong centralized controls. To prevent such mishaps, the fund created the new position of "independent risk oversight officer." The fund also set up new risk-management committees, one of which is at the board level. Its custodian, Mellon Trust, developed online software that checks for violations of investment policies. To reduce operational risk, the fund also cut the number of active managers and custodial agreements.

Such occurrences have moved the pension fund industry toward centralized risk management. VAR systems provide a central repository for all positions. Independent reconciliation against manager positions makes fraud a lot more difficult. VAR systems also allow users to quickly catch deviations from stated policies.

17.3.2 Using VAR to Design Guidelines

VAR systems also can be used to design better investment guidelines. Managers' guidelines generally are set up in an ad hoc fashion to restrict the universe of assets in which the manager can invest and, to some extent, to control risk. Typically, guidelines include limits on duration gaps (between fixed-income portfolios and their benchmarks), maximum sector weight deviations for equities, limits on currency notionals, and so on. Guidelines often are not updated for years.

Says Leo de Bever, risk manager at Ontario Teachers, "Typically, you control positions by saying, `Thou shalt not have more than X million of this.' When you do that, you end up with a whole bunch of rules on what you can and cannot do, but not a handle on how much you might lose on any given day."

Another problem is that the spirit of these limits can be skirted with new financial instruments. For example, a manager may not be allowed to trade in futures that may be viewed as too "risky," such as futures contracts. Instead, investments may be allowed in high-grade medium-term notes, often viewed as safe because they have no credit risk. The problem is that these notes can be designed as *structured* notes with as much market risk as futures contracts. Hence detailed guidelines, like government regulations, are one step behind continuously changing financial markets. Traditional guidelines cannot cope well with new instruments or with leverage. They also totally ignore correlations.

This is precisely what VAR attempts to measure. Instead of detailed guidelines, plan sponsors could specify that the anticipated volatility of tracking error cannot be more than 3 percent, for instance. Position limits can be set consistently across markets.

17.3.3 Using VAR to Monitor Risk

With a VAR system in place, investors can monitor their portfolio risk better. Consider, for instance, an investor who "chases" investment funds with the highest returns, switching monies to the best performers. This investor may not realize that these funds may have high returns because they are all exposed to the same risk factors. The top 5 percent funds, for instance, may all have a heavy exposure to the high-technology industry. If so, the reallocation may substantially increase the portfolio risk. To avoid this imbalance, the investor could either compute the sector exposure of the prospective portfolio or, more simply, compute its VAR.

Investors also can react to a sudden increase in the reported VAR of their portfolio. The key is to identify the reason for the jump. Several explanations are possible, requiring different actions.

- *Different managers taking similar bets.* This can happen, for instance, when all managers increase their allocation to a particular sector, which is perhaps becoming more attractive. Because active managers operate in isolation, such a problem can be caught only at the portfolio level. To decrease the portfolio risk, managers can be given appropriate instructions.
- *More volatile markets.* VAR can simply increase if the current environment becomes more volatile. The plan sponsor will then have to decide whether it is worth accepting greater volatility. If the risks are deemed to be too large, positions can be cut. Increased volatility, however, is often associated with falls in asset prices leading to correspondingly higher expected returns. Thus the rebalancing decision involves a delicate tradeoff between risk and return.
- *A trader deviating from the guideline.* A VAR system can help to catch policy deviations quickly. If significant, the infraction must be corrected at once.

More generally, VAR can be reverse-engineered to understand where risk is coming from using the VAR tools we lay out in Chapter 7. Measures of marginal and component VAR can be used to identify where position changes will have the greatest effect on the total portfolio risk.

17.3.4 The Role of the Global Custodian

The philosophy behind VAR is centralized risk management. The easiest path to centralization is to use one global custodian only.

This explains why many investors are now aggregating their portfolio holdings with a single custodian. With one global custodian, position reports directly give a consolidated picture of the total exposure of the fund. Custodians become the natural focal point for this analysis because they already maintain position information and have market data. The next level of service is to combine the current position with forward-looking risk measures.

Not all agree, however, that the risk-measurement function can be delegated to the custodian. Some larger plans have decided to develop their own internal risk-management system. Their rationale is that they have tighter control over risk measures and can better incorporate VAR systems into operations. Larger plans also benefit from economies of scale, spreading the cost of risk-management systems over a large asset base, and also require tighter control when their assets are partly managed internally.

These clients are the exception, however. Most investors may be content with risk-management reports developed by custodians. Such systems, however, are not cheap to develop. As a result, the trend will be toward fewer custodians that can provide more services. Already, large custodian banks such as Deutsche Bank, Chase, Citibank, and State Street are providing risk-management products. State Street, for instance, is already providing a Web-based system, called *VAR Calculator*, that allows users to perform VAR calculations on demand. Firms that cannot provide such services are in danger of becoming marginal players.

17.3.5 The Role of the Money Manager

On the money management side, managers are now under pressure from clients to demonstrate that they have in place a sound risk-management system. More and more clients are explicitly asking for risk analysis, because they are no longer satisfied with quarterly performance reports. They want risks to be considered before the fact, not after a bad loss has happened.

Increasingly, clients are asking their managers, "What is your risk-management system?" Leading-edge investment managers have already adapted VAR systems into their investment-management process. Managers who do not have comprehensive risk-management systems put themselves at a serious competitive disadvantage.

Box 17–4 presents an example of a money manager who has developed a new function, risk management and product control, to serve clients better.[5]

17.4 USING VAR TO MANAGE RISKS

17.4.1 Strategic Asset Allocation

As explained earlier, the strategic asset allocation decision is the first and most important step in the investment process for pension funds. It is usually based on a mean-variance optimization that attempts to identify the

---

5. I am grateful to Todd Wolter, of CSAM, for writing this box.

B O X   17–4

RISK MANAGEMENT AT CRÉDIT SUISSE ASSET MANAGEMENT

Structure of Risk Management and Product Control Organization. The risk management (RM) and product control (PC) function at Crédit Suisse Asset Management (CSAM) is central to the control process of both investment and noninvestment risks. Established as an independent global function, it provides formal oversight through monthly local committee meetings reviewing, for example, ex ante risk reports and ex post performance reports on the investment process. The committee includes senior personnel from all functions and is chaired by the local head of RM&PC. Local functions report to the global head of RM&PC, who in turn reports to the global chief financial officer and the CSAM global operating committee.

Value Added. The primary function of the product control team is to ensure that the business delivers the product that it has been mandated by the client. Whether this is a specific, segregated institutional mandate or a pooled retail product, it has predefined risk and return characteristics. This requires consistency of performance, closely aligned to the mandate objectives. Consequently, risk limits are established with the intent of achieving active risk, or tracking error, in line with the client's expectation.

Each portfolio has an explicitly defined tracking-error target. Although many may view a tracking error lower than the stated target as desirable, clients are paying fees with the expectation that managers will generate a positive alpha. As a consequence of this, through proprietary measures, managers at CSAM are penalized not only for active risk in excess of their stated target but also for active risk that is significantly lower than a client's expectations.

Key to the implementation of a comprehensive risk-management initiative is transparency to the managers that are being measured. Therefore, in addition to periodic committee meetings, the risk reports are published regularly to the company's intranet so that managers can review their tracking error and style or sector bets that are contributing to or reducing their active bets.

It is through this focus on delivering consistent returns, tailored to each client's risk appetite, that the risk-management function adds value for CSAM clients.

portfolio with the best risk-return tradeoff using a set of long-term forecasts for various asset classes.

In practice, the optimization is usually constrained in an effort to obtain solutions that look "reasonable." This adjustment, however, partly defeats the purpose of portfolio optimization and fails to recognize the effects of marginal adjustments from the selected portfolio.

Since value at risk is, after all, perfectly consistent with a mean-variance framework, VAR tools also can be used to allocate funds across asset classes. Box 17–5 shows how incremental VAR can yield useful insights into the risk drivers for a pension fund.

17.4.2 VAR as a Guide to Investment Decisions

VAR systems, of course, will not tell you where to invest. Rather, they allow users to evaluate the risk-adjusted performance of alternative investments.

Analysts are paid to take bets. Presumably, they developed skills in one dimension of the risk-return space. They are expected to identify expected returns on various investments. While expected returns can be estimated on an individual basis, assessing the contribution of a particular stock to the total portfolio risk is much less intuitive. Even if analysts could measure the individual risk of the particular stock they are considering, they cannot possibly be aware of the relationships between all existing positions of the fund. This is where VAR systems help.

For each asset to be added to the portfolio, analysts should be given a measure of its marginal VAR. If two assets have similar projected returns, the analyst should pick the one with the lowest marginal VAR, which will lead to the lowest portfolio risk. Assume, for instance, that the analyst estimates that two stocks, a utility and an Internet stock, will generate expected return of 20 percent over the next year. If the current portfolio is already heavily invested in high-tech stocks, the two stocks will have a very different marginal contribution to the portfolio risk. Say the utility stock has a portfolio beta of 0.5 against 2.0 for the other stock, leading to a lower marginal VAR for the first stock. With equal return forecasts, the utility stock is clearly the preferred choice. Such analysis is only feasible within the context of a fund-wide VAR system.

BOX 17-5

VAR AND CURRENCY HEDGING

Bankers Trust (now Deutsche Bank) recently provided its RAROC 2020 risk-management system to the Chrysler pension fund. The system provides measures of total and incremental VAR for the various asset classes in which the fund is invested. It can be used, among other things, to evaluate the effectiveness of hedging strategies. For example, the fund was considering adding a currency hedge to protect the currency position of its foreign stock and bond investments.

The RAROC system showed that the "individual" risk of a $250 million currency position was $44 million at the 99 percent level over 1 year, which appears substantial. However, the pension fund realized that the "incremental" contribution to total risk of a passive currency hedge program was only $3 million. Currency risk was already largely diversified in the current portfolio. The fund decided not to hedge its currency exposure, thereby saving hefty management fees. These savings more than offset the modest cost of the RAROC system, which is priced around $50,000 per year.

This result parallels the discussion in the academic literature, where currency hedging initially was advocated as a "free lunch," i.e., lower risk at no cost.* Indeed, currency hedging reduces the volatility of individual asset returns, but this is not the relevant issue. Absent currency views, what matters is total portfolio risk. Empirically, total risk is generally affected little by currency hedging if the proportion of assets invested abroad is small.

The fund also considered implementing a $250 million equity hedge account. This had absolute risk of $38 million and incremental risk of $35 million. An equity hedge therefore was found to be much more effective than a currency hedge. Of course, this comes at a cost. The stock market returns a positive risk premium (historically 6 percent per annum in the United States), and therefore, a short position in equity futures would be expected to lose this risk premium. The issue is whether this performance penalty is worth accepting in return for lower risk.

---

*As in Pérold and Schulman (1988). Jorion (1989), however, argues that the benefit of hedging must be viewed in the context of total portfolio risk.

FIGURE 17–1

Schedule of performance fees.

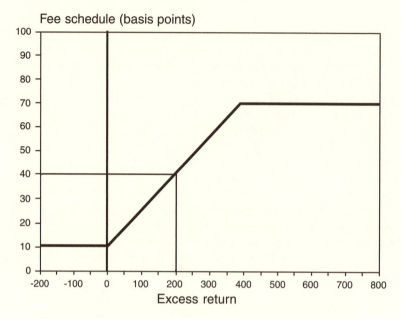

Fee schedule (basis points)

Excess return

17.4.3 VAR for Risk-Adjusted Returns

We have seen in Chapter 16 how VAR can be used for active management of financial market risks. A widespread application was the evaluation of trader performance, where the return is explicitly adjusted for the
assumed risk, using a VAR measure.

The same idea can be used to create a reward system whereby asset managers are compensated for their profits in excess of the benchmark
but are also penalized for their relative VAR.

Indeed, the investment-management industry has employed *performance fees* that compensate the manager based on the fund's performance.[6] As Figure 17–1 shows, a typical structure starts with a base
fee that is less than the manager's normal fee. In exchange, a greater compensation could come from a bonus that is related to the excess performance over the benchmark.

6. For a good introduction to the major issues with performance fees, see Davanzo and Nesbitt
   (1987), Grinold and Rudd (1987), and Kritzman (1987).

This system can be set up with an objective of outperforming the benchmark by 200 basis points. If so, the normal ("flat") fee would be 40 basis points applied to the current asset pool, paid annually. Instead, a performance-fee schedule would start at 10 basis points and grow at a rate of 0.15 times the excess return, with a cap of 70 basis points. Thus, provided the target outperformance is met, the total fee would still be 40 basis points. With a greater performance, the fee will be higher.

The rationale for this structure is to have the client and asset manager share the risk of deviations from the benchmark. This compensation system, however, is similar to the bonus payments for Wall Street traders and can be fraught with the same dangers.

Optionlike payments create a natural incentive to modify the risk of the position. For example, a portfolio manager whose initial performance is below par could decide to take on more risk in a "catchup" attempt. Alternatively, a manager with a very good initial performance could decide to bring the portfolio back to the benchmark to "lock in" the management fee. Perhaps this explains the general reluctance of pension funds and managers to use performance fees, which are not widespread in the industry.

Nonetheless, some features of performance fees do alleviate the moral hazard problem that prevails with trader compensation on Wall Street. The fee can be capped, which avoids extreme risk-taking. The fee also can be paid over a longer horizon, decreasing the number of times the fees could be "gamed." Most important, it is widely recognized that the threat of manager termination serves as a powerful incentive to maintain consistent performance. Termination is much more costly to an ongoing business such as an investment-management firm than to a trader.

More generally, as in the case of Wall Street traders, the best defense against excessive risk-taking is close monitoring of the manager's risk profile. Incentives should be rewards for superior active management at agreed-on risk levels. Before the advent of VAR, measuring risk from historical data was dubious at best. Now that VAR can be used to control the risk of managers, perhaps there will be greater interest in performance fees.

17.4.4 Risk Budgeting

The latest application of VAR in pension funds is the *risk-budgeting concept*. This extends the allocation of economic risk capital to an investment-management environment.

The first step is to determine how much risk the fund is willing to take. Say, for instance, that the plan-wide active management VAR has been determined to be $1,800 million. The fund can then parcel out "risk units" to its managers, taking into account correlations across asset classes and managers. The VAR allocation would be, for instance, $400 million for its active equity managers.

Each manager is then charged to earn the highest return on these risk units. The target value added would be set at a fixed percentage of the VAR, say, 10 percent. Hence active equity managers would be expected to return $40 million over the benchmark. This system is markedly different from the usual target excess return over the benchmark, which ignores risks.

One advantage of this approach is that it avoids micromanaging the investment process. As long as managers stay within their risk guidelines, they can execute new transactions without requiring approval of senior management.

This assumes, however, that all the relevant risks are captured by the risk-management system. The inherent limitations of the VAR methodology are described in a later chapter. Suffice it to say that for pension funds, risk cannot be measured easily for some important asset classes such as real estate or venture capital, which are not mark-to-market. Other series may have very short histories, such as emerging markets, or none at all, like initial public offerings. In some cases, the missing series can be replaced by a proxy. The challenge is to construct a plan-wide VAR system that successfully integrates most of the risks the fund is exposed to. Box 17–6 gives an example of a pension fund that has totally embraced VAR.

17.5 THE RISK STANDARDS

In November 1996, a working group representing institutional investors drafted the first formal set of "Risk Standards" for institutional investment managers and institutional investors. Together, the Risk Standards Working Group represented 11 major institutions with more than $250 billion in total assets. Its purpose was to update risk-management policies, practices, and procedures in an evolving investment industry.

The report started from the G-30 "best practice" recommendations, and enlarged to a much wider array of assets than derivatives. It also focused on the special fiduciary responsibility in pension plans, which include the board of directors, trustees, plans sponsors, and chief investment officers.

BOX 17—6

ONTARIO TEACHERS' PENSION PLAN AND VAR

The Ontario Teachers' Pension Plan Board (OTPPB) has been at the forefront of applying VAR techniques among institutional investors. OTPPB is the biggest pension fund in Canada, with about C\$60 billion (US\$41 billion) in assets in 1998.

The plan is required to deliver defined benefits to Ontario's teachers during their retirement years. Its stated objective is to earn a high rate of return, at least as great as the rate of inflation plus 4.5 percent per annum, while minimizing the risk of a contribution increase. One particular feature of the fund is that it makes extensive use of swaps to transform a large position in nonmarketable debt into an equity exposure.

In 1996, OTPPB purchased a firm-wide risk-management system sold by Sailfish that cost about \$500,000. The software uses the historical simulation method, which was selected because it could handle nonnormal market movements. The system loads more than 10,000 positions on a daily basis, which are combined with 13 years of history for about 1300 time series. Management has access to daily risk reports. The board now receives risk reports in its monthly information package.

The next step was to set "active management" VAR limits for each asset class and individual portfolios. Each active manager is then expected to produce an added value that is a fixed percentage of his or her "risk budget." The fund found that the target return for the top quartile of active managers is around 0.65σ, where σ is the volatility of tracking error. The corresponding downside risk is estimated at 2.6σ, using a 99 percent quantile based on historical data. This implies an expected return-to-risk ratio of $0.65/2.6 = 25$ percent at the fund level and of 10 percent at the manager level, taking into account correlations. If, for instance, an active equity manager is allocated a risk budget of \$300 million, the corresponding expected return would be \$30 million.

The fund has found that the system proved to be quite useful in "motivating people to do the right thing." The VAR system has reduced the number of investment rules and has facilitated the closer supervision of risks.

The "Risk Standards" are grouped into various categories, management, measurement, and oversight.

In particular, "Risk Standard" number 12 deals with "risk measurement and return attribution analysis." It states that the "Fiduciaries should measure the total risk in the overall portfolio, individual portfolio, and each instrument. Then, they should perform attribution analyses to determine the various risks and returns posed by each instrument or port-folio." Analysis of the sources of outperformance is important as it enables investors to identify the types of risk they are exposed to.

The report next discusses how VAR can be used to measure market risk. VAR is described as "widely used method for creating a common unit of measurement risk." In fact, VAR is more than this, since it provides an aggregate measure of total portfolio risk.

Another noteworthy "Risk Standard" is number 13, which advocates comparing managers using risk-adjusted returns, using the Sharpe ratio, the Treynor ratio, or the information ratio.[7] It argues, for instance, that an outperformance of 200 basis points should be viewed differently for a manager investing in U.S. Treasuries and another investing in distressed emerging debt.

Two years later, a survey by Capital Market Risk Advisors (CMRA) identified a shift toward risk management. The survey indicates that the "Risk Standards" are starting to be widely used as a best-practice risk-management guide. It also reveals that an increasing proportion of pension funds are now turning toward risk-adjusted return measurement (47 percent in 1998, up from 6 percent in 1996). Managers are also actively bringing their risk oversight to the level of industry best practices (71 percent in 1998, up from 50 percent in 1996). The report also notes that manager differentiation is increasingly created by providing risk-management services to clients.

17.6 CONCLUSIONS

Centralized risk-management systems, by now widely adopted on Wall Street, are also taking hold in the investment-management industry. Even though institutional investors have a longer-term horizon than bank trading departments, they also greatly benefit from the discipline provided by VAR systems.

Traditionally, risk has been measured using historical returns or as the occurrence of a big loss. While useful for some purposes, these risk measures have severe shortcomings because they are backward-looking. In contrast, VAR provides forward-looking measures of risk, using a combination of current positions with risk forecasts.

---

7. The information ratio is a simple extension of the Sharpe ratio to the excess return on the portfolio over its benchmark. It is equal to the average excess return divided by the standard deviation of the tracking error.

When implemented at the level of the total plan, VAR allows improved control of portfolio risk and of managers. It cuts through the maze of diversification rules, benchmark portfolios, and investment guidelines. VAR systems allow analysts to make better risk-return tradeoffs. The goal, of course, is not to eliminate risk but rather to get the just reward for risk that managers elect to take.

Such risk-management systems are spreading quickly among pension funds, changing the face of the industry. They are also affecting the custody business, forcing custodians to offer risk-management reporting capabilities. Managers are affected, too. Those who do not have a risk-management system put themselves at a serious competitive disadvantage.

It is somewhat ironic that the investment-management industry, which has long relied on modern portfolio theory, is only now turning to fund-wide risk-measurement systems. These systems have been developed by "quants" on Wall Street who were originally trying to get a grip on their short-term derivatives risk. What we are learning now is that these methods can be usefully extended from the short-term trading environment to the longer-term framework of patient investors.

This turn of events was inevitable. Since advances in technology and communications create almost instantaneous flows of information across the globe, plan sponsors cannot continue to rely on monthly or quarterly hard-copy reports on their investments.

CHAPTER 18

The Technology of Risk

Dealers that have integrated their derivatives risk management systems with their back-office systems have found that the integration enhances operating efficiency and reliability.

Group of Thirty Report

Value-at-risk (VAR) systems range from simple spreadsheet applications to full-blown *enterprise-wide risk-management* (ERM) systems. ERM represents the control of risk across all locations and products for the highest-level corporate entity. ERM systems capture all trades, store the information in a global data warehouse, and provide sophisticated risk reporting and management capabilities.

The risk-management revolution of the 1990s has created an army of software developers that offer ready-made solutions to the measurement of value at risk. A recent compilation in the magazine *Derivatives Strategy,* for instance, lists more than 120 product entries. The issue confronting institutions is how to choose the product that best suits their needs.

For some users, such as companies with a small number of positions and simple products, a spreadsheet may be sufficient. For global financial institutions, however, a firm-wide risk-management system has become a necessary component of doing business. Having a central repository for trades, positions, and valuation models allows institutions to measure and manage their risk profile from a central location most efficiently. It also offers some protection against operational risks and rogue traders.

While most information technology (IT) spending is focused on routine areas, technology is now increasingly used for what is called *strategic IT spending,* which supports strategic business initiatives. These are investments that increase competitiveness and help the institution expand into new markets. In recent years, enterprise-wide risk-management systems have become a key area for strategic IT investments. ERM systems have evolved from risk-control systems to drivers of corporate value. A portfolio approach to risk produces diversification benefits, leading to tighter allocation of capital.

This chapter discusses the IT challenge created by the need for comprehensive risk-management systems. As Section 18.1 shows, measuring an institution's VAR requires integrating the front and back offices with a newly created "middle office." The need for integration is discussed in Section 18.2. Section 18.3 provides a bird's-eye view of the rapidly evolving risk-management software industry. Next, Section 18.4 shows how to structure VAR reports. Section 18.5 illustrates with an application. Finally, Section 18.6 provides some concluding thoughts.

18.1 SYSTEMS

Implementing a global risk-management system can be a major technological challenge. The software that supports trading at financial institutions falls into three areas:

- *Trading systems* (or front-office systems) used by traders to price deals and to track current positions
- *Back-office systems* used to settle transactions (i.e., validating trades and communicating accounts to be debited and credited) and confirm new transactions into the bank's books
- *Risk-control systems* (also called *middle-office systems*) used by an independent risk-control unit to monitor traders and the global risk exposure of the firm (This term also covers a collection of departments such as internal audit, accounting, and product control.)

These systems typically operate on different platforms, a *legacy* of disparate systems having grown out of widely different requirements. Typically, front offices, which directly generate profits, have the most modern application systems installed on decentralized platforms, generally powerful PCs or workstations. In contrast, unglamorous back offices usually have older systems, such as mainframes.

Back offices suffer from the perception that they do not contribute directly to the bottom line. This perception is seriously mistaken, since many institutions have suffered losses that could have been avoided by decent back-office support. The $1.1 billion loss incurred by Daiwa, for instance, has been partly blamed on an inadequate back-office system that prevented the bank from getting a complete overview of its position.

The third category, risk-control systems, is relatively recent. Such systems range from humble spreadsheets to firm-wide risk-management systems that also include front- and back-office functions. Enterprise-wide risk management really came into existence after 1994.

There is some functional overlap for these three systems. Trading desks also require some risk-management capabilities such as hedging and portfolio risk measurement. Traders do need to verify that their portfolio profile complies with their risk guidelines in real time. These risk-management capabilities are essentially local and may be quite specific to the instrument traded.

Risk control, in contrast, aggregates all the positions across the firm and should be general enough to cover the whole range of products traded within the firm. It is crucial for risk control to operate independently and to have oversight of traders. Whenever risk control identifies a situation to be corrected, e.g., a trader position exceeding its limit, it should flag the problem but should not recommend a specific action, lest it become too involved with trading decisions. The logistical aspect of firm-wide risk control, however, makes it difficult to implement intraday risk calculations.

Figure 18–1 describes the typical structure of a risk-management system, which is composed of three parts. The *analytics* platform collects and filters market data. Market data can be pulled either from traditional data research services, such as Datastream or Bloomberg, or from online data sources, such as Reuters, that now increasingly provide *digital feeds,* as opposed to analog or video feeds. With digital feeds, the data can be retrieved online in a computer-readable format for use in valuation models for securities and risk forecasts.

The *positions* platform serves as a global repository for all trades, which are received from the front office and transmitted to the back office. Ideally, this should be done with *straight-through processing,* which ensures timely and accurate recording of transaction data. Next, deals are decomposed into component positions. This process, known as *mapping,* involves delicate choices. Simplifications of complicated positions are often necessary for manageability and consistency. This may be acceptable, since risk-measurement systems are not intended to be used as traders' pricing systems. However, too much simplification can create blind spots in the risk-measurement system.

FIGURE 18–1

Components of a risk-management system.

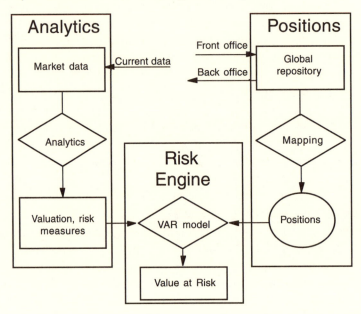

The third platform, *risk engine*, integrates analytics and positions with a VAR model to create a measure of market or credit risk or both.

18.2 THE NEED FOR INTEGRATION

For most banks, the problem is not that they have no system but that they have too many disparate ones. Typically, a bank will have separate risk-management systems for foreign currencies, bonds, money market instruments, derivatives, and equities.

The challenge is to integrate these systems, front, middle, and back offices. Integration involves automating the flow of data for each transaction, sending it to the settlement and risk-management units for verification and bookkeeping.

Integration is made easier by the rising capabilities of PCs and workstations, along with their falling costs. The trend to integration will be helped by two developments:

- *Object-oriented tools* allow firms to develop new programs with parts of old ones. Chunks of application logic are constructed as separate "objects" with well-defined functions and interfaces. Programs are built by combining objects. Individual objects can be used in many programs or in the design of other objects, which speeds up development time. This approach is particularly important for derivatives, which evolve very fast and constantly require new software. With object-oriented tools, new software can be constructed with pieces of existing programs that price simpler derivatives.

- *Relational databases* are organized collections of items of data, like all databases, but information is organized into *tables* that enable users to sift through large amounts of data for specific information. They provide a centralized location for trade positions and live data feeds that can be accessed by a wide variety of programs. The interface with relational databases consists of a query language with one in particular, Structured Query Language (SQL) being a de facto standard, which allows easy transfers of data between different databases.

Ideally, a firm-wide risk-management system should manage market, credit, and operational risk across the institution globally. At the heart of such systems is a global repository, a *data warehouse* that contains all positions. The data warehouse consolidates all the relevant information about each transaction and counterparty into a centralized database.

This leads to a flexible system that can be queried when traders need credit approval for a trade, for instance. In the old days, a credit officer would check the trade against counterparty credit limits. With an ERM system, the marginal credit risk impact of the trade can be assessed quickly, allowing traders to price deals more finely than before. This frees up precious capital, thus increasing returns.

Figure 18–2 illustrates a centralized risk-management architecture, which has been kindly provided by Meridien Research, a consulting firm. All the relevant databases are accessible for market and credit risk calculations. Valuations of market exposures are also fed into the credit risk-measurement system. This allows integrated management of market risk, credit risk, and associated limits.

Integration of systems provides other advantages. It enables banks to take full advantage of netting. Offsetting exposures to the same counterparty is only possible with a global reporting system. Integration also imposes discipline on traders whose positions can be compared regularly with their limits. This can help avoid breakdowns in controls such as

FIGURE 18–2

Centralized risk-management architecture.
(Meridien Research.)

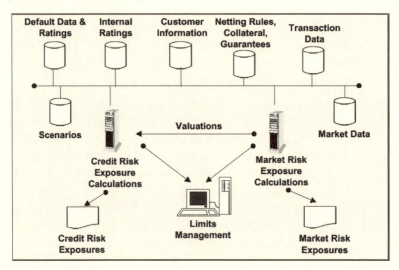

happened to Barings. Finally, integration ensures that a single source is used for price quotes, which ideally should be completely independent of the trading desk. Independent prices and valuation models sharply reduce the likelihood of traders reporting fictitious profits.

Admittedly, comprehensive risk-management systems can never completely eliminate operational risks. Rogue traders can always feed false data or violate trading limits. However, redundant systems, double checks, and automation should reduce the chances of catastrophes. As Box 18–1 shows, the Barings failure would most likely have been avoided by a simple separation of trading and back-office functions.

Additional types of safeguards also can be implemented. Another approach, decidedly low tech, is to provide incentives for employees to inform on colleagues who exceed trading limits. Such a system has been used by Bear Stearns with success. Rotation of trading staff also may help. In the case of Daiwa, for example, Toshihide Igushi was able to conceal losses for 11 years because he was hired as a "local" instead of an expatriate staff member, which would be rotated every 3 to 5 years. In 1993, Daiwa instituted a new mandatory 2-week consecutive vacation policy, under direction from U.S. regulators. This made it increasingly difficult

BOX   18–1

BARINGS'S RISK MISMANAGEMENT

The Barings case is a case in point of lack of trader controls. A good risk-management system may have raised the alarm early and possibly avoided most of the $1.3 billion loss.

Barings had installed in London a credit risk-management system in the 1980s. The bank was installing a market risk-management system in its London offices. The system, developed by California-based Infinity Financial Technology, has the capability to price derivatives and to support VAR reports. Barings's technology, however, was far more advanced in London than in its foreign branches. Big systems are expensive to install and support for small operations, which is why the bank relied heavily on local management.

The damning factor in the Barings affair was Leeson's joint responsibility for front- and back-office functions which allowed him to hide trading losses. In July 1992, he created a special "error" account, numbered 88888, which was hidden from the trade file, price file, and the London gross file. Losing trades and unmatched trades were parked in this account. Daily reports to Barings's Asset and Liability Committee showed Leeson's trading positions on the Nikkei 225 as fully matched. Reports to London therefore showed no risk. Had Barings used internal audits to provide independent checks on inputs, the company might have survived.

for Igushi, who dug a $1.1 billion hole, to hide his losses, and he finally confessed. In this case as in many others, an independent risk-management system would have provided additional safeguards against operational risks.

Unfortunately, integration is not a one-step process. It can be bogged down by existing equipment, which performs its function well in isolation but not across platforms. In addition, there may be organizational resistance to integration, since departmental rivalries may create conflicting objectives.

All this will not come cheap. Implementation costs are illustrated in Table 18–1. The average cost of total implementation is $12 million for large institutions (defined as those with assets greater than $100 billion) and ranges from $7.5 to $100 million. Most of these firms develop their own internal systems because they view financial risk management as the

TABLE 18-1

Expenditures on Enterprise Risk Technology (Millions of Dollars per Institution)

	Average Annual Spending	Average Total Cost	Range of Total Cost
Large institutions	$7 million	$12 million	$7–100 million
Midsized institutions	$0.75 million	$1.5 million	$0.5–5 million

Source: Williams (2000), Meridien Research.

keystone of their competitive advantage. For midsized institutions, however, average costs are lower, at $1.5 million.

As a whole, the market for ERM systems is large and growing. According to Meridien Research, total spending on enterprise-level risk-management systems amounted to $2.6 billion in 1999, with an additional $8 billion on front- and middle-office systems. By 2004, total spending is projected at $17 billion.

18.3 THE RISK-MANAGEMENT INDUSTRY

After having decided to implement a risk-management system, a major issue is whether to develop the system in-house or to purchase an off-the-shelf system provided by an outside vendor. This "build or buy" choice is crucial because it will determine operational costs as well as the level of competitive advantage.

In-house systems offer more flexibility and integration with existing systems. Some institutions view risk as a "strategic" aspect of their business that has to be kept in-house. However, in-house systems can be extremely expensive to develop (sometimes 10 times more than a vendor-supplied system); they require long development periods; and in the end, there is no guarantee the system will be completed on time. Box 18–2 compares successful and not-so-successful internal systems.

Outside systems, in contrast, offer immediate functionality. When institutions do not have the necessary expertise in key technologies, outsourcing is cheaper, due to the fact that outside firms have developed economies of scale. Generally, only large institutions that need a high level of customization develop in-house systems. Even so, they may purchase some components from outside vendors.

BOX 18–2

TECHNOLOGICAL SUCCESSES AND FAILURES

In the late 1970s, Morgan Stanley decided it needed to bring back-office support in-house. The new system, called TAPS (for Trade Analyis and Processing System), was installed in 1986 after 5 years of development and a cost of $60 million.

TAPS was superbly planned, paying attention to using cost-efficient technologies. For example, the system was built on a mature platform (IBM mainframes running the MVS operating system) that offered ready-made and stable solutions. At the same time, the system did not eschew developing innovations that were essential to back-office support. TAPS was one of the earliest systems to use a relational database. It also was Wall Street's first foray into online processing, where input data are fed directly into the database from networked terminals. The system incorporated technological advances only when necessary. As a result, TAPS allowed fast trade capture, fewer errors, and rapid access to positions. With the system in place, Morgan Stanley later doubled its trading business without increasing costs and kept better controls on its traders than competitors. TAPS has been widely viewed as a success.

Many other in-house systems, however, have not been so successful. Integrated front- and back-office systems at CS First Boston and Salomon have been plagued with delays and cost overruns, with total costs exceeding $100 million each. But the biggest technological disaster in finance has been Taurus, an electronic share-settlement system backed by the London Stock Exchange, which collapsed after costing $630 million. The system did not start with narrowly focused objectives, evolved in response to conflicting requirements, and ran into major technological difficulties.

An intermediate solution consists of *custom-made systems,* built to specifications by firms such as the consulting practices of the Big Five accounting firms. This route is cheaper than wholly in-house systems but may be still too expensive for small institutions, which are more likely to rely on off-the-shelf analytical tools.

Off-the-shelf systems can be usefully classified by functionality:

- *Front- to back-office systems* usually started as pricing and deal capture systems and evolved into complete front-to-back office solutions for companies typically handling large volumes of derivatives. Such systems can be quite expensive. They can easily cost above $1 million for large banks.

- *Middle-office systems* offer independent risk-management reporting and usually were designed from the ground up for this purpose. These systems are also expensive, costing above $300,000.
- *Front-office systems* focus on market analysis, valuation, sensitivity analysis, and some trader risk-management functions. At the low end, they consist of spreadsheet add-ons, costing as little as $2000.

The sharpest distinction is between middle-office systems and front-office systems, where analytics are targeted to different users. Risk managers require firm-wide coverage of all instruments. Front-office users require systems that can price the latest instruments with great precision.

A sample of representative systems is described in Table 18–2. The table lists the company, the product, the operating system (Unix, Windows

TABLE 18–2

Risk-Management Systems

Company	Software	Operating System	Credit Risk	Value-at-Risk Implementation
Front-to-Back Office				
Brady plc	Trinity	Unix, NT		V-cov, hist, MC
Infinity/ Sunguard	Panorama	Unix	Integrated	V-cov, hist, MC
Summit Systems	Summit	Unix, NT	Integrated	V-cov, hist, MC
Theoretics	Targa	Win		V-cov, MC
Middle Office				
Algorithmics	RiskWatch	Unix	Integrated	V-cov, hist, MC
Axiom	RiskMonitor	Unix, Win	Integrated	V-cov, hist, MC
MKIRisk	CARMA	Unix, NT	Integrated	V-cov, hist, MC
Reuters	Sailfish	Unix, Win		V-cov, hist
Front Office				
RiskMetrics	Fourfifteen	Excel		V-cov
Fin.Engin.Assoc.	Outlook	Excel		V-cov, MC
MBRM	Universal	Excel		V-cov, MC

FIGURE 18–3

Commerzbank risk-management system.
(Meridien Research.)

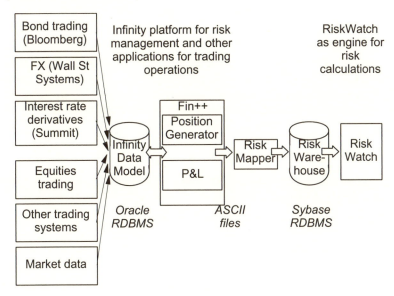

NT, or Windows 98 and above), whether the system integrates credit and market risk, and the VAR implementation (variance-covariance, historical simulation, Monte Carlo).

Figure 18–3 describes the actual system implemented by Commerzbank, Germany's fourth largest bank. Note the multiplicity of systems, with various front-office systems, an Infinity platform, a warehouse, and a RiskWatch engine for firm-wide risk measurement. The system includes the two major data storage vendors, Sybase and Oracle.

The risk-management software industry is in a state of flux. Developing ERM software presents technical challenges that can best be tackled by global firms with substantial resources. This explains why the past years have been characterized by a flurry of acquisitions and marketing agreements. In the future, it is likely that the firm-wide risk-management software business will be dominated by a few well-capitalized firms. In contrast, vendors of front-end systems can still thrive by providing specialized services and extending their product coverage.

As the technology of risk matures and the market for risk-management application broadens, new entrants appear. Some, like Statistical Analysis Systems Institute (SAS), leverage their installed base of users and emphasize the integration of statistical analysis with risk management. Suppliers of *enterprise resource planning* (ERP) systems such as SAP, Baan, and PeopleSoft are also entering the market. These large integrated ERP systems link accounting systems with manufacturing, transportation, supply, and human resources. The goal is to expand the corporate treasury module to mark-to-market derivatives and to measure VAR numbers, as required by the FASB and SEC rules.

18.4 HOW TO STRUCTURE VAR REPORTS

VAR systems aggregate a lot of data and perform numerous computations. The challenge is to present results in an appealing fashion. Since a major purpose of VAR is to communicate risks effectively, VAR reports should be easy to interpret by their intended users.

When the reports contain a lot of information, visual and colorful displays can be effective. "Heat" maps, for instance, use warm colors to indicate greater numbers, which helps users to get to anomalies very quickly. Software vendors are also providing interactive "drill down" capabilities, where users click on a particular point in the report, which then expands into the next level of detail, by department, book, counterparty, trader, or transaction.

VAR reports should only present information directly targeted to the user. Table 18–3 indicates the level of detail appropriate to various users.

- *Senior managers* require firm-wide reporting of profits and losses (P&L) as well as global VAR. Ideally, numbers should be placed in the perspective of previous reports so that anomalies can be detected easily. Also, the level of detail should be kept to a small number of risk factors.

- *Risk managers* require much more detailed capabilities. Besides P&L, position, and VAR reporting, they need a system that flags positions beyond their notional or VAR limits. They also require the capability to "drill down" VAR reports to investigate the positions having the greatest influence on a firm's VAR or the source of an exceedance of a trading limit. Risk managers also need to provide daily VAR reports that comply with capital adequacy requirements and are subject to regular backtesting.

TABLE 18–3

Types of VAR Reports

Users	Level of Detail	Information	Main Features	Timing
Senior managers	Firm-wide	P&L, positions, VAR	Clarity and brevity, few factors, firm-wide scenarios	Daily; weekly
Risk managers	Firm-wide, dept.-wide, books	P&L, positions, VAR, limits	Drill-down capability, scenarios, sensitivity analysis, regulatory reports	Daily, intraday
Traders	Book level	P&L, positions, limits, VAR	Single-deal analysis, pricing, hedging, marginal VAR	Real time

- *Traders* require real-time information on a great deal of detail in their positions. They also need to examine the pricing and hedging of potential deals. Naturally, the system also should automatically warn them of violations of trading limits.

18.5 AN APPLICATION

As an example, we now illustrate the application of a global risk-management system, using RiskWatch, a firm-wide risk-management software provided by Algorithmics, Inc. Users have the option of choosing one of three VAR methods and therefore can assess whether the results are sensitive to the methodology.

This application represents a global bank with operations in seven geographic locations. The portfolio consists of more than 200 instruments, including fixed-rate bonds, floating-rate notes, interest rate swaps, FRAs, caps and floors, FX forwards, FX options, common stocks, and equity options. The mark-to-market value of the portfolio is $1.4 billion. The issue is, How much could this portfolio lose over a day?

We first measure a hypothetical profit and loss series using the historical simulation method. Figure 18–4 displays the time series of simulated portfolio returns for a hundred days of data. The portfolio returns range from a loss of $7 million to a gain of $10 million. Users can expand or narrow the sample period as desired. In addition, the system

FIGURE 18–4

Algorithmics system: historical simulation.

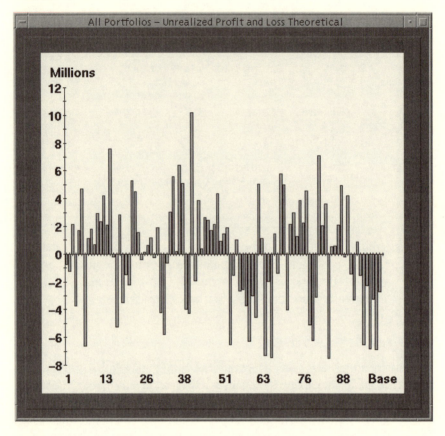

provides "drill down" capabilities, which allow users to examine in more detail the drivers of a particularly bad loss.

Next, Figure 18–5 summarizes the distribution of profits and losses using both the historical simulation and delta-normal methods. The empirical distribution yields a 95 percent daily VAR of $7.32 million. The normal VAR is based on the RiskMetrics forecasts and gives a similar number, at $7.51 million. Apparently, the many sources of risk average out to an empirical distribution that is close to the normal.

Finally, Figure 18–6 provides a breakdown of the VAR by asset class and by geographic location. The graph shows individual VAR numbers of $1.9 million, $6.8 million, and $4.5 million for each asset class, interest rates,

FIGURE 18–5

Algorithmics system: distribution of returns.

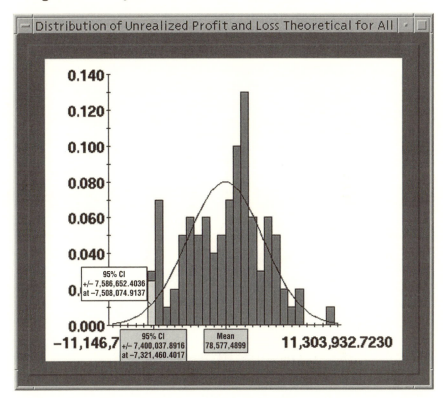

currencies, and equities, respectively. These numbers add up to about $13 million, which is the undiversified VAR. The portfolio VAR of $7.5 million is lower, reflecting diversification benefits. The graph also breaks down VAR by geographic location, in the local currency. Here, Tokyo is exposed primarily to equity risk; New York, to interest rate risk. Based on this visual information, top management can get a better sense of their risk profile.

18.6 CONCLUSIONS

The technical challenges involved in producing firm-wide risk-control systems are considerable. Perhaps the most difficult part of the process is the integration of disparate components into a centralized warehouse, which feeds into an analytical system with its risk engine.

FIGURE 18-6

Algorithmics system: VAR breakdown.

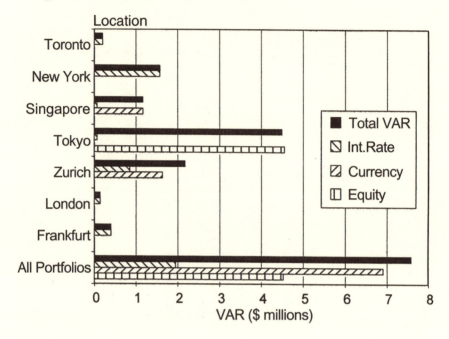

The benefits from integrated systems, however, are also substantial. ERM systems allow users to have better control of their financial risks and to exploit diversification effects fully, hence gaining a competitive advantage in terms of pricing deals. In short, ERM systems move the application of VAR from defensive control to the active management of financial risks.

CHAPTER 19

Operational Risk Management

[A]n informal survey . . . highlights the growing realization of the significance of risks other than credit and market risks, such as operational risk, which have been at the heart of some important banking problems in recent years. The Committee is proposing to develop capital charges for such other risks.

Basel Committee on Banking Supervision (June 1999)

Operational risk is perhaps the most pernicious form of risk, since it is indirectly responsible for numerous failures in financial institutions. Recognition of operational risk is relatively new, however. For a long time, institutions have narrowly focused on a subset of operational risk, which involves transaction processing, ignoring other aspects of operational risk. This is slowly changing.

For the first time, the industry is attempting to measure operational risks on a systematic basis. We are learning to quantify these risks using tools borrowed from the insurance industry and to manage such risks using the tools of market risk management. Once quantified, operational risk can be subject to controls and capital charges using value-at-risk (VAR) techniques.

As in the case of market risk, the increased focus on operational risk management should give some comfort to senior management, boards, and investors that risk is being monitored. This increased scrutiny of operational risk has been, as in the case of credit and market risks, also spurred by bank regulators who are mulling new capital charges as a further incentive to control operational risks.

Section 19.1 motivates the recent interest in operational risk. While our knowledge of market and credit risk has matured, operational risk management is still in its infancy. There is not even complete agreement on definitions, which are covered in Section 19.2. Section 19.3 discusses various approaches to operational risk.

We are making some progress in the quantitative measurement of operational risk, as shown in Section 19.4. The body of knowledge that has grown from the management of market risk readily applies to operational risk. Once risk is measured, it can be controlled and allocated for better performance. Section 19.5 discusses the management of operational risk. Finally, Section 19.6 contains some concluding comments.

19.1 THE IMPORTANCE OF OPERATIONAL RISK

Many of the great financial fiascos can be traced to a combination of market or credit risk and failure of controls—in other words, they involve some form of operational risks. The biggest such risk is unauthorized trading. Indeed, the biggest fear of banks is to have their name end up in the hall of infamy, along with the likes of Barings, Daiwa, and Sumimoto. While shareholders understand that the very function of trading is to take financial risk, thus leading once in a while to trading losses, few are willing to forgive losses due to lack of supervision, which are viewed as entirely avoidable.

This recognition, along with the pace of change in the industry, leading to bigger and more complex business operations, is bringing greater interest in operational risk. At the same time, we are witnessing advances in the quantitative measurement of operational risk, leading to software offerings to evaluate this risk.

Armed with improved measures of operational risk, senior management will be able to compare financial risks across business lines. Box 19–1 illustrates the case of an asset-management business, which is traditionally viewed as relatively safe because it creates no market or credit risk for the owners. Yet a compliance failure led to a huge operational loss.

As in the case of market and credit risk, the industry is also being prodded into action by bank regulators. Indeed, the Basel II document issued in June 1999 proposes to establish capital charges for operational risks in exchange for lowering capital charges for credit risk. The 8 percent charge of the 1988 Capital Accord implicitly accounts for operational risk. The view of regulators is that the current level of global bank capital is adequate, having been "stress tested" through some tumultuous recent times. Thus it will be up to the industry to convince regulators that their capital can be reduced further. The issue is important because squeezing capital down will increase shareholder returns.

B O X   19—1

DEUTSCHE MORGAN GRENFELL'S RISK

In September 1996, the investment bank Deutsche Morgan Grenfell (DMG) announced it had suspended a star fund manager, Peter Young, in its asset-management unit. DMG also halted trading on its three main European equity funds, worth some $2.2 billion.

Apparently, Peter Young had breached the limit of 10 percent that such funds can invest in unlisted securities. This limit is imposed due to the difficulty of confirming market values for these securities. While the funds he managed had a stellar performance in 1995, they ranked dead last in their category in the first half of 1996.

Deutsche Bank, the German owner of DMG, agreed to compensate the shareholders in the funds. It later announced it had set aside some $720 million to cover the total losses. The total cost must have been even higher as a result of the lost business due to tarnished reputation.

Figure 19–1, for example, shows that different financial activities have very different risk profiles. Most of the risk of commercial banking comes from credit and operational risks. Investment banking with proprietary trading and treasury management has greater exposure to market risk. In contrast, activities such as retail brokerage and asset management are mainly exposed to operational risk.

In practice, reporting of these risks varies widely, as shown by a recent Ernst & Young risk-management survey of top 100 U.S. banks. Figure 19–2 reveals that risk measurement is more widespread at longer reporting intervals. On a monthly basis or better, 94 percent of banks measure market risk, 100 percent measure credit risk, and only 69 percent measure operational risk.

19.2 DEFINING OPERATIONAL RISK

There is currently no universally agreed-on definition of *operational risk.*[1] Too often the industry is using definitions that are inconsistent or overlapping, generating much confusion. We can broadly distinguish four approaches.

---

1. A recent survey by the Basel Committee (1998d) provides some definitions and discusses current practices. For a good review of operational risk definition and techniques, see Jameson (1998a, 1998b) and Ceske and Hernandez (1999).

FIGURE 19-1

Breakdown of financial risks. (After Robert Ceske.)

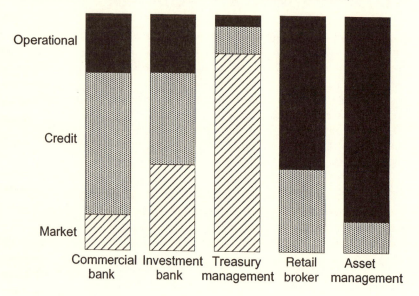

FIGURE 19-2

Reporting of financial risks.

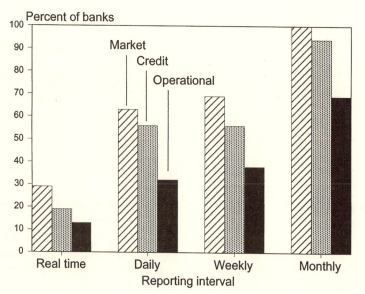

The first, wider-ranging approach defines *operational risk* as any financial risk *other than market and credit risk.* This broad net, however, makes it difficult to measure and manage all the risks that are identified. It also includes business risk, which the firm is supposed to assume to create shareholder value.

At the other extreme is a second, much narrower approach, which defines *operational risk* as *risk arising from operations.* This involves transactions processing and systems failures, for example. While these risks are easiest to control, they miss significant risks such as fraud.

A third, slightly broader approach views *operational risk* as *any risk over which the institution has control.* This would include, for instance, internal fraud but would exclude external events such as the influence of regulators or natural disasters.

The industry, however, seems to be converging on a fourth approach, which is *the risk of direct and indirect loss resulting from failed or inadequate process, systems, or people or from external events.* This still excludes business risk but includes external events such as political/regulatory risk, disaster risk, counterparty risk, security breaches, and so on. These fall under the general umbrella of *event risk* and are detailed in the next chapter.

A set of definitions for internal risks has been provided by Cooper's & Lybrand, which classifies operational risk into transaction risk, operational controls risk, and systems risk. *Transactions risk* results from errors in the processing of transactions. *Operational controls risk* results from breakdowns in the controls around the front-, middle-, and back-office activities. *Systems risk* is due to errors or failures in systems support. Table 19–1 summarizes these definitions.

The definition of operational risk is far from an academic exercise. Proper definitions are essential to assign responsibilities and risk capital. In recent years, an increasing number of banks have appointed specialist operational risk managers, with the rank equivalent to heads of credit risk and market risk, who report directly to committees in charge of overall risk. To avoid overlaps or holes in the coverage of various risks, each of these functions needs to be well defined. Further, one cannot measure operational risk without first defining it.

19.3 APPROACHES TO OPERATIONAL RISK

Tools used to manage operational risk can be categorized as follows, listed in order of increasing sophistication.

TABLE 19–1

Operational Risk According to GARP

Categories of Operational Risk		
Transactions Risk	**Operational Controls Risk**	**Systems Risk**
Execution error	Exceeding limits	Systems failure
Booking error	Rogue trading	Model error
Settlement error	Fraud	Mark-to-market error
Commodity delivery	Money laundering	Management information failure
Documentation risk	Security risk	Programming error
	Key personnel risk	Telecommunication failure
	Processing risk	Contingency planning failure

Source: Generally Accepted Risk Principles (GARP), Cooper's & Lybrand.

- *Audit oversight,* where an external audit department reviews business processes to identify weaknesses
- *Critical self-assessment,* where each department submits a *subjective* evaluation of sources of operational risk, as well as their expected frequency and costs
- *Key risk indicators,* where a centralized unit develops *subjective* risk forecasts through risk indicators, which are compared across the organization
- *Formal quantification,* where operational risk managers measure an *objective* distribution of losses due to operational risk from an event database

It is only very recently that institutions are building systems for the attribution and capital allocation of operational risks. One of the early proponents was Wilson (1995), who argued that traditional VAR techniques can be applied readily to the management of operational risk.

19.4 MEASURING OPERATIONAL RISK

Unlike market and credit risk, where the source of uncertainty lies outside the firm, operational risk is created by sources internal to the firm. Thus there may be more scope for minimizing the occurrences and size of such losses. To decide how to control or manage operational risk, however, it is essential to have some measure of its cost.

19.4.1 Top-Down versus Bottom-Up Approaches

Operational risk measurement is still a developing art form. Some take a *top-down* approach, which estimates risk based on firm-wide data. These models are easier to apply than bottom-up models but are not sensitive to the actual implementation to the business process.

One example is overall *earnings volatility*. If one views operational risk as any risk that is not captured by market or credit risk, then subtracting the component of earnings due to the other two risk categories should reveal the effect of operational risk. This "rear mirror" approach, however, does not provide a current measure of risk, nor does it shed much light on sources of operational risk or ways to control it better. In addition, much of the variability in earnings can be ascribed to business risk, involving macroeconomic fluctuations, instead of operational risk.

In contrast, *bottom-up* models provide a structural approach that is much more useful to understand causes of operational risk. Bottom-up models involve the mapping of workflows at the business unit level, which is used to identify potential failures and associated losses.

The contrast between these two approaches is akin to that between historical versus VAR measures of market risk. Historical measures are backward-looking and provide little information on the current portfolio risk. In contrast, VAR measures are forward-looking and provide a process by which risk exposures can be controlled. A bottom-up approach is also the only method that can incorporate operational risk into the pricing of products. It also helps to measure the effect of process improvements.

19.4.2 Loss Distributions

In both cases, the distribution of losses can be measured using *actuarial models*. Actuarial science has its roots in the study of mortality rates. Life insurance companies, for instance, set their insurance premiums as a function of the average mortality rate for their portfolio. Due to the law of large numbers, insurance models provide rather good approximations of average mortality rates.

Actuarial losses due to operational risk can be ascribed usefully to a combination of two separate random variables, the loss frequency and the loss severity when it occurs. The *loss frequency* is a measure of the number of loss events over a fixed interval of time. The *loss severity* is a measure of the size of the loss once it occurs. The advantage of this break-down into two sources of risk, as compared with directly modeling loss distribution, is that it gives more insights into the causes and effects of losses.

Risk managers need to estimate probability distribution functions (pdfs) for loss frequencies and severities. Loss severities can be tabulated, for instance, from historical data, in which case historical measures of the loss severity y_k, at time k, would have to be adjusted for inflation and some measure of current business activity. Define P_k as the consumer price index at the time the loss was recorded and V_k as a real business activity measure such as the number of trades. We can assume that the loss sever-ity is proportional to the volume of business V, for example. The *scaled* loss is then measured as of time t as

$$x_t = y_k \times \frac{P_t}{P_k} \times \frac{V_t}{V_k} \tag{19.1}$$

Now, define n as the number of occurrences of losses over the horizon, generally taken to be 1-year. Define the pdf for this random variable as

$$\text{pdf of loss frequency} = f(n) \qquad n = 0, 1, 2, \ldots \tag{19.2}$$

Next, if x is the loss severity when a loss occurs, we define its pdf as

$$\text{pdf of loss severity} = g(x \mid n = 1) \qquad x \geq 0 \tag{19.3}$$

The total loss is then the summation of these random losses over a ran-dom number of occurrences:

$$S_n = \sum_{i=1}^{n} X_i \tag{19.4}$$

Table 19–2 provides a simple example of two such distributions.

Assuming that X and N are independent considerably simplifies the analysis. If we need just the expected total loss, we can find it simply as the product of the expected frequency and severity, which is here $E(S) = E(N) \times E(X) = 0.7 \times \$13,600 = \$9520$. Similarly, the assumption of in-dependence leads to the variance $V(S) = E(N) \times V(X) + V(N) \times E(X)^2$. To find the quantile, however, we need to recover the full distribution.

Assuming that the frequency and severity are independent, the two distributions can be combined into a probability distribution of aggregate

TABLE 19-2

Sample Loss Frequency and Severity Distributions

Frequency Distribution		Severity Distribution	
Probability	Frequency	Probability	Severity
0.5	0	0.6	$1,000
0.3	1	0.3	$10,000
0.2	2	0.1	$100,000
Expectation	0.7	Expectation	$13,600

loss through a process known as convolution. *Convolution* aggregates the two distributions into that of the sum of independent losses over a fixed period.

Convolution can be implemented through a variety of methods. We illustrate here the process through tabulation. *Tabulation* consists of systematically tabulating all possible combinations with their probability. This is only feasible with a small number of combinations, however.

Table 19–3 illustrates use of the tabulation method. We can have at most two occurrences of a loss. Thus we start with a situation with no loss, which has probability 0.5. Next, we go through all occurrences of one loss. A loss of $1000 can occur with probability of $P(n = 1) \times P(x = \$1000) = 0.3 \times 0.6 = 0.18$. After that, we compute the probability of a one-time loss of $10,000 and $100,000. Next, we go through all occurrences of two losses. A loss of $1000 can occur twice, with a probability of $0.2 \times 0.6 \times 0.6 = 0.072$. And so on. Finally, we collect all total loss occurrences and their associated probabilities.

The distribution is summarized in Figure 19–3. Note that even with only three possible values for N and X, the loss distribution is quite rich. From this we can compute the expected loss, which is $9520, as found previously, and the 95 percent quantile, which is $68,000. Hence the VAR measure would be about $58,500.

This operation is equivalent to finding the loss pdf as the integral of

$$\text{pdf of loss} = h(s) = \int g_s(s \mid n) f(n) \, dn \qquad (19.5)$$

where g_s is the pdf of a sum of severity variables. For some combinations of the functions f and g we can find a closed-form analytical solution for $h(s)$, as illustrated in the appendix to this chapter. If not, we have to

TABLE 19-3

Tabulation of Loss Distribution

Number of Losses	First Loss	Second Loss	Total Loss	Probability
0	0	0	0	0.5
1	1,000	0	1,000	0.18
1	10,000	0	10,000	0.09
1	100,000	0	100,000	0.03
2	1,000	1,000	2,000	0.072
2	1,000	10,000	11,000	0.036
2	1,000	100,000	101,000	0.012
2	10,000	1,000	11,000	0.036
2	10,000	10,000	20,000	0.018
2	10,000	100,000	110,000	0.006
2	100,000	1,000	101,000	0.012
2	100,000	10,000	110,000	0.006
2	100,000	100,000	200,000	0.002

FIGURE 19-3

Finding the loss distribution.

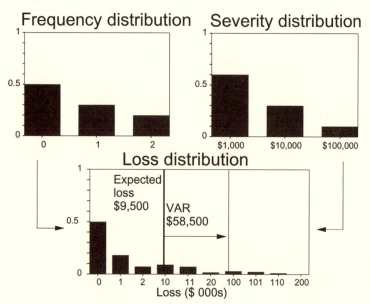

resort to simulation methods. Note that the integration of the variables, as well as the concept of loss severity, is conceptually similar to the tools of credit risk, i.e., event of default and recovery rate when default occurs.

The next step is to aggregate operational risk across product or business lines for the whole institution. Figure 19–4 provides an example of such a distribution from RiskOps, a system for operational risk management provided by NetRisk. The graph shows the distribution of losses as well as a classification by cause.

19.4.3 The Data Challenge

Perhaps the greatest challenge to the measurement of operational risk is the collection of relevant data. Unlike market and credit risk, the sources of operational risk are internal to the firm. Within each firm, experience with large losses is rare (fortunately). Hence the challenge is to build a database of operational losses and their associated factors. In practice, these have to be built from both internal and external data.

Internal data provide a history of occurrences of losses due to operational failures, such as errors in transactions processing or losses due to system failures or personnel turnover. These would be divided into loss estimates, e.g., penalties paid for not fulfilling a transaction, and frequency indicators, e.g., error rates and associated transaction volumes. Model risk also can be assessed by periodically sampling the portfolio and checking the size of errors using an independent valuation model. Such *high-frequency/low-value losses* lend themselves well to statistical analysis.

Ideally, one should collect not only loss data but also their characteristics. The goal should be to establish causal relationships between, say, the frequency of losses and the age of computer systems. Changing the characteristics should then directly affect the loss distribution, creating a tool for balancing the cost of process improvement with their benefits.

At the other end of the spectrum are *low-frequency/high-value losses.* For these, one needs to cull *external data,* ideally from comparable institutions. This raises several issues.

The first one is that not all losses are publicly disclosed. Institutions may be understandably reluctant to reveal failures in their internal systems.[2] Thus the database may be biased toward public information such

---

2. This is also a problem within a bank. Barclays Bank, for instance, encourages its managers to reveal their mistakes by calling them "process-improvement opportunities."

FIGURE 19-4

An example of loss distribution.

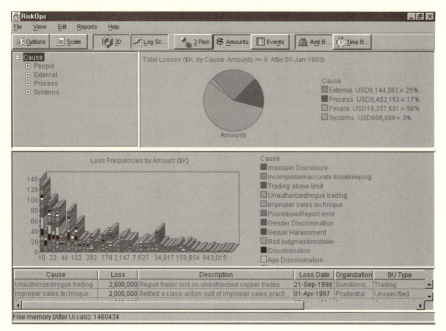

as legal settlements and ignore technological failures, which are rarely ac-
knowledged.

Another problem is that external losses could correspond to different business profiles and internal controls and may not be directly applicable to another institution. In the words of some observers, external data
should allow some "marking-to-operations," i.e., adapting the loss distribution for different internal controls.

Finally, as in the case of market risk, the data may not contain any
instance of situations that are nonetheless likely to appear in the future,
thus potentially biasing the loss distributions. Particularly dangerous are
transitory situations that historically have been associated with substantial losses. The Basel Committee (1998a) lists these as (1) changed operating environment, (2) new personnel, (3) new or revamped information
systems, (4) activities experiencing rapid growth, (5) new technology,
(6) new products or activities, (7) corporate restructurings, and (8) ex-
pansions abroad.

Prodded by regulators, the industry is slowly moving toward centralized databases such as those used by the insurance industry. There are some initiatives in that direction, such as the Multinational Operational Risk Exchange (MORE) Consortium. This is no easy matter, since banks may not be quite willing to report their own internal failures, which is necessary for building a complete database.

In light of these problems, many banks think that current methods are not sufficiently developed for bank supervisors to mandate guidelines specifying particular measurement methodologies or quantitative limits on operational risks. Thus it is probably going to take a while before we can have formal VAR-based risk charges for operational risks.

Instead, shortcuts are adopted. Some banks, for instance, set up a charge as a percentage of some business volume measure, e.g., cash flows. Others, like Bank of America, charge 25 percent of fixed costs and 50 percent of noninterest expenses. The assumption is that historical loss experience provides a good measure of prospective losses.

The problem with these shortcuts is that they do not account for the quality of the control processes and may have perverse consequences. For instance, a unit that wanted to improve its risk management by purchasing a new computer would see its costs go up and hence would be charged more capital. As a result, it would have no incentive to invest in process improvements.

Thus it is important to account for the quality of controls. One may devise, for instance, a scheme where the capital charge is set as

$$\text{Capital charge} = \text{business volume} \times \text{business line multiplier} \times k \quad (19.6)$$

where k would be a regulator score of the business environment, akin to the Basel multiplier for the market risk charge.

19.5 MANAGING OPERATIONAL RISK

Once operational risk has been measured, it can be better controlled, financed, and managed. The probability distribution of losses reveals, for each business unit, an expected loss as well as a VAR-type worst loss at some confidence level. The apparatus for risk-adjustment methods, such as RAROC, also applies.

Table 19–4 compares methods to manage market, credit, and operational risks. In each case, we need to define risk and measure the distribution of risk factors and exposures so as to calculate a VAR figure.

TABLE 19-4

Steps in the Management of Financial Risk

Step	Market Risk	Credit Risk	Operational Risk
Define risk categories	Interest rate Equity Currency Commodity	Default Downgrade	Transactions Operational controls Systems
Measure risk factors	Volatility Correlations	Default and recovery distributions	Loss frequency
Measure exposure	Duration Delta Mapping	Current and potential exposure	Loss distribution
Calculate risk	Market VAR	Credit VAR Expected loss	Operational VAR Expected loss

19.5.1 Expected versus Unexpected Losses

In the first step, a capital charge should be allocated for expected operational losses. These charges will reveal vulnerabilities and measure gains from improved controls. Armed with this information, the institution can evaluate the cost and benefit of investments in process improvements. At a broader, firm-wide level, these charges should lead to more informed strategic decisions. Top management may then discover that a particular business line that looks attractive without considering operational risk is actually barely profitable once expected operational losses are factored in. In the second step, the institution must choose how to fund unexpected losses.

19.5.2 Controlling Operational Risk

Operational risk can be better controlled with measures of the costs and benefits of *alternative actions.* Once vulnerabilities are identified, corrective actions can be framed in the following terms:

- *Loss reduction,* or reduction in the severity of the losses when they occur
- *Loss prevention,* or reduction in the frequency of occurrences

■ *Exposure avoidance,* which is an extreme form of the latter, where the activity is completely avoided

Loss prevention can be achieved by purchasing better equipment that will decrease failure rates or restructuring processes to make them less prone to errors. Like "total quality management" or "six-sigma quality control systems" in manufacturing firms, measuring operational risk in itself should pave the road for process improvements. *Redundant and automated control systems* are other loss-prevention measures. "Straight through" processing, for instance, interfaces the front- and back-office systems so that deals entering the front-office system are automatically sent to the back office, which eliminates manual intervention and the potential for human errors. Some systems now require double validations for trades above certain thresholds.

Loss reduction can be achieved by strategies that mitigate the cost of operational errors. One sample is *contingency planning.* While insurance can be purchased as protection against natural disasters such as fire, floods, and earthquakes, it may only cover physical structures. Loss of business activity may be substantial if disaster strikes without an institution having adequate backup facilities.

More generally, the key to controlling operational risk lies in *control systems* and *competent managers.* In fact, many of the recommendations of the G-30 report help to establish a safe internal environment. Institutions should start from clear policies on risk and have independent risk-management functions with authority to set and monitor risk limits. In itself, the implementation of market risk-management systems should provide some protection against operational controls risks such as rogue trading or fraud.

19.5.3 Funding Operational Risk

Once the appropriate control structure is in place, the next aspect of operational risk management is the *financing of unexpected losses.* The decision can be viewed in terms of a choice of *preloss financing* or *postloss financing.*

Postloss financing simply uses the available capital to absorb a loss after it occurred. Preloss financing builds up a reserve in anticipation of risk of losses. This risk can be *retained* or *transferred.*

Institutions can decide to guard against unexpected losses by *self-insurance,* i.e., putting aside capital in an internal reserve fund against

BOX 19–2

ROGUE TRADER INSURANCE

Insurance policies can now be bought for protection against rogue trader losses. Chase Manhattan was reported to be the first bank to have purchased such a policy. The underwriter, a subsidiary of Lloyd's of London, provided insurance for up to $300 million in losses at a cost of about $2 million per year. More recently, other firms have offered coverage over a broader array of risks.

The issue, of course, is the pricing of rogue trader risk. Initially, insurance companies are charging a high premium to compensate for the unknown. Over the period 1997–1999, they have netted around $50 million in premiums, without a claim. Eventually, competition should drive down the premium to a level that reflects actuarial estimates.

such losses (retaining risk). Alternatively, they can purchase external insurance (transferring risk). When considering external insurance (see Box 19–2), the obvious issue is whether the insurance premium is reasonably priced.[3] One could argue that self-insurance should be cheaper. After all, capital allocations based on internal loss histories should prove more accurate than insurance companies' best guesses. Such questions can only be addressed systematically with quantitative measures of loss distributions.

19.6 CONCLUSIONS

Operational risk has only very recently come under close scrutiny by the financial industry. Indeed, institutions and regulators now realize that many financial disasters can be traced to a fatal combination of operational risk with some other form of financial risk.

In response, institutions anxious to avoid the fates of Barings, Daiwa, and DMG recently have begun to develop a framework for explicitly measuring and monitoring operational risks. This quantification should allow them to understand their risks better and to control and manage their risks more efficiently.

---

3. Another, unrelated issue is that insurance payouts often involve litigation, thus creating legal uncertainty.

For quantification purposes, however, the collection of relevant data presents a major stumbling block. Unlike market and credit risk, operational risk is internal to the firm. Since firms are understandably not eager to reveal their failings, public data on losses caused by operational risk are nowhere as rich as for other forms of risk. Methodologies for measuring operational risk are also still evolving.

As a result, there are still wide differences of opinion as to the applicability of operational risk measures. It is fair to predict, however, that this area of financial risk management will undergo profound changes in the coming years.

FURTHER INFORMATION

Reports on Risk Management

One of the earliest documents, still regarded as the "bible" of risk management, is the G-30 report, *Derivatives, Practices and Principles* (1993). Available at the IFCI Web site, risk.ifci.ch.

The Basel Committee on Banking Supervision (BCBS) also has issued relevant documents, including *Risk Management Guidelines for Derivatives* (1994), and *Operational Risk Management* (1998). Available at www.bis.org.

Britain's Financial Services Authority has issued a report entitled, *Allocating Regulatory Capital for Operational Risk* (1999). Available at www.fsa.gov.uk.

The Federal Reserve Board has written a useful in-depth guide, *Trading and Capital Markets Activities Manual* (1998). Available at www.bog.frb.fed.us.

The Risk Standards Working Group has established a set of standards for institutional investors, *Risk Standards for Institutional Investment Managers* (1996). Available at www.cmra.com.

Operational Risk Web Information

The Multinational Operational Risk Exchange (MORE) is a recently established consortium whose goal is to pool operational risk data. Available at www.morexchange.org.

APPENDIX: CONSTRUCTING LOSS DISTRIBUTIONS

The purpose of this appendix is to illustrate analytical methods for modeling loss distributions. The risk manager could tabulate a distribution of relevant losses from historical data, but this is unlikely to be smooth, especially with limited sample sizes. Instead, we can fit the pdf for the loss frequency from a parametric distribution.

Take, for instance, the geometric distribution for the loss frequency n,

$$f(n) = p(1 - p)^{n-1} \qquad n = 1, 2, \ldots \qquad (19.7)$$

where the parameter p must be $0 < p \leq 1$. For instance, with $p = 0.5$, we have $f(1) = 0.5$, $f(2) = 0.25$, and so on. So the probability decreases geometrically. The expected loss frequency is then $E(N) = 1/p$ and its variance $V(N) = (1 - p)/p^2$. Other frequency distributions include the Poisson and negative binomial, of which the geometric is a special case.

Next, the pdf for the loss severity x can be taken from an exponential distribution

$$g(x) = \lambda e^{-\lambda x} \qquad x \geq 0 \qquad (19.8)$$

which is characterized by the parameter $\lambda > 0$. This implies a probability of a loss that decreases exponentially with the size of the loss. The expected value and standard deviation of the loss are given by $E(X) = SD(X) = 1/\lambda$. Other severity distributions include the log-normal, Weibull, and gamma distribution, of which the exponential is a special case.[4]

We seek to find the distribution of the total losses over the period, which is $S_n = \Sigma_{i=1}^{n} X_i$. This is the sum *of a random number* of random variables. We assume that n is independent of the realizations X.

The total probability of observing a sum less than s is then

$$P(S \leq s) = \sum_{n=1}^{\infty} P(S_n \leq s \mid n) f(n) \qquad (19.9)$$

Next, we use the fact that a sum of i.i.d. exponential random variables has a gamma distribution of

$$P(S_n \leq s \mid n) = \int_0^s \frac{1}{(n-1)!} \lambda^n u^{n-1} e^{-\lambda u} \, du \qquad (19.10)$$

After integration, we find that

$$P(S \leq s) = 1 - e^{-\lambda p s} \qquad (19.11)$$

or that the loss has itself an exponential distribution with parameter λp:

$$h(s) = (\lambda p) e^{-(\lambda p) s} \qquad (19.12)$$

---

4. Cruz et al. (1998) show how to fit an extreme value distribution to losses from a fraud database with more than 3000 events collected by a major U.K. bank over 5 years.

From this we can compute the expected loss as well as the worst deviation at some confidence level. The expected loss is $E(S) = (1/\lambda p)$, which is indeed the product of the two expected distribution values. The VAR at the c level of confidence is then $s^* - E(S) = (1/\lambda p)[\ln(1/c) - 1]$.

Other distributions are feasible but may not combine analytically as easily as these do. If so, we could approximate the loss distribution by running simulations from processes sampled from $f(n)$ and $g(x)$.

CHAPTER 20

Integrated Risk Management

> Is it an accident that banks are now looking for growth in areas where they do not directly allocate capital and where risk is difficult to manage, rather than in basic trading and lending where businesses now have to pay their own way?

Anonymous quote reported in Euromoney (September 1996)

The revolution in risk management that started with value-at-risk (VAR)-based measures of financial market risk is now spreading to firm-wide risk management. This stems from the recognition that once market and credit are quantified, financial risks tend to slip toward areas where they are not measured. Ideally, risk-management systems should provide comprehensive views of firm-wide risks.

Integrated risk management has other advantages. It could help to stabilize earnings, whose volatility appears to worry corporate CFOs, by careful neutering of undesirable risks. More usefully, integrated risk management has the potential to reduce the cost of hedging. If the risks facing institutions are uncorrelated, a piecewise approach provides unnecessary coverage. Instead of hedging risks individually, considerable cost savings could be achieved by hedging only *net* risks. This is nothing more than an extension of the VAR approach to market risk, whose essence is centralization, to firm-wide risks. Thus the ideas behind the VAR revolution are quickly spreading to enterprise-wide risk management.

Section 20.1 presents a classification of firm-wide risks. This book has already covered market risk, credit risk, and operational risk. Section 20.2 then discusses remaining risks, including legal, reputational, disaster, political, and regulatory.

Section 20.3 then turns to the recent topic of firm-wide risk management. It is only recently that institutions have been able to evaluate their risks on a firm-wide basis, which can lead to considerable cost savings. The benefits of firm-wide reduction in volatility are discussed in Section 20.4. We discuss why risk management can add value to corporations, leading to recent findings that firms with a risk-management program have a market value 5 percent higher than others. Finally, Section 20.5 provides some concluding comments.

20.1 THE GALAXY OF RISKS

We first provide a broad description of the risks facing financial and other institutions. Figure 20–1 classifies the risks facing institutions into business and nonbusiness risks, the latter being further classified into event risks and financial risks. Admittedly, these classifications are somewhat arbitrary, since some of these risks overlap categories.

Business risks generally are defined as those the corporation willingly assumes to create a competitive advantage and add value for shareholders. This risk pertains to the product market in which a firm operates and includes product design and sales. The product market creates implicit exposure to *macroeconomic risks,* which result from economic cycles or fluctuations in incomes and monetary policies, and the *risk of technological innovations.* Business risk is symmetrical in that it can create

F I G U R E   20–1

Firm-wide risks.

both gains and losses. In some sense, corporations are "paid" to take business risk.

Financial risks generally are associated with the effect of financial variables. Among these, we have so far covered market, credit, and liquidity risks. These risks are also symmetrical because they can create both gains and losses. Institutions are "paid" to manage financial risks. This leaves us with operational risk, which is examined in Chapter 19.

Event risks generally can be ascribed to other, negative events outside the control of the institution. Event risks only create losses, some of which can be covered by traditional insurance. Institutions "pay" to mitigate event risks. These risks are further detailed in the next section. Because these risks are more encompassing in nature, it is likely that they will be assumed at the highest level. Some definitions of operational risk, however, also include event risk.

20.2 EVENT RISKS

20.2.1 Legal Risk

Legal risk reflects the possibility of losses due to the fact that contracts are not legally enforceable or are documented incorrectly. This risk can be limited through policies developed by the institution's legal counsel, as approved by senior management. Legal risk is sometimes classified within financial risk because it occurs regularly due to market or credit losses suffered by clients.

Prior to engaging in trades, institutions should ensure that their counterparties have the legal authority to do so and that the terms of the contracts have a sound basis. Even so, contracts that lead to large losses for counterparties often end up in a lawsuit. Such contracts are invariably claimed *unsuitable* to the client's needs or level of expertise. Losing parties often claim a form of *financial insanity;* i.e., they were temporarily unable to judge financial contracts. Here, VAR can provide additional protection, as Box 20–1 shows.

The financial industry is also working to reduce legal risks through the use of standardized contracts such as master netting agreements. The language in such contracts has been formulated carefully so as to reduce mistakes and misunderstanding. Even when there are differences of interpretation, the use of such standardized contracts makes it more costly for a financial institution to renege on them unilaterally. Such behavior

BOX 20–1

USING VAR TO CONTROL LEGAL RISKS

VAR is now used to control legal risks. *Suitability* can now be defined in terms of VAR limits.

Some banks now require their traders to obtain signatures from counterparties based on VAR limits. Above a VAR level of $1 million, for instance, the deal must be approved by the finance director of the client institution. Above some other level, say, $5 million, the deal also must be signed off by a senior manager. This makes it more difficult for clients to claim financial insanity later.

---

would be badly received by the rest of the community and actually increase the cost of entering future contracts.

20.2.2 Reputational Risk

Reputational risk can be viewed as the damage, in addition to immediate monetary losses, caused to the ongoing business of an institution due to a damaged reputation. It is particularly important for banks because the nature of their business requires maintaining the confidence of the marketplace.

One such example is the story of Bankers Trust (Box 20–2), which before 1994 was widely admired as a leader in risk management but at some point became a victim of the backlash against derivatives.

20.2.3 Disaster Risk

Disaster risk includes natural disasters such as earthquakes, floods, tornadoes, and fires, as well as war. They generally can be covered by external insurance. Their effect can be mitigated through contingency planning and backup facilities.

20.2.4 Regulatory and Political Risk

Political risks arise from actions taken by policymakers that significantly affect the way an organization runs its business. It seems that big finan-

BOX 20-2

BANKERS TRUST'S STRATEGIC RISKS

Charles Sanford transformed Bankers Trust from a sleepy commercial bank into a financial powerhouse using risk management as a competitive tool. In 1994, however, the bank became embroiled in a high-profile lawsuit with Procter & Gamble that badly damaged the bank's name. Many customers shied way from the bank after the bad publicity.

In an attempt to restore its reputation, the bank brought in a new chief executive, Frank Newman, in 1996. Mr. Newman, a well-respected former deputy secretary of the U.S. Treasury, quickly reached an out-of-court settlement with P&G and attempted to deemphasize the bank's trading activities.

The bank also recognized that its profit-driven culture often placed the bank's profit before the client's interest. Focusing on financial risks can become harmful only if it detracts from the client relationship, which is still an important part of the banking business. Bankers Trust later implemented changes in its compensation schemes to reward salespeople for improving relationships with customers. It also turned its risk-management savvy into new products, such as its RAROC 2020 system.

The new plan was to create a full-service investment bank serving growth companies in the U.S. market. The strategic transformation of Bankers Trust failed to take hold, however. By October 1998, the bank's stock price was back at its level of early 1996, underperforming its peer group. In November 1998, Bankers Trust announced it had agreed to an acquisition by the German behemoth Deutsche Bank. The price was right, at $9.2 billion, or 2.1 times Bankers Trust's book value.

---

cial losses, either attributed to derivatives or to hedge funds, regularly lead to threats of legislative intervention. The private sector has then to demonstrate that self-policing is preferable to new laws.

Regulatory risks are the result of changes in regulations or interpretation of existing regulations that can negatively affect a firm. For instance, as a result of the Bankers Trust case, the Commodities and Futures Trading Commission (CFTC) and Securities and Exchange Commission (SEC) have extended their jurisdiction over market participants by declaring swaps to be "futures contracts" and "securities," respectively. The bank agreed to pay $10 million to settle charges brought by regulators.

20.3 INTEGRATED RISK MANAGEMENT

The financial risk-management revolution is spreading well beyond market risk. Indeed, more and more companies are taking a comprehensive look at the risks they take. The goal of the new internal risk models is to incorporate business, event, and financial risks.

Enterprise-wide risk management (ERM), or integrated risk management, aims at measuring, controlling, and managing the overall risk of the institution across all risk categories and business lines. This is slowly made possible by a convergence in methods used to quantify financial risk.

20.3.1 Measuring Firm-Wide Risk

The first step is the measurement of overall risk. Once capital charges have been set up for the various classes of risk, the overall charge can be totted up from the various components. Figure 20–2 illustrates the process for financial risk, which consists of market/liquidity risk, credit risk, and operational risk. In theory, this process can be extended to all the other

FIGURE 20–2

Setting up a firm-wide charge for financial risks.

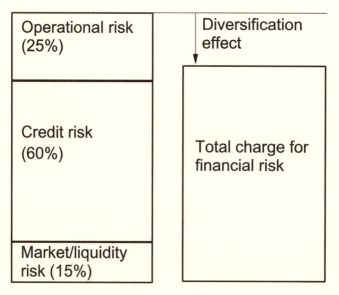

risks facing the institution. A key result is that the overall charge will be less than the total, due to diversification effects.

20.3.2 Controlling Firm-Wide Risk

The first benefit of firm-wide risk management is better control over global risks. This is becoming essential as businesses are becoming more complex, with more products that reach across various risk categories.

Financial institutions in particular are discovering complex and unanticipated interactions between their risks. Most disturbingly, it seems that risk has a way of moving toward areas where it is not well measured.

Attempts at controlling one type of risk often end up creating another one. The syndicated eurodollar loan, described in Box 3–3, provides an interesting illustration of how market risk can be transformed into credit risk. Banks made short-term dollar loans to Latin American countries that had no market risk but created credit risk. Box 20–3 also shows another important example of such interactions, sometimes called *wrong-way trades*.

B O X   20–3

WRONG-WAY TRADES

Wrong-way trades are those where credit and market risk amplify each other. An example is cross-currency swaps with Asian counterparties during the Asian currency crisis of 1997.

A number of Asian institutions had borrowed in U.S. dollars to take advantage of low nominal interest rates and to invest in the local currency, in particular the Thai baht or Korean won, at higher rates.

At initiation, the contracts had little market and credit risk. As the local economies deteriorated, however, these Asian currencies devalued sharply, creating large losses on the contracts. At the same time, most Asian institutions suffered large operating losses due to the contraction in local business activity.

This combination led to numerous defaults. Basically, this was due to the fact that the counterparties were using the swaps to speculate instead of hedging. Had they been hedging, losses on the contracts would have been offset by operating gains.

Similarly, the increasing practice of marking-to-market OTC swaps decreases credit risk, but at the expense of more frequent collateral payments that increase operational risk. Conversely, operational risks also can lead to market and credit risk. For example, an operational problem in a business transaction, such as a settlement "fail," can create market risk and credit risk, since the cost may depend on movements in market prices.

Finally, an increasing number of instruments now mix different types of risks. Credit derivatives, for instance, involve both market and credit risk. So do tradeable loans. These *risk interactions* create a need for integrated risk-management systems.

20.3.3 Managing Firm-Wide Risk: The Final Frontier

Integrated risk-management systems should allow institutions to manage their risk much better. Even if some risks are difficult to quantify, the process itself creates insights into a company's overall risk. This will create a better allocation of capital.

An immediate benefit of ERM is the discovery of *natural hedging*. Some firms have discovered that some risks offset each other. For instance, a California telecommunications company found that the losses of uninsured phone masts during a 1994 earthquake were offset by the increased call volume as worried families called relatives. Enron is selling weather derivatives, which cannot be hedged individually but rather are aggregated into the large pool of risks that the company manages. The company is also taking advantage of correlations between electricity and weather products. By now, there is a large market in electricity derivatives, which can be used to hedge weather products because their pricing is also affected by weather conditions.

Perhaps the most tangible benefit is *cost reduction* for insurance against firm-wide risks. By treating their risks as part of a single portfolio, institutions do not need to buy separate insurance against each type of risk, thereby taking advantage of diversification benefits.

Some companies have taken the cost saving one step further by cutting down on the purchase of external insurance. British Petroleum, for instance, after carefully reviewing its portfolio of risks, has decided to discontinue all purchase of external insurance, except when required by law. This saves a bundle in insurance premiums. In response, insurance companies are now developing ERM-based insurance products, as seen in Box 20-4.

B O X   20–4

MULTIPLE-RISK INSURANCE

The insurance industry is starting to respond to the threat of internal risk-management systems by creating contracts that provide coverage for a broad range of risks. Honeywell, the U.S. controls-technology company, entered in June 1997 a 3-year insurance program that covers currency risk along with property and liability coverage. Losses beyond $30 million a year are underwritten by AIG, the U.S. insurance giant. In the past, Honeywell had been hedging currency risks by using forwards and options contracts. By blending together these risks, Honeywell estimates that it saved at least 25 percent on annual premiums.

These programs, which are coming in vogue with CFOs anxious to stabilize corporate earnings, are also known as *holistic risk, enterprise risk,* and *insuritization risk.* This last term probably will take a while before being widely used. Also, since these insurance contracts embed some derivatives, they have been dubbed, less gracefully, "derivatives in drag."

Even more tangibly, centralized risk management can help to save transactions costs. Up to the mid-1990s, hedging systems consisted of focusing on sources of risk one at a time and perhaps covering risks individually. For instance, multinationals would evaluate their transaction risks in various currencies and hedge them individually. The problem with this approach is that it is inefficient because it ignores correlations that exist among financial variables. Transaction costs can be saved if the hedging problem is viewed on a company-wide basis.

20.4 WHY RISK MANAGEMENT?

Through better control of their risks, firm-wide risk management can help corporations stabilize their cash flows or earnings. The question is, Why bother?

20.4.1 Why Bother?

This is not as obvious as it seems, for in the absence of market "frictions," investors in corporations should be able to replicate whatever risk-management action the firm is taking. Hence it is not clear that risk management should add value. Indeed, the Modigliani-Miller (M-M) theorem (1958) states that under these conditions, the value of a firm should be

F I G U R E   20–3

VAR and corporate hedging.

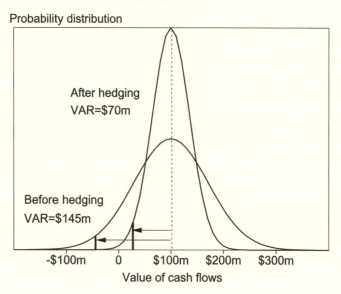

Probability distribution

After hedging
VAR=$70m

Before hedging
VAR=$145m

-$100m   0 $100m $200m $300m

Value of cash flows

unaffected by its financial policies. Thus risk management is supremely irrelevant.

We give the example of Mobil in Chapter 15. The company is heavily exposed to oil price risk. Investors, however, are perfectly aware of this. Some may even buy Mobil to acquire exposure to oil prices. Others may decide to cover the risk of their investment in Mobil by selling oil futures. Either way, it is not obvious that risk reduction at Mobil adds value to the firm.

To understand the effect of hedging with VAR, Figure 20–3 gives an example of cash-flow distributions. Without hedging, the 95 percent VAR is $145 million. If the firm decides to hedge with derivatives, VAR provides a consistent measure of the effect of hedging on total risk, including correlations. This is a significant improvement over traditional hedging programs, which typically focus on individual transactions only.

Assume, for instance, that the firm has decided to hedge with linear contracts, such as forwards or swaps. As shown in the figure, hedging narrows the distribution of cash flows. Say that, after hedging, the VAR number is reduced to $70 million. Even if hedging reduces risk, however, it does not change the mean of the distribution when the contracts are fairly priced. Thus, without market imperfections, hedging does not add value.

20.4.2 Why Hedge?

The real usefulness of the M-M theorem is not its conclusion of irrelevance but rather the focus it brings on market imperfections. Since then, finance researchers have identified conditions under which hedging, meaning activities that lower the volatility of cash flows or firm value, should add value.[1]

- *Hedging can lower the cost of financial distress.* As Figure 20–3 shows, hedging reduces the probability of unfavorable left-tail outcomes. This is valuable if financial distress has *deadweight costs,* such as legal fees and costs incurred because the firm cannot be managed efficiently when undergoing bankruptcy proceedings.[2] Some of these costs may take place earlier, as soon as a firm's situation becomes unhealthy. For example, potential customers may become reluctant to deal with an ailing firm, leading to lost business.

- *Hedging can lower taxes.* Greater earnings stability also can reduce average taxes paid when the firm's tax function is convex. Tax rates start at zero for negative incomes and then grow positive and higher for increasing levels of income.[3] The schedule of the tax authority is akin to a perpetual call option on profits. By lowering volatility, the firm can lower the value of this option, thereby enhancing firm value.

- *Hedging can lower agency costs.* Corporations can be viewed as delicate collections of contracts between stakeholders, such as shareholders, bondholders, and managers. Shareholders necessarily delegate decisions to managers. This, however, creates *agency costs,* due to the fact that the agents' interests (management) are not aligned with those of the shareholders. Some managers may be incompetent, wasting firm value. Shareholders,

---

1. Smithson's (1998) book provides a good survey of why firms should hedge. For a more systematic approach, see Stulz (2000).
2. Weiss (1990) finds that direct bankruptcy costs average about 3 percent of total assets.
3. With a convex tax function, taxes paid when income is really high are not offset by a tax refund when a loss is incurred (there may be limited carryforwards, however).

of course, are perfectly aware of this situation and are continually trying to assess the performance of managers, by watching earnings, for example. The problem is that earnings can fluctuate due to factors outside the control of the firm. By making earnings less volatile through hedging, risk management makes earnings more informative, which should lead to better performance assessment.

- *Hedging can facilitate optimal investment.* Some companies need steady cash flows to invest in research and development (R&D) programs. It would be impractical to cut down R&D programs whenever the firm incurred a temporary financial loss only to restart them later. Firms also may need cash to take advantage of new projects. In all these cases, companies could go to external markets, e.g., borrow funds from banks or bondholders to raise cash when needed. If, however, external financing proves more costly than internal sources of funds, hedging may add value to the firm.

These theories predict that hedging financial risks should add value to the firm. In addition, risk management should allow institutions to achieve better risk-return tradeoffs.

There is now tentative evidence that this is the case. Allayannis and Weston (2000) find that market valuations are higher for firms that make use of foreign currency derivatives to hedge. The value added is significant: Hedging firms have, on average, market values that are 4.9 percent higher than others. With a median market capitalization of $4 billion in their sample, this translates into an average value added of $200 million for each firm with a risk-management program. This is powerful evidence that risk management does increase shareholder value.

20.5 CONCLUSIONS

The last few years have been unusually rich in lessons for risk management. Mainly, we are learning that institutions should take a comprehensive approach to risk management. A piecemeal approach can miss significant risks or worse, push risks into places less visible, creating a misleading sense of safety.

In response, institutions have embarked on ambitious programs to quantify their financial risks systematically and comprehensively. The trend is toward combined capital charges for market, credit, and operational risks.

The bright side of this vast effort is a better understanding of risks facing institutions, leading to improved control and risk management. The trend toward firm-wide risk management brings substantial benefits. At a minimum, hedging costs can be lowered through pruning unnecessary transactions and taking advantage of diversification. Even more striking is the evidence that active firm-wide risk management can increase shareholder value substantially.

PART FIVE

The Risk-Management Profession

CHAPTER 21

Risk Management: Guidelines and Pitfalls

Risk management is asking what might happen the other 1 percent of the time.

Richard Felix, chief credit officer at Morgan Stanley

The impetus for today's risk-management industry can be traced to the financial disasters of the 1990s. While unfortunate, these derivatives disasters have led to useful lessons. If one document must be singled out as having shaped the risk-management profession, it must be the landmark review published by the Group of Thirty (G-30) in July 1993. The G-30 laid out a series of "best practices" that included measuring value at risk (VAR). These recommendations, however, have wider applicability than just derivatives and have become a benchmark for prudent management of all financial risks.

This chapter shows how the industry has responded to episodes of financial distress by periodically improving risk-management techniques and, sometimes belatedly, realizing their limitations. Some limitations are, or should be, obvious. Other side effects may be more subtle. Due to the complexity of the process leading to VAR, some users have a mistaken impression of absolute precision in the VAR number. This is not the case. VAR gives a first-order magnitude of financial risks and has, like all approximations, limitations. Users must be aware of these limitations when interpreting the data. The saga of Long-Term Capital Management (LTCM) is an example of what can happen to VAR models.

Section 21.1 summarizes milestone documents in risk management. Section 21.2 then discusses VAR limitations. It reviews standard drawbacks of VAR, which should be well recognized. These include the risk of exceptions, the risk of changing positions, event and stability risks, and model risks. Section 21.3 turns to more fundamental side effects with VAR. These are illustrated in the context of the Long Term Capital Management story in Section 21.4. Finally, Section 21.5 provides some concluding comments.

21.1 MILESTONE DOCUMENTS IN RISK MANAGEMENT

We now review the defining documents that shaped the risk-management profession. These include the 1993 Group of Thirty (G-30) recommendations for managing derivatives, the Bank of England report on the Barings failure, and the Counterparty Risk Management Policy Group Report on LTCM.

21.1.1 "Best Practices" Recommendations from G-30

The G-30 best practices report has been hailed as a milestone document for risk management. Initially developed to deal with derivatives, the G-30 recommendations, however, are much more general and truly apply to any investment portfolio.

The report provides a set of 24 sound management practices, the most important of which are summarized as follows (using the original G-30 numbering method):

1. *Role of senior management.* Policies governing derivatives should be clearly defined at the highest level.[1] Senior management should approve procedures and controls to implement these policies, which should be enforced at all levels. In other words, derivatives activities merit the attention of senior management because they can generate large profits or losses. Senior management, the board of directors, or the board of trustees is the first point of responsibility.

2. *Marking-to-Market.* Derivative positions should be valued at market prices, at least on a daily basis. This is the only valuation technique that correctly measures the current value of as-

---

1. Ignoring derivatives does not solve the problem, since companies have been sued for not using derivatives. In 1992, for instance, an Indiana grain co-op suffered losses when grain prices fell. The directors were sued and found liable for retaining a manager inexperienced in derivatives.

sets and liabilities. Marking-to-market should be implemented regardless of the accounting method used. Even firms that use accrual accounting should establish a separate set of books to measure market risks.

5. *Measuring market risk.* Dealers should use a consistent measure to calculate daily the market risk of their position, which is best measured with a *value-at-risk* (VAR) approach. Once a method of risk measurement is in place, market risk limits must be set based on factors such as tolerance for losses and capital resources.

6. *Stress simulations.* Users should quantify market risk under adverse market conditions. VAR systems usually are based on normal market conditions, which may not reflect potential losses under extreme market environments. Stress simulations should reflect both historical events and estimates of future adverse moves.

8. *Independent market risk management.* Dealers should establish market risk-management functions to assist senior management in the formulation and implementation of risk-control systems. These risk-management units should be set up with clear independence from trading and should have enforcement authority. They should establish risk-limit policies, measure value at risk, perform stress scenarios, and monitor whether actual portfolio volatility is in line with predictions.

10. *Measuring credit exposure.* Users should assess the credit risk arising from derivatives activities based on frequent measures of current and potential exposure. Current exposure is the market value, or replacement cost, of existing positions. Potential exposure measures probable future losses due to default over the remaining term of the transaction.

11. *Aggregating credit exposure.* Credit exposure to each counterparty should be aggregated taking into account netting arrangements. Credit risk can be reduced by broadening the use of multiproduct master agreements with closeout netting provisions.

12. *Independent credit risk management.* Users should establish oversight functions for credit risks with clear authority, independent of the dealing function. These units should set credit limits and monitor their uses.

16. *Professional Expertise.* Users should authorize only professionals with the requisite skills and experience to transact. These professionals include traders, supervisors, and those responsible for processing and controlling activities.

All these recommendations are still applicable. Nowadays, however, firms tend to integrate their market, credit, and operational risk functions due to the relationship between these risks.

21.1.2 The Bank of England Report on Barings

The Barings failure served as a powerful object lesson in risk management. By one estimate, Barings had ignored half the G-30 recommendations.

But new lessons also were learned from this fiasco. The Bank of England's report mentioned for the first time *reputational risk.* This relates to the risk to earnings arising from negative public opinion. Reputational risk can expose an institution to litigation or financial loss due to the disruption of relationships.

The report also identified several lessons from this disaster:

- *Management teams have a duty to understand fully the businesses they manage.* Top management at Barings did not have (or claimed so) a good understanding of Leeson's business, despite the fact that it was apparently creating huge profits for the bank.
- *Responsibility for each business activity must be clearly established.* Barings was using a "matrix" reporting system (by region and product) that left ambiguities in Leeson's reporting lines. These problems were compounded by the transition into a new organizational structure.
- *Clear segregation of duties is fundamental to any effective risk-control system.* Indeed, the failure has been ascribed to the fact that Leeson had control over both the front and back offices. The Barings affair demonstrated once and for all the need for independent risk management.

21.1.3 The CRMPG Report on LTCM

The Counterparty Risk Management Policy Group (CRMPG) was formed in the wake of the LTCM near failure to strengthen risk-management practices in the industry.[2] As with the G-30, this private-sector initiative also aimed at forestalling heavy-handed regulation of financial markets.

Indeed, the brokerage industry had come under fire for allowing LTCM to build up so much leverage. Chase Manhattan, for example, had a $3.2 billion exposure to LTCM, equivalent to 13 percent of the bank's equity. Apparently, much of this *current* exposure was collateralized, since the loans were marked-to-market. There was no margin, or haircut, though, to provide further protection. Had LTCM been forced into default, the *potential* credit exposure could have been quite large, with total losses to brokers estimated at up to $6 billion. Brokers had underestimated the interactions between credit risk, market risk, and liquidity risks.

In its defense, the brokerage industry argued that it did not have a complete picture of LTCM's positions, since the hedge fund maintained a religious secrecy about its positions, even to its own investors. Yet a report by the President's Working Group on Financial Markets (1999) found "serious weaknesses in how firms used what information they did have."

In response, the CRMPG report provides a set of recommendations, summarized as follows[3]:

1. *Information sharing.* Financial institutions that engage in dealings likely to entail significant credit exposures should assess capital conditions and market and liquidity risk of their counterparty. Since some of this information is considered confidential, institutions should have in place policies governing the use of proprietary information.

2. *Integrated view of risk.* Financial institutions should apply an integrated framework to evaluate market, liquidity, and credit risk, especially for highly leveraged counterparties.

3. *Liquidation-based estimates of exposure.* Institutions should measure their credit exposure not only using current exposure but also using potential exposure assuming liquidation of positions. This is especially important when exposures are large or illiquid.

4. *Stress testing.* Institutions should stress test their market and credit exposure, taking into account concentration risk to groups of counterparties and the risk that liquidating positions could move the markets.

---

2. The LTCM fiasco was followed by a flurry of reports, which are summarized in the International Monetary Fund (1999), Annex IV.

3. Parts of the CRMPG report that deals with liquidity risk are described in Chapter 14.

5. *Harmonization of documentation.* The report identified areas
for improvements in standard industry documents, which
should help to ensure that netting arrangements are carried out
in a timely fashion.

The appendices to the report provide an analytical framework for
evaluating the effects of leverage on market liquidity and credit risk.
Several measures are also proposed to evaluate funding liquidity risk,
some of which are explained in Chapter 14.

The LTCM affair has forced financial institutions to recognize that
credit risk and market risks are related. Indeed, a survey by Capital
Markets Risk Advisors revealed that the proportion of institutions having
integrated the two functions rose from 9 percent before 1998 to 64 percent after the crisis. Similarly, the number of firms making adjustments
for large or illiquid positions rose from 25 percent of respondents to 58
percent. Finally, many more institutions now perform systematic stress
tests. Thus the industry is belatedly learning from this episode and moving toward better risk-management practices.

21.2 LIMITATIONS OF VAR

Although VAR provides a first line of defense against financial risks, it
is no panacea. Users must understand the limitations of VAR measures.
These drawbacks can be classified into limitations of the system that are
(or should be) generally recognized and more fundamental criticisms,
which are explored in the next section.

21.2.1 Risk of Exceedences

The most obvious limitation of VAR is that it does not provide a measure of the absolute worst loss. VAR only provides an estimate of losses
at some confidence level. Hence there will be instances where VAR will
be exceeded. The lower the confidence level, the lower is the VAR measure, but the more frequently we should observe exceptions. This is why
backtesting is an essential component of VAR systems. It serves as a reminder that exceptions are expected to occur, hopefully at a rate that corresponds to the selected confidence level.

21.2.2 Changing Positions Risks

VAR also assumes that the position is fixed over the horizon. This also
explains why the typical adjustment from 1-day to multiple-day horizons

uses the square root of time factor. This adjustment, however, ignores the possibility that trading positions may change over time in response to changing market conditions.

There is no simple way to assess the effect of changing positions on the portfolio VAR, but it is likely that prudent risk-management practices create less risk than that measured by conventional VAR numbers. For instance, the enforcement of loss limits should gradually decrease the exposure as losses accumulate (assuming liquid markets). This is similar to a long position in an option, which can be dynamically replicated by buying more of the asset as its price moves up or selling as its price decreases. This dynamic trading pattern is thus similar to purchasing an option, which creates a skewed distribution with limited downside potential. It is also possible, however, as Barings has demonstrated, that traders who lose money increase their bets in the hope of recouping their losses.

21.2.3 Event and Stability Risks

Another drawback of VAR models based on historical data is that they assume that the recent past is a good projection of future randomness. As always, there is no guarantee that the future will not hide nasty surprises that did not occur in the past.

Surprises can take two forms, either one-time events (such as a devaluation or default) or structural changes (such as going from fixed to floating exchange rates). Situations where historical patterns change abruptly will cause havoc with models based on historical data.

In particular, changing correlation coefficients can lead to drastically different measures of portfolio risk. Recent work now extends portfolio optimization to scenarios where the market can be quiet, with normal correlation patterns, and more "hectic" periods, with correlations breaking down.[4]

Stability risk can be evaluated by *stress testing,* which aims at addressing the effect of drastic changes on portfolio risk. To some extent, structural changes also can be captured by models that allow risk to change through time or by volatility forecasts contained in options. An example of structural change is the 1994 devaluation of the Mexican peso, which is further detailed as follows.

---

4. See, for instance, Chow et al. (1999).

VAR and the Peso's Collapse

In December 1994, the emerging market play turned sour as Mexico devalued the peso by 40 percent. The devaluation was widely viewed as
bungled by the government and led to a collapsing Mexican stock market. Investors who had poured money into the developing economies of
Latin America and Asia faced large losses as the Mexican devaluation led
to a widespread decrease in emerging markets all over the world.

Figure 21–1 plots the peso/dollar exchange rate, which was fixed at
around 3.45 peso for most of 1994 and then jumped to 5.64 by mid-
December.

Apparently, the devaluation was widely unanticipated. This was despite a ballooning current account deficit running at 10 percent of
Mexico's GDP and a currency widely overvalued according to purchasing power parity. A conventional VAR system would not have anticipated
the magnitude of the devaluation. Based on an exponential volatility forecast, Figure 21–2 shows that the 35 percent devaluation was way outside
the 95 percent confidence band. After December, the forecasts seem to
capture reasonably well the turmoil that followed the devaluation. This
was poor solace for investors caught short by the devaluation.

FIGURE 21–1

Peso/dollar exchange rate.

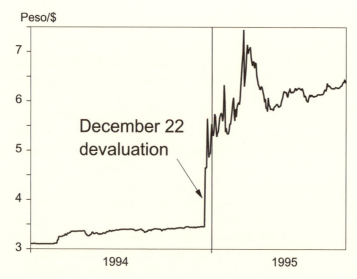

FIGURE 21–2

Peso/dollar volatility.

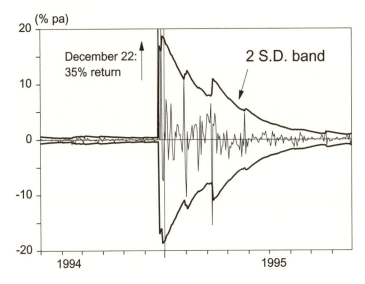

This episode indicates that especially when price controls are left in place for long periods, VAR models based on historical data cannot capture potential losses. These models must be augmented by an analysis of economic fundamentals and stress testing. Interestingly, shortly after the devaluation, the Mexican government authorized the creation of currency futures on the peso. It was argued that the existence of forward-looking prices for the peso would have provided market participants, as well as the central bank, an indication of market pressures. In any event, this disaster was not blamed on derivatives.

21.2.4 Transition Risk

Whenever there is a major change, a potential exists for errors. This applies, for instance, to organizational changes, expansion into new markets or products, implementation of a new system, or new regulations. Since existing controls deal with existing risks, they may be less effective in the transition.

Transition risk is difficult to deal with because it cannot be modeled explicitly. The only safeguard is increased vigilance in times of transition.

21.2.5 Data-Inadequacy Risks

Problem positions are in a category similar to transition. All the analytical methods underlying VAR assume that some data are available to measure risks. For some securities, such as infrequently traded emerging market stocks, private placements, initial public offerings, and exotic currencies, meaningful market-clearing prices may not exist, however.

Without adequate price information, risk cannot be assessed from historical data (not to mention implied data). Yet a position in these assets will create the potential for losses that is difficult to quantify. In the absence of good data, educated stress testing appears as the only available method to assess risks.

21.2.6 Model Risks

Model risk can be defined as the risk of loss occurring from the use of inappropriate models for valuing securities. This can result in misvaluation of the portfolio and hence of its risks. Model risk usually falls under the umbrella of operational risks.

Models are just abstractions of reality. As Emanuel Derman, head of quantitative strategies at Goldman Sachs, states, "A model is just a toy, though occasionally a very good one, in which case people call it a theory." Models can fail for a number of reasons: (1) the input data can be wrong, (2) the parameters of the model can be incorrectly estimated, (3) the model can be incorrect, and (4) the model can be incorrectly implemented. This taxonomy is presented in Figure 21–3, adapted from Crouhy et al. (1998). Each of these is now examined in turn.

Data Input Risk
Models rely on input data such as deal data and market data. At the most basic level, models can go wrong if the input data are flawed.

Estimation Risk
Errors in model outputs can be due to errors in inputs, even if the model is correct. For instance, the Black-Scholes model requires inputting the implied volatility. Using wrong values can lead to major losses, as shown in NatWest's case in Box 21–1.

Also known as *parameter risk,* this risk stems from the imprecision in the measurement of parameters from historical data. Even in a perfectly

FIGURE 21–3

Model risk.

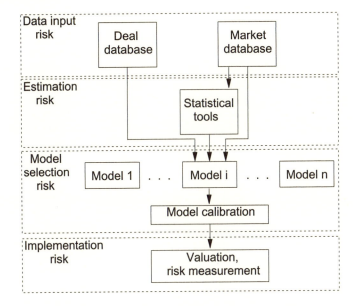

stable environment, we do not observe the true expected returns and volatilities. Thus some random errors are bound to happen just because of sampling variation.

One could formally assess the effect of estimation risk by replacing the sample estimates by values that are statistically "equivalent." An alternative method consists of sampling over different intervals. If the risk measures appear to be sensitive to the particular choice of the sample period, then estimation risk may be serious.

The problem of estimation risk is often ignored in VAR analyses. Users should realize the fundamental tradeoff between using more data, which leads to more precise estimates, and focusing on more recent data, which may be safer if risk changes over time.

Unfortunately, the data may not be available for very long periods. Only very limited histories are available, for instance, for emerging markets or exotic currencies. All the more reason to remember that VAR numbers are just estimates.

Even worse, the available histories may give a distorted picture of risk merely due to the *survival* of the series. Survivorship is an issue when

BOX 21-1

NATWEST'S MODEL RISK

On February 28, 1997, National Westminster Bank announced a loss of £77 million ($127 million) due to mispricing derivatives. This revelation was shocking because NatWest, the biggest bank in the United Kingdom, was assumed to have a sophisticated risk-management system. The size of its interest rate option book alone was enormous, £267 billion in 1996.

NatWest said that a junior interest rate trader, Kyriacos Papouis, "covered up losses and created false profits over a period of 2 years." The trader had been dealing in long-dated OTC interest rate options. Such options are used by companies, for instance, that borrow at a floating rate and purchase a "cap" on interest payments. Mr. Papouis would sell the cap and charge a premium presumably high enough to cover the bank's risk.

The difficulty lies in valuing these options when they are relatively illiquid. Valuing options essentially reduces to estimating their implied volatility, which is easy to do for liquid at-the-money options that have a ready market. For out-of-the-money options, however, estimating volatility involves extrapolation.

Mr. Papouis calculated the price of these options by feeding his own estimates of volatility. Apparently, he overestimated the volatility and thus the model value of the options he had been selling, creating fictitious profits that built up over time. In addition, losses were concealed by unauthorized transfers. This was convenient, because large profits translated into large bonuses.

To get an idea of the effect of mispricing, consider a typical £1 million 3-month cap starting in 1 year with a cap rate 1 percent higher than the current rate. Using Black's model, the value of this cap is £520 with a 20 percent volatility. With a 25 percent volatility, the value grows to £805. Assuming that these prices are representative and extrapolating the difference to a £267 billion portfolio create an error of £76 million, on the order of the reported loss.

NatWest was relying primarily on its internally developed system. As a backup system, it also used the Oberon software, developed by Lombard Risk Systems. The source of the problem, however, was not in the analytics but in the model inputs. It is not clear why NatWest's risk managers accepted the trader's volatility estimates. Observers have speculated that the bank's culture made it difficult for financial controllers to question what traders were doing. One even said, "Little squirts in the middle office earning £20,000 a year don't stand in the way of a producer earning £200,000 or £2 million." This incident reflected badly on controls at the bank. Six managers resigned. Martin Owen, the chief executive of NatWest Markets, initially announced that he would give up £200,000 from his £500,000 bonus. He resigned soon thereafter.

This episode has been largely interpreted as an illustration of model risk due to faulty input data. Top management also failed to instill a culture of independent checks and balances in the capital markets group.

an investment process only considers series, markets, stocks, bonds, or contracts that are still in existence. The problem is that assets that have fared badly are not observed. Analyses based on current data therefore tend to project an overly optimistic image or display certain characteristics.

Survivorship effects are akin to the "peso problem" in the foreign exchange market. Before the devaluation of 1982, the Mexican peso was selling at a large discount in the forward market (the forward price of the peso was well below the price for current delivery). This discount rationally anticipated a possible devaluation of the peso. An observer analyzing the discount before 1982 would have concluded that the market was inefficient. The failure, however, was not that of the market but rather of the observer, who chose a sample period where the data did not reflect any probability of a devaluation.

More generally, unusual events with a low probability of occurrence but severe effects on prices, such as defaults, wars, or nationalizations, are not likely to be well represented in samples and may be totally omitted from survived series. Unfortunately, these unusual events are very difficult to capture with conventional risk models.

Model-Selection Risk

Most people interpret model risk as model-selection risk. This is the form of model risk that most observers refer to. Valuation errors can arise if the particular functional form chosen for valuing a security is incorrect.

The Black-Scholes model, for instance, relies on a rather restrictive set of assumptions (geometric brownian motion, constant interest rates, and volatility). For conventional stock options, departures from these assumptions may not be consequential.

However, there are situations where the model is totally inappropriate, such as options on short-term interest rate instruments. For these, one needs to model an interest rate process first, perhaps with a one-factor model. The option value can then be estimated by numerical or analytical models, when possible. But again, what may be satisfactory for these instruments may not be appropriate for another class of options, such as options on the slope of the term structure, which require more richness in the dynamics of interest rates.

Model risk also grows more dangerous as the instrument becomes more complicated. Pricing CMOs requires heavy investments in the development of models, which may prove inaccurate under some market conditions.

The model can be incorrect due to *data mining,* a most insidious form of risk. This occurs when various models are reviewed and only the one that gives good results is reported. This is particularly a problem with nonlinear models (such as neural-network models), which involve searching not only over parameter values but also over different functional forms.

Data mining also consists of analyzing the data until some significant relationship is found. Take, for instance, an investment manager who tries to find "calendar anomalies" in stock returns. The manager tries to see if stock returns systematically differ across months, weeks, days, and so on. So many different comparisons can be tried that in 1 case out of 20 one would expect to find "significant" results at the usual 5 percent level. Of course, the results are only significant because of the search process that discards nonsignificant models. Data-mining risk manifests itself in overly optimistic simulation results. Often, results break down outside the sample period because they are fallacious.

Data mining risks can be best addressed by running *paper portfolios,* where an objective observer records the decisions and checks how the investment process performs on actual data.

Implementation Risk

Even if the model and its parameters are correct, implementation may be fraught with problems. With numerical methods, for instance, the solution may be badly approximated. Bugs can creep into the software and hardware. Even with the same program, *user risk* arises when different users obtain different solutions.

Some of this risk is a direct result of the model approximation. For instance, regression models never produce a perfect fit. Predictions will then inevitably produce some errors, which can create significant hedging risks.

To get a sense of the magnitude of these problems, Marshall and Siegel (1997) surveyed 10 vendors of VAR software. The vendors were asked to report VAR numbers for standardized portfolios using the RiskMetrics approach. Table 21–1 reports the variations in vendor's estimates.

For the portfolio of forwards, for example, the median VAR across vendors was $425,800, with a standard deviation of $4800. This range is quite narrow, since it represents only 1 percent of the median. The narrow range reflects the fact that forward contracts are easy to map and are linear in the risk factors.

TABLE 21-1

Implementation Risk

				Portfolio			
	Forwards	Money Market	FRAs	Global Bonds	Interest Rate Swaps	FX Options	Interest Rate Options
Notional (gross)	$130 million	$46 million	$375 million	$350 million	$311 million	$374 million	$327 million
1-day 95% VAR:							
Median	$425,800	$671,300	$79,000	$3,809,100	$311,100	$804,200	$416,700
SD	$4,800	$60,700	$7,500	$652,800	$66,600	$198,800	$115,200
Ratio (SD/Med.)	1%	9%	10%	17%	21%	25%	28%

As the products become increasingly more complicated, however, there is less agreement in VAR numbers. The most complicated products are interest rate options (caps and floors), which are nonlinear and require modeling the term structure and its dynamics. Here, the standard deviation of VAR is 28 percent of the median. Model risk is greatest for the most complicated instruments.

There is no easy solution to model risk. As the industry moves toward more complex models, there is also a greater risk of mistakes. This is why modeling has become multidisciplinary and requires a good understanding of the process, from model development to coding and user interface. Modelers, programmers, and users need to work together to minimize model risk.

21.3 SIDE EFFECTS OF VAR

21.3.1 The "Man in the White Coat" Syndrome

It has been argued that the widespread use of VAR is not only useless but even harmful because it gives a false impression of accuracy. Hence the "man in the white coat," which refers to what has been called a misguided scientific approach to risk measurement.

This criticism of VAR is developed in Box 21–2, where Nassim Taleb, a veteran options trader, discusses his view of VAR.

The gist of this argument is that VAR is useless because it is not perfect, unlike measures in the physical sciences. As discussed in the preceding section, VAR is indeed not perfect. There is no way to provide an estimate of the absolute worst outcome, since the tails of continuous probability distributions are theoretically unlimited. Nor should we expect, however, an institution to be protected against all possible losses. In defense of VAR, one might argue that our world is constructed by engineers, not physicists. This is why engineering has been described as the "art of the approximation." The same definition may apply to VAR, one of the tools used by "financial engineers."

Admittedly, risk managers must be aware of the limitations of VAR. It also behooves them to avoid creating an impression of undue precision when discussing VAR. Observers who claim risk management to be a "science" do a disservice to the profession. Risk management is much more an art form than a science.

BOX 21–2

NASSIM TALEB'S ASSAULT ON VAR

Derivatives Strategy. *What do you think of value at risk?**

VAR has made us replace about 2500 years of market experience with a covariance matrix that is still in its infancy. We made *tabula rasa* of years of market lore that was picked up from trader to trader and crammed everything into a covariance matrix. Why? So that a management consultant or an unemployed electrical engineer can understand financial market risks.

To me, VAR is charlatanism because it tries to estimate something that is not scientifically possible to estimate, namely, the risks of rare events. It gives people misleading precision that could lead to the buildup of positions by hedgers. It lulls people to sleep. All that because there are financial stakes involved.

To know the VAR, you need the probabilities of events. To get the probabilities right you need to forecast volatility and correlations. I spent close to a decade and a half trying to guess volatility, the volatility of volatility, and correlations, and I sometimes shiver at the mere remembrance of my past miscalculations. Wounds from correlation matrices are still sore.

Derivatives Strategy. *Proponents of VAR will argue that it has its shortcomings but it's better than what you had before.*

That's completely wrong. It's not better than what you had because you are relying on something with false confidence and running larger positions than you would have otherwise. You're worse off relying on misleading information than not having any information at all. If you give a pilot an altimeter that is sometimes defective, he will crash the plane. Give him nothing and he will look out the window. Technology is only safe if it is flawless.

**©Derivatives Strategy* (January 1997), reprinted with kind permission. The magazine followed up this interview with the "Jorion-Taleb" (April 1997) debate on the pros and cons of VAR.

21.3.2 Traders Gaming the System

A potentially more serious danger of VAR systems is that it could induce traders to try to "game" the system. If a risk manager uses a VAR system for risk control or performance evaluation, traders may have an incentive to evade their risk limits. This is what Bob Kopprasch, of Salomon Smith Barney, has called VAR arbitrage.

VAR arbitrage

The deliberate creation of risky trades that appear to be low risk in a VAR framework.

For instance, traders could move into markets or securities that appear to have low risk for the wrong reasons. Currency traders could take large positions in pegged currencies, which have low historical volatility but high devaluation risk.

Historical simulation methods also create problems. For instance, if the window is very short, a dropoff day can create a VAR measure of risk that is predictably lower than the true or implied risk. Traders could then arbitrage by going long the asset and short options. If the window is too long, it will be slow to respond to increases in the true risk. Traders could then arbitrage in the same fashion.

Analytical methods also may invite option trades. Traders exposed to a delta-normal VAR could take short straddles with zero delta (like Barings's Leeson). Such positions appear profitable, but only at the expense of future possible losses that may not be captured by VAR. More generally, a trader may be aware of measurement errors in the covariance matrix used to judge him or her. If so, he or she may overweight assets that have low estimated risk, knowing full well that this will result in a downward-biased risk measure.

Ju and Pearson (1999) provide estimates of this potential bias, assuming *normal* distributions. Suppose a trader is subject to a constraint on estimated VAR. If the trader knows the true covariance matrix, he or she will try to maximize the expected return on the position subject to this constraint. The true VAR, however, will be higher than the estimated VAR. Table 21–2 shows the ratio of true VAR to the estimated VAR for various number of observations (T) and number of assets (N). For instance, with 100 days and 50 assets, the true VAR is 201 percent, or twice the estimated VAR. The bias increases as the number of assets increases relative to the number of observations, reflecting increased measurement error in the covariance matrix.

With an exponential model for forecasting risk, the number of effective observations is quite small, leading to very serious biases. With a decay factor of 0.94 and 50 assets, the true VAR is nearly 5 times the estimated VAR. This explains why the Basel Committee disallows the use of such models and requires a long period for the estimation of VAR.

In the context of portfolio management, gaming by traders can be compared with the general problem of in-sample portfolio optimization,

TABLE 21-2

Bias in VAR: Ratio of True to Estimated VAR

	Number of Assets (N)			
Model	10	20	50	100
Moving-average:				
50	123%	164%		
100	110%	124%	201%	
200	105%	111%	133%	199%
1000	101%	102%	105%	111%
Exponential	135%	185%	485%	2174%

Note: The table reports the mean ratio of true VAR to estimated VAR assuming that the trader knows the true covariance matrix and maximizes expected return subject to a constraint on VAR. Because the trader may not know the true matrix, these numbers represent worst-case estimates of the bias. The exponential model uses 100 data points and a decay factor of 0.94.

Source: Adapted from Ju and Pearson (1999).

which is well known to create biased views of risk. This danger lies in relying on the same covariance matrix (i.e., in-sample) to perform the portfolio optimization and to measure risk.[5]

This behavior can be even more dangerous in the presence of *options,* or asymmetrical return distributions. Basak and Suleyman (1999) analyze the optimal behavior of managers subject to VAR limits and find that these managers incur large losses when losses occur. A manager with a 95 percent VAR limit of $10 million, for instance, may choose positions with losses that exceed VAR only 5 percent of time, but by a very large amount. In essence, the problem is that this simple VAR limit does not distinguish between expected losses beyond VAR of $20 million or $100 million. This simply reflects the fact that quantile-based measures are not "coherent," as we saw in Chapter 5. The solution is to look not only at one quantile but also at the whole distribution. Alternatively, the risk manager could compute the expected loss conditional on exceeding VAR.

---

5. Michaud (1989), for instance, argues that mean variance optimizers are in effect "error maximizers" when using historical data. In other words, the optimizer will overweight assets with high recent average returns, whereas most of this performance may simply reflect luck. Derman is also skeptical of optimization, because it "tends to accentuate" much of the misspecification.

This is indeed a serious issue with VAR systems. This is why risk management is not simply a black box but a dynamic process where a competent risk manager must be aware of the human trait for adaptation.

21.3.3 Dynamic Hedging

Some take a more extreme view of the effects of risk-management systems. The argument is that "attempts to measure risk in financial markets may actually be making them riskier."[6]

Take, for instance, another high-tech computer-driven portfolio management technique, portfolio insurance. *Portfolio insurance* was developed in the mid-1980s as an application of the Black-Scholes model, which showed that a position in an option is equivalent to a dynamically adjusted position in the underlying asset. Hence the idea of replicating a long protective put strategy simply by buying "delta" of the asset. Variations in delta are such that as the asset falls in price, one would need to sell more of the asset to provide the protection.

In practice, these abstract models totally ignore liquidity. The problem is that as one starts selling large amounts in a falling market, the strategy can exacerbate price swings, thus amplifying volatility. Indeed, portfolio insurance has been widely blamed for having triggered the stock market crash of October 1987.[7] Note that the problem does not arise from automatic trading per se but rather from the practice of placing large sell orders in a falling market. More primitive trend-following systems, which have been used for a long time, also can be described as "destabilizing" speculation.

A similar argument has been made with VAR systems. Supposedly, VAR systems encouraged banks to take on bigger risks due to the "false sense of precision." Then, as volatility spiked up after the Russian default in August 1998, driving VAR higher, risk managers faced with binding VAR-based capital requirements could either increase the amount of capital or cut the size of positions.[8] The claim is that the widespread reduction of positions by the banking sector in 1998 reduced liquidity further.

---

6. See, for instance, *The Economist:* "Risk Management: Too Clever by Half" (November 14, 1998), and "The Price of Uncertainty" (June 12, 1999).

7. See the Brady Report (1989).

8. On the other hand, the market risk charge adjusts slowly to increased volatility, as shown in Chapter 3. It is set at the maximum of three times the average VAR over the last 60 days and yesterday's VAR. Hence we would need a rather drastic movement for yesterday's VAR to become binding. As for the first term, a temporary spike in volatility would be diluted through the 60-day averaging.

These arguments are hard to verify, since they are based primarily on anecdotal evidence. They also reflect different interpretations of these events. Large price changes can be due to reassessment of economic fundamentals or to failures in the market-making function due to the volume of trading. We do know that after the Russian default of 1998, there was a broad-scale reassessment of credit risk across global markets. And once the extent of LTCM's problems became public, it was not clear that financial intermediaries would be able to weather an outright default by LTCM. This uncertainty was one of the causes of the widening of credit spreads that ensued. Thus the volatility of market could have been due to fundamentals.

Despite the turmoil of 1998, the market risk-management systems of financial institutions seemed to have worked better than expected. As Howard Davies (1999), chairman of the United Kingdom's Financial Services Authority put it,

> It is fair to say . . . that—overall—financial institutions in the developed world survived the turmoil of '97 and '98 remarkably well. So their risk management systems cannot have been as bad as all that.

Indeed, the Basel Committee (1999c) surveyed the performance of 40 banks during the second half of 1998. The report showed that although some banks experienced "yellow zone" exceptions, i.e., 5 to 10 exceptions in a 250-day period, none suffered a trading loss that exceeded its capital requirement. A few banks had large trading losses, but none was seriously threatened. Considering the turbulence of 1998, this is a remarkable achievement. In other times and other countries, such events would have wiped out a few banks.

21.4 RISK-MANAGEMENT LESSONS FROM LTCM

21.4.1 LTCM's Risk Controls

The story of LTCM provides useful risk-management lessons.[9] As described in Chapter 14, the core strategy of LTCM consisted of convergence-arbitrage trades, trying to take advantage of small differences in prices among near-identical bonds. Compare, for instance, a corporate bond yielding 7.5 percent and an otherwise identical Treasury bond with

---

9. This section is based on Jorion (1999).

a yield of 6 percent. The yield spread of 1.5 percent represents some compensation for credit risk, including an actuarial expected loss and some risk or liquidity premium. In the absence of default, a trade that is long the corporate bond and short the Treasury bond would be expected to return 1.5 percent. In the short term, the position will be even more profitable if the yield spread narrows further. The key is that eventually the two bonds must converge to the same value. Most of the time, this will happen, barring a default or market disruption.

The problem with such strategy is that it only provides tiny returns. Thus the portfolio had to be leveraged to create the 30 to 40 percent returns investors were hoping for. However, without some constraint on risk, leverage could become immense.

LTCM chose to limit its risk by targeting a level of volatility similar to that of an unleveraged position in U.S. equities, i.e., about 15 percent per annum. Applying this number to an equity base of $4.7 billion, we find a monthly dollar volatility of 4700×15 percent$/\sqrt{12} = \$204$ million. In other words, the positions were allocated so as to maximize expected returns subject to the constraint that the fund's perceived risk was no greater than that of the stock market. At least, in theory.

21.4.2 Portfolio Optimization

To understand how portfolio optimization was used to set up LTCM's positions, this section presents a stylized example based on mean-variance optimization with two highly correlated assets. We use a government and a corporate bond portfolio series and assume the investor maximizes expected returns subject to the constraint that the annual volatility is 15 percent.

Table 21–3 presents a worked-out example of a portfolio optimization with two risky assets, a BAA-rated corporate bond series and a Treasury-note series. The data are taken from the 5-year period 1993–1997, using yields as estimates of expected returns. Note that the two bonds have very high correlation, at 0.9654. Expected returns are simply taken as yields on December 1997. With a credit yield spread of 1.53 percent and no allowance for defaults, the optimization should identify an "arbitrage" strategy.

Indeed, the portfolio takes a very large position in the corporate bond, $10.5 for every $1 of equity, offset by a large short position of $8.3 in the Treasury bond. The sum of the bond positions is $2.2, which implies

TABLE 21–3

Portfolio Optimization with Two Assets

Input Data	Corporate Bond	Treasury Bond	Risk-Free Asset
Expected return-yield (%pa)	7.28%	5.75%	5.36%
Volatility of return (%pa)	5.47%	6.58%	
Correlation	0.9654		
Output data			
Position (for $1 equity)	$10.5	−$8.3	−$1.2

Optimal Portfolio	Monthly	Annual
Expected return	1.9%	22.2%
Volatility of return	4.3%	15.0%

a loan of $1.2 at the risk-free rate. The expected return on the portfolio is 1.9 percent per month, which translates into 22 percent per annum. This optimization is illustrated in Figure 21–4.

This simple exercise captures the essence of LTCM's so-called arbitrage strategy. The leverage ratio is very high, above 10, which leads to a high expected return of 22 percent. What is the problem with this strategy?

For every dollar invested, the annual volatility is supposed to be 15 percent, assuming the correlation stays at the high level of $\rho = 0.9654$. The problem is that this high number is likely to have been measured with some error, probably positive. In addition, the correlation may change over time, more likely down because it is already so high.

The issue is the sensitivity of the estimate of the portfolio risk to changes in this crucial parameter, the correlation coefficient. This stress-testing exercise is performed in Figure 21–5, which examines changes in the portfolio volatility as the correlation coefficient decreases.

We start with a volatility of 15 percent for the estimated correlation of 0.965. If the correlation drops to 0.80, however, the portfolio volatility rises sharply, to 36 percent.

In fact, this correlation, which had been high in the recent past, dropped sharply to 0.80 in 1998, explaining why the convergence strategy suddenly went bad. Indeed, the portfolio returns were −$325 million in May, −$440 million in June, and −$1,850 million in August. It was

FIGURE 21–4

Portfolio optimization.

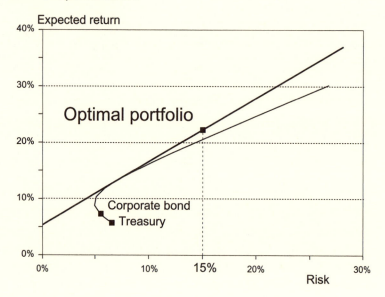

FIGURE 21–5

Effect of changing correlation on portfolio risk.

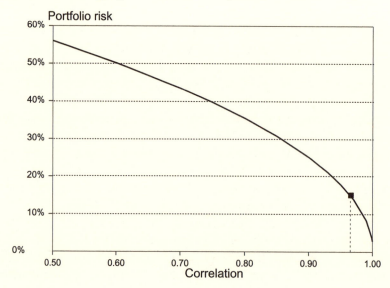

unlikely that these numbers could have resulted from a distribution with a volatility of $204 million.

More likely, the portfolio risk had been underestimated, due to biases from portfolio optimization. As this exercise demonstrated, risk measures derived from an optimization are extremely sensitive to errors in input parameters.

21.4.3 LTCM's Short Option Position

In addition, the payoff profile of LTCM was strongly asymmetrical. The fund took large positions in interest rate swaps. Up to 1998, swap spreads had sharply narrowed. As a result, the distribution of these spreads had to be strongly asymmetric, since swap spreads cannot go below zero. Thus LTCM was exposing itself to large losses in case of spreads widening.

LTCM also had taken a position in Russian bonds and other emerging market debt. These provide high yields, but at the expense of a possibility of a large loss in case of default. Again, the distribution is asymmetrical.

LTCM also had short positions in option-implied volatilities. Volatilities are asymmetrically distributed, since they cannot go below zero but can increase greatly. Here again, the distribution is asymmetric.

To make it even worse, the LTCM portfolio also was exposed to liquidity risk, due to its huge size. As we learned from Chapter 14, liquidity is positively correlated with volatility.

All these positions added up to a rather undiversified portfolio with a distribution strongly skewed to the left, as shown in Figure 21–6. Based on history up to 1997, the 95 percent portfolio VAR would have been about minus 5 percent. Instead, the portfolio delivered several very large negative returns, culminating in an 80 percent loss in September of 1998.

Overall, the near failure of LTCM can be ascribed to inappropriate use of risk-management tools. LTCM was not diversified in terms of strategy. Its payoff profile was strongly asymmetric, like a short position in a gigantic option, invalidating the use of volatility as a measure of risk. When positions involve infrequent events, risk cannot be measured from recent data only. All these mistakes explain why LTCM's performance turned from stellar to disastrous in short order.

Overall, the LTCM episode was an aberration. It was the largest hedge fund in the industry by far, with an unprecedented leverage. It was so big that like a wounded tanker heading for a reef, it was unable to

FIGURE   21–6

Distribution of LTCM's monthly returns.

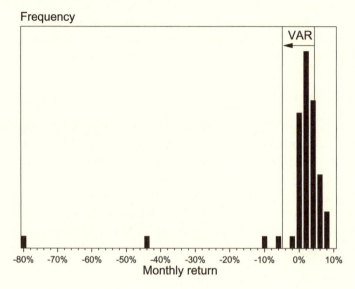

alter its positions after having lost half its capital. Hopefully, financial institutions and regulators will have learned their lesson and not allow this
disaster to happen again.

21.5 CONCLUSIONS

While current risk-management practices represent a huge step forward
from unbridled risk-taking, the experiences of the last few years have shown
that we still have much to learn in the application of risk-management
models.

In particular, users should beware of limitations of VAR measures.
VAR measures do not attempt to pinpoint the worst loss. The expectation
is that they will be exceeded regularly. VAR also typically assumes some
stability in the portfolio composition and, if based on historical data, in
the risk measures. Finally, VAR is subject to model risk, which involves
the choice of models, of parameters, and their implementation.

VAR systems also may have more subtle, and perhaps dangerous,
side effects. The technique may give users a false sense of accuracy, lulling
portfolio managers into taking bigger positions than they might otherwise.

Traders also may attempt to game the system, exploiting flaws in VAR risk measures. Sometimes, as we have seen in the extreme case of LTCM, this involves positions equivalent to large sales of options, providing regular profits at the expense of being exposed to rare but huge losses.

This is why risk management will never be a science. Instead, it should be viewed as an evolving art form where we still have much to learn. We did learn that risk management should promote a comprehensive approach to risk. Otherwise, a piecemeal approach can miss significant risks or worse, create a misleading sense of safety. As we have seen, ideally, we should measure market, credit, operational, and hopefully other risks in a comprehensive fashion. We also learned that formal risk-management models cannot substitute for judgment and experience.

As James Leach (1998), chairman of the House Banking and Financial Services Committee that conducted hearings on the LTCM affair, put it,

> The fact that [modern financial engineering] failed does not mean that the science of risk management is wrong-headed; just that it is still an imperfect art in a world where the past holds lessons but provides few reliable precedents.

CHAPTER 22

Conclusions

[Risk managers] . . . The New Emperors of Wall Street.

Risk Magazine, *March 1999*

The risk-management industry has truly experienced a revolution since the early 1990s. Once the domain of a few exclusive pioneers, risk management is now wholly embraced by the financial industry. It is also spreading fast among the corporate world. As a result, the financial risk-manager function is now acquiring strategic importance within the corporate structure. Risk managers must be proficient in an amazing variety of topics, ranging from the practical knowledge of financial markets to derivatives pricing, probability, and even actuarial insurance modeling.

An essential part of their tool kit is value at risk (VAR). VAR provides a forward-looking view of a portfolio's overall risk. The strength of VAR is that it assigns a probability boundary to a dollar amount of loss occurring. VAR provides a prospective measure of a portfolio's risk profile determined in a comprehensive and consistent fashion. By now, VAR is widely used to quantify and control price risk. Some firms also use it as the basis for the allocation of capital. The VAR methodology is now even being extended to other forms of risk besides market risk, i.e., credit risk and operational and liquidity risk.

Without a doubt, the impetus behind the growth of the risk-management industry was the series of derivatives debacles of the 1990s. At that time, it seemed that the technology behind the creation of ever-more complex financial instruments had advanced faster than our ability to control it. This has been in large part corrected by risk-management techniques, which give users a better understanding of financial instruments.

Another major factor behind the advent of risk management is the perverse incentive structure or moral hazard problem. Profit-based compensation, as well as government insurance schemes, create incentives to take on extra risk, in some cases unwarranted risks. Risk management has grown as a counterbalancing factor to such problems.

But the explosive growth in risk management simply could not have evolved from these essentially defensive applications. The industry now realizes that risk management is a centerpiece of all financial market activity. Risk management, which grew up on a desk-by-desk basis, is now applied at the level of the whole corporation.

This chapter provides some concluding thoughts on VAR and risk management. Section 22.1 reflects on the evolution of risk management, which evolved from accrual methods to marking-to-market to VAR measures to optimization. Section 22.2 then discusses the newly established position of risk manager. Finally, Section 22.3 provides concluding comments on VAR.

22.1 THE EVOLUTION OF RISK MANAGEMENT

The steps leading us to VAR provide an interesting reflection on the evolution of modern financial management, as described in Figure 22–1.

VAR's antecedents can be traced to asset/liability management systems in place in the 1980s. At the time, banking institutions carried most of their financial assets and liabilities on the balance sheet using *accrual methods;* i.e., transactions were booked at historical costs with adjustments for accruals. Some items, such as those held for the purpose of trading, were carried at market values.

The problem was that these accounting methods insulated the value of balance sheet items from their economic reality. Sometimes, forecasts of future rates were used to project income over long periods, in a manner somewhat similar to what we describe as *scenario analysis.* Such accounting methods contributed to the great savings and loan debacle because it allowed institutions to present balance sheets that were in accordance with accounting rules but were hiding large losses.

Later, with the trend toward mark-to-market, some balance sheets started to be reported at market values. Once market values are available, the next logical step is to assess risk. A simple method for computing VAR, for instance, consists of keeping track of the market value of all securities over a selected time interval, which gives an idea of the possible range of values for a trading portfolio. Thus the combination of positions,

FIGURE 22–1

Modern financial management.

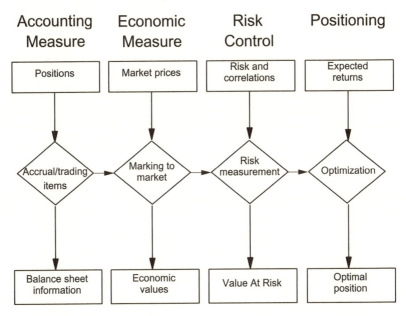

marking-to-market, and fluctuations in market values naturally leads to the concept of value at risk (VAR).

The next step consists of using the risk-control system as a feedback mechanism to evaluate business units. VAR provides a framework to compare the profitability of various operations on a risk-adjusted basis. Firms can then make informed decisions about maintaining or expanding lines of business or whether to hedge financial risks at the firm level.

More generally, optimization makes the best use of return forecasts, combined with risk and correlations, to find the set of portfolios or businesses that provide the best tradeoff between risk and return. Thus risk management is now poised to take full advantage of Markowitz's portfolio theory.

22.2 THE ROLE OF THE RISK MANAGER

22.2.1 Controlling Trading

The impetus behind the rise of the risk manager was the realization of the perverse effects of compensation incentives. On the one hand, profit-based

compensation pushes traders to do their very best and weeds out inefficient ones. On the other hand, the design of contracts with risk-taking
agents gives them incentives to engage in activities that may not be in the
best interest of their firm.

One of the lessons of these many financial disasters is the fundamental asymmetry, or convex profit pattern, in payoffs to traders. Absent
fraud, a losing bet just means a lost job and some reputational damage.
In contrast, a winning bet can lead to lifetime wealth.

Senior management in financial institutions is coming to realize that
the negative effects of these convex patterns should be offset by some
concave functions of profits. This can take the form of risk-based adjustment, such as RAROC, or by hiring risk managers. Obviously, the decision to implement risk-management systems must come from the top of
the institution.

22.2.2 Organizational Guidelines

Senior managers bear a particular responsibility because they define objectives, procedures, and controls. They also can foster safe or unsafe environments, through the choice of organizational structure.

Risk-management practices vary widely. As described in Table 22–1,
less advanced companies may operate a credit risk committee only and
generally aggregate their risks at the business level only. More advanced
institutions have global risk committees for credit and market risk and use
quantitative measures of risk.

TABLE 22–1

Risk-Management Practices

Stage of Development	Risk Policy Committees	Aggregation Level	VAR Analysis
Leaders	Integrated credit, market, and operational	Company-wide	Yes
Followers	Credit, yes Market, sometimes Operational, no	Business unit level	Sometimes
Laggards	Credit risk only	None	No

F I G U R E   22–2

Organizational structure for risk management.

Generally, banks in industrialized countries appear to have the most developed risk-management systems. For a while, U.S. commercial banks actually were ahead of U.S. investment banks in terms of global risk-management practices, somewhat perversely due to the imposition of strict capital requirements by regulators.

Figure 22–2 describes one implementation of a control model. The key to this flowchart is that the risk-management unit is independent of the trading unit. Risk managers should not report to anybody whose compensation is linked to the success of a trading unit but rather should report directly to top management. Also, the compensation of risk managers and auditors cannot be associated with how well traders perform. In this structure, each unit has segregated duties and no overlapping management at lower levels. This provides for a system of checks and balances.

The implementation of risk-management systems is spreading slower than one would wish, however, particularly outside industrialized markets. Besides the cost and intellectual development needed to develop the technological support for risk management, there is often a conflict of culture between the trading area and traditional bankers. Whereas most traders typically are well versed in derivatives pricing and attendant risk measures, traditional loan officers are often less familiar with these concepts. The challenge is to convince the whole organization of the benefits from better control and pricing of risks. Faster-moving financial markets, regulatory pressure, and lessons from recent financial disasters should all prod global banking into better management of financial risks. Clearly, the impetus for change must come from the top of the institution.

22.2.3 Risk Managers

Unfortunately, there is a great temptation to cut corners on risk management and controls. Unlike traders, these units do not contribute directly to the bottom line of the firm. Jobs in back and middle offices are unglamorous jobs. In particular, risk managers serve a function similar to *selling an option:* At best, nothing happens; at worst, they fail to detect a problem, and they may be out of a job. This is the opposite of traders, for whom the performance bonus link is similar to *buying an option.*

Risk managers are a special breed.[1] They must be thoroughly familiar with financial markets, with the intricacies of the trading process, and with financial and statistical modeling. Box 22–1 describes the profile of a well-known risk manager.

Risk managers must be attentive to details, because they continually put their reputations on the line. To be effective, they need to develop positive relationships with traders, convincing them of the usefulness of active risk management. As we have seen in Chapter 7, the VAR methodology also can assist portfolio managers in making strategic decisions by measuring the impact of a trade on portfolio risk. While traders are paid to take bets in various markets, it is certainly less intuitive to estimate the marginal contribution to risk. The challenge for risk managers is to convince traders that risk management can help them too.

Yet risk managers cannot receive huge bonuses as traders do. Their compensation is a delicate issue. Institutions that try to skimp on the remuneration of back- and middle-office personnel will fail to attract qualified staff. A recent G-30 survey, for instance, finds that there is "some concern that the development of staff in support areas lags behind."

This is where senior management again plays an important role. Strong internal controls are in the best interests of the institution, since perceptions of a counterparty's integrity are vital to the continuous flow

---

1. For interesting views, see Shirreff (1998), "The Rise and Rise of the Risk Manager," and Dunbar (1999), "The New Emperors of Wall Street."

BOX 22-1

PROFILE OF A RISK MANAGER

Lev Borodovsky's career illustrates how a background in finance and mathematics can lead to a senior risk-management function.* His family emigrated from Tashkent, Uzbekistan, into the United States in 1978, when he was fourteen. With a strong background in mathematics, Mr. Borodovsky's went to the University of Oklahoma to study physics.

By the time he graduated, in 1986, the oil and defense industries were in a slump, so he looked for a job on Wall Street. He landed his first position at J.P. Morgan, where he developed a commodity derivatives system. Four years later he moved to Crédit Suisse, where he became global head of foreign exchange and money market risk management, directing 60 people.

In the spring of 1996, Borodovsky and Marc Lore, who was also working at Crédit Suisse First Boston, decided to set up an industry association, the *Global Association of Risk Professionals* (GARP), initially run by volunteers only. What seemed to be a far-fetched idea at the time developed into the voice of the global financial risk-management community, with over 10,000 members in more than 90 countries.

Lev Borodovsky's view of risk management is "You don't want the decimal point—you want the order of magnitude."

---

*See also *Risk Professional* (March 1999).

of business. Effective oversight also reduces the likelihood that an institution will be exposed to litigation, financial loss, or reputational damage. The spectacular failures of institutions that lacked internal controls should serve as a powerful object lesson in the need for risk management.

Risk managers now have increasing responsibilities in the best institutions. No longer perceived as ex-traders tired of their job, they are given the power to allocate capital and, in some cases, even trader bonuses. As Box 22–2 shows, they are now viewed as crucial to the survival of the institution.

22.3 VAR REVISITED

The history of finance is littered with financial disasters. These expensive lessons have led the industry to adopt VAR as a universal benchmark for managing financial risk. VAR integrates market risk across all assets,

BOX 22–2

RISK MANAGEMENT AT CHASE

Chase Manhattan was one of the few U.S. banks that emerged relatively unscathed from the summer of 1998. The bank had lost $78 million in the fourth quarter of 1997, due to the Asian crisis. While not life-threatening, this loss prodded the bank into augmenting its risk-management system with stress testing.

In particular, the stress tests allowed the bank to evaluate a scenario where credit spreads—then at historical lows—would widen again. The bank positioned its portfolio accordingly and suffered minimal losses despite a hectic summer. Marc Shapiro, Chase's vice chairman and head of risk management, is convinced that the market risk team "saved the bank from disaster."

---

derivatives, stocks, bonds or commodities. As we have seen, VAR also can be adapted to account for credit risk, liquidity risk, and operational risk.

Admittedly, VAR is no panacea. As we have seen, VAR makes no attempt to measure the losses beyond the specified limit. Even with a 99 percent confidence interval, unusual events happen, and they sometimes do so with a vengeance. Historical-based methods also have shortcomings. This is why VAR must be augmented by stress testing, which aims at assessing the effect of unusual market conditions. While VAR techniques are firmly grounded on a scientific basis, their interpretation remains more of an art than a science.

Thus VAR should be considered only as a first-order approximation. The fact that the value is generated from a statistical method should not hide the fact that it is only an estimate. Users should not be lulled into a state of complacency but rather recognize the limitations of VAR, which have been amply documented in this book. As Steven Thieke, chairman of J.P. Morgan's risk-management committee says, "There has to be a point where this stops being a risk measurement methodology and becomes a management issue—what is the level of experience of the people in this business, and the firm's tolerance for risk."

Appropriate use of VAR, however, may have avoided some of the spectacular debacles of recent years, where investors had, or claimed to have, no idea of their exposure to financial risks. In addition, the implementation of VAR forces integration of the front office (trading desk), of the back office, and of a newly created middle office, which performs a risk-management function. This integration, although not necessarily easy in terms of logistics, has the side benefit that it provides some protection against operational risk and is the only consistent approach to credit risk measurement.

This explains why VAR has become the new benchmark for managing financial risks. But clearly, the process of getting to VAR is as important as the number itself.

REFERENCES

Alexander, Carol, 1998, "Volatility and Correlation: Measurement, Models and Applications," in Alexander, C., ed., *Risk Management and Analysis,* Wiley, Chichester, England.

Allayannis, George, and James Weston, 2000, "The Use of Foreign Currency Derivatives and Firm Market Value," *Review of Financial Studies* (forthcoming).

Almgren, Robert, and Neil Chriss, 1999, "Optimal Execution of Portfolio Transactions," working paper, University of Chicago, Chicago.

Artzner, Philippe, Freddy Delbaen, Jean-Marc Eber, and David Heath, 1999, "Coherent Measures of Risk," *Mathematical Finance* 9 (July), 203–228.

Bair, S., and S. Milligan, 1996, "Voluntary Efforts to Provide Oversight of OTC Derivatives Activities," in Klein, R., and J. Lederman, eds., *Derivatives Risk and Responsibility,* Irwin, Chicago.

Bangia, Anil, Frank Diebold, Til Schuermann, and John Stroughair, 1999, "Liquidity on the Outside," *Risk* 12 (June), 68–73.

Bank of England, 1995, *Report of the Board of Banking Supervision Inquiry into the Circumstances of the Collapse of Barings,* HMSO Publications, London.

Basak, Suleyman, and Alex Shapiro, 1999, "Value-at-Risk Based Risk Management: Optimal Policies and Asset Prices," working paper, Wharton School, University of Pennsylvania, Philadelphia.

Basel Committee on Banking Supervision, 1988, *International Convergence of Capital Measurement and Capital Standards,* BIS, Basel, Switzerland.

Basel Committee on Banking Supervision, 1995a, *An Internal Model-Based Approach to Market Risk Capital Requirements,* BIS, Basel, Switzerland.

Basel Committee on Banking Supervision, 1995b, *Public Disclosure of the Trading and Derivatives Activities of Banks and Securities Firms,* BIS, Basel, Switzerland.

Basel Committee on Banking Supervision, 1995c, *Basel Capital Accord: Treatment of Potential Exposure for Off-Balance-Sheet Items,* BIS, Basel, Switzerland.

Basel Committee on Banking Supervision, 1996a, *Supervisory Framework for the Use of "Backtesting" in Conjunction with the Internal Models Approach to Market Risk Capital Requirements,* BIS, Basel, Switzerland.

Basel Committee on Banking Supervision, 1996b, *Amendment to the Basel Capital Accord to Incorporate Market Risk,* BIS, Basel, Switzerland.

Basel Committee on Banking Supervision, 1998a, *Framework for the Evaluation of Internal Control Systems,* BIS, Basel, Switzerland.

Basel Committee on Banking Supervision, 1998b, *Amendment to the Basel Capital Accord of July 1988,* BIS, Basel, Switzerland.

Basel Committee on Banking Supervision, 1998c, *Enhancing Bank Transparency,* BIS, Basel, Switzerland.

Basel Committee on Banking Supervision, 1998d, *Operational Risk Management,* BIS, Basel, Switzerland.

Basel Committee on Banking Supervision, 1999a, "Capital Requirements and Bank Behaviour: The Impact of the Basel Accord," working paper, BIS, Basel, Switzerland.

Basel Committee on Banking Supervision, 1999b, *Credit Risk Modelling: Current Practices and Applications,* BIS, Basel, Switzerland.

Basel Committee on Banking Supervision, 1999c, *A New Capital Adequacy Framework,* BIS, Basel, Switzerland.

Basel Committee on Banking Supervision, 1999d, *Performance of Models-Based Capital Charges for Market Risk: 1 July–31 December 1998,* BIS, Basel, Switzerland.

Basel Committee on Banking Supervision, 1999e, *Recommendations for Public Disclosure of Trading and Derivatives Activities of Banks and Securities Firms,* BIS, Basel, Switzerland.

Basle Committee on Banking Supervision, 1994, *Risk Management Guidelines for Derivatives,* BIS, Basel, Switzerland.

Bates, D., 1995, "Testing Option Pricing Models," *NBER Working Paper* 5129, Cambridge, Mass.

Baumol, William, 1963, "An Expected Gain-Confidence Limit Criterion for Portfolio Selection," *Management Science* 11, 174–182.

Beder, T., 1995, "VAR: Seductive But Dangerous," *Financial Analysts Journal* 51, 12–24.

Beder, Tanya, Michael Minnich, Hubert Shen, and Jodi Stanton, 1998, "Vignettes on VAR," *Journal of Financial Engineering* 7 (September), 289–309.

Berkowitz, Jeremy, 2000, "A Coherent Framework for Stress Testing," *Journal of Risk* 2 (Winter), 5–15.

Bickel, P., and D. Freedman, 1981, "Some Asymptotic Theory for the Bootstrap," *The Annals of Statistics* 9, 1196–1271.

Black, F., 1976, "The Pricing of Commodity Options," *Journal of Financial Economics* 3, 167–179.

Black, F., and M. Scholes, 1973, "The Pricing of Options and Corporate Liabilities," *Journal of Political Economy* 81, 637–659.

Blejer, Mario, and Liliana Schumacher, 1999, "Central Bank Vulnerability and the Credibility of Its Commitments: A Value-at-Risk Approach" *Journal of Risk* 2 (Fall), 37–55.

Bliss, Robert, and David Smith, 1998, "The Elasticity of Interest Rate Volatility," *Journal of Risk* 1 (Fall), 21–46.

Blume, M., and D. Keim, 1991, "Realized Returns and Defaults on Low-Grade Bonds: The Cohort of 1977 and 1978," *Financial Analysts Journal* 47, 63–72.

Board of Governors of the Federal Reserve System, 1995, *Request for Comment on the Pre-Commitment Approach for Market Risks,* Board of Governors of the Federal Reserve System, Docket No. R-0886, Washington, D.C.

Bollerslev, T., 1986, "Generalized Autoregressive Conditional Heteroskedasticity," *Journal of Econometrics* 31, 307–327.

Bollerslev, T., R. Chou, and K. Kroner, 1992, "ARCH Modelling in Finance: A Review of the Theory and Empirical Evidence," *Journal of Econometrics* 52, 5–59.

Bookstaber, Richard, 1997, "Global Risk Managment: Are We Missing the Point?" *Journal of Portfolio Management* 23 (Spring), 102–107.

Boudoukh, J., M. Richardson, R. Stanton, and R. Whitelaw, 1995, "A New Strategy for Dynamically Hedging Mortgage-Backed Securities," *Journal of Derivatives* 2 (Summer), 60–77.

Boudoukh, Jacob, Matthew Richardson, and Robert Whitelaw, 1998, "The Best of Both Worlds," *Risk* 11 (May), 64–67.

Boyle, P., 1977. "Options: A Monte Carlo Approach," *Journal of Financial Economics* 4, 323–338.

Boyle, Phelim, Mark Broadie, and Paul Glasserman, 1997, "Monte Carlo Methods for Security Pricing," *Journal of Economic Dynamics and Control* 21, 1267–1321.

Brady Report, 1989, "Presidential Task Force on Market Mechanisms," in *Black Monday and the Future of Financial Markets,* Irwin, Homewood, Ill., pp.127–203.

Bralver, C., and A. Kuritzkes, 1993, "Risk Adjusted Performance Measurement in the Trading Room," *Journal of Applied Corporate Finance* 6, 104–108.

Brennan, M., and E. Schwartz, 1979, "A Continuous-Time Approach to the Pricing of Bonds," *Journal of Banking and Finance* 3, 133–155.

Brinson, Gary, Randolph Hood, and Gilbert Beebower, 1986, "Determinants of Portfolio Performance," *Financial Analysts Journal* 51 (July), 39–72.

Brinson, Gary, Brian Singer, and Gilbert Beebower, 1991, "Determinants of Portfolio Performance II: An Update," *Financial Analysts Journal* 47 (May), 40–48.

Butler, J. S., and Barry Schachter, 1998, "Estimating Value at Risk with a Precision Measure by Combining Kernel Estimation with Historical Simulation," *Review of Derivatives Research* 1, 371–390.

Campa, José Manuel, and Kevin Chang, 1998, "The Forecasting Ability of Correlations Implied in Foreign Exchange Options," *Journal of International Money and Finance* 17, 855–880.

Caouette, John, Edward Altman, and Paul Narayanan, 1998, *Managing Credit Risk: The Next Great Financial Challenge,* Wiley, New York.

Ceske, Robert, and José Hernandez, 1999, "Operational Risk: Where Theory Meets Practice," *Risk* (November), S17–20.

Chow, George, Eric Jacquier, Marc Kritzman, and Kenneth Lowry, 1999, "Optimal Portfolios in Good Times and Bad," *Financial Analysts Journal* 55 (May), 65–73.

Christoffersen, P. F., 1998. "Evaluating Interval Forecasts," *International Economic Review* 39, 841–862.

Considine, Jill, 1998, "Pilot Exercise—Pre-Committment Approach to Market Risk," *FRBNY Economic Policy Review* (October), 131–136.

Cooper's & Lybrand, 1996, *Generally Accepted Risk Principles,* Cooper's & Lybrand, London.

Counterparty Risk Management Policy Group, 1999, *Improving Counterparty Risk Management Practices,* CRMPG, New York. At www.counterparty.org.

Cox, J., S. Ross, and M. Rubinstein, 1979, "Option Pricing: A Simplified Approach," *Journal of Financial Economics* 7, 229–263.

Cox, J., J. Ingersoll, and S. Ross, 1985, "A Theory of the Term Structure of Interest Rates," *Econometrica* 53, 385–407.

Crnkovic, Cedomir, and Jordan Drachman, 1996, "Quality Control," *Risk* 9, 139–143.

Crouhy, Michel, Dan Galai, and Robert Mark, 1998, "Key Steps in Building Consistent Operational Risk Measurement and Management," in *Operational Risk and Financial Institutions,* Risk Books, London.

Crouhy, Michel, Stuart Turnbull, and Lee Wakeman, 1999, "Measuring Risk-Adjusted Performance," *Journal of Risk* 2 (Fall), 1–31.

Cruz, Marcelo, Sydney Coleman, and Gerry Salkin, 1998, "Modeling and Measuring Operational Risk," *Journal of Risk* 1 (Fall), 63–72.

Culp, C., and J. Overdahl, 1996, "An Overview of Derivatives: Their Mechanics, Participants, Scope of Activity, and Benefits," in Kirsch, C., ed., *Financial Services*

2000 A.D.: The Dissolving Barriers Among Banks, Mutual Funds and Insurance Companies, Irwin, Chicago.

Culp, C., and M. Miller, 1995, "Metallgesellschaft and the Economics of Synthetic Storage," *Journal of Applied Corporate Finance* 7 (Winter), 62–76.

Danielsson, Jon, and Casper de Vries, 1997, "Value-at-Risk and Extreme Returns," *LSE Financial Markets Group Discussion Paper 273,* London School of Economics.

Davanzo, Lawrence E., and Stephen Nesbitt, 1987, "Performance Fees for Investment Management," *Financial Analysts Journal* 43 (January), 14–20.

Davies, Howard, 1999, "Remarks at the IMF/World Bank Seminar: Dealing with Volatility: The Role of Risk Management," Financial Services Authority, London.

De Grauwe, Paul, 1997, *The Economics of Monetary Integration,* Oxford University Press, New York.

Derivatives Policy Group, 1995, *A Framework for Voluntary Oversight,* Derivatives Policy Group, New York.

Derman, Emanuel, 1996, "Valuing Models and Modeling Value," *Journal of Portfolio Management* 22 (Spring), 106–114.

Dimson, Elroy, and Paul Marsh, 1995, "Capital Requirements for Securities Firms." *Journal of Finance* 50, 821–851.

Dornbusch, Rudiger, 1998a, "Capital Controls: An Idea Whose Time Is Gone," working paper, Massachusetts Institute of Technology, Cambridge, Mass. At www.mit.edu/rudi/.

Dornbusch, Rudiger, 1998b, "After Asia: New Directions for the International Financial System," working paper, Massachusetts Institute of Technology, Cambridge, Mass. At www.mit.edu/ rudi/.

Duan, J.-C., 1995, "The GARCH Option Pricing Model," *Mathematical Finance* 5, 13–32.

Duffie, D., and M. Huang, 1996, "Swap Rates and Credit Quality," *Journal of Finance* 51, 921–949.

Dunbar, Nicholas, 1999, "The New Emperors of Wall Street," *Risk* 12 (March), 26–33.

Efron, B., 1979, "Bootstrap Methods: Another Look at the Jackknife," *The Annals of Statistics* 7, 1–26.

Embrechts, P., Claudia Klupperlberg, and Thomas Mikosch, 1997, *Modelling Extremal Events for Insurance and Finance,* Springer, Berlin, Germany.

Engle, R., 1982, "Autoregressive Conditional Heteroskedasticity with Estimates of the Variance of United Kingdom Inflation," *Econometrica* 50, 987–1007.

Engle, R., and C. Granger, 1991, *Long-Run Economic Relationships,* Oxford University Press, New York.

Engle, R., D. Lilien, and R. Robins, 1987, "Estimating Time-Varying Risk Premia in the Term Structure: The ARCH-M Model," *Econometrica* 55, 391–407.

Estrella, A., D. Hendricks, J. Kambhu, S. Shin, and S. Walter, 1994, "The Price Risk of Options Positions: Measurement and Capital Requirements," *Federal Reserve Bank of New York Quarterly Review* 19, 27–43.

European Union, 1989, *Council Directive 89/647/EEC of 18 December 1989 on a Solvency Ratio for Credit Institutions,* EU, Brussels. At europa.eu.int/eur-lex/en/lif/dat/1989/en_389L0647.html.

European Union, 1993, *Council Directive 93/6/EEC of 15 March 1993 on the Capital Adequacy of Investment Firms and Credit Institutions,* EU, Brussels. At europa.eu.int/eur-lex/en/lif/dat/1993/en_393L0006.html.

European Union, 1979, *Council Directive 79/267/EEC of 5 March 1979 on the Coordination of Laws, Regulations and Administrative Provisions Relating to the Taking Up and Pursuit of the Business of Direct Life Assurance,* EU, Brussels. At europa.eu.int/eur-lex/en/lif/dat/1979/en_379L0267.html.

FSA Informal Working Party, 1999, *Allocating Regulatory Capital for Operational Risk,* Financial Services Authority, London. At www.fsa.gov.uk.

Financial Accounting Standards Board, 1998, *Statement No. 133: Accounting for Derivative Instruments and Hedging Activities,* FASB, Norwalk, Conn.

Finnerty, J., 1988, "Financial Engineering in Corporate Finance: An Overview," *Financial Management* 17, 14–33.

Fisher, L., 1966, "An Algorithm for Finding Exact Rates of Return," *Journal of Business* 39, 111–118.

French, K., W. Schwert, and R. Stambaugh, 1987, "Expected Stock Returns and Volatility," *Journal of Financial Economics* 19, 3–29.

Froot, K., and J. Stein, 1998, "Risk Management, Capital Budgeting and Capital Structure Policy for Financial Institutions: An Integrated Approach," *Journal of Financial Economics* 47, 55–82.

Garman, Mark, 1996, "Improving on VAR," *Risk* 9 (May), 61–63.

Garman, Mark, 1997, "Taking VAR to Pieces," *Risk* 10 (October), 70–71.

General Accounting Office, 1994, *Financial Derivatives: Actions Needed to Protect the Financial System,* U.S. GAO, Washington, D.C. At www.gao.gov/reports.htm.

General Accounting Office, 1996, *Financial Derivatives: Actions Taken or Proposed Since May 1994,* U.S. GAO, Washington, D.C. At www.gao.gov/reports.htm.

General Accounting Office, 1998, *Risk-Based Capital: Regulatory and Industry Approaches to Capital and Risk,* U.S. GAO, Washington, D.C. At www.gao.gov/reports.htm.

Giovannini, A., and P. Jorion, 1989, "The Time-Variation of Risk and Return in the Foreign Exchange and Stock Markets," *Journal of Finance* 44, 307–325.

Glasserman, Paul, Philip Heidelberger, and Perwez Shahabuddin, 1999, "Variance Reduction Techniques for Estimating VAR," working paper, Columbia University, New York.

Gluck, J., 1996, "Measuring and Controlling the Credit Risk of Derivatives," in Klein, R., and J. Lederman, eds., *Derivatives Risk and Responsibility,* Irwin, Chicago.

Gnedenko, B. V., 1943, "Sur la Distribution Limite du Terme Maximum d'une Série Aléatoire," *Annals of Mathematics* 44, 423–453.

Golub, Bennett and Leo Tilman, 2000, *Risk Management: Approaches for Fixed-Income Markets,* Wiley, New York.

Gordy, Michael, 2000, "A Comparative Anatomy of Credit Risk Models," *Journal of Banking and Finance* 24, 119–149.

Greenspan, Alan, 1996, "Remarks at the Financial Markets Conference of the Federal Reserve Bank of Atlanta," Board of Governors of the Federal Reserve System, Washington, D.C.

Grinold, Richard, and Andrew Rudd, 1987, "Incentive Fees: Who Wins? Who Loses?" *Financial Analysts Journal* 43 (January), 27–38.

Group of Thirty, 1993, *Derivatives: Practices and Principles,* Group of Thirty, New York.

Harlow, W., 1991, "Asset Allocation in a Downside Risk Framework," *Financial Analysts Journal* 47 (September), 28–40.

Heath, David, Robert Jarrow, and Andy Morton, 1992, "Bond Pricing and the Term Structure of Interest Rates: A New Methodology," *Econometrica* 60, 77–105.

Heston, S., 1993, "A Closed-Form Solution for Options with Stochastic Volatility with Applications to Bond and Currency Options," *The Review of Financial Studies* 6, 327–343.

Hsieh, D., 1988, "The Statistical Properties of Daily Foreign Exchange Rates: 1974–1983," *Journal of International Economics* 24, 129–145.

Hull, John, 2000, *Options, Futures, and Other Derivatives,* Prentice-Hall, Upper Saddle River, N.J.

Hull, John, and Alan White, 1998, "Incorporating Volatility Updating into the Historical Simulation Method for Value-at-Risk," *Journal of Risk* 1 (Fall), 5–19.

International Swap and Derivatives Association, 1995, *Public Disclosure and Risk Management Activities Including Derivatives,* ISDA, New York. At www.isda.com.

International Swap and Derivatives Association, 1998, *Credit Risk and Regulatory Capital,* ISDA, New York. At www.isda.com.

International Monetary Fund, 1999, *International Capital Markets,* IMF, Washington, D.C. At www.imf.org.

Jackson, Patricia, David Maude, and William Perraudin, 1997, "Bank Capital and Value-at-Risk," *Journal of Derivatives* 4 (Spring), 73–90.

James, Chris, 1996, "RAROC-Based Capital Budgeting and Performance Evaluation: A Case Study of Bank Capital Allocation," working paper, Wharton Financial Institutions Research Center, Philadelphia, PA.

Jameson, Rob, 1998a, "Operational Risk: Playing the Name Game," *Risk* (October), 38–42.

Jameson, Rob, 1998b, "Operational Risk: Getting the Measure of the Beast," *Risk* (November), 38–41.

Jamshidian, Farshid, and Yu Zhu, 1997, "Scenario Simulation: Theory and Methodology," *Finance and Stochastics* 1 (January), 43–68.

J.P. Morgan, 1995, *Riskmetrics Technical Manual,* J.P. Morgan, New York.

Jordan, J., and G. Morgan, 1990, "Default Risk in Futures Markets: The Customer-Broker Relationship," *Journal of Finance* 45, 909–933.

Jorion, Philippe, 1989, "Asset Allocation with Hedged and Unhedged Foreign Stocks and Bonds," *Journal of Portfolio Management* 15 (Summer), 49–54.

Jorion, Philippe, 1995a, "Predicting Volatility in the Foreign Exchange Market," *Journal of Finance* 50, 507–528.

Jorion, Philippe, 1995b, *Big Bets Gone Bad: Derivatives and Bankruptcy in Orange County,* Academic Press, San Diego, Calif.

Jorion, Philippe, 1996, "Risk^2: Measuring the Risk in Value-at-Risk," *Financial Analysts Journal* 52 (November), 47–56.

Jorion, Philippe, 1997, *Value at Risk: The New Benchmark for Controlling Market Risk,* McGraw-Hill, New York.

Jorion, Philippe, 1999, "Risk Management Lessons from Long-Term Capital Management," mimeo, University of California at Irvine. At www.gsm.uci.edu/~jorion.

Ju, Xiongwei, and Neil Pearson, 1999, "Using Value-at-Risk to Control Risk Taking: How Wrong Can You Be?" *Journal of Risk* 1, (Winter) 5–36.

Kendall, M., 1994, *Kendall's Advanced Theory of Statistics,* Halsted Press, New York.

Klein, R., and J. Lederman, 1996, *Derivatives Risk and Responsibility,* Irwin, Chicago.

Koyluoglu, Ugur, and Andrew Hickman, 1999, "Reconcilable Differences," in *Credit Risk: Models and Management,* Risk Publications, London.

Kritzman, Mark, 1987, "Incentive Fees: Some Problems and Some Solutions," *Financial Analysts Journal* 43 (January), 21–26.

Kupiec, Paul, 1995, "Techniques for Verifying the Accuracy of Risk Measurement Models," *Journal of Derivatives* 2 (December), 73–84.

Kupiec, Paul, 1998, "Stress Testing in a Value at Risk Framework," *Journal of Derivatives* 6 (Fall), 7–24.

Kupiec, Paul, 1999, "Risk Capital and VAR," *Journal of Derivatives* 7 (Winter), 41–52.

Kupiec, Paul, and James O'Brien, 1995, "A Pre-Commitment Approach to Capital Requirements for Market Risk," *FEDS Working Paper No. 95-34,* Federal Reserve Board, Washington, D.C.

Kupiec, Paul, and James O'Brien, 1997, "The Pre-Commitment Approach: Using Incentives to Set Market Risk Capital Requirements," *FEDS Working Paper No. 97-14,* Federal Reserve Board, Washington, D.C.

Lawrence, Colin, and Gary Robinson, 1997, "Liquidity, Dynamic Hedging and Value at Risk," in *Risk Management for Financial Institutions,* Risk Publications, London, pp. 63–72.

Leach, James, 1998, *The Failure of Long-Term Capital Management: A Preliminary Assessment,* House Banking and Financial Services Committee, Washington, D.C.

Leeson, Nicholas, 1996, *Rogue Trader: How I Brought Down Barings Bank and Shook the Financial World,* Little, Brown, Boston, Mass.

Lev, Baruch, 1988, "Toward a Theory of Equitable and Efficient Accounting Policy," *Accounting Review* 63 (January), 1–22.

Linsmeier, Thomas, and Neil Pearson, 1997, "Quantitative Disclosures of Market Risk in the SEC Release," *Accounting Horizons* 11 (March), 107–135.

Litterman, Robert, 1996, *Hot Spots and Hedges,* Goldman Sachs, New York.

Longin, François, 1996, "The Asymptotic Distribution of Extreme Stock Market Returns," *Journal of Business* 69, 383–408.

Longin, François, 2000, "From Value at Risk to Stress Testing: The Extreme Value Approach," *The Journal of Banking and Finance* 24, 1097–1130.

Longin, François, and B. Solnik, 1995, "Is the Correlation in International Equity Returns Constant, 1960–1990?" *Journal of International Money and Finance* 14, 3–26.

Lopez, José, 1999, "Regulatory Evaluation of Value-at-Risk Models," *Journal of Risk* 1 (Winter), 37–63.

Macaulay, F., 1938, *Some Technical Problems Suggested by the Movements of Interest Rates, Bond Yields and Stock Prices in the United States Since 1856,* National Bureau of Economic Research, New York.

McNeil, Alexander, 1999, "Extreme Value Theory for Risk Managers," in *Internal Modelling and CADII,* Risk Publications, London, pp. 93–113.

McNeil, Alexander, and R. Frey, 1998, "Estimation of Tail-Related Risk Measures for Heteroscedastic Financial Time Series: An Extreme Value Approach," working paper, ETH, Zurich.

Margrabe, W., 1978, "The Value of an Option to Exchange One Asset for Another," *Journal of Finance* 33, 177–186.

Markowitz, H., 1952, "Portfolio Selection," *Journal of Finance* 7, 77–91.

Markowitz, H., 1959, *Portfolio Selection: Efficient Diversification of Investments,* Wiley, New York.

Marshall, Chris, and Michael Siegel, 1997, "Value At Risk: Implementing a Risk Measurement Standard," *Journal of Derivatives* 4, 91–110 .

Matten, Chris, 1996, *Managing Bank Capital: Capital Allocation and Performance Measurement,* Wiley, Chichester, England.

Merton, R., 1973, "Theory of Rational Option Pricing," *Bell Journal of Economics and Management Science* 4, 141–183.

Merton, R., 1974, "On the Pricing of Corporate Debt: The Risky Structure of Interest Rates," *Journal of Finance* 29, 449–470.

Merton, R., and P. Samuelson, 1974, "Fallacy of the Log-Normal Approximation to Portfolio Decision-Making Over Many Periods," *Journal of Financial Economics* 1, 67–94.

Michaud, Richard, 1989, "The Markowitz Optimization Enigma: Is Optimized Optimal?," *Financial Analysts Journal* 45, 31–42.

Miller, M., 1986, "Financial Innovations: The Last Twenty Years and the Next," *Journal of Financial and Quantitative Analysis* 21, 459–471.

Modigliani, Franco, and Merton Miller, 1958, "The Cost of Capital, Corporation Finance and the Theory of Investment," *American Economic Review* 48, 261–297.

Mood, Alexander, Franklin Graybill, and Duane Boes, 1974, *Introduction to the Theory of Statistics,* Wiley, New York.

Moro, B., 1995, "The Full Monte," *Risk* 8 (February), 57–58.

Muralidar, Arun, and Ronald Van Der Wouden, 2000, "Optimal ALM Strategies for Defined Benefit Pension Plans," *Journal of Risk* 2 (Winter), 47–69.

Nelson, C., and A. Siegel, 1987, "Parsimonious Modelling of Yield Curves," *Journal of Business* 60, 473–490

Nelson, D., 1990, "ARCH Models as Diffusion Approximations," *Journal of Econometrics* 45, 7–38.

Office of the Comptroller of the Currency, 1993, *Banking Circular BC-277: Risk Management of Financial Derivatives,* Comptroller of the Currency, Washington, D.C.

Ong, Michael, 1999, *Internal Credit Risk Models,* Risk Publications, London.

Overdahl, J., and B. Schachter, 1995, "Derivatives Regulation and Financial Management: Lessons from Gibson Greetings," *Financial Management* 24, 68–78.

Papageorgiou, A., and S. Paskov, 1999, "Deterministic Simulation for Risk Management," *Journal of Portfolio Management* (May), 122–127.

Parkinson, M., 1980, "The Extreme Value Method for Estimating the Variance of the Rate of Return," *Journal of Business* 53, 61–65.

Parkinson, Patrick, 1998, "Commentary," *FRBNY Economic Policy Review* (October), 155–159.

Paskov, S., and J. Traub, 1995, "Faster Valuation of Financial Derivatives," *Journal of Portfolio Management* 22, 113–120.

Pérold, A., and E. Schulman, 1988, "The Free Lunch in Currency Hedging: Implications for Investment Policy and Performance Standards," *Financial Analysts Journal* 44 (May), 45–50.

Picoult, Evan, 1997, "Calculating Value at Risk with Monte Carlo Simulation," in *Risk Management for Financial Institutions,* Risk Publications, London, pp. 73–92.

Powers, M., 1992, "The Day the IMM Launched Financial Futures Trading," *Futures* (May), 52–58.

President's Working Group on Financial Markets, 1999, *Hedge Funds, Leverage, and the Lessons of Long-Term Capital Management,* PWGFM, Washington, D.C. At www.treas.gov.

Press, W. H., S. A. Teulosky, W. T. Vetterling, and B. P. Flannery, 1992, *Numerical Recipes: The Art of Scientific Computing,* Cambridge University Press, Cambridge, England.

Rawnsley, J., 1995, *Total Risk: Nick Leeson and the Fall of Barings Bank,* Harper, New York.

Rebonato, R., 1996, *Interest Rate Option Models,* Wiley, New York.

Rebonato, Riccardo, and Peter Jäckel, 2000, "The Most General Methodology to Create a Valid Correlation Matrix for Risk Management and Option Pricing Purposes," *Journal of Risk* 2 (Winter), 17–27.

Redington, F. M., 1952, "Review of the Principles of Life-Office Valuations," *Journal of the Institute of Actuaries* 78, 286–340.

Risk Publications, 1995, *Derivative Credit Risk: Advances in Measurement and Management,* Risk Publications, London.

Risk Standards Working Group, 1996, *Risk Standards for Institutional Investment Managers,* RSWG, New York. At www.cmra.com.

Roy, Andrew D., 1952, "Safety First and the Holding of Assets," *Econometrica* 20, 431–449.

Sarig, O., and A. Warga, 1995, "The Risk Structure of Interest Rates," *Journal of Finance* 44, 1351–1360.

Saunders, Anthony, 1999, *Credit Risk Measurement,* Wiley, New York.

Scott, D., 1992, *Multivariate Density Estimation: Theory, Practice and Visualization,* Wiley, New York.

Securities and Exchange Commission, 1997, *Disclosure of Accounting Policies for Derivative Financial Insturments and Derivative Commodity Instruments and Disclosure of Quantitative and Qualitative Information about Market Risk Inherent in Derivative Financial Instruments, Other Financial Instruments, and Derivative Commodity Instruments,* Release 33-7386, SEC, Washington, D.C. At www.sec.gov/rules/final/33-7386.txt.

Securities and Exchange Commission, 1998, *Review of the First Phase of Filings of Disclosures of Quantitative and Qualitative Information about Market Risks Inherent in Derivative Instruments and Other Financial Instruments,* SEC, Washington, D.C. At www.sec.gov/rules/final/33-7386.txt.

Sharpe, W., 1964, "Capital Asset Prices: A Theory of Market Equilibrium Under Conditions of Risk," *Journal of Finance* 19, 425–442.

Sharpe, William F., 1966, "Evaluating Mutual Fund Performance," *Journal of Business* 39, 119–138.

Shiller, R., and H. McCulloch, 1987, "The Term Structure of Interest Rates," *NBER Working Paper 2341,* Washington, D.C.

Shimko, David, ed., 1999, *Credit Risk: Models and Management,* Risk Books, London.

Shirreff, David, 1998, "The Rise and Rise of the Risk Manager," *Euromoney* (February), 56–60.

Silber, W., 1981, "Innovation, Competition and New Contract Design in Futures Markets," *Journal of Futures Markets* 1, 123–156.

Smith, Clifford, and René Stulz, 1985, "The Determinants of Firms' Hedging Policies," *Journal of Financial and Quantitative Analysis* 20, 341–406.

Smithson, C., 1999, *Managing Financial Risk Yearbook,* CIBC School of Financial Products, New York.

Smithson, Charles, and Clifford Smith, 1998, *Managing Financial Risk: A Guide to Derivative Products, Financial Engineering, and Value Maximization,* McGraw-Hill, New York.

Stahl, G., 1997, "Three Cheers," *Risk* 10 (October), 67–69.

Stoughton, Neal, and Josef Zechner, 1999, "Optimal Capital Allocation Using RAROC and EVA," working paper, University of California at Irvine.

Studer, Gerold, 1999, "Market Risk Computation for Nonliner Portfolios," *Journal of Risk* 1 (Summer), 33–53.

Stulz, René, 2000, *Financial Engineering and Risk Management,* Southwestern Publishing, New York.

Treynor, Jack L., 1965, "How to Rate Management Investment Funds," *Harvard Business Review* 43, 63–75.

Turner, Chris, 1996, "VAR as an Industrial Tool," *Risk* 9 (March), 38–40.

United States Congress, 1993, *Safety and Soundness Issues Related to Bank Derivatives Activities,* U.S. Congress, Washington, D.C.

Vasicek, Oldrich, 1977, "An Equilibrium Characterization of the Term Structure," *Journal of Financial Economics* 5, 177–188.

Wakeman, Lee, 1998, "Credit Enhancement," in Alexander, C., ed., *Risk Management and Analysis,* Wiley, Chichester, England.

Wee, Lieng-Seng, and Judy Lee, 1999, "Integrating Stress Testing with Risk Management," *Bank Accounting and Finance* (Spring), 7–19.

Weiss, Lawrence, 1990, "Bankruptcy Resolution: Direct Costs and Violations of Priority of Claims," *Journal of Financial Economics* 27 (October), 285–314.

Williams, Deborah, 2000, "Selecting and Implementing Enterprise Risk Management Technologies," in Marc Lore and Lev Borodovsky, eds., *The Professional Handbook of Risk Management,* Butterworth, London.

Wilson, Duncan, 1995, "VAR in Operation," *Risk* 8 (December), 24–25.

Wilson, Tom, 1994, "Debunking the Myths," *Risk* 7 (April), 67–72.

Zaik, E., J. Walter, G. Kelling, and C. James, 1996, "RAROC at Bank of America: From Theory to Practice," *Journal of Applied Corporate Finance* 9, 94–113.

Zangari, Peter, 1996, "A VAR Methodology for Portfolios That Include Options," *RiskMetrics Monitor* (first quarter), 4–12.

Ziemba, William, and John Mulvey, 1998, *Worldwide Asset and Liability Modeling,* Cambridge University Press, Cambridge, England.

INDEX

Locators in **bold** indicate additional display matter.

Absolute risk, 15–16, 411
Absolute VAR, 109
Acceleration methods, Monte Carlo simulation, 301–302
Accrual methods, 512
Accumulated benefit obligations, 413
Active application, VAR, 362
Active management risk, 411–413
Active risk management, 383–405
   and economic capital, 383–384, 403–405
   firm-wide performance measurement, 394–398, **397**
   RAPM methods, 391–394
   risk-adjusted performance measurement, 387–389
   and risk capital, 383–387
   as a strategic tool, 398–402
Actual return, 131
Actuarial methods, 21, 318, 453–454
Actuarial risk, 74
Add-on factor, credit risk, 334–335
Agency costs, 477
Aggregation, time, 102–106, 252
Ahrens, Kent, 417
AIG insurance, 475
AIMR (Association for Investment Management and Research), 48
Algorithmics, Inc., 443, **444, 445, 446**
Alternative action, operational loss, 460
Amortizaton effect, 324
Analytics platform, risk-management technology, 433, **434**
Annual report, 373
Anticipated exposures, 366, 368
Antithetic variable technique, 301
Arbitrage, VAR, 499–500
Arbitrage models, 311
Arithmetic rate of return, 98
Asian crisis, xxiv
Askin, David, 19
Asset-based VAR, 391
Asset liquidity risk, 17, 340–342, 343–351, **350,** 355, 357
Asset managers and VAR adoption, xxiv
Asset returns, 99–102, 151
Asset risk, 411
Association for Investment Management and Research (AIMR), 48
Asymmetric information, 345, 372
Asymmetric return distributions, 501

AT&T, 414
Automated control systems, operational loss, 461

Back-office risk-management systems, 432–433, 434, 439, **440**
Backtesting models, 129–145
   Basel Rules, 136–140, **139**
   conditional coverage models, 140–142
   criteria for, 119
   defined, 129
   distribution forecast models, 142–143
   method comparison, 144–145
   parametric models, 143
   setup for, 130–132
   verification and failure rates, 132–136
Bad loans, 35
Bank of America, 387, 388
Bank of England report on Barings, 486
Bankers Trust, 96, 377–379, 390, 423, 471
Barings failure, 36–38, 42–43, 58, 165–167, **166,** 215–219, 437, 486
Basel Accord (1988), 52, 55–60, 68, 70, 334–336, 448
Basel Committee, 17, 119–122, 129–130, 231, 371–373, 458, 503
Basel II, 70, 448
Basel penalty zones, 137–138
Basel Rules, 136–140, **139**
Basis risk, 16, 39, 262
Benchmarking, portfolio, 271–274, **275**
Bernoulli trials, 133
Best hedge, 158
"Best Practices" G-30 recommendations, 484–486
Beta (β), 16, 82, 155
Beta mapping, 175, 176, **176**
Beta model, 288
Bear Stearns, 354, 436
Bever, Leo de, 418
Bias in VAR, 500, **501**
Bid-ask spread cost, 344–346
Binomial distribution, 91, 133
Black Monday (1987), 242, **243,** 244
Black-Scholes (BS) model, 92, 112, 216, 285, 403, 405, 502
Bonds:
   credit exposure, 323–325
   credit risk, 16
   financial instability of, 5
   market crisis in (1994), 5, 19
   returns correlation matrix, 174

Bonds (*cont.*)
   risks and correlations for, 17, **173**
   unit-level VAR adjustment, 379–381, **380**
   (*See* also Interest rates)
Bonus structure, trading, 392–393, 394
Bootstrapping, 221, 296–298
Borodovsky, Lev, 517
Bottom-up approach, operational risk, 453
Brownian motion model, geometric (GBM),
   292–295, **294**
BS (Black-Scholes) model, 92, 112, 216, 285,
   403, 405, 502
Buffett, Warren, 394
"Bulletproofing" by LTCM, 353
Business risks, 3–4, 468–469
"Buy side" investors, 408, **409**

Capital, defined, 73
Capital asset pricing model (CAPM), 155, 400
Capital charge, 400–401, 459
Capital Market Risk Advisors (CMRA), 428, 488
CAPM (capital asset pricing model), 155
CAR (credit-at-risk), 326
Cardano, Girolamo, 86
Cash-flow-at-risk (CFAR), 366, 368–369
Cash-flow/funding liquidity, 342
Cash-flow mapping, 264
Cash-flow risk, 18, 19, 415
Cash liquidity, 351
Central limit theorem (CLT), 91
Centralized risk management, 363–364, 435,
   436
CFAR (cash-flow-at-risk), 366, 368–369
Chase Manhattan Bank, 402, 462, 487, 518
Chebyshev's inequality, 120
Chemical Bank, 402
Chicago Mercantile Exchange (CME), 237
Cholesky Factorization, 304–305
CIR (Cox, Ingersoll and Ross) model, 309
Citron, Bob, 40
Cleaned return, 132
CLT (central limit theorem), 91
Cluster, volatility, 183
CME (Chicago Mercantile Exchange), 237
CMO (collateralized mortgage obligation), 19
CMRA (Capital Market Risk Advisors), 428
Co-integrated time-series, 310
Collateral, 327
Collateralized mortgage obligation (CMO), 19
Commerzbank risk-management system, 441
Commodities and Futures Trading Commission
   (CFTC), 471

Commodity forwards, 278–279
Commodity risk, 82
Common Fund, 416, 417
Compliance, VAR to check, 416–417
Component VAR, 159–161, **162**, 395–396, **397**
Computation, VAR, 107–128
   computing, 108–116
   precision assessment, 122–128
   quantitative factor choice, 116–122
Conditional coverage models, 140–142
Conditional loss, 97
Conditional scenario analysis, 240, **241,** 242
Conditional variance, 188
Confidence, credit risk, 334, 385–387
Confidence-based risk measures, 115, 118,
   124–127
Construction of loss distributions, operational
   risk, 463–465
Contingency planning, operational loss, 461
Contracted cash flows, 366
Contraction risk, 62
Control systems, operational loss, 461
Controlling trading, 513–514
Convenience yield, 278
Conventional option pricing model, 19
Convexity, 16, 82, 212
Convolution, loss distribution, 455
Cooke Ratio, 55–57
Cooper's & Lybrand, 451
Cornish-Fisher expansion, 213, 217
CorporateMetrics, 29, 310
Correlations:
   correlated returns and time aggregation,
     104–105
   correlation coefficient, 150–153
   financial crashes, 198–199
   internal model approach, 64
   portfolio credit risk models, 336–337
   (*See* also Forecasting risks and correlations)
Counterparty Risk Management Policy Group
   (CRMPG), 340, 351, 484, 486–488
Coupon payment, 278
Covariance, 90, 102
Covariance matrix approach, 147
Cox, Ingersoll and Ross (CIR) model, 309
CR (credit reserve), 333
CRC (credit risk charge), 57
Credit-at-risk (CAR), 326
Credit derivatives, 58
Credit event, 16
Credit exposure, 316, 323–327, 334, 485
Credit ratings, 70–71, 118
Credit reserve (CR), 333, 393

Credit risk, 313–338
    Basel Accord, 55, 60, 334–336
    credit exposure, 323–327
    default risk, 318–323, **319**
    defined, 16–17, 313
    as financial risk, **450,** 451, **472**
    G-30 Best Practices, 485
    legal risk, 20
    management, 333–334, 363–364
    measurement, 329–333
    nature of, 314–318
    netting arrangements, 327–329
    operational risk, 18
    portfolio credit risk models, 336–338
    and risk interactions, 473–474
    telescoping of, 63
Credit risk charge (CRC), 57
Credit Risk Revisions (1999), Basel Accord,
    68, 70–72
Crédit Suisse Asset Management, 421, 517
CreditMetrics, 29, 45, 323, **337**
CreditPortfolioView, **337**
CreditRisk+, **337**
CRMPG (Counterparty Risk Management
    Policy Group),340, 351, 484, 486–488
CTFC (Commodities and Futures Trading
    Commission), 471
Cumulative default rates, **319,** 320
Cumulative standard normal distribution
    function, 112–113
Currency:
    common currency and volatility, 9–10
    delta-normal VAR implementation,
        257–259
    Mexican peso devaluation, 489–491, 495
    unit-level VAR adjustment, 379, **380**
    (*See* also Exchange rates)
Current exposure, 487
Custom-made risk-management systems, 439

Daily marketing-to-market, 327
Daiwa failure, 41–43, 436–437
Data, operational risk, 457–459
Data-inadequacy risk, 492
Data input model risk, 492, **493**
Data mining, model-selection risk, 496
Davies, Howard, 503
DBL Group (Drexel Burnham Lambert
    Group), 317
Deadweight costs, 477
Decay factor, 193
Decomposition, risk, 159, 161–162, **163**

Deep markets, 340
Default probability, 314
Default risk, 118, 318–323, **319**
Default VAR, 330
Defensive application of VAR, 362
Defined-benefit plans, 75
Degrees of freedom, 93
Delta (Δ), 16
Delta-gamma approximations, 211–214, **215,**
    216, 228
Delta-gamma-delta method, 213, **215**
Delta-gamma-Monte Carlo method, 213–214,
    215, 218
Delta-normal valuation method, 147,
    206–209, 214, **215,** 219–221, 227–230
Delta-normal VAR implementation, 255–289
    currency application, 257–259
    equity portfolios, 287–289
    fixed-income portfolios, 264–274, **268, 272**
    linear derivatives, 274–285, **281, 283, 284**
    options, 285–287
    overview, 256–257
    "primitive" securities, choosing, 259,
        260–261, 262–264
Deposit insurance, 53
Deregulation, 7
Derivatives:
    credit exposure, 323–325
    credit risk, 16–17, 328–329, 334–336,
        337–338
    defined, 11–12
    delta-normal VAR implementation,
        274–285, **281, 283, 284**
    global risk management, 363
    markets of, 12–15
    OTC dealers, 73
    risk measurement, 82
    (*See also* Hedging with derivatives)
Derivatives, losses, 32–36, 49–50
    Barings, 36–38, 42–43, 58, 165, **166,** 167,
        215–219, 437, 486
    Daiwa, 41–43, 436–437
    Metallgesellschaft (MG), 38–40, 42–43
    Orange County, 40–41, 42–43
    private-sector responses to, 43–45
    public-sector, regulatory response to, 45–48
Derivatives Policy Group (DPG), 43–44, 231,
    235
Derivatives Strategy (magazine), 431, 499
Derman, Emanuel, 492
Determinants, Monte Carlo simulation, 304
Deterministic simulation, Monte Carlo method,
    306–307

Deutsche Bank, 423, 449, 471
Deutsche Morgan Grenfell (DMG), 449
Diagonal model, 169–170, 175, **176**
Diffusion effect, 324
Digital feeds, risk-management technology,
    433, **434**
Dimensional scenario analysis, 235–245
Directional risks, 16
Disaster risk, 470
Disclosure, risk management, 371–376
Discount rate, 400–401
Discrete rate of return, 98
Dispersion, risk as, 95
Distributions:
    forecast models, 142–143
    identically and independently distributed
        (iid) returns, 101–103, **104**
    loss and operational risk, 453–457, **458,**
        463–465
    marginal, 90
    mean of, 87, 91, 101, 105–106, 123–125
    mode of, 87
    normal, 91–94, 110–114, 500
    parametric, 91–94, 110–113, 121–122
    probability distribution function (pdf),
        86–94
    student t, 93–94
    VAR for, 109–116
Diversification:
    Basel Accord, 60, 70–71
    and risk, 62, 152, 365, **472,** 473
    unit-level VAR adjustment, 379–381, **380**
    VAR measurement of, 150, 152
Diversified component RAPM measure, 396
Dividend yield, 278
DMG (Deutsche Morgan Grenfell), 449
Documentation, risk management, 484–488
DPG (Derivatives Policy Group), 43–44, 231, 235
Drexel Burnham Lambert Group (DBL Group),
    317
Duration, 16, 62, 82, 206, 207
Duration mapping, 264, 266–271, **268**
Dynamic hedging, 502–503

Earnings-at-risk (EAR), 368, 389
Earnings-based RAPM methods, 389–391
Earnings volatility, 453
EC (economic capital), 383–385, 403–405
ECE (expected credit exposure), 325–327
ECL (expected credit loss), 329–330
Econometrics (*See specific topics*)
Economic capital (EC), 383–385, 403–405

Economic exposures, 368–369
Economic risk, 415
Economic risk capital, 52
Economic value added (EVA), 399, 401, 402
EDF (estimated default frequency), 318
Education of a Speculator (Niederhoffer), 234
Efficient markets, 103
Eigenvalue, 179
Eigenvector, 179
Employee Retirement Income Security Act
    (ERISA), 75
EMS (European Monetary System), 196, 201
Enterprise resource planning (ERP), 442
Enterprise risk, 475
Enterprise risk technology, 434–438
Enterprise-wide risk-management (ERM)
    systems, 431–432, 435, 438, 446, 472, 474
Equity capital, 117–121, 384
Equity coverage, 386
Equity portfolios, 287–289
Equity reserve, 333–334
Equity risk, 82
ERISA (Employee Retirement Income Security
    Act), 75
ERM (enterprise-wide risk-management)
    systems, 431–432, 435, 438, 446, 472, 474
ERM (Exchange Rate Mechanism), 239
Ernst & Young risk-management survey, 449,
    450
ERP (enterprise resource planning), 442
Error-correction term, 310
Errors:
    measurement and estimation, 122–126
    type 1 and 2, 133–135, **136,** 137, 138
Estimated default frequency (EDF), 318
Estimation model risk, 492–495
European Monetary System (EMS), 196, 201
EVA (economic value added), 399, 401, 402
Event risk, 451, 469–471
EVT (extreme value theory), 233
EVT theorem, 250
EWMA (exponentially weighted moving
    average), 193
Exceedences, risk of, 130, 488
Exceptions in VAR models, 130, 138, **139,**
    141, 145
Exchange Rate Mechanism (ERM), 239
Exchange rates:
    exchange rate risk, 82
    settlement risk, 17
    volatility in, 5, **6,** 9–10, **83,** 183, 184–186
    (*See also* Currency)
Exchange-traded derivative instruments, 13, **14**

Exercise price, 286
Expectations, properties of, 89–91
Expected credit exposure (ECE), 325–327
Expected credit loss (ECL), 329–330
Expected operational losses, 460
Expected shortfall, 97
Exponential averages method, 197–198, 500
Exponentially weighted moving average (EWMA), 193
Exposure, 16, 327, 487
Extension risk, 62
External data, operational risk, 457
External performance measurement, 396
Externalities, 53
Extreme value theory (EVT), 233, 249–253

Factor analysis, 173
Factor models, covariance matrix, 171–175, **173**
Factor push method scenario analysis, 240
Failure rates, backtesting, 132–136
Fair value, 46
FASB (Financial Accounting Standards Board), 46–47
Fat tails, 220–221, 225
Federal Deposit Insurance Corporation (FDIC), 75
Federal Deposit Insurance Corporation Improvement Act (FDICIA), 57
Financial Accounting Standards Board (FASB), 46–47
Financial insanity, legal risk, 469
Financial institutions:
    costs of insolvencies, 35–36
    globalization of, 7
    information sharing, 487
    regulation of, 75–77
    VAR adoption by, xxi
    (*See also* Derivatives, losses)
Financial letters of credit, 326
Financial management, modern, 512–513
Financial market stability, 372
Financial risk:
    asset returns, 99–102
    defined, 4
    integrated risk management, 469, 472–473
    and market volatility, 4–7
    origin of risk, 7–10
    tools for risk management, 10–11
    types, 16–21, 449, **450**
    VAR as benchmark, 116–118
Financial Risk Manager Certification Program, 45

Financial risk measurement, 81–106
    asset returns, 99–102
    market risks, 82, **83–84,** 85
    probability distribution functions (pdf), 86–94
    risk, 95–99, **98**
    time aggregation, 102–106
Financial statement section, annual report, 373
Finer granularity, 310
Firm-wide integrated risk management, 468–475, 472–475
First Capital Strategies, 417
Fixed-income market, 82
Fixed-income portfolios, 264–274, **268, 272**
Forecasting risks and correlations:
    modeling correlations, 196–199
    options data, 199–202
    time-varying risk, 184–196
Foreign interest rate, 278
Forward contracts, 274–278
Forward rate agreements (FRA), 279–282, **281**
Fraud, 18
Freedom, degrees of, 93
Frequency distribution, 86, **87,** 454, **456**
Front-to-back risk-management systems, 439, **440**
Front-office risk-management systems, 440
Full Monte Carlo model, 216, **312**
Full valuation methods, 201, 209–210, **211, 214, 215,** 223, **312**
Funding liquidity risk, 17, 18, 42, 351–352, 355, 357
Funding operational risk, 461–462
Funding risk, 413–414
Futures contracts, 262–264
Futures market, 12–13

G-10 (Group of Ten), 55
G-30 (Group of Thirty), 43, 231, 426, 483, 484–486
Gambling and probability, 86
Gamma (γ), 16
GAO (General Accounting Office), 46
GARCH (generalized autoregressive heteroskedastic) model, 187–189, **190, 191,** 192, **193,** 297–298
GARP (Global Association of Risk Professionals), 45, 517
Gauss, Karl F., 91
GBM (geometric brownian motion model), 292–295, **294**

GED (generalized error distribution), 94
General Accounting Office (GAO), 46
General distribution, 109–110, 114
General market risks, 168
Generalized autoregressive heteroskedastic
    (GARCH) model, 187–189, **190, 191,** 192,
    193, 297–298
Generalized error distribution (GED), 94
Generalized Pareto distribution, 250
Geometric brownian motion (GBM) model,
    292–295, **294**
Geometric rate of return, 98–99
Ghosting, moving averages, 187
Glass-Steagall Act, 76–77
Global Association of Risk Professionals
    (GARP), 45, 517
Global custodian, 419–420
Global portfolio equity report, 163, **164,** 165
Global risk management, 361–365, 432–438,
    473
Globalization of financial institutions, 7
Goldman Sachs, 376, 381, 492
Gonzalez, Henry, 31
The "Greeks" methods, 211–214, 217
Greenspan, Alan, 54, 71
Grid Monte Carlo method, 210, **215**
Gross-position approach, 73
Gross replacement value (GRV), 328–329
Group of Ten (G-10), 55
Group of Thirty (G-30), 43, 231, 426, 483,
    484–486
GRV (gross replacement value), 328–329
Guldimann, Till, 22, 29

Haircut, 343, 353
Half-life, liquidation, 348
Heavy tails, 250
Hedging with derivatives:
    best hedge, 158
    dynamic, 502–503
    and investment management, 409
    natural, 474
    uses of, 12
    with VAR, 476–478
    volatility measure, 16
    (*See also* Derivatives)
Herstatt Bank, 17
High-frequency/low-value losses, 457
Histogram, 23, **24**
Historical scenario analysis, 232, 242–245,
    243

Historical simulation method, 210, 215,
    221–224, **227,** 229, **230,** 500
Holistic risk, 475
Homogeneity, risk measure, 115
Honeywell, 475
Horizon, investment:
    credit risk, 334
    investment management, 408, 409
    liquidity risk, 343
    time aggregation, 102–106
    time-varying risk, 184–196
    VAR modeling, 117–119, 131, 215,
        223, 225
Hot Spots, 163
Hypothetical return, 132
Hysteria factor, internal model approach, 64

IAS (International Accounting Standards), 47
Identically and independently distributed (iid)
    returns, 101–103, **104**
Igushi, Toshihide, 41, 436–437
i.i.d. (identically and independently distributed)
    returns, 101–103, **104**
Immediate liquidation, 346
Implementation risk, **493,** 496–498, **497**
Implementation shortfall, liquidation, 348
Implied standard deviation (ISD), 200–202
Implied volatility, 200
Importance sampling techniques, 302
In-house risk-management systems, 438
In-the-money option, 316
Incentive-compatible approach, 65
Incremental VAR, 155–159, 161, **162**
Index mapping, 175, **176**
Individual mapping, 176
Individual VAR, 150
Industry mapping, 176
Information-reporting tool, VAR as, 370–376
Information technology (IT), 431–432
    (*See also* Technology of risk)
Institutional investors, 408
Instruments and global risk management, 365
Insurance and risk, 53, 461–462, 474–475,
    502
Insurance company regulation, 74–75
Insuritization risk, 475
Integrated risk management, 467–479
    event risk, 469–471
    firm-wide, 472–475, 487
    reasons for, 475–478
Integration of risk technology, 434–438

Interest rates:
  and market risk, 16
  risk from, 62, 63
  swaps of, 282, **283, 284,** 285, 324
  volatility in, 5–6, **7, 83,** 183
Internal data, operational risk, 457
Internal models approach, 63–67, 70, 119, 137, 313
Internal performance measurement, 396
International Accounting Standards (IAS), 47
International Swaps and Derivatives Association (ISDA), 327
Inventory-carrying costs, 345
Investment guidelines, VAR to design, 417–418
Investment management:
  applicability of VAR, 408–409, 428–429
  regulation, 75
  risk management, 420–426
  risk monitoring and control, 415–420
  risk standards, 426–428
  risks in, 410–415
  VAR in, 407–429
ISD (implied standard deviation), 200–202
ISDA (International Swaps and Derivatives Association), 327
IT (information technology), 431–432

Japanese futures and Barings's collapse, 36–38, 42–43, 58, 165, **166,** 167, 215–219
J.P. Morgan, 28

Kopprasch, Bob, 499
Krieger, Andy, 390
Kurtosis, 93, 102

Leach, James "Jim," 31, 509
Lee, John, 59
Leeson, Nicholas, 37–38, 165, 167, 215–219, 437, 486
Leeson's Straddle, 215–219
Legal risk, 20–21, 469–470
Lending (*See* Credit risk)
Letter of credit, 326
Leverage:
  liquidity risk, 342
  LTCM, 353–355
Leveraged instrument, derivatives as, 12
LGD (loss given default), 314

Linear derivatives, delta-normal VAR implementation, 274–285, **281, 283, 284**
Liquidation, price impact of, 349–351, **350**
Liquidation-based estimates of exposure, 487
Liquidation period, 117
Liquidity-adjusted value-at-risk (LVAR), 348–349
Liquidity risk:
  asset liquidity risk, 343–351, **350**
  defined, 340–343
  as financial risk, 17–18, 339–357, **472**
  funding of, 351–352
  LTCM lessons, 352–357, **356**
  and VAR systems, 502
Local valuation methods, 201–209, 205, **215, 312**
Long-Term Capital Management (LTCM):
  CRMPG report on, 486–488
  liquidity risk, 340, 352–357, **356,** xix
  risk management, lessons from, 503–508, **506**
Loss distributions, operational risk, 453–457, **458,** 463–465
Loss given default (LGD), 314, 321
Losses (*See* Derivatives, losses)
Low-frequency/high-value losses, 457
LTCM (See Long-Term Capital Management (LTCM))
LVAR (liquidity-adjusted value-at-risk), 348–349

MA (moving averages), 186–187, 196–197
McDonough, William, 58–59
Macroeconomic risks, 4, 8–9, 468
"Man in the White Coat" syndrome, 498–499
Management:
  asset managers and VAR adoption, xxii
  "Best Practices" G-30 recommendations, 484–486
  discussion and analysis section, annual report, 373
  operational loss avoidance, 461
  risk management role, 513–517
Mapping:
  fixed-income portfolios, 264, 266–269, **268**
  risk-management technology, 433, **434**
  securities, 168, 175–178, 255
Margin calls, 18, 19
Marginal default rates, 320
Marginal distribution, 90
Marginal RAPM, 395
Marginal VAR, 154–155, **162,** 395
Market discipline, 372

Market impact effect, 340
Market neutral funds, 19
Market/product liquidity risk, 17–18, 340
Market risk:
   Basel Accord, 60–61
   change in, 62, 64
   credit risk source, 314
   defined, 15–16
   disclosure, 373–374
   as financial risk, 42–43, **450**, 451, **472**
   G-30 Best Practices, 484–485
   measurement of, 82, **83–84**, 85
   quantified by VAR, 21
   and risk interactions, 473–474
   volatility and financial risks, 4–7
Marking-to-market G-30 policy, 484–485
Marking to model, 19
Markowitz, Harry, 10, 114, 115, 147, 513
Martingale valuation, 27
Mathematical reserves, 74
Matrix multiplication, 178–179
Matrix notation, 149
Maximum-loss criterion, 245
Maxwell, Robert, 416
MC simulation method (*See* Monte Carlo (MC)
   simulation method)
Mean of distribution, 87, 91, 101, 105–106,
   123–125
Mergers, 77
Meridien Research, 435, **436,** 438
Merrill and global risk management, 364
Merton model, 323, 403
Metallgesellschaft (MG), 38–40, 42–43
Methods, VAR, 205–229
   delta-normal valuation, 147, 206–209, 214,
   215, 219–221, 227–230
   empirical comparisons among, 227–229
   exponential averages, 193, 197–198, 500
   full valuation, 201, 209–210, **211,** 214, **215,**
   223, **312**
   historical simulation, 210, 215, 221–224,
   227, 229, **230,** 500
   local vs. full valuation, 201–209, 205, **215,**
   312
   Monte Carlo, 210, **215,** 224–226, 228,
   229–230
   partial, 214
   (*See also* Monte Carlo (MC) simulation
   method; Scenario analysis; *specific
   methods*)
Mexican peso devaluation, 489–491, 495
MG (Metallgesellschaft), 38–40, 42–43
MG Refining & Marketing (MGRM), 38–40

MGRM (MG Refining & Marketing), 38–40
Mid price, price function, 340
Middle-office risk-management systems, 432,
   433, 434, 440
Miller-Modigliani (MM) theorem, 400,
   475–476
Mobile Corporation, 376, 476
Mode of distribution, 87
Model parameters, 245, 246
Model risk, 18–19, 120, 226, 492–498,
   497
Model selection risk, **493,** 495–496, 498
Model validation, 129
Models, VAR (*See specific models*)
Modified duration, 206, 207
Modigliani-Miller (MM) theorem, 400,
   475–476
Money manager, 420, 421
Monotonicity, risk measure, 115
Monte Carlo (MC) simulation method,
   291–312
   as common VAR method, 210, **215,**
   224–226, 228, 229–230, 291–292
   deterministic simulation, 306–307
   model choice, 309–311
   multiple variables, 302–305
   one random variable, 292–299, **294**
   scenario simulation, 307–308
   speed vs. accuracy, 299–302
Moral hazard, 53–54
MORE (Multinational Operational Risk
   Exchange) Consortium, 459
JP Morgan, 28, 44–45
Morgan Stanley (MS), 349, 351, 439
Moving averages (MA), 186–187, 196–197
Moving window, 186
   estimation of variance, 224
MS (Morgan Stanley), 349, 351
Mu (μ), 87
Multidimensional scenario analysis, 239–245
Multinational Operational Risk Exchange
   (MORE) Consortium, 459
Multiplicative factor, internal model approach,
   64

Narrow stress loss (NSL), 240
National Association of Insurance
   Commissioners (NAIC), 74
National Westminster Bank, 494
Natural hedging, 474
NatWest model risk, 494
Net-position approach, 73

Net present value (NPV), 398
Net replacement value (NRV), 328–329
Net-to-gross ratio (NGR), 335
NetRisk, 457
Netting, 60, 327–329
Newman, Frank, 471
Niederhoffer, Victor, 234
Nikkei and Barings's collapse, 36–38, 42–43, 58, 165, **166,** 167, 215–219
Nonbank regulation, 50, 72–77
Nonbusiness risks, 3, 4
Nondirectional risks, 16
Nonfinancial corporations, xiii–xxiv, 366, 368–370
Normal distribution, 91–94, 110–114, 500
Normal market size, 340
Notational exposure, derivative contracts, 11, 13, 14, 379
Null hypothesis, 134–135

Object-oriented tools, 434–435
October 1987 stock market crash, 242, **243,** 244
Off-balance-sheet items, 46
Office of Thrift Supervision (OTS), 236–237
Oil price volatility, 5, 6, **8, 84,** 85
Ontario Teachers' Pension Plan Board (OTPPB), 418, 427
Operating cash flows, 368, **369**
Operational controls risk, 451, **452**
Operational risk, 18–20, 42, **472,** 473–474
Operational risk management, 447–465
    approaches to, 451–452
    defined, 449–451, **450**
    importance of, 448–449
    management, 459–462
    measurement, 452–453
    top-down vs. bottom-up approaches, 453–459, **456**
Optimization, portfolio, 504–507, **506**
Options:
    buying and selling, 516
    delta-normal VAR implementation, 285–287
    forecasting risks and correlations, 199–202
    market for, 12, 16
    short options, 316, 507–508
Orange County, 40–41, 42–43
Order-processing costs, 345
OTC (over-the-counter) market, 12–13, **14**
OTPPB (Ontario Teachers' Pension Plan Board), 418, 427
OTS (Office of Thrift Supervision), 236–237

Outside risk-management systems, 438
Over-the-counter (OTC) market, 12–13, **14**
Overall economic capital, 394
Owen, Martin, 494

Paper portfolios, model-selection risk, 496
Papouis, Kyriacos, 494
Parameter risk, 492
Parametric backtesting models, 111, 143
Parametric distribution, 91–94, 110–113, 121–122
Pareto distribution, generalized, 250
Partial simulation method, 214
Pascal, Blaise, 86
Passive application, VAR, 361–362
PBGG (Pension Benefit Guarantee Corporation), 75
PC (principal components), 180
PC (product control), 421
Pdf (probability distribution function), 86–94
Peak credit exposure, 316
Pension Benefit Guarantee Corporation (PBGC), 75
Pension funds (*See* Investment management)
Percent VAR, 396, **397**
Percentiles, 95
Peregrine Investment Holdings, 59
Performance (*See* Risk-adjusted performance measurement)
Performance fees, 424
Persistence parameter, 188–189, 192, **193**
Peso devaluation, 489–491, 495
P&L (profit and loss) measures, 117, 131
Plus factor, 64–65
Policy mix risk, 411–413
Political risk, 470–471
Portfolio:
    approach, derivatives, 363
    benchmarking, 271–274, **275**
    credit models, 71
    credit risk, 316–318, 332–333
    credit risk models, 336–338
    insurance for, 502
    optimization of, 504–507, **506**
Portfolio risk analysis, 148–177
    construction of, 148–153
    covariance model simplification, 167–177, **173**
    examples, 162–167
    tools, 153–162
Position limits, 342
Position platform, risk-management technology, 433, **434**

Position risks, 488–489
Positive-definiteness, 168
Postloss financing, 461
Potential exposure, 317, 487
Potential loss measure, 117
Precommitment Model, 65–68
Predicted stress loss, 240
Present value of expected credit losses
  (PVECL), 330–331
Present value of unexpected credit losses
  (PVUCL), 331
President's Working Group on Financial
  Markets, 487
Price discovery, 200
Price elasticity, 369
Price function, and asset liquidity risk,
  340–341
Price volatility, equity, 5, **9, 84,** 85, 183
Pricing credit risk, 330–331
Pricing method, Monte Carlo system, 298–299
"Primitive" securities, delta-normal VAR
  implementation, 259, **260–261,** 262–264
Principal components (PC), 180
  analysis, 172, 179–181
Principal mapping, 264
Private-sector responses to derivative losses,
  43–45, 49–50
Probability distribution function (pdf), 86–94
Probability distributions, 86
Probability theory, 86–88
Product control (PC), 421
Professional expertise as G-30 Best Practices,
  486
Profit and loss (P&L) measures, 117, 131
Proprietary trading activities, 60, 365–366,
  367
Prospective scenario analysis, 232, 239
Public-sector responses to derivative losses,
  45–48, 50
PVECL (present value of expected credit losses),
  330–331
PVUCL (present value of unexpected credit
  losses), 331

Qualitative parameters, internal model
  approach, 64
Quantiles in risk measurement:
  computation, 95, 97–99, **98**
  VAR estimation errors, 115, 125–126, 127
Quasi-Monte Carlo method, 306–307

Random numbers, creation of, 295–296
Random walk, 103
RAPM (*See* Risk-adjusted performance
  measurement)
RAROC (risk-adjusted return on capital), 96,
  389, 399, 401, 402, 423–425, xxi
R&D (Research and Development), 478
Reality checks, 129
Receivables, credit risk, 326
Recouponing, 327
Recovery rates, 16, 321, 336–337
Recursive estimator, 194
Redundant control systems, operational loss, 461
Regulatory capital standards:
  approach comparisons, 51–77, 66–68, **69**
  Basel Accord, 52, 55–60, 68, 70
  Internal Models Approach, 63–67, 70
  Precommitment Model, 65–68
  reasons for regulation, 52–55, 75–77
  Standardized Method, 61–63, 66
Regulatory issues:
  derivative risks, 45–48, 50
  regulatory arbitrage, 58
  regulatory risk, 470–471
  VAR adoption, xxi
Relational databases, 435
Relative risk, 15–16, 411
Replacement value, 328
Replications, Monte Carlo simulation, 300–301
Reporting, VAR, 442–443
Reputational risk, legal risk, 470, 486
Research and Development (R&D), 478
Retained operational risk, 461
Return-on-assets (ROA), 383
Return-on-book equity (ROE), 383
Returns:
  arithmetic rate of, 98
  asset returns, 99–102, 151
  correlated, and time aggregation, 104–105
  geometric rate of, 98–99
  iid returns, 101, 102–103, **104**
  RAROC, xxiii, 96, 389, 399, 401, 402,
    423–425
  in VAR modeling, 131–132
Risk:
  defined, 4–5, 81, 85, 86, 411
  factors of, 149, 264, **265**
  managers of, 516–517
  measurement of, 95–99, **98,** 114–116
  VAR as risk-control tool, 361–362,
    376–381, **380**
  (*See also specific topics*)

Risk, technology of (*See* Technology of risk)
Risk-adjusted performance measurement
    (RAPM):
    active risk management, VAR for, 383,
        387–389
    earnings-based methods, 389–391
    firm-wide performance measurement,
        394–398, **397**
    VAR-based methods, 391–394
Risk-adjusted return on capital (RAROC), 96,
    389, 399, 401, 402, 423–425, xxi
Risk-based capital charges, 51
Risk-budgeting concept, 425–426
Risk capital, 383–387
Risk capital weights, 56–57
Risk-control systems software, 432–434
Risk decomposition, 159, 161–162, **163**
Risk drivers, 336–337
Risk engine platform, 434
Risk interactions, 474
Risk management (RM), 3–29
    Basel Accord risk-mitigation techniques, 60
    centralized, 363–364, 435, **436**
    criticism of, 502–503
    defined, 3
    derivatives, 11–15
    disclosure, 371–376
    documentation, 484–488
    evolution of, 10–11, 25–29, 512–513
    financial risks, 3–11, 16–21
    industrial technology for, 432–434, 438–442
    and investment management, 420–426
    LTCM lessons, 503–508, **506**
    Monte Carlo system, 298–299
    organizational guidelines, 514–516
    reports, 463
    role of manager, 513–517
    and VAR, 21–29
    VAR limitations, 488–498, **497**
    VAR side effects, 498–503
    (*See also* Active risk management;
        Operational risk management)
Risk managers, VAR reporting, 442, **443**
Risk-neutral world, 403
Risk Standards, 426–428
RiskMetrics, 28–29, 44–45, 172, 193–196,
    201–202, 496
RiskOps, 457
RiskWatch, 441, 443–445
RM (*See* Risk management)
ROA (return-on-assets), 383
ROE (return-on-book equity), 383

Rogue traders, 36–38, 41–43, 416, 417, 436,
    462
Rohatyn, Felix, 31
Rolling hedge, 39
Russian credit default, 244–245, 248, 502

Sailfish, 427
Salomon Brothers, 394, 439
Salomon Smith Barney, 499
Sampling distribution, 123
Sampling variability, 226, 300
Sanford, Charles, 471
SAS (Statistical Analysis Systems Institute),
    442
SBC (Swiss Bank Corporation), 381
Scaled loss distribution, 454
Scenario analysis:
    conditional, 240, **241,** 242
    defined, 231–232
    factor push method, 240
    historical, 232, 242–245, **243**
    Monte Carol method, 307–308
    multidimensional, 239–245
    prospective, 232, 239
    SPAN system (Standard Portfolio Analysis
        of Risk), 237–239
    stress testing, 235–245
    stylized, 235–239
    systematic, 245
    unidimensional, 235–239
    (*See also* Methods, VAR)
Securities and Exchange Commission (SEC),
    47–49, 471
Securities firms regulation, 72–74
Securities vs. derivatives, 11
Securitization, 58
Self-insurance, operational losses, 461–462
"Sell side" banks, 408, **409**
Senior managers, VAR reporting, 442, **443**
Sensitivity analysis, 245–246
Settlement risk, 17
Severity, loss distribution, 454, **456**
Shapiro, Marc, 518
Shareholder value added (SVA), xxiii,
    398–399, 401–402
Sharpe, William, 394
Sharpe ratio, 394–395, 428
Short option, 316, 507–508
Short straddle, 215–216
Sigma (σ), 82, 88
Simulation methods (*See* Methods, VAR)

Singular value decomposition, 179–180
Skewness, 93, 102
Slope, 174
Sobol procedure, 306
Software, risk-control systems, 432–434
Solution, portfolio credit risk models, 336–337
Soundness, 52
Sovereign risk, 17
SPAN (Standard Portfolio Analysis of Risk)
   system, 237–239
Specific risks, 168
Sponsor risk, 414–415
Spreadsheet program and VAR, 431
SQL (Structured Query Language), 435
Stability risks, 489–491
Standard deviation, 82, **83–84**, 85, 88, 111,
   126, 200
Standard normal distribution function, 92
Standard Portfolio Analysis of Risk (SPAN)
   system, 237–239
Standardized Method, 61–63, 66
State of Wisconsin Investment Board, 410
Statistical Analysis Systems Institute (SAS),
   442
Stochastic programming, 414
Straddle, 209, 215–219
Straight-through processing, risk-management
   technology, 433, **434**
Strategic asset allocation, 420, 422, 423
Strategic IT spending, 431
Strategic options, 370
Strategic risks, 4, 31–32
Stress testing, 231–253
   CRMPG report, 487
   defined, 231
   extreme value theory (EVT), 233,
      249–253
   G-30 Best Practices, 485
   management of, 247–248
   model parameters, 245–247
   operational risk, 448
   reasons for, 232–235, 248–249
   scenario analysis, 235–245
   stability risks, 489–491
Structural breaks, 223
Structure effects, 60
Structured Query Language (SQL), 435
Student *t* distribution, 93–94
Stylized scenario analysis, 235–239
Subadditivity, risk measure, 115
Suitability, legal risk, 470
Surplus-at-risk, 413–414
Survivorship, estimation risk, 493

SVA (shareholder value added), 398–399,
   401–402
Swap derivative instruments, 1, 3, **14,** 17
Swaps, interest rate, 282, **283, 284,** 285, 324
Swiss Bank Corporation (SBC), 381
Syndicated Eurodollar loan, 63
Systematic risk, 82
Systematic scenario analysis, 245
Systems risk, 53, 451, **452**

Tabulation, loss distribution, 455, **456**
Tail conditional expectation, 97
Tail loss, 97
Taleb, Nassim, 498, 499
TAPS (Trade Analysis and Processing System),
   439
Taurus in-house risk-mangement system, 439
Taylor approximation, 212–214
Technical errors, 18
Technology of risk, 431–446
   application of, 443–445
   global risk-management systems, 432–434
   integration, need for, 434–438, 487
   risk management industry, 438–442
   VAR report structuring, 442–443
Techological innovation, risk of, 468
Telescoping of credit and interest rate risk, 63
Thieke, Steven, 518
Thin markets, 340
Time (*See* Horizon, investment)
Time aggregation, 102–106, 252
Time effects, credit risk, 316–318
Time-varying risk, forecasting, 184–196
TMCC (Toyota Motor Credit Corporation),
   371
Top-down approach, operational risk, 453
Total risk charge (TRC), 68, **69**
Toyota Motor Credit Corporation (TMCC), 371
Tracking error, 16
Trade Analysis and Processing System (TAPS),
   439
Trade credits, 326
Trading and traders:
   controlling, 513–514
   gaming the VAR system, 499–502
   rogue, 36–38, 41–43, 436, 462
   strategies, 346–349, 392–393, 394
   trading systems software, 432–434
   VAR reporting, 443
Transaction-by-transaction approach, credit
   risk, 317–318, 335–336
Transaction risk, 451, **452**

Transferred operational risk, 461
Transition risk, 491
Translation invariance, risk measure, 115
TRC (total risk charge), 68, **69**
Treynor ratio, 395, 428
Type 1 and 2 errors, 133–135, **136,** 137, 138

UCL (unexpected credit loss), 330
Unconditional coverage model, 140
Undiversified conventional RAPM measure, 396
Undiversified VAR, 152
Unexpected credit loss (UCL), 330
Unexpected operational losses, 460, 461
Unidimensional scenario analysis, 235–239
Uniform liquidation, 346
User risk, implementation risk, 496

Validation, model, 129
Valuation methods, 201, 209–210, **211,** 214, **215,** 223
Value added, risk management as, 421
Value at risk (VAR) and systems:
    application and usage, 361–370, **367,** 381–382, 517–519, xx–xxiii
    criticism of, 498–499
    defined, xxii, 15, 21–25, 108
    forecasting risks and correlations, 184–196
    as information-reporting tool, 370–376
    as investment decision guide, 422
    and investment guideline design, 417–418
    portfolio risk analysis, 148–177
    as risk-control tool, 361–365, 376–381, **380**
    SEC required analysis, 48

success of, 407–408
    VAR Calculator, 420
    (*See also specific topics*)
Variance, 88–91, 101, 104, 123–125, 224
Vasicek model, 309
Vega risk, 222
Verification and failure rates, backtesting, 132–136
Volatility:
    adjusting firm-wide and unit-level VAR, 377-381, **380**
    computation, 88, 89, 101
    earnings, 453
    exchange rates, 5, **6,** 9–10, **83,** 183, 184–186
    and global risk management, 363
    implied, 200
    interest rates, 5–6, **7,** 16, **83,** 183
    as measure of risk, 82
    and VAR, 183, 419
    volatility risk, 16

Warehoused derivatives, 363
WCE (worst credit exposure), 326–327
Wisconsin Investment Board, 410
Worst credit exposure (WCE), 326–327
Wrong-way trades, 473

Young, Peter, 449

Zero VAR measures, covariance matrix, 168–171

Philippe Jorion is currently Professor of Finance at the University of California, Irvine. He has also taught at Columbia University, Northwestern University, the University of Chicago, and the University of British Columbia. He received his M.B.A. and Ph.D. from the University of Chicago, and a master's degree in engineering from the University of Brussels.

Dr. Jorion has written two books, *Big Bets Gone Bad: Derivatives and Bankruptcy in Orange County* (Academic Press, 1995) and *Financial Risk Management: Domestic and International Dimensions* (co-authored with S. Khoury; Blackwell, 1995), and more than 50 publications directed to academics and practitioners on the topics of risk management and international finance. His recent work addresses the issue of forecasting risk and return in global financial markets. He is on the editorial board of a number of finance journals and is editor-in-chief of the *Journal of Risk.*

Dr. Jorion has received prestigious academics awards and has served as a consultant to various institutions. He is a frequent speaker at academic and professional conferences.